T0392116

Kings in All but Name

Kings in All but Name

The Lost History of Ōuchi Rule in Japan, 1350–1569

THOMAS D. CONLAN

OXFORD
UNIVERSITY PRESS

OXFORD
UNIVERSITY PRESS

Oxford University Press is a department of the University of Oxford. It furthers
the University's objective of excellence in research, scholarship, and education
by publishing worldwide. Oxford is a registered trade mark of Oxford University
Press in the UK and certain other countries.

Published in the United States of America by Oxford University Press
198 Madison Avenue, New York, NY 10016, United States of America.

CIP data is on file at the Library of Congress

ISBN 978-0-19-767733-9

DOI: 10.1093/oso/9780197677339.001.0001

Printed by Integrated Books International, United States of America

MIX
Paper
FSC FSC® C183721

To the Ōuchi and their scholars

Contents

Acknowledgments

A visit to Yamaguchi and a glimpse of its Rurikōji pagoda in the fall of 1995 served as the inspiration of the book. Once I returned from my travels, on 10.22.1995, I wrote to my adviser Jeffrey Mass, "I learned so many fascinating things about the Ōuchi which have come to light over the past few years that I am tempted to devote my next research project to the Ōuchi (but of course, I must first finish the current dissertation!)." As late as 2004, however, I had only drafted a single page sketch of this study. Attendance to the conference "Pieces of Sengoku: Interpreting Historical Sources and Objects from Japan's Long Sixteenth Century" at Princeton on 4.27.2009, convinced me to embark on this endeavor. After many years, and the support of many people, this research came to fruition. I cannot adequately thank everyone who has helped me.

I was fortunate to have received a Japan Foundation Fellowship in 2011–12, where I spent a year in Japan, and an American Council of Learned Societies grant in 2018–19, which allowed me to complete my research. A 2017 Princeton Humanities Council Magic Grant also helped me to analyze samples of Naganobori slag.

In Japan I benefited greatly from the pathbreaking research of a myriad of remarkable scholars, first among them Hirase Naoki, who opened me to the world of the Ōuchi and has been an invaluable guide, showing me the city of Yamaguchi and important artifacts and historical sites, and introducing me to researchers in the field, first in 1995 and again in 2011–12 and 2015. Without his guidance and support, this project would have been impossible to complete.

I am extremely grateful to the erudite Wada Shūsaku, who generously answered so many questions about the Ōuchi and their sources and led me on informative and enjoyable tours of Kudamatsu, Taineiji, Sue castles, Iwakuni, and the Nakatsu coin hoards (which were explained by Miura Narihisa, Fujita Shin'ichi, and Kanzaki Susumu), the route of Ōuchi Teruhiro's invasion of Yamaguchi, and important sites linked to the Yoshimi. I learned more from him than words can convey.

Yamaguchi's remarkable team of archaeologists, including Kitajima Daisuke, Satō Chikara, and Mashino Shinji, taught me much about Ōuchi ethnicity, roof tiles, trade, the founding of Yamaguchi, and experiments in metallurgy. Always ready to share their time and knowledge, they have enriched this project immensely. I am particularly grateful to Kitajima Daisuke for his explanations of Ryōunji, and a memorable visit to Kōnomine and Tōshunji. In addition, Maki Takayuki explained Kōryūji Hikamisan, the Yamaguchi shrines, and changes in architecture and urban planning to both me and my students and was always an informative guide and source of good cheer. I have also learned much from Itō Kōji and Saeki Kōji about Kyushu, trade, and the Ōuchi. Both also provided me with valuable monographs, sources, and references.

I owe a great debt to Yoshikawa Shinji, who taught me much about the sources of the Japanese court. His enthusiasm and unstinting support means spurred me on as I researched the attempt to move Japan's capital to Yamaguchi. He too introduced me to Ikeda Yoshifumi, whose knowledge of Naganobori and its copper has proved transformative and who has generously allowed me to analyze samples of slag and ore. Likewise, our trip to Mishima, Fukawa, and the beaches of Yuigahama, with Hara Hidesaburō and Kuroha Ryōta, will remain a fond memory.

I was able to visit Masuda, the mines at Tsumo, and Iwami Ginzan in June 2015 thanks to the efforts of Hirase Naoki. There I first met Nakatsuka Ken'ichi, indispensable guide to Masuda, Tsumo, and the sources and history of Iwami. Nakano Yoshifumi and Yamate Takeo explained much about the Iwami Silver Mines, and I remember vividly the tours provided by Shinkawa Takashi, who helped me to fully appreciate the remarkable mines and their secret harbors, and Mr. Hasegawa, tour guide to the Ōkubo mine shafts (*mabu*). I have learned from and received support many more, and cannot adequately convey my debt, but I list them here—Ōzaki Chika, Egaitsu Michihiko, Furuya Yūko, Arikawa Nobuhiro, Kawamura Shōichirō, Amino Yukari, Ebara Masaharu, Kurushima Noriko, Matsui Naoto, Hagihara Daisuke, Harada Masatoshi, Nagasawa Kazuyuki, Nakagi Sayumi, Itō Hajime, Mori Michihiko, Hori Daisuke, and Minami Takao.

Horikawa Yasufumi, while here at Princeton, advised me in translating Ōuchi laws, while Patrick Schwemmer provided invaluable insights and translated the Portuguese version of the 1552 document. Special thanks too to Christina Lee. Furthermore, Horikawa Yasufumi and Oka Mihoko of the Historiographical Institute, the University of Tokyo, and Lucio de Sousa of the Tokyo University of Foreign Studies helped me to secure images of this record, and Benita Ferreira transmitted them to me, for which I am grateful.

My knowledge of sixteenth-century culture sources and insights into sources would not be complete without many informative discussions with Andrew Watsky. He and Alexandra Curvelo helped me to better understand much about Sakai. Likewise, Peter Shapinsky helpfully introduced me to the *Riben Yijian*. Christopher Mayo has been an invaluable resource for all things pertaining to the Ōtomo. Peter Kornicki informed me of Korean books with an Ōuchi King of Japan seal (9.5) and I want to thank him, Kate Wildman Nakai, Linda Grove, and Shinozaki Yōko for all their help in securing these images. For other image permissions, I am grateful to Wada Shūsaku of the Yamaguchi monjokan, Kitajima Daisuke of the Yamaguchi-shi kyōiku iinkai, Harayama Eiko of the Masaki Museum of Art, Yamada Minoru of the Yamaguchi Prefectural Museum of Art, and Inoue Mayu of the Yonezawa-shi Uesugi Museum. Special thanks to Mikami Yasushi for showing the statues of Yōkōji, Anne Rose Kitagawa and Carrie Simonds for giving me the opportunity to view the 1510 *Tale of Genji* album in person in 2005, Rachel Sanders for insights into silk used for this album, Dorinda Neave for her research about the monk Chikai, Xiaojin Wu for explaining the value of bamboo paper, Shimao Arata for the Ōuchi role in disseminating Chinese paintings to the Ashikaga, Louise Cort for pottery found in Hagi, and, in the seas near Bermuda, the first mate of the *Celebrity Summit* for insights about stars and navigation.

Crafting this narrative has proved time-consuming, and in reading an early draft of my manuscript, my debt to three friends is especially great. Email exchanges about caltrops led to a fruitful partnership with Royall Tyler. From discussing translations to exploring issues of style and interpretation in this text, which he read repeatedly, I have learned much from Royall, who is an exemplar in so many ways. Also, I would like to thank Philippe Buc and Jaqueline Stone for reading earlier versions of this manuscript and providing excellent advice. Philippe taught me to approach Japan from a comparative perspective and appreciate aspects of Japan I would have otherwise overlooked. Jacqueline Stone, with her deep knowledge and good cheer, is an inspiration.

David Lurie helped me with my understanding of ancient *kabane*, and thanks to Michael Como, I came to appreciate the importance of immigrants to ancient and medieval Japan. Morgan Pitelka, David Spafford, and Noda Taizō have encouraged me to explore Warring States history, while David

Robinson has taught me much about Ming military and diplomatic history. Ashton Lazarus offered insights concerning passages of the *Kanmon nikki*. Nam-lin Hur of the University of British Columbia is a wellspring of information regarding Japanese and Korean connections. During my years at Bowdoin, I was fortunate to have stimulating intellectual exchanges with John Holt, Allen Wells, Olufemi Vaughan, Sree Padma, Lawrence Zhang, Ya Zou, and Paul Friedland. Adam Clulow has imparted his knowledge of maritime trade and offered me encouragement at important times. Suzanne Gay and James Dobbins have also immeasurably improved this work. Special thanks too to Bridget St. Clair for giving me the opportunity to explore Japan and Korea in the *Le Soléal* and to better understand the Ōuchi realm from the seas. Finally, I want to thank Nancy Toff, Cynthia Read, and Chelsea Hogue at Oxford University Press for their invaluable help in publishing this manuscript and Mary Mortensen for indexing this work.

I had the opportunity to present my preliminary findings at Princeton's East Asian Department Colloquium Series, a Works in Progress lecture at the Davis Center, IAS Princeton, as well as the University of Cambridge, Yale University, Columbia University, the Seattle Art Museum, the University of Pennsylvania, the University of British Columbia, the University of Vienna, and the Central European University at Budapest, and at Yamaguchi for the thirteenth *Ōuchi shi rekishi bunka kenkyūkai* lecture. I am grateful to the many who invited me and attended these talks and regret that I do not have the space to personally thank them all in these acknowledgments. In particular, I would like to thank Benjamin Elman, who encouraged me to use the model of a "segmented polity," Federico Marcon, who taught me much about coins, currency, and the concept of the historian as a redeemer of the past, as well as Sue Naquin and Jennifer Rampling for insights on matters related to metallurgy and alchemy. Brian Steininger and Tom Hare provided many insights regarding Japanese literature and culture and Bryan Lowe has been a great resource for ancient Japan. Helmut Reimitz and Willard Peterson helped me to hone my understanding of Ōuchi identity, Ksenia Chizhova introduced important Korean sources and concepts, Amy Borovoy gave the gift of a rare Ōuchi related book, Sheldon Garon provided probing comments on chapter 5, Xin Wen and Buzzy Teiser illuminated the world of Central and East Asia, and William Chester Jordan imparted upon me the wise words of Lawrence Stone, to "make sure that history is never boring."

Princeton's graduate students have provided me with great intellectual stimulation, and here let me thank those who directly aided me in this project. Megan Gilbert, David Romney, and Nate Ledbetter have taught me more than they can know. Megan, for her skepticism, erudition, critical spirit, and precision in writing; David, for his immense knowledge of things relating to Yoshida Shinto; and Nate, an intrepid explorer of the military documents of Kyushu. I would also like to especially thank Gina Choi for her great help in translating articles about copper and for teaching me much about Ōuchi/Korean interactions in the 1540s. I am deeply indebted to Soojung Han, who helped me to use Korean databases and taught me much about Korean history and notions of East Asian ethnicity.

At Princeton, Setsuko Noguchi helped me to purchase two Ōuchi Yoshioki documents for Princeton's library, as well as a treatise on copper smelting. Hyoungbae Lee aided me in explaining the principles of Korean romanization and checking over my transliterations. I received great help in translating my research into Japanese thanks to the efforts of Yoshikawa Itsuko in Japan and Megumi Watanabe at Princeton. And I am grateful to my son George, who helped me to scale the steep slopes of Kōnomine and shared so many important journeys, my wife Yūko for her patience and good cheer, and our dog Rosie, my loyal and happy companion to the end.

Conventions

Macrons will not be used for common place names (Honshu, Kyushu, Kyoto) unless they are part of official titles, names of books, articles, and publishers.

Dates will be reproduced in the month, date, year format, with years in the CE format. Dates from the lunar calendars of Japan and Korea will not be translated to the Julian or Gregorian calendar, but will be referred to numerically (first month, second month).

Chinese characters (*kanji*) will not be used unless the meaning of the character is particularly difficult to decipher for researchers proficient in Japanese.

All ages will be according to the traditional Japanese count, where year one begins at the time of birth and the second year is determined by the new year. Thus, a child born on New Year's Eve would be two years old on New Year's Day.

The McCune-Reischauer system will be used for romanizing Korean, Pinyin will be used for Chinese, and Modified (Revised) Hepburn will be used for Japanese.

Unless otherwise indicated, the place of publication is Tokyo.

Introduction

The Lost History of Ōuchi Rule

Much that was has been forgotten. The vicissitudes of time, the fragility of sources, and the destruction of regimes, institutions, and cultures have caused much of the human past to disappear. This story of the Ōuchi, a family all but extinct, attempts to recover one such lost history.

The Ōuchi ruled western Japan for centuries, until a 1551 coup led to the death of nearly all the Ōuchi and their core supporters. After 1569, memories of all facets of Ōuchi rule—their culture, modes of governance and ritual practice, trade policies and international ties, and even their distinct ethnic identity—faded. Nevertheless, enough Ōuchi architectural monuments, cultural artifacts, and administrative documents survived to afford, through determined effort, a glimpse into their world.

This book traces the history of the Ōuchi and explores how they amassed power and influence from the fourteenth through the mid-sixteenth centuries. It is organized on biographies of Ōuchi leaders to reveal the structural advantages and limitations each ruler confronted and aims to show how they variously met with success, failure, and, almost invariably, unintended consequences. Focus on these individuals allows for the creation of a totalizing history, as coverage of both long-term processes and specific events can be combined in a single, encompassing narrative. However, it is neither a familial nor a regional history. Rather, it takes the Ōuchi as a starting point to investigate neglected areas and to revise received understandings of the history of medieval Japan. It aims to destabilize the standard political narrative of medieval Japanese history that portrays Kyoto, Japan's capital, as the economic, cultural, and political center of Japan. The intent is not to show how a "periphery" interacted with a "center," but rather to suggest that the political and economic core of Japan migrated from the capital to the western tip of Honshu during the fifteenth and sixteenth centuries.[1] This approach affects

[1] For example, concerning greater Ōuchi access to more quantity of specie than the center, and

Kings in All but Name. Thomas D. Conlan, Oxford University Press. © Oxford University Press 2024.
DOI: 10.1093/oso/9780197677339.003.0001

accepted views of Japan and East Asia. Japan has, for most of its history, been portrayed as a relatively isolated polity, but this new view from the west shows that Japan was politically, culturally, and economically integrated with the rest of East Asia. The study will explore the cultural, economic, and political underpinnings of Ōuchi rule, highlighting the unique features of their culture, institutions, and policies, and emphasizing a new understanding of Japan's political history.

The Ōuchi founded the settlement Yamaguchi in the fourteenth century, at a time when urbanization was rare in Japan. Whereas earlier efforts at urban development had been limited to the establishment of capitals such as Kyoto or Nara in the eighth century, or the organic rise of regional and trading outposts that grew up around important shrines located near excellent harbors in the eleventh and twelfth (Kamakura and Hakata), Yamaguchi was not linked to either. Instead, it was founded around the dwelling of the Ōuchi lord. Previously, no one had planned a comparable settlement, laying out its roads asymmetrically at an unremarkable crossroads, far from a useful harbor or an old and prominent site of worship.[2] This city was the first of several palace settlements, which would be founded throughout Japan over the course of the fifteenth and sixteenth centuries, although in terms of size, age, and influence, Yamaguchi was unique.[3]

Yamaguchi had access via river and road to the Japan Sea in the north, and the Inland Sea in the south. Roads from the east led to silver mines, while those to the west ran by copper mines. All ended at serviceable harbors. The site was selected to facilitate exchange and trade. It is located on the western tip of Honshu, thirteen miles north of Ogōri, the nearest harbor on the Inland Sea, twenty-four miles to the south of the nearest port on the Japan Sea, forty-two miles to the east of the Straits of Shimonoseki, the western tip of Honshu (Figure I.1).

their pioneering efforts to regulate currencies, see Kuroda Akinobu, "Copper Coins Chosen and Differentiated: Another Aspect of the 'Silver Century' in East Asia," *Acta Asiatica* 88 (2005), p. 78. Kuroda first explains how shroffing edicts first appeared in Kyoto in 1500, but then notes that the first reforms happened fifteen years earlier in Ōuchi domains.

[2] To be sure, Taira Kiyomori (1118–81) had attempted to move Japan's capital to Fukuhara, an important harbor, for six months in 1180, but he abandoned this effort.

[3] For this process, and a high degree of urbanization by the end of the sixteenth century, see Wayne Farris, *Japan's Medieval Population: Famine, Fertility, and Warfare in a Transformative Age* (Honolulu: University of Hawaii Press, 2006), pp. 151–53, 245–46 and Morgan Pitelka, *Reading Medieval Ruins: Urban Life and Destruction in Sixteenth-Century Japan* (Cambridge: Cambridge University Press, 2022), pp. 6–15. For the characterization of palace settlements, see Pitelka, pp. 13–15, 27–43.

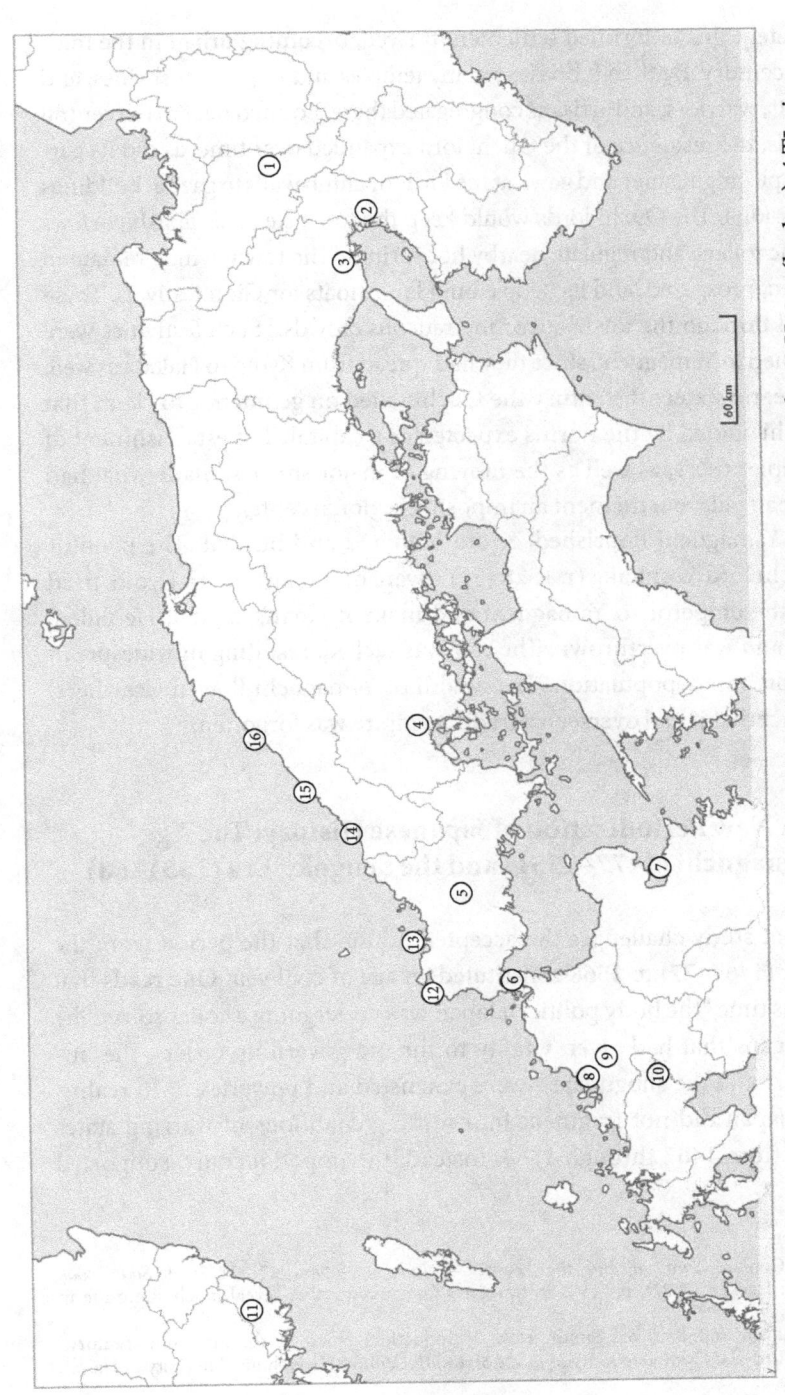

Figure I.1 Map of Major Cities and Harbors of Central, Western Japan, and Korea. 1.Kyoto, 2.Sakai, 3.Hyōgo (harbor), 4.Tōsai (harbor), 5.Yamaguchi, 6.Moji (harbor), 7.Funai (city and harbor), 8.Hakata (city and harbor), 9.Dazaifu, 10.Kanzaki (harbor), 11.Pusan (city and harbor), 12.Hijū (harbor), 13.Senzaki (harbor), 14.Masuda (harbor and city), 15.Hamada (harbor and city), 16.Nima (harbor).

Ultimately, this unfortified settlement thrived, becoming urban in the mid-fifteenth century. By then it boasted many temples and important shrines, and merchants, warriors, and artisans congregated there. Located next to the central crossroads, the residence of the Ōuchi lord expanded over time, as did its gardens. People might enter and gawk at the lords or climb walls to gaze at buildings or processions. The Ōuchi lords would keep the town clean, establish curfews and public toilets, and regulate nearby hot springs. The town, which remained unfortified, prospered, and its people built large floats for Gion festivals. These circulated through the town, attracting raucous crowds.[4] Such festivities were not confined to Yamaguchi, since they had spread from Kyoto to Hakata as well.

In the early sixteenth century the Ōuchi relied on geomancy to claim that Yamaguchi abided by the norms expected of a capital. The establishment of large temples there, as well as the moving of major shrines, made what had been a small palace settlement an imposing regional center.

While Yamaguchi flourished, Kyoto withered and burned. The penultimate Ōuchi lord Yoshitaka (r. 1528–51), aware of the turmoil in Kyoto, tried to bring the emperor to Yamaguchi and make it Japan's capital. He failed, however, and was overthrown. The city was sacked, resulting in widespread destruction and depopulation. The wealth of Yamaguchi flowed elsewhere, and the fact that it had overseen a trading empire was forgotten.

A New Periodization of Japanese History: The Age of Yamaguchi (1477–1551) and the Sengoku Era (1551–68)

The present study challenges the accepted notion that the period from the Ōnin War (1467–77) to 1568 constituted an age of civil war. One reads that during this time "the body politic of Japan was undergoing a collapse" as "the central organs that had given vitality to the old governing order—the imperial court and the shogunate—were exhausted and powerless."[5] In reality, however, Japan did not fragment into shifting coalitions of warring states (*sengoku*) from 1467 through 1568. Instead, the imperial court, supported

---

[4] Thomas Conlan, *Samurai and the Warrior Culture of Japan, 471–1877: A Sourcebook* (Indianapolis: Hackett, 2022), pp. 194–98 translates Ōuchi codes that reveal much about life in Yamaguchi.

[5] George Elison and Bardwell Smith, eds., "Introduction: Japan in the Sixteenth Century," *Warlords, Artists, and Commoners: Japan in the Sixteenth Century* (Honolulu: University of Hawaii Press, 1981), p. 2.

by the Ōuchi, functioned well until 1551. During the Ōuchi heyday, Japan constituted a segmented polity, governed by two complementary cities, the trading city of Yamaguchi, which served as the economic core of Japan, and Kyoto, the old capital, which remained the focus of emperor-centered rites. For this reason, much of the era hitherto classified as the Sengoku Age could better be seen as the Age of Yamaguchi.

This focus on the two complementary cities of Yamaguchi and Kyoto rehabilitates the role of a court long thought to have been politically supine and economically enervated.[6] It suggests that the court, which became a junior governing partner with the Ashikaga bakufu (1338–1573), rebounded after the implosion of that warrior government during the latter half of the fifteenth century. Court officials reached out to the Ōuchi to ensure that the rites of state would continue to be performed, albeit increasingly in the Ōuchi territories rather than the Kyoto region. In turn, the Ōuchi first occupied Kyoto for a decade (1508–18) in order to stabilize central Japan. They then abandoned that endeavor and, in 1551, attempted to move the court to their city of Yamaguchi, thereby making it the capital of Japan.

Most studies of this period focus on the turmoil of the mid-sixteenth century. John Hall, for example, argued that "it is clear that by 1550 Japan had reached a state of political and social instability that could only be brought under control by a militarily powerful autocrat."[7] This study does not dispute Hall's statement, but instead of seeing 1550 as the nadir of a long period of decline, it suggests that the Ōuchi controlled areas of western Japan experienced relative stability, and then all of Japan experienced a sudden political collapse in 1551. It argues that the Yamaguchi heyday lasted until 1551, and that the period of intense civil war, which is usually thought to have lasted until about 1568, began only then. The Sengoku era was a century shorter than has commonly been assumed.

---

[6] For example, Victor Lieberman, *Strange Parallels: Southeast Asia in Global Context, c. 800–1830*, vol. 2, *Mainland Mirrors: Europe, Japan, China, South Asia, and the Islands* (Cambridge: Cambridge University Press, 2012), p. 411, characterizes Japan's warrior government as being "nearly as powerless as the imperial court." For a study of the economic difficulties of courtiers after the Ōnin War, see Lee Butler, "The Struggle to Survive," in *Emperor and Aristocracy in Japan: Resilience and Renewal* (Cambridge, MA: Harvard East Asia Monographs, 2002), pp. 21–68.

[7] John W. Hall, "Japan's Sixteenth Century Revolution," in Elison and Smith, *Warlords, Artists, and Commoners*, p. 8. See also Elison and Smith, "Introduction," p. 2.

Trade, Mining, and Sea Power

Although most accounts of Japan, or for that matter of East Asian history, focus on the centrality of agriculture for economic development, the Ōuchi prospered most remarkably through trade, thanks to their access to copper and silver—two commodities in great demand throughout Asia. They controlled mines, promoted new techniques for mining and smelting copper and silver, and oversaw a dramatic expansion in the export of these metals to Korea and China.

They also mediated the entry of materials and ideas into Japan.[8] Responsible as they were for major exports of metal, the Ōuchi also welcomed Korean roof-tile craftsmen to Yamaguchi and imported finished materials such as Buddhist or Confucian texts and works of art. They largely monopolized this trade and, in addition, engaged in independent diplomatic relations with Korea and China. After 1518, the Ōuchi relied on the title of "King of Japan," which had been the prerogative of the Ashikaga shoguns from 1404, to justify their trade with Ming China through 1557. Their possession of the "King of Japan" seals allowed them to oversee lucrative trade in the form of tribute to the Ming emperor. By being able to act as if they were Japan's kings, they were indeed kings in all but name.

Most studies of medieval Japanese history focus on land taxes because these records survive in abundance; hence accounts focus more on the landed nature of the polity. This bias remains one of the most durable tropes of early English-language histories of Japan.[9] An important correction occurred when scholars such as Amino Yoshihiko turned away from the centrality of land and taxation per se to focus on nonagrarian activities, and on the importance of trade and merchants, as well as other activities not linked necessarily to local governance.[10] Innovative studies have arisen from this approach, but Amino sees change as fundamentally occurring from below. This study suggests the opposite. Large-scale trading and mining required considerable political authority since many people had to be mobilized to

[8] For suggestions of Japan's relative isolation and cultural homogeneity, see Lieberman, *Mainland Mirrors*, p. 378.

[9] The trope of Japan as being agricultural is very old. For example, James Murdoch writes, "Old Japan was almost entirely an agricultural country." *A History of Japan*, vol. 1 (London: K. Paul, Trench, Trubner, 1925), p. 17. For an important corrective on the overemphasis of agriculture in studies of the past, see James Scott, *Against the Grain: A Deep History of the Earliest States* (New Haven: Yale University Press, 2017).

[10] Amino Yoshihiko, *Rethinking Japanese History* (Ann Arbor: University of Michigan Center for Japanese Studies, 2012).

extract and ship valuable commodities. The court and the Ōuchi played a crucial role in promoting both mining and trade.

Recently, scholars have focused on "peoples of the seas" rather than solely on land-based activity.[11] This approach supersedes that of earlier English work on Ōuchi rule, which assumes that powerful lords focused on governing lands, and only lands, leaving the sea to others.[12] The present study shows that the Ōuchi were as much lords of the sea as lords of the land. Control of the Straits of Shimonoseki allowed them to fuse their rule over parts of two islands, Honshu and Kyushu, as well as over distant harbors that served as their outposts—harbors accessible only by sea from their core domains. Indeed, trade and money from abroad, particularly when funneled through the Ōuchi, could influence political change, particularly during the late fifteenth and the early sixteenth centuries.

Likewise, later narratives of Japanese history emphasize internal disunity and adopt the characterization of term *Sengoku jidai*, the "Warring States Era." The phrase, when taken to its extreme, suggests that competing regions within Japan behaved as autonomous entities capable of diplomatic interactions. In fact, the only prominent regional leaders within Japan capable of engaging with foreign states and directly influencing them were the Ōuchi.

The Ōuchi dominated maritime commerce, and their collapse in the 1550s reverberated throughout East Asia; for once their trading monopoly ceased, a variety of armed groups strove to replace them. These armed traders, known as *wakō*, were pirate groups of sailors from the Japanese islands and the Asian continent.[13] When the Ōuchi weakened, the *wakō* moved in.

The allegiances of these *wakō* have been debated. Some have suggested alliance with the kings of Ryūkyū, others Ōuchi control.[14] This study disproves the idea of Ōuchi control; to the contrary, *wakō* influence in the seas of western Japan was inversely proportional to Ōuchi authority. They were, in other words,

---

[11] Amino argues this in *Rethinking Japanese History*. The concept is skillfully developed by Peter Shapinsky, *Lords of the Sea: Pirates, Violence, and Commerce in Late Medieval Japan* (Ann Arbor: University of Michigan Center for Japanese Studies, 2014).

[12] Peter Arnesen, *The Medieval Japanese Daimyo: The Ōuchi Family's Rule in Suō and Nagato* (New Haven: Yale University Press, 1979).

[13] For the *wakō*, Mark Hudson, *Ruins of Identity: Ethnogenesis in the Japanese Islands* (Honolulu: University of Hawaii Press, 1999), pp. 242–43. For a revisionist study about a wide-reaching Ryūkyū Empire, which was purportedly linked to the *wakō*, see Gregory Smits, *Maritime Ryūkyū* (Honolulu: University of Hawaii Press, 2018).

[14] For the former view, see Smits, *Maritime Ryūkyū*. For the latter, see Takekoshi Yosaburō, *Economic Aspects of the History of the Civilization of Japan*, vol. 1 (London: George Allen & Unwin,

traders who were often hostile to Ōuchi networks, but unable to effectively compete against them because they lacked the military power and diplomatic connections of the Ōuchi. Although some *wakō* would join Ōuchi networks during their period of dominance, they only gained influence when the Ōuchi were otherwise incapacitated. It is no coincidence that the period of their greatest activity, the Jiajing *wakō* raids, whereby armed Chinese merchants such as Xu Hai (d. 1556) and Wang Zhi (d. 1560) gained control of shipping networks between Japan and East and Southeast Asia, peaked in 1555, just as Ōuchi power faded, and they continued through the 1560s, as the seas and trade routes remained contested in the aftermath of the Ōuchi destruction.[15]

The Ōuchi, Korea, and the Question of "Ethnicity"

Ōuchi ties to Korea, strengthened by ties of blood and trade, proved to be particularly deep and binding. Able to hold high rank and position in Japan and to wield influence also in Korea, the Ōuchi drew the two together. No doubt extensive Chinese influence has been long recognized, but the importance of interaction with Korea, and of ties between Korea and western Japan, has largely passed unnoticed.

A history of the Ōuchi provides insight into the question of ethnicity and identity during Japan's middle period.[16] The notion of a multiethnic Japan seems at first far-fetched. Modern social scientists see Japan and Korea as among the most ethnically homogenous states in the world.[17] The idea that a combined Japanese/Korean identity existed appears unlikely because by the eighteenth century, at the very latest, Korean or indeed any "non-Japanese" identities or origins had become a source of stigma and discrimination.[18]

1930), p. 346, and Kazuo Miyamoto, *Vikings of the Far East* (New York: Vantage Press, 1975), pp. 29–32.

[15] For the Jiajing raids, see Bernhard Scheid, "Hachiman Worship among Japanese Pirates (*wakō*) of the Medieval Period: A Preliminary Study," in *The Sea and the Sacred in Japan: Aspects of Maritime Religion* (New York: Bloomberg Academic, 2018), p. 92. For how the turmoil led to a reduction in the number of dwellings in Hakata from ten thousand to three thousand during the 1570s, see Pitelka, *Reading Medieval Ruins*, p. 210.

[16] For a summary of this middle period, see Hudson, *Ruins of Identity*, pp. 242–43.

[17] Alberto F. Alesina, William Easterly, Arnaud Devleeschauwer, Sergio Kurlat, and Romain T., Wacziarg, *Fractionalization* (6.2002). Available at SSRN: https://ssrn.com/abstract=319762.

[18] David Howell, "The Geography of Civilization," and "Modernity and Ethnicity," in *Geographies of Identity in Nineteenth Century Japan* (Berkeley: University of California Press, 2005), pp. 131–53, 197–204.

By the turn of the eighteenth century, ethnic identity served to demarcate the boundaries of the Japanese state, but in the middle period ethnic boundaries did not correspond to political ones.[19] Scholars have argued, however, that a very early cosmopolitan identity fused into a shared common ethnic notion among political elites in the 700s. This notion came to be accepted by even regional officials throughout the archipelago by 900.[20] Because a durable, monolithic Japanese identity was thought to exist in the Japanese core homeland, scholars interested in the question of identity have explored geographically peripheral groups, be they the Emishi "barbarians" of the north, or *wakō* pirates plying the East China seas.[21]

This focus on ethnicities and Japan's boundaries overlooks the fact that a prominent, centrally connected lord could claim descent from a Korean (Paekche) prince and have this descent recognized by officials in Japan and Korea. The Ōuchi emphasized their Korean heritage along with their Japanese identity. This unique identity was desirable enough that some prominent families, such as the Munakata of Kyushu, who had no demonstrable genealogical ties to the Ōuchi, sought to adopt it. The same idea was also so widespread in Ōuchi territories that claims of Paekche ancestry were essential for the wielding of political power. For example, the last Ōuchi ruler established his authority by mimicking the perceived actions of the Paekche prince progenitor. Although the unique identity and ancestry of the Ōuchi has attracted much research recently in Japan, starting with the scholarship of Mori Shigeaki and continuing with the seminal work of Itō Kōji, Suda Makiko, and Wada Shūsaku, it has been largely dismissed in in Western-language scholarship, which has treated the Ōuchi as being irreducibly Japanese people who sometimes "pretended" to be Korean.[22]

In order to clarify what is meant by ethnicity, this monograph adopts the conceptual framework of Walter Pohl, who argues for ethnic identification requiring (1) the personal act of expressing allegiance to a social group;

[19] David Howell, "Ainu Ethnicity and the Boundaries of the Early Modern Japanese State," *Past and Present* 142 (1994), pp. 69–93. See also his "The Geography of Civilization," and "Modernity and Ethnicity."

[20] Bruce Batten, *To the Ends of Japan: Premodern Frontiers, Boundaries, and Interactions* (Honolulu: University of Hawaii Press, 2003), pp. 87–114ff.

[21] Batten, *To the Ends of Japan*, pp. 103–120. These people did not, in the view of Batten, develop an ethnic identity. See also Hudson, *Ruins of Identity*, pp. 242–43.

[22] Mori Shigeaki, "Ōuchi shi no kōryū to sosen denju," *Yamaguchi kenshi kenkyū*, no. 11 (3.2003), pp. 93–117; Suda Makiko, *Chūsei nitchō kankei to Ōuchi shi* (Tokyo daigaku shuppankai, 2011); Itō Kōji, "Chūsei saikoku shoshi no keifu ninshiki," in *Kyōkai aidentiti* (Kyūshū shigakukai, 2008) and "Chūsei bushi no keifu—Suō Ōuchi shi no jirei to shite," *Rekishi to chiri Nihonshi no kenkyū*, no. 717 (9.2018), pp. 33–38; and Wada Shūsaku, "Ōuchi shi no sōsho kankei o megutte," in Kage Toshio, ed.,

(2) the collective self-representation of a group through its speakers or as a whole; and (3) the classification of social groups by outsiders.[23] By these standards, the Ōuchi and their branch families possessed a distinct ethnic identity. They identified as a social group, the Tatara, descended from Prince Imsŏng (circa 577?–657?), an imagined immigrant from Paekche who never actually existed. Their identity was recognized by outsiders, both Japanese courtiers, who sometimes suggested that they were not truly "Japanese," and Korean officials, who noted an unusual affinity with them. Both Japan and Korea tolerated multiple ethnicities, even among their elite, but a more monolithic ethnic sense permeated the archipelago and the Korean peninsula after the Ōuchi collapse. Throughout the sixteenth century, other families such as the Takahashi would claim descent from non-Japanese progenitors, including Chinese Latter Han Dynasty emperors, but such claims of foreign origins later became disadvantageous and were largely abandoned.[24]

Religion and Rule

Japan remained a cohesive and ritually (hence politically) functioning entity through 1551. The court continued to be essential as a locus for governance, and its rituals worked to make claims of power "real," for the notion endured that ritual served not as a "theater of state" but rather had practical effect. It functioned as a language of power in a society where people believed that

---

Ōuchi to Ōtomo: Chūsei nishi Nihon no nidai daimyō (Bensei shuppan, 2013). For a study from the perspective of art history, see Sangnam Lee, "The Jeoson Court and the Ōuchi Clan: A Case Study of the Interregional Circulation of Material Culture," *Artibus Asiae* 78.2 (2018), pp. 151–80. By contrast, some historians discount this issue entirely. Peter Arnesen, *The Medieval Japanese Daimyo*, only looks at their position within the confines of Japan, while Jurgis Elisonas portrays Ōuchi ancestral claims as being fictional. In his words, "The Ōuchi family, which itself pretended to a royal Korean ancestry, had a long history of diplomatic and economic relations with Korea and a long history of borrowing from overseas." See "Christianity and the Daimyo," in John Whitney Hall, et al., eds., *The Cambridge History of Japan* (New York: Cambridge University Press, 1991), p. 314.

[23] Walter Pohl, "Introduction: Strategies of Identification—a Methodological Profile," in *Strategies of Identification: Ethnicity and Religion in Early Medieval Europe* (Turnhout: Brepols, 2013), pp. 1–64, and Eirik Hovden, Christina Lutter, and Walter Pohl, eds., *Meanings of Community across Medieval Eurasia: Comparative Approaches* (Leiden: Brill, 2016). For a complementary view, see Batten, "What Is "Ethnicity," in *To the Ends of Japan*, pp. 87–90.

[24] Howell, *Geographies of Identity*, pp. 144, 201–3 for stigma attached to Korean identity. See also p. 138 for thinkers such as Nishikawa Joken (1648–1724), who saw Korean and Chinese civilization as differing fundamentally from Japan. Luke Roberts, *Performing the Great Peace: Political Space and Open Secrets in Tokugawa Japan* (Honolulu: University of Hawaii Press, 2012), insightfully analyzes contradictory claims and overlapping identities in later Japanese history. For the Takahashi, see Itō Kōji, "Chūsei saikoku shoshi no keifu ninshiki."

supramundane forces influenced human affairs.[25] Ritual allowed the Ōuchi to order and control their domains, and ensured that the state itself continued to function, since its rites were thought to order the realm and the cosmos. This meant that the imperial court governed until at least 1551, even if some of its critical rituals were performed in Yamaguchi rather than in Kyoto. The imperial center did not collapse. Rather, its functions were gradually absorbed by the Ōuchi. In short, the core rituals of the Japanese polity functioned through 1551.

Focus on the Ōuchi provides new insight into Japanese religion during the middle period, first because of the Ōuchi practice of transforming state institutions into ones devoted to their own family. This practice involved several of the most important shrines in Japan. It also meant that the Ōuchi imposed their deities on, or linked them to, the tutelary deities of the imperial family and the Ashikaga shoguns (Figure I.2).

They also favored the "One and Only Shinto" (*yuiitsu shintō*) of Yoshida Kanetomo, with its renewed focus on the centrality of Japan's gods, although for the Ōuchi the malleability of this new system, and its usefulness as a means of legitimating their position, undoubtedly contributed to its appeal.[26] By patronizing Yoshida Shinto, the Ōuchi were able to perform remarkable feats, including the only time that Japan's most sacred (and hitherto immobile) Ise shrines were moved. Yoshida religious specialists, with the support of the Japanese emperor, transferred the gods of Ise, the tutelary deities of the imperial family, to Yamaguchi, an act of enormous socioreligious significance that has nonetheless been almost forgotten. The Yoshida also helped the Ōuchi to deify one of their rulers. Previously, wronged spirits might be deified, but not successful leaders. This pattern changed, however, when Ōuchi Norihiro (1420–65) was enshrined as a god in 1485. His apotheosis became a template for deifying leaders, such as the late sixteenth-century "unifier" Toyotomi Hideyoshi, and as one of the most significant methods of politically legitimating rulers of Japan in later ages.[27]

---

[25] See Conlan, *From Sovereign to Symbol: An Age of Ritual Determinism in Fourteenth Century Japan* (New York: Oxford University Press, 2011). For more on supernatural powers, sovereignty, and transcendentalism, see Alan Strathern, *Unearthly Powers: Religious and Political Change in World History* (New York: Cambridge University Press, 2019).

[26] For an excellent overview of Kanetomo and Yoshida Shinto, see Helen Hardacre, *Shintō* (New York: Oxford University Press, 2016), pp. 209–25.

[27] Thomas Conlan, "When Men Become Gods: Apotheosis, Sacred Space, and Political Authority in Japan 1486–1599," *Quaestiones Medii Aevi Novae*, no. 21 (2016), pp. 89–106.

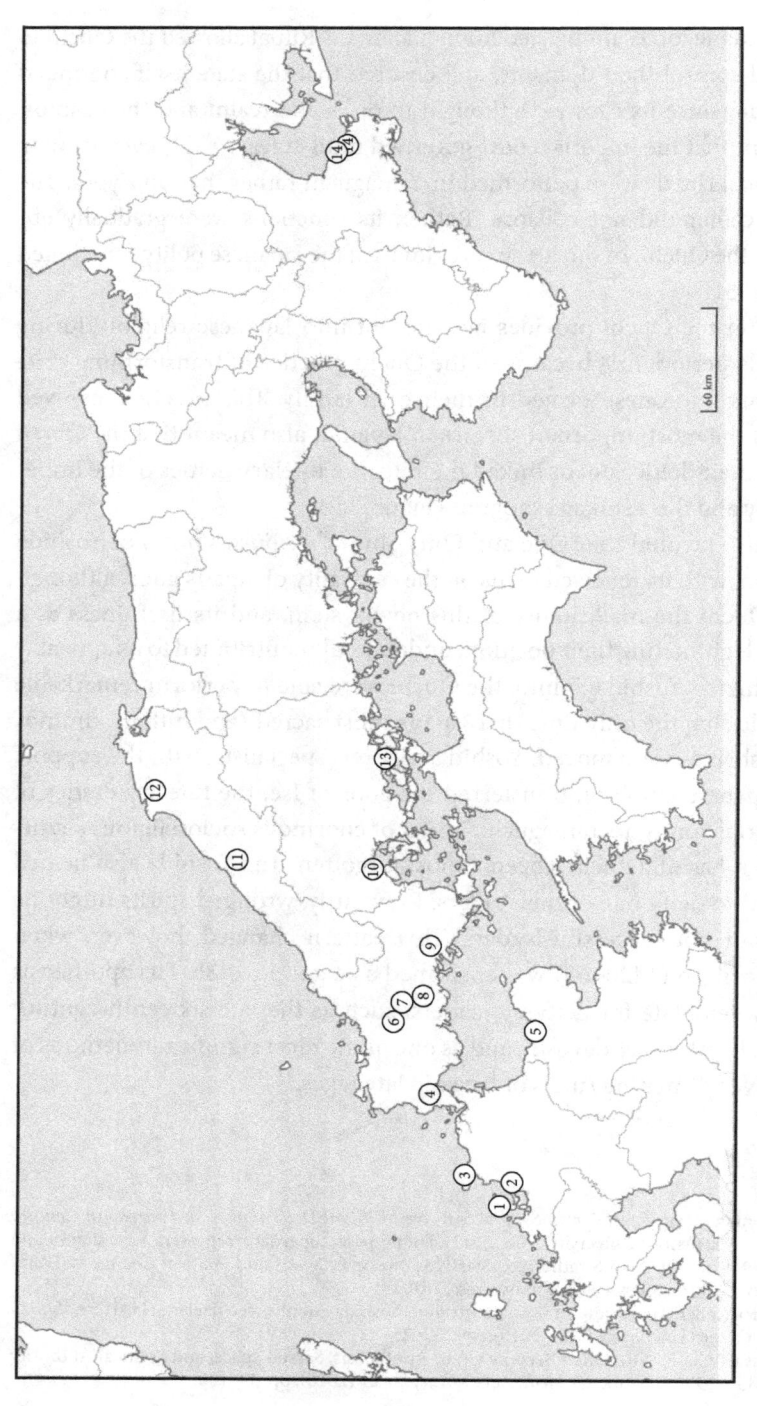

Figure I.2 Map of Major Shrines of Central and Western Japan. 1. Shikaumi Shrine, 2. Hakozaki Shrine, 3. Munakata Shrine, 4. Sumiyoshi Shrine, 5. Usa Hachiman Shrine, 6. The Kōnomine (Ise) Shrines of Yamaguchi, 7. Myōken Hikamisan, 8. Hōfu Tenmangū Shrine, 9. Kudamatsu Myōken Shrine, 10. Itsukushima Shrine, 11. Iwami Hachiman Shrine, 12. Izumo Shrine, 13. Ōyamazumi Shrine, 14. The Ise (Inner and Outer) Shrines.

60 km

The Ōuchi attempted to control institutions for the worship of deities of the stars and the seas.[28] Many families, particularly those involved in trade and navigation, favored the same gods, but Ōuchi possessiveness was unique. Early on, competing Ōuchi branches families tried to monopolize their deities, particularly Myōken, the Buddhist conception of the North Star. They relied upon yearly rites to formalize their lordship ties, and as their power expanded, they ensured that state rites too would be performed in Yamaguchi.

Through patronage and economic power, the Ōuchi took widely revered gods and made them their own familial deities, a process first apparent in the case of Kōryūji Hikamisan, their temple shrine complex dedicated to Myōken. Their policy is most manifest, however, with the case of Usa Hachiman in the early fifteenth century, when the Ōuchi co-opted a state-sponsored deity into their ancestral cult, but not before relying heavily on state funds to repair the shrine. They also forced others to pay for these institutions, which they appropriated, going so far as to request funds from Korea in the case of Kameyama Hachiman shrine. Finally, they transferred deities to highlight their familial prestige. At times that involved establishing new shrines to Myōken in the Kyoto region, or even inserting these deities into the shrines of their Ashikaga rivals.

Individuals and Institutions

In order to explain the significance of the Ōuchi, this monograph adopts what may seem an antiquated narrative, since it is structured around the genealogy of the Ōuchi family. Rather than using institutions or political or social orders as the basis for analysis, it focuses on the lives of Ōuchi lords from the years 1350 through 1569. This approach is required because individual leaders' resourcefulness, skill, and beliefs determined their achievements more than the office that they held. Ōuchi ideas, policies, and overall influence can best be understood when focusing on the powerful individuals who influenced their governance, institutions, and patronage.

Japanese- and English-language scholarship on this topic tends to focus less on individuals than on the definition and significance of the office of *shugo*, or protector. This office became influential once its holder was able

---

[28] For a pioneering study of their star worship, see Hirase Naoki, *Ōuchi shi no ryōgoku shihai to shūkyō* (Hanawa shobō, 2017).

to use half of a province's revenue for military provisions, which became possible after 1350. The Ōuchi held the post of *shugo* for a varying number of provinces, most notably Suō, Nagato, and Buzen, for much of the period of their rule. They also more fleetingly held this post for other provinces. However, they also made some provinces all but ungovernable by any *shugo*.

John Hall championed a view of the *shugo* as incipient regional magnates, the crucial institutional figures of their age, who oversaw a devolution of power from the court to the provinces, where they ruled with autonomy.[29] Peter Arnesen's *The Medieval Japanese Daimyo: The Ōuchi Family's Rule in Suō and Nagato*, the only major study of the Ōuchi in English, argued that their offices mattered more for their authority than direct control of the land. In his work, Arnesen focuses more on the role of *shugo* as officers of the state rather than autonomous domanial, or feudal, lords. To Arnesen, they used privileges of their office to attract followers, rather than personal authority or grants of land. He goes against the grain of earlier scholarship by arguing that the office, rather than control of land, which the Ōuchi did not possess in great amounts, was central to their lordship.[30]

For all the interest of his pathbreaking work, Arnesen was criticized for not clarifying how representative the Ōuchi were. By relying on the office of *shugo* for his analysis, he created a seamless narrative that did not fully explore ruptures or explain the relative strength of *shugo* vis-à-vis the Ashikaga shogunate or their followers.[31] On the other hand, some Japanese scholars have focused on relations with the center. Among them, Kawaoka Tsutomu most cogently argued for Ōuchi support of the central polity, at least through the 1460s, while others such as Matsuoka and Fujii have stressed their autonomy.[32]

[29] John W. Hall, "Foundations of the Modern Japanese Daimyō," *Journal of Asian Studies* 20.3 (1961), pp. 317–29.

[30] Arnesen, *The Medieval Japanese Daimyo*. Arnesen takes issue with his mentor John Hall about a typology of regional rule, suggesting that two ideal types, the *shugo* daimyo and the warring states (sengoku) daimyo were not that dissimilar. Arnesen recognized that the Ōuchi were a rich topic for study, stating: "One might, for example, choose to focus on the immense role which the Ōuchi played in Japan's trade with China and Korea during the Muromachi period, on their equally significant role in the patronage of art and literature, or on the tempestuous history of their relationship with the Ashikaga shoguns." Nevertheless, the central focus on their role, in his view, was their position as *shugo* and sengoku daimyo. See p. 23.

[31] Mary Elizabeth Berry, "Public Official or Feudal Lord?," *Monumenta Nipponica* 36.2 (Summer 1981), pp. 187–93.

[32] Kawaoka Tsutomu, "Muromachi bakufu shugo taisei to saikoku shugo," *Saikoku no kenryoku to senran* (Seibundō shuppan, 2010), pp. 37–66. By contrast. Matsuoka Hisatō, "Ōuchi shi no hatten to sono ryōgoku shihai," in *Ōuchi shi no kenkyū* (Seibundō, 2011), pp. 88–94, argues for the autonomy and power of the Ōuchi. This view is favored too by Fujii Takashi, *Muromachiki daimyō kenryokuron* (Dōseisha, 2013).

These studies of *shugo* have proved insightful; however, a focus on debates about *shugo* authority has caused much to be lost. Arnesen, for example, does not explore, or even clearly acknowledge, their presence in the dimension of trade, and he treats only their "home" provinces of Suō and Nagato, ignoring their authority over northern Kyushu, Aki, and Iwami. That they promoted urbanization in Yamaguchi, funded political rites in Kyoto, and claimed to be of a unique ethnicity is all but ignored in his book, as are most of their actions in the fifteenth and sixteenth centuries. Finally, in terms of important institutions, the district (*kōri*) mattered more than the province (*kuni*). The Ōuchi administered some provinces as *shugo*, while their control of certain districts and harbors prevented rivals from governing others.

Study of the Ōuchi reveals the disproportionate influence leaders had in shaping policies and actions and legitimating social structures and laws underpinning their rule. In the early years of Ōuchi dominance, the notion of a powerful lord proved so durable that times of succession were marked by intense skirmishes, leading to the death of many defeated candidates. Lordship was won, or determined through ability and military prowess, rather than primogeniture. A move toward more orderly succession, with heirs linked to Myōken, the polestar deity, followed during the last century of Ōuchi rule. At the same time, as Ōuchi influence expanded, a single lord proved unable to govern directly. This led to the rise of core administrators, who maintained consistency even in times when rulers were incapacitated or killed. Ōuchi policies and organs of governance proved durable, sophisticated, and skilled. After their final destruction, those who still remembered how they had governed complained of the relative incompetence of their successors, the Mōri. In terms of institutions of administration, economic policies, court affairs, and trade, the situation in western Japan, and indeed the whole archipelago, did not "progress" or improve during the decades of turmoil that accompanied the Ōuchi fall.

The Forgetting

The collapse of the Ōuchi resulted in great destruction. The main line died out, as too most of their collateral lineages, while the city of Yamaguchi would burn down three times between 1551 and 1569, and the main Ōuchi archives would be destroyed.

Most of the plotters involved in the coup of 1551, too, would perish. The Mōri, who were marginally implicated in the coup, moved their headquarters from Yamaguchi to Hagi. Even after the final fires of 1569, many Ōuchi temples still stood, but the Mōri dismantled and moved many of the grandest buildings to places as far afield as Hakata, Hiroshima, and Ōtsu, to the east of Kyoto. In the end, only one large pagoda remained. The Mōri also had an important role in writing the histories of their area in compiling sources, and they subtly de-emphasized the grandeur of the Ōuchi.

Unfortunately, precious little survives about the lives and influence of Ōuchi women, although some tantalizing clues remain. The wives and mothers of some Ōuchi leaders are known, particularly those who were from Kyoto, or the daughters of prominent warriors. A few letters survive from Ōuchi Kuniko, who played a crucial role in directing the defense of Yamaguchi during the Ōnin War (1465–78), but the destruction of the main Ōuchi archives was so complete that unfortunately her significance, and that of many others can be little more than guessed at.

The world changed radically after the Ōuchi fall. After the hegemon Toyotomi Hideyoshi twice invaded Korea in 1592 and 1597, relations between Korea and Japan fractured, and never recovered. Although the Tokugawa, the successors to Hideyoshi, received Korean embassies, they consistently emphasized the foreignness of Korea, and gradually Korean identity and origins became a social stigma in Japan. That a powerful lord could claim descent from Korean kings came to be seen as exotic, or quixotic, in a far more uniform Japan.

During the Tokugawa era (1603–1867), trade with the continent went from being normal to exceptional, as ships and individuals were prohibited from leaving Japan, and most trade was confined to the port of Nagasaki. All other harbors along the Japan Sea coast of northern Kyushu, or western Honshu, were cut off from Korea once they came more firmly under Tokugawa control. Although the characterization of Japan as a "closed country" (sakoku) has been shown to be exaggerated, and continued trading and intellectual exchanges have been documented, it remains true that for many regions, particularly the western reaches of Honshu, the onset of Tokugawa rule led to isolation.[33]

---

[33] For the revision undermining the notion of sakoku, see Ronald Toby, State and Diplomacy in Early Modern Japan: Asia in the Development of the Tokugawa Bakufu (Princeton: Princeton University Press, 1984). For a study showing how the Tokugawa gained control of harbors and limited travel on the Japan (Genkai) Sea, see Noell Wilson, Defensive Positions: The Politics of Maritime Security in Tokugawa Japan (Cambridge, MA: Harvard University Asia Center, 2015).

Tokugawa era attitudes profoundly shaped understandings of the past. After 1615 and 1635, Tokugawa limits on people traveling abroad or departing from harbors other than Nagasaki distorted the understanding of the past, emphasizing Kyushu harbors over those in western Honshu. The idea that Japanese craft six times the size of those allowed by the Tokugawa plied the seas, full of ore, became inconceivable. The Tokugawa saw agricultural production as the basis for revenue and for Japan's currency exchanges, and the trading polity of earlier ages was largely forgotten. Few could imagine that the town of Yamaguchi had been the center of a great trading network. It became incomprehensible that early examples of rare, imported texts should be found in Yamaguchi temples like Tōshunji.

Likewise, the notion that politics centered on the court rather than on warrior governments per se was obscured during the Tokugawa era. During the Tokugawa era, the idea that court rituals were the essence of governance withered. As a result, the Ōuchi, especially Yoshitaka, were seen as preoccupied by mere courtly dilettantism. The court's increasing power vis-à-vis the Ashikaga in the early decades of the sixteenth century was downplayed. That an Ōuchi lord might rule on behalf of an emperor and rely solely on the institutions of the court to do so, undermined the very concept of a warrior government (*bakufu*). The radical attempt to move Japan's capital was erased from memory and the meaning of such an act forgotten.[34] Likewise, local histories of the Ōuchi omitted Yoshitaka's attempt to move the court to Yamaguchi.[35] Yoshitaka's attempt to transfer the capital, which was known in the decades after the Ōuchi collapse, was censored in nineteenth-century chronicles.[36]

To the Tokugawa, the court was dangerous, and it is no coincidence that when the constraints on it loosened, it became the vehicle for the destruction of the Tokugawa regime. The first thing the new leaders, many of whom came from the old Ōuchi domains, did was to move the capital from Kyoto, only this time eastward to Tokyo.

---

[34] Pierre Souyri, "The Sengoku Period: Warriors Seeking Power," in *The World Turned Upside Down: Medieval Japanese Society* (New York: Columbia University Press, 2001), p. 212, portrays Ōuchi exchanges with the court as being merely limited to the cultural sphere. "Warlords who fancied themselves men of culture sometimes extended the hospitality of their capitals to nobles. The Ōuchi in Yamaguchi . . . attempted in this way to recreate the atmosphere of Kyoto in its prime in the main town of their principalities."

[35] Thomas Conlan, "The Failed Attempt to Move the Emperor to Yamaguchi and the Fall of the Ōuchi," *Japanese Studies* 35.2 (September 2015), pp. 14–15.

[36] Conlan, "Failed Attempt," pp. 14–15.

Certain religious institutions had a vested interest in emphasizing the turmoil of Japan's so-called Sengoku era. This is most striking in the case of the Ise shrines, which were patronized by the Tokugawa and became a focal point of pilgrimage. The Tokugawa deified their founder, Tokugawa Ieyasu, but in doing so they used rituals designed by a Tendai monk named Tenkai, rather than the Yoshida specialists, who had deified Toyotomi Hideyoshi as the Toyokuni Daimyōjin in 1599.[37] They allowed the Yoshida to maintain power over many shrines, but not Ise, and so with the Ise resurgence under Tokugawa patronage, there was a tendency to ignore entirely the fact that Ise, transferred to Yamaguchi, had survived the civil wars.[38]

Early Scholarship

After the passing of the Ōuchi and the death of most of their supporters, the destruction of the Ōuchi archives and the city of Yamaguchi caused much about the Ōuchi to become obscure. Few chronicles survive that laud the exploits of the Ōuchi. Some, such as the *Chronicle of Ōnin*, downplay the Ōuchi role in that war because it was politically expedient to do so in the early sixteenth century, while chronicles about Ōuchi Yoshitaka, the penultimate lord, were likewise also altered to hide his unsuccessful plan to move the capital in 1551.[39] Only Yoshihiro, the third Ōuchi lord, appears as a major character in two popular war tales, and he has attracted considerable fame, arguably beyond his actual significance, while his more historically significant siblings, ancestors, and descendants have languished in relative obscurity.

Fortunately for later historians, the Mōri encouraged the copying of sources in their domains, leading to an unusually strong tradition of rigorous inspection and evaluation of documents. Bucking the trend of ignoring the Ōuchi and surviving the turmoil that followed the fall of the Tokugawa, the

---

[37] For a pathbreaking work, see Herman Ooms, *Tokugawa Ideology: Early Constructs, 1570–1680* (Princeton: Princeton University Press, 1985) and Bernhard Scheid, "Shinto as a Religion for the Warrior Class: The Case of Yoshikawa Koretaru," *Japanese Journal of Religious Studies* 29.3–4 (2002), pp. 299–324.

[38] Yoshida Kanetomo, too, was portrayed as relying on forged edicts to delegitimate tenets of Yoshida control. For a recent assertion to that effect, see Inoue Tomokatsu, *Kinsei no jinja to chōtei ken'i* (Yoshikawa kōbunkan, 2007), pp. 31–36.

[39] For more on the complex narrative of the *Chronicle of Ōnin*, see Conlan, "The 'Ōnin War' as Fulfillment of Prophecy," *Journal of Japanese Studies* 46.1 (Winter 2020): 31–60.

scholar Kondō Kiyoshi (1833–1916) went from researching sources in his domain to continuing the same work with the new Meiji government. He led the first efforts to collect and compile surviving materials on the Ōuchi. One compilation, entitled *Ōuchi shi jitsuroku* (*The Veritable History of the Ōuchi*), remains vital. Some of the material he relied upon, the equally valuable *Ōuchi shi jitsuroku dodai*, has recently been digitized and is readily accessible.

In the early twentieth century some scholars, particularly economic historians such as Takekoshi Yosaburō, recognized the importance of the Ōuchi.[40] Kobata Atsushi's many works on mining and trade also gave the Ōuchi a prominent place. The impressive number of surviving Ōuchi artifacts became evident in the 1989 exhibit at the Yamaguchi Prefectural Museum, *Ōuchi bunka no ihōten* (*Surviving Cultural Artifacts of the Ōuchi*), while important discoveries were made with the 2012 Kita Kyūshū Natural History Museum's exhibit *Ōuchi bunka to Kita Kyūshū* (*Ōuchi Culture and Northern Kyūshū*). The most remarkable developments over the past thirty years include the lengthy and careful excavation of the site of the Ōuchi mansion (1980–2014) and the publication of numerous sources, many appearing in print for the first time, in the volumes *Yamaguchi kenshi shiryō hen chūsei* (*The Sources of Yamaguchi Prefecture*) and the sister volumes *Yamaguchi shishi shiryōhen Ōuchi bunka* and *Yamaguchi shishi shiryōhen chūsei* (*The Sources of Yamaguchi City*). The publication of sources pertaining to the Masuda in Iwami as well as the introduction of new documents from Fukuoka are invaluable for an understanding of Ōuchi power in Iwami and Hakata. Finally, Ōuchi sources have been compiled in Wada Shūsaku's magisterial *Sengoku ibun Ōuchi shi hen* (*Warring States Sources: The Ōuchi*), which chronologically reproduces their documents from 1467 through the mid-sixteenth century.

Once Ōuchi sources in Yamaguchi prefecture and elsewhere became readily accessible, together with remarkable archaeological discoveries, interest in the Ōuchi and related research expanded greatly.[41] This development comes at a historical moment where transnational and global histories are favored more than narrow national accounts. In this way too, people are more receptive to researching and learning about a multiethnic Japan.

---

[40] See Takekoshi, *Economic Aspects*.
[41] The scholarship of Itō Kōji, Suda Makiko, Hirase Naoki, Wada Shūsaku, Maki Takayuki, and Kitajima Daisuke, among others, has proved remarkably influential and informative.

The idea that the Ōuchi were mere regional lords inhibited scrutiny of the archives of the Kyoto court for information relevant to them. However, recent discoveries and transcriptions of documents from the Imperial Archives have revealed the process by which Ōuchi Norihiro was deified, as well as the central Ōuchi role in the negotiations that ended the Ōnin War. Likewise, the publication of documents pertaining to the lowest-ranking people of the court, who built structures and tended the braziers and torches, provided decisive evidence for the attempt to move the court to Yamaguchi in 1551.[42] These archives are central to this narrative. Thanks to these many discoveries of sources relating to the Ōuchi, and to advances in scholarship, the Ōuchi story can be told.

The Structure of This Book

The depth of coverage varies among chapters. The first chapter covers centuries, but the later ones cover decades, with the span of years ranging from fifteen to fifty. Chapter 1 provides an overview of the Tatara, who immigrated to Japan by, at the very latest, the seventh century, and recounts conflicts among competing lineages through the mid-fourteenth century. Chapter 2 explores the rise of Ōuchi Hiroyo, who overshadowed his competing relatives. He conquered the province of Nagato, established control over the strategic Straits of Shimonoseki, and seized important mines. Yoshihiro, a noted general, was closest to the court and the Ashikaga. He also reached out to Korea to learn about Ōuchi identity, claimed descent from Paekche kings, and died attacking Ashikaga Yoshimitsu (chapter 3). Moriakira (chapter 4), oversaw trade with Korea as well as innovations in mining, and appropriated what had been national shrines. The short rule of three brothers brought turmoil but also increasing trade and institutionalization of Ōuchi rule (chapter 5).

Norihiro amassed great wealth and ultimately attempted to create his own warrior government in the west (chapter 6). As a result of his ambitions, a decade-long war broke out between his son and the forces of Ashikaga Yoshimasa. Masahiro, Norihiro's son, fought in the capital for over a decade. He abandoned his father's dreams of establishing an independent warrior regime but made Yamaguchi the de facto capital of Japan and ensured that

---

[42] Suegara Yutaka, ed., *Kyōto gosho Higashiyama gobunko shozō Jige monjo* (Yagi shoten, 2009).

his father's deification (chapter 7). Masahiro's son Yoshioki sheltered an Ashikaga shogun ousted in a coup and advanced to the capital, restoring order there for a decade. By the time he departed in 1518, he had transferred Japan's most sacred shrines to Yamaguchi and also seized the King of Japan seals of the Ashikaga, which allowed him to monopolize the China trade (chapter 8). The rule of Yoshitaka (chapter 9), who oversaw a trading empire and experienced the zenith of Ōuchi power, is covered at the greatest length. There follow the six years of his successor, Yoshinaga (chapter 10), and the ten-day rebellion by Yoshiteru in 1569 (epilogue). The final two chapters show that the year 1551 was a year of rupture: the beginning of the end for the Ōuchi organization, and a period coinciding with the onset of Japan's descent into "Warring States."

The endpoint of Ōuchi rule, 1569, came as this spasm of political violence began to recede. During the previous year, Oda Nobunaga had entered Kyoto and embarked upon a radical transformation of Japan, one continued by his successor Toyotomi Hideyoshi. Nobunaga, Hideyoshi, and Tokugawa Ieyasu, the last of whom established a warrior government in 1603, live on in historical memory and consciousness, and so have supplanted memories of what existed before. For example, while the Kenkun shrine in the Funaoka area of contemporary Kyoto is devoted to Oda Nobunaga, behind it, fenced off from visitors, there is sanctuary dedicated to Myōken. Worshiped there by the Ōuchi, it harks back to a time now obscured by later writings on "unification" and warrior rule.

1

The Origins of the Ōuchi

Waves of immigrants fled the internecine wars on the Korean peninsula to the islands of the Japanese archipelago. Among them were refugees from Kaya (J. Mimana), a region at south-central tip of the peninsula, bordering the Nakdong River, that is rich in iron ore deposits. Here, settlements of skilled iron workers and weapon makers gained wealth and influence, trading in objects coming from as far away as the Black Sea.[1] By the turn of the fifth century, they came under increasing pressure from two nearby states, Silla and Paekche, and their polity ceased to exist in the sixth. Many fled to the seas, whose currents brought them to a fertile and mineral-rich archipelago.

Travel was easy enough, as currents allowed for anyone setting out from the ports on the south of the Korean peninsula to reach the islands, later known as Japan. Linguistically, the inhabitants of the peninsula and the Japanese archipelago spoke similar languages, described by some as Peninsular Japonic and Insular Japonic.[2] In these early centuries, people from both regions would most likely have understood each other.

The Yamato polity, which dominated the islands, had long traded for Kaya iron.[3] Metalworkers in turn traveled to the Japanese isles, maintaining distinctive settlements in the western reaches of Honshu from the fifth through seventh centuries. They landed on the western tip of the main Japanese island of Honshu, an area rich in copper and iron ores. Miners would gravitate to

---

[1] Mark Byington, *Early Korea: The Rediscovery of Kaya in History and Archaeology* (Cambridge, MA: Korea Institute, Harvard University, 2012), pp. 125, 141, 152–55. See also C. Aikins, Gina Barnes, and Song-nai Rhee, *Archaeology and History of Toraijin: Human, Technical, and Cultural Flow from the Korean Peninsula to the Japanese Archipelago c. 800 BC–AD 600* (Oxford: Archaeopress Publishing, 2021), pp. 102–4.

[2] See, for example, Alexander Vovin, "Origins of the Japanese Language," in *Oxford Research Encyclopedia: Linguistics* (2017) (accessed 11.13.2019), https://oxfordre.com/linguistics/view/10.1093/acrefore/9780199384655.001.0001/acrefore-9780199384655-e-277.

[3] Pankaj Mohan, "The Controversy over the Ancient Korean State of Gaya [Kaya]: A Fresh Look at the Korea–Japan History War," in *"History Wars" and Reconciliation in Japan and Korea: The Roles of Historians, Artists and Activists* (Palgrave Macmillan US, 2016), p. 111.

Kings in All but Name. Thomas D. Conlan, Oxford University Press. © Oxford University Press 2024.
DOI: 10.1093/oso/9780197677339.003.0002

Japan because of these rich deposits of ore but maintain their continental customs.[4] Telling evidence comes from a settlement of metalworkers, specializing in copper, who left behind artifacts unique to the Korean peninsula.[5]

One such immigrant group, the Tatara from Kaya, crossed 120 miles of sea sometime during the fifth through seventh centuries.[6] Little is known about them, but the name Tatara means "bellows" and suggests involvement in metallurgy. They settled in a variety of locales along Japan's Inland Sea or in central Japan, in the vicinity of the capital, where metalworkers were in demand.[7]

The province of Suō, located in western Honshu, was a popular area for these immigrants. A seventh-century Chinese envoy commented on how "civilized" the region of Suō was, referring to its awareness of continental cultural norms, in contrast to other regions of Japan.[8] The Tatara of Suō prospered, and some became low-ranking provincial officials.

An influential group settled in the harbors of Kudamatsu and Sabaryō on the Inland Sea, where they worshiped the North Star bodhisattva Myōken, a cult they presumably brought with them, but which also was widely shared throughout East Asia, including the archipelago.[9]

Some Tatara later settled inland in the Yoshiki district of Suō at a place known as Ōuchi. Although they temporarily favored an alternate site after 1309, when they were employed as functionaries in the capital, they returned to the Ōuchi region in 1333. There they worshiped their own shrine dedicated to Myōken, only to see it burned by their more powerful Tatara relatives in 1341. This chapter recounts the origins and rivalries of these groups over control of religious institutions.

This study of the Tatara and their rise to power reveals several truths that are misunderstood in most narratives of Japanese history. The first is that the

---

[4] One settlement, that of Kokushū, was inhabited by miners from Korea. Activity there reached a peak during the fifth through the seventh and eighth centuries, then suddenly declined.

[5] See http://www.y-maibun.jp/2015/04/ for reference to an earthenware cup, manufactured in Silla, that was discovered at the Kokushū site.

[6] See Saeki Arikiyo, *Shinsen Shōjiroku no kenkyū*, 10 vols. (Yoshikawa kōbunkan, 2001), *Honbunhen* (vol. 1), p. 311, and *Ju'i hen* (vol. 10), pp. 262–64, and Ōta Akira, *Seishi kakei daijiten*, 3 vols. (1934), vol. 2, pp. 3474–75.

[7] Tatara also resided in Sanuki and Iyo of Shikoku, and Iga. For an excellent overview of this source and the Tatara, see Mori Shigeaki, "Ōuchi shi no kōryū to sosen denju," *Yamaguchi kenshi kenkyū* 11 (3.2003), pp. 106–7.

[8] Ichihara Michihiro, *Shintei Gishi Wajinden* (Iwanami bunko, 1994), p. 71, and Ryūsaku Tsunoda, *Japan in the Chinese Dynastic Histories: Later Han through Ming Dynasties*, ed. L. Carrington Goodrich (South Pasadena, CA: Perkins, 1951), p. 32.

[9] The North Star itself is prominently displayed in the wall paintings found in tombs such as Takamatsu, which date from the seventh century.

Japanese polity tolerated multiethnicity, in that not all its inhabitants, or even its most exalted and powerful ones, needed to claim they were "Japanese." The second point, particularly true for western Japan, is that wealth did not simply stem from agriculture, but depended greatly on mining and trade. Finally, for the early Tatara authority was intensely personal, and not invariably dependent upon institutional prerogatives. Ties were forged and maintained through the creation and repeated performance of religious rites, which formed the bedrock of their authority, although they were capable of effectively mobilizing and relying on military force as well.

During the seventh and eighth centuries, the Japanese archipelago was governed by a powerful administrative state, which organized its territory into distinct units and collected varied taxes. The population of Japan expanded as waves of immigrants arrived on its shores.

Until the latter half of the seventh century Korea was composed of three competing kingdoms. During that century, two of the three Korean states, including Koguryŏ, located in the north, and Paekche, located in the southwest, collapsed. Only the state of Silla in the southeast survived. Most immigrants to Japan were from the state of Paekche, or from the old Kaya lands, but refugees came from other regions as well.

An ill-fated attempt to restore Paekche resulted in disaster for the Yamato polity in 663, when its forces were decimated along with Paekche remnants at the Battle of Paekchon River. The institutions and finances of the Yamato state were reorganized, and these far-reaching transformations were accompanied by changes in dress and diet.[10] At this time, the King of Yamato took the title of Emperor (*tennō*) of Japan, portraying the two defunct kingdoms of Koguryŏ and Paekche as tributary states of Japan, and according privileges to immigrants from these states to encourage them to support this notion.[11] Although the notion represents a legal fiction of sorts, it also established as a fundamental principle that Japan was not a monolithic ethnic state but rather a multiethnic polity, composed of residents from Yamato as well as refugees from Paekche and Koguryŏ.

The most exalted of the immigrant families, descendants of the crown prince of Paekche, telegraphed their royal origins with the name Kudara no Konikishi ("The Kingly House of Paekche"), and they initially settled in the

---

[10] See Bruce Batten, "Foreign Threat and Domestic Reform: The Emergence of the Ritsuryō State," *Monumenta Nipponica* 41.2 (Summer 1986), pp. 199–219, and Yoshikawa Shinji, "Tenmu jūnenkan no tenkan," in *Asuka no Miyako* (Iwanami shoten, 2011), pp. 142–55.

[11] Torquil Duthie, *Man'yōshū and the Imperial Imagination in Early Japan* (Leiden: Brill, 2014), pp. 49–56 ff.

Naniwa (Ōsaka) region. Over the course of a century this family gained appointment to provincial governor posts. They notably appear in the historical record in 749, for Kudara no Konikishi Kyōfuku (697–776) was governor of Mutsu when gold was discovered there.[12] Likewise, this family found great favor during the reign of Emperor Kanmu (737–806, r. 781–806).[13] Some members of this family maintained this prestigious name for centuries. In the case of the province of Suō, as late as 1.28.997 a deputy governor, upper sixth rank, was named Kudara no Konikishi Tametaka.[14]

A wooden slip (*mokkan*) excavated from the site of the Suō provincial headquarters contains a reference to Tatara *no kimi* Ite, a local official (*zaichō kanjin*). This Ite's *kabane* rank of "*kimi*" was lower than the *ōmi* or *muraji* of the greatest families.[15] Nothing more is known of him, but a certain Tatara *no kimi* Okihito seems to have had a connection with Tōdaiji, for he appears several times in their documents, and can be documented as copying records in 748, when he was forty years old. The near contemporaneous existence of Tatara with the same *kabane* rank of *kimi* reveals that this line was tied to Tōdaiji and was connected to both Suō and the capital region.[16] Such a connection is unsurprising because the Naganobori mine in Nagato, located to the west of Suō, had such rich ore deposits that it became the primary source for the nearly 490 tons (739,560 *kin*) of copper used between 745 and 752 to cast the Great Buddha of Tōdaiji.[17]

---

[12] *Shoku Nihongi*, Sixth month Tenpyō-jingo 2 (776), for the obituary of Kudara no Konikishi Kyōfuku.

[13] Nadia Kanagawa, "Making the Realm, Transforming the People: Foreign Subjects in Seventh-through Ninth-Century Japan," PhD dissertation, University of Southern California, 2019, pp. 123–27, 194–98, 234.

[14] *Yamaguchi kenshi shiryōhen kodai* (Yamaguchi, 2001), docs. 758–59, pp. 334–35 of 997 (Chōtoku 3). See also Ueno Toshizō, "'Kudara ōke Mimatsu shi keizu' no shiryō kachi ni tsuite," *Ritsuryō jidai no kikajin no kisoteki kenkyū* (Keiō daigaku hōgakubu, 10.1983), pp. 385–407.

[15] *Hōfu shishi tsūshi* I *Genshi kodai chūsei* (Hōfu shishi hensan iinkai, comp. Hōfu shi, 2004), p. 232. For photos and analysis of this *mokkan*, see Yanagi Tomoko, "Nisennen shutsudo no mokkan: Yamaguchi Suō kokufu no ato," *Mokkan kenkyū*, no. 23 (11.2001), pp. 145–48. All the early Tatara maintained the rank (*kabane*) of *kimi*. *Kabane* were hereditary noble titles that denoted rank and standing. They were revised during the sixth and seventh centuries, and gradually faded from use during the ninth and tenth centuries.

[16] A search of the Historiographical Institute Database (4.17.2015) reveals that Okihito's name appears five times. *Dainihon komonjo hennen monjo*, 25 vols. (Tōkyō daigaku shuppankai, 1901–40), vol. 9, p. 39, mentions Okihito being forty years old on 1.17 Tenpyō 20 (748), and copying sutras early in the first through the fourth months of that year. See also *Dainihon komonjo hennen monjo*, vol. 3, pp. 69, 152, and vol. 10, pp. 1–2. He is also documented as neglecting these duties for nine consecutive months twice. See *Dainihon komonjo hennen monjo*, vol. 24, p. 520, and, for the last reference dating from 752 (Tenpyō shōhō 4), *Dainihon komonjo hennen monjo*, vol. 12, p. 376.

[17] This is according to the "Hitsuden" section written by the monk Kangon, in Tsutsui Eshun, ed., *Tōdaiji yōroku* (Ōsaka: Zenkoku shobō, 1944), pp. 34–35. The figures were calculated based on the

By the year 799, confusion became so commonplace throughout Japan regarding the genealogies and perceived origins of many families, in particular immigrant groups, that they were required to submit their genealogies to the court for inspection.[18] The *Shinsen shōjiroku* (*New Record of Hereditary Titles and Familial Names*), a genealogical compendium, was created and presented to Emperor Saga (786–842, r. 809–823) in 815 so as to prevent falsehoods and errors from creeping into familial histories and genealogies.[19] The Tatara were listed, one of only nine families hailing from Kaya (J. Mimana).[20] The creation of the *Shinsen shōjiroku* coincided with a period of great linguistic changes in Korea, as Peninsular Japonic would die out in the ninth century, making communication between Korea and Japan more difficult than before.[21]

At some time, the Tatara of Suō confused their origins, forgetting that they came from Kaya, and instead coming to believe that they were descended from the Kingly House of Paekche. The Tatara would have known of the Kingly House of Paekche as they had resided in Suō while a certain Kudara no Konikishi Tametaka served as a deputy governor of that province, but they had no apparent connection to this illustrious house. This garbled memory would linger in the absence of any supporting evidence and despite the contradictory claims of the *Shinsen shōjiroku*.

A 908 register of the inhabitants of Kuga district, in the far eastern part of the province of Suō, some thirty miles east of the provincial headquarters, lists a certain Tatara *no kimi* Akio, aged sixty-six.[22] Akio almost certainly was related to Tatara *no kimi* Ite and Okihito, since he had the same surname and rank (*kabane*), although the two surnames were written in different characters. This was one of the last times that their *kabane* rank of *kimi*

---

fact that one *kin* equals six hundred grams. For more on the Naganobori mine, see Ikeda Yoshifumi, "Kodai no Mine," in *Mitōchō shi Tsūshi hen* (Mitō-chō, 2004), pp. 72–90.

[18] Kanagawa, "Making the Realm," pp. 199–205.

[19] For more on this source, see Michael Como, "Immigrant Gods on the Road to Jindō," in Bernard Faure, Michael Como, and Iyanaga Nobumi, eds., "Rethinking Medieval Shintō," *Cahiers d'Extrême-Asie* 16 (2009), pp. 25–28, and Torquil Duthie, *Man'yōshū and the Imperial Imagination in Early Japan* (Leiden: Brill, 2014), pp. 77–78.

[20] Of the 326 families of foreign origin recorded in this source, 163 were from China, 104 from Paekche, 41 from Koguryŏ, 9 from Silla, and 9 from Kaya.

[21] See, for example, Alexander Vovin, "Origins of the Japanese Language" in the *Oxford Research Encyclopedia: Linguistics* (2017) (accessed 11.13.2019), https://oxfordre.com/linguistics/view/10.1093/acrefore/9780199384655.001.0001/acrefore-9780199384655-e-277.

[22] *Heian ibun*, vol. 1, doc. 199, 908 (Engi 8) Suō no kuni Kuga gō *koseki*, 289–305. See p. 293 for reference to the "ancient" Tatara Kin'aki, aged sixty-six. For more on this document, Suō no kuni kuga gun kuga gō *engi hachinen koseki zankan*, see Ōta Akira, *Seishi kakei daijiten*, pp. 3474–75.

was used for them. The next record comes from 1152 and suggests some official connection to Tōdaiji, for several individuals named Tatara added their monogram to a document concerning Tōdaiji affairs.[23]

Over the course of the twelfth century, the most prominent members of the Tatara lineage in Suō resided at Washizu estate in Kudamatsu, a site fifteen miles southwest of Kuga.[24] Kudamatsu was an important site for mariners on the Inland Sea, for a certain Washizu (Eagle Head) mountain, a far steeper and more difficult climb than its 243-meter height would imply, looms over the coast and serves as an important navigation marker.

The beaches in front of Washizu Mountain were known as Kudamatsu. A shrine dedicated to Myōken was apparently founded in the seventh century, during the reign of Suiko (554–628, r. 592–628), but the mountain has yet to be excavated, although old traces of pottery exist on the mountain and probably predate the fifteenth century, when the shrine can be documented as being reconstructed.[25] This area would become the site of Myōken worship starting from the time that the Tatara resided in this region, or sometime during the ensuing decades.[26]

Star Cults and Myōken

Stars, and particularly comets and meteors, have inspired worship. Meteors were thought to be messengers of the stars, and the materials from meteors

[23] *Heian ibun*, vol. 6, doc. 2763, 8.1.1152 (Ninpei 2) Suō no kuni *zaichōkanjin kudashibumi*, pp. 2295–96. The Tatara name appears twice, once with a monogram, on p. 2296. See also *Yamaguchi kenshi shiryōhen kodai*, doc. 1318, p. 610.

[24] Wada Shūsaku, "Ōuchi shi no sōsho kankei o megutte," in Kage Toshio, ed., *Ōuchi to Ōtomo: Chūsei nishi Nihon no nidai daimyō* (Bensei shuppan, 2013), pp. 51–52. See also his "Chūsei no Washizu shi ni tsuite," *Kudamatsu chihōshi kenkyū* 50 (4.2014): 3–26.

[25] On 6.8.2015, the author climbed this mountain and discovered *hajiki* pottery fragments that date from the medieval period. A greater antiquity is quite possible but currently unknowable. This shrine was rebuilt in 1478 by Ōuchi Masahiro. See Wada Shūsaku, "Ōuchi shi no sōsho kankei o megutte," pp. 51–52. See also Nakatsuka Ken'ichi, "Ōuchi tōshugawa kinsō no keisei to tenkai," in Kage Toshio, *Ōuchi to Ōtomo*, p. 118. For a summary of the Ōuchi Myōken cult in English, see Bernard Faure, *The Fluid Pantheon: Gods of Medieval Japan*, vol. 1 (Honolulu: University of Hawaii Press, 2016), p. 71.

[26] The pronunciation of Kudamatsu recalls the Japanese name for Paekche (Kudara), and this may explain why descendants from the Mimana region would later make such claims about their descent from this kingdom. See *Kadokawa Nihon chimei daijiten, Yamaguchi*, "Tatarahama," Japan Knowledge (accessed 12.11.2013). These myths are difficult to decipher, as the oldest source, the *Rokuonin Saikoku gekōki*, has been shown by Mori Shigeaki to date from 1479. See Mori Shigeaki, "Ōuchi shi no kōryū to sosen denju," p. 100. A 1486 Ōuchi genealogy, which makes these claims, appears in Yamaguchi kenshi hensanshitsu, comp., *Yamaguchi kenshi shiryōhen chūsei*, 4 vols. (Yamaguchi, 1996–2008), vol. 1, p. 740. Wada Shūsaku, "Ōuchi shi no sōsho kankei o megutte," pp. 28–29.

were carefully polished into swords. Chou Dynasty swords exist that were made from meteorites; as Edward Schafer recognized, "Since the Chinese believed that meteors were star messengers, each with its unique message and that usually of war, the natural destiny of a meteor was to take the shape of a sword of power."[27] This concept was transmitted to Japan, for one sword found in the Shōsōin repository prominently displays the seven stars of the Big Dipper.

The fact that the two outer stars of the bowl of the Big Dipper point to the North Star caused this constellation, and Polaris, the North Star itself, to attract worship. Polaris is the key referential star, as it does not rotate in the heavens, but rather sits to the north. This makes it the most important of the fifty-seven navigation stars that are readily visible with a magnitude of one to three in the night sky. Polaris has held this position for the past fourteen thousand years, when it supplanted the star Vega, which previously would have been the North Star visible from the earth.[28]

The North or Pole Star, widely venerated in East Asia, came to be seen in the Buddhist world as the bodhisattva Myōken, although Myōken was also linked to the seven stars of the Big Dipper and to Alcor, a barely visible double star located in the handle of the Big Dipper star known as *hosei*, the auxiliary star.[29] As Alcor is not a well-known star, and the whole constellation is linked to the North Star, Myōken will be described as the North Star throughout this manuscript.

In esoteric Buddhism Myōken became a protector deity of the state and was worshiped in a number of guises and under various names, including Sonjō-ō (Venerable Star King).[30] Outside the Buddhist realm, this deity was also known as Chintaku Reifujin and was linked to one of Japan's oldest gods, Ame no Minaka Nushi no Kami.[31] Scholars studying images of this deity have noted that Chintaku Reifujin closely resembles the Daoist Zhengwu Dadi, making it a "composite deity," with all forms loosely linked to the North

---

[27] Allan Grapard, *Mountain Mandalas: Shugendō in Kyushu* (New York: Bloomsbury, 2016), p. 108, and Edward Schafer, *Pacing the Void* (Berkeley: University of California Press, 1977), pp. 103, 148–59.
[28] Vega will again become the North Star in twelve thousand years.
[29] Faure, *The Fluid Pantheon*, pp. 64–65 for Myōken's association with the North Star, Big Dipper, and Alcor (J. *hosei*, Ch. *fuxing*).
[30] For more on astral worship, see Lucia Dolce, "The Worship of Celestial Bodies in Japan: Politics, Rituals, and Icons," *Culture and Cosmos: A Journal of the History of Astrology and Cultural Astronomy* 10.1–2) (2006), pp. 12–17. See also Hayashi On, "Myōken Bosatsu," *Myōken Bosatsu to hoshi mandara. Nihon no bijutsu*, no. 377 (Chibundō, 1997), pp. 48–51, and Faure, *The Fluid Pantheon*.
[31] Yoshihiro Nikaidō, "Cultural Interaction: Myōken Bosatsu and the God Zhenwu," in *Asian Folk Religion and Cultural Interaction* (Göttingen: Vandenhoech & Ruprecht, 10.2015), pp. 115–16.

Star.[32] Some scholars have indeed described Myōken as "essentially a Daoist deity in Buddhist garb."[33]

Although images of Myōken as a martial deity were linked to thirteenth-century Chinese iconography, the cult itself proved far older. Myōken was widely spread throughout East Asia, and ships from Southern China, which sometimes arrived in Japan, had an image of the North Star carved into the joint of the main beam of the ship.[34] Myōken had obvious links to navigation, and other lore suggests that worship of the stars aided one's fortunes in battle. Allegedly, one warrior went so far as to name seven moles on his arm after the seven stars of the Big Dipper, attributing his skill in archery and good luck in avoiding injury on the battlefield to these marks.[35]

By the twelfth century, and around the time the Tatara adopted Kudamatsu as their core territory, if not before, the North Star became their ancestral deity.[36] Certainly people widely worshiped the North Star and tended to amalgamate these various forms. The geography of Kudamatsu, with its Washizu Mountain being so important to navigation, suggests that Tatara consolidation of this region coincided with the rise of syncretic North Star worship.

Three Tatara Lineages in Suō

By establishing Kudamatsu as their chief residence, the Tatara also emphasized their ties to central Japan, as Kudamatsu would be the first stopping point in Suō for a boat coming from the capital. Unsurprisingly, these

---

[32] Nikaidō, "Cultural Interaction," p. 121. For his notion of a composite deity, see p. 128. For more on the resemblance to Zhenwu, see Hirase Naoki, *Ōuchi shi no ryōgoku shihai to shūkyō* (Hanawa shobō, 2017), pp. 277–79.

[33] Faure, *The Fluid Pantheon*, p. 60.

[34] For evidence of this see Yiwen Li, "Networks of Profit and Faith: Spanning the Sea of Japan and the East China Sea, 838–1403," PhD dissertation, Yale University, 2017, p. 174, and Yamagata Kinya, *Rekishi no umi o hashiru: Chūgoku zōsen gijutsu no kōseki* (Nōsan gyoson bunka kyōkai, 2004), pp. 182–86.

[35] *Gukanshō*, in Okami Masao and Akamatsu Toshihide, eds., *Nihon koten bungaku taikei* (Iwanami shoten, 1967), p. 222. For an English translation, see Delmer Brown, trans., *The Future and the Past: Translation and Study of the Gukanshō* (Berkeley: University of California Press, 1979), p. 103. In this passage from 1220, a Kyushu warrior named Shigesada explained that his ability to accurately shoot Fujiwara Yorinaga, a famous rebel of the 1156 Hōgen Disturbance, and remain protected in war came from these seven moles that represented seven stars (*nanatsu hoshi*).

[36] Hirase Naoki, *Ōuchi shi no ryōgoku shihai to shūkyō*, p. 15, argues, however, for the difficulty in ascertaining an exact timeline of Myōken worship.

links led to new attention from the center, something not always welcome, for in 1178, four members of the Tatara family, led by a certain Moriyasu, were accused of an attempted coup against Taira no Kiyomori (1118–81).[37] Kiyomori had been a client of the sovereign (*chiten no kimi*) Go-Shirakawa (1127–92), but after an attempted assassination attempt in 1177, he engineered an attempt to oust Go-Shirakawa from power, which he accomplished in a coup in 1179. The fact that Moriyasu and his companions were banished, and later pardoned, attests to their local significance, which caused them to gain the attention of people at the court.

Perhaps unsurprisingly, when a civil war erupted, fought nominally between the supporters of the Taira and their Minamoto rivals (the Genpei war, 1180–85), Tatara Moriyasu took it upon himself to assert local authority as an acting deputy governor of Suō, for he signed a document with the title Tatara *gon no suke*, which implied that he was the acting deputy of the province, a title that was commonly asserted rather than appointed.[38]

The Taira happened to have a stronger base in the west, but because of Moriyasu's earlier banishment, the Tatara of Suō turned against them quite early, and distinguished themselves as one of two prominent families from the west to do so. Although the original documents do not survive, one can infer from reliable references that some personally received edicts from Minamoto Yoritomo, which would have meant that they had gained formal rights to their lands in Kudamatsu.[39]

Yoritomo gained power by attacking central authority and establishing the post of *jitō*, which was a durable right to the land. Yoritomo mostly rewarded warriors in the east, close to where he was rebelling. He rarely issued such edicts for western warriors. Hence the Tatara prized the fact that they had a

---

[37] *Gyokuyō*, 10.8.1178 (Jishō 2) in *Yamaguchi kenshi shiryōhen kodai*, doc. 1449, pp. 689–90. Wada Shūsaku has explained how Moriyasu was the most prominent member of the Tatara lineage at this time. See "Ōuchi shi no sōsho kankei o megutte," pp. 51–52, and Wada Shūsaku, "Chūsei no Washizu shi ni tsuite."

[38] *Heian ibun*, vol. 8, doc. 4023, 4.28.1182 (Yōwa 2) Nodera Sō Benkai *mōshijō an*, pp. 3059–62, and *Yamaguchi kenshi shiryōhen kodai*, doc. 1469, Nodera Sō Benkei *mōshijō an*, pp. 707–710. Hirase Naoki explains how other mid-twelfth-century warriors adopted the title of *suke* in his *Ōuchi Yoshihiro* (Minerva shobō, 2017), pp. 11–12.

[39] A fragmentary judicial document, adjudicated by Kamakura, refers to the Ōuchi as receiving lands since the time of Yoritomo. *Kamakura ibun*, vol. 24, Shō-ō (1288–93) Kantō *gechijō an*, pp. 36–37. It is not clear who received the edicts. One written in the 1540s stated that the individual was Mitsumori. See Conlan, "Shiryō shōkai: Yoshida Kanemigi ga utsushita Ōuchi keizu," *Yamaguchi kenshi kenkyū* 21 (3.2013), pp. 65–70. Others claim that a certain Hiromori and Morifusa received the edict. See *Yamaguchi shishi shiryōhen Ōuchi bunka* (Yamaguchi, 2010) (hereafter *Ōuchi bunka*), pp. 16–18 and 22. For reference to the Kōno family likewise receiving Yoritomo's edicts, the *Yoshōki*, *Gunsho ruijū*, vol. 21, *Kassenbu*, p. 520. The copied documents in this genealogy are relatively reliable.

personal connection with the victorious Yoritomo. One of their genealogies claims that a certain Mitsumori received a letter "in Yoritomo's hand," but further information about this person and his exact relationship to Yoritomo remains unclear.[40] One can find, however, a reference in the *Azuma kagami* to a document dated the second month of 1187 written by thirteen local officials (*zaichō kanjin*) of Suō, the most illustrious of whom, a certain *gon no suke* Tatara *sukune*, can be verified as being in the capital of Kyoto at the time.[41] Siding so quickly with the ultimate victor in the civil war, well before their compatriots, won the Tatara considerable rewards. In addition to consolidating their control over Kudamatsu, they received at least two other lands, each of which would become a core holding of one of three distinct branches of their lineage (Figure 1.1).

A document dating from 1294 provides a clear sense of the Tatara holdings. In addition to the Washizu, it refers to the *jitō* post at Sabaryō, which is on the coast of the Inland Sea, some twenty miles to the west of Kudamatsu. Sabaryō was an important locale, and site of the Suō provincial headquarters. Another *jitō* post was at a place called Ōuchi, located inland some ten miles northwest of Tatara and slightly over thirty miles northwest of Washizu.[42] A fourth estate, that of Yokoyama, was also granted to Tatara Hiromori because of his service against the Taira.[43]

As early as 1192, tension appears to have existed among the brothers and nephews who had received or inherited *jitō* posts after the Genpei wars. The *jitō* office entailed the right to manage territory and was the most desirable and unassailable of all land rights at the time. One major event of that war was the Taira burning Tōdaiji. It influenced the Tatara in Suō. The main line, at Kudamatsu, sided with Tōdaiji and demanded that Hiromori, of a branch lineage of Tatara,

[40] If this had occurred, the mostly likely candidate would be the Washizu main Ōuchi heir Moriyasu, who had been exiled to Izu. See *Ōuchi bunka*, p. 18 for the claims regarding Mitsumori. See also p. 22 for reference to a phonetically written (*kana*) letter in Yoritomo's hand, and confusion concerning whether he "received" Nagato during the 1180s or the 1221 Jōkyū War.

[41] *Yamaguchi kenshi shiryōhen chūsei*, vol. 1, Azuma kagami, 3.1.1187 (Bunji 3), pp. 494–95. A mere five years later, one sees the dominant Ōuchi being referred to as Ōuchi *no suke*, a sign that they started preferring another surname. See *Yamaguchi kenshi shiryōhen chūsei*, vol. 1, Azuma kagami, 1.19.1192 (Kenkyū 3), p. 499.

[42] See the *Kadokawa Nihon chimei daijiten*, Kudamatsu, Washizu, accessed from the Japan Knowledge and *Kamakura ibun*, vol. 24, doc. 18673, 10.10–13.1294 (Einin 2) Hōjō Sanemasa *shigyōjō an*, p. 195.

[43] Miyata Itsumi, "Hironaka shi ni tsuite," in Iwakuni-shi Kyōiku iinkai, comp., *Nakatsu kyokan ato II* (Iwakuni-shi, 2016), pp. 78–79. For analysis of Ōuchi landholdings of the Tatara, see Hirase Naoki, "Nanbokuchō ki Ōuchi shi ni miru chiiki shakai kenryoku no kakuritsu," *Kamakura ibun kenkyū*, no. 34 (10.2014), pp. 41–56, pp. 43–44 for Tatara (Ōuchi) holdings in the Kamakura era, including Yokoyama. This roster appears in *Tōdaiji monjo*, doc. 1-24-211 and in *Yamaguchi shishi shiryōhen chūsei* (Yamaguchi, 2016), doc. 108, p. 125.

Figure 1.1 Map of Notable Sites in Suō Province. 1. Kudamatsu, 2. Sabaryō (Hōfu), 3. Hiraijō, 4. Yokoyama, 5. Ōuchi (Yoshiki district), 6. Shōgoji.

provide timber for the reconstruction of the temple.[44] Ultimately, Hiromori acquiesced and signed an oath that served to strengthen the authority of the Tatara chieftains, but Hiromori seems to have here favored the name "Ōuchi," which was a region within the Yoshiki district of Suō.[45] The oldest use of the Ōuchi surname dates from this time in 1192.[46]

The most powerful Tatara lineages controlled the sites of Kudamatsu and Sabaryō on the coast. Kudamatsu, the headquarters for the Washizu, was where Myōken, the ancestral deity of the Tatara, was worshiped. Sabaryō, currently known as Hōfu, is located on the coast. There, close to the Suō provincial headquarters, a mounded keyhole-style tomb survives. Known to posterity as Kuruma-zuka, it constituted the tomb of a powerful local figure of whom little is known.[47] Very few artifacts exist for this tomb, making an accurate dating impossible, but it seems most likely that this tomb, with its very unusual large anterior chamber, dates from the mid- to late seventh century.[48] It was the easternmost tomb of a type that resembled others along the Inland Sea, suggestive of the significance of the deceased in linking Kyushu, Central Japan (the Kinai), and the Inland Sea.[49] Tatarahama, or Tatara beach, located here, became remembered in the fifteenth to sixteenth centuries as the site where the Tatara landed in Japan, while the mound became associated with the immigrant ancestor of the Tatara.[50] The Tatara activity broadly resembled that of other families, such as the Masuda, who emphasized the clan name of Mikamoto to emphasize the direct descent from the gods of the main line of their lineage.[51]

[44] *Yamaguchi kenshi shiryōhen chūsei*, vol. 1, Azuma kagami, 1.19.1192 (Kenkyū 3), p. 499. Hiromori was counted as an Ōuchi progenitor. See Conlan, "Shiryō shōkai," pp. 66, 68.

[45] *Kamakura ibun*, vol. 2, p. 405, doc. 1163, 11.1200 (Shōji 2) Suō no kuni *zachōkanjin okibumi*, pp. 405–10, and docs. 1164–65, pp. 410–22. See also *Yamaguchi kenshi shiryōhen chūsei*, vol. 2, Amidaji monjo, doc. 30, 7.19.1480 (Bunmei 12) Suō no kuni *mokudai zaichō kanjin okibumi an narabini mokudai* [Sanemasa] *okugaki*, pp. 355–56.

[46] *Yamaguchi kenshi shiryōhen chūsei*, vol. 1, Azuma kagami, 1.19.1192 (Kenkyū 3), p. 499, first refers to an Ōuchi *no suke*, a sign that some Tatara started preferring this surname.

[47] For this characterization, see *Hōfu shishi shiryōhen II Kōko shiryō* (Hōfu shishi hensan iinkai, comp., Hōfu, 2004), pp. 110–13.

[48] *Hōfu shishi tsūshi I Genshi kodai chūsei*, p. 39.

[49] *Hōfu shishi tsūshi I*, pp. 37–39, and for the significance of the buried individual, *Hōfu shishi shiryōhen II Kōko shiryō*, pp. 110–13

[50] Tatara remained significant enough to the Ōuchi that the final lord Yoshinaga would land here in an attempt to replicate the actions of his ancestor. See Suda Makiko, *Chūsei nichō kankei to Ōuchi shi* (Tōkyō daigaku shuppan, 2011), p. 235, and *Chūgoku chiranki, Shinkō Gunsho ruijū*, vol. 17 (Naigai kabushiki kaisha, 1930), p. 440.

[51] Inoue Kenji, ed., *Shiryōshū Masuda Kanemi to sono jidai Masuda ke monjo ga kataru chūsei no Masuda* (Masuda, 1994), pp. 174–80 for the 8.10.1383 (Eitoku 3) Masuda Shōken *okibumi an*, and for more analysis, p. 183. See also Matsuoka Hisatō, comp., *Nanbokuchō ibun Chūgoku Shikoku hen*, 6 vols. (Tōkyōdō shuppan, 1987–95) (hereafter NBIC), vol. 6, doc. 4813, 8.10.1383 (Eitoku 3) Masuda

When the Tatara became separate families is not clearly known, but Wada Shūsaku has shown that as early as 1275 the main line of this lineage group started naming themselves Washizu. However, they also used the name Ōuchi, an apparent, albeit contested prerogative of the dominant Tatara lineages.[52] As late as 11.27.1289, the Washizu could expect to enforce their dominance over other branch lineages by requesting that they fund rites offered on their behalf. At that time, one styled Ōuchi Hiroie, of Sabaryō, commended two horses for memorial (*kuyō*) ceremonies at Amidaji on behalf of the head of the main (Washizu) line.[53] He demonstrated his fealty to the Washizu, although he still adopted the name Ōuchi. Eventually, however, the Sabaryō descendants would gain some autonomy from the Washizu. They adopted the name Migita, but would split again and constitute two families, the Migita and the Sue.[54]

The Ōuchi Region

The Ōuchi region of Yoshiki district in Suō was the least cultically significant site and the least desirable locale. In contrast to Sabaryō, with its Tatara beach, access to provincial headquarters, and grave mounds, and Kudamatsu, the site of Washizu Myōken shrine, the Ōuchi region possessed no important links to Tatara ancestry. Nevertheless, this south-facing area afforded easy access to the Inland Sea and the port areas of Sabaryō, some twenty miles distant, and Kudamatsu, which is logical based on Ōuchi origins and historical ties.

Ōuchi regional lore was prosaic, and later compilations of legend merely stressed the agricultural productivity of the area, and mention that the most

---

Shōken (Kanemi) *okibumi jōjō*, pp. 13–16. For the similarity to the Tatara, see Hirase Naoki, *Ōuchi Yoshihiro*, p. 14.

[52] Wada Shūsaku, "Chūsei no Washizu shi ni tsuite," p. 3. For the original documents, see Ebina Nao and Fukuda Toyohiko, "Shiryō shōkai: 'Rokujō Hachimangū *zōei chūmon*' ni tsuite," *Kokuritsu rekishi minzoku hakubutsukan kenkyū hōkoku*, 45 (12.1992), p. 387. This document, dating from the fifth month of 1275 (Kenji 1) refers to the legacy (*ato*) of Washizu Chikuzen *zenshi*. The Ōuchi *no suke* mentioned in this document was most likely Ōuchi Hironari.

[53] *Kamakura ibun*, vol. 21, doc. 16044, 11.27.1286 (Kōan 9) Ōuchi Hiroie *hōgajō*, pp. 160–61 and *Yamaguchi kenshi shiryōhen chūsei*, vol. 2, Amidaji monjo doc. 38, 11.27.1286 (Kōan 9) Ōuchi Hiro'ie *hōgajō*, p. 364.

[54] See Matsuoka, *Ōuchi shi no kenkyū*, pp. 53–54. The Migita would maintain lands in this region. For a sixteenth century roster of Migita Takatoshi's lands, see *Yamaguchi kenshi shiryōhen chūsei*, vol. 2, Kokubunji zō monjo, doc. 108, 4.27.1558 (Kōji 4) Migita Takatoshi *honryō tōchigyō sashidashi an*, pp. 432–33 and doc. 109, 6.2. Migita Takatoshi *fuchigyō chūmon*, p. 433.

notable object in the region was a massive cherry tree that many would enjoy on a spring day, as it was so wide that seventy or eighty mats (jō) could be spread out underneath its shade.[55]

Tatara Hirosada is the first identifiable Tatara with close ties to the Ōuchi area, for on 11.27.1257 he commissioned a bell for Kōryūji, a temple located in Ōuchi mihori, an area in Yoshiki district of some importance, as the name suggests that the region was surrounded by a moat, or contained irrigation canals.[56] This is one of the earliest references to what would become the lineage temple (ujidera) of the Ōuchi lords, but tellingly, at this time Hirosada did not use the Ōuchi name, which was the prerogative of the dominant Washizu lineage, and would remain so through the mid-fourteenth century.[57] Although Hirosada could not force the Migita or the Washizu to contribute to rituals that he had performed at his new temple of Kōryūji, he still had enough wealth to commission a bell for it.[58]

Hirosada's wealth, and that of his descendants, did not stem from the intrinsic wealth of their locale, but rather his ties to the capital. Hirosada served as a counselor (hyōjoshū) for the Rokuhara tandai, a judicial organ of Japan's warrior government, the Kamakura bakufu, a regime founded by Minamoto Yoritomo. The tandai, Kamakura's western appellate office, was established in 1221.[59] Surviving evidence suggests that a certain Hirosada had one of his retainers, Saigō Jirō, transmit an appeal by the court noble Nakanomikado Shōshō to Kamakura, where the suit was dismissed.[60] Hirosada's son Hiroie wrote to the Shōni, arguably the most powerful warrior family in northern Kyushu. Hiroie consulted with them concerning shrines and added monograms to wills to show Rokuhara's approval of a bequest.[61] Hirosada's

---

55 Bōchō fūdo chūshin an, vol. 12 Yamaguchi saiban jō (Yamaguchi, 1960), p. 341.

56 For the bell, see Ōuchi bunka, 11.27.1257 (Shōka 1), p. 858. Genealogies are opaque concerning the actual relationship of heirs of Hiromori. The sheer number of heirs between Hiromori, his son Mitsumori, and Hirosada suggests lateral succession among cousins or siblings. Conlan, "Shiryō shōkai," pp. 65–70.

57 Wada Shūsaku, "Ōuchi shi no sōsho kankei o megutte," pp. 28–29. Hirase Naoki too has argued that dominant members of this family adopted the title Ōuchi no suke which had links already to worship of Myōken. Hirase Naoki, "Muromachiki ni okeru Ōuchi shi no Myōken shinkō to sosen densetsu," Shirin 97.5 (9.2014), particularly pp. 35–51.

58 Ōuchi bunka, p. 858, and Wada Shūsaku, "Ōuchi shi no sōsho kankei o megutte," pp. 28–29.

59 Kamakura ibun, vol. 10, doc. 7368, 10.7.1251 (Kenchō 3) Rokuhara mikyōjo an, p. 269, and 12.13.1251 (Kenchō 3) Rokuhara mikyōjo an, p. 280. For the genealogical references to Ōuchi Shigehiro serving this function see Ōuchi bunka, pp. 8, 11–12. See also Matsuoka Hisatō, Ōuchi Yoshihiro (Jinbutsu ōraisha, 1966), pp. 41–44.

60 Kamakura ibun, vol. 11, doc. 8417, 10.18 [(Shōgen 1) 1259] Shōni Kagesuke shojō an, p. 362.

61 Kamakura ibun, vol. 10, doc. 7624, 10.13.1253 (Kenchō 5) Gen Yakushi kasane mōshijō, pp. 393–94 for reference to the Ōuchi monogramming a document, and vol. 21, doc. 16044, 11.27.1286 (Kōan 9) Ōuchi Hiroie hōkajō, pp. 160–61 for actual evidence of such a monogram. This document was signed with the surname Tatara. For examples of the new name Ōuchi no suke appearing in the Azuma

widow appears to have resided in Kyoto, and this connection contributed to the relative prosperity of what would otherwise be the most obscure Tatara lineage.[62]

Although the Washizu remained dominant in Suō, Hirosada's son Shigehiro gained power and influence because of his connection to Kyoto and the Rokuhara appellate office.[63] Documents dating from 1317–18 reveal that Shigehiro was involved in a dispute with the monks of Tōdaiji.[64] The points of contention concerned access to the important port at of Hyōgo, as well as tax levies for Tōdaiji. Shigehiro had apparently torched temple lands and "illegally" imprisoned monks, justifying his actions because of the need to fund court rituals (*kuge no chōgi*).[65] Because of his close links to Rokuhara, Shigehiro could readily transmit information and quickly appeal to Kamakura, and thus thwart any complaints.[66]

Little else is known about Shigehiro, save that in 1312, some eight years before his death, he founded Jōfukuji, one of the oldest Zen temples in the Ōuchi region.[67] He is also the first of his line that can explicitly be linked, through lore at least, to residing in the Ōuchi area of central Suō.[68]

Nevertheless, this area was not the inevitable, or even the preferred, site for his direct descendants, since in 1309 his son Hiroyuki founded Yōkōji, located twenty miles to the east of Kudamatsu, near the boundary of Suō and Aki provinces. By living there, Hiroyuki could travel directly to the

kagami, see *Yamaguchi kenshi shiryōhen chūsei*, vol. 1, Azuma kagami, 1.19.1192 (Kenkyū 3), p. 499, and 3.1.1250 (Kenchō 2), p. 502. For other references to their service in this body, see *Kamakura ibun*, vol. 10, doc. 7368, 10.7.1251 (Kenchō 3) Rokuhara *mikyōjo an*, p. 269, and 12.13.1251 (Kenchō 3) Rokuhara *mikyōjo an*, p. 280.

[62] *Kamakura ibun*, vol. 24, Shō-ō (1288–93) Kantō *gechijo an*, pp. 36–37 refers to Hirosada's widow being a person of the capital, while the 10.27.1295 (Einin 3) document reveals that the Ōuchi relied on their Kyoto connections regarding a court case about Shinano's Kawawa estate. See *Kamakura ibun*, vol. 25, doc. 18917, 10.27.1295 (Einin 3) Muromachi in *ryōji an*, p. 141, and *Ōuchi Yoshihiro*, p. 42. Matsuoka argues that the Ōuchi engaged in investigation concerning litigation by 1259. See pp. 42–43.

[63] See Wada Shūsaku, "Chūsei no Washizu shi ni tsuite," particularly pp. 12–14 for their influence in Suō during the Kamakura era.

[64] For a good overview, see Matsuoka, p. 44.

[65] *Kamakura ibun*, vol. 34, doc. 26093, 2.10.1317 (Bunpō 1) Ryōkei Jōshin *renshojō*, p. 127, and vol. 35, doc. 26910, 12.26.1318 (Bunpō 2) Tōdaiji *shutora rensho kishōmon*, pp. 71–73. Implicit in this document is that Shigehiro's capital connections made him relatively immune. The latter document reveals more about the nature of the dispute.

[66] *Kamakura ibun*, vol. 34, doc. 26093, 2.10.1317 (Bunpō 1) Ryōkei Jōshin *renshojō*, p. 127. For analysis of this episode, see Matsuoka, "Kamakura makki Suō no kuni kokugaryo shihai no dōkō to Ōuchi shi," in *Ōuchi shi no kenkyū*, pp. 121–48.

[67] *Ōuchi bunka*, p. 969, and *Jōfukuji ato* I (Yamaguchi, 2001), p. 4.

[68] *Bōchō fūdo chūshin an*, vol. 12, p. 341.

capital without interference from the Washizu. During the second and third decades of the fourteenth century, Hiroyuki seems to have favored this residence, which was closer to Kyoto than even Kudamatsu. In addition, it had access along the nearby Nishiki River to the nearby harbor of Tōsai and the mineral-rich region of Iwami. The spot seems to have been propitious for trade. Recently, the remains of an impressive residence have been discovered, together with forty to fifty thousand coins, the latest of which dates from the early fourteenth century.[69]

A Yakushi statue survives at Yōkōji. It was created in the fourteenth century. It is of such high quality that it must have been made by Kyoto craftsmen, which points to a link to Hiroyuki, whose father had ties to Rokuhara.[70] Most likely, this region of Yokoyama, located twenty miles to the east of Kudamatsu, rather than the more distant Ōuchi, served as Hiroyuki's headquarters until the 1330s.[71] As a sign of Hiroyuki's deep ties to the region, his mortuary temple is listed as Yōkōji in the oldest surviving Ōuchi genealogies.[72]

The Struggle for Survival, 1331–50

The civil war that erupted in 1331, when the emperor Go-Daigo (1288–1339) attempted to overthrow the Kamakura regime, buffeted Tatara fortunes. The main line navigated the turmoil initially most successfully. Washizu Nagahiro, the heir of the Washizu line, initially reinforced Kamakura forces when they were first attacked by partisans allied with Go-Daigo.[73] With

---

[69] For the best sources, see *Nakatsu kyokan ato: Kyū kaya izuminokami kyokan'ato*, vols. 1–2 (Iwakuni-shi Kyōiku iinkai, 2012–16). Analysis of the coins appears in the second volume of this work. See also Kanzaki Zen, "Nakazu kyokan ato hakkutsu chōsha ni tsuite," *Yamaguchi ken chihōshi kenkyū* 112 (10.2014): 58–61.

[70] Viewed 6.13.2016. For an image, see *Fudōsan Yōkōji no jihō* (Iwakuni, 2010), pp. 14–16.

[71] Thereupon the region would be controlled by the Hironaka, a trusted retainer family of the Ōuchi. The Hironaka can only be documented as having ties to this region from 1347 (Jōwa 3). See Wada Shūsaku, comp., *Sengoku ibun Ōuchi shi hen*, vol. 2 (Tōkyōdō shuppan, 2017), doc. 1179, 4.28.1503 (Bunki 3) Shirasaki Hachimangū *munafuda mei*, pp. 80–81. See also Miyata Itsumi, "Hironaka shi ni tsuite," p. 79, and p. 84 n. 4 for reference to Aramaki Daisetsu, *Yamaguchi jukkyōshi kō* (Yamaguchi, Sakura purinto, 1999), pp. 30–39. Aramaki suggests that another Yōkōji was built in Yamaguchi in approximately 1367 near Furukuma and the Fushino River region. See *Ōuchi bunka*, pp. 534–35.

[72] Conlan, "Shiryō shōkai," pp. 65–70, p. 66. This source appears in *Yamaguchi shishi shiryōhen chūsei* (Yamaguchi 2016), Sengoku zenki, doc. 789, Ōuchi shi *keizu*, p. 710. The Yōkōji associated with Hiroyuki is identified by the editors as being in Kuga district, in current day Iwakuni, rather than Yamaguchi.

[73] Hyōdō Hiromi, ed., *Taiheiki (Seigen'in bon)*, 6 vols. (Iwanami bunko, 2014–16), vol. 1, maki 6, Tōgoku sei jōraku no koto, p. 299.

Kamakura's collapse, Nagahiro not only survived, but remarkably, he was somehow appointed as the *shugo*, or protector of Suō, by Go-Daigo's Kenmu regime (1333–36).[74] This post proved significant as it gave Nagahiro policing powers over the province. The collateral lines navigated the turmoil less successfully. Two generations of the Migita, the Tatara lineage based at Sabaryō, were killed when Kamakura's Nagato branch (*tandai*) was annihilated in 1333.[75] This devastated their fortunes.

The line of Shigehiro and Hiroyuki, being less powerful than the Washizu, and more closely tied to Kamakura, was also thoroughly eclipsed. Nevertheless, Hiroyuki survived what for him would have been difficult times due to his Kyoto connections. The victorious Go-Daigo designated Jōfukuji, which had been founded by Shigehiro in 1312, as an imperial prayer temple in 1334, quite an honor for such a recently established institution.[76] Hiroyuki took Buddhist vows thereafter, renouncing his political ambitions, no doubt because of his deep ties with the discredited and destroyed Kamakura regime.[77] That Jōfukuji had been designated as an imperial prayer temple suggested that Shigehiro's son Hiroyuki retained some influence in Go-Daigo's regime.

Around the time when Jōfukuji was established as an imperial prayer temple, Hiroyuki took the tonsure and adopted the name Myōgon.[78] Although Hiroyuki founded Yōkōji, he abandoned the Yokoyama region in favor of the Ōuchi region, where Jōfukuji was located, in the aftermath of Kamakura's collapse. Yokoyama's former advantages, such as closeness to the capital, no longer applied, and with the prominence of the Washizu, residing in a location to their immediate east would not allow for any autonomy.

Washizu Nagahiro was nevertheless more skilled than Hiroyuki in navigating the treacherous political waters of the 1330s. Nagahiro transferred his allegiance again from Go-Daigo to Ashikaga Takauji, who rebelled against the sovereign during the waning days of 1335. Takauji, whose early attempt to occupy Kyoto ended in defeat in the first month of 1336, fled west. Nagahiro, in his role as *shugo* of Suō, along with forces of the *shugo*

---

[74] For the best summary, see *Yamaguchi kenshi tsūshihen chūsei* (Yamaguchi, 2012), pp. 319–20.

[75] Wada Shūsaku, "Suō Migita shi no sōden monjo ni tsuite," *Yamaguchi ken monjokan kenkyū kiyō* 41 (3.2014), p. 94. See also *Yamaguchi kenshi shiryōhen chūsei*, vol. 1, Shōkyō ranrishi, p. 66 for events of the third month of 1333.

[76] *Yamaguchi kenshi shiryōhen chūsei*, vol. 2, Jōfukuji monjo doc. 1, 4.2.1334 (Kenmu 1) Go-Daigo *tennō rinji*, p. 840.

[77] Fukuo Takeichirō, *Ōuchi Yoshitaka* (Yoshikawa kōbunkan, 1959), p. 24.

[78] *Yamaguchi kenshi shiryōhen chūsei*, vol. 3, Kōryūji monjo, doc. 206, *urū* 4.15 Ōuchi Myōgon (Hiroyuki) *shojō*, pp. 312–13.

of Nagato, Kotō Takezane, rescued Takauji by supplying five hundred ships, or so the chronicles claim, when he desperately needed to flee to the west.[79] Takauji regrouped and managed to recapture Kyoto during the summer of 1336. Thereupon he rewarded Nagahiro with the *shugo* post of Suō province, which he would maintain from 1336 through 1349.[80]

Nagahiro could not consolidate his control over Suō because he could not defeat Go-Daigo's partisans, who supported his Southern Court (1336–92); he required the aid of warriors from the neighboring province of Nagato, under the command of the *shugo* of that province, Kotō Takezane. Both Nagahiro and Takezane fought a battle at Shikiyama Castle in Sabaryō.[81] What happened to the Tatara in this region in 1336 is not clear, but they seem to have followed Nagahiro, who ultimately administered much of Suō. In addition, Nagahiro's son Hirokazu commanded military forces against the Southern Court.[82]

Hiroyuki (Myōgon) aroused the ire of Nagahiro, who burned down Kōryūji in 1341. No surviving sources explain this action. Perhaps Hiroyuki had allied himself with the Southern Court, or perhaps his patronage of Kōryūji as a site of Myōken worship threatened Washizu authority. Hiroyuki would later lament how wicked it was for descendants of "this house" to burn "an unparalleled site of ancestral worship."[83] By burning Kōryūji, however, the Washizu demonstrated that Myōken's star shone brighter on Kudamatsu than on the Ōuchi lands in interior Suō.[84]

Hiroyuki, who had access to lands and wealth, attempted to discredit the Washizu through the fervor of his support of Myōken. He repeatedly

[79] Yashiro Kazuo and Kami Hiroshi, eds., *Baishōron Gen'ishū* (Gendai shichōsha, 1975), p. 93. The *Taiheiki* refers to the Ōuchi as aiding Takauji when he fled to the west along with the Ōtomo and Kotō. *Taiheiki* (*Seigen'inbon*), vol. 2, maki 15, "Minatogawa kassen no koto," p. 478.

[80] Satō Shin'ichi, *Muromachi bakufu shugo seido no kenkyū*, vol. 2 (Tokyo daigaku shuppan, 1988), p. 168. See also *Yamaguchi kenshi tsūshihen chūsei*, p. 335. Takezane would also be appointed as the *shugo* of Nagato.

[81] NBIC, vol. 1, doc. 431, 7.1336 (Kenmu 3) Nagatomi Suemichi *dai shisoku* Sueari *gunchūjō*, p. 176, and *Nagato no kuni shugo Kotōshi hakkyū monjo* (Yamaguchi monjokan, 2014), pp. 22–23.

[82] NBIC, vol. 1, doc. 1031, 12.12.1340 (Ryakuō 3) Washizu (*sic*) Hirokazu *chūshinjō*, p. 359. See also *Yamaguchi kenshi shiryōhen chūsei*, vol. 2, Amidaji monjo, 3.11.1347 (Jōwa 3) Ōuchi Nagahiro *kishinjō*, p. 342.

[83] *Yamaguchi kenshi shiryōhen chūsei*, vol. 3, Kōryūji monjo, doc. 206, *uru* 4.15 Ōuchi Myōgon (Hiroyuki) *shojō*, pp. 312–13. For analysis of how this enemy was most likely Ōuchi Nagahiro, see Fukuo Takeichirō, *Ōuchi Yoshitaka*, pp. 24–25.

[84] For more on iconoclasm, see Fabio Rambelli, "Iconoclasm and Religious Violence in Japan: Practices and Rationalizations," in Fabio Rambelli and Eric Reinders, eds., *Buddhism and Iconoclasm in East Asia: A History* (New York: Bloomsbury Academic, 2012), pp. 47–88, and Alan Strathern, "The Many Meanings of Iconoclasm: Warrior and Christian Temple-Shrine Destruction in Late Sixteenth Century Japan," *Journal of Early Modern History* (2020), pp. 1–31.

commended lands on the second intercalary month of 1344, and again on 10.23.1348 for the reconstruction of Kōryūji, with the caveat that "Myōgon's descendants should not have enmity (*Myōgon no shishi sonson tekitai no gi ni arazu*)."[85] Hiroyuki apparently rebuilt the temple in the eleventh month of 1349, but a lack of resources delayed the ceremonies to celebrate its reconstruction and dedication (*kuyō*) for over half a century.[86] At the same time that Hiroyuki was bolstering his familial authority through commendations, the *shugo* Nagahiro in turn attempted to assert authority over the Tatara kin group by demanding that the oaths of unity dating from 1200 be upheld.[87]

After Kōryūji was destroyed by forces allied to the more powerful Washizu in 1341, Hiroyuki did not attempt to rebuild it. Instead, he patronized and restored the main hall of a nearby temple, called Ninpeiji.[88] Ninpeiji was an ancient Tendai temple, dating from the Heian era (794–1185), with grand buildings, occupying considerable territory and supporting at least thirty monks. Ninpeiji dwarfed Kōryūji, the temple devoted to Myōken and founded by Hiroyuki's ancestors.[89] Because the temple was old and its upkeep the responsibility of whoever governed Suō, Hiroyuki's restoration of this structure served to re-establish his influence in Suō affairs despite the hostility of the *shugo* Washizu Nagahiro.[90]

Both Kōryūji and Ninpeiji were located on a road that led directly to Sabaryō. Conveniently for the Ōuchi, and less so for the Washizu, Sabaryō was located only two miles from Kōryūji and was not a site of Myōken worship. In addition, the vicinity of Ninpeiji also constituted the homelands of the Toida and the Uno, collateral Tatara descendants who also served as the deputy *shugo* of Suō.[91] Hiroyuki's sponsoring of

---

[85] *Yamaguchi kenshi shiryōhen chūsei*, vol. 3, Kōryūji monjo, doc. 204, *urū* 2.21.1343 (Kōei 3) Ōuchi Myōgon (Hiroyuki) *kishinjō*, pp. 311–12 and doc. 205, 10.23.1348 (Jōwa 4) Ōuchi Myōgon (Hiroyuki) *kishinjō*, p. 312.

[86] See Maki Takayuki, "Suō no kuni Ōuchi shi to sono ujidera Kōryūji no shitsuteki henyō," in Kawaoka Tsutomu and Koga Nobuyuki, comps., *Saikoku no bunka to gaikō* (Seibundō, 2011), p. 90. Ōuchi Moriakira had these performed in 1404. See chapter 4.

[87] *Yamaguchi kenshi shiryōhen chūsei*, vol. 2, Amidaji monjo, doc. 8, 3.11.1347 (Jōwa 3) Ōuchi Nagahiro *kishinjō*, p. 342.

[88] For the best overview of Ninpeiji, and excellent analysis of these Suō rites, see Maki Takayuki, "Suō no kuni Ōuchi shi to sono ujidera Kōryūji no shitsuteki henyō."

[89] For this document describing the rebuilding of Ninpeiji, which survives by chance in the Kōryūji collection, see *Yamaguchi kenshi shiryōhen chūsei*, vol. 3, Kōryūji monjo doc. 82, Ninpeiji *hondō kuyōki*, pp. 262–68 and Maki Takayuki, "Suō no kuni Ōuchi shi to sono ujidera Kōryūji no shitsuteki henyō," p. 111. See also p. 122 for how these Ninpeiji rites would later be dwarfed by those performed at Kōryūji in the early fifteenth century.

[90] *Yamaguchi kenshi shiryōhen chūsei*, vol. 3, Kōryūji monjo, doc. 1, Kōryūji hondō *kuyō nikki*, p. 231.

[91] *Yamaguchi kenshi shiryōhen chūsei*, vol. 3, Kōryūji monjo, doc. 81 Tatara Kidōmaru Hikamisan Myōken Jōgū *sankei mokuroku*, p. 265 for the Toida and p. 268 for the Uno.

Ninpeiji rites proved uncontroversial, because this temple had long been of regional importance in Suō. Still, these rites and Hiroyuki's position remained tenuous. Emblematic of the turmoil of the time, special seats for guests (*zashiki*) were not completed, but the rites were nevertheless of considerable magnitude.[92]

The Ninpeiji rites provided a vehicle for allowing some supporters of the *shugo* Washizu Nagahiro to shift to Hiroyo. One Toida Hiroari appeared as a representative of the *shugo* and was accorded a position of unusual respect, along with the Uno.[93] Hiroari attended these ceremonies even though the Ōuchi were concurrently attacking their Washizu rivals. Instead of lending support to the Washizu, who were under attack by Hiroyuki's son, they forged new allegiances at Ninpeiji.

On 3.6.1352, two days before the performance of the climactic Ninpeiji rites, and through stress, exhaustion, or illness, Hiroyuki suddenly died. The ceremonies had to be delayed for a week,[94] but they then went forward on a considerable scale, lasting for over two days. Dances (*warabe mai*) performed by costumed children can be documented at this time, and they would later become a staple of annual Ōuchi rites for Myōken.

Conclusion

From the seventh through the mid-fourteenth centuries, descendants of the Tatara shared common assumptions regarding the worship of Myōken. They founded and destroyed temples to demonstrate the political and ritual authority of their respective lineages. The most junior line, which settled in the region called Ōuchi, would gain enough power and wealth to found Kōryūji and cast a giant bell for it. Even after the destruction of this temple, the use of an alternate site at Ninpeiji for major rites served to forge, among the Tatara,

---

[92] Reference to the Ninpeiji rites can be known from a single document that survives by chance in the Kōryūji collection and is transcribed in *Yamaguchi kenshi shiryōhen chūsei*, vol. 3, Kōryūji monjo doc. 82, Ninpeiji *hondō kuyōki*, pp. 262–68. See p. 268 for reference to the attendance of the provincial governor's representative, as well as the deputy *shugo*, for these elaborate rites, which reveals that they garnered the support of public authorities in addition to Ōuchi Hiroyuki and his son Hiroyo.

[93] *Yamaguchi kenshi shiryōhen chūsei*, vol. 3, Kōryūji monjo doc. 82, Ninpeiji *hondō kuyōki*, p. 268.

[94] For the death of Hiroyuki, see *Yamaguchi kenshi shiryōhen chūsei*, vol. 3, Kōryūji monjo doc. 82, Ninpeiji hondō *kuyōki*, p. 262, and Fujii Takashi, "Nanbokuchōki Nagato no kuni ni okeru Kotō shi kenryoku to Hiroyo ki Ōuchi shi kenryoku," *Kamakura ibun kenkyū* 21 (4.2008), p. 67. See also *Ōuchi bunka*, p. 12 for the Ōuchi genealogy and Hiroyuki's death.

personal bonds of allegiance that ultimately caused the eclipse of their main Washizu line.

By the mid-fourteenth, century, the Tatara had become prominent in Suō. With prosperity, different lineages increasingly became rivals. By the 1350s, one branch of the Tatara, which adopted the name Ōuchi, was embroiled in open warfare with the dominant Washizu lineage. In the political turmoil of the 1330s, Ōuchi Hiroyuki abandoned the seemingly more promising region of Yōkōji, an apparently misguided decision since his temple of Kōryūji was destroyed by his Washizu rivals. Undeterred, Hiroyuki promoted rites for Ninpeiji, nearby. These did not attract the ire of the Washizu and distantly related collaterals, still allied with the Washizu, were able to attend. The participants forged a new organization that would survive the turmoil and allow Hiroyuki's descendants to gain prominence and dominance, an outcome Hiroyuki probably never imagined. In any case, he died suddenly, leaving the troubled fortunes of his line to his son Hiroyo.

2

The Founder Ōuchi Hiroyo

Ōuchi Hiroyo (1325–80) established the basis for Ōuchi rule, forcing rival relatives into submission, seizing neighboring provinces, and exerting influence across the seas. He also encouraged the development of mines, solidified a new ritual order for organizing his territories, and founded the city of Yamaguchi.

Hiroyo was a visionary. He took advantage of the civil wars of the fourteenth century to defeat his Tatara relatives in Suō, first by abandoning the Northern Court for the rival Southern Court in 1352, and then by surrendering again to the Northern Court in 1363. He also conquered the province of Nagato on the western tip of Honshu. It would remain a core Ōuchi domain for centuries, and Hiroyo prospered thanks to his control of its mines. He also identified and seized crucial districts (*kōri*) in neighboring provinces and conquered choke points such as the Straits of Shimonoseki, which connected the Sea of Japan to the Inland Sea and separated the island of Honshu from Kyushu. In addition, he used the powers of the office of *shugo* to forge some provinces into core Ōuchi territories, while he made others ungovernable for rivals. In addition to promoting Myōken worship, Hiroyo patronized shrines that were dedicated to the gods of the seas.

Hiroyo also founded Yamaguchi, a planned settlement located to the north of Kōryūji, the site of Myōken worship for his lineage. Hiroyo first built his mansion three hundred yards to the north of an important, albeit sparsely settled, crossroads. He then laid out the town of Yamaguchi, with the central point of this planned community being an intersection at southwestern corner of his dwelling, linking the old north–south highway of Tatekōji to a newly created "Great Lord's Road" (*ōdono ōji*), an east–west road that served as the southern boundary of his property.

Under the watchful eyes of Hiroyo and his successors, this town of Yamaguchi thrived with its good access to transportation along roads,

Kings in All but Name. Thomas D. Conlan, Oxford University Press. © Oxford University Press 2024.
DOI: 10.1093/oso/9780197677339.003.0003

rivers, and seas. In later centuries, other planned settlements would be founded by competing lords, but Hiroyo's town preceded these efforts by over a century. Hiroyo was the first in Japan to establish a town that was neither an organically arising trading entrepôt, like Hakata in northern Kyushu, nor a capital city laid out on a grid-like pattern, the previous template for planned cities.

Origins

Little is known about Hiroyo's youth. He was born in 1325, making him seven years old when the civil war erupted, and nine when the Kamakura shogunate was destroyed. He may have accompanied his father Hiroyuki, a functionary for the shogunate's Rokuhara branch office in Kyoto, when Hiroyuki fled to the west in the aftermath of the warrior regime's destruction in 1333. Experiencing such turmoil at a young age may have helped Hiroyo to respond effectively to uncertainties in ways that others could not, or perhaps he was simply more intelligent and decisive than others, for he saw possibilities and capitalized on them in ways that most of his compatriots did not.

Hiroyo first appears in the sources in 1350 when, at the age of twenty-five, he fought on behalf of the Ashikaga along with Washizu Hirokazu, the son of Nagahiro, the *shugo*, scion of the chief line of the Tatara, and acknowledged leader of Suō.[1] Nagahiro ruled at a time when the Ashikaga were overpowering their Southern Court adversaries. A few short weeks after this campaign ended, however, the Ashikaga split into two warring factions, one allied with Takauji, the first shogun and leader of the regime, and the other with the forces of Takauji's brother Tadayoshi, who was their chief lawmaker. This uprising, known as the Kannō Disturbance of 1350–55, led to the death of many generals, including Tadayoshi himself.

During the chaos of Kannō, Hiroyo abandoned both Ashikaga factions and instead sided with the Southern Court. On 2.19.1352 he attacked Washizu Nagahiro. In battles that lasted over the next six weeks, Hiroyo killed several

---

[1] See Matsuoka Hisatō, comp., *Nanbokuchō ibun Chūgoku Shikoku hen*, 6 vols. (Tōkyōdō shuppan, 1987–95) (hereafter NBIC), vol. 2, doc. 1921, 12.25.1350 (Jōwa 6) Naitō Tokuekimaru *dai* Shinkaku *mōshijō utsushi* pp. 371–72. See also Matsuoka, *Ōuchi Yoshihiro* (Jinbutsu ōraisha, 1966), p. 56.

of the Washizu, as well as Naitō Morikiyo, one of their prominent supporters.[2] After a string of defeats, the Naitō would join Hiroyo's forces.[3]

Hiroyo's attacks occurred at the same time Hiroyo's father Hiroyuki was conducting the Ninpeiji rites in Suō. This allowed him to attract the support of other warriors who had been allied to the Washizu. During his campaigns, Hiroyo undermined the Washizu and Migita by co-opting their core supporters. In the case of the Migita, who had suffered the loss of two generations of leaders in 1333, Hiroyo engineered the defection of a junior line of their family, known by the name of Sue. Although the Migita would continue to resist Hiroyo for fifteen years, they never could reestablish their autonomy or former power. The Sue in turn abandoned their homelands, located at Shōgoji in Yoshiki district (kōri), not far from Sabaryō, to a more defendable site further to the east, at Hirajō. From Hirajō they could check both the Migita to the southwest and the Washizu to the east (see Figure 1.1).[4]

The Washizu could not be so easily conquered, and Hiroyo did not defeat them outright, although he subjugated the Naitō, their retainers. Even after the defection of the Naitō, the Washizu continued to resist Hiroyo and his descendants, who would only fully control the Washizu homelands, and their Kudamatsu shrine dedicated to Myōken, over a century later.[5]

A combination of patronage, ritual performance, and conquest enabled Hiroyo to consolidate his authority in Suō. He was most effective in absorbing the Sabaryō region, where the Migita had long held sway, relying on patronage of its major shrine, known retrospectively as Hōfu Tenmangū, and

---

[2] NBIC, vol. 3, doc. 2338, 8.1352 (Kannō 3) Naitō Fujitoki gunchūjō utsushi, p. 124, for the death of a Nagayoshi supporter named Morikiyo. For another document describing Hiroyo in open warfare with the forces of Nagayoshi's second son Sadahiro in the second intercalary month of 1352, see NBIC, vol. 3, doc. 2537, 11.18.1353 (Bunwa 2) Ōuchi Sadahiro chūshinjō utsushi, pp. 182–83. For overviews of Hiroyo and the Washizu, see Matsuoka, Ōuchi Yoshihiro, pp. 54–60. For Hiroyo's expansion into Nagato, see pp. 60–64, and Fujii Takashi, "Nanbokuchōki Nagato no kuni ni okeru Kotō shi kenryoku to Hiroyo ki Ōuchi shi kenryoku," Kamakura ibun kenkyū 21 (4.2008), p. 67.

[3] For the last petition describing the Naitō fighting for Washizu Sadahiro, against Hiroyo, and suffering considerable casualties, see NBIC, vol. 3, doc. 2537, 11.18.1353 (Bunwa 2) Ōuchi Sadahiro chūshinjō utsushi, pp. 182–83.

[4] Nothing remains of Sue dwellings in the Hirajō area. A school was built over the area, but in the Shōgoji region traces of where the Sue mansion was located are evident, including impressive earthen walls. According to Wada Shūsaku, the Sue moved to the Hirajō region shortly before the Kannō Disturbance of the 1350s. For more on the Sue, see Nakatsuka Ken'ichi, "Sue shi no ryōshu zaisei 1," Shigaku kenkyū 265 (8.2009), pp. 37–52 and Nakatsuka Ken'ichi, "Sue shi no ryōshu zaisei 2," Shigaku kenkyū 266 (9.2009), pp. 1–14. Finally, for a good overview and analysis of the Ōuchi retainers, see Hirase Naoki, "Nanbokuchō ki Ōuchi shi ni mieru chiiki shihai kenryoku no kakuritsu," Kamakura ibun kenkyū, no. 34 (10.2014), pp. 47–52.

[5] Ōuchi Masahiro rebuilt the Myōken shrines there in 1478. Wada, "Ōuchi shi no sōsho kankei o megutte," pp. 51–52. See also Nakatsuka Ken'ichi, "Ōuchi tōshugawa kinsō no keisei to tenkai," p. 118.

on the performances of prayers there in 1352 for peace, health, and the prosperity of his descendants.[6] Hiroyo's influence in the region increased, and by 1365 he had rebuilt this Hōfu shrine devoted to the deified god of learning Sugawara Michizane, relying partly on contributions from Sabaryō families and thus fusing ritual with rebuilding efforts and political union.[7]

Hiroyo's political and military success also bolstered the prestige of Kōryūji, the Myōken temple burned by his Washizu relatives in 1341. In 1353, the Southern Court designated his otherwise nondescript temple as an imperial prayer temple (goganji).[8] In 1354 Hiroyo levied taxes throughout the province to fund the rebuilding of Kōryūji and the performance of its essential rites.[9] Political authority allowed for religious institutions to be rebuilt, and in turn the needs of these institutions justified taxation and other methods of control. Hiroyo established regulations for Kōryūji on 1.7.1357, thereby consolidating his control of Suō.[10] He also prohibited the shugo from the province (the Washizu) from encroaching on Kokubunji temple lands in 1362.[11] Ninpeiji, to the contrary, experienced no such largesse, and it ultimately fell into ruin. Records of the 1352 rites survive only by chance at Kōryūji.

The Conquest of Nagato

Rather than attempt to annihilate residual Washizu opposition, Hiroyo astutely directed his attention to Nagato, located to the west of Suō. He had no ties with Nagato, but he took advantage of the Kannō Disturbance to attack the Kotō, shugo of Nagato province since 1336, who had lost two generations

---

Although presumably these shrines go back to the seventh century, to date only medieval traces have been discovered.

[6] Yamaguchi kenshi hensanshitsu, comp., Yamaguchi kenshi shiryōhen chūsei, 4 vols. (Yamaguchi, 1996–2008), vol. 2, Hōfu Tenmangū monjo, doc. 8, 11.3.1352 (Kannō 2) Ōuchi Hiroyo sodehan ategaijō, p. 476.

[7] NBIC, vol. 4, doc. 3399, 6.11.1365 (Jōji 4) Tenjin sha munafuda utsushi, pp. 116–17.

[8] Bōchō fūdo chūshin an, vol. 12 Yamaguchi saiban jō (Yamaguchi, 1960), 9.22.1353 (Shōhei 8) Ashikaga Tadafuyu mikyōjo utsushi, p. 122. Ultimately this temple would be made an imperial prayer temple (chokuganji) by Emperor Go-Kashiwabara (1462–1526, r. 1500–1526), but this would not occur until 1501–4. See p. 143.

[9] See Bōchō fūdo chūshin an, vol. 12, p. 97, for a 1.18.1354 (Shōhei 9) Ōuchi Hiroyo mikyōjo.

[10] NBIC, vol. 3, doc. 2864, 1.7.1357 (Shōhei 12) Ōuchi Hiroyo jōjō kotogaki, p. 278.

[11] Yamaguchi kenshi shiryōhen chūsei, vol. 2, Kokubunji monjo, doc. 32, 3.1362 (Jōji 2) Ōuchi Hiroyo kinzei an, p. 410. This copy of Hiroyo's document was confirmed by his son Moriakira (Tokuyū) on 8.25.1419 (Ōei 26).

of leaders in three years (1348–51) and were in no position to respond effectively to the turmoil.[12]

Hiroyo invaded Nagato in 1355, and by 1358 he had gained control of the province. When he initiated his Nagato campaign, Hiroyo relied on the shrines of the province for support to pacify the Kotō, "rebels" who had, in fact, governed the province for twenty years.[13] In 1358 he killed yet another leader of the Kotō, which was a loss that they could ill afford.[14] That same year the Southern Court appointed Hiroyo as the *shugo* of Nagato, well after he had occupied the province.[15] Hiroyo seized the Nagato provincial capital on 6.23.1358, a victory that he underscored by worshiping on the same day at the two most important shrines of the province. Military control was confirmed and justified through worship at these shrines.[16]

Although Hiroyo's ancestors had long worshiped Myōken, the move into Nagato led him to favor the gods of the province, which were associated with the sea.[17] He particularly relied upon the two most important shrines in the province to establish his authority. One, the Ichinomiya ("First Shrine") of Nagato, was dedicated to Sumiyoshi, a god of the sea. It had fallen into

[12] Two of their chiefs, Takezane, and Takemura, perished in 1348 and 1351. See *Dainihon shiryō* (hereafter DNSR), ser. 6, vol. 12, pp. 72–73, for Takezane's death on 11.9.1348 (Jōwa 4). See also p. 74 for references to Takemura's death on 10.10.1351 (Kannō 2) and DNSR ser. 6, vol. 15, p. 499.

[13] Inoue Hiroshi, *Nihon Chūsei kokka to shokoku Ichinomiya sei* (Iwata shoin, 2009), p. 215, NBIC, vol. 3, doc. 2835, 9.20 Ōuchi Hiroyo *kansū henji*, p. 270, doc. 2844, 10.16 Ōuchi Hiroyo *shojō utsushi*, p. 272, and doc. 2908, 7.13.1357 (Shōhei 12) Ōuchi Hiroyo *gansho utsushi*, pp. 291–92.

[14] Satō Shin'ichi, *Muromachi bakufu shugo seido no kenkyū* 2 (Tokyo daigaku shuppan, 1988), p. 173. This would most likely be Takenao, the third generation of Kotō leaders to die in the span of a decade. For Takenao's 11.20.1353 (Bunwa 2) death according to the Kotō genealogy, see *Yamaguchi kenshi tsūshihen chūsei* (Yamaguchi, 2012), p. 345. In fact, he last issued an order on 11.27.1356 (Enbun 1). See 11.27.1356 (Enbun 1) Kotō Takenao *kakikudashi*, *Nagato no kuni shugo Kotōshi hakkyū monjo* (Yamaguchi-ken chihōshi gakkai, 2014), pp. 38–39.

[15] Satō Shin'ichi, *Muromachi bakufu shugo seido no kenkyū* 2, p. 173, and Kondō Kiyoshi, *Ōuchi shi jitsuroku* (Yamaguchi, 1885, 3rd reprint ed., Tokuyama: Matsuno shoten, 1984), p. 23.

[16] *Yamaguchi kenshi shiryōhen chūsei*, vol. 1, Nagato no kuni shugo daiki, p. 606. See also Fujii, "Nanbokuchōki Nagato no kuni ni okeru Kotō shi kenryoku to Hiroyo ki Ōuchi shi kenryoku," pp. 67–68. For how this was remembered in Ōuchi lore, see *Hagi han batsuetsu roku* (Yamaguchi, 1994), vol. 2, maki 65, Mitsui Zenbei monjo, doc. 11, 3.1514 (Eishō 11) Mitsui ke *yuisho*, p. 538. See also Inoue Hiroshi, *Nihon Chūsei kokka to shokoku Ichinomiya*, pp. 243–44, and "Chūsei shokoku Ichinomiyasei no rekishiteki kōzō to toskushitsu: Chūsei kōki Nagato no kuni no jirei o chūshin ni," *Kokuritsu rekishi minzoku hakubutsukan kenkyū hōkoku*, no. 148 (12.2008), pp. 200–203. https://rekihaku.repo.nii.ac.jp/?action=pages_view_main&active_action=repository_view_main_item_detail&item_id=1671&item_no=1&page_id=13&block_id=41.

[17] See the pathbreaking research on sea gods by Fabio Rambelli, ed., *The Sea and the Sacred in Japan: Aspects of Maritime Religion* (Bloomsbury, 2018), particularly his "Sea Theologies: Elements for a Conceptualization of Maritime Religiosity in Japan," pp. 181–99. Inspiration for this analysis came from a lecture by Bernard Faure, "Divine Land, Demonic Seas: Another Look at Japanese Religion," Columbia University, 3.2019.

Figure 2.1 The Sumiyoshi Shrine is a rare example of five gabled fourteenth-century architecture. Photograph by Thomas Conlan.

disrepair, and Hiroyo started rebuilding it in the sixth month of 1367. The endeavor required four years.[18]

It is a sign of his wealth that he could initiate this construction a mere two years after he rebuilt the Hōfu Tenmangū shrine in Suō. The repair cost fifteen thousand *kanmon*, a princely sum.[19] The original building still survives

[18] *Yamaguchi kenshi shiryōhen chūsei*, vol. 4, 6.1367 (Jōji 6) Ōuchi Hiroyo *ganmon utsushi*, pp. 209–10, NBIC, vol. 5, doc. 4443, 8.25.1378 (Eiwa 4) Nagato Ichinomiya *munafuda mei*, p. 199, and *Yamaguchi kenshi shiryōhen chūsei*, vol. 4, Sumiyoshi jinja monjo doc. 234, 3.11.1370 (Ōan 3) Ōuchi Yoshihiro *ganmon* and doc. 235, 8.10.1371 (Ōan 4), p. 453. See also Fujii Takashi, "Nanbokuchōki Nagato no kuni ni okeru Kotō shi kenryoku to Hiroyo ki Ōuchi shi kenryoku," pp. 73–74, for analysis of this prayer and Hiroyo's rebuilding of the shrine, which helped him to erase traces of earlier authorities in the region, such as the Nagato *tandai* of the Kamakura regime and the Kotō family.
[19] Fujii has shown that to rebuild the Nagato Iminomiya shrine required three thousand *kanmon* and estimates that the repairs and rebuilding in Nagato alone constituted fifteen thousand *kanmon*. Fujii, "Nanbokuchōki Nagato no kuni ni okeru Kotō shi kenryoku to Hiroyo ki Ōuchi shi kenryoku," pp. 75–76. For a 11.7.1309 (Engyō 2) reference to the Iminomiya shrine requiring three thousand *kanmon*, see *Kamakura ibun*, vol. 31, doc. 23801, 11.7.1309 (Engyō 2) Kantō *mikyōjo*, p. 189. Fujii also mentions a 1320 document that reveals that the Munakata shrine required seven hundred *kanmon* to rebuild a smaller shrine within the precincts in 1320; see *Kamakura ibun*, vol. 36, doc. 27618, 10.30.1320 (Gentoku 2) Tokusō ke *bugyōnin rensho hōsho*, p. 37.

and is remarkable for its single, long roof decorated with five curved gables (*chidori hafu*), a rare and impressive style (see Figure 2.1).[20]

Hiroyo patronized another shrine, the Ninomiya ("Second Shrine") of Nagato, which was in the provincial capital, and close to the Straits of Shimonoseki. It was dedicated to the ancient rulers of Japan, Chūai (r. 192–200?), Jingū (r. 201–69?), and Ōjin (r. 270–310?), who were associated with Japan's imaginary conquest of Korea. As the Sumiyoshi sea gods had aided these mythical rulers in their conquest, this shrine was paired with that of Sumiyoshi.[21] Moriya, the Sannomiya ("Third Shrine"), was likewise located at the Straits of Shimonoseki and dedicated to the same three divinities of Jingū, Chūai, and Ōjin.

Hiroyo proved to be an able leader. He adopted two distinct patterns of religious ritual and control in two disparate provinces. In the case of Suō, Hiroyo relied on Myōken rites focused at Kōryūji to consolidate his authority and establish ties of lordship over a diverse band of men. In Suō Province, the process of conquest proved gradual, but Nagato presented a vacuum that allowed him to quickly establish effective rule. There, Hiroyo's rapid conquest enabled him to pacify the province by honoring and dominating its shrines, which had been central to governance of the province for centuries. Although Hiroyo confirmed holdings of temples in that province as well, it was his conquest, made real through exclusive worship at these shrines, which established a lasting political authority.

Hiroyo thus ruled Nagato thanks to control of a network of shrines, most of them located near the Nagato provincial headquarters.[22] In 1359 he confirmed the customary exemptions from "public duties" accorded to the commoners of the Ninomiya holdings and the holdings of its shrine attendants.[23] What these duties entailed is not well known, but later sources reveal that provincial (*zaichō*) warriors were responsible for performing a variety of rites at the Ichinomiya and Ninomiya shrines throughout the year.[24]

---

[20] This shrine has five gables and was devoted to the worship of Sumiyoshi, Hachiman, Kōra daimyōjin, Jingū kōgo, and Suwa daimyōjin, See *Bōchō jisha yurai*, vol. 7 (Yamaguchi, 1986), p. 494.

[21] Emily Simpson, "An Empress at Sea: Sea Deities and Divine Union in the Legend of Empress Jingū," *The Sea and the Sacred in Japan: Aspects of Maritime Religion* (New York: Bloomberg Academic, 2018), pp. 65–78. For Hiroyo's prayers to the Iminomiya shrine, see *Yamaguchi kenshi shiryōhen chūsei*, vol. 4, 6.1367 (Jōji 6) Ōuchi Hiroyo *ganmon utsushi*, pp. 209–10.

[22] Inoue Hiroshi, *Nihon Chūsei kokka to shokoku Ichinomiya sei*, pp. 215–16, 241–44.

[23] Inoue, *Nihon Chūsei kokka to shokoku Ichinomiya sei*, pp. 215–16, NBIC, vol. 3, doc. 3009, 4.10.1359 (Shōhei 14) Ōuchi *bugyōnin rensho hōsho* and doc. 3010, 4.10.1359 (Shōhei 14) Ōuchi Hiroyo *andojō*, p. 319.

[24] Inoue, *Nihon Chūsei kokka to shokoku Ichinomiya sei*, pp. 220–22.

The Kotō, the previous *shugo*, and supporters of Ashikaga Takauji had long levied taxes for the performance of rites at shrines.[25] These rites remained important enough that the Kotō continued offering prayers at Nagato's Ninomiya shrine. Their claims to authority hinged upon their ability to protect these shrines, and their last surviving record, dating from late 1368, constitutes a confirmation of these shrine lands.[26]

The Ninomiya shrine was located at the heart of the Nagato provincial headquarters, and therefore had a political and, increasingly, a cultic significance that transcended that of Ichinomiya for control of the province.[27] In Nagato, nearly all the major shrines where important rites were performed were located in the vicinity of the provincial headquarters and the Ninomiya shrine complex.[28] Thus a governor could conduct all of the important rites while still remaining near the provincial headquarters.

So essential were these shrines to Ōuchi governance that the Ichinomiya ("First"), Ninomiya ("Second"), and Sannomiya ("Third") shrines all survive for this province, which is unusual, as in most of Japan's provinces, Sannomiya shrines fell into ruin for lack of resources and patronage.[29] Hence, Hiroyo's Nagato success enhanced his authority and enabled him to further solidify control over Suō. Ultimately Hiroyo and his descendants would control the two westernmost provinces of Honshu, Suō and Nagato, for the next two centuries.

Controlling the Straits of Shimonoseki

Not content with taking these two western provinces, Hiroyo engaged in a more difficult campaign that proved decisive for Ōuchi wealth and authority.

[25] As early as 1326, for example, Kamakura had requested that the Second Shrine of Nagato be rebuilt, and as *shugo*, Kotō Takezane ensured that these levies would take place. See the 9.15.1326 (Karyaku 1) Kotō Sūsai *jungyōjō*, in *Nagato no kuni shugo Kotōshi hakkyū monjo*, pp. 8–9. This document has not been transcribed in *Kamakura ibun*. These levies would again be issued in 1342. See 8.28.1342 (Kōei 1) Kotō Sūsai *jungyōjō* in *Nagato no kuni shugo Kotōshi hakkyū monjo*, pp. 30–31.

[26] Both records date from when the Kotō were fighting for the Southern Court. NBIC, vol. 4, doc. 3294, 6.13.1364 (Shōhei 19) Kotō Yoshitaka *kakikudashi*, p. 84 and doc. 3680, 12.13.1368 (Shōhei 23) Kotō Yoshitaka *ategaijō*, p. 246. See also *Nagato no kuni shugo Kotōshi hakkyū monjo*, doc. 17, 6.13.1364 (Shōhei 19) Kotō Yoshitaka *kakikudashi*, pp. 40–41, and doc. 18, 12.23.1368 (Shōhei 23) Kotō Yoshitaka *ategaijō*, pp. 42–43.

[27] Inoue, *Nihon Chūsei kokka to shokoku Ichinomiya sei*, p. 223.

[28] Inoue, *Nihon Chūsei kokka to shokoku Ichinomiya sei*, pp. 241–44. There were exceptions of course, as the Ichinomiya shrine was located elsewhere, while the Sannomiya shrine was located near the Straits of Shimonoseki.

[29] Remarkably, in the case of Suō, a Shinomiya "Fourth Shrine," the Akada Shinomiya, survives. Shinomiya remain in eleven of Japan's sixty-six original provinces: Suō, Higo, Harima, Izumi, Suruga, Izu, Sagami, Musashi, Kai, Kōzuke, and Echizen.

Figure 2.2 This fortified hilltop, Moji, dominated the narrowest part of the Straits of Shimonoseki. Photograph by Thomas Conlan.

This expansion brought him wider influence. Before annihilating the Kotō, he crossed the Straits of Shimonoseki, a narrow, turbulent, and treacherous body of water, just over two thousand feet wide at its narrowest point, into Kyushu. He attacked the castle at Moji in the third month of 1361 and captured it in the seventh month of 1362, thereby securing this strategic waterway.[30] Moji, formerly controlled by leaders of the Kamakura shogunate through 1333, came under the authority of the warrior family who had adopted the name of the place. The Moji apparently controlled both sides of the straits, and their support proved vital.[31] Hiroyo's conquest of the Straits of Shimonoseki gave him the upper hand in the west, and the Ashikaga, victorious elsewhere, enticed him into the fold by recognizing his gains as well as his position as the *shugo* of Suō and Nagato (Figure 2.2).[32]

Hiroyo sided with the Ashikaga prior to the third month of 1363.[33] His allegiance to the dominant regime consolidated his authority, but the fact that he gave it from a position of strength meant that the Ashikaga would never

---

[30] Seno Sei'ichirō, comp., *Nanbokuchō ibun Kyūshū hen* (7 vols. Tōkyōdō shuppan, 1985–92), vol. 4, doc. 4530, 3.1364 (Jōji 3) Moji Chikahisa *gunchūjō*, pp. 273–74. See also *Moji monjo* (Kita Kyūshū shiritsu shizenshi rekishi hakubutsukan, 2005), doc. 17, 3.1364 (Jōji 3) Shimōsa Chikahisa *gunchūjō*, pp. 27–28.

[31] Kawazoe Shōji, *Chūsei bungei no chihōshi* (Heibonsha, 1982), "Sōgi no mita Kyūshū," p. 261. The straits had been held by the main (*tokusō*) line of the Hōjō family from the period of 1303–5. What happened after their collapse is not clear, and when precisely the Moji first gained control of both sides of the straits is not known either. For the best compilation of Moji sources, see Yagita Ken, *Shiryō ni miru Chūsei no Moji* (Kita Kyushu, revised printing, 2010).

[32] Satō Shin'ichi focused merely on how the Shiba and other *bakufu* officials enticed Hiroyo to join their cause in the spring of 1363. See *Nanbokuchō no dōran* (Chūō kōronsha, 1974), p. 345.

[33] NBIC, vol. 4, doc. 3221, 3.1363 (Jōji 2) Ōuchi Hiroyo (Dōkai) *kinzei an*, p. 58. See also Seno Sei'ichirō, *Ashikaga Tadafuyu* (Yoshikawa kōbunkan, 2005), pp. 171–72.

trust either him or his descendants. Pro-Ashikaga narratives could not paper over this situation. The *Taiheiki* recounted this process as follows:

> Ōuchi *no suke* [Hiroyo], long allied with the [Southern] Court forces, pacified both provinces of Suō and Nagato, and all feared [his power]. For some reason, however, in the spring of 1363 he suddenly had a change of heart. He notified the shogun that if he were to receive both provinces, he would perform military service, and this would be the foundation of stability in the west. In the end he therefore received the rewards he desired.[34]

Hiroyo crossed into Kyushu sometime between the seventh and the eleventh months of 1363 (Jōji 2), and he completed a successful campaign there in the twelfth month of that year.[35] He had defeated the Kikuchi, a former ally and a Southern Court stalwart. This caused "great joy" among Ashikaga supporters, although Hiroyo's offensive "encountered difficulties" when he returned to Suō shortly thereafter.[36] Pro-Ashikaga forces could now gain access to northern Kyushu and maintain authority there through the goodwill of Hiroyo.

Ritual Bonds of Lordship

Hiroyo's influence in the region increased over time, and by 1365 he had rebuilt the Hōfu Tenmangū shrine, relying partly on contributions from Sabaryō families and thus fusing ritual with rebuilding efforts and political union. At the same time, he enticed Migita Hirotada, the main surviving Migita of the Sabaryō region, to accept the position of deputy *shugo* in the

[34] The Konshō'inbon version of the *Taiheiki* correctly mentions Hiroyo's surrender as occurring in the third month of 1363 (Jōji 2) but most other versions incorrectly state that it happened in 1364. See Imai Kōsai et al., eds., *Sankō Taiheiki* (revised ed., Kokusho kankōkai, 1943), p. 569. For the other version, see Hyōdō Hiromi, ed., *Taiheiki* (Seigen'inbon, 6 vols., Iwanami bunko, 2014–16), vol. 6, maki 39, "Ōuchi no suke kōsan no koto" pp. 139–40 and Koakimoto Dan et al., eds., *Kōtei Kyōdaibon Taiheiki* (Bensei shuppan, 2011), vol. 2, pp. 1333, 1464.

[35] 2.17.1364 (Jōji 3) Ashikaga Yoshiakira *gohan mikyōjo utsushi*, in Wada Shūsaku, ed., "Furoku Sasaki Shichibei no suke Yoshiie no honkoku to shōkai," *Yamaguchi monjokan kiyō*, no. 39 (2012), p. 125. For his *shugo* appointment, see Satō, *Muromachi bakufu shugo seido no kenkyū*, vol. 2, p. 168. Simultaneously he would receive the *shugo* post of Nagato. See p. 175.

[36] For the joy of the Shimazu, Ashikaga supporters from Southern Kyushu, when Hiroyo first attacked the Kikuchi, see the *Yamada Shōei jikki*, which is accessible on DNSR ser. 6, vol. 25, p. 43. See also *Yamada Shōei jikki* (Kagoshima: Kagoshima kenritsu toshokan, 1967), p. 63.

distant province of Iwami.[37] The Migita, who had not participated in the 1365 rebuilding of Hōfu, now joined forces with Hiroyo—an alliance that contrasted with the still hostile Washizu at Kudamatsu. Hiroyo continued to favor Hōfu Tenmangū, since reconstruction efforts lasted from 1364 through 1375.[38]

Hiroyo's patronage of Hōfu Tenmangū provided a way to emphasize the cultic importance of the Sabaryō region of Suō by changing the region's religious focus from the cult of Myōken to that of Tenman Tenjin, the deified form of the courtier Sugawara Michizane. While adding another deity to the Ōuchi pantheon of protector deities, this change also, later on, enabled Hiroyo to strengthen his home temple of Kōryūji as the crucial site of Myōken worship without wholly bypassing Sabaryō.

Once Hiroyo had established effective control over Sabaryō, he removed the casket of the purported Ōuchi progenitor from Kuruma-zuka, an ancient tumulus (*kofun*) in Hōfu, to Jōfukuji, a temple located not far from Kōryūji.[39] By doing so, Hiroyo made his headquarters in the Ōuchi the preeminent site of Tatara ancestor worship. Accordingly, the Ōuchi region fully supplanted the cultic significance of Sabaryō.[40]

Study of Hiroyo suggests the steady accumulation of authority, but his success was by no means obvious, nor did it invariably translate into continued authority and influence for his followers. A comparison of the Ninpeiji rosters of 1352 and the Hōfu list of 1365 shows that only three prominent families, the Toida, Uno, and Niho, appear on both, while eight families appearing in the earlier roster are omitted in 1365.[41] Thus, Hiroyo's followers were not a cohesive bloc, since only a few remained with him during the intervening

[37] For a somewhat later document of Hironao as deputy, see *Masuda ke monjo*, vol. 2 (Tōkyō daigaku shuppankai, 2003), doc. 517, 8.10. 1395 (Ōei 2) Iwami no kuni *shugo dai* Migita Hironao *jungyōjō*, pp. 260–61.

[38] *Sengoku ibun Ōuchi shi hen*, vol. 2 (Tōkyōdō shuppan, 2017), doc. 1876, 9.29.1526 (Daiei 6) Matsuzaki *tenmangū shigyōsō chō-ō mōshijō utsushi*, pp. 321–23.

[39] *Bōchō fūdo chūshin an*, vol. 9, *Mitashiri jō* (Yamaguchi, 1960), p. 592 for how the casket was transferred. This source also contains a sketch of the interior of the tomb.

[40] For later Ōuchi narratives of this transfer, see Tatara metsubō shidai, *Yamaguchi kenshi shiryōhen chūsei*, vol. 1, p. 743.

[41] Compare *Yamaguchi kenshi shiryōhen chūsei*, vol. 3, Kōryūji monjo, doc. 82, Ninpeiji hondō *kuyō nikki*, p. 268, with NBIC, vol. 4, doc. 3399, 6.11.1365 (Jōji 4) Tenjin sha *munafuda utsushi*, pp. 116–17. Close analysis of the photograph reveals significant discrepancies with printed versions such as *Nanbokuchō ibun*, so photographs and transcriptions, most conveniently found in *Hōfu Tenmangūten: Nihon saisho no Tenjin-sama: Matsugasaki Tenjin engi emaki nanahyakunen kinen* (Yamaguchi bijutsukan, 2011), pp. 41, 126–27, should be consulted. Technically, this document is not a copy, but an accurate tracing, or *anmon*. See also *Yamaguchi shishi shiryōhen Ōuchi bunka* (Yamaguchi, 2010) (hereafter *Ōuchi bunka*), pp. 773–75.

fifteen years. Of course, this comparison overstates the dislocation, since two local families—the Saigō and the Sanai—who consistently followed Hiroyo appear on both lists as well.[42] Apparently lordship was forged and focused by performing rites and rebuilding temple and shrine structures in specific regions. However, these allegiances remained limited in scope.

In his rebuilding of Hōfu Tenmangū, Hiroyo relied upon his standing as the "great patron" (daiganshu). This allowed him to claim the title of Ōuchi no suke, the senior member of his lineage, and suggested that all taking part in these rites accepted his primacy. In consonance with his influence and prestige, the rebuilding required the technical expertise of craftsmen from the capital, as well as of several monks from the powerful Tōdaiji of Nara.[43] Likewise, these rites and the placement of names on the roster revealed the hierarchy among Hiroyo's followers, with more powerful warriors carefully distinguished from lower-ranking administrators.[44]

Repeated ritual performances and reconstruction of religious institutions ultimately solidified Hiroyo's band of followers. A roster of donors for Kōryūji lists the names of forty-three men who donated one horse each to Kōryūji during an 8.10.1374 ceremony.[45] The durable Sanai and Saigō, who appear on the 1352 and 1365 rosters, remain. The Ōuchi collaterals appearing in 1365—the Toida, Sue, Suetaka, and Kurokawa—all appear, as do the Migita. One difference, however, and a sign of Hiroyo's increasing authority, was the inclusion of warriors from further afield, most notably the Masuda of western Iwami, who would retain complex relations with the Ōuchi for centuries; the Sugi, who would become prominent in Kyushu; and the Hironaka warriors from the eastern boundary of Suō.

After incorporating such shrines as Hōfu Tenmangū into his ritual and political network, Ōuchi Hiroyo established a ritual hierarchy in which Kōryūji and its contiguous shrine at Hikamisan, some three hundred meters from

---

[42] The Saigō served Hiroyo's ancestors as far back as 1256, when a Saigō Jirō acted as a messenger for Tatara Hirosada. Kamakura ibun, vol. 11, doc. 8417, 10.18 [(Shōgen 1) 1259] Shōni Kagesuke shojō an, p. 362. According to Hirase, the Sanai had long lived in what became the Yamaguchi region. For more on them see Hirase Naoki, "Nanbokuchōki Ōuchi shi no honkyochi: Hiroyo ki o chūshin ni," Nihon rekishi 810 (11.2015), p. 48 and Hirase Naoki, Ōuchi Yoshihiro, p. 41.

[43] One group, called the banjō, was composed of Tōdaiji craftsmen with thirteen followers (shoku) who incidentally are omitted from transcriptions of the document. Likewise, in addition to shrine attendants, two monks, Ryūson and Ryū'in, were most likely from Tōdaiji.

[44] Hirase Naoki, "Nanbokuchōki Ōuchi shi no honkyochi," pp. 47–49.

[45] Yamaguchi kenshi shiryōhen chūsei, vol. 3, Kōryūji monjo, doc. 79, 8.10.1374 (Ōan 7) Hikamisan Myōken Jōgū jōtō jinme kishin chūmon, pp. 257–58, and NBIC, vol. 5, doc. 4071, Hikamisan Jōgū jōtō jinme chūmon, pp. 18–19.

the temple at the top of a nearby hill, constituted the premier site of Myōken and Ōuchi ancestral worship. He enhanced the prestige of these shrines by installing two Hie deities on Hikamisan in 1369, where he established seven shrines—the number of the seven stars of the Big Dipper (*hokuto shichisei*). In this way he had the constellations represented as shrines around Yamaguchi. He further enhanced Hikamisan by building a large Niōmon gate (1373) and an "Upper" shrine in the hills (1374–75).[46]

The Mines of Iwami

Hiroyo expanded into the mineral-rich province of Iwami. In 1367, he confirmed the holdings of the Misumi, a prominent Southern Court supporter, thereby removing the greatest challenge to his authority in Iwami.[47] Having consolidated his rule over his core territories and established a capable group of retainers, Hiroyo focused his attention on controlling strategic harbors. He was particularly interested in the port at Nima in Iwami. Located near the mouth of the Ushio River, it was a good harbor. Hills to the west protected it against storms, which tended to arise from that direction. The terrain made it comparable to the harbor of Hakata in northern Kyushu, although there are so many good harbors in Iwami that it is considered only the second best in the province.[48] The presence of an arable plain made its region one of three in Iwami capable of supporting larger-scale agriculture production, the others being the regions of Hamada and Masuda. Nevertheless, the primary

[46] Maki, "Suō no kuni Ōuchi shi to sono ujidera Kōryūji no tokushitsu henyō," pp. 107–10. The sources he refers to date from the Edo era, but unpublished writings of Yoshida Kanemigi dating from the 1540s reveal that these seven shrines were significant sites of worship at Hikamisan; see *Bōchō fūdo chūshin an*, vol. 12, pp. 96–97, for Hiroyo constructing an upper shrine in 1374 (Ōan 7), and a list of names including the Migita. See also p. 96 for reference that the main shrine was rebuilt in 1375. For a confirmation of Hikamisan lands by Hiroyo, see the 10.13.1377 (Eiwa 3) Ōuchi Dōkai (Hiroyo) *andojō*. See also p. 144, for reference to Hiroyo (Dōkai) rebuilding Jōfukuji in 2.1378 (Eiwa 4). Sūnin, the third head of the temple, praised the construction for being in a great (*bigyō*) and proper (*shōfū*) kingly style (*ōke*).

[47] See Tanaka Hiroki, Nakajima Keiichi, Nakatsukasa Ken'ichi, Nishida Tomohiro, and Watanabe Hiroki, eds., "Masuda Saneuji shozō shinshutsu chūsei monjo no shōkai," *Kokuritsu rekishi minzoku hakubutsukan kenkyū hōkoku* 212 (12.2018), pp. 101–66, doc. 2, 3.5.1367 (Jōji 6) Ashikaga Yoshiakira *gohan mikyōjo*, p. 106 where Ashikaga Yoshiakira directs Hiroyo to confirm Misumi lands.

[48] For the comparison, see Ōba Yasutoki, "Hakata to Iwami ginzan-minato no shiten kara," *Iwami ginzan Iwami ginzan iseki te-ma betsu chosa kenkyū hōkokusho* 1 (3.2011), pp. 97–110. The best harbor is Hamada, which was controlled by the Sufu, followed by the Nima, then the Masuda.

advantage of the harbor is that it is roughly a four-hour walk from a site exceptionally rich in copper and silver: the silver mines of Iwami.[49]

Commerce requires products or commodities in demand, and copper and silver were particularly prized. Hiroyo would have known that when he directed campaigns in Iwami in 1366 and led local warriors, such as the Kuri, against the Nima, another major family in the region, in their contest for local supremacy.[50] The triumphant Hiroyo, who served for a decade as the *shugo* of Iwami, was able to supplant both the Nima and the Kuri and dominate this region.[51] He appointed Migita Hirotada, a collateral holdout from the Sabaryō region, to the position of deputy *shugo* of Iwami, thus at once attracting a former regional rival and converting him into an able subordinate.[52]

Hiroyo conquered northern Nagato and Iwami, an area of plentiful copper and silver ore, with rich veins located near the surface, embedded in soft, readily excavated rock.[53] Evidence of small-scale copper smelting and mining has been uncovered in two separate regions of Iwami. Copper slag dating from the late thirteenth century has been discovered at the Kobuyama region of Ōmoriza, now known as the Iwami silver mine (Iwami *ginzan*).[54] In addition, copper slag has been uncovered at the Ōtoshi no moto site of Masuda, where mountains open out into a broader field. Here, copper ore was hauled from Tsumo and smelted in a few small pits (see Figure 2.3).[55]

[49] Shinkawa Takashi, "Tōjiki kara mita Iwami ginzan shūhen chiiki Nima chō shutsudo shiryō o chūshin ni," *Sekai isan Iwami ginzan iseki no chōsa kenkyū* 3 (3.2013), pp. 1–15. Shinkawa Takashi explained on a tour of the region on 6.11.2015 that travel from the mines to Tomogaura required over four hours by foot and entailed traversing a steep mountain, while Yunotsu, used by the Mōri, required six to seven hours. The harbor witnessed two peaks of activity, one in the eleventh and twelfth centuries and the other in the fifteenth and early sixteenth centuries.

[50] *Yamaguchi kenshi shiryōhen chūsei*, vol. 4, Kuri ke monjo, doc. 15, 4.1353 (Bunwa 2) Akanami Shigefusa *gunchūjō*, p. 844, for battles between the Kuri and Nima Yatarō in 1353, and doc. 16, 8.1366 (Jōji 5) Kuri Chō'a *gunchūjō*, pp. 844–45, for conflicts during the later year.

[51] For more on the debates of the timing of Ōuchi control, see Itō Kenji, "Ōuchi shi no Iwami no kuni shihai no Nimagun bungun chigyō," *Yunotsu chōshi jōkan* (Yunotsu chō, 1994), pp. 595–615, and Itō Kenji, "Suō Ōuchi shi no Iwami no kuni Nimagun bungun chigyō," *Nanbokuchō ibun Chūgoku Shikoku hen*, vol. 2, *furoku*, 1989, pp. 3–6, for the suggestion that it happened in the mid-fourteenth century. See Kitajima Daisuke, "Chūsei Yamaguchi ni okeru kinzoku seisan," *Ōuchi shi kanren machinami iseki* 8 (Yamaguchi shi kyoiku iinkai, 2014), p. 258, for the suggestion that this occurred after 1366.

[52] For a somewhat later document of Migita Hironao as deputy, see *Masuda ke monjo*, vol. 2, doc. 517, 8.10. 1395 (Ōei 2) Iwami no kuni *shugo dai* Migita Hironao *jungyōjō*, pp. 260–61.

[53] Conversation Yasukuni Ryōichi, Sumitomo shiryōkan, 6.25.2018.

[54] Nakano Yoshifumi, the head of the Iwami ginzen shiryōkan, informed me of this discovery on 6.10.2015. For the excavations at Ōmoriza, see *Iwami ginzan iseki hakkutsu chōsa gaiyō Kobuyamatani Munaoka jūtaku machinami hozon chiku*, vol. 23 (3.2015), p. 61, although the excavation results at Kobuyama were not specifically mentioned.

[55] Copper slag excavated from the Ōtoshi no moto region provides proof of copper mining during the late fourteenth and early fifteenth centuries.

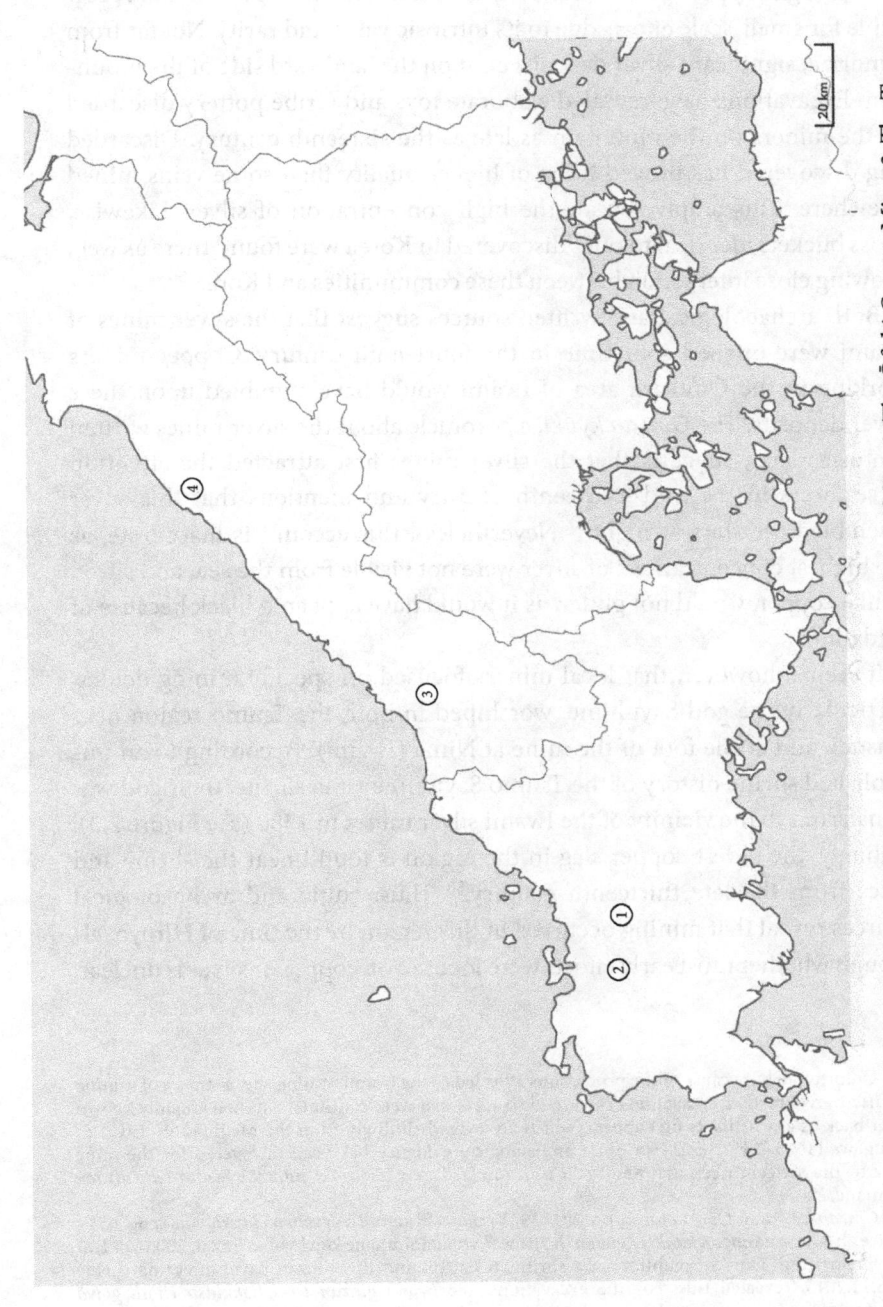

Figure 2.3 Map of Major Mines in Nagato and Iwami. 1. The Naganobori Copper Mine, 2. The Ōfuki Copper Mine, 3. The Tsumo Copper Mine, 4. Iwami Ginzan (Ōmoriza).

Although copper could be mined on a small scale, silver proved more profitable for small-scale efforts due to its intrinsic value and rarity. Not far from Ōmoriza, significant silver deposits exist on the landward side of the mountain. Excavations have revealed elaborate toys and Oribe pottery discarded by the miners on the mountain as late as the sixteenth century. Discarded slag discovered has proved to be of higher quality than some veins mined elsewhere. This amply reveals the high concentration of silver. Likewise, dross buckets identical to ones discovered in Korea were found there as well, showing close interaction between these communities and Korea.[56]

Both archaeological and written sources suggest that the silver mines of Iwami were opened sometime in the fourteenth century. Copper miners working in the Ōmoriza area of Iwami would have stumbled upon these silver deposits. The *Ginzan kyūki*, a chronicle about the silver mines written centuries later, suggests that the silver mines first attracted the attention of seafarers in the mid-fourteenth century and mentions that this silver resembled the stars at night.[57] Nevertheless, this account is inaccurate, as the highest concentrations of silver were not visible from the sea, and silver, unlike copper, would not glitter, as it would have appeared black because of oxidation.

It seems, however, that local miners focused on specific mining deities, particularly the god Sayuhime, worshiped in both the Tsumo region near Masuda and at the foot of the mine at Nima (Iwami). According to an unpublished shrine history of the Tsumo Sayuhimeyama shrine, their god was transferred to the vicinity of the Iwami silver mines in 1380 (see Figure 2.3). Tellingly, the oldest copper slag in the region is found near the shrine and dates from the late thirteenth century.[58] Thus, cultic and archaeological sources reveal that mining occurred in this region by the time of Hiroyo, although whether most early efforts were focused on copper or silver is unclear.

---

[56] Unfortunately, because of the protections afforded to the Iwami mining site, as traces of mining are discovered, further excavation ceases, and so areas that were continually mined are only known as far back as any artifacts first appear, which are overwhelmingly from the Meiji (1868–1912) or Tokugawa (1603–1867) eras. No other archeological evidence has been uncovered for the mine prior to the sixteenth century. See *Sekai isan toroku kinen Kagayaki futatabi Iwami Ginzan ten* (Shimane, 2007).

[57] *Ginzan kyūki*, in *Ōuchi bunka*, pp. 231–35, *Yamaguchi kenshi shiryōhen chūsei*, vol. 1, pp. 651–58. See also *Iwami Ginzan kankei hennen shiryō mokuroku* (Shimane ken kyoiku iinkai, 2003), p. 1.

[58] Exploration Tsumo Sayuhimeyama shrine, 6.9.2015, and the Ginzan Sayuhimeyama shrine on 6.11.2015, revealed this. For the excavations, see *Iwami ginzan iseki hakkutsu chōsa gaiyō Kobuyamatani Munaoka jūtaku machinami hozon chiku* (Shimane, 3.2015), p. 61. Kobuyama is located close to the Sayuhime shrine.

Ties with the Court

After early years spent consolidating authority in the provinces, Hiroyo did not return to Kyoto until 1363, roughly a generation after he had fled with his father at the age of seven. He made quite an impression on the residents of Kyoto when he visited in 1363, for according to the penultimate volume of the *Taiheiki*, he overawed them by liberally distributing the equivalent of millions of dollars—tens of thousands of *kan*—along with countless "newly imported Chinese [Tang] goods (*karamonotō*) from the continent," to warriors, monks and prostitutes.[59] *Taiheiki* is prone to exaggeration, but Hiroyo did rebuild multiple shrines for fifteen thousand *kanmon* each around this time, so he was undoubtedly capable of largesse. He was appointed to the fifth rank lower, making him a full member of the court nobility late in 1365, an honor uncommon for even warriors appointed to the powerful post of *shugo*, and took religious vows in the following year.[60]

Hiroyo's return to the capital was undoubtedly facilitated by nobles with Southern Court sympathies who resided in Suō under his protection, in spite of his having joined the rival Ashikaga. For example, the 1365 list of people who donated to the reconstruction of the Hōfu shrine included the Itsutsuji advisor (*jijū*) and novice (*nyūdō*), the only person given the honorific ("honorable") *dono* title.[61] The man in question was either Itsutsuji Toshiuji, who attained the third rank before retiring in 1336, and who returned to Kyoto with briefly resurgent Southern Court forces on 1.10.1353,[62] or Toshiuji's son Toshikazu, who also renounced the world. It is probably the latter who resided in Suō under Hiroyo's protection in 1365.[63] Thus Hiroyo maintained connections with Southern Court supporters, thereby revealing influence with the capital and a certain residual distance from the Ashikaga.

---

[59] Koakimoto Dan et al., eds., *Kōtei Kyōdaibon Taiheiki*, vol. 2, pp. 1333, 1464.

[60] *Yamaguchi kenshi tsūshihen chūsei*, CD-ROM Kengai shiryō, Tōkyō daigaku shiryōhensanjo *Kuzen rinji inzen mikyōjo an*, doc. 5, 12.20.1365 (Jōji 4) Go-Kōgon tennō *kuzen an utsushi*, p. 434.

[61] The Itsutsuji, descended from Kazan'in Kanemasa (d. 1216), were related to the family of Emperor Go-Daigo's mother. *Kokushi daijiten* (Yoshikawa kōbunkan, 1979), vol. 1, p. 684. For the Itsutsuji genealogy, see *Sonpi bunmyaku* (Yoshikawa kōbunkan, 1964), vol. 1, p. 201.

[62] *Kugyō bunin*, vol. 2 (Yoshikawa kōbunkan, 1964), pp. 535, 553, 558, and most importantly 562 for Toshiuji's rank and renouncing the world in 1336. For Toshiuji's return to the capital, *Dazaifu shishi chūsei hen* (Dazaifu, 2002), pp. 459–61, 464, and *Entairyaku*, vol. 4 (Zoku gunsho ruijū kanseikai, 1971), 1.10.1353 (Bunwa 2), p. 273.

[63] *Sonpi bunmyaku*, vol. 1, p. 201.

Court rank enabled Hiroyo to fraternize with the court nobility and facilitated a match with the daughter of a courtier.[64] One of his consorts was the daughter of Sanjō Kintada, the author of *Gogumaiki*. She bore his sixth son, Rokurō, the future Moriakira (1377–1431), at a residence near the Imakōji and Rokujō intersection in Kyoto in 1377.[65] Because of these court ties this son was treated differently than Hiroyo's third and fifth sons, for example, who were removed from succession and became retainers.[66]

Hiroyo's consort remained a conduit to the court, since Kintada's diary refers to receiving a letter from the "Bōshū [Suō] Ōuchi woman," an expression without honorifics that probably refers to his daughter.[67] Some accounts suggest that Hiroyo founded a settlement, which became known as Yamaguchi, just to the north of Kōryūji, and made it resemble Kyoto so as to please this same daughter, but such assertions are unverifiable, although they do suggest her influence.[68]

The Planned Settlement of Yamaguchi

Ōuchi Hiroyo decided to settle nearly three miles to the north of Kōryūji Hikamisan to establish his headquarters. He crossed a small ridge of hills and settled near a crossroads, with the only notable structure being Ima Hachiman, a shrine dedicated to Hachiman.[69] The site possessed natural advantages. It

[64] Other matches to the Jimyōin family of low-ranking nobles existed previously, and Kōno Moronao fathered Moroka by abducting a woman of the Nijō family, but this match between Hiroyo and the Sanjō appears to have been an unprecedented example of a *shugo* regional warrior marrying into the nobility. See Mizuno Tomoyuki, *Muromachi jidai kōbu kankei no kenkyū* (Yoshikawa kōbunkan, 2005), p. 226.

[65] *Ōuchi bunka*, p. 26, for the detailed Ōuchi genealogy in the Mōri archives. See also *Bōchō fūdo chūshin an*, vol. 13, *Yamaguchi saiban ge* (Yamaguchi, 1961), pp. 373–74, for how this connection led to a street with the same name being established in Yamaguchi. It also discusses the establishment of the "four cardinal directions for the city (*shijin sō-ō*). For analysis of Ōuchi dwellings in Kyoto during the late fourteenth and early fifteenth centuries, see Suda Makiko, "Ōuchi shi no zaikyō katsudō," *Ōuchi to Ōtomo*, pp. 101–2.

[66] *Hagi han batsu etsu roku*, vol. 3 maki 102–2 Reizen Gorō, doc. 128, pp. 235–36, which states that the Reizen were descended from Ōuchi Gorō Hiromasa, the fifth son of Hiroyo, and ultimately a prince (Imsŏng) from Korea, which we shall explain more fully in chapter 4. See also Matsuoka, *Ōuchi shi no kenkyū* (Seibundō, 2011), p. 81 for the Reizen. Their genealogy, from the Naikaku bunko, appears most conveniently in *Ōuchi bunka*, pp. 49–51.

[67] *Gogumaiki*, vol. 2 (Iwanami shoten, 1984), 4.22.1378 (Eiwa 4), p. 265.

[68] For these claims, see Koga Nobuyuki, "Bōshū Yamaguchi ni okeru shiro, tate, tera," in *Chūsei toshi kenkyū*, comp., *Toshi no kyūshin roku* (Shinjinbutsu ōraisha, 2000), p. 100.

[69] *Bōchō fūdo chūshin an*, vol. 13, pp. 278–79, also reveals that an Ima Hachiman shrine predated Hiroyo's settlement. Located near the Tatekōji road, it may partially explain why Hiroyo settled in this region, just as Tsurugaoka Hachiman became the core of Kamakura. Conversation with Hirase Naoki, 10.2011.

was convenient for transportation and trade, and a valley basin some four-teen miles long placed it at a crossroads: one road led north to the Japan Sea through what is now Hagi, and another, east–west, led to Iwami and its copper and silver mines.[70] Kyushu was not far to the west, and a north–south road meant that fish and produce from both the Inland Sea and the Japan Sea could be shipped. The site was therefore a natural hub for trade.[71] Likewise, this residence was a mere seven miles to the northeast of Itsukushima shrine, located on the intersection of the Fushino River and the Sanyōdō western highway, which at the time would have been located on the coast.

The city of Yamaguchi did not arise in a haphazard manner. It was rather a planned settlement laid out around Hiroyo's original dwelling. The major roads of Yamaguchi themselves were aligned with the peaks of surrounding hills.[72] Likewise, Hiroyo created a new road, the east–west "Great Lord's Road" (ōdono ōji). It passed from the front of his mansion, some three hundred yards north of the old intersection, and linked the old highway to Iwami and its mines, and Tatekōji, a north–south route that ran from the Inland Sea to the Japan Sea.[73]

Recent archaeological excavations show that Hiroyo's dwelling there first came into use in the latter half of the fourteenth century,[74] and the Ming ambassador Zhao Zhi mentions visiting his "new dwelling" in 1373.[75] It was around this time that Hiroyo transferred the casket of the purported Ōuchi

---

[70] Kitajima Daisuke, "Ōuchi yakata to Yamaguchi," *Saikoku no kenryoku to senran*, p. 185, for the connection to Iwami, and how Yamaguchi is only eight and a half miles from the mouth of the Fushino River, which connects to the Inland Sea. For the best overview of Yamaguchi, and the varying historical, geographic and archaeological analysis of the site, see Mashino Shinji, "Chūsei no Yamaguchi," in Kage Toshio, ed., *Ōuchi to Ōtomo* (Bensei shuppan, 2013), pp. 245–84, and Koga Nobuyuki, "Bōshū Yamaguchi ni okeru shiro, tate, tera," p. 100, for the convenient selection of the Yamaguchi valley, which was just over twelve miles in length, with its links to the Japan Sea and Inland Sea, and roads to Iwami and the Suō provincial headquarters.

[71] Koga Nobuyuki, "Bōshū Yamaguchi ni okeru shiro, tate, tera," p. 100.

[72] The roads so constructed included Ōdono ōji Tsukiyama kōji, Ise ōji, Shimo kōji, Nakadono kōji, Itomai kōji, and Babadono kōji. Kitajma Daisuke, "Ōuchi shi no machi zukuri: Chūsei toshi Yamaguchi no 'genten' no hakken," in Kage Toshio, ed., *Sengoku daimyō no doboku jigyō* (Ebisu kōshō, 2018), pp. 124–42. For the lining up of the roads, see pp. 137–39.

[73] For a pioneering study, see Hirase Naoki, "Chūsei toshi no kūkan kōzō—Suō no kuni Yamaguchi o chūshin ni," *Hokuriku toshi shigaku kaishi* 8 (2001), p. 4. See also Yamamura Aki, "Chūsei toshi no kūkan kōzō," in *Yamaguchi kenshi tsūshihen chūsei*, pp. 670–98, and Kitajima "Ōuchi yakata to Yamaguchi," p. 185.

[74] For more recent excavations and a timeline by Kitajima Daisuke, see *Ōuchi yakata hōkokusho* 11 (Yamaguchi shi maizō bunka chōsa hōkoku no. 101, 2010), pp. 175–258, 259–63, and 13 (2012), pp. 7–8.

[75] This is the *Unmon ikkyoku* by the Ming ambassador Zhao Zhi reproduced in *Ōuchi bunka*, pp. 535–48. See also pp. 537, 540, 542–43.

Figure 2.4 Early Ōuchi *Hishi* (Water Chestnut Flower) Crest. Photograph and permission courtesy Yamaguchi-shi kyōiku iinkai

progenitor from Kuruma-zuka to Jōfukuji in Yamaguchi.[76] A well-known map of Yamaguchi (Figure 8.3) claims that the region was settled in 1360.[77]

James McClain has pointed out how "from the 14th century onward, an increasing number of towns began to dot the Japanese mapboard. Strung necklace-like around Kyoto were satellite communities," while "further afield were local towns that often specialized in particular products."[78] The towns that McClain describes arose organically, but Yamaguchi differed in that it was a planned settlement, designed to be convenient for trade and suited for Ōuchi supervision and control. Epitomizing this, Ōuchi rooftiles graced not only their mansion, but could be found decorating structures in the town with the distinctive Ōuchi *hishi* crest (see Figures 2.4 and 2.5).[79]

---

[76] *Bōchō fūdo chūshin an*, vol. 9, *Mitashiri jō* (Yamaguchi, 1960), p. 592.

[77] For this map, see Figure 8.3 and *Ōuchi bunka*, supplementary map (*fuzu*), Yamaguchi *kozu*. See also *Bōchō fūdo chūshin an*, vol.13, *Yamaguchi saiban ge* (Yamaguchi, 1961), p. 214. For skepticism regarding some aspects of this map, such as the date of Yamaguchi's founding, see Kitajima Daisuke, "Ōuchi shi no machi zukuri," p. 125.

[78] James McClain, "Japan's Pre-modern Urbanism," in *The Oxford Handbook of Cities in World History* (New York: Oxford University Press, 2013), p. 330.

[79] *Ōuchi shi yakata ato* 15 (Yamaguchi, 2014), pp. 235–54, for analysis and dating of the rooftiles. The crest depicted above exhibits older stylistic traits than one Ōuchi *hishi* crest from Jōfukuji, Hiroyo's mortuary temple, which likely dates from the late fourteenth century. Yamaguchi kyōiku iinkai, comp., *Yamaguchi shi maizō bunkazai chōsa hōkokusho*, no. 121, *Ryōunji ato*, vol. 2 (Yamaguchi: Yamaguchi kyōiku iinkai, 2019), p. 232. This example, discarded in the sixteenth century, resembles others from the Ōuchi mansion that had been thrown away in a well around the same time as well. For those tiles, see *Ōuchi shi yakata ato* V (Yamaguchi shi maizō bunkazai chōsa hōkokusho no. 16, Yamaguchi shi kyōiku iinkai, 1983), p. 17. For more on Jōfukuji, see chapter 3.

Figure 2.5 Later Style Ōuchi *Hishi* Crest. Photograph by Thomas Conlan

Ōuchi genealogies mention that Hiroyo transferred still further deities from the capital to Yamaguchi, since he purportedly founded religious institutions named after Kiyomizu and Atago, two important Kyoto sites.[80] Other sources describe him founding a Gion shrine in 1369 and the Furukuma shrine, which housed the deified Sugawara Michizane, in 1373.[81] These shrines, linked to Kitano and Gion, were established in the new city proper.[82] Gion festivals started to be performed at Yamaguchi from that time. Hiroyo is reported also to have wished to model Yamaguchi on the Mibu region of Kyoto, where he had lived.[83] Nevertheless, despite this large number of shrines, the early Yamaguchi

[80] *Ōuchi bunka*, p. 25.

[81] *Bōchō fūdo chūshin an*, vol. 13, p. 53, for how Hiroyo had the deity of Yasaka (Gion) transferred (*kanjō*) to Yamaguchi in 1369 (Ōan 2). See also *Ōuchi yakata* 12, p. 5, for references to a Gion shrine in Yamaguchi. See also *Ōuchi bunka*, pp. 653–54, for how Furukuma shrine was founded through the transfer of the Tenjin deity from Kitano Tenmangū in 1373. See also p. 650 for Hiroyo's construction of Yasaka shrine in 1370.

[82] *Ōuchi bunka*, p. 650, for reference to how Hiroyo transferred the deity (*kanshin*) of Yasaka shrine there in 1370 (Ōan 3). For Furukuma shrine being linked to Kitano, and that this name dates from 1373 (Ōan 6), see pp. 653–54.

[83] *Bōchō fūdo chūshin an*, vol. 13, p. 51. See pp. 51–53 for a description of the Gion festival in Yamaguchi through the time of Ōuchi Yoshinaga (d. 1557).

settlement basically consisted of the Ōuchi dwelling complex and several religious institutions, rather than of an extensive urban center.[84] That town would
become more expansive in the fifteenth century.

Turmoil of the 1370s

It is in 1366 that Hiroyo took the tonsure, and sometime between the eighth
and ninth months of that year he became a lay priest under the name of
Dōkai.[85] He nevertheless continued expanding his influence, focusing on the
province of Aki, located to the east. Like Iwami, it was rich in ore.

Hiroyo had conquered regions based on their wealth and terrain rather
than their administrative boundaries. Northern Aki was close to Iwami, so
a natural target. He originally was not *shugo* of that province, but he used a
brief appointment with great success until he was divested of the office; he
then used his authority to make the province of Aki, and Iwami, ungovernable by later *shugo* successors.

By the seventh month of 1367, Hiroyo can already be documented as
attacking "rebel" Southern Court forces in Aki.[86] Not long thereafter, in the
following year, he was appointed as *shugo* of Aki, a post he would hold until
early in 1371.[87] During that time, he confirmed the lands of such Aki warriors
as Naitō Michiyasu, from the Itsukushima region, and adjudicated disputes.[88]

---

[84] Mashino Shinji, "Chūsei no Yamaguchi," p. 273.

[85] This has been noted by Kondō Kiyoshi, Ōuchi shi jitsuroku, p. 24, as occurring between the sixth
and ninth months of 1366. Compare petitions signed by Hiroyo for the Kuri and the Masuda in the
eighth and ninth months of 1366 (Jōji 5). See NBIC, vol. 4, doc. 3484, 8.1366 (Jōji 5) Kuri Chō'a
gunchūjō, p. 189, and doc. 3489, 9.3.1366 (Jōji 5) Masuda Kanemi gunchūjō, p. 190.

[86] NBIC, vol. 4, doc. 3565, 10.1367 (Jōji 6) Bō gunchūjō, p. 213.

[87] This appointment is not mentioned in Satō Shin'ichi, Muromachi bakufu shugo seido no kenkyū
2, pp. 151, 157. Surviving documents reveal, however, that Hiroyo and not a Takeda was appointed to
this position. See Yamaguchi kenshi tsūshihen chūsei, CD-ROM Kengai shiryō, Tōji hyakugō monjo
(Kyōto furitsu sōgō shiryōkan zō), doc. 66, 6.1379 (Kōryaku 1) Saishōkōin kata hyōjō hikitsuke,
pp. 475–76, for hitherto unacknowledged proof that Hiroyo served as the Aki shugo. This document
explains how "the shugo Ōuchi no suke Zenmon [Dōkai/Hiroyo] claimed that Tōji's Miwa estate
constituted lands dedicated for military provisions and had entrusted them to his followers since
1369 (Ōan 2)." Kawamura Shōichi follows Satō in arguing that no evidence exists for Hiroyo as shugo
even though "he acted like one." Aki Takeda shi (Ebisu kōshō, 2010), pp. 58–59. Matsuoka, as well,
provides considerable evidence of Hiroyo acting as if he were shugo from 1368 through 1371. See
Ōuchi shi no kenkyū, pp. 221–23, for reference to Hiroyo's shugo-like status (shugoteki chi'i).

[88] For Hiroyo's activities and confirmations, see NBIC, vol. 4, doc. 3635, 8.16 Ōuchi Dōkai shojō,
p. 233, doc. 3636 8.28 Dōkai azukejō, p. 233, doc. 3643, 9.24 Ōuchi Dōkai shojō, p. 235, and doc. 3644,
Ōuchi Dōkai urafu Ashikaga Tadayoshi saikyojō, pp. 235–36. For his confirmations of Tōji rights,
see doc. 3724, 6.12.1369 (Ōan 2) Muromachi bakufu mikyōjō an, p. 262, doc. 3726, 6.22.1369 (Ōan
2) Muromachi bakufu mikyōjō, p. 262, doc. 3811, 10.13.1370 (Ōan 3) Muromachi bakufu mikyōjō,
p. 293, and doc. 3815, 11.3.1370 (Ōan 3) Ōuchi Dōkai (Hiroyo) ukebumi utsushi, p. 294.

Hiroyo was an effective commander. He launched an offensive into Northern Aki, where he defeated Southern Court supporters: something that the previous *shugo*, a member of the Takeda family, had been unable to accomplish.[89] Mōri Chikahira, for example, admitted that he surrendered because Hiroyo had entered the province.[90] Likewise, Hiroyo's absence in 1372, when he crossed over to Kyushu, caused this offensive against Southern Court supporters in Aki to sputter.[91]

Hiroyo had access to what was for the time a considerable army of four thousand troops. By contrast, his son Yoshihiro commanded only three hundred in 1375.[92] Both contemporary documents and chronicles such as the *Sakaiki* consistently mention Hiroyo's army of four thousand, which was not large enough to wage successful campaigns simultaneously in Aki and Kyushu.[93]

Hiroyo's military effectiveness stemmed thus not from military manpower but, in part, from his ability to occupy and distribute lands in Aki, which can be documented as happening during and after his tenure as *shugo*, from the tenth month of 1368 through 1371.[94] He did not fight only for Ashikaga interests but constructed his own power base as well. He built castles in the Itsukushima region and attacked his "old enemy" but nominal ally, the Takeda.[95]

[89] For the best analysis, see Kawamura Shōichi, *Aki Takeda shi*, pp. 58–59.

[90] Kawamura Shōichi, *Aki Takeda shi*, p. 59, and Tōkyō daigaku shiryōhen sanjo, comp., *Mōri ke monjo*, vol. 1 (Tōkyō daigaku shuppankai, 1920), doc. 15, 5.1376 (Eiwa 2) Mōri Motoharu *jihitsu kotogaki an*, pp. 18–34, and doc. 13-9, 7.10.1374 (Ōan 7) Mōri Motoharu *gunchūjō an*, pp. 11–12. See also NBIC, vol. 5, doc. 4262, 3.1376 (Eiwa 2) Mōri Motoharu *gunchūjō an*, p. 85, for how Hiroyo colluded with Chikahira to take over Motoharu's lands.

[91] This was evident by the eight month of 1372 (Ōan 5). NBIC, vol. 5, doc. 4065, 7.1374 (Ōan 7) Mōri Motoharu *gunchūjō an*, pp. 16–17.

[92] NBIC, vol. 5, doc. 4252, 1.23 [(Eiwa 2) 1376] Imagawa Ryōshun *shojō utsushi*, pp. 80–81.

[93] Kansai daigaku chūsei bungaku kenkyūkai, ed., *Sonkeikaku bunko zō Sakaiki* (Izumi shoin, 1990), pp. 47–48, and Royall Tyler, *Fourteenth-Century Voices III: Iwashimizu Hachiman in War and Cult* (Blue Tongue Books, 2017), "Ōeiki," pp. 113–30, p. 116, for a translation of a variant text. The *Sakaiki* mentions that Yoshihiro only had three hundred under his command, a figure that meshes with the Imagawa letter of 1.23.1376. For a list of other texts that refer to this same number, see *Ōuchi shi jitsuroku*, p. 25 for 10.7.1371 (Ōan 4).

[94] *Yamaguchi kenshi tsūshihen chūsei*, CD-ROM Kengai shiryō (*Chūsei bōchō shōen shiryō*), Tōji hyakugō monjo (Kyōto furitsu sōgō shiryōkan zō), doc. 54, 10.7.1368 (Ōan 1) Muromachi shōgun ke Ashikaga Yoshimitsu *mikyōjo an*, p. 468, doc. 56, 6.12.1369 (Ōan 2) Muromachi shōgun ke Ashikaga Yoshimitsu *mikyōjo an*, p. 469. Hiroyo apparently repeatedly and consistently ignored these edicts. See doc. 61, 9.1373 (Ōan 6) Tōji *zasshō* Raiken *kasane mōshijō*, p. 473. One of these complaints appears in doc. 64, Saishōkōin kata *hyōjō hikitsuke*, p. 474.

[95] NBIC, vol. 4, doc. 3983, 7.19.1373 (Ōan 6) Muromachi bakufu *saikyōjō utsushi*, pp. 357–58, p. 358. The narrative is not clear, but the events took place after Hiroyo entered Aki and before the eleventh month of 1370.

As Hiroyo expanded into Aki he adjudicated various disputes regarding its lands in 1370.[96] He thus continued the process, evident elsewhere, of fusing patronage of shrines with consolidation of his authority in the province. In Aki, however, he was checked in 1371 when Imagawa Ryōshun (1326–1420) was dispatched to the west in that year and appointed *shugo* of Aki in his stead. Ryōshun, who explicitly announced this appointment in documents addressed to local Aki warriors, thus displaced Hiroyo.[97]

The relationship between the two commanders became tense. Hiroyo, briefly involved in a campaign in Kyushu, crossed the sea on 12.19.1371 and achieved success before returning to western Honshu during the eighth month of 1372, but he remained embroiled in Aki affairs.[98]

Hiroyo flouted Ashikaga authority in judicial cases immediately after his appointment as the *shugo* of this province.[99] In the seventh month of 1374, having abandoned the Kyushu campaign, he invaded Aki again with a powerful force, directly attacking Imagawa Ryōshun, his successor as Aki *shugo*. Among other things he confiscated the lands of Mōri Motoharu and built fortifications, which prevented Motoharu from exercising authority for three years.[100] In 1376 Motoharu later complained bitterly that Hiroyo's allegiances were suspect, arguing that Hiroyo's surrender to the Ashikaga was merely nominal and that he "still harbored deep ambition and remained in contact with the Kyushu prince [Kaneyoshi], and the Kikuchi."[101] One might take this to be slander, but in fact Hiroyo did long protect Southern Court princes in his territories.

It made sense, therefore, that the Ashikaga suspected Hiroyo of being in sympathy with the Southern Court and relieved him of his Iwami *shugo* post

---

[96] Matsuoka, *Ōuchi shi no kenkyū*, pp. 222–24. The most significant documents were those in which the *shugo* demanded compliance to orders to cease the occupation of lands, which can be verified for 1368 and 1369. See *Yamaguchi kenshi tsūshihen chūsei*, CD-ROM Kengai shiryō (*Chūsei bōchō shōen shiryō*), Tōji hyakugō monjo (se), doc. 54, 10.7.1368 (Ōan 1) Muromachi shōgun ke (Ashikaga Yoshimitsu) *mikyōjo an*, p. 468, and doc. 56, 6.12.1369 (Ōan 2) Muromachi shōgun ke (Ashikaga Yoshimitsu) *mikyōjo an*, p. 469.

[97] See NBIC, vol. 4, doc. 3860, 4.16 [(Ōan 4) 1371] Imagawa Ryōshun (Sadayo) *shojō*, p. 314 and Kawazoe Shōji, *Imagawa Ryōshun* (Yoshikawa kōbunkan, 1964), pp. 88–89. Ryōshun effectively began exercising this authority on 3.21.1371. See NBIC, vol. 4, doc. 3853, 3.21.1371 (Ōan 4) Imagawa Ryōshun (Sadayo) *azukejō an*, p. 312.

[98] This is most evident in the 7.1374 (Ōan 7) Mōri Motoharu *gunchūjō an*, NBIC, vol. 5, doc. 4065, pp. 16–17, and doc. 4665, 7.1374 (Ōan 7) Mōri Hirofusa *kasenegaki an*, reproduced in the 1.13.1381 (Kōryaku 3) document, pp. 273–277, p. 274.

[99] NBIC, vol. 4, doc. 3983, 7.19.1373 (Ōan 6) Muromachi bakufu *saikyōjo utsushi*, pp. 357–58. This describes more the dispute over Aki lands with Kobayakawa and Itsukushima *zasshō*.

[100] NBIC, vol. 5, doc. 4665, 1.13.1381 (Kōryaku 3) Mōri Hirofusa *kasanegaki an*, pp. 273–77, p. 276.

[101] NBIC, vol. 5, doc. 4269, 5.1376 (Eiwa 2) Mōri Motoharu *jihitsu kotogaki an*, pp. 125–32; p. 129. See also p. 131 for reference to Hiroyo as being a grave enemy with great ambitions.

in the fourth month of 1376. At the same time, however, cognizant of durable Ōuchi authority further west, they expressly confirmed his Suō and Nagato *shugo* appointments.[102]

A warrior who had spent much of his life conquering diverse regions, Hiroyo was not constrained by administrative boundaries or official appointments. To the contrary, in order to wield authority in these provinces he established a pattern of rule independent of such offices as that of *shugo*. Even after losing his *shugo* appointments in Aki and Iwami he maintained control over the most vital district in both provinces: the harbors of Nima and Tōsai. Located in central administrative regions, these were the economic and political heart of each province, as well as important ports.[103] Thus, even by the latter half of the fourteenth century, not all provinces could be governed by the office of *shugo*, particularly in cases where magnates like Hiroyo and his successor were able to establish direct authority in districts in provinces that he did not nominally govern.

Soon after being dismissed as *shugo* of Aki, and shortly before losing the same post in Iwami, Ōuchi Hiroyo granted the Masuda autonomy from all *shugo* authority in the latter province, thus extending privileges that he had granted the Masuda in 1371.[104] Imagawa Ryōshun, Hiroyo's successor as *shugo* of Aki, tried to assert control over the province and demanded that Hiroyo cease occupying districts within it.[105] Hiroyo ignored him, and his descendants maintained in these provinces a presence that prevented *shugo* from exercising effective administrative control of both provinces.

---

[102] *Gogumaiki*, vol. 2, intercalary (*urū*) 7.16.1376 (Eiwa 2), p. 212 for Hiroyo's divestment of his Iwami post, and reconfirmation by the *kanrei* Hosokawa Yoriyuki of his *shugo* posts for Suō and Nagato. See also NBIC, vol. 5, doc. 4665, 1.13.1381 (Kōryaku 3) Mōri Hirofusa *kasanegaki an*, p. 276, Matsuoka, *Ōuchi shi no kenkyū* p. 247, and Satō Shin'ichi, *Muromachi bakufu shugo seido no kenkyū* 2, pp. 69–73.

[103] For reference to Hiroyo's links to Tōsai dating from 1374, see NBIC, vol. 5, doc. 4075, 9.6.1374 (Ōan 7) Ōuchi Yoshihiro *andojō*, p. 20. This mistakenly refers to Yoshihiro but is most likely Hiroyo confirming these lands in his position as *shugo*. See also *Yamaguchi kenshi tsūshihen chūsei* 1, p. 359, showing how Hiroyo's control over Tōsaijō began at around 1370, the first summer of the Ōan era.

[104] NBIC, vol. 4, doc. 3862, 4.27.1374 (Ōan 4) Shami Seishū *hōsho*, p. 314. Notably, Hiroyo granted these rights to the Masuda coterminous with Ryōshun exercising *shugo* rights to Aki. Compare doc. 3860, 4.16 Imagawa Ryōshun Sadayo *shojō*, p. 314. See also NBIC, vol. 4, doc. 3883, 8.12.1371 (Ōan 4). Shami Seishū *ukebumi*, p. 321, and Inoue Hiroshi, *Shiryōshū Masuda Kanemi to sono jidai: Masuda ke monjo no kataru chūsei no Masuda* 1 (Masuda kyōiku iinkai, 1994), doc. 42, 4.27.1371 (Ōan 4) Shami Seishū *hōsho*, p. 73.

[105] *Yamaguchi kenshi tsūshihen chūsei*, Kengai shiryō CD-ROM (*Chūsei bōchō shōen shiryō*), Tōji hyakugō monjo, doc. 65, 3.16.1379 (Eiwa 5) Imagawa Ryōshun (Sadayo) *hōsho*, p. 475. See also doc. 67, 2.24.1380 (Kōryaku 2) Muromachi shōgun ke Ashikaga Yoshimitsu *mikyōjo*, p. 476, for complaints that the Ōuchi lay priest (*nyūdō*) continued to occupy districts (*gō*) and *jitō* posts of Aki.

Hiroyo's de facto authority in Iwami and Aki worked through a network of roads, ports, and informal bonds of affiliation.[106] His spirit was amply reflected in the Ōuchi pattern of rule in these regions, since it paid little attention to formal authority, instead emphasizing control over strategic resources and, at the same time, the creation of a powerful alliance of shared interests. Ōuchi and local warrior resistance to *shugo* authority made for a durable, but informal network of governance. Over time, Hiroyo and his descendants were well placed to absorb prominent warriors from both provinces, such as the Yoshimi of Iwami, who became incorporated into their organization.[107] The Yoshimi may have eluded formal Ōuchi control, but they firmly remained part of the Ōuchi network of authority.

Hiroyo, who had fared poorly with his *shugo* appointments and in dealing with the Ashikaga in general, in 1376 dispatched a plenipotentiary named Hirai Dōjo or alternately Shōjo, a Kyoto resident, to serve as a conduit for information to and from Yamaguchi.[108] Wada Shūsaku characterizes Hirai's role as dealing with Ashikaga administrators, aiding with land confirmations, and engaging in negotiations with capital authorities. Hirai, who also transmitted works of literature, was involved in trade with the continent and in negotiations and promotions. He remained permanently in the capital but was known for his erudition as far afield as Korea.[109] Having someone like Hirai Dōjo proved helpful, as the late 1370s witnessed instability, political change, and the rise to power of Yoshimitsu, the unpredictable third Ashikaga shogun.[110]

---

[106] For an informative article on the rich network of roads linking Aki and Iwami, see Akiyama Nobutaka, "Muromachi Sengokuki ni okeru Aki Iwami kōtsū," *Shigaku kenkyū* 218 (10.1997), p. 8, where he reveals that western Iwami was closely linked to Hatsukaichi and the Itsukushima area of Aki. His sources date from the fifteenth century but describe routes that had existed earlier.

[107] *Tsuwano chōshi*, vol. 1 (Tsuwano chō, 1970), pp. 412–13.

[108] For research on Ōuchi representatives (*zasshō*) in the capital, see Wada Shūsaku, "Ōuchi shi no ryōgoku shihai soshiki to jinzai tōyō," in Kishida Hiroshi, ed., *Mōri Motonari to chiiki shakai* (Hiroshima: Chūgoku shinbunsha, 2007), p. 206. See also Suda Makiko, "Ōuchi shi no zaikyō katsudō," p. 104. For a good overview of the role of the representative in Kyoto for the Ōuchi, albeit during the fifteenth century, see Kobayashi Takeo, "Sengoku daimyō ke zaikyō zasshō o megutte: Ōuchi shi no bai," *Komazawa shigaku* nos. 39–40 (9.1988), pp. 225–38.

[109] Wada Shūsaku, "Ōuchi shi no ryōgoku shihai soshiki to jinzai tōyō," pp. 206–7. Wada postulates that Hirai was most likely related to retainers of the same name who were affiliated with the Kyōgoku, a *shugo* of Ōmi province and this explains why they aided Yoshihiro in the 1399 disturbance. According to Wada, Hirai appears in the Korean sources as Minamoto Shōjo and is described as a famous official of the provinces (*kuni no meishi*). See p. 206 and chapter 3. For more analysis, see Hagihara Daisuke, "Chūsei kōki Ōuchi shi no zaikyō," *Nihon rekishi* 786 (11.2013), pp. 18–19, including documents issued to Tōji and the Masuda.

[110] Hirai Dōjo, after serving Hiroyo, would also be an agent of his son Yoshihiro. See chapter 3.

Nevertheless, Hiroyo's loss of the Aki and Iwami *shugo* posts caused a dispute to fester within the Ōuchi organization as to where to concentrate their effort toward expansion—Iwami, Aki and further east, or Kyushu to the west. Hiroyo and his younger son Mitsuhiro favored maintaining control in Iwami and Aki even if doing so entailed a rift with the Ashikaga. Hiroyo's eldest son and designated successor Yoshihiro advocated advancing into Kyushu, where he had fought in 1375, and strongly supporting the Ashikaga. Hiroyo, by contrast, conspicuously failed to support Imagawa Ryōshun in his hour of need in 1375. Ryōshun himself would recount how father and son were not in accord when Yoshihiro crossed the sea with three hundred men to Bungo province in Kyushu.[111]

Hiroyo remained active in Yamaguchi in his last years, crafting laws concerning the governance of Kōryūji and founding more temples and shrines.[112] In the eighth month of 1379, in the immediate aftermath of the political upheaval that witnessed the ouster of Hosokawa Yoriyuki, the powerful chancellor (*kanrei*) of Ashikaga Yoshimitsu, Hiroyo was again appointed *shugo* of Iwami, a position that he would hold for only three months, until he was replaced by his son and heir Yoshihiro.[113] Mitsuhiro, his deputy in Iwami, continued to act on his behalf even after Yoshihiro's appointment.[114] Hiroyo and Mitsuhiro acted in alliance with the Masuda, to whom Hiroyo had granted considerable rights.[115] In fact, Mitsuhiro appears to have acted as the actual *shugo* of Iwami and Nagato later that year. This led to warfare within the Ōuchi organization during the last year of Hiroyo's life, resulting in Yoshihiro's ultimate victory.[116]

---

[111] Hirase Naoki, *Ōuchi Yoshihiro* (Minerva shobō, 2017), p. 26. For Ryōshun's complaint, see *Aso monjo*, vol. 2 (Tōkyō daigaku shuppankai, 1933), Aso ke *utsushi*, 7, 1.23 [(Eiwa 2) 1376] Imagawa Ryōshun *shojō*, pp. 167–69.

[112] Momose Kesao et al., eds., *Chūsei hōsei shiryōshū*, vol. 4, *buke hō* 2 (Iwanami shoten, 1998), doc. 91, p. 78. See also Iwasaki Toshihiko *Kōryūji monjo o yomu*, vol. 1 (Ōuchi shi kabegaki kenkyūkai, 2004), pp. 49–52.

[113] See Satō Shin'ichi, *Muromachi bakufu shugo seido no kenkyū*, vol. 2, pp. 71–73. See also NBIC, vol. 5, doc. 4543, 9.12.1379 (Kōryaku 1) Ōuchi shi *bugyōnin rensho hōsho*, p. 227 for documentary proof that Hiroyo served in this position. For Hiroyo and Suō and Nagato, see Satō Shin'ichi, *Muromachi bakufu shugo seido no kenkyū*, vol. 2, pp. 158–75. For more on the upheaval of 1379, see Conlan, *From Sovereign to Symbol* (New York: Oxford University Press, 2011), pp. 169–70.

[114] Satō Shin'ichi, *Muromachi bakufu shugo seido no kenkyū*, vol. 2, pp. 72–73, for Yoshihiro's appointment. For Mitsuhiro as deputy from the time that Hiroyo was Iwami *shugo*, and how he worked in Hiroyo's interests, see Inoue, *Shiryōshū Masuda Kanemi to sono jidai*, pp. 147–49.

[115] Inoue, *Shiryōshū Masuda Kanemi to sono jidai*, pp. 147–49.

[116] Inoue, *Shiryōshū Masuda Kanemi to sono jidai*, pp. 148–53, and Matsuoka, *Ōuchi Yoshihiro*, pp. 104–11. For Mitsuhiro documents revealing his position as *shugo* of Nagato, see NBIC, vol. 5, doc. 4647, 10.13.1380 (Kōryaku 2) Ōuchi Mitsuhiro *ategaijō utsushi*, and doc. 4648, 10.26.1380 (Kōryaku 2) Ōuchi Mitsuhiro *ategaijō utsushi*, p. 267. See also *Yamaguchi kenshi shiryōhen chūsei*, vol. 2, Ono ke monjo, doc. 15, 6.13.1380 (Kōryaku 2) Ōuchi Mitsuhiro *azukejō*, pp. 1018–19.

As a fitting coda to Hiroyo's life of conquest and consolidation, in 1380, just months before his death, three members of the Washizu were killed in battle, thus ending Washizu autonomy. According to *Taiheiki*, the Kotō, who had been the *shugo* of Nagato, perished as well.[117] The Washizu survivors had no choice but to follow the Ōuchi line of Hiroyo and his sons.[118] By the time of Hiroyo's death it had become evident that no collaterals could challenge his dominance in the core lands Suō and Nagato, although his descendants' final control of over the Washizu homeland of Kudamatsu would not be cemented until the late fifteenth century, when Hiroyo's great-grandson Masahiro would rebuild the shrine at Kudamatsu and forge documents making Hikamisan, not Kudamatsu, the primary site of Ōuchi Myōken worship.[119]

Hiroyo died on 11.15.1380, and Jōfukuji became his mortuary temple.[120] His legacy proved profound. He had fully realized the opportunities provided by the turmoil of the 1350s and ensured that his authority over Suō and Nagato remained unchallenged. His conquest of Nagato gave him initial access to mines, and from there he began attempting to control and pacify the nearby seas. His expansion into Iwami and Aki allowed him to amass great wealth and to incorporate Suō, Nagato, and Iwami warriors into his forces. His relatively brief tenure as *shugo* in Aki (four years) and Iwami (ten years) also helped him to establish links to the most strategic regions of both provinces, including the Straits of Shimonoseki and the Aki harbor of Tōsai.

Yamaguchi, a new core settlement, linked by road to the Japan and Inland Seas, as well as to Iwami and Suō, also represents something remarkable and new. No other comparable new settlement arose during the fourteenth century. Hiroyo's focus on the east would be replaced by renewed interest in the west—Kyushu, the major port of Hakata, and territories in northern Kyushu that would become core Ōuchi holdings through the mid-sixteenth

---

[117] *Yamaguchi kenshi shiryōhen chūsei*, vol. 1, Kaei sandaiki, 5.18.1380 (Koryaku 2), p. 505, and Hyōdō Hiromi, ed., *Taiheiki*, vol. 6, maki 39, "Ōuchi no suke kōsan no koto" p. 139, for a lament regarding the fate of the Kotō. As this is absent from other texts, like the Kyōdaibon (Koakimoto Dan et al., eds., *Kōtei Kyōdaibon Taiheiki*, vol. 2, pp.1333, 1464) the reference may reflect Hosokawa sympathies.

[118] The Washizu sided with Michihiro over Yoshihiro in a succession dispute in Hiroyo's late years, with three being killed in Aki. Ultimately, Washizu Hirotada was appointed as the deputy *shugo* of Nagato province, but he was killed in 1448. See chapter 6.

[119] See chapter 7.

[120] *Ōuchi shi jitsuroku*, pp. 26–27.

century. With this foothold in Kyushu and access to the port at Hakata, trade and contacts with Korea and the Asian continent would flourish. Yoshihiro, Hiroyo's successor, saw greater opportunity than did his father in advancing west, across the sea, in order to control Kyushu. His vision would build and define the core Ōuchi territories for the next century and a half. It is to this man, and the dangers that he invited, that we now turn.

3

Ōuchi Yoshihiro and the Forging
of Ōuchi Identity

Ōuchi Yoshihiro (1356–99), the eldest child of Ōuchi Hiroyo (1325–80), gained fame through war, ritual, and diplomacy. He sought knowledge about his ancestry from the Chosŏn Dynasty (J. Chōsen, 1392–1897), claiming descent from Korean kings, and strove to reconstruct his forgotten lineage so as to enhance his status and prestige. Several anonymous chronicles describe his exploits, which has meant that he is much studied and remains one of the more famous Ōuchi lords.[1]

Yoshihiro, a man of undeniable valor, was selected as heir by his father Hiroyo at the age of ten, and by sixteen he was old enough to lead men into battle. Despite or perhaps because of his position as undisputed heir, he increasingly disagreed with Hiroyo over how best to expand the Ōuchi domains. Unlike his father, who tried to occupy Aki and Iwami provinces to the east, Yoshihiro favored expansion westward into Kyushu, and close alliance both with the Ashikaga and with officials of the newly founded Chosŏn Dynasty.

Yoshihiro successfully established control over portions of northern Kyushu, which allowed him to move some Kyushu warriors to Nagato and consolidate authority over this province. He was initially appointed as the *shugo* of the core provinces of Suō and Nagato, and later, Buzen in northern Kyushu. At the same time, he had yearly rituals dedicated to Myōken performed at Kōryūji. His warriors were required to travel to Yamaguchi, to

---

[1] For two excellent biographies of Ōuchi Yoshihiro, see Matsuoka Hisatō, *Ōuchi Yoshihiro* (Jinbutsu ōraisha, 1966) and Hirase Naoki, *Ōuchi Yoshihiro* (Minerva shobō, 2017). Yoshihiro appears in two chronicles, the *Meitokuki* and *Ōeiki*, both of which have been translated expertly by Royall Tyler, in *Fourteenth-Century Voices*, vol. 3, *Iwashimizu Hachiman in War and Cult* (Blue Tongue Books, 2017). Finally, it is telling that even in later popular histories devoted to Japan, Yoshihiro alone of the Ōuchi figures merits a prominent role in the narrative. See Rai Sanyō, *Nihon gaishi*, vol. 2 (Iwanami shoten, 2016), pp. 65–67.

Kings in All but Name. Thomas D. Conlan, Oxford University Press. © Oxford University Press 2024.
DOI: 10.1093/oso/9780197677339.003.0004

view and sometimes participate in these annual rites. As a sign of the signif-icance of Myōken, he transferred the deity to the distant central provinces of Izumi and Kii in 1392, when he was appointed as *shugo* of these provinces.

Yoshihiro reached out to Korea, as he was active at the time when the Koryŏ Dynasty (J. Kōrai 918–1392) was collapsing and the new Chosŏn Dynasty was being established. Scattered sources suggest that he in fact spoke Korean, and further evidence of close contact stems from the arrival of Koryŏ roof-tile makers in Yamaguchi. During his time, then, Yoshihiro and at least some others in Yamaguchi were bilingual.

Yoshihiro was aided by having the continued help of his father's skilled representative, Hirai Dōjo, in the imperial capital, and this may account for why he, of all the Ōuchi lords, became famous and became a protagonist in two major war tales. He also became a trusted and valued ally of the shogun Ashikaga Yoshimitsu. In contrast to his father, who kept his distance from the Ashikaga, Yoshihiro attempted to gain power and influence by closely allying with the wily Ashikaga leader, although in the end—like many other great lords—he was goaded into rebellion. He attempted unsuccessfully to destroy Yoshimitsu, taking the battle to central Japan, and died while fighting at the port city of Sakai late in 1399. Nonetheless, he had strengthened the foundations of Ōuchi power to the point where it could weather his demise.

Quelling "Pirates" and Kyushu Enemies

Yoshihiro was probably born around 1356, but little is known about his birth or his early years. He was given the name Magotarō, meaning that he was Hiroyo's eldest son, and he was officially designated as Hiroyo's heir in 1365.[2] At sixteen, Yoshihiro apparently crossed the Straits of Shimonoseki in an at-tempt to pacify northern Kyushu.[3] From 2.21.1372 he and his father fought near Dazaifu, which they captured on 8.11.1372.[4] Dazaifu, established in the

[2] Matsuoka Hisatō, comp., *Nanbokuchō ibun Chūgoku Shikoku hen*, 6 vols. (Tōkyōdō shuppan, 1987–95) (hereafter NBIC), vol. 4, doc. 3399, 6.11.1365 (Jōji 4) Tenjinsha *munafuda utsushi*, pp. 116–17.

[3] *Dainihon shiryō* (hereafter DNSR), ser. 6, vol. 34 (Tōkyō daigaku shuppankai, 1964), pp. 470–71. Kondō Kiyoshi, *Ōuchi shi jitsuroku* (Yamaguchi, 1885, 3rd reprint ed., Tokuyama: Matsuno shoten, 1984), p. 28, provides a useful summary of multiple chronicles according to which Yoshihiro first went to Kyushu when he was sixteen. For a convenient overview of his life, see Yamaguchi kenshi hensanshitsu, comp., *Yamaguchi kenshi shiryōhen chūsei*, 4 vols. (Yamaguchi, 1996–2008), vol. 1, Ōuchi Yoshihiro den, pp. 748–49.

[4] *Dazaifu Dazaifu Tenmangū shiryō*, vol. 12 (Dazaifu Tenmangū, 1984), pp. 214–15 for a Shōni Fuyutsuke letter to Shimazu Chikatada dating from 2.21 [(Ōan 5) 1372] as well as when he captured

seventh century, was Japan's official portal to the continent, and the administrative center for all of Kyushu. It was a significant prize. There he met an ambassador of the newly founded Ming Dynasty (1368–1644)—or rather, this Zhao Zhi was forced to meet him.[5]

The Ming had just adopted a trade policy radically different from that of the previous Yuan Dynasty (1271–1368). They preferred to funnel all exchanges through the political mechanism of tribute, whereby goods would be granted to foreign rulers who in turn would recognize Ming suzerainty. Trade itself was not allowed, and this prohibition had soon led to an upswing in "piracy" by seafarers and armed merchants. Therefore, prior to Yoshihiro's conquest of Dazaifu, the Ming had sent emissaries to Dazaifu to request that these pirates be chastised. Prince Kaneyoshi (1329–83) of the Southern Court had dominated northern Kyushu since 1352, and as he promised to stamp out piracy, the Ming invested him with the title of King of Japan in 1369, in recognition of his efforts. This title entailed nominal subservience to the Ming, and in turn for this recognition of universal Ming authority, and quelling pirates on their behalf, the person invested with the post of King of Japan would receive considerable profits and rewards.

With the fall of Dazaifu in 1372 to the pro-Ashikaga forces of Imagawa Ryōshun (1326–1420) and Ōuchi Yoshihiro, the Ming ambassador Zhao Zhi tried instead to travel to Kyoto in 1373 to visit the Ashikaga. He was apprehended, presumably by the Ōuchi, had his tributary goods confiscated, and was forced to remain in Hiroyo's mansion in Yamaguchi. There Zhao Zhi spent several months with the eighteen-year-old Yoshihiro.[6] Perhaps this exposure influenced Yoshihiro, because he would remain far more interested in Hakata and Kyushu than his father.

Yoshihiro's father, Hiroyo, fell out with Imagawa Ryōshun, the overall commander of the Kyushu campaign, abandoned his cause, and left for Aki with his four thousand-strong army. In the seventh month of 1374, he attacked rivals there.[7] Nevertheless, Yoshihiro decided to remain and fight with

---

the Dazaifu on 8.11 (*Dazaifu Dazaifu Tenmangū shiryō*, vol. 12, pp. 224–25). See also NBIC, vol. 4, doc. 3945, Sufu Shidō *gunchūjō utsushi*, p. 345, and vol. 5, doc. 4132, 2.1374 (Ōan 8) Tahara Ujiyoshi *gunchūjō*, pp. 42–45.

[5] Gregory Smits, *Maritime Ryūkyū* (Honolulu: University of Hawaii Press, 2018), pp. 62–66, provides an overview of Ming, Japanese, and Ryūkyū relations, including the actions of early envoys like Zhao Zhi.

[6] Hirase Naoki, *Ōuchi shi no ryōgoku shihai to shūkyō* (Hanawa shobō, 2017), pp. 55–56.

[7] Matsuoka, *Ōuchi Yoshihiro*, pp. 84–85, and Imagawa Ryōshun's reference to an argument with Ōuchi Hiroyo regarding command in Kyushu. NBIC, vol. 5, doc. 4259, 3.11 [(Eiwa 2) 1376] Imagawa Ryōshun *shojō*, pp. 83–84. For Hiroyo in Aki, see NBIC, vol. 5, doc. 4262, 3.1376 (Eiwa

Ryōshun in northern Kyushu. He was widely credited with rallying troops and achieving an impressive victory over Southern Court supporters on 3.3.1375.[8] Yoshihiro's close ties with the Imagawa lord stemmed in part from his marriage to Ryōshun's niece.[9] Yoshihiro continued to fight with Ryōshun even after Ryōshun had assassinated Shōni Fuyutsuke (1333–75), the *shugo* of Chikuzen province in northern Kyushu, at a banquet on 8.26.1375—an act that most contemporaries found reprehensible.[10]

Yoshihiro fell out with his father in 1375. As late as the ninth month of 1374, Hiroyo still recognized Yoshihiro as his heir and had him make ritual offerings on his behalf to the Sumiyoshi shrine in Nagato.[11] By the eighth month of 1375, however, Hiroyo ignored his son when taking credit for reroofing the Tenjin shrine, which suggests that he had second thoughts about him.[12] In 1376, Yoshihiro abandoned his father in Aki and once again crossed over into northern Kyushu with only three hundred followers.[13] There, he and his small band decisively defeated Prince Kaneyoshi, killing more than a hundred men in all, including another Southern Court prince, on 8.12.1377.[14]

After this victory in Kyushu, Yoshihiro became more estranged from his father. The two had rival visions of the core Ōuchi territories. They also disagreed over how to expand their authority, with Hiroyo relying solely on military conquest, and Yoshihiro favoring gaining influence through conquest and cooperation with the Ashikaga.

---

2) Mōri Motoharu *gunchūjō an*, p. 85, and doc. 4269, 5.1376 (Eiwa 2) Mōri Motoharu *jihitsu kotogaki an*, pp. 125–133. For how Hiroyo's departure allowed Southern Court forces to gain dominance in Kyushu, see NBIC, vol. 5, doc. 4665, 1.13.1381 (Kōryaku 3) Mōri Hirofusa *kasanegaki an*, pp. 273–77, p. 274.

[8] See the *Ōuchi shi jitsuroku*, "Yoshihiro," pp. 28–29. See also the *Ōunki, Kaitei shiseki shūran*, vol. 3 (2nd printing, Kondō Keizō shuppanbu, 1906), maki 10, p. 48, and *Nanzan junshūroku, Kaitei shiseki shūran*, vol. 4, maki 21 (3rd printing, 1906), p. 498.

[9] For these ties, see Momosaki Yūichirō, *Muromachi no hasha: Ashikaga Yoshimitsu* (Chikuma shobō, 2020), p. 184.

[10] For this episode, see Conlan, "Largesse and the Limits of Loyalty in the Fourteenth Century," in Jeffrey P. Mass, ed., *The Origins of Japan's Medieval World: Courtiers, Clerics, Warriors, and Peasants in the Fourteenth Century* (Stanford: Stanford University Press, 1997), p. 39.

[11] NBIC, vol. 5, doc. 4084, 9.1374 (Ōan 7) Ōuchi Hiroyo Yoshihiro *rensho hōgajō utsushi*, p. 22.

[12] NBIC, vol. 5, doc. 4163, 8.10.1375 (Eiwa 1), Tenjingū *munafuda utsushi*, p. 53.

[13] NBIC, vol. 5, doc. 4252, 1.23 [(Eiwa 2) 1376] Imagawa Ryōshun *shojō utsushi*, pp. 80–81.

[14] *Nanzan junshūroku*, p. 505. See also *Ōuchi shi jitsuroku*, p. 29, Seno Sei'ichirō, comp., *Nanbokuchō ibun Kyūshū hen* (7 vols. Tōkyōdō shuppan, 1985–92) (hereafter NBIK), vol. 5, doc. 5826, 7.1384 (Kōwa 4) Kikuchi Taketomo *mōshijō utsushi*, p. 381 for reference to Yoshihiro and his brother being part of an army that consisted of several thousands. Although this is a later copy, its evidence is verifiable in other sources. See also Sanjō Kintada, *Gogumaiki*, vol. 2 (Iwanami shoten, 1984), 9.1.1377 (Eiwa 3), p. 248.

By 8.1378 Hiroyo no longer recognized Yoshihiro as his heir, favoring instead his third son Mitsuhiro (d. 1397).[15] Around that time Yoshihiro and Mitsuhiro commanded competing armies. The battle-hardened Yoshihiro had the advantage, having long commanded men in war. He could even conscript rowers from Nagato for missions to Korea, and he also dispatched an emissary to Koryŏ along with a contingent of 186 warriors to attack Tsushima "pirates" in support of the tottering Koryŏ Dynasty.[16]

Yoshihiro's close connections with the Japanese court, epitomized by relatively high court rank, and with the Ashikaga constituted a further advantage.[17] His commendations or confirmations had greater weight because they could be easily upheld by documents issued either by the shogunal chancellor (kanrei), Shiba Yoshimasa (1350–1410), or by the shogun Ashikaga Yoshimitsu (1358–1408, shogun 1368–94) himself.[18]

Mitsuhiro, believing that surprise could compensate for his disadvantages, launched an attack against Yoshihiro at Sakariyama, a Nagato fort about four miles north of the Straits of Shimonoseki, on 5.10.1380. His forces killed Sugi Chisei, Yoshihiro's deputy shugo, and some twenty-seven followers of Yoshihiro.[19] Mitsuhiro then confirmed lands to Naitō Shigekane, an Aki warrior, in an attempt to increase his support.[20] During the conflict, Hiroyo seems to have been fighting with Mitsuhiro, but his actions during the last few months of his life are not clearly known.

---

[15] NBIC, vol. 5, doc. 4443, 8.25.1378 (Eiwa 4) Nagato Ichinomiya munafuda mei, p. 199, where Hiroyo omitted Yoshihiro's name from a description of repairs to Nagato's Ichinomiya shrine. Ōuchi Mitsuhiro was also named Saburō, which reveals that he was Hiroyo's third son. See NBIC, vol. 5, doc. 4615, 6.13.1380 (Kōryaku 2) Ōuchi Mitsuhiro azukejō, p. 259.

[16] Yamaguchi kenshi shiryōhen chūsei, vol. 1, Kōraishi, pp. 862–63. Yoshihiro dispatched an emissary on intercalary (urū) 4.25.1379 (5.25 in the Korean calendar). See also Richō jitsuroku, 3.3.1397 (T'aejo 5), p. 863. For his mobilization of Nagato warriors for rowing, see Yamaguchi kenshi shiryōhen chūsei, vol. 4, Iminomiya jinja monjo, doc. 134, 4.16 [(Eiwa 4) 1378] Ōuchi shi bugyōnin rensho hōsho, and doc. 235, 4.17 [(Eiwa 4) 1378] Bō kakikudashi, p. 210. For analysis of these levies, see Suda Makiko, Chūsei Nichō kankei to Ōuchi shi (Tōkyō daigaku shuppan, 2011), pp. 48–50.

[17] See letter addressed to Ōuchi sakyō gon daibu. NBIC, vol. 5, doc. 4456, 10.15 [(Eiwa 4) 1378] Ashikaga Yoshimitsu gohan mikyōjo utsushi, p. 204. This letter is attributed to 1378, but its context suggests 1379. See NBIC, vol. 5, doc. 4554, 11.2.1379 (Kōryaku 1) Ōuchi Yoshihiro kakikudashi, pp. 230–31. For his appointment as the Sakyō daibu of the fifth rank upper, see Yamaguchi kenshi tsūshihen chūsei (Yamaguchi, 2012), CD-ROM Kengai shiryō (Chūsei bōchō shōen shiryō), Tōkyō daigaku shiryōhensanjo Kuzen rinji inzen mikyōjo an, doc. 6, 8.18.1379 (Kōryaku 1) Go-Enyū tennō kuzen an utsushi, p. 434.

[18] For the former, NBIC, vol. 5, doc. 4623, 7.19.1380 (Kōryaku 2) Muromachi bakufu mikyōjo utsushi, p. 261; for the latter, doc. 4639, 9.8.1380 (Kōryaku 2) Ashikaga Yoshimitsu gokan mikyōjo an, pp. 264–65.

[19] Yamaguchi kenshi shiryōhen chūsei, vol. 1, Kaiei sandaiki, p. 505. See also the Yamaguchi kenshi tsūshihen chūsei, pp. 367–38.

[20] NBIC, vol. 5, doc. 4607, 5.10.1380 (Kōryaku 2) Ōuchi Mitsuhiro azukejō, p. 256.

Yoshihiro countered first by offering immunities to the Masuda, a major Iwami warrior family.[21] Shortly thereafter he attacked the interior regions of Aki, closest to Iwami, on 5.18.1380 and secured a great victory, resulting in the death of over two hundred Mitsuhiro supporters, including five members of the Washizu family, as well as associates of families who had long supported his father Hiroyo, including the Sanai, Suyama, Suetaka, Toida, and Niho.[22] The Toida and Niho would survive the debacle, but the Sanai, Sueyama, and Suetaka were severely weakened.

Both Mitsuhiro and Yoshihiro struggled to attract the support of Iwami and Nagato warriors. When Mitsuhiro issued a flurry of confirmations to Iwami and Nagato men,[23] Yoshihiro countered by granting immunities to the Sufu, a major Iwami family, and promised, as he had to the Masuda on 9.12.1380, that no *shugo* could encroach on their lands. Although this bolstered his support, it also meant that future *shugo* of Iwami would remain ineffective because they could not readily govern the province.[24]

Yoshihiro, who was also the *shugo* of Buzen in Kyushu,[25] surmounted the stalemate in Nagato and Iwami by dispatching warriors from northern Kyushu to attack Sakariyama during the sixth month of 1380.[26] He defeated more Mitsuhiro supporters, captured fifty Niho rivals during the ninth month of that year, and reconquered Sakariyama castle in the tenth. Some thirty supporters of Mitsuhiro then committed hara kiri there.[27]

[21] NBIC, vol. 5, doc. 4608, 5.14.1380 (Kōryaku 2) Ōuchi Yoshihiro *kakikudashi*, p. 256 for Yoshihiro's confirmation for Masuda Kanemi. See also Inoue Hiroshi, ed., *Shiryōshū Masuda Kanemi to sono jidai: Masuda ke monjo no kataru chūsei no Masuda* (Masuda kyōiku iinkai, 1994), pp. 148–50.

[22] *Yamaguchi kenshi shiryōhen chūsei*, vol. 1, Kaei sandaiki, 5.18.1380 (Kōryaku 2), p. 505. See also *Yamaguchi kenshi tsūshihen chūsei*, pp. 367–68.

[23] NBIC, vol. 5, doc. 4614, 6.8.1380 (Kōryaku 2) Ōuchi Mitsuhiro *andojō utsushi*, p. 258, and doc. 4615, 6.13.1380 (Kōryaku 2) Ōuchi Mitsuhiro *azukejō*, p. 259.

[24] NBIC, vol. 5, docs. 4633–34, 8.15 [(Kōryaku 2) 1380] Ōuchi Yoshihiro *shojō utsushi*, p. 263 for the Sufu letters describing the wars, and doc. 4640, 9.12 [(Kōryaku 2) 1380] Ōuchi Yoshihiro *shojō utsushi*, p. 265 for the Sufu being granted immunity from *shugo* entering their lands. In the 8.15 letters, Ōuchi Yoshihiro praises the Sufu, another Iwami family, for coming to his aid against the Masuda and also mentions the Hirai. The Sufu became Yoshihiro's primary ally in Iwami. See *Shiryōshū Masuda Kanemi to sono jidai*, p. 150.

[25] Satō Shin'ichi, *Muromachi bakufu shugo seido no kenkyū*, 2 vols. (Tōkyō daigaku shuppankai, 1988), vol. 2, pp. 249–52. Matsuoka asserts that Yoshihiro's appointment to Buzen may date from 1374. See Matsuoka Hisatō, "Ōuchi shi no Buzen no kuni shihai," in *Ōuchi shi no kenkyū* (Seibundō, 2011), p. 186. Only eight of Yoshihiro's documents survive that pertain to Buzen and they date from 1383 (Eitoku 3) through 1399 (Ōei 6). See pp. 187–88.

[26] *Usa jingūshi shiryōhen* vol. 8 (Usa, 1991), p. 751 for 6.20 Ōuchi Yoshihiro *shojō* revealing that he was dispatching a representative to Nagato's Sakariyama castle to Buzen. The editors believe that this dates from 1379, but *Kumamoto ken shiryō chūsei*, vol. 2 (Kumamoto, 1962), p. 181, Sata ke monjo, doc. 35, 6.20 Ōuchi Yoshihiro *shojō* correctly attributes this document to 1380.

[27] NBIC, vol. 5, doc. 4639, 9.8.1380 (Kōryaku 2) Ashikaga Yoshimitsu *gokan mikyōjo an*, pp. 264–65 and doc. 4646 10.8 [(Kōryaku 2) 1380] Ōuchi Yoshihiro *shojō utsushi*, p. 267 for reference to

The confiscation of lands from rebellious warriors in favor of more reliable Kyushu followers, such as the Buzen warrior Sugi Shigeaki, allowed Yoshihiro to consolidate his authority in Nagato.[28] He did not confine his largesse to Kyushu warriors, since on 8.18.1380 he rewarded Tairako Sadashige of Suō with Abu district lands, located on the Japan Sea coast of Nagato province.[29] These grants displaced the older Nagato warriors. Yoshihiro also encouraged trade by establishing new way stations (yado) in Nagato.[30] Thanks to these grants, he also knitted provinces separated by the Straits of Shimonoseki into a distinct political and cultural region. To cite one example, Sugi Shigeaki received grants of Suō lands in 1385 and 1387, and confirmations of Buzen lands in northern Kyushu, on the opposite sides of the straits, in 1390.[31]

The Ōuchi patriarch Hiroyo died on 11.15.1380, and ultimately the two brothers reached a settlement in 1381. Mitsuhiro recognized Yoshihiro's primacy as the Ōuchi chief (sōryō) and, in exchange, was appointed shugo of Iwami.[32] As shugo, Mitsuhiro administered the province in 1381.[33] Nevertheless, Yoshihiro served as the conduit between Iwami warriors like the Masuda, and the authorities in the capital.[34] Epitomizing his superiority

thirty men being captured and thirty committing hara-kiri at Sakariyama. See also Yamaguchi kenshi tsūshihen chūsei, pp. 367–68, and Matsuoka, Ōuchi Yoshihiro, pp. 106–7. NBIC, vol. 5, doc. 4639, 9.8.1380 (Kōryaku 2) Ashikaga Yoshimitsu gokan mikyōjo an, pp. 264–65, also refers to some fifty being killed at Niho by Tairako Sadashige.

[28] Inoue Minoru, Hagi Hakubutsukan kitaku Sugi ke monjo, Hagi hakubutsukan kenkyū hōkoku no. 3 (3.2008): 1–20; pp. 1–2 for a newly discovered letter from Yoshihiro to Sugi Shigeaki dating from 2.21.1383 (Eitoku 3), whereby he bestowed upon Shigeaki the Nagato lands of the late Yaji Hizen no kami. Inoue's compilation supersedes the earlier study on the Sugi, Tamura Tetsuo, "Ōuchi no bushō Sugi shi monjo ni tsuite," Yamaguchi chihōshi kenkyū, no. 16 (11.1966), pp. 28–37.

[29] NBIC, vol. 5, doc. 4635, 8.18.1380 (Kōryaku 2) Ōuchi Yoshihiro azukejo utsushi, p. 264. According to Tairako lore, they moved to Yamaguchi and followed Yoshihiro at this time. See Hagi han batsu etsu roku, vol. 2 (Yamaguchi ken monjokan, 1994), maki 45 no. 1 Miura Matauemon monjo, doc. 59, Kōya (Takano) Ken'ei (Shigekata) Zenmon yuisho, pp. 175–77. For more on the tribulations of the Tairako, see the informative Tokubetsuten Kamakura gokenin Tairako shi no seisen • hokusen (Yokohama: Yokohama shi rekishi hakubutsukan, 2003).

[30] NBIC, vol. 5, doc. 4698, 4.23.1381 (Eitoku 1) Ōuchi Yoshihiro kakikudashi an, p. 285.

[31] Inoue Minoru, Hagi Hakubutsukan kitaku Sugi ke monjo for the for the 2.21 [(Eitoku 3) 1383] Ōuchi Yoshihiro shōjō, the 10.1.1385 (Shitoku 2) and 5.7.1387 (Shitoku 4) Suō grants, and the Buzen grants on 9.17 and 10.18.1390 (Meitoku 1). For published transcriptions of some of these documents, see NBIK, vol. 6, docs. 6142–43, 9.17.1390 (Meitoku 1) Ōuchi Yoshihiro ategaijō utsushi, pp. 98–99. These documents do not appear in NBIC.

[32] For the settlement, see NBIC, vol. 5, doc. 4610, 6.2 Imagawa Ryōshun shōjō, pp. 256–58, p. 257, and doc. 4621, 6.24 Ōuchi Yoshihiro shōjō utsushi, pp. 260–61. Both letters are listed as being from 1380, but as Matsuoka's own research reveals they date from 1381. For the situation in Iwami, see Inoue, Shiryōshū Masuda Kanemi to sono jidai, p. 153, and Matsuoka's pioneering "Nanbokuchō Muromachiki Iwami no kuni to Ōuchi shi," Ōuchi shi no kenkyū, pp. 245–75.

[33] NBIC, vol. 5, doc. 4726, 11.3.1381 (Eitoku 1) Ōuchi Mitsuhiro andojō utsushi, p. 296.

[34] See Ōuchi Yoshihiro's confirmations of intercalary (urū) 1.12.1382 (Eitoku 2). See NBIC, vol. 5, doc. 4736, urū 1.12.1382 (Eitoku 2) Ōuchi Yoshihiro kyojō, p. 300.

to Mitsuhiro, and his better ties to the capital, Yoshihiro endorsed Mitsuhiro's confirmations to Iwami warriors and attested to their legitimacy in the eyes of the Ashikaga.[35] His status was enhanced with his 10.13.1382 appointment to junior fourth rank lower, far higher than Mitsuhiro or, for that matter, most provincial figures. Yoshihiro had now joined the upper nobility.[36]

Yoshihiro most effectively governed provinces where he served as *shugo*. In Buzen, his authority was uncontested; three short years after his appointment as *shugo* there, his control was beyond challenge.[37] The situation in Aki and Iwami was more complex. Yoshihiro relied on personal power and connections to overrule the appointed *shugo* of Iwami, and although not the *shugo* of Aki, he also confirmed the lands of warriors there.[38]

Now firmly in control of Iwami, Yoshihiro managed in 1385 to strip his brother Mitsuhiro of the office of *shugo* in the province in favor of another brother, Moriakira (1377–1431). Moriakira would become the next Ōuchi lord after Yoshihiro's death. At some time thereafter Mitsuhiro was made either *shugo* or deputy *shugo* of Buzen, where he can be verified as governing in 1396.[39]

Yoshihiro appointed Migita Hironao, an Ōuchi relative whose ancestors hailed from Sabaryō, as deputy *shugo* of Iwami. Hironao would occupy this post from 1385 through 1399.[40] His core territory was the central district at

---

[35] NBIC vol. 5, doc. 4776, 12.8 Ōuchi Yoshihiro *shojō*, p. 313. Although a slip of paper was added to this document stating that it was from 1382, it could plausibly date also from 1381. Ultimately, Yoshimitsu followed it with a confirmation on 2.15.1383 (Eitoku 3) for the Masuda. NBIC, vol. 6, doc. 4783, 2.15.1383 (Eitoku 3) Ashikaga Yoshimitsu *sodehan mikyōjo*, p. 4.

[36] *Yamaguchi kenshi tsūshihen chūsei*, CD-ROM *Kengai shiryō* (*Chūsei bōchō shōen shiryō*), Tōkyō daigaku shiryōhensanjo *Kuzen rinji inzen mikyōjo an*, 10.13.1382 (Eitoku 2) Go-Komatsu tennō *kuzen an utsushi*, p. 434. See Wada Shūsaku, "Ōuchi shi no sōsho kankei o megutte," in Kage Toshio, ed., *Ōuchi to Ōtomo: Chūsei nishi Nihon no nidai daimyō* (Bensei shuppan, 2013), p. 30 for evidence that Mitsuhiro achieved the rank of fifth rank lower only in 1397 (Ōei 4).

[37] Numerous records survive revealing Yoshihiro's governance of Buzen. NBIK, vol. 5, doc. 5829, 8.7 [(Shitoku 1) 1384] Ōuchi shi *bugyōnin rensho hōsho*, p. 383, and NBIK, vol. 6, doc. 5995, 11.16 [(Shitoku 3) 1386] Ōuchi shi *bugyōnin rensho kakikudashi*, pp. 45–46. See also NBIC, vol. 5, doc. 4716, 7.25 [(Eitoku 1) 1381] Nawa Shigefuyu *shojō*, pp. 291–93, p. 293 for Yoshihiro's military victories in the province.

[38] NBIC, vol. 5, doc. 4731, 12.14.1381 (Eitoku 1) Ōuchi Yoshihiro *andojō*, p. 297.

[39] Wada Shūsaku, "Ōuchi shi no sōsho kankei o megutte," p. 30 for how Mitsuhiro (fifth rank lower), served as either *shugo* or deputy *shugo* of Buzen. The source for this is *Usa jingūshi shiryōhen*, vol. 9 (Usa, 1992), 12.13.1396 (Ōei 3) Omotoyama *kane no mei*, pp. 27–28. It is not clear when he received this appointment, but it apparently happened after his divestment of the Iwami post.

[40] For evidence that the Migita served as the deputy *shugo* of Iwami, see NBIC, vol. 5, doc. 4637, 8.27 [(Kōryaku 2) 1380] Ōuchi Yoshihiro *shojō utsushi*, p. 264, and doc. 4638, 9.2 [(Kōryaku 2) 1380] Ōuchi Yoshihiro *shojō utsushi*, p. 264. See also Wada Shūsaku, "Suō Migita shi no sōden monjo ni tsuite," *Yamaguchi ken kenkyū kiyō* 41 (3.2014), p. 94. For the appointment of Moriakira as Iwami *shugo*, see Wada Shūsaku, "Ōuchi shi no sōsho kankei o megutte," p. 30.

Nima, a strategic harbor located near important mines.[41] Sometime around this time, Yoshihiro managed to tax the Naka district in Iwami, which, along with Nima, and the Yoshika part of Kanoashi district, would remain an important Ōuchi holding in the province. Furthermore, at some time before 1393 he even briefly confiscated lands from the Masuda.[42] Yoshihiro levied a *hanzei* half tax, which was a *shugo* prerogative and meant that half of a province's revenue would be used for military provisions.

Enshrining Authority

To formalize his band of retainers, Yoshihiro relied on the Second Month rites at Kōryūji. The Toida, who had first participated in these rites a generation earlier, had one of their family serve in the important role of primary archer (*yumi tarō*), who would show off his skills in archery during the opening of the rites performed there in 1382.[43] These yearly rites served to incorporate the various Ōuchi factions into an encompassing body whose members experienced these shared rituals. Since some of this collateral lineage of the Toida had died in 1380, fighting for Mitsuhiro and Hiroyo, this ritual inclusion helped to establish new, lasting bonds among the survivors.[44] The fact that participation in the ceremonies was determined not by "ability" or age, but merely by lot (*kuji*), highlighted the unity of the group rather than divisions within it.[45]

Furthermore, the expenses associated with the yearly enactment of these rites were drawn from tax revenues drawn from specific districts, rather than provinces or individual retainers under Ōuchi control. This process ensured

---

[41] See Yamaguchi shi kyōiku iinkai, comp., *Ōuchi shi kanren machinami iseki* 8 (Yamaguchi shi kyōiku iinkai, 2014), p. 258.

[42] See Nakatsukasa Ken'ichi, "Chūsei kōki Iwami no kuni kokujin dōkō to Muromachi bakufu, daimyō," in *Iwami no chūsei ryōshu no seisui to Higashi Ajia kai-iki sekai* (Tottori ken kodai bunka sentaa kenkyū ronshū no. 18. Tottori, 3.2018), p. 66 for a Yoriie *shojō* (also reproduced in *Masuda ke monjo* as doc. 82, Yoriie *shojō*) recounting the *hanzei* in Yoshika, the southwestern spur of Iwami, part of Kanoashi district, which was closest to Yamaguchi. For the Masuda confiscation, see *Masuda ke monjo*, vol. 1, doc. 75, 12.27.1393 (Meitoku 4) Ōuchi Yoshihiro *andojō*, p. 71, and doc. 76, 12.27.1393 (Meitoku 4) Ōuchi *bugyōnin rensho hōsho*, pp. 71–72. See also Nakatsukasa, "Chūsei kōki Iwami no kuni kokujin dōkō," pp. 66, 76.

[43] NBIC, vol. 5, doc. 4743, 2.13.1382 (Eitoku 2) Ōuchi Yoshihiro *nigatsu-e iteyaku sashijō*, p. 302.

[44] Yoshihiro had forced them to give up Iwami lands to Kikkawa Yoshimi on 8.29.1379 (Kōryaku 1) and this may have accounted for the Toida later supporting (and dying for) Mitsuhiro in 1380. See NBIC, vol. 5, doc. 4540, 8.29.1379 (Kōryaku 1) Toida Tadayoshi Sohara Hiromitsu *rensho uchiwatashijō*, p. 227.

[45] NBIC, vol. 5, doc. 4743, 2.13.1382 (Eitoku 2) Ōuchi Yoshihiro *nigatsu-e iteyaku sashijō*, p. 302.

that the burden of the ceremonies was spread evenly throughout the territories. Not only did each district so selected have ample time to plan to secure adequate funding, but their selection served to solidify regions under Ōuchi control. Mostly the districts were from regions where the Ōuchi served as *shugo*, but that was not invariably the case, as some crucial districts in neighboring provinces of other *shugo* were nevertheless administered by the Ōuchi. Through ritual and cultic imperatives, Ōuchi authority over regions was asserted.

Yoshihiro's success in uniting warriors from two of Japan's largest islands stemmed in part from the offerings he made to important shrines on both islands. He also confirmed grants of land by local warriors to the Ichinomiya ("First") shrine of Nagato, dedicated to the sea god Sumiyoshi, thus giving these grants legal force that enhanced his authority.[46] After commending administrative rights in the form of a managerial (*jitō*) post to the Itsukushima shrine in Aki, to commemorate his victory over his brother,[47] he turned his attentions to the Usa Hachiman shrine.

Usa Hachiman, in Buzen, was a crucial cultic site, with strong ties to deities of the stars and the seas. Hachiman was the deification of Emperor Ōjin (reigned c. 270–310), who was a *kami* and had also been granted the status of bodhisattva by the court in 781.[48] This shrine owned land in many provinces. One of its elaborate rites, lasting over fifteen days, used model boats manned with puppets (*kugutsu*) to re-enact the imagined third-century conquest of Korea by the female "emperor" Jingū, Ōjin's mother, after his death.[49] However, such rites lapsed during the fourteenth century. In 1309 the Usa complex suffered a major fire, and although some structures were rebuilt in 1323, other Usa buildings were destroyed in 1327.[50] Imagawa Ryōshun's attempt to rebuild Usa in 1386 failed.[51] By then a century had passed since the last rebuilding, which

[46] NBIC, vol. 5, doc. 4697, 4.23.1381 (Eitoku 1) Ōuchi Yoshihiro *andojō utsushi*, p. 285. For a prohibition protecting shrine lands, see NBIC, vol. 5, doc. 4734, 1.11.1382 (Eitoku 2) Ōuchi Yoshihiro *kinzei*, p. 298.

[47] NBIC, vol. 5, doc. 4710, 7.1.1381 (Eitoku 1) Ōuchi Yoshihiro *kishinjō*, p. 290.

[48] For this overview, I am indebted to Jacqueline Stone.

[49] Tamura Masataka, "Muromachiki ni okeru Usa no miya no saiki zōei saikō," *Chūsei shi kenkyū* 32 (2007), p. 120. Although Jingū may have existed, she would in the parlance of the time at best be considered as a "king" and her purported conquest of Korea was a myth. Jingū too was worshiped at Usa Hachiman along with Himegami, a heavenly deity who descended to the earth, and thus had links to star worship.

[50] Matsumoto Takuya, "Chūsei Usagū no zōei shisutemu to Ōuchi shi," *Kamakura ibun kenkyū*, no. 31 (4.2013), pp. 64–66.

[51] Matsumoto, "Chūsei Usagū no zōei shisutemu to Ōuchi sh," pp. 67–68.

Figure 3.1 The Main Hall (*honden*) of the Usa Shrine (Usa Jingū) is one of three contiguous buildings that are dedicated to Hachiman. The North Star (*hokushin*) is worshipped at the small shrine to the left. Photograph by Thomas Conlan

was supposed take place every thirty-three years.[52] By 1397 Yoshihiro had ousted Imagawa Ryōshun and gained sole authority over Usa.[53] The rebuilding of the shrine accorded with his patronage of sea gods, but in practice the task would be accomplished under the direct supervision of his brother Mitsuhiro. Yoshihiro became entangled in the politics of Kyoto, where he resided, serving near Ashikaga Yoshimitsu. He ran afoul of the third Ashikaga shogun, attempted a rebellion, and died some three years later (Figure 3.1).

Yoshihiro in the Capital

Another reason for Yoshihiro's success was easy communication with the capital. Hirai Dōjo resided in Yoshihiro's Kyoto residence and served as his

[52] Matsumoto, "Chūsei Usagū no zōei shisutemu to Ōuchi shi," pp. 57ff. for the thirty-three-year rebuilding of Usa.

[53] See *Usa jingūshi shiryōhen*, vol. 9, 4.11 [(Ōei 4) 1397] Ōuchi Yoshihiro (?) *andojō an*, pp. 34–35. And also see Nagata Tadayasu, "Chūsei kōki ni okeru Buzen Ichinomiya Usagū no dōkō-Ōuchi shi to no kankei o chūshin ni," *Kokuritsu rekishi minzoku hakubutsukan kenkyū hōkoku*, no. 148 (12.2008), p. 242

plenipotentiary.[54] As we have seen in chapter 2, Dōjo had been dispatched by the aged Hiroyo in 1376 to oversee affairs in the capital and negotiate with the Ashikaga.

Dōjo disseminated news of Yoshihiro's victories, giving him credit for killing a Southern Court prince and a hundred supporters on 8.12.1377 and ignoring the important role of Imagawa Ryōshun, the titular commander.[55] Dōjo also facilitated communication with the capital concerning the ownership of Suō estates and served as a conduit to Korea.[56] Korean records mention him by name.[57]

The shogun Ashikaga Yoshimitsu visited western Honshu in 1389, undoubtedly as part of an attempt to keep an eye on lords such as Yoshihiro, but also because of a professed interest in Yoshihiro's attempt to rebuild Usa.[58] With his visit, Yoshimitsu swept Yoshihiro into his orbit and encouraged the Ōuchi leader to return with him to the capital, where Yoshihiro would remain for most of his final years.[59] These years would encompass two short conflicts. In the Meitoku disturbance of 1392, Yoshihiro vanquished the Yamana, who sought to challenge Yoshimitsu's power, while in the conflict of 1399 Yoshihiro himself tried and failed to supplant the Ashikaga leader.

[54] Wada Shūsaku, "Ōuchi shi no ryōgoku shihai soshiki to jinzai tōyō," in Kishida Hiroshi, ed., *Mōri Motonari to chiiki shakai* (Hiroshima: Chūgoku shinbunsha, 2007), pp. 197–223; Suda Makiko, "Ōuchi shi no zaikyō katsudo," in Kage Toshio, *Ōuchi to Ōtomo*, pp. 97–114; Hagihara Daisuke, "Chūsei kōki Ōuchi shi no zaikyō," *Nihon rekishi* 786 (11.2013), pp. 17–32; and Tamura Masataka, "Ōuchi shi Hirai kashin Hirai Dōjo kō," *Nanakuma shigaku* 17 (3.2015), pp. 23–40.

[55] *Nanzan junshūroku*, p. 505, and Sanjō Kintada, *Gogumaiki*, vol. 2, 9.1.1377 (Eiwa 3), p. 248.

[56] *Yamaguchi kenshi tsūshihen chūsei*, CD-ROM *Kengai shiryō* (*Chūsei bōchō shōen shiryō*), *Tōji hyakugo monjo* (Kyoto furitsu sōgō shiryōkan zō), doc. 69, 10.27.1383 (Eitoku 3) Saishōkōin *hyōjō hikitsuke*, p. 478. For how Hirai Dōjo conveyed the information in an edict, see doc. 71, 3.20 Ōuchi Yoshihiro *shojō*, p. 479. Finally, for a recent study of Dōjo's cultural proclivities, see Ogawa Takeo, *Ashikaga Yoshimitsu* (Chūkō shinsho, 2012), pp. 186–90.

[57] *The Veritable Records of King Sejong*, vol. 80, 2.19.1438 (Sejong 20), http://sillok.history.go.kr/id/wda_12002019_002, accessed 6.12.2022, retrospectively describes Hirai (Bishū *no kami* Minamoto Shōjo) as a noted figure (*kuni no meishi*). See also Ogawa Takeo, *Ashikaga Yoshimitsu*, pp. 188–89. Hirai even owned and disseminated maps of Ōuchi lands and Japan to Korean emissaries such as Pak Tonji. Kenneth R. Robinson, "Pak Tonji and the Vagaries of Government Service in Koryŏ and Chosŏn, 1360–1412," *Korean Studies* 40 (2016), pp. 94–96.

[58] Matsumoto Takuya, "Chūsei Usagū no zōei shisutemu to Ōuchi," pp. 67–68.

[59] Imagawa Ryōshun wrote the best account of this visit, his *Rokuon'in dono Itsukushima mōdeki*, and tells how Yoshimitsu traveled to Itsukushima before returning to Kyoto. *Yamaguchi kenshi shiryōhen chūsei*, vol. 1, pp. 667–70. Another oft-relied-upon source for this meeting, the *Rokuon'in saikoku gekōki*, has been shown by Mori Shigeaki to be an unreliable fifteenth-century glorification of these events. Mori Shigeaki, "Ōuchi shi no kōryū to sosen denju," *Yamaguchi kenshi kenkyū*, no. 11 (3.2003), pp. 93–117. See also *Yamaguchi kenshi shiryōhen chūsei*, vol. 1, Shiryō kaidai, p. 37.

The disturbance of 1392 is recounted in *Meitokuki* and that of 1399 in *Ōeiki*, two war tales. The former makes of Yoshihiro a hero whose service Yoshimitsu praised as "beyond compare,"[60] although later versions of the same war tale portray him more negatively, reflecting the tensions that later arose between the two.[61]

Yoshimitsu accorded Yoshihiro the privileges of an Ashikaga family member, an unprecedented honor, but his gesture also implied that Yoshihiro's lineage was inferior to that of Yoshimitsu.[62] However, Yoshihiro was not cowed. On the contrary, he strove to lift his standing further and to privilege his gods, as he expanded his influence into central Japan.

Yoshihiro was appointed *shugo* of Kii and Izumi in the first month of 1392, thus assuming control of regions that had constituted the core of the Southern Court's domain, and he administered them skillfully for the next seven years.[63] Once appointed, he transferred Myōken to these new provinces. He brought Myōken to Izumi, where he now resided, immediately after the festivals of the second month.[64] Myōken belief was widespread in Japan, but Yoshihiro desired to transplant and explicitly worship his lineage's Myōken from Kōryūji Hikamisan.

The transfer of Ōuchi tutelary deities (*ujigami*) served his claim of lasting authority. The movement of gods had a permanence that appointments as *shugo* did not. Although Yoshihiro controlled Izumi province for only a few years, he transformed it, promoted Myōken belief there, and ensured that memories of Ōuchi rule would linger there for over a century.[65]

---

[60] Tyler, *Iwashimizu Hachiman*, pp. 46–47. For the original passage, see Tomikura Tokujirō, ed., *Meitokuki* (Iwanami bunko, 1941), pp. 51–52, and Wada Hidemichi, "Kunaichō shoryōbuzō Meitokuki honkoku," *Atomi gakuen joshi daigaku kiyō* 12 (3.1979), p. 48. See also Tyler, *Iwashimizu Hachiman*, p. 90, and Tomikura, pp. 135–37 for his praise.

[61] See Nozuki Michio, "Meitokuki to shugo daimyō," *Yagoto bunka* 4 Chūkyō daigaku chūsei bungaku kenkyūkai (3.1998), p. 34 for analysis of how the language used in the *Meitokuki* to describe Yoshihiro subtly changed in later and more widely disseminated texts such as the Yōmei version.

[62] Tōkyō daigaku shiryōhen sanjo, comp., *Ninagawa ke monjo*, vol. 1 (Tōkyō daigaku shuppankai, 1981), doc. 9, 12.13 [(Meitoku 4) 1393] Shōgun Ashikaga Yoshimitsu *gonaisho an*, pp. 11–12. See also NBIC, vol. 6, doc. 5575, 12.13 [(Meitoku 4) 1393] Ashikaga Yoshimitsu *gonaisho an*, p. 335. For relations between Yoshimitsu and Yoshihiro, see Ogawa Takeo, *Ashikaga Yoshimitsu*, pp. 181–82.

[63] Satō, *Muromachi bakufu shugo seido no kenkyū*, vol. 1, p. 28 for Izumi and vol. 2, p. 186 for Kii. The other provinces where the Southern Court retained influence, such as Kawachi and Nara (through 1393), were governed by the Hatakeyama, while the Akamatsu and Yūki served alternately as the *shugo* of Settsu. For Yoshihiro's records pertaining to Kii province, see Fujii Takashi, *Muromachiki daimyō kenryokuron* (Dōseisha, 2013), pp. 82–87.

[64] NBIC, vol. 6, doc. 5397, 1.29 [(Meitoku 3) 1392] Ōuchi Yoshihiro shojō, p. 273. See also *Yamaguchi kenshi shiryōhen chūsei*, vol. 3, p. 236, and doc. 23, 9.19.1386 (Shitoku 3), p. 237.

[65] A sixteenth-century account (*engi*) suggests that Yoshihiro also relied on a Tenman shrine located in Izumi's Ihara estate for support and promised to reward it generously if he met with success on the battlefield. *Shinshū Izumi Sanno shishi*, vol. 4, Shiryōhen kodai chūsei 1 (Seibundō, 2004), pp. 352–55, and *Shinshū Izumi Sanno shishi*, vol. 1, Tsūshihen shizen chūsei (Seibundō, 2008), pp. 398–99.

The intertwined nature of political, judicial, and sacerdotal authority appears in an oath to Mōri Hirouchi dating from 8.5.1392. Yoshihiro forced Mōri Hirouchi to serve in his army and insisted that Hirouchi remain in Izumi, promising to support Hirouchi in an oath to Myōken, Tenjin, Kumano deities of Kii, and all the great, lesser, and middling gods of Japan. That he wrote this oath on Kumano paper also suggests his control over Kii.[66]

Oaths to Myōken underpinned Ōuchi authority and imprinted Ōuchi rule in Izumi. Likewise, the research of Satō Hiroo suggests that the oaths used for punishment had to be addressed to local deities, so that by bringing his gods to Izumi and Kii, and relying heavily on the local Kumano shrines, Yoshiro could more effectively assert ritual and political control in the provinces.[67]

In Kii province Yoshihiro effectively created a network of castles that served to check the Southern Court, which had ruled part of the province since 1336.[68] He also directly conscripted laborers from Nagusa district villages to aid his army.[69] From Nagusa, Yoshihiro could attack Uda district, in Yamato, one of the Southern Court's last strongholds.[70]

In the negotiations concerning the ultimate surrender of the Southern Court, which put an end to sixty years of civil war, Yoshihiro was a crucial figure. He played a major role in bringing them to a successful conclusion over the course of the tenth month of 1392. He was present in Kyoto at the surrender ceremonies and performed the role of guarding the regalia, the sword, mirror, and jewel that, according to the Southern Court, justified its claims to being the legitimate imperial branch.[71] When the Southern Court

---

[66] Tōkyō daigaku shiryōhen sanjo, comp., *Mōri ke monjo*, vol. 4 (Tōkyō daigaku shuppankai, 1924), doc. 1334, 8.5.1392 (Meitoku 3) Ōuchi Yoshihiro *kishōmon*, pp. 250–51.

[67] Satō Hiroo, "Wrathful Deities and Saving Deities," in Mark Teeuwen and Fabio Rambelli, eds., *Buddhas and Kami in Japan: Honji Suijaku as a Combinatory Paradigm* (New York: Routledge, 2003), pp. 95–114.

[68] NBIC, vol. 6, doc. 5396, 1.25.1392 (Meitoku 3) Ōuchi shi *bugyōnin rensho kinzei*, p. 273.

[69] NBIC, vol. 6, doc. 5436, 7.19 Ōuchi Yoshihiro *shojō an*, p. 293.

[70] Fujii, *Muromachiki daimyō kenryokuron*, pp. 83–84.

[71] A genealogy in the Agari archives states that Yoshihiro was a messenger who helped negotiate peace between the Northern and Southern Courts. *Agari ke monjo* (Nagato shi shitei bunkazai, 1995), doc. 13, Ōuchi ke *ryaku keizu*, p. 9. Likewise, see Hirase Naoki, *Ōuchi Yoshihiro*, p. 72 for a reference to the unpublished *Yūsokushō*, mentioning Yoshihiro's role as a crucial negotiator on behalf of the Ashikaga. These sentiments also appear in Kansai daigaku chūsei bungaku kenkyūkai, ed., *Sakaiki* (Sonkeikaku bunkozō) (Ōsaka: Izumi shoin, 1990), p. 48, and Tyler, "Ōeiki," in *Iwashimizu Hachiman*, p. 116. See also the *Kongōji kōki utsushi*, located most conveniently in *Yamaguchi kenshi shiryōhen chūsei*, vol. 1, p. 588, and *Nanpō kiden*, *Kaitei shiseki shūran*, vol. 3 (3rd printing, 1932) maki 11, p. 36 for the tenth month of 1392. For the veracity of these later accounts, see Mori Shigeaki, *Yami no rekishi Gonanchō* (Kadokawa shoten, 1997), pp. 52–55.

officials passed these objects to the Ashikaga, they relinquished all Southern Court claims, thus ending sixty years of war in favor of the Ashikaga and their Northern Court. This, together with his earlier victories in Kyushu and against the Yamana, gave Yoshihiro the reputation as "the greatest warrior in the realm."[72]

At first, in the aftermath of the end to the civil war, Yoshihiro enjoyed close ties with Yoshimitsu. These peaked midway through 1395, when he was allowed to take the tonsure at the same time as the Ashikaga lord.[73] Close ties notwithstanding, Yoshihiro's position proved precarious. One the one hand, he furthered Ashikaga interests, while on the other, he used his influence to bolster his position and local power, which served to enhance his ability to engage in trade. Too slavish support of Yoshimitsu risked undermining Ōuchi autonomy, while too much resistance could result in an armed conflict with the powerful Ashikaga lord.

Initially, Yoshihiro proved successful in bolstering his authority in Kyushu. He maneuvered to have Imagawa Ryōshun recalled, thus leaving his own preeminence in northern Kyushu unchallenged.[74] Thereafter he controlled Jutenji and Seifukuji, two important Zen temples in Hakata, whose monks were core figures for diplomatic exchanges with the continent.[75] In 1397–98 he expanded his authority into Chikuzen province, the western part of northern Kyushu, a crucial staging ground for ships traveling to Asia.[76] Finally, and most significantly, he allied himself with the families of the Munakata shrine and their network of followers. Munakata control over strategic islands off the coast of Kyushu, including Okinoshima (equidistant between Korea and Japan), cemented his ability to control the sea lanes north

---

[72] Yoshimitsu so referred to Yoshihiro just before Yoshihiro's death. *Sakaiki*, p. 75.

[73] *Yamaguchi kenshi shiryōhen chūsei*, vol. 1, Tsunetsugu kōki, 7.24.1395 (Ōei 2), p. 76. The others allowed to take vows included Hosokawa Yorimoto and Isshiki Akinori.

[74] *Dazaifu Dazaifu Tenmangū shiryō*, vol. 12, pp. 449–66 for sources pertaining to his divestiture during the seventh intercalary month of 1395 (Ōei 2).

[75] Hyakuda Masao, "Ōuchi Yoshihiro bōdaiji kōsekiji no jūzō," *Yamaguchi ken monjokan kenkyū kiyō* no. 26 (1999), pp. 57–72. See also Itō Kōji, "Chūsei kōki chiiki kenryoku to taigai kōshō to zenshū monha, Ōuchi shi to Tōfukuji shō-ichi ha no kakawari o chūshin ni," *Komonjo kenkyū* no. 48 (1998), pp. 20–40.

[76] Saeki Kōji, "Ōuchi shi no Chikuzen no kuni shihai—Yoshihiro ki kara Masahiro ki made," *Kyūshū chūseishi kenkyū* 1 (1978), pp. 245–47. Saeki shows how Yoshihiro made inroads into Shōni lands after Imagawa Ryōshun was ousted. For negotiations with Korea over the importation of the Tripiṭaka, see Kenneth R. Robinson, "Treated as Treasures: The Circulation of Sutras in Maritime Northeast Asia from 1388 to the Mid-Sixteenth Century," *East Asian History* 21 (6.2001), pp. 38–39.

of Kyushu. Yoshihiro rewarded the Munakata with lands in Saigō district, seized from the shrine's rivals, the Shōni.[77]

In 1392, the year when the war between the Northern and Southern Courts ended, the Chosŏn Dynasty came to power in Korea after a successful coup against the earlier Koryŏ Kingdom. Yoshihiro reached out to this new regime and secured a Korean printed copy of the Buddhist canon (the Tripiṭaka), which Ryōshun had failed to do.[78] Receiving each set of these five thousand facsimiles was not an easy task, for they were rare, difficult to transport, and prized in the Buddhist world as both a source of merit and a means of enabling more powerful Buddhist rites.[79]

Nonetheless, Yoshihiro was overshadowed by Ashikaga Yoshimitsu, who, after 1395, increasingly acted ritually as Japan's sovereign.[80] Yoshimitsu also built a variety of remarkable structures to demonstrate his authority, such as Shōkokuji, a Zen temple complex that unfortunately burned down in 1394.[81] Undeterred, Yoshimitsu had it rebuilt by the sixth month of 1396, although its 360-foot (*shaku*) tower was not finished until 1399. At that time, a thousand monks participated in the celebratory rites commemorating its completion.[82] Yoshimitsu also constructed the famous Kinkakuji, a structure initially coated in lacquer before being covered in either gold leaf or gold

[77] Saeki, "Ōuchi shi no Chikuzen no kuni shihai," pp. 246–47 for the first evidence of the Munakata supporting the Ōuchi in 1398 (Ōei 5).

[78] Imagawa Ryōshun was the point person for Korean relations from 1375 until his dismissal in 1395. See Suda Makiko, *Chūsei Nichō kankei to Ōuchi shi*, pp. 43–52. For how he requested copies of the Tripiṭaka from 1388 until 1392, see p. 143, and *Dazaifu Dazaifu Tenmangū shiryō* vol. 12, pp. 446–47 for Ryōshun's return of 570 prisoners the year before he lost his office, as mentioned in a Ming historical account dating from 1395 (Ōei 2).

[79] For the significance and desirability of the Tripiṭaka, see Richard Bowring, *The Religious Traditions of Japan, 500–1600* (New York: Cambridge University Press, 2005), pp. 227–29, and Mimi Hall Yiengpruksawan, *Hiraizumi: Buddhist Art and Regional Politics in Twelfth-Century Japan* (Cambridge, MA: Harvard East Asian Monographs, 1998), pp. 80–86.

[80] Conlan, *From Sovereign to Symbol: An Age of Ritual Determinism in Fourteenth Century Japan* (New York: Oxford University Press, 2011), chap. 7, "The Ashikaga Emperor."

[81] *Nihon rekishi chimei taikei*, JapanKnowledge Lib (accessed 10.12.2015). The temple was largely completed by 1385. For references to the first fire that destroyed Shōkokuji, see *Daijōin nikki mokuroku*, in *Daijōin jisha zōjiki* (Kyoto: Rinsen shoten, 2003), vol. 12, 8.1.1394 (Meitoku 5), p. 296.

[82] See Imaeda Aishin, "Ashikaga Yoshimitsu no Shōkokuji sōken," in *Chūsei zenshūshi no kenkyū* (Tokyo daigaku shuppan, 1970) and Harada Masatoshi, "Mannen-san Shōkoku Jōtenzen-ji Ekō narabini sho to Ashikaga Yoshimitsu," *Kansai daigaku Tōzaigakujutsu kenkyū*, no. 46 (4.2013), pp. 17–31. For the height of the pagoda, see Keijo Shūrin's *Kanrin goroshū sansetsu*, excerpts of which appear in *Koji ruien*, *Shūkyōbu*, vol. 3 (Koji ruien kankōkai, 1927), p. 387, and *Nanpō kiden*, in DNSR, ser. 7, vol. 4 (Tōkyō daigaku shuppankai, 1931), 9.15.1399 (Ōei 6), p. 37 for the estimate of 360 feet. Fragments of the finial were discovered in 2016. See Matthew Stavros and Tomishima Yoshiyuki, "The Shōkokuji Pagoda: Building the Infrastructure of Buddhist Kingship in Medieval Japan," *Japanese Journal of Religious Studies* 45.1 (2018), pp. 125–44, and Stavros, "Monuments and Mandalas in Medieval Kyoto: Reading Buddhist Kingship in the Urban Plan of Ashikaga Yoshimitsu," Harvard Journal of Asiatic Studies 77.1 (12.2017), pp. 321–61.

dust, and modeled himself after the Chinese monk Dōgi (Ch. Dàoyì), who had purportedly built a temple with the same name centuries earlier during the Tang Dynasty.[83] Kinkakuji was erected near a beautiful lake and set near a graceful line of hills, known as Kitayama. The cost was estimated at over a million *kanmon*, approximately two billion current dollars.[84] Yoshimitsu could readily pay for such projects, as his receipt of the title of King of Japan allowed him access to lucrative trade, in the form of tribute exchanges, with the Ming.[85]

Ashikaga Yoshimitsu made demands of corvée labor on the *shugo* for his various projects. Ōuchi Yoshihiro provided funds and laborers for the project through levies on Izumi and Kii provinces. Nevertheless, he balked in using his warriors for these projects, stating that his men were practitioners of the way of the bow and arrow rather than laborers. He refused to allow them to haul earth for the expansion of gardens around Kinkakuji, a feat that entailed the moving of a mountain of earth to level a steep incline, a project unparalleled in medieval Japan.[86] Among the *shugo* lords, only Yoshihiro dared to refuse Yoshimitsu.

In 1397 an uprising by the Shōni of Chikuzen and by the Kikuchi, die-hard Southern Court supporters, exacerbated tensions between Yoshihiro and Ashikaga Yoshimitsu. Yoshihiro remained in the capital and relied on Mitsuhiro and Moriakira, his brothers, to quell it. Mitsuhiro was killed and the Ōuchi forces were routed late in 1397.[87] According to some

[83] It is telling, however, that the thirty-eight-year-old Yoshimitsu did not take the new name when he initially renounced the world, on 6.20.1395 (Ōei 2), but rather some five months later. See Yutani Yūzō, "Kinkakuji wa Kinkakuji to shite taterareta: 'Nihon kokuō Minamoto Dōgi' koto Ashikaga Yoshimitsu to Godaisan (Wu-Tai-Shan) no Bukkyō setsuwa," *Nagoya gaikokugo daigaku kokugo gakubu kiyō* 42 (2.2012), pp. 3–10.

[84] For the estimate of this price see DNSR, ser. 7, vol. 2, *Gaun nikkenroku* 8.19.1448 (Bunan 5), p. 780. This contemporary equivalent to purchasing power with a *kanmon* roughly equal to $2,000 at the turn of the fifteenth century is based on a conversation with Maki Takayuki, Yamaguchi, 12.17.2011.

[85] For the best overview, see Charlotte von Verschuer, "Ashikaga Yoshimitsu's Foreign Policy 1398–1408: A Translation from *Zenrin Kokuhō ki*, the Cambridge Manuscript," *Monumenta Nipponica*, 62.3 (2007), pp. 261–97.

[86] See DNSR, ser. 7, vol. 2, 4.16.1397 (Ōei 4), p. 780 for the *Gaun nikken roku*, 8.19.1448 (Bunan 5). See also Momosaki Yūichirō, *Muromachi no hasha: Ashikaga Yoshimitsu*, pp. 185–86. I learned of archaeological evidence about the movement of the earth through conversations with Hori Daisuke and Minami Takao at excavations at the site of the southern boundary of the lake, 5.29.2017. Pottery discovered at this site on 5.26.2017 reveals that a large area was leveled during the time of Yoshimitsu, and yet the area never held water, suggesting that this great project was abandoned before the lake was ever expanded. See also *Kyoto shinbun*, "Kinkakuji ni Ashikaga Yoshimitsu ga zōei shita maboroshii no ike," (accessed 10.11.2018), https://headlines.yahoo.co.jp/hl?a=20181011-00000050-kyt-l26.

[87] *Dazaifu Dazaifu Tenmangū shiryō*, vol. 12, pp. 487–91. See also *Yamaguchi shishi shiryōhen Ōuchi bunka* (Yamaguchi, 2010), p. 64 (hereafter *Ōuchi bunka*), for the Mōri-ke bunko genealogy reference to Mitsuhiro.

accounts, Yoshimitsu's failure to compensate Yoshihiro for Mitsuhiro's death contributed to the rift between the two and moved the latter to contemplate rebellion.[88]

Imagawa Ryōshun later wrote that Yoshihiro had started plotting rebellion against Ashikaga Yoshimitsu sometime between late 1395 and early 1396.[89] Whether he really did so or not is hard to know, since Ryōshun's account is self-serving and obscures his own role in the uprising.[90] Recently discovered sources suggest that Yoshimitsu still supported Yoshihiro, for he paid the Yoshida for prayers on behalf of Yoshihiro on 10.16.1398, the day that he departed for Kyushu to pacify the Shōni and the Kikuchi.[91] Although other accounts suggest, to the contrary, that Yoshihiro rebelled after discovering a plot by Yoshimitsu to frame and destroy him, no evidence exists for Yoshimitsu's duplicity.[92] No doubt in connection with his plan to move against Yoshimitsu, Yoshihiro reasserted descent from the royal lineage of Paekche (18 BCE–660 CE), claiming descent from the Paekche founder Onjo (18 BCE–29 CE).[93]

[88] *Dazaifu Dazaifu Tenmangū shiryō*, vol. 12, p. 487. See *Sakaiki*, pp. 49–50, and Tyler, *Iwashimizu Hachiman*, p. 116 for Yoshihiro complaining of a lack of recognition for Mitsuhiro's death.

[89] *Nantaiheiki*, pp. 318–20. See also Tyler, *Fourteenth-Century Voices*, vol. 2, *From Baishōron to Nantaiheiki*, pp. 229–30, 257–60. For detailed analysis of this passage, see Matsuoka, *Ōuchi Yoshihiro*, pp. 147–50. Ryōshun in the *Nantaiheiki* states that his conversation with Yoshihiro happened "the year before when Ōtomo Chikayo departed for Kyushu," which would be sometime between the seventh month of 1395 and the third month of 1396. See also Hirase Naoki, *Ōuchi Yoshihiro*, pp. 147–52.

[90] In the crucial passage itself in the *Nantaiheiki*, pp. 320–21, and Tyler, *From Baishōron to Nantaiheiki*, p. 258, Ryōshun suggests that the conversation with Yoshihiro happened in the capital, but then Ryōshun laments not being able to travel up to the capital to defend himself. The account is at variance with other historical developments. Yoshimitsu assumed that Ryōshun was deeply implicated in the rebellion and demanded his death. See a letter dispatched to the Uesugi in *Niigata kenshi shiryōhen 3 chūsei* 1 (Niigata, 1982), doc. 637, 1.18 [(Ōei 7) 1400] Ashikaga Yoshimitsu *shojō*, pp. 397–98. For the best overview, see Ogawa Takeo, *Ashikaga Yoshimitsu*, pp. 198–204. Ryōshun ultimately had a humiliating audience with Yoshimitsu during the ninth month of 1400. See the *Yoshida ke hinamiki* 10.7.1400 (Ōei 7), reproduced in Ogawa, *Ashikaga Yoshimitsu*, pp. 202–3. For a contrary view, see Tyler, *From Baishōron to Nantaiheiki*, p. 230.

[91] Kirita Takashi, "'Kyōto gotaiji gokōmon' ni mieru Ashikaga Yoshimitsu no jingi kitō," *Komonjo kenkyū* 90 (12.2020), p. 53. For Yoshimitsu's payment of six thousand *hiki* for prayers to Yoshida Kaneatsu on 10.16.1398 (Ōei 5), see Kirita Takashi, "Tenri daigaku fuzoku toshokan shozō 'Kyōto gotaiji gokōmon,'" *Shintōshi kenkyū* 69.1 (2021), doc. 16, 10.16 [(Ōei 5) 1398] Nakayama Chikamasa *hōsho utsushi*, p. 116. For a transcription of the prayer by Yoshimitsu against the Kikuchi and Shōni issued on the following day, see doc. 13, 10.17.1398 (Ōei 5) Ashikaga Yoshimitsu *kōmon utsushi*, pp. 115–16. I am indebted to David Romney for these references. See also Matsuoka, *Ōuchi Yoshihiro*, pp. 182–83, and *Dazaifu Dazaifu Tenmangū shiryō* vol. 12, p. 497.

[92] *Sakaiki*, pp. 49–50, and Tyler, *Iwashimizu Hachiman*, p. 116. See also Takeda Osamu, ed., *Ashikaga Yoshimitsu to Tōji* (Kyōto furitsu sōgō shiryōkan rekishi shiryōkan, 2004), p. 32. For reference to the Shōni having documents calling for the death of Yoshihiro, see *Sakaiki*, p. 49, and Matsuoka, *Ōuchi Yoshihiro*, pp. 176–78.

[93] *Yamaguchi kenshi shiryōhen chūsei*, vol. 1, Richō jitsuroku, 7.10.1399 (Chŏngjong 1)/7.9.1399 (Ōei 6), p. 864, and Suda Makiko, *Chūsei Nichō kankei to Ōuchi shi*, pp. 216–18.

Crafting Ōuchi Identity

Keenly interested as he was in his genealogy, already by 1378 Yoshihiro had contacted officials of the failing Koryŏ Dynasty and claimed ancestry from the founder of the ancient kingdom of Paekche.[94] In 1399 his emissary to the newly founded Chosŏn Dynasty declared that the Japanese (*Nihon kokujin*) did not know that he was descended from the Paekche founder and boasted both of his conquest of Kyushu and of his control of six Japanese provinces. After relating how he had quelled the brigands of Tsushima, Yoshihiro requested through the emissary, in recognition of his service and heritage, restoration of his patrimonial lands in the southwestern region of Wansan, which "had for some reason been confiscated."[95] This region would have been in the Paekche heartland.[96]

Chosŏn officials balked at Yoshihiro's request, but they promised other rewards, including (as we have seen when discussing his religious pursuits) a complete copy of the Buddhist canon, the Tripiṭaka.[97] They also recognized Yoshihiro's claim of royal descent and provisionally referred to him with the surname Kō (Kr. Ko) in 11.1399. Ko was the royal surname of rulers of the Koguryŏ Dynasty (37 BCE–668 CE), rather than Paekche kings, who used the name Puyŏ, but the two royal lines were loosely related.[98] In 11.7.1399, their official *Veritable History* identified Yoshihiro accordingly as a Ko.[99]

---

[94] *Yamaguchi kenshi shiryōhen chūsei*, vol. 1, Kōraishi, pp. 862–63. For analysis, see Suda Makiko, *Chūsei Nichō kankei to Ōuchi shi*, pp. 44, 50.

[95] Itō Kōji has argued that this was an attempt by Yoshihiro to show within Japan his closeness to Korea, and perhaps to seek a base in Korea. Itō Kōji, "Chūsei saikoku shoshi no keifu ninshiki," in *Kyokai aidentiti* (Kyūshū shigakukai, 2008), p. 118.

[96] *Yamaguchi kenshi shiryōhen chūsei*, vol. 1, Richō jitsuroku, 863–65. His quelling of pirates and request for a Tripiṭaka are mentioned on 3.1397 (T'aejo 5)/(Ōei 3), p. 863. For more analysis of this, see Suda Makiko, *Chūsei Nichō kankei to Ōuchi shi*, pp. 143, 216–18, and Maeda Yūya, "Ōuchi Yoshihiro to Chōsen," *Kōgakkan shigaku* no. 24 (3.2009), pp. 69–94. Maeda, p. 72, suggests that the account could have been used to denigrate the Korean king, who favored this request, in favor of glorifying his advisors. See pp. 88–89.

[97] Suda Makiko, *Chūsei Nichō kankei to Ōuchi shi*, p. 217 for their recognition of his claims. For the grant of the Tripiṭaka, see *Yamaguchi kenshi shiryōhen chūsei*, vol. 1, p. 865.

[98] *Yamaguchi kenshi shiryōhen chūsei*, vol. 1, Richō jitsuroku, 7.10.1399 (Chŏngjong 1)/7.9.1399 (Ōei 6) p. 864. This surname was noted by Suda, *Chūsei Nichō kankei to Ōuchi shi*, pp. 216–18. She does not comment on the fact that Ko was not a Paekche royal surname. For the actual royal surname of the Paekche kings, Puyŏ, or at times Yŏ, see Jonathan Best, *A History of the Early Korean Kingdom of Paekche, together with Annotated Translation of the Paekche Annals of the Samguk sagi* (Cambridge: Harvard University East Asia Center, 2007), pp. 11, 52. The distinction is less significant than it might seem, as Koguryŏ leaders also claimed descent from the Puyŏ, and Paekche rulers recognized that their ancestors had branched off from the Koguryŏ. See, for example, Best, pp. 20–21.

[99] *Yamaguchi kenshi shiryōhen chūsei*, vol. 1, Richō jitsuroku, 11.7.1399 (Chŏngjong 1) /7.9.1399 (Ōei 6), p. 866, and Suda, p. 217.

Figure 3.2 Jōfukuji *Tekisui* Roof Tile of Dragon 乗福寺滴水瓦 B 一9. These tiles (Figures 3.2 and Figure 3.3) were made in Yamaguchi by Korean artisans who used local clay. Photograph and permission courtesy Yamaguchi-shi kyōiku iinkai

Sometime between 1379 and 1399, Yoshihiro had Jōfukuji, the mortuary temple of his father Hiroyo located in Yamaguchi, built in the style of Korean royalty, with roof tiles in the *tekisui* dragon-and-phoenix pattern used solely for palaces and temples associated with Koryŏ kings. Archaeological evidence suggests that a Koryŏ craftsman traveled to Yamaguchi to make these tiles.[100] It is possible that they were originally meant for a larger monastic complex (Figures 3.2 and 3.3).[101]

The Ōuchi were not unique in claiming descent from continental kings or emperors. For the warriors of the west, status mattered more than the geographic origins of their ancestors. One family, the Takahashi, claimed descent variously from Emperor Guangwudi (5 BCE–57 CE), the founder of the Latter Han, who allegedly made his way to Japan and lived in the Okura

---

[100] Ko Jyonyon, "Yamaguchi Jōfukuji ato shutsudo kawara no kentō," in *Kitani Yoshinobu sensei koki kinen ronshū* (ed. Kitani Yoshinobu sensei koki kinen ronshūkai, 2006), pp. 437–450. For the archaeological reports of this temple, see *Jōfukuji ato*, Satō Tsutomu, "Jōfukuji no kawara to Tomitajō no kawara," *Yamaguchi daigaku kokogaku ronshū* (Yamaguchi, 2003), pp. 321–38, and *Ōuchi bunka*, pp. 969–74. See also Suda Makiko, *Chūsei Nichō kankei to Ōuchi shi*, pp. 17, 31, and Itō, "Chūsei saikoku shoshi no keifu ninshiki," pp. 116–17.

[101] For more recent analysis of these roof tiles, see Satō Chikara, "Suō no kuni Jōfukuji ato shutsudo kawara no saikentō," in Kage Toshio, *Ōuchi to Ōtomo*, pp. 367–98.

Figure 3.3 Jōfukuji *Tekisui* Roof Tile of Phoenix 乗福寺滴水瓦 B 一10.
Photograph and permission courtesy Yamaguchi-shi kyōiku iinkai

valley of Chikuzen; while Takahashi Akitane more generally asserted that his
family was descended from the Liu emperors of the Han.[102]

Royal origins were prized, and enemies were castigated not for being "foreign" but, rather, for being descended from villains, which involved recasting
older lineages as being "evil." Thus, the Kotō, who had been *shugo* of Nagato,
were descended from an old lineage of warriors, the Mononobe, which had
largely been eclipsed in the sixth century, but whose descendants remained
throughout Japan.[103] To counter this, the Ōuchi recast the Kotō as stemming

---

[102] Itō, "Chūsei saikoku shoshi no keifu ninshiki," p. 113. For the sources, see *Miyazaki kenshi shiryōhen kinsei,* vol. 1 (Miyazaki, 1991), Takahashi *buke denrai shojō an,* doc. 69, Takahashi ke *oboegaki,* pp. 73–74 for an explanation of descent from the founder of the Latter Han. For Takahashi Akitane's spurious document claiming descent from the Liu, see *Miyazaki kenshi shiryōhen kinsei,* vol. 1, doc. 71, Takahashi Akitane *okibumi,* p. 75.

[103] For Kotō claims of Mononobe descent, see a convenient copy of their genealogy in *Hagi han batsu etsu roku,* vol. 4, Bōchō jisha shōmon, pp. 132–33.

from Mononobe Moriya (d. 587), who had resisted Buddhism and had been killed by the Buddhist sage Prince Shōtoku (574–622).[104] The Ōuchi later crafted links in their genealogy to Prince Shōtoku and, by extension, to his patronage of Buddhism. The Kōno, Ōuchi rivals from western Shikoku, emphasized divine descent, claiming ties to an Iron Man who defeated, among others, a Paekche king.[105]

Nevertheless, in contrast to rivals, Yoshihiro seems to have had knowledge of the Korean language, in and of itself an important ethnic marker. For example, he contacted the ritual specialist Yoshida Kaneatsu about a myth found in the Japanese history *Nihon shoki* and asked whether the horses described as springing from the body of Ukemochi, a fertility goddess, were Korean. Although Yoshida Kaneatsu denied the claim and asserted that the horses came from central Japan, Yoshihiro's question reveals an awareness of an ancient Korean linguistic correspondence, for the terms for each body part and each horse were phonetically related in that language, but not in Japanese.[106]

Yoshihiro's construction of a royal genealogy in 1399 allowed him to claim a status equal, if not superior, to the lineage of the Ashikaga. His assertions of Paekche royal identity had the added advantage of aiding diplomatic and economic exchanges with Korea. Bolstered by this claim, as well as by his long record of battle prowess and ample wealth, and moved by suspicion of Yoshimitsu's motives and intentions, Yoshihiro embarked on an attempt to overthrow the Ashikaga leader in 1399.

The Ōei Disturbance (1399)

Resenting lack of compensation for his brother Mitsuhiro's death and believing in Yoshimitsu's plan to have him killed in battle, Yoshihiro

---

[104] For the Ōuchi as later portraying their rival, the Kotō as being of the Mononobe descent, see their genealogy, located in *Ōuchi bunka*, p. 16. For how this represents the first Ōuchi attempt to create a lineage linked to this prince, see Suda Makiko, *Chūsei Nichō kankei to Ōuchi shi*, pp. 201–47, particularly pp. 215–18. The Mononobe did exist in Suō from ancient times. See *Heian ibun*, vol. 1 (Tōkyōdō shuppan, 1963), doc. 199, Engi 8 (908) Suō no kuni *kuga gō koseki*, pp. 289–305.

[105] *Yoshōki, Gunsho ruijū*, vol. 21, kassenbu, pp. 497–98, 509–10.

[106] For the question, *Yamaguchi kenshi shiryōhen chūsei*, vol. 1, Kaneatsu assonki, 7.16–18.1398? (Ōei 5?), p. 77. For the linguistic correspondences, see Michael Como, *Weaving and Binding: Immigrant Gods and Female Immortals in Ancient Japan* (Honolulu: University of Hawaii Press, 2009), p. 189. Worship of the deity Ukemochi was also linked to the Outer Shrine of Ise and may account for later Ōuchi interest in this shrine.

attempted to forge an alliance capable of bringing down the Ashikaga lord. He garnered widespread support. His confederates included Ashikaga Mitsukane, who as the *Kantō kubō* (Lord of the East) was responsible for governing Kamakura and eastern Japan;[107] Nijō Morotsugu, *kanpaku* (Regent) from 3.27.1398 through 5.22.1399; and the Zen monk Setsudō Sōboku, of Myōshinji.[108] He was also in contact with a variety of *shugo*, as well as with Miidera, the Buddhist institution that controlled the Seta bridge and the approaches to the capital from the east.[109]

Difficulties in coordinating eastern and western Japan contributed to the failure of the coup. Yoshihiro was in Kyushu, while Mitsukane was in eastern Japan. Nijō Morotsugu, who could have linked the two, was divested of his position in the fifth month of 1399. This impeded communication.

During the seventh month of 1399, the courtier Yoshida Kanehiro recounted Mitsukane's "crazed" preparations to attack Kyoto.[110] On 7.25.1399 Mitsukane issued to the monks of Kōfukuji a manifesto against Yoshimitsu, stating that the mandate of heaven (*tenmei*), a Chinese concept not generally used to argue for political change in Japan, demanded Yoshimitsu's destruction for the sake of peace in the realm and the welfare of the people.[111] He apparently sent this document to Yoshihiro. But Yoshihiro kept it under wraps for months, a silence that may explain Mitsukane's agitation.

Ultimately Yoshihiro left the west for central Japan. He reached the port of Sakai on 10.13.1399, but his intentions remained unclear.[112] While in Sakai he negotiated with several representatives of Yoshimitsu. The first was a

---

[107] For the best overview, see *Kanagawa kenshi tsūshi hen genshi kodai chūsei* (Kanagawa, 1981), "Ashikaga Mitsukane no jidai," pp. 799–806, particularly pp. 800–802. The remonstrance of Uesugi Norisada caused Mitsukane to turn back after Yoshihiro's death. For a recent study of Mitsukane, and the seriousness of this rebellion against Yoshimitsu, see Ishibashi Kazuhiro, "Ashikaga Mitsukane to Muromachi bakufu," in Kuroda Motoki, ed., *Ashikaga Mitsukane to sono jidai* (Ebisu kōshō, 2015), pp. 6–23.

[108] Ogawa Takeo, "Ryōshin kara mita Ashikaga Yoshimitsu," *ZEAMI Chūsei no geijutsu to bunka: Tokushū: Ashikaga Yoshimitsu no jidai roppyaku nen kikinen* (Shinwasha, 2007), p. 158, and p. 170 n. 5. For Setsudō and Myōshinji, Ueda Jun'ichi, *Ashikaga Yoshimitsu to zenshū* (Kyoto: Hōzōkan, 2011), p. 12. Setsudō was connected to Yoshihiro because he held office at Kannonji, a temple in Izumi. See Tamamura Takeji, "Shoki Myōshinjishi no ni, san giten," *Nihon zenshū shi ronshū ge* (Kyoto: Shibunkaku, 1981), pp. 279–80.

[109] See the *Sakaiki*, pp. 63, 65. This passage does not appear in the variant of the *Ōeiki* tale translated by Tyler in *Iwashimizu Hachiman*.

[110] Ishibashi Kazuhiro, "Ashikaga Mitsukane to Muromachi bakufu," pp. 8–9 for references to Kanehiro's *Yoshida ke hinamiki*, 7.2–7.17.1399.

[111] *Yamaguchi kenshi shiryōhen chūsei*, vol. 1, Jimon no koto jōjō kikigaki, p. 80, and *Ōuchi bunka*, p. 128.

[112] Tyler, *Iwashimizu Hachiman*, p. 113. For more on Yoshihiro and Sakai, see Itō Kōji, "Ōuchi shi no Nichimin bōeki to Sakai," *Chūsei Nihon no gaikō to zenshū* (Yoshikawa kōbunkan, 2002), pp. 210–13.

Tendai monk dispatched by Sondō, the princely head of Shōren'in, while the second was the Rinzai Zen monk Zekkai Chūshin. These discussions continued until just before Yoshihiro openly rebelled.[113]

Yoshihiro confronted the messengers with a document, claimed to be written in Yoshimitsu's own hand that called for his destruction; he had seized it from the Kikuchi after defeating them.[114] Yoshihiro stated that this potential divestment as *shugo* of Kii and Izumi provinces was the main reason for his attempted rebellion. The lack of acknowledgment for Mitsuhiro's death is the second reason for his unwillingness to surrender. Finally, he mentioned that he was aware of rumors that he might be killed in Kyoto. In addition, Yoshihiro boasted of his many victories and his diplomatic triumphs.[115]

Consequently, Yoshihiro appealed to favored gods to help him maintain control of Kii and Izumi provinces. For example, he can be documented as praying to Matsuzaki Tenmangū, stating that he would further patronize this shrine dedicated to Sugawara Michizane, a god favored by Yoshihiro's father Hiroyo, if he was successful in battle.[116]

Some of Yoshihiro's trusted followers were not sanguine about their prospects in this conflict and attempted to order their affairs before an almost certain death. Sugi Shigeaki, one of Yoshihiro's generals, purchased lands in Suō province shortly before the uprising in two installments on 10.15 and 10.20.1399, immediately after arriving in Sakai.[117] Perhaps he did so to strengthen his ties to this province, but his motives remain unknown. Shigeaki and Yoshihiro remained in communication with Ashikaga Yoshimitsu and the shogunal chancellor (*kanrei*) as the paperwork for legitimating the transfer of these lands continued in parallel to military preparations.

---

[113] *Sakaiki*, pp. 44–50 for reference to these negotiations. See also Tyler, *Iwashimizu Hachiman*, pp. 113–17. Sondō is not mentioned in the *Ōeiki*.

[114] *Yamaguchi kenshi shiryōhen chūsei*, vol. 1, Jimon no koto jōjō kikigaki, p. 80.

[115] *Sakaiki*, pp. 49–50.

[116] *Shinshū Izumi Sanno shishi*, vol. 4, *Shiryōhen kodai chūsei* 1, pp. 352–55. See also *Shinshū Izumi Sanno shishi*, vol. 1, *Tsūshihen shizen chūsei*, pp. 398–99.

[117] Shigeaki paid 650 *kanmon* and 30 *kanmon* on 10.15 and 10.20.1399 for lands in Kuga estate. *Sugi ke monjo, Hagi Hakubutsukan kenkyū hōkoku* no. 2 (Hagi hakubutsukan 2007), doc. 11, 2.7.1399 (Ōei 6) Ashikaga Yoshimitsu *sodehan mikyōjo*, and docs. 12–13, dated 10.13 and 10.17.1399 for the confirmations by the *kanrei* and Yoshihiro. For the remaining documents of sale, see docs. 14–15 of 10.15 and 10.20.1399. See also Fujii, *Muromachiki daimyō kenryokuron*, pp. 87–88. As Fujii notes, Yoshihiro continued to confirm Yoshimitsu's documents even though he was preparing to be attacked at Sakai.

By 10.27.1399, the die was cast. Mitsukane called the eastern warriors to arms.[118] On 10.28, Yoshihiro dispatched to Kōfukuji Mitsukane's document of the seventh month, which argued that Yoshimitsu had "lost the mandate of heaven."[119] Here Yoshihiro, like Ashikaga Mitsukane, ineffectively attempted to hold Ashikaga Yoshimitsu to this Chinese standard.

On the opposite side, Yoshimitsu called warriors to arms on that same day, demanding the chastisement of Yoshihiro.[120] He also issued various maledictions, some of which appealed to North Star worship, and others that were directed to the twenty-two shrines of Japan, so as to check Yoshihiro ritually as well as politically.[121] They were commissioned on the same day that Yoshimitsu mobilized warriors, although the Yoshida prayers themselves were offered on the following day.[122]

In contrast to the inflamed rhetoric of Ashikaga Mitsukane, Yoshihiro remained cautious and calculating.[123] He decided to hold onto documents and to release them at a time of his choosing. Just as he had withheld Mitsukane's declaration of war for nearly three months, so too he kept hold of administrative records from the Ashikaga. Knowing that war was imminent, he issued a flurry of documents immediately before his open rebellion, while he still held the uncontested post of *shugo* of his provinces.

Yoshihiro had kept documents of the tenth month confirming Sugi Shigeaki's purchase, issued by Ashikaga Yoshimitsu and the shogunal chancellor (*kanrei*) Hatakeyama Motokuni. In addition, he kept similar records confirming the holdings of reliable supporters such as the Mikita of Izumi and the Koyama of Kii. Yoshihiro completed their paperwork since a *shugo* signature was necessary, so that there could be no procedural excuse, whatever might happen to himself, for undoing these grants or confirmations.[124]

---

[118] *Hagi han batsu etsu roku*, vol. 1, maki 17, Kodama Saburō Uemon doc. 85, 10.27 [(Ōei 6) 1399] Kamakura dono Mitsukane *gunzei saisokujō*, p. 492, and maki 19, Kodama Shirō Hyōei, doc. 81, 10.27 [(Ōei 6) 1399] Kamakura dono Mitsukane *gunzei saisokujō*, p. 529. For more analysis, see Ishibashi "Ashikaga Mitsukane to Muromachi bakufu," p. 9.

[119] *Yamaguchi kenshi shiryōhen chūsei*, vol. 1, Jimon no koto jōjō kikigaki, p. 80.

[120] *Hagi han batsu etsu roku*, vol. 1, Fukuhara Tsushima 8 no. 2, 10.28.1399 (Ōei 6) Ashikaga Yoshimitsu *sodehan gunzei saisokujō*, p. 157.

[121] DNSR, ser. 7, vol. 4, 7.20.1399 (Ōei 6) p. 6 for *Daihokutohō* rites at Tenryūji, and 10.27.1399 (Ōei 6), pp. 162–64 for more generalized five altar maledictions. For how Yoshimitsu also prayed to the core twenty-two shrines, see Kirita Takashi, "'Kyōto gotaiji gokōmon' ni mieru Ashikaga Yoshimitsu no jingi kitō," pp. 53–54.

[122] Kirita Takashi, "Tenri daigaku fuzoku toshokan shozō 'Kyōto gotaiji gokōmon,'" doc. 14, 10.29.1399 (Ōei 6) Ashikaga Yoshimitsu *kōmon utsushi*, p. 116.

[123] Fujii, *Muromachiki daimyō kenryokuron*, pp. 88–90.

[124] See Fujii, *Muromachiki daimyō kenryokuron*, pp. 87–90, and *Hagi Hakubutsukan kitaku Sugi ke monjo, Hagi hakubutsukan kenkyū hōkoku* no. 3 (3.2008), p. 3 for these newly discovered documents, which include a 2.7.1399 (Ōei 6) Ashikaga Yoshimitsu *sodehan mikyōjo*, a 10.13.1399

Some scholars have argued that Yoshihiro ultimately realized that he could not defeat Yoshimitsu, but intended, rather, through his actions to encourage the shogun to modify his behavior. In the end, however, Yoshihiro's mindset is not knowable, although his actions were interpreted by contemporaries in this way.[125]

Sakai

Yoshihiro entrusted the Ōuchi lands in the west to his younger brother Moriakira, entreating him to "guard the provinces that are yours" regardless of what might happen in Sakai.[126] Debate then raged as to whether Yoshihiro should travel to Kii and garner the support of local warriors or remain at Sakai, a harbor named "the boundary" because it was located at the boundary of Izumi, Settsu, and Kawachi provinces. His brother Hiroshige argued that with good access to the ports of Sakai and Shimizu, in Kii, they could occupy the castle of Tsuchimochi and "remain there for fifty years." However, Hirai Dōjo felt that they would soon lose support if they were to leave Sakai, and ultimately his advice prevailed.[127]

These debates within the warrior group reveal something about Ōuchi understanding of ports and terrain. Shimizu and Sakai were important harbors, and Tsuchimochi castle was located close enough to the coast to be resupplied. Shimizu, located further south than Sakai, allowed good access to the Inland Sea via Awa province in Shikoku; or one could avoid the Inland Sea in a time of war and travel to the west via southern Shikoku and southern Kyushu.[128]

Sakai proved significant, but not because it was a good port. The area around Sakai, located at the mouth of the Yamato River, frequently silted

(Ōei 6) Muromachi bakufu *kanrei hōsho*, and a 10.17.1399 (Ōei 6) Ōuchi Yoshihiro *jungyōjō*. For the Mikita document of 11.6.1399 (Ōei 6), see DNSR, ser. 7, vol. 4, p. 180. See also pp. 188–89 for the 11.15.1399 (Ōei 6) Koyama confirmation.

125 Momosaki Yūichirō, *Muromachi no hasha: Ashikaga Yoshimitsu*, pp. 188–89.

126 Tyler, *Iwashimizu Hachiman*, p. 120, and *Sakaiki*, pp. 58–59. For an excellent overview of the conflict, and relevant sources, see Hirase Naoki, "Ōei no ran to sakai: Ōuchi Yoshihiro no kyoten ni tsuite," *Hokuriku toshi shigakukaishi* 18 (8.2012), pp. 10–18.

127 *Sakaiki*, pp. 55–57 for these negotiations; see also Tyler, *Iwashimizu Hachiman*, pp. 119–20. See also Shimatani Kazuhiko, "Chūsei Sakai no kangō o meguru shomondai," in Chūsei toshi kenkyūkai, comp., *Toshi o kiru* (Yamakawa shuppan, 2010), p. 114.

128 *Sakaiki*, p. 56. I owe much of this insight regarding the Shimizu sea lanes to Hirase Naoki. Discussion, Kanazawa, Japan, 4.27.2012.

up.[129] Large ships could not land at this shallow anchorage, but instead had to unload their cargo onto small boats that could travel over the sandbars.[130] Sakai's great advantage was not in its anchorage, but rather in its access to three major roads: the Kumano ōdō, Takauchi kaidō, and Nagao kaidō. In the fourteenth century goods moving to and from Nara were also transported through Sakai.[131] Excavations have revealed that Sakai mattered because of its transport access to other regions, so that its storehouses were designed to store goods temporarily.[132] Of the medieval harbor itself, little is known.[133]

Located on the coast, with no natural barriers, Sakai was not easy to defend, but the experienced Yoshihiro made the most of it. He fortified the city, constructed moats, and built numerous towers for archers, although their number is undoubtedly exaggerated in the chronicles.[134] His ally Ashikaga Mitsukane left Kamakura on 11.21.1399, but he was too far away to help in a meaningful way.[135]

Kitabatake Akiyasu and Mitsuyasu departed from Ise to attack Yoshihiro on 11.3–7.1399.[136] Yoshimitsu himself led another army, which left Tōji on 11.13 and arrived near Sakai the following day. Yoshihiro issued his final

[129] Shimatani Kazuhiko, "Chūsei Sakai no kangō o meguru shomondai," p. 104. Michelle Damien, "Late Medieval Japan's Seto Inland Seascape: Shipping, Sailors and Seafaring," PhD dissertation, University of Southern California, 5.2015, p. 178, would recognize that large ships landed at Hyōgo and then shipped objects to Sakai. For more on ports on the inland sea, see p. 63ff. See also Richard Pearson, "Japanese Medieval Trading Towns: Sakai and Tosaminato," *Japanese Journal of Archaeology* 3 (2016), pp. 99–106.

[130] See *Sakai shishi*, vol. 1 (Sakai, 1929), pp. 20–25. I confirmed this situation with Hirase Naoki. Conversation 10.14.2011. See also Yoshida Yutaka, "Chūsei no Sakai," *Kōwan to chūsei toshi Sakai Masuda Takamatsu Ōsaka* 12.23.2011 Symposium, Ōsaka rekishi hakubutsukan, pp. 29–35. Frois commented on the shallowness of Sakai as a harbor, and how Hyōgo was preferable for docking in his *History of Japan (Nihonshi)*. Matsuda Kiichi and Kawasaki Momota, trans., *Zenyaku Furoisu Nihonshi Shōgun Yoshiteru no saigō oyobi jiyū toshi Sakai: Oda Nobunaga hen*, vol. 1 (Chūō kōron shinsha, 2000), p. 45. Joao Rodrigues described it as "a sandy plain surrounded to the west by a rough coast." *This Island of Japon: Joao Rodrigues' Account of 16th Century Japan*, trans. Michael Cooper (Rutland, VT: Tuttle, 1973), p. 275.

[131] *Ōsaka fushi*, vol. 3, *chūseihen 1* (Ōsaka fu, 1979), pp. 864–65. For an excellent overview of Sakai, see Hirase Naoki, *Ōuchi Yoshihiro*, pp. 161–63. Some of the earliest sources refer to Kasuga shrine people buying and selling fish and shellfish at Sakai and transporting them along the Yoshino Road. *Kasuga jinja monjo*, vol. 4 (Kasuga shrine, 1984), doc. 799, 6.11.1337 (Kenmu 4) Ashikaga Takauji mikyōjo, pp. 121–22.

[132] Conversation Hirase Naoki.

[133] Shimatani Kazuhiko, "Chūsei Sakai no kangō o meguru shomondai," pp. 104–6. Hyōgoshima, to the contrary, consisted of a far better port, although it was ruined during the Ōnin War. Nagashima Fukutarō, *Ōnin no ran* (Shibundō, 1968), pp. 148–49. For more on supply, see Nagashima, pp. 136–38.

[134] Tyler, *Iwashimizu Hachiman*, pp. 119–20, 130 for descriptions of the fortifications, described improbably as forty-eight watchtowers and seventeen hundred (!) archery towers.

[135] DNSR, ser. 7, vol. 4, pp. 190–93.

[136] *Yamaguchi kenshi shiryōhen chūsei*, vol. 1, Jimon no koto jōjō kikigaki, p. 80. Yoshimitsu also mobilized Satsuma warriors on this day. See *Sakaishi* vol. 4, p. 35 for a 11.3.1399 (Ōei 6) Ashikaga Yoshimitsu mikyōjo. See also *Hagi han batsu etsu roku*, vol 2, maki 37.1, Nakagawa Yōemon, doc. 54, 11.7.1399 (Ōei 6) Ashikaga Yoshimitsu sodehan gunzei saisokujō, p. 25.

document of confirmation on 11.15, but from then on, his forces were essentially cut off in Sakai.

Kitabatake Mitsuyasu, Akiyasu's son, led the first attack on 11.29.1399, but his forces were repulsed and Mitsuyasu (named after Ashikaga Yoshimitsu) was killed.[137] A second battle took place on 12.21.1399. The Ashikaga attackers burned Sakai to the ground. The oldest archaeological evidence reveals a layer of ash corresponding to the burning of the fortified port, which at the time had a moat and stood at the crossroads of Daidō *tsuji* and Ōshōji.[138]

Yoshihiro perished along with Sugi Shigeaki and several hundred followers.[139] Hopeless though his cause was, it was a testament to his leadership and organization that numerous Kii warriors, such as the Tomita who served under him for a few years, and perhaps as many as two hundred Iwami warriors fought with him to the end.[140] His forces were decimated, but many died for the Ashikaga as well.[141] Nor did all of the defenders perish. Yoshihiro's younger brother Hiroshige, known in the chronicles as *shinsuke*, which implied that he was the new deputy governor of the province, and by extension the Ōuchi heir, as well as Hirai Dōjo were, in a turn of events regarded by contemporaries as being most unusual (*kidai no koto*), captured alive.[142]

Legacies

With Yoshihiro's death, and the surrenders of his younger brother Hiroshige and Hirai Dōjo, the rebellion petered out quickly. Imagawa Ryōshun fled to the east, where Yoshimitsu demanded that he be killed "for the sake of the realm." Ryōshun surrendered and at the age of seventy-five had with Yoshimitsu an audience that saved his life.[143] Later on he would write his

---

137 For Mitsuyasu's death, see DNSR, ser. 7, vol. 4, pp. 196–201.

138 Shimatani Kazuhiko, "Chūsei Sakai no kangō o meguru shomondai," p. 107 for the remains of the moat and crossroads, and p. 114 for evidence of this city burning in the fourteenth century.

139 For the best summary, see the 12.1399 (Ōei 6) Tokuda Akimitsu *gunchūjō*, in DNSR, ser. 7, vol. 4, pp. 224–25. For other petitions and documents describing this encounter, see pp. 223–63. See also *Yamaguchi kenshi shiryōhen chūsei*, vol. 1, Jimon no koto jōjō kikigaki, p. 80.

140 *Yamaguchi kenshi shiryōhen chūsei*, vol. 1, Ōeiki, p. 787.

141 For the latter quotation, see the *Iwashimizu Hachimangū kiroku*, DNSR, ser. 7, vol. 4, p. 241. For documentary evidence of one Hongō Tokiyasu perishing there, see pp. 226–27.

142 *Yamaguchi kenshi shiryōhen chūsei*, vol. 1, Jimon no koto jōjō kikigaki, p. 80.

143 The Jimon no koto jōjō kikigaki refers to the situation being unresolved even after Yoshihiro perished. See *Yamaguchi kenshi shiryōhen chūsei*, vol. 1, p. 80. For the Uesugi document see *Niigata*

Nantaiheiki, in an attempt to rehabilitate the Imagawa. Yoshimitsu regretted Mitsukane's involvement in the rebellion.[144] Although long established in Musashi province in the east, Mitsukane quit his campaign and apologized to Yoshimitsu for leading a great army, cementing his apology with a prayer to the Mishima shrine.[145] Like Ryōshun, Mitsukane peacefully ended his rebellion, meaning that he, too, would be spared.

Not all were so lucky. Nijō Morotsugu incurred Yoshimitsu's censure in the fourth month of 1399, lost his post as Regent, and starved to death in the eleventh month of that year. Ogawa Takeo suggests that he may have been complicit in Yoshihiro's plot.[146] Setsudō Sōboku was placed under "temple arrest" by the Shōrenin *monzeki*, the most important of the five noble cloisters of the Tendai temple Enryakuji, and his temple, Myōshinji, was abolished.[147] Hiroshige attempted to return to Yamaguchi and assert his position as the Ōuchi heir, but as we shall see, he was killed by Moriakira, who had remained behind to defend the territories.

Yoshihiro became the hero of two war tales, but this last revolt became the object of parody. A picture scroll, the *Jūnirui kassen emaki*, mocked the disturbance by depicting it as a dispute between warring animals. Yoshimitsu was represented as a victorious dragon, while Yoshihiro was portrayed as a brave wolf, who advocated attacking the enemy directly but died quickly. The fox who promises to come but did not was Mitsukane, while Hirai Dōjō was the old kite, who had lost too many feathers to fly and was unaccustomed to wearing armor, but who nevertheless "flew around and spread the word in appropriate places," advocated building fortresses for defense, just as he was portrayed as doing in the *Ōeiki*, and who treacherously switched sides after the wolf's death.[148] Yoshimitsu undoubtedly enjoyed this parody and

kenshi shiryōhen 3 *chūsei* 1, doc. 637, 1.18 [(Ōei 7) 1400] Ashikaga Yoshimitsu *shojō*, pp. 397–98. For the best overview, see Ogawa Takeo, *Ashikaga Yoshimitsu*, pp. 198–204. As an indispensable source for Imagawa Ryōshun, see Kawazoe Shōji's *Imagawa Ryōshun* (Yoshikawa kobunkan, 1964); for his involvement in the Ōei disturbance, see pp. 208–30.

[144] *Niigata kenshi shiryōhen* 3 *chūsei* 1, doc. 638, 12.29 [(Ōei 6) 1399] Ashikaga Yoshimitsu *shojō*, p. 398 for Yoshimitsu's lament. For Mitsukane's attitude, see Tanabe Hisako, *Uesugi Norizane* (Yoshikawa kōbunkan, 1999), pp. 42–43.

[145] *Shizokuka kenshi chūsei shiryō*, vol. 2 (Shizuoka, 1994), doc. 1275, 6.15.1400 (Ōei 7) Kantō kubō (Ashikaga Mitsukane) *ganmon*, p. 630.

[146] Ogawa Takeo, "Ryōshin kara mita Ashikaga Yoshimitsu," *ZEAMI*, p. 158, and p. 170 n. 5.

[147] See Ueda Jun'ichi, *Ashikaga Yoshimitsu to zenshū*, p. 12. See also Tamamura Takeji, "Shoki Myōshinjishi no ni, san gimon," pp. 279–80. For more on the importance of this *monzeki*, see Mikael Adolphson, *The Gates of Power* (Honolulu: University of Hawaii Press, 2000), pp. 71, 73.

[148] See Sarah E. Thompson, "The War of the Twelve Animals," in Keller Kimbrough and Haruo Shirane, eds., *Monsters, Animals and Other Worlds: A Collection of Short Medieval Japanese Tales* (New York: Columbia University Press, 2018), pp. 385–416. The passages that refer to the wolf, wild

his triumph over Yoshihiro, but the intervening years would unfold less to his liking, for the Ōuchi capably resisted him. Nevertheless, his selection of Hiroshige as an heir suggests that he too recognized Ōuchi rights to Suō and Nagato, and while he tried to maintain these hereditary Ōuchi control of these regions, he desired to keep them fractured and their heir ultimately beholden to him.

Ōuchi Yoshihiro's legacy proved ambivalent. He successfully fused northern Kyushu and western Honshu into an integrated political sphere and increased ties to Korea. He gained influence and power in central Japan by supporting central authority,[149] and he played a large role in the politics of the fourteenth century, defeating the Yamana and engineering the surrender of the Southern Court, for which he received control of the fledgling town and port of Sakai, as well as control over the provinces of Izumi and Kii. He transferred Myōken to Izumi, ensuring that memories of Ōuchi rule would remain there. He may have failed in central Japan, but he ensured a lasting ritual and administrative consolidation of authority in western Honshu and northern Kyushu. With his death there arose another contest for hegemony between Hiroshige, the Ōuchi heir designated heir by Ashikaga Yoshimitsu, and Moriakira, whom Yoshihiro had left behind in Yamaguchi. Ultimately, Moriakira would defeat Hiroshige, secure Yoshimitsu's acquiescence, and preserve autonomy under the umbrella of Ashikaga hegemony. It is to this remarkable brother that we now turn.

dog, dragon, and kite appear on pp. 396–401 of the translation. For the view of this as a parody, I am indebted to Sarah E. Thompson, "The War of the Twelve Animals (*Jūnirui kassen emaki*): A Medieval Japanese Illustrated Beast Fable," PhD dissertation, Columbia University, 1999, pp. 283–94ff. Some difference in interpretation exists, in that Thompson suggests that the raccoon (*tanuki*) may be an amalgamation of Ryōshun and Yoshihiro, while I see it as being Ryōshun. I believe that Yoshihiro is not the kite, as Thompson suggests, but rather the brave wolf. Hirai Dōjo, who would have been well known to contemporaries and was more aged, better fits with the portrayal of the kite.

[149] For the early part of his career, he did follow the model envisioned by Kawaoka Tsutomu, "Muromachi bakufu shugo taisei to saikoku shugo," in *Saikoku no kenryoku to senran* (Seibundō shuppan, 2010), who argued that western *shugo* supported the Ashikaga politically.

4

The One Who Could See Stars

The Unlikely Rule of Ōuchi Moriakira

Ōuchi Moriakira (1377–1431) never expected to rule, yet he rule he did, long and well. He enriched his family and followers, and his wealth funded rituals that helped to reinforce the cohesion of the Ōuchi domains. Yearly rites for Myōken were supplemented with memorial rites and biannual readings of imported sutra collections. Moriakira awed his rivals and resisted, then supported, the central government of the Ashikaga, leveraging his influence from close interactions with the shoguns to gain prerogatives that further enhanced his authority. He was successful first in resting the powerful shogun Yoshimitsu (1358–1408), and then he manipulated the later shoguns Yoshimochi (1386–1428, shogun 1394–1423) and Yoshinori (1394–1441, shogun 1429–41) to enact policies that fundamentally served his interests. Finally, he relied upon central authorities to help finance the reconstruction of the Usa shrine, which he then monopolized, thereby repurposing a formerly national shrine for Ōuchi ends.

Born the sixth of nine sons, Moriakira deferred to his older brothers Yoshihiro (1356–99) and Mitsuhiro (d. 1397), being too young to hope ever to succeed them. However, the unexpected deaths of all of his older brothers made him the chief of the Ōuchi after all. In time he, like his elder brothers, died in battle, ambushed by a rival. So ended thirty years of successful rule.

Moriakira promoted extensive mining of copper. He seems to have overseen the introduction of new smelting techniques, but it is his ability to mobilize men to mine the copper and to secure adequate timber for the furnaces required to smelt the ore that most directly accounts for this expansion. The copper so extracted facilitated trade and, in particular, closer ties with Korea. Likewise, through the support of officials from the Chosŏn Dynasty, he successfully advertised and broadcast his royal Korean ancestry.

Kings in All but Name. Thomas D. Conlan, Oxford University Press. © Oxford University Press 2024.
DOI: 10.1093/oso/9780197677339.003.0005

Nevertheless, Moriakira remains an obscure figure, far less famous than his brother Yoshihiro, but far more important for the Ōuchi. Rather than amass public fame, he built institutions, patronized rites, and participated in cultural salons. Until recently, even the correct pronunciation of his name (盛見) was forgotten.[1] His name is a curious one and literally means one of abundant vision, who by implication could see stars.[2] The link to Myōken is clear, for in Esoteric Buddhism it was associated with a barely visible double star (Alcor) located in the handle of the Big Dipper star known as *hosei*, the auxillary star.[3] True to his name, Moriakira fervently worshiped Myōken, and the stars, but also was practitioner of Zen and worshiped the sea gods as well.

Moriakira left a lasting imprint on the Ōuchi. He preserved their autonomy after fighting Ashikaga Yoshimitsu to a standstill, although Yoshimitsu had defeated all other opponents. He alone checked the powerful Ashikaga leader, and, as already noted, he forged the Ōuchi into a community united by repeated ritual performances. He also left a lasting imprint on the ritual and political framework of Japan. Through deft negotiations, he used state funds for the upkeep and reconstruction of Usa, a major shrine, but he privatized its rituals and used them for his ends.

Early Life and Lordship

Moriakira was born in 1377 at a residence located at the corner of Imakōji and Rokujō Streets in Kyoto.[4] His father, Hiroyo (1325–80), would then have been fifty-two and his brother Yoshihiro twenty-one. His mother was the daughter of Sanjō Kintada, mentioned at the end of chapter 2 as a courtier and an important diarist. The prestige of his maternal line gave the young Moriakira, known in youth as Rokurō ("Sixth Son"), a privileged position. Hiroyo's third and fifth sons were given surnames and relegated to the status of retainers whose descendants were ineligible to succeed as heirs to the main

[1] Many have read his name as Morimi, although some have preferred Moriharu, but recently discovered sources reveal that it was read as Moriakira. See Conlan, *Shiryō shōkai: Yoshida Kanemigi ga utsushita Ōuchi keizu*, *Yamaguchi kenshi kenkyū* 21 (3.2013), p. 66.

[2] For this point, I am indebted to Maki Takayuki. Conversation, 12.17.2011.

[3] Bernard Faure, *The Fluid Pantheon: Gods of Medieval Japan*, vol. 1 (Honolulu: University of Hawaii Press, 2016), pp. 64–65.

[4] *Yamaguchi shishi shiryōhen Ōuchi bunka* (Yamaguchi, 2010) (hereafter *Ōuchi bunka*), p. 26 for the detailed Ōuchi genealogy in the Mōri archives. See *Bōchō fūdo chūshin an*, vol. 13, *Yamaguchi saiban ge* (Yamaguchi, 1961), pp. 373–74 for how streets in Yamaguchi were later given the same names as those near Moriakira's birthplace. See also Suda Makiko, "Ōuchi shi no zaikyō katsudō," in *Ōuchi to Ōtomo* (Bensei shuppan, 2013), pp. 101–2.

Ōuchi line.[5] That Moriakira, a still younger son, remained an Ōuchi attests to his mother's social prominence and his father's support.

Moriakira became the *shugo* of Iwami at the age of nine. This appointment occurred because of a dispute between Yoshihiro and Mitsuhiro, his two older brothers, regarding the governance of Iwami. Moriakira's investiture with this *shugo* post served as a compromise, preventing either of the brothers from gaining uncontested control over this mineral-rich province.[6] Moriakira relied on his deputy, Migita Hidenao, an Ōuchi collateral from Sabaryō, to govern the province, about which he nonetheless learned enough to serve him well later on.[7]

In his twenty-first year (1397) he fought with Mitsuhiro in northern Kyushu against the Shōni and Kikuchi. The Ōuchi forces were defeated, Mitsuhiro was killed, and Moriakira fled.[8] Even in defeat, however, he had the presence of mind to reinforce Moji, the castle guarding the Straits of Shimonoseki, thereby retaining control of this critical choke point.[9]

When Yoshihiro departed for Sakai and rebelled against Ashikaga Yoshimitsu (1358–1408), he left the twenty-two-year-old Moriakira in charge of Yamaguchi and the lands to the west, namely the provinces of Suō, Nagato, Iwami, and Buzen.[10] As Yoshihiro's successor, Moriakira claimed jurisdiction over the "three major crimes" of murder, arson, or rebellion, which transcended rights of sanctuary.[11] He also claimed preeminent legal

---

[5] According to the Mōri genealogy, Hiromasa (Gorō), fought and died in Kyoto during the Meitoku disturbance, and his descendants founded the Reizen branch of the Ōuchi. *Ōuchi bunka*, the Mōri ke bunko Ōuchi genealogy (*keizu*), p. 26. See also *Hagi han batsu etsu roku*, vol. 3 (Yamaguchi ken monjokan, 1994), maki 102.2 Reizen Gorō collection, for a 1717 (Kyōho 2) postscript appearing immediately after doc. 128, 8.13 Ise Sadataka *shojō*, pp. 234–36.

[6] Wada Shūsaku, "Ōuchi shi no sōsho kankei o megutte," in *Ōuchi to Ōtomo*, p. 30. Thereupon, in 1397 Mitsuhiro served as the *shugo* of Buzen.

[7] Migita Hironao can be documented as being the deputy of Iwami from Meitoku 4 (1393). See, for example, *Masuda ke monjo*, vol. 1 (Tōkyō daigaku shuppankai, 2000), doc. 76, Ōuchi shi *bugyōnin rensho hōsho*, pp. 71–72. For evidence of Moriakira as Iwami *shugo* as late as 1398 (Ōei 5), see *Masuda ke monjo*, vol. 1, doc. 62, 8.10.1398 (Ōei 5) Iwami *no shugo* Ōuchi Moriakira *kakikudashi*, p. 62. For more on the Migita as the deputy *shugo* of Iwami, see Fujii Takashi, "Kōryaku naisen ni kansuru shomondai," *Muromachiki daimyō kenryokuron* (Dōseisha, 2013), pp. 55–68, 80–82.

[8] *Dazaifu Dazaifu Tenmangū shiryō*, vol. 12 (Dazaifu Tenmangū 1984), pp. 487–91. *Ōuchi bunka*, p. 64, reproduces the Mōri ke bunko genealogy reference to Mitsuhiro. For more on Moriakira fighting in Kyushu, see the Sonkeikaku bunkozō *Sakaiki* (Ōsaka: Izumi shoin, 1990), pp. 49–50.

[9] *Moji monjo* (Kita Kyūshū shizenshi rekishi hakubutsukan, 2005), doc. 46, 11.1 Ōuchi Moriakira *shojō*, p. 63. The monogram has been shown by Wada Shūsaku to date from 1398.

[10] *Sakaiki*, pp. 58–59. See also Yamaguchi kenshi hensanshitsu, comp., *Yamaguchi kenshi shiryōhen chūsei*, 4 vols. (Yamaguchi, 1996–2008), vol. 1, p. 784 for an alternate version of this text. Moriakira also received an unidentified memento (*katami*) from Yoshihiro.

[11] *Sengoku ibun Ōuchi shi hen*, vol. 1 (Tōkyōdō shuppan, 2016), doc. 454, 9.21.1479 (Bunmei 11) Ōuchi shi *kokugaryō hatto*, pp. 134–35. These laws were issued in 1399 and would be repeatedly reissued with the accession of new Ōuchi lords.

authority in his domains even though he was technically a rebel against the state, and he reaffirmed the judgments of Yoshihiro's time. Through the repeated promulgation of laws, Moriakira attempted to assert that he governed his domains.[12]

Sorely tested, Moriakira tried to strengthen his support among Iwami warriors, some of whom he rewarded in 1399. Many others, however, turned against him when Yoshihiro's defeat became clear.[13] To make matters worse, another brother, Hiroshige (d. 1401), survived the battle at Sakai, surrendered, and was recognized as the Ōuchi heir by Ashikaga Yoshimitsu. This encouraged one of Moriakira's younger brothers, Dōtsū (d. 1403), and his cousin Mitsuyo (d. 1433), the son of Mitsuhiro, to join Hiroshige's army.[14] Nevertheless, Yoshimitsu also weakened Hiroshige by divesting him of the *shugo* posts for all Ōuchi provinces except the core ones of Suō and Nagato.[15]

Hiroshige departed Kyoto on 7.11.1400 and on 7.21 advanced into Bitchū, midway between Kyoto and the Ōuchi lands.[16] The Ashikaga attempted to bolster Hiroshige's support among Iwami warriors and issued an order demanding that they join him.[17] Here Yoshimitsu's refusal to appoint Hiroshige as the *shugo* of Iwami made coordination more difficult and hampered Hiroshige's ability to attract the support needed to overthrow his brother Moriakira.

---

[12] Kawaoka Tsutomu, *Yamana Sōzen* (Yoshikawa kōbunkan, 2009), p. 89, also argues that the Ōuchi promulgated laws for their surrounding territories.

[13] *Yamaguchi kenshi shiryōhen chūsei*, vol. 3, Izuwa ke monjo, doc. 20, 11.1398 (Ōei 5) Izuwa Yūnao *gunchūjō*, p. 161. For more on the Izuwa, see Hirase Naoki, "Kyū chōshū hanshi Izuwa ke monjo oyobi Naitō ke monjo," *Yamaguchi monjokan kenkyū kiyō* 22 (1995), pp. 69–81.

[14] *Masuda ke monjo*, vol. 1, doc. 71, 7.13 Tokugen *shojō*, pp. 67–68; doc. 12, 7.6.1400 (Ōei 7) Ashikaga Yoshimitsu *gohan mikyōjo*, p. 28; doc. 69, 7.7 [(Ōei 7) 1400] Ōuchi Hiroshige *shojō*, pp. 65–66 for further evidence of the plot to entice Mitsuyo; and doc. 70 of 7.13 Ōuchi Hiroshige *shojō*, p. 67 for Mitsuyo's departure from Kyoto. See also *Masuda ke monjo*, vol. 2 (Tōkyōdō shuppan, 2003), doc. 513, 7.13 Ōuchi Mitsuyo *shojō*, pp. 256–58. Ogawa Makoto, *Ashikaga ichimon shugo hattenshi no kenkyū* (Yoshikawa kōbunkan, 1980), pp. 696–97, correctly dates these Masuda documents to 1400 (Ōei 7). *Ōuchi bunka*, Ōuchi *keizu* (Mōri ke bunko), p. 26, refers to Hiroshige as being the legitimate heir and provides information about the hapless Dōtsū.

[15] Buzen's *shugo* post was granted to Shibukawa Mitsuyori, a rival. Fujii, *Muromachiki daimyō kenryokuron*, p. 111. *Kumamoto ken shiryō chūsei*, vol. 2 (Kumamoto, 1962), Sata monjo, doc. 45, 4.27 Shibukawa Mitsuyori *shojō*, pp. 186–87. The document dates from 1400.

[16] *Masuda ke monjo*, vol. 1, doc. 69, 7.7 [(Ōei 7) 1400] Ōuchi Hiroshige *shojō*, pp. 65–66 for Hiroshige explaining his plans to leave on 7.11, and doc. 70, 7.13 Ōuchi Hiroshige *shojō*, p. 67 for his actual departure on this day as planned. For his arrival in Bitchū, see *Masuda ke monjo*, vol. 1, doc. 72, 7.21 Ōuchi Hiroshige *shojō*, p. 68.

[17] *Masuda ke monjo*, vol. 1, doc. 11, 7.2.1400 (Ōei 7) Muromachi bakufu *mikyōjo*, p. 27. See also doc. 12, 7.6.1400 (Ōei 7) Ashikaga Yoshimitsu *gohan mikyōjo*, p. 28, and doc. 69, 7.7 [(Ōei 7) 1400] Ōuchi Hiroshige *shojō*, pp. 65–66.

Iwami warriors were loath to accept the orders of any person without knowing who served as the *shugo* or his deputy.[18] Hirai Dōjo conveyed Yoshimitsu's anger (*onrippuku tachi sōrō*) and admonished these warriors to conquer Suō and Nagato before worrying about administrative authority, but they continued to chafe regarding the unclear authority in Iwami.[19] A few Iwami warriors, such as the weakened Sueyama, who had supported Hiroyo and Mitsuhiro in 1380 in their conflict with Yoshihiro, became ardent Hiroshige supporters, but others, such as the Sugi, joined Moriakira.[20]

Having nothing to lose, since they had already been punished for Yoshihiro's rebellion, most Ōuchi warriors supported Moriakira against the Ashikaga. All affiliated with the rebellion had their lands confiscated, even if their paperwork was in order. For example, Sugi Shigeaki (d. 1399) had purchased lands and had the sale confirmed by Ashikaga Yoshimitsu and Ōuchi Yoshihiro, but because he fought and died in Ōuchi Yoshihiro's rebellion, these lands were appropriated by the Ashikaga.[21] Shigeaki's heirs unsurprisingly sided with Moriakira. Hiroshige tried to appease them by granting lesser rights to their estates, but they refused his offer.[22]

Moriakira, by contrast, upheld the confirmations of Yoshihiro.[23] Being a rebel gave him the advantage of not needing to negotiate with the Ashikaga or being limited by other legal claims to the land. He rewarded his followers and endeared himself to them, and as a sign of affection the warriors who

---

[18] Commonly the *shugo* of Iwami was thought to be Kyōgoku Takanori from 1399 until 1401, when the Yamana took over, but Masuda documents reveal that two competing *shugo* attempted to govern the province. See *Masuda ke monjo*, vol. 3 (Tōkyōdō shuppan, 2006), doc. 592 7.7 Shōjo *shojō*, pp. 60–61, doc. 593, 7.26 Shōjo *shojō*, pp. 61–62, and vol. 2, doc. 508, 7.25 Yusa Nanagori *shojō*, p. 251.

[19] *Masuda ke monjo*, vol. 2, doc. 508, 7.25 Yusa Nanagori *shojō*, p. 251, and vol. 3, doc. 593, 7.26 Shōjo *shojō*, pp. 61–62. For the situation festering, see doc. 594, 62–64, 8.12 (Ōei 7) Shōjo *shojō*, pp. 62–64.

[20] *Yamaguchi kenshi shiryōhen chūsei*, vol. 1, Nagato no kuni shugo daiki, p. 607 for the Sueyama and Sugi appointments. For evidence of the Sueyama Takanaga as governing Nagato, see *Yamaguchi kenshi shiryōhen chūsei*, vol. 2, Ono ke monjo, doc. 18, 4.22 Ōuchi Hiroshige *shojō utsushi*, p. 1019, and doc. 19, 5.1 Ōuchi Hiroshige *shojō utsuji*, pp. 1019–20. Both documents date from 1401 (Ōei 8). For more on the Sueyama, see Fujii, *Muromachiki daimyō kenryokuron*, p. 112.

[21] Inoue Minoru, *Hagi Hakubutsukan kitaku Sugi ke monjo*, *Hagi hakubutsukan kenkyū hōkoku* no. 3 (3.2008), doc. 16, 2.17.1400 (Ōei 7) Ashikaga Yoshimitsu *sodehan mikyōjo*, p. 3 (hereafter *Sugi ke monjo*).

[22] *Sugi ke monjo*, doc. 17, Ōuchi Hiroshige *daikan shiki ategaijō*, 9.12.1400 (Ōei 7), p. 3. This was confirmed by the shogunal chancellor (*kanrei*) on 11.19.1400 (Ōei 7). See doc. 18, Muromachi bakufu *kanrei hōsho*, p. 3. Ultimately Moriakira was able to force the sale to go through, enabling Sugi Yoriaki to receive their lands. See doc. 21, 4.19.1410 (Ōei 17) Shami Zenyō *saribumi*, p. 4, who also received a *jitō shiki* of Hongō, designating comprehensive rights for these lands on 8.22.1413 (Ōei 20). See doc. 22, on 8.22.1413 (Ōei 20) Ōuchi Moriakira *chigyō andojō*, p. 4.

[23] For one such example, see *Shimonoseki shishi shiryōhen* 6 (Shimonoseki, 2001), Chōfu Mōri ke monjo tekagami, doc. 15, 12.13.1403 (Ōei 10) Ōuchi Moriakira *andojō*, p. 10.

fought for him addressed him not by his surname or court title, but simply as Rokurō.[24] The only comparable figures who fought and survived without court legitimacy were Minamoto Yoritomo (1147–99) in 1180–83 and Ashikaga Takauji (1305–58) in 1335–36. Both went on to establish their own warrior regimes.

On 12.26.1401 Moriakira sailed from northern Kyushu to Nagato, where he fought a decisive battle at the Nagato provincial headquarters, killing or capturing nearly all the Hiroshige supporters there.[25] Having occupied the provincial headquarters, Moriakira immediately issued protections for the Nagato Ninomiya shrine.[26] His reconquest of the province hinged upon protecting its cultic sites, and here his actions resembled those of Hiroyo when Hiroyo first conquered Nagato a half century before. Moriakira then attacked Hiroshige's inadequately defended main camp. Three days later, on 12.29.1401, he killed Hiroshige at Sakariyama.[27] After twelve more days spent consolidating control in southern Suō and Nagato, he triumphantly entered Yamaguchi on the eleventh day of the first month of 1402.[28]

Moriakira survived and prospered because by 1400 the Ōuchi had created a cohesive administrative organization, in control of sufficient resources to resist central authority. His supporters continued to resist on his behalf because they believed that he could win, and that he most deserved to govern the Ōuchi in the aftermath of Yoshihiro's defeat.

After Hiroshige's death, late in 1402, Ashikaga Yoshimitsu dispatched Ōuchi Dōtsū in another attempt to defeat Moriakira.[29] Yoshimitsu also relied on *chōbuku hō*, Buddhist rites to subdue one's enemy, to further his cause, and he ordered Kyoto's most prominent monks to engage in star rites directed against Moriakira.[30]

---

[24] Both Takano Shin'uemon, a Bungo warrior who moved to Nagato, and a Shōkokuji monk named Nakatsu, who fought on his behalf, refer to him on such terms. *Miura ke monjo* (Tōkyō daigaku shuppankai, 1937), doc. 26, Takano Ken'ei Shigekata *zenmon yurai*, pp. 318–21 for the history and actions of the Takano who were rewarded by Moriakira. For the Shōkokuji monk, see the 7.27 Nakatsu *shojō* in *Dainihon shiryō*, ser. 7, vol. 5 (Tōkyō daigaku shuppankai, 1934), p. 77, which refers to repeated noted service (*kōmyō chūsetsu*) for Ōuchi Rokurō on 7.27.1401 (Ōei 8).

[25] *Yamaguchi kenshi shiryōhen chūsei*, vol. 1, Nagato no kuni shugo daiki, p. 607.

[26] *Yamaguchi kenshi shiryōhen chūsei*, vol. 4, 12.26.1401 (Ōei 8) Ōuchi Moriakira *kinzei*, p. 208.

[27] *Yamaguchi kenshi shiryōhen chūsei*, vol. 1, Nagato no kuni shugo daiki, p. 607.

[28] *Yamaguchi kenshi shiryōhen chūsei*, vol. 1, Nagato no kuni shugo daiki, p. 607.

[29] *Masuda ke monjo*, vol. 1, doc. 14, 12.6 Tokugen *shojō*, p. 29. See Fujii, *Muromachiki daimyō kenryokuron*, pp. 113–114, and *Yamaguchi kenshi tsūshihen chūsei* (Yamaguchi, 2012), pp. 376, 441 for references to his actions and accidental death. This brother was also referred to as the *shinsuke* novice (*nyūdō*).

[30] *Tōji nijūikku kusōkata hyōjō hikitsuke*, vol. 1 (Kyoto: Shibunkaku, 2002), 2.11, 2.16.1402 (Ōei 9) Suisei *onkitō no koto*, pp. 54–57.

These efforts met with limited success. In the spring of 1403, Ashikaga Yoshimitsu tried again to coerce Aki warriors into chastising Moriakira, commanding them to follow Ōuchi Dōtsū.[31] However, his plan soon failed when the hapless Dōtsū drowned at the Kamadoseki port of eastern Suō.[32] Sometime before the second month of 1404, Mitsuyo, the last Ōuchi supporter of Yoshimitsu, joined forces with Moriakira and participated in Kōryūji rites in Yamaguchi.

While fighting Moriakira, Yoshimitsu faced still other problems closer to home. A lighting strike caused the massive nine-story Shōkokuji pagoda to burn down on 6.3.1403.[33] Yoshimitsu immediately set about rebuilding it, and on 4.3.1404, groundbreaking ceremonies for the new pagoda were held at Kitayama, where Yoshimitsu was putting the finishing touches on his Gold Temple (Kinkakuji).[34] His focus on the reconstruction meant fewer resources for anti-Ōuchi curses and less interest in cobbling together another expeditionary force. The ensuing delay enabled Moriakira to further consolidate his position.

Moriakira solidified his authority despite Yoshimitsu's active opposition by patronizing cultic sites and emphasizing his ties to the gods. Having made donations to the Nagato shrines and to Usa, the powerful Hachiman shrine vital for the control of Kyushu's Buzen province, he next exempted Kōryūji from taxes in the fourth through sixth month of 1402.[35] Likewise, he issued several commendations for the Hōfu Tenmangū shrine from 6.1 to 6.3.1402, thus strengthening his position in the Hōfu (Sabaryō) region.[36]

---

[31] Tōkyō daigaku shiryōhen sanjo, comp., *Mōri ke monjo*, vol. 1 (Tōkyō daigaku shuppankai, 1920), doc. 23, 4.28.1403 (Ōei 10) Ashikaga Yoshimitsu *mikyōjo* (*kirigami*), p. 39. See *Yamaguchi kenshi tsūshihen chūsei*, p. 441 for the correct identification as Dōtsū. For a genealogical reference to Dōtsū, see *Ōuchi bunka*, p. 64. He is described as Bō Shirō *shinsuke*, who was dispatched by Ashikaga Yoshimochi (*sic*) to attack Moriakira. He failed and died at the Kamado barrier (*seki*). That harbor is currently known as Kaminoseki.

[32] *Ōuchi bunka*, pp. 25–26 for the Mōri edition Ōuchi genealogy. Fujii, *Muromachiki daimyō kenryokuron*, pp. 113–14.

[33] *Daijōin nikki mokuroku, Daijōin jisha zōjiki* (Kyoto: Rinsen shoten, 2003), vol. 12, 6.3.1403 (Ōei 10), p. 301. According to the *Kanmon gyōki*, this pagoda also burned down in 1400 (Ōei 7), but the date seems to be a mistake for 1403. *Kanmon gyōki* (Fushimi no miya Sadafusa; Go-Sukō'in) (Zoku gunsho ruijū kanseikai, 1930), *hoi*, vol. 1, 1.9.1416 (Ōei 23), p. 2.

[34] *Daijōin nikki mokuroku, Daijōin jisha zōjiki*, vol. 12, 4.3.1404 (Ōei 11), p. 301.

[35] *Yamaguchi kenshi shiryōhen chūsei*, vol. 3, doc. 218, 4.13.1402 (Ōei 9) Ōuchi Moriakira *kakikudashi*, p. 317 for Hikamisan not being responsible for public duties, doc. 86, 6.23.1402 (Ōei 9) Ōuchi shi *bugyōnin rensho hōsho*, p. 271, doc. 89, 6.5.1402 (Ōei 9) Ōuchi shi *bugyōnin rensho hōsho*, p. 272, and doc. 216, 8.19.1402 (Ōei 9) Ōuchi Moriakira *azukejō*, p. 316 for the grant of Suō lands to Hikamisan.

[36] *Yamaguchi kenshi shiryōhen chūsei*, vol. 2, Hōfu Tenmangū monjo, doc. 13, 6.1.1402 (Ōei 9) Ōuchi Moriakira *kishinjō*, pp. 477–78, and docs. 14–17 for the 6.1 to 6.3.1402 (Ōei 9) Ōuchi shi *bugyōnin rensho hōsho*, pp. 478–79.

Devoted as he was to Tenjin, Moriakira recorded dreams in which Tenjin came to him and offered active support precisely at this time.[37] He also commissioned a portrait of Tenjin that still survives at the Furukuma shrine, where Tenjin was worshiped in Yamaguchi, and planted many plum trees, favored by this divinity, in Hizen and Suō.[38] Other sources show that he rebuilt a bell tower at the Matsuzaki shrine at Hōfu and donated a copy of the Tripiṭaka there as well.[39]

Copper Mines and Trade

Moriakira's control of the Nagato copper mines allowed him to fund these rituals in Yamaguchi, reward followers, and patronize religious institutions. He first exercised control over the mines in 1400, when he commended a *jitō* post in Ōda district, site of the mines to Kokushōji, his future mortuary temple.[40]

Moriakira's construction of such a prominent mortuary temple during his lifetime suggested that he perceived himself as maintaining influence in this life and the next, and this led to tensions between him and his heirs, and the sons of Yoshihiro. Exemplifying this, early as 1404 a dispute arose over territory between the monks of his temple and those affiliated with Kōshakuji, Yoshihiro's mortuary temple.[41]

Ōda district was the site of the Naganobori copper mines, which had provided copper for Tōdaiji in the eighth century. However, the Naganobori

[37] He commissioned an image of Tenjin, which still survives, at the Egara shrine in Kamakura. Kamakura kokuhōkan, ed., *Egara Tenjinsha kyūhyakunen* (Yokohama hōsōkyoku, 2004), p. 8, Jinenju Tenjin *ritsuzō*.

[38] *Hōfu Tenmangūten* (Yamaguchi, 2001), pp. 72 and 138–39, and *Kokuhō Tenjin sama* (Fukuoka: Kyūshū National Museum, 2008), pp. 124, 205 for the portrait. For the planting of plum trees, see Yonehara Masayoshi, *Ōuchi Yoshitaka* (Jinbutsu ōraisha, 1967), pp. 40–41, and Mori Shigeaki, "Suō no kuni Hikamisan Kōryūji shunigatsu-e ni tsuite no ikkōsatsu," *Fukuoka daigaku jinbun ronsō* 30.3 (no. 118, 12.1998), pp. 46–47.

[39] *Sengoku ibun Ōuchi shi hen*, vol. 2 (Tōkyōdō shuppan, 2017), 9.26.1526 (Daiei 6) Matsuzaki Tenmangū *shikōsō Jūo mōshijō utsushi*, p. 322.

[40] *Yamaguchi kenshi shiryōhen chūsei*, vol. 3, Jōeiji monjo, doc. 42, 8.1.1400 (Ōei 7) Ōuchi Moriakira *kishinjō*, p. 348, and, for another version, *Hagi han batsu etsu roku*, vol. 4, Bōchō jisha shōmon, *Kōzan Jōeiji ge*, doc. 47, 8.1.1400 (Ōei 7) Ōuchi Moriakira *kishinjō*, p. 225.

[41] *Yamaguchi kenshi shiryōhen chūsei*, vol. 3, Jōeiji monjo, doc. 54, 2.10.1404 (Ōei 11) Ōuchi Moriakira *jōsho utsushi*, p. 351, and doc. 55, 2.11.1404 (Ōei 11) Ōuchi Moriakira *kakikudashi utsushi*, p. 351. See also Maki, "Suō Ōuchi shi to sono ujidera Kōryūji," pp. 130–31. This temple lost its privileged position after Moriakira passed away (see pp. 131–32). Epitomizing the changing fortunes, temples such as Kōshakuji would later receive their own copies of the Tripiṭaka. Suda Makiko, *Chūsei Nichō kankei to Ōuchi shi* (Tokyo daigaku shuppan, 2011), p. 149. Kōshakuji received one before 1443.

mines lost their earlier prominence when large-scale mining gave way to small-scale mining in the eleventh and twelfth centuries. The next upswing occurred in the late fourteenth and early fifteenth centuries.

The reason for the change is that previously the old miners smelted cuprite, an oxidized copper that was found in rich concentrations, but they were unable to smelt sulfurized copper (copper pyrites), which had lower concentrations of copper. This type of copper is common near volcanic regions, and the smelting of this material was thought to have occurred in Japan only starting late in the sixteenth century.[42]

Research suggests the appearance of new smelting techniques that allowed exploitation of previously unminable deposits of copper pyrites. The conclusion is supported by the accumulation of sulfur in stalactites and stalagmites, related to the release into the atmosphere of sulfuric acid in the process of smelting copper. This increase in sulfur residue coincides with a change in the appearance of slag, which became flatter, and is visually distinct from eighth-century samples.[43] This new smelting technique would seem to account for what Delmer Brown characterized as a "definite increase in the total copper output" of Japan in the fifteenth century as "copper became a major item of export at a time when the total volume of trade was increasing by leaps and bounds."[44]

A single source, the Kodō zuroku, describes the process of smelting and refining copper from copper pyrites.[45] Ore was crushed, creating a matte,

---

[42] Sung-il Ch'ung, "Chosŏn ŭi dongjŏn kwa Ilbon ŭi ŭnhwa: hwap'ye ŭi yut'ong ŭl t'onghae bon 15~17 segi HanIl gwan'gye (Korean Copper and Japanese Silver Money: Korean-Japanese Relations and the Circulation of Money between Chosŏn Korea and Japan from the Fifteenth Century to the Seventeenth Century)," HanIl gwangyesa yŏngu (Korea-Japan Historical Review) 20 (4.2004), p. 26. I am grateful to Gina Choi for translating this article. For more on smelting copper pyrites, see https://chem.libretexts.org/Bookshelves/Inorganic_Chemistry/Supplemental_Modules_(Inorganic_Chemistry)/Descriptive_Chemistry/Elements_Organized_by_Block/3_d-Block_Elements/1b_Properties_of_Transition_Metals/Metallurgy/The_Extraction_of_Copper. By contrast, for the earlier analysis of cuprites, being found with malachite, see https://www.mindat.org/min-1172.html.

[43] Yoshimura Kazuhisa and Ikeda Yoshifumi et al., Akiyoshidai Naganobori dōzan Ogirikō seki ni kiroku sareta ryūka kōseiren," Gekkan Chikyū 35.10 (2013), pp. 598–99 for evidence of a prominent spike in the amount of sulfur coinciding with the year 1400. This has also been published in English. See Yoshimura Kazuhisa et al., "Sulfide Ore Smelting at the Naganobori Copper Mine Recorded on Speleothems from the Ogiri No. 4 Pit on the Akiyoshi-dai Plateau, Yamaguchi, Japan," ISIJ International (Iron and Steel Institute of Japan) 54.5 (5.2014), pp. 1147–54. Recent Japanese scholarship has noted the importance of these new techniques for mining and smelting copper and silver. Sakurai Eiji, "Chūsei no gijutsu to rōdō," in Iwanami kōza Nihon rekishi, vol. 4 (Iwanami shoten, 2015), pp. 279–314.

[44] Delmer Brown, Money Economy in Medieval Japan: A Study in the Use of Coins (Institute of Far Eastern Languages, Yale University, 1951), p. 34. Brown pointed out that a trade mission to China in 1451 carried 154,500 kin of copper (102 tons), while another in 1539 transported 298,500 kin, or 197 tons, of copper.

[45] At least sixty-two copies of this manuscript survive. Sumitomo Shiryōkan, comp., Kodō zuroku no kenkyū-Shoshi to keifu (Sumitomo Shiryōkan, 2015), pp. 7–26, analyzes sixty-one surviving texts,

which was in turn roasted, causing the sulfur to be driven off; then the melted ore was roasted by a strong blast. Conclusive evidence of a fifteenth-century transformation in smelting techniques, based on changes in the chemical composition of the slag itself, remains elusive, since the crucial sulfuric residue would be found in the environment and not the slag.[46]

Copper mining required thousands of individuals to mine the ore, to collect enough wood for charcoal to smelt it on site, and to transport the ingots. Perhaps even more important than improvements in mining techniques would be the ability to mobilize the necessary labor force. From the time of Moriakira's 1404 commendation, the monks of Kokushōji, his mortuary temple, oversaw mining at Naganobori.[47] Moriakira assisted the temple, since temple lands were immune from shugo encroachment, and laborers could not be requisitioned from them. In other words, the temple provided the manpower for mining and smelting. These laborers were too valuable to be conscripted for other services and were exempted from labor taxes.[48]

Copper was in high demand in Chosŏn Korea, where officials noted that neither it, nor iron, was mined in their territories. This seems to have been the case for all the fifteenth century, although the clearest expression was found in a statement by the Chosŏn official Yi Kŭk-pae (1422–95) on 9.28.1490.[49] This demand explains why Moriakira developed harbors to the north of his lands, on the Japan Sea, and also why the Chosŏn officials were so eager to engage with him.[50]

Moriakira shipped copper to Korea over a route that passed west from Yamaguchi through Mine, the site of the Naganobori mines, and then traveled west to Ōfuki, the site of a second mine, before going north to Senzaki,

while the sixty-second of these texts, which is among the twenty oldest surviving copies (early nineteenth century) exists at the Princeton East Asian library.

[46] Under the auspices of a Magic Grant over thirty samples of copper were analyzed to find out if changes in smelting techniques could be ascertained by analyzing slag, but the data is inconclusive.

[47] For insightful analysis of the link between this temple and copper mining, see Kitajima Daisuke, "Chūsei Yamaguchi ni okeru kinzoku seisan," in Yamaguchi shi maizō bunkazai chōsa hōkoku 112 Ōuchi shi kanren machinami iseki 8 (Yamaguchi shi kyōiku iinkai, 2014), pp. 256–57.

[48] Hagi han batsu etsu roku, vol. 4, Bōchō jisha shōmon, Kōzan Jōeiji ge, doc. 50, 2.18.1404 (Ōei 11), Hironaka ichizoku rensho ukebumi, p. 225; doc. 51, 2.18.1404 (Ōei 11) Naitō Morisada ukebumi, p. 225–26; doc. 52, Migita Yoshinobu hoka nime rensho ukebumi, 2.18.1404 (Ōei 11), p. 226; and doc. 53, p. 226, Yasutomi Hironori hoka nime rensho ukebumi, p. 226.

[49] Chosŏn wangjo sillok, vol. 245, 9.28.1490 (Seonjong 21) (tongchŏl pulsan at'o) (accessed 12.3.2019), http://sillok.history.go.kr/id/wia_12109128_001.

[50] Likewise, in 1494, Ōuchi Masahiro recognized that Chosŏn Korea was lacking in copper and iron (tongchŏl). See Chosŏn wangjo sillok, vol. 296, 11.4.1494 (Seonjong 25) (accessed 12.3.2019), http://sillok.history.go.kr/id/wia_12511004_001.

a good harbor from which ships could easily set out for Korea. A second harbor of Hijū, at the western tip of Honshū, to the west of Senzaki, also came into use. Locals attribute the opening of the harbor to Moriakira's time (See figures I.1 and 2.3).[51]

Moriakira also established control over the Nima district, with its excellent harbor and access to the Iwami mines, sometime between 1401 and 1403.[52] The proximity of the mines made Nima vital, and Iwami warriors vied, many successfully, to acquire rights there independent of their main holdings.[53] Moriakira did not dominate the Masuda region, site of a mine and harbor in western Iwami, but a proliferation of mines in Nagato and Iwami, all with nearby harbors, amply attests to the increase of mining and its significance in trade.

Kingly Status

Having established his administration in Suō and Nagato, as well as control over Nima and the Straits of Shimonoseki, Moriakira moved to affirm a standing worthy of one capable of fighting the Ashikaga shoguns. He did so by reaching out to Korea in order to confirm his royal descent. Building on the efforts of his brother Yoshihiro, Moriakira was able to identify his Korean ancestor, who was in fact the imaginary Prince Imsŏng (J. Rinshō), a purported third son of the Paekche King Sŏngmyŏng (523–53).[54] He also

---

[51] Yamaguchi kyōiku iinkai, comp., Yamaguchi shi maizō bunkazai chōsha hōkokusho, no. 121, Ryōunji ato, vol. 2 (Yamaguchi: Yamaguchi kyōiku iinkai, 2019), pp. 206–8. For insights into the port of Hijū dating from Moriakira's time, I am indebted to Kitajima Daisuke, discussion, 5.26.2019. Kitajima suggests that the name of this region possesses a name suggestive of smelting (e.g., bellows blow greatly [ōfuki]).

[52] Inoue Hiroshi, "Suō Ōuchi shi no Iwami gun Nima gun bun chigyō," Nanbokuchō geppō (1.1989), pp. 3–6 for how Moriakira received lands Nima between 1401 and 1403 and Yunotsu shi (Yunotsu chō, 1994), p. 598. Inoue argues that this patrimony came into Moriakira's possession while he was battle with Hiroshige and Dōtsū in 1401–3 (Ōei 8–10). See p. 4. See also Manzei jugō nikki (2 vols. Zoku gunsho ruijū hōi 1. Zoku gunsho ruijū kanseikai, 1928), vol. 2, 9.3.1431 (Eikyō 3), p. 287–88 for for Morakira's testament, which mentions Nima. The oldest surviving sources referring to Nima as Ōuchi-controlled territory dates from 1425. See "Nanbokuchō Muromachiki Iwami no kuni to Ōuchi shi," Ōuchi shi no kenkyū (Seibundō, 2011), editor's note, p. 275 n. 9.

[53] Inoue Hiroshi, "Suō Ōuchi shi no Iwami gun Nima gun bun chigyō." A 1395 (Ōei 2) list of families with holdings in Nima included not only local families such as the Kuri, but also major Iwami families such as the Masuda, Fukuya, and Sufu.

[54] Ōuchi bunka, 2.1404 (Ōei 11) Kōryūji hondō kuyō ganmon, p. 355, and Kenneth Robinson, "Treated as Treasures: The Circulation of Sutras in Maritime Northeast Asia from 1388 to the Mid-Sixteenth Century," East Asian History 21 (6.2001), pp. 50–53.

commissioned a statue of Prince Imsŏng that was placed in the mortuary temple of Jōfukuji, thereby making his descent from Imsŏng tangible.[55]

By claiming kingly descent, Moriakira could avoid reliance on the lineage or status of the Ashikaga, as Yoshihiro had briefly done.[56] Thanks to his mother's birth, Moriakira secured support from the Japanese court as well, even though he remained at war with Ashikaga Yoshimitsu. A "doctor of letters" (*hakase*) and a yin yang specialist determined the time to offer at Kōryūji an invocation that praised Moriakira and his leadership. These officials kept their support quiet and did not sign their names, to avoid Yoshimitsu's wrath.[57] However, a draft of the prayer was explicitly written by a senior secretary of the Council of State (*daigeki*) from Moriakira's natal family, the Sanjō. To the surprise of all, its final version was written by none other than Sanjō Sanefuyu, a Grand Minister of the first rank and the highest-ranking courtier of his day.[58] The fact that Ōuchi Mitsuyo surrendered to Moriakira by attending ceremonies linked to Ōuchi ancestral rites is further evidence that Moriakira consolidated his military success through ritual means.[59]

In invocations for these ceremonies, Moriakira explained how he had, through military prowess, defeated enemies of the court and as a result garnered several provinces, an honor that "exceeded his status."[60] Alluding to the disorder of 1399 and his lack of experience, Moriakira tried to unite all through these rites. He also expressed the hope that the Tatara line would prosper for ten thousand generations and ably govern the realm, and that

[55] Until late in 2011, this statue was universally considered to be a creation of the Edo era, but in fact it was created in the late fourteenth or early fifteenth century. See *Ōuchi bunka to Kita Kyūshū* (1.2012), p. 42. Although the catalog states that this statue dates from the late fourteenth century, Furuya Yūko and others present at the exhibit stated that a fifteenth-century date is equally plausible. Furthermore, Itō Kōji, "Chūsei saikoku shoshi no keifu ninshiki," in *Kyokai aidentiti* (Kyūshū shigakukai, 2008), pp. 124–28, argues that myths about Imsŏng and Shōtoku myth were created during the time of Moriakia.

[56] This represents a situation somewhat analogous to the process by which nonkings raised their status through creating semantic distinctions, such as when dukes claimed that in their Duchy of Prussia they were kings *in* Prussia, which became a springboard for later assertions of royal authority. See, for example, Christopher Clark, *Iron Kingdom* (Cambridge: Harvard University Press, 2006), and Neil MacGregor, *Germany: Memories of a Nation* (New York: Vintage Books, 2014), pp. 47–50.

[57] *Yamaguchi kenshi shiryōhen chūsei*, vol. 3, Kōryūji monjo, doc. 1, Kōryūji hondō *kuyō nikki*, pp. 226–31. For the reference to a Kyoto specialist (*hakase*) writing this, see p. 227. Maki analyzes this in his "Suō no kuni Ōuchi shi to sono ujidera Kōryūji no shitsuteki henyō," p. 120.

[58] *Yamaguchi kenshi shiryōhen chūsei*, vol. 3, Kōryūji monjo, doc. 1, Kōryūji hondō *kuyō nikki*, p. 228. Sanefuyu was referred to as the Sanjō Minister of the Right (*udaijin*), which was his rank from 1396 to 1399. By 1404 (Ōei 11), Sanefuyu was the Grand Minister of State (*Daijō daijin*) of the first rank.

[59] *Yamaguchi kenshi shiryōhen chūsei*, vol. 3, Kōryūji monjo, doc. 1, Kōryūji hondō *kuyō nikki*, p. 227.

[60] *Ōuchi bunka*, 2.1404 (Ōei 11) Kōryūji hondō *kuyō ganmon*, pp. 355–56.

Ōuchi valor would be known far and wide. Finally, he promised good fortune to all present and wished them rebirth on the ninth level of the Pure Land.[61]

The death of Hirai Dōjo, Yoshihiro's representative in the capital and a stalwart supporter of Hiroshige's candidacy, allowed for a rapprochement between Yoshimitsu and Moriakira. The Ashikaga first confiscated Hirai's lands, then the shogunal chancellor (kanrei), Hatakeyama Motokuni, recognized Moriakira by name, addressing him not by a title, as was customary in such documents, but as "The Honorable Ōuchi Rokurō."[62] This style of salutation continued for at least a month, starting late in the sixth month of 1404, when Ashikaga Yoshimitsu contacted "Ōuchi Rokurō" to complain about how his followers, the Sugi, Hironaka, and Kutsuya had occupied Iwashimizu lands in Suō since 1402.[63]

Sometime in 1403 Yoshimitsu acquiesced, recognized Moriakira's legitimacy, accepted him as the Ōuchi heir, and granted him shugo posts in Suō, Nagato, and, in a further concession, Buzen.[64] By the seventh month of 1404, emissaries dispatched to China by the "King of Japan" Minamoto Dōgi (Yoshimitsu) included gifts from Ōuchi Tatara Moriakira, thus confirming the alliance between the two.[65] Late in 1405 Moriakira was promoted to the fifth rank lower, which gave him the ability to enter the palace and be counted as a member of the court nobility, an honor possible only with the acquiescence of the Ashikaga and the court.[66]

In exchange for these offices and this consolidation of his position, Moriakira protected the estates belonging to central proprietors, such as

---

[51] *Yamaguchi kenshi shiryōhen chūsei*, vol. 3, Kōryūji hondō *kuyō nikki*, p. 231 for a 3.1408 (Ōei 11) *ganmon*. Admittedly the ninth level was the lowest level for those who barely entered due to the power of their last *nenbutsu*. I am grateful to Jacqueline Stone for this observation.

[62] *Kobayakawa ke monjo*, vol. 1 (Tōkyō daigaku shuppankai, 1927), doc. 32, 5.28.1404 (Ōei 11) Ashikaga Yoshimitsu *gohan mikyōjo*, p. 20, and doc. 33, 5.30.1404 (Ōei 11) *Kanrei* Hatakeyama Tokugen (Motokuni) *shigyōjō*, p. 20.

[63] *Yamaguchi kenshi tsūshihen furoku* CD-ROM, Tanaka ke monjo, doc. 17, 6.24.1405 (Ōei 12), Muromachi shōgun ke *mikyōjo utsushi*, p. 689. The content seems right, but this copy apparently has the wrong date, and should be 1404 (Ōei 11) because in 1405 (Ōei 12) Moriakira already had his position as *shugo* confirmed and was fighting on behalf of the Ashikaga. In this same document collection, doc. 18, *urū* 6.8.1406 (Ōei 13) Muromachi shōgun Ashikaga Yoshimitsu *mikyōjo*, p. 689, Moriakira is referred to as the governor of Suō (Suō *no kami*).

[64] Suda Makiko suggests that Moriakira gained the position as head of Suō and Nagato midway through 1403 (Ōei 10). See *Nichō kankei to Ōuchi shi*, p. 191 n. 22. I believe, however, that this estimate is premature. *Yamaguchi kenshi tsūshihen chūsei*, p. 377, reveals that Morakira became *shugo* sometime prior to 1406 (Ōei 13). Moriakira became *shugo* of Buzen before 8.27.1408 (Ōei 15).

[65] *Yamaguchi kenshi shiryōhen chūsei*, vol. 1, p. 866, Richō jitsuroku 7.30.1405 (T'aejong 4)/ (Ōei 11).

[66] *Yamaguchi kenshi tsūshihen furoku* CD-ROM, Kuzen rinji inzen mikyōjo an, doc. 8, 12.28.1406 (Ōei 13) Go-Komatsu tennō *kuzen an utsushi*, p. 434. A copyist's error has the document dating from 1406 (Ōei 13), but it in fact dates from 1405 (Ōei 12).

Ninnaji's Aio Futajima, located on the boundary between the coast and the Fushino River, just to the south of Yamaguchi.[67] He also garnered support from officials of the Munakata shrine in northern Kyushu and from the Shibukawa of Kyushu, who had attacked anti-Ashikaga rivals early in 1405.[68] Moriakira crossed over to Buzen at the head of one army in the fifth month of 1405, while the Shibukawa led another.[69]

Northern Kyushu had long remained turbulent, and Moriakira's attempt to re-establish control there proved costly. Several Ōuchi affiliates perished, among them Sue Dōrin (Hironaga), the deputy *shugo* of Nagato. Late in 1405 another otherwise unknown figure named the Echigo lay priest (*nyūdō*) died at Inotake, a strategic locale in Buzen.[70] Despite suffering these casualties, the victory at Inotake allowed Moriakira to consolidate Ōuchi rule in northern Kyushu.[71]

After the battle at Inotake, Moriakira commended lands to Buzen's Kōkokuji for the sake of prayers for the realm and for the salvation of one of his followers who had died in the battle.[72] He also repurposed Kokubunji, in Suō, and confirmed that it was a prayer site for the realm in the third month of 1406. At this time, he apparently took the tonsure and became known as Dōyū.[73] In an attempt to pacify the sea gods and promote links between Yamaguchi and the Inland Sea, in 1406 he opened a new site of worship in Yamaguchi and transferred the Itsukushima deity there from the nearby shrine in Fushino. He also offered extensive and ongoing prayers at Usa.[74]

---

[67] *Yamaguchi kenshi tsūshihen furoku* CD-ROM, Ninnaji monjo, doc. 22, referring to a 5.6.1407 (Ōei 14) Muromachi shōgun ke Ashikaga Yoshimitsu *mikyōjo an*, p. 786. See also doc. 23, 8.10.1407 (Ōei 14), pp. 786–87, and doc. 24, 10.15.1407 (Ōei 14), Muromachi shōgun ke Ashikaga Yoshimitsu *mikyōjo an*, p. 787. This estate was located to the south of the Itsukushima shrine of Fushino River that was mentioned in chapter 2.

[68] *Dazaifu Dazaifu Tenmangū shiryō*, vol. 12. For references to Ōuchi aid on 1.26.1405 (Ōei 12), see pp. 556–57. For Shibukawa Mitsuyori commending lands in support of an offensive against Kyushu rebels, see 1.23.1405 (Ōei 12) Shibukawa Mitsuyori *kishinjō*, p. 548.

[69] *Dazaifu Dazaifu Tenmangū shiryō*, vol. 12, 5.10 Shibukawa Mitsuyori *shojō*, pp. 550–51, and 5.19 [(Ōei 12) 1405] Shibukawa Mitsuyori *shojō*, p. 551.

[70] *Dazaifu Dazaifu Tenmangū shiryō*, vol. 12, 9.28 Shibukawa Mitsuyori *shojō*, p. 553 for continued turmoil in Buzen. See pp. 556–57 for Sue Dōrin's death on 12.5.1405 (Ōei 12). A member of the Munakata died in Buzen the following year. See p. 559. For other deaths in that battle, see *Buzen Agano Kōkokuji Kyūshū no jisha shirizu* no. 17, *Kyūshū rekishi shiryōkan* (3.2000), Kōkokuji monjo, doc. 41, 4.17.1406 (Ōei 13) Suō no kami Ōuchi Moriakira *kishinjō*, p. 24.

[71] Arikawa Nobuhiro, "Buzen Kōkokuji no rekishi," in *Buzen Agano Kōkokuji Kyūshū no jisha shirizu no. 17 Kyūshū rekishi shiryōkan*, pp. 27–28.

[72] *Buzen Agano Kōkokuji Kyūshū no jisha shirizu*, Kōkokuji monjo, doc. 38, 4.17.1406 (Ōei 13) Suō no kami Ōuchi Moriakira *kishinjō*, p. 23, and doc. 41, 4.17.1406 (Ōei 13) Suō no kami Ōuchi Moriakira *kishinjō*, p. 24.

[73] *Yamaguchi kenshi shiryōhen chūsei*, vol. 2, Kokubunji monjo, doc. 30, 3.5.1406 (Ōei 13) Ōuchi Dōyū *andojō*, p. 409. His first tonsured name was Dōyū.

[74] *Usa jingūshi shiryōhen*, vol. 9 (Usa, 1993), p. 86, 3.10, for the completion of Usa prayers.

Briefly, for some reason, Moriakira seems to have laicized himself in the fourth month of 1406, but he then renounced the world again shortly thereafter, this time adopting the name Tokuyū (Figure 4.1).[75]

Tripiṭaka (Buddhist Canon)

After his reconciliation with Moriakira, Yoshimitsu could more easily send emissaries to Korea and Ming China. One ship passed through Akamaseki on the tenth day of the sixth intercalary month of 1406,[76] and an intensification of "official" exchanges occurred, with eight embassies visiting Korea between 1407 through 1409.[77] 1n 1407, Moriakira successfully obtained a copy of the Buddhist canon (Tripiṭaka) from Chosŏn Korea for Kōryūji.[78] In 1408 he also had the laws of his domains recopied, since his position had become stabilized after his earlier rebellion.[79]

Although Moriakira had earlier offered prayers on behalf of all in his realm, the Tripiṭaka served further to draw the realm together and ensure their salvation. Twice a year, the complete Tripiṭaka, or portions thereof, would be ritually read (tendoku), with over 164 monks flipping sections of

[75] To avoid confusion, he will continue to be referred to as Moriakira. His brief renouncing of his tonsure is curious. Although he confirmed Kokubunji privileges as a lay monk named Dōyū on 3.5.1406 (Ōei 13), his Kōkokuji commendations of 4.17.1406 (Ōei 13) are signed as "Suō no kami Tatara ason Moriakira." Compare Yamaguchi kenshi shiryōhen chūsei, vol. 2, Kokubunji monjo, doc. 30, 3.5.1406 (Ōei 13) Ōuchi Dōyū andojō, p. 409, with Buzen Agano Kōkokuji Kyūshū no jisha shirizu, Kōkokuji monjo, doc. 38, 4.17.1406 Suō no kami Ōuchi Moriakira kishinjō, p. 23, and doc. 41, 4.17.1406 (Ōei 13) Suō no kami Ōuchi Moriakira kishinjō, p. 24. He seems to have once again taken the tonsure and changed this name to Tokuyū by 7.13.1406 (Ōei 13). See Hagi han batsu etsu roku, vol. 4, Bōchō jisha shōmon, Kōzan Jōeiji ge, doc. 55, 7.13.1406 (Ōei 13) Ōuchi Tokuyū (Moriakira) kishinjō p. 226. Likewise, Kokubunji documents show him as using this name Tokuyū in 1407. See Kokubunji monjo, doc. 31, 10.18.1407 (Ōei 14) Ōuchi Tokuyū kishinjō, pp. 409–10. Conversely, documents dating from 1405 reveal that Moriakira had not yet taken the tonsure. Hagi han batsu etsu roku, vol. 4, Bōchō jisha shōmon, Kōzan Jōeiji ge, doc. 54, Ōei 12.8.4 Moriakia kishinjō, p. 226.

[76] Yamaguchi kenshi shiryōhen chūsei, vol. 1, urū 6.10.1406 (Ōei 13) Noritoki kyōki, p. 81.

[77] Yamaguchi kenshi shiryōhen chūsei, vol. 1, pp. 866–67 for contacts during the years 1407–09 on 2.26.1407 (Ōei 14), 7.22.1407 (Ōei 14), 8.30.1407 (Ōei 14), 5.21.1408 (Ōei 15), 7.5.1408 (Ōei 15), 8.1.1408 (Ōei 15), 4.16.1409 (Ōei 16), 4.25.1409 (Ōei 16). There were two missions to Korea before 1407, one with Moriakira cooperating with Ashikaga Yoshimitsu on 7.30.1404 (Ōei 11), and another 2.12.1403 (Ōei 10) which is shrouded in obscurity. For these exchanges, see Kenneth Robinson, "Treated as Treasures: The Circulation of Sutras in Maritime Northeast Asia from 1388 to the Mid-Sixteenth Century," East Asian History 21 (6.2001), pp. 49–50.

[78] Yamaguchi kenshi shiryōhen chūsei, vol. 3, Kōryūji monjo, doc. 202, pp. 310–11. Three Zen monks from Hakata facilitated this exchange and compared their version of the Tripiṭaka with one imported by Yoshihiro. Itō Kōji, "Ōuchi shi to Hakata," Shishi kenkyū Fukuoka, no. 8 (3.2013), pp. 11–12.

[79] Sengoku ibun Ōuchi shi hen, vol. 1, doc. 454, 9.21.1479 (Bunmei 11) Ōuchi shi kokugaryō hatto, pp. 134–35.

Figure 4.1 Ōuchi Moriakira Statue. Permission Tōshunji. Image provided by Yamaguchi-shi kyōiku iinkai

the text, so that the merit of reading the sutras might accrue to all, or at least to the 868 people who directly contributed to the acquisition of the Tripiṭaka (Figure 4.2).[80]

---

[80] Maki Takayuki, "Suō Ōuchi shi to sono ujidera Kōryūji," pp. 123–27. See also *Yamaguchi kenshi shiryōhen chūsei*, vol. 3, Kōryūji monjo, docs. 154, 202–3, pp. 294, 310–11 and docs. 237–38, Kōryūji issaikyō kanjinchō, pp. 322–26, and *Ōuchi bunka*, pp. 365–68. See also Suda Makiko, *Chūsei Nichō kankei to Ōuchi shi*, pp. 154–60.

Figure 4.2 Originally from Moriakira's Kokushōji, the Ōuchi Tripiṭaka was transported to Miidera in 1602. Photograph by Thomas Conlan

Equally important, the 868 direct contributors were memorialized in a text, which, based on its composition, was created sometime between 1406 and 1407.[81] Moriakira himself was a driving force for importing the Tripiṭaka from Korea and expressly notified followers throughout his lands of his intent to do so.[82]

The roster of donors (*kanjinchō*) was signed personally by most. The amount of their donations was checked and, in one case, corrected.[83] The fact that these names were bound in a book meant that the participants could be known in later ages and that their names would be part of the memorial ceremonies to be performed yearly. The sutras themselves would be ritually

[81] The range of dates stems from the fact that one of the signatures, Sue Saburō Morinaga, succeeded his father, who died on 12.5.1405. Moriakira's monogram is also consistent with the year 1406. Email exchange, Wada Shūsaku, 11.12.2019. I am indebted to Philippe Buc for highlighting the significance of these documents.

[82] *Yamaguchi kenshi shiryōhen chūsei*, vol. 3, Kōryūji monjo, doc. 219, 2.21 Ōuchi Moriakira *shojō*, p. 317, which is addressed to the people of the province of Nagato (*Nagato no kuni no hitobito*).

[83] I viewed the original manuscript at the Yamaguchi monjokan, 6.14.2015.

read twice during the spring and autumn equinoxes (*higan*), during yearly memorial ceremonies performed on auspicious days, at the same time that court dances (*bugaku*) for Second Month (*nigatsu-e*) rites would be held at Hikamisan. In addition to these ongoing rites, a special ceremony would be held for visits by Korean officials.[84] Being part of such a group of donors to so important a project fostered ties of community and discouraged those in future generations who might think about rebelling against their Ōuchi lord.[85]

These rituals bound all into a community capable of continuing them and importing more copies of the Tripiṭaka. Ultimately Moriakira requested six to seven copies of the Buddhist canon and received five or six.[86] These were distributed to important religious institutions, starting with Kōryūji and then Kokushōji, which oversaw the copper mines, and then Yōkōji, located near Kudamatsu, where Moriakira's grandfather Hiroyuki had lived. Moriakira also gave copies to the important shrines of Hōfu Tenmangū, devoted to Tenjin worship, at Sabaryō.[87] He also gave at least a portion, if not the whole Tripiṭaka, to a subshrine in the Usa Hachiman complex linked to Myōken.[88] Thus, he linked crucial geographic areas in his domains. In addition, he provided Tripiṭaka copies to the mortuary temples (*bodaiji*) of Ōuchi Hiroyo, Yoshihiro, and Hiroyuki.[89]

Ashikaga Rapprochement

Moriakira's reputation rose after the sudden death of Ashikaga Yoshimitsu on 5.6.1408, since he, alone of the despot's rivals, remained unbowed. Yoshimochi, Yoshimitsu's successor as shogun, abandoned most of Yoshimitsu's assertions

[84] *Yamaguchi kenshi shiryōhen chūsei*, vol. 3, Kōryūji monjo doc. 203, Kōryūji *issaikyō kuyō jōsho dodai*, p. 311 for an explanation of when these sutras would be "flipped and read." See also Suda Makiko, *Chūsei Nichō kankei to Ōuchi shi*, pp. 151–53.

[85] In this sense, they very much resemble the confraternity books or Books of Life in the European context. See Gerd Althoff, *Family, Friends and Followers: Political and Social Bonds in Medieval Europe* (Cambridge: Cambridge University Press, 2004), pp. 20–21.

[86] Suda Makiko, *Chūsei Nichō kankei to Ōuchi shi*, pp. 143–66 and Suda Makiko, "Chūsei koki ni okeru Ōuchi shi no daizōkyō yunyū," *Nenpō chūseishi kenkyū* 32 (2007), pp. 102–16.

[87] Suda Makiko, *Chūsei Nichō kankei to Ōuchi shi*, p. 149.

[88] See Suda, *Chūsei Nichō kankei to Ōuchi shi*, pp. 144–45 for a helpful database of all the imported Tripiṭaka. Itō, "Usanomiya Genki," in *Shintō taikei*, vol. 47 (Shintō taikei hensankai, 1989), p. 480, provides evidence for one portion of the Daihannya (*Mahā prajñā*) sutra being granted to the northern hall (*hokushinden*) at Usa on 12.13.1422 (Ōei 29).

[89] *Yamaguchi kenshi shiryōhen chūsei*, vol. 3, Jōeiji monjo, doc. 55, 2.11.1404 (Ōei 11) Ōuchi Moriakira *kakikudashi utsushi*, p. 351. Two more verified temples include Yoshihiro's *bodaiji* at Kōshakuji in 1443 and Nagato's Ankokuji sometime before 1479. Suda, *Chūsei Nichō kankei to Ōuchi shi*, pp. 144–45.

of sovereign authority.[90] He repudiated Yoshimitsu's practice of governing as a courtier or sovereign, and preferred acting simply as shogun.[91] In the following year (1409) Yoshimochi abandoned Kitayama with its Kinkakuji, and moved to a shogunal residence in central Kyoto at Sanjō bōmon.[92]

Yoshimochi also invited Moriakira, his father's great enemy, to Kyoto, assuring him that Kokushōji would be designated as a prayer temple for the realm.[93] Moriakira traveled to Kyoto in the winter of 1409, to celebrate what the Zen monk Kiyō Hōshū described as "the accession of the new lord of Japan," referring to Yoshimochi in terms normally reserved for the emperor, showing that it took some time for Yoshimochi's more limited conception of Ashikaga authority to take hold.[94] Moriakira remained in Kyoto for the next sixteen years as a confidant of the Ashikaga shoguns. Moriakira also cultivated his knowledge of Japanese poetry and had himself initiated into some of its secrets.[95] He composed poems in the company of courtiers connected with the Southern Court, but he was also close to Yoshimochi, who frequently visited him.[96]

The world had changed greatly with the death of Yoshimitsu, and Yoshimochi proved less interest in maintaining the intricate web of tributary and trading relations than his father. Epitomizing this shift, late in 1408, a mere months after Yoshimitsu's death, Yoshimochi turned away a black Sumatran elephant, six feet tall, a gift for the King of Japan from Shi Jinqing (d. 1421), the newly installed pacification superintendent of Palembang. Yoshimochi professed no need for it, and instead regifted it to the King of Korea. There, the expenses of feeding it proved great, and after it trampled a man to death, it was banished to an island, where it starved.[97]

[90] Conlan, *From Sovereign to Symbol* (New York: Oxford University Press, 2011), pp. 187–89. See also Itō Kiyoshi, *Ashikaga Yoshimochi* (Yoshikawa kōbunkan, 2008), pp. 16–18.

[91] Itō Kiyoshi, *Ashikaga Yoshimochi*, pp. 52–55 for Yoshimochi's increased distance from the court.

[92] Akamatsu Toshihide, "Jishi," in *Rokuon*, p. 28 .

[93] *Yamaguchi kenshi shiryōhen chūsei*, vol. 3, Jōeiji monjo, doc. 41, 12.11.1409 (Ōei 16) Ashikaga Yoshimochi *gohan mikyōjo utsushi*, p. 348.

[94] See *Funiikō*, reproduced most conveniently in *Ōuchi bunka*, p. 279. For further analysis of this passage see Ueda Jun'ichi, *Ashikaga Yoshimitsu to zenshū* (Kyoto: Hōzōkan, 2011), p. 154.

[95] One example is that of Tō no Tsuneyori's *Kokinshumonsho. Tenri toshokan hisho mokuroku Wakansho no bu dai ni*, pp. 125–26. See also Yoshizawa Hajime, "Ōeiki ni okeru Totō Tenjin setsuwa no tenkai," *Shigaku zasshi* 120.10 (2011), pp. 50, 58.

[96] Yanbe Kōki, "Muromachi bakufu shugo no zaikyō to zaikoku," *Rekishi to chiri* 527 (1999), pp. 18–25 for how Moriakira retained close links to Southern Court emperors and courtiers. For Yoshimochi's visits, see note 106.

[97] Kunihara Misako, "Jūgo seiki no nichōkan de juju shita sanju," *Shiron*, no. 54 (2001), pp. 129–32; Momosaki Yūichirō, *Muromachi no hasha Ashikaga Yoshimitsu* (Chikuma shoin, 2020), p. 204, and "Wakasa no kuni Saisho Imatomi myō ryōshu daidai shidai," *Gunsho ruijū*, vol. 4, *buninbu*, 6.22.1408, p. 352. For more on this episode, see Isao Soranaka, "Obama: The Rise and Decline of a Seaport," *Monumenta Nipponica* 52.1 (Spring, 1997), p. 90.

Yoshimochi unsurprisingly abandoned Yoshimitsu's policy of relying on the title of "King of Japan" to oversee tributary exchanges sometime prior to the ninth month of 1411.[98] That title had enabled the Ashikaga to engage in lucrative trade in exchange for nominal subservience to Ming suzerainty. Yoshimochi's decision to abandon it has long been seen either as xenophobic or as an assertion of Japanese sovereignty. Certainly, it represented an abandonment of Ashikaga preeminence in Chinese relations. This ending of formal tributary relations disrupted the flow of goods from China and caused Korea to matter even more as a conduit for trade. In this regard the Ōuchi benefited, since they had a crucial role as intermediaries between Chosŏn officials and the Ashikaga.[99] And they made sure that objects more prized than Sumatran elephants would be exchanged.

Moriakira mediated not only material resources but also areas of culture. He headed a Zen cultural salon, where he introduced new painting styles from the continent. Yoshimochi, who has been described as being one of the first rulers deeply versed in Zen, also valued Moriakira as an interlocutor who introduced him to new teachings and objects from the continent.[100]

Sometime before 1415 Moriakira received a painting, the *Mountain Villa* (*Sansōzu*), with inscriptions by eight Zen monks, comparing Moriakira's retreat to those of the reclusive T'ang poet Wang Wei or the Daoist sages on mount Penglai.[101] This work and the 1413 *Hidden Cottage by a Mountain Stream* by Minchō, in the Song Academy Landscape Style, became influential among Japanese artists of the next generation.[102] Thus, the "Muromachi style" of ink painting came first to the Ōuchi, whose ties to the continent gave them access to its newest trends (Figure 4.3).

---

[98] For the best summary, see Ueda, *Ashikaga Yoshimitsu to zenshū*, pp. 150–57. See also Tanaka Takeo, ed., *Zenrin kokuhōki* (Shūeisha, 1995), pp. 138–41, 150–51, and 558–59 for the diplomatic exchanges, as well as Yoshimochi's rational dating from 7.20.1419 (Ōei 26), and Verschuer, *Across the Perilous Sea: Japanese Trade with China and Korea from the Seventh to the Sixteenth Centuries* (Ithaca, NY: Cornell East Asia Series, 2006), pp. 122–23.

[99] Ueda Jun'ichi, *Ashikaga Yoshimitsu to zenshū*, pp. 156–57, *T'aejong sillok*, 10.1411 (T'aejong 11/Ōei 18). This source is reproduced most conveniently in *Yamaguchi kenshi shiryōhen chūsei*, vol. 1, p. 867.

[100] Tamamura Takeji, "Ashikaga Yoshimochi no zenshū shinkō ni tsuite," Tamura Takeji, ed., *Nihon zenshūshi ronshū ge* no. 2 (Kyoto: Shibunkaku, 1981), pp. 57–84. See also Ueda, *Ashikaga Yoshimitsu to zenshū*, p. 158.

[101] For the characterization of this work, see John Parker, *Zen Buddhist Landscape Arts of Early Muromachi Japan (1336–1573)* (Albany: SUNY Press, 1999), p. 102. See also *Ōuchi bunka*, p. 820 for this image.

[102] Ōta Takahiko, "Masaki bijutsukan zō 'Sansōzu' ni tsuite," *MUSEUM* (Tōkyō kokuritsu hakubutsukan), no. 450 (9.1998), pp. 4–12.

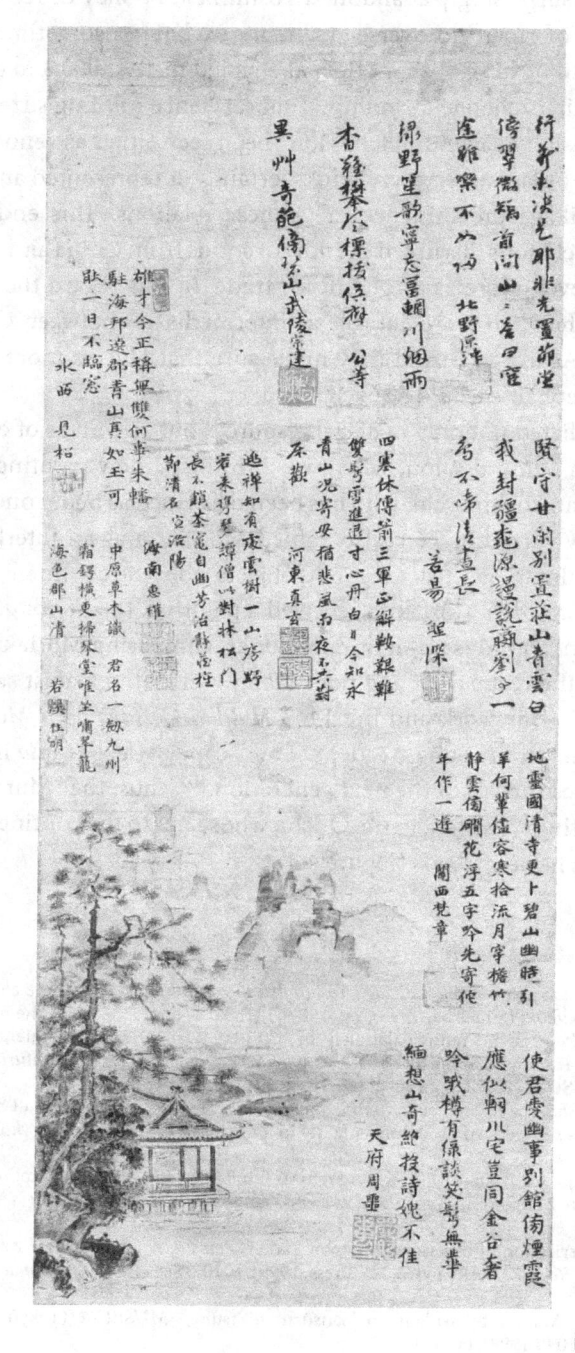

Figure 4.3 Predating 1415, "Mountain Villa (*Sanshōzu*)" is one of the oldest examples of ink paintings in the Song Academy Landscape style in Japan. Its colophons praise Moriakira. Photograph and permission courtesy Masaki Museum of Art

Moriakira introduced to Ashikaga Yoshimochi information about Totō Tenjin, a form of the deified Sugawara Michizane, represented as a traveler to China.[103] He also promoted the cult of Tenjin, invited Yoshimochi to a Zen temple (Shōzen'in), and gave him an image of the deity.[104] This is the same image, dating from 1417, for which the Zen monk Daishū Shūchō (1348–1419) of Shōkokuji provided the inscription.[105]

Yoshimochi visited Moriakira's mansion in Kyoto repeatedly from 1413 to 1418 as well as in 1424.[106] This was unusual, since visitors usually came to the shogun. He so favored Moriakira that he wrote the nameplate for Moriakira's two Kyoto dwellings in his own hand, a great honor.[107] Yoshimochi and Moriakira's Zen salon would include most of the major warlords of their day.[108] The two went together on pilgrimage to Ise, and Moriakira also visited Iwashimizu Hachiman with Ashikaga Yoshikazu, Yoshimochi's heir.[109] These close interactions aided him greatly. For example, he was able to establish Yoshihiro's grave at Mt. Kōya on 3.22.1417—a sign of Yoshihiro's rehabilitation in the eyes of the Ashikaga.[110]

[103] Yoshizawa Hajime, "Ōei ki ni okeru Totō Tenjin setsuwa no tenkai," pp. 48–50 for Moriakira's relationship with Yoshimochi and the upswing in Totō Tenjin worship in the Ōei era (1394–1428). See also Miyajima Shin'ichi, "Tosoku Tenjinzō to Totō tenjinzō," *Bungaku kaishaku to kanshō* 67.4 (4.2002), pp. 148–156. See also Hashimoto Yū, *Chūka Gensō: Karamono to gaikō no Muromachi jidaishi* (Bensei shuppan, 2011), pp. 57–90.

[104] *Yamaguchi kenshi shiryōhen chūsei*, vol. 1, pp. 175–76. These reminiscences date from 5.7.1466 (Bunshō 1) and were recorded in the *Gaun nikken roku batsuyū*. This would be reciprocated by Yoshimochi when Moriakira left on a campaign. See Yoshizawa, pp. 45–47 for the image in Furukuma shrine in Yamaguchi dating from 11.13.1429 (Eikyō 1).

[105] It still survives at the Egara shrine in Kamakura. The Shōkokuji monk Daishū later added an explanation of the image in 1417 (Ōei 24), explaining how Moriakira had this dream "a decade and some odd years later," which would place this event at the time when Moriakira was fighting against Yoshimitsu. *Egara Tenjinsha kyūhyakunen*, p. 8, *Jinenju Tenjin ritsuzō*.

[106] *Yamaguchi kenshi shiryōhen chūsei*, vol. 1, Manzei jugō nikki, 3.23, 4.19, 8.22.1413 (Ōei 20), 3.2.1414 (Ōei 21), 3.28.1415 (Ōei 22), and 11.1.1418 (Ōei 25), pp. 83–84. See also *Kanenobu kōki* (Hirohashi Kanenobu) (Zoku gunsho ruijū kanseikai, 2012), vol. 2, 2.9.1424 (Ōei 31), p. 101.

[107] *Yamaguchi kenshi shiryōhen chūsei*, vol. 4, Hisentei no shi narabi ni jō, p. 781. For Moriakira having two dwellings, see Yoshizawa, p. 49, and Kawai Masaharu, "Muromachi dono no buke shakai to bunka," in *Chūsei buke shakai no kenkyū* (Yoshikawa kōbunkan, 1973), p. 221.

[108] Moriakira, along with several important *shugo*, took Zen names. Moriakira was known as Daisen Tokuyū *koji*, and he interacted with Hosokawa Mitsumoto (Etsudō Dōkan *koji*), Hatakeyama Mitsuie (Chokugen Dōkan *koji*), Yamana Tokihiro (Kyosen Jyōki *koji*), and Akamatsu Yoshinori (Enrei Seishō *koji*). *Zenrin gasan*, p. 296, and Ōta Takahiko, "Masaki Bijutsukan zō 'Sansōzu' ni tsuite," p. 8. See also Melissa McCormick, "Genji Goes West," *Art Bulletin* 85.1 (3.2003), p. 59.

[109] Kondō Kiyoshi, *Ōuchi jitsuroku* (3rd reprint ed., Tokuyama: Matsuno shoten, 1984), p. 49 for his trip to Ise on 11.13.1421 (Ōei 28) from the *Kaei sandai jitsuroku*. For the Hachiman pilgrimage, see Tamura Masataka, "Muromachiki ni okeru Usa no miya no saiki zōei saikō," *Chūsei shi kenkyū* 32 (2007), p. 130.

[110] *Ōuchi jitsuroku*, p. 49 for the establishment of Yoshihiro's grave at Mt. Kōya on 3.22.1417 (Ōei 24).

Tombs, Kings, and Ōuchi Ethnicity

As we have seen, Moriakira had reached out to Korea and received recognition of descent from Prince Imsŏng. He later turned his attention to the Kuruma-zuka, Prince Imsŏng's purported tomb in Tatara, in order to worship his ancestor better. As previously noted, the casket in this tomb had been moved to Jōfukuji in Yamaguchi, and Moriakira installed a statue of this prince as well.

This appeal to a common ancestor served to cement a sense of Ōuchi ancestry from a royal progenitor from Korea, and it further emphasized Ōuchi special identity by focusing on Tatara, the place where this prince landed in Japan, as the site of the family's origins as immigrants. This location would have an enduring meaning for the Ōuchi and their followers since it was also the site where the last Ōuchi lord landed after the coup of 1551 (see chapter 10). Thus, the Ōuchi established their special descent, highlighted the site of their origins, and as evidence concerning Yoshihiro suggests, maintained some knowledge of the Korean language.[111]

Moriakira took the unprecedented step of restoring Kuruma-zuka.[112] As stated in chapter 1, this was indeed an old tomb but had no link in fact to Imsŏng. Although some barrows had served as graves for a few centuries after their construction, lingering taboos protected most from being plundered, even if strapped armies at times in the mid-fourteenth century dug up valuables from them.[113] This restoration of the Kuruma-zuka, which began in 1414, entailed building and maintaining a moat 195 yards in length and planting trees along the perimeter.[114] Paddy land in the district was mapped, and a levy of five feet of moat per two acres (*chō*) of paddy

[111] As we have seen, Yoshihiro was aware of Korean pronunciations when questioning the horses named concerned with the Ukemochi myth. Yoshitaka, the great-great-grandson of Moriakira, also imported Korean editions of Confucian texts. See Figures 9.2, 9.5 and Peter Kornicki, "Korean Books in Japan: From the 1590s to the End of the Edo Period," *Journal of the American Oriental Society* 133.1 (2013), pp. 72–73, which suggests Ōuchi facility with the language.

[112] For the rarity of restoring *kofun*, I am indebted to Yoshikawa Shinji, conversation 12.27.2011.

[113] Kō no Moroyasu (d. 1351) plundered such tombs for gold and other valuables while conducting a campaign in Yoshino. *Entairyaku*, vol. 2, 2.3.1348 (Jōwa 4), p. 300. See also Conlan, *State of War* (Ann Arbor: University of Michigan Center for Japanese Studies, 2003), p. 95.

[114] *Hōfu shi shi tsūshi I genshi kodai chūsei* (Hōfu shi, 2004), pp. 37–39, p. 521, "Kurumatsuka Myōken," and "Tatara miyabori no chikuzō," pp. 281–83. For more analysis, see Matsuoka, *Ōuchi shi no kenkyū*, pp. 6, 155–58, and Suda, *Chūsei Nichō kankei to Ōuchi shi*, pp. 215, 237. The length of the moat was 117 *jin*. One *jin* equals five *shaku*, or approximately five feet, giving the moat a total length of 585 feet, or 195 yards.

was assessed, although some temples, such as Amidaji, were made exempt.[115] Overgenerosity with exemptions led to a shortfall, since taxes were assessed on 234 *chō* and 7 *tan* (nearly 234 acres), enough for only 108 *jin* (540 feet). This left 45 feet (9 *jin*) unfunded. Moriakira's deputies warned local officials that delays in planting trees near the moats would force them to complain to Moriakira of their negligence, and this spurred on efforts to complete the reconstruction quickly.[116] Moriakira meant not only to restore this tomb, but to transform it into a cultic site glorifying the kingly Korean ancestry that he claimed. The Kuruma-zuka tomb was renamed as the Tatara shrine in 1418. This would lead to claims within Japan, expressed later in the century during the ascendancy of Moriakira's grandson Masahiro (1446–95), that the Ōuchi were not Japanese. Recognition of Ōuchi difference was linked too to the sense that their origins were bound to their landing at the beaches of Tatara, in Suō.[117] The Ōuchi were capable of writing letters in the proper epistolary and diplomatic format of both Japan and Korea, but their sense of ethnic difference was known to some nobles in Japan. The Ōuchi demonstrated awareness of spoken Korean, built temples in the Korean royal style to emphasize their Korean descent, and highlighted their origins as immigrants from Tatara. This ethnic awareness not only permeated the Japanese court, but existed in Korea as well, where the Ōuchi were described as being unusually close,[118] even though the ancestor (Prince Imsŏng) that they claimed descent from was fictional.

Given these asserted affinities, Ōuchi links with Korea and their sense of a distinct ethnicity would strengthen over time. The impact of these bonds would be felt almost immediately, since Moriakira reached out to Korea while he was rebuilding the Kuruma-zuka tomb. In 1419, Moriakira's support, or at least acquiescence, aided Korean attempts to restrain the *wakō* plying the seas near Tsushima.

---

[115] *Yamaguchi kenshi shiryōhen chūsei*, vol. 2, doc. 71, 11.10.1416 (Ōei 23) Ōuchi shi *bugyōnin rensho hōsho an*, p. 374.

[116] Paraphrased from *Yamaguchi kenshi shiryōhen chūsei*, vol. 2, Amidaji monjo, doc. 64, 1.22 [(Ōei 25) 1418], Ōuchi shi *bugyōnin rensho hōsho an*, p. 372.

[117] *Yamaguchi kenshi shiryōhen chūsei*, vol. 1, Daijōin jisha zōjiki, 5.27.1472 (Bunmei 4), p. 209.

[118] Shin Sukchu, *Kaitō shokokuki*, ed. Tanaka Takeo (Iwanami bunko, 1991), p. 150.

Conflict, Korean Ties, and Trading Networks

In 1419, the Chosŏn court launched a ten-day campaign against Tsushima Island, apprehending many islanders as "pirates" before returning to their shores.[119] The Korean sources suggest that some two years earlier, in 1417, Moriakira or perhaps Mitsuyo was involved with discussions about the likelihood of a Korean attack on Tsushima and the Sō family, seafarers who dominated this island.[120] The campaign caused a stir in the capital and led to reports of miraculous portents presaging Japanese victory at shrines such as Izumo, Iwashimizu Hachiman and Ise.[121]

The Ōuchi proved effective at promoting their interests as being those of the gods themselves. During these moments of tension, they reported that an oracle from Tenjin had revealed that an Ōuchi-led force had defeated the Ming with the support of Kitano.[122] Moriakira's Kitano allies portrayed the invasion as coming from China, while the Shōni, their rivals from northern Kyushu, argued correctly that the attack came from Korea. Families closely allied to the Shōni, such as the Fukabori, criticized the Ōuchi as being unreliable, claiming that the Ōuchi had aided the Mongols when they attempted to invade Japan in 1281.[123] In the end, the coordination between Moriakira and Chosŏn officials served to constrain *wakō* rivals from Tsushima.

Chosŏn Dynasty sources dating from 12.3.1429 (J. intercalary 11.3.1429) show recognition by the ambassador Pak Sŏ-saeng that the Ōuchi could stop the flow of "pirates" through the Straits of Shimonoseki, while the Ashikaga were, to the contrary, ineffective.[124] After Moriakira's conquest of Hakata,

---

[119] Itō Kōji, "Ōei no gaikō o meguru kaii genshō," in *Nichō kōryū to sōkoku no rekishi* (Asakura shobō, 2009), pp. 191–208. For an initial study, see Nakamura Hidetaka, *Nichō kankeishi no kenkyū jō* (Yoshikawa kōbunkan, 1965).

[120] *Yamaguchi kenshi shiryōhen chūsei*, vol. 1, p. 869, 12.19.1417 (T'aejong 17)/(Ōei 24) for reference to an attack on Tsushima. For the activities of Mitsuyo, see p. 870, 10.2.1420 (Sejong 2)/ 10.1.1420 (Ōei 27), p. 870.

[121] Itō Kōji, "Ōei no gaikō o meguru kaii genshō," p. 199.

[122] *Yamaguchi kenshi shiryōhen chūsei*, vol. 1, Kanmon gyōki, 6.29.1419 (Ōei 26), p. 122 for a passage describing how the Ōuchi, with the support of Kitano, destroyed a Ming expedition.

[123] *Ōuchi bunka*, p. 23 for a reference to how the Ōuchi led Paekche warriors in 1281, a fact all the more remarkable because Paekche had collapsed six hundred years before the Mongol invasions.

[124] *Yamaguchi kenshi shiryōhen chūsei*, vol. 1, 12.3.1429 (Sejong 11)/urū 11.3.1429 (Eikyō 1), p. 874. See also Hirase Naoki, *Ōuchi shi no ryōgoku shihai to shūkyō* (Hanawa shobō, 2017), pp. 224–27. For coverage in English, see Etsuko Hae-Jin Kang, *Diplomacy and Ideology in Japanese-Korean Relations: From the Fifteenth to the Eighteenth Century* (London: Palgrave Macmillan, 1997), pp. 65–66, and Peter Shapinsky, *Lords of the Sea: Pirates, Violence, and Commerce in Late Medieval Japan* (Ann Arbor: University of Michigan Center for Japanese Studies, 2014), pp. 201–2.

Korean officials feared that he might gain control of the Chosŏn sea lanes and potentially lead an invasion, relying on his ships in the Inland Sea.[125] Moriakira desired to continue trading with the Chosŏn Dynasty, since the conquest of Kyushu was also integrally linked to his attempt to quell the "pirates" of Tsushima. However, Chosŏn officials complained of his repeated requests for goods such as leopard skins.[126] Although they maintained trade, they did not seek close political relations with Moriakira, despite his claim of Korean ancestry. Nevertheless, the Chosŏn scholar and official Yi Ye (1375–1445) would write in 1439 that "the Ōuchi had faithfully served the Chosŏn court" since the time of Yoshihiro, and "there should be no doubt about the clan's loyalty to the Chosŏn."[127]

In tandem with his closer ties to Korea and assertions of Korean ancestry, Moriakira's ships increasingly plied the seas between the ports of Senzaki, Hijū, and Nima, on the one hand, and Korea on the other, loaded with copper and silver. This activity brought Moriakira in contact with, and ultimately competition against, what Gregory Smits has described as "The East China Sea Network" stretching from Ningbo through the Okinawa Islands, to Tsushima, Cheju, and Korea.[128] Centered in this area were *wakō*, peoples of the seas, drawn from a variety of regions, who were forced to become armed traders because of restrictive Ming policies. These *wakō* were particularly active in Korea, Cheju island, Tsushima, and the Okinawan islands, although their activities would diminish around 1420, when Moriakira, in cooperation with Korea, successfully limited them.[129] From the 1420s onward, some Korean merchants lived in Hakata, traveling from there back to Korea or to Ming China, where they disseminated Japanese information and goods.[130]

[125] *Yamaguchi kenshi shiryōhen chūsei*, vol. 1, 5.19.1430 (Sejong 12)/5.20.1430 (Eikyō 2), p. 874; Shapinsky, *Lords of the Sea*, pp. 201–2; and Hirase Naoki, "Shugo daimyō Ōuchi shi to kaihen no busō seiryoku: kaizoku, keigoshū, wakō," *Yamaguchi ken chihōshi kenkyū* 71 (6.1994), p. 29.

[126] *Yamaguchi kenshi shiryōhen chūsei*, vol. 1, *urū* 12.13.1430 (Sejong 12)/12.12.1430 (Eikyō 12), p. 875. See also *Ōuchi bunka*, Ōuchi Yoshioki *toijō sūhentō*, p. 589, and Suda, *Chūsei Nichō kankei to Ōuchi shi*, pp. 60–61.

[127] Translation from Sangnam Lee, "Traces of a Lost Landscape Tradition and Cross-Cultural Relationships between Korea, China, and Japan in the Early Joseon Period (1392–1550) (PhD diss., University of Kansas, 2014), pp. 190–91. See also *Sejong sillok*, vol. 48, 5.19.1430 (Sejong 12).

[128] Gregory Smits, *Maritime Ryūkyū, 1050–1650* (Honolulu: University of Hawaii Press, 2018), pp. 15–18.

[129] For an excellent recent overview, see Smits, *Maritime Ryūkyū*, pp. 40–42.

[130] Saeki Kōji, "Muromachiki no Hakata shōnin Sōkin to Higashi Ajia," *Shien* 136 (1999), pp. 106–21. For another Korean merchant, active from 1453 through 1473, see Saeki Kōji, "Muromachi kōki no Hakata shōnin Dōan to Higashi Ajia," *Shien* 140 (2003), pp. 31–49.

Figure 4.4 Cast by Korean craftsmen, the Mishima Island Sanukibō Bell (1413) was patronized by Munakata shrine officials from Kyushu and warriors from the island. Photograph by Thomas Conlan

Moriakira's encroachment on the earlier trading networks of *wakō* led to unprecedented prosperity in regions under his control. For example, the residents of Mishima Island, located off the coast of Nagato, cast bells and gongs of great size and manufactured with great skill.[131] One bell, cast in the

---

[131] Kawamura Kimiaki, *Hagi Abu no chūsei fūdoki* (Hagi: Mashiyama insatsu, 2010), pp. 117–18 for the bells and the importance of Mishima for trade.

Korean style, and thus made by Korean craftsmen, had an inscription written by two local warriors (*jitō*) who had ties to an individual from Munakata shrine, showing how Nagato, Kyushu, and Korea were linked in a lucrative trade and close collaboration (Figure 4.4).[132] One sign of the strength of Korean trade with the Ōuchi is that 250 entries in the *Chosŏn wangjo shillok* refer to them, their commerce, and trade between the years 1392 and 1553.[133]

The Nagato and Iwami regions were a natural focus for trade with Korea, but they have been overlooked by scholars who tend to focus on the large port of Hakata. Ocean currents flowed from the Pusan region of southern Korea to the Iwami region, and Korean sailors frequently washed ashore on the Iwami coast. There, in at least one instance, they were given provisions and cash (forty *koku* of rice and one hundred *kan* of cash) and allowed to return.[134] The Ōuchi had access to and awareness of numerous ports on the Japan Sea, and this enabled them to transmit and receive goods and information directly from the continent. These exchanges went largely undetected by others within Japan, particularly the Ashikaga. Moriakira did not trade only with Korea. His ships also plied the Inland Sea, providing him with information and goods from Kyoto.[135]

Moriakira's access to copper also benefited him greatly. Chosŏn sources praise his wealth, as well as his cordial relations with Korea, in connection with his request for yet another Tripiṭaka in 1408.[136] That year he also received tiger and leopard skins, both of which he collected.[137] He requested more tiger and leopard pelts in 1424 and 1430.[138] Korean

---

[132] This information is written on the Sanukibō bell inscription, dating from 1413 (Figure 4.4). Viewed 5.30.2016, Mishima. A large gong (*waniguchi*) at the entrance of the Shōkannon temple likewise reveals the wealth of the area. It dates from 1406, and is much larger than another, dating from 1387, which appears at the other harbor. Both amply attest to the wealth of these two *jitō*, each of whom controlled a harbor on the island.

[133] Sangnam Lee, "Traces of a Lost Landscape Tradition," p. 190; for an overview of the items exchanged, see pp. 195–98.

[134] Inoue Atsushi, "Rigei (Yiye) to Iwami no tsunagari: Chosŏn kōchō jitsuroku, Dōbunikō, Hyōnin ryōraitōroku (Pyo-In Yong-Nae Dung-nok) o tegakari to shite," *Hokutō AJIA Kenkyū* 27 (3.2016), p. 27 for the cash in 1408, and for how Nima served as a pipeline to Korea, p. 33.

[135] *Yamaguchi kenshi tsūshihen furoku* CD-ROM, doc. 115, Saishō kōin kata *hyōjo hikitsuke*, pp. 505–6 for references to Moriakira dispatching a messenger from Kyoto on 2.13.1419 (Ōei 26) and receiving forty *kanmon* of cash at the port of Hyōgo.

[136] *Yamaguchi kenshi shiryōhen chūsei*, vol. 1, 5.22.1408 (T'aejong 8)/5.21.1408 (Ōei 15), pp. 866–67.

[137] Few Chosŏn original documents survive, but a letter dating from around 1597 by King Sŏnjo (r. 1567–1608) to a court woman (*sug-ui*) recounts sending her a leopard skin as a special gift. The letter is privately held, but an image appears in Kim Ilgŭn, *Ch'inp'il ŏn'gan ch'ongnam* (Seoul: Unknown Publisher, 1974), pp. 10–11. I am indebted to Ksenia Chizhova for this reference.

[138] *Yamaguchi kenshi shiryōhen chūsei*, vol. 1, p. 866 for reference to an imported Tripiṭaka on 9.1.1407 (T'aejong 7)/8.30.1407 (Ōei 14), and 8.1.1408 (T'aejong 8)/(Ōei 15), p. 867 for his receipt

visitors lauded Kokushōji, while Zen monks not only praised Moriakira for his abilities, martial and otherwise, but also admired Kokushōji and Yamaguchi.[139]

Although sources describing trade with Korea are fragmentary, it appears that the Ōuchi domains provided porters (*okuribu*) and packhorses (*denma*) for it. Such levies were standard by 1423 and were linked to Moriakira's ability to assess a *hanzei*, or half tax of all revenue of the province, for military provisions. He could even do this for Iwami, although he was not *shugo* of that province.[140] Thus, with his control of ports, mines, and superior administrative abilities, Moriakira assumed a central role in trade with Korea to the detriment of the *wakō* plying the East China seas. This process would then lead his heirs to sponsor and build great trading ships that dominated the ocean trade in the ensuing decades.

Ōuchi Administrative and Ritual Authority

Under Moriakira, the Ōuchi developed effective institutions of governance. A coterie of officials resided in Yamaguchi. Responsible for governing provinces as deputy *shugo*, or districts such as Nima, they debated policy and transmitted missives to underlings at the district level. Conversely, these officials would screen local disputes at Yamaguchi before transmitting the most significant ones to the capital.[141]

Moriakira relied upon many officials to help him negotiate affairs in Kyoto and govern his territories from afar. This body was more generously staffed than during the time of Yoshihiro.[142] Naitō Chitoku (d. 1439), who had served as an official (*mokudai*) in Chikuzen and then acted as the deputy

---

of tiger and leopard skins, and part of the Tripiṭaka. Other shipments which can be verified on 8.20.1416 (T'aejong 16)/(Ōei 23), p. 869. See also p. 872 for references to tiger and leopard skins (1.9 and 2.7.1424 (Sejong 6)/(Ōei 31).

[139] For this insight, I am indebted to Andrew Watsky. Conversation 8.25.2015.

[140] *Yamaguchi kenshi shiryōhen chūsei*, vol. 4, Inomiya monjo, doc. 224, 8.9.1443 (Kakitsu 3) Ōuchi shi *bugyōnin rensho hōsho*, p. 207, signed by Ida Hideie, Naitō Moriyo, and Sugi Shigenobu, which refers to these shrine exemptions existing since 9.3.1423 (Oei 30). For how the 1423 developments were linked to the *hanzei* in Izumi, see Mimura Kōsuke, "Ōuchi shi no hanzeisei," *Komonjo kenkyū* 56 (11.2002), pp. 2–3.

[141] Wada Shūsaku, "Ōuchi shi no ryōgoku shihai soshiki to jinzai tōyō," p. 208.

[142] Okamoto Nin, "Nanbokuchō Muromachi shoki Ōuchi shi no shihai kōzō hōsha no bunseki o chūshin to shite," *Yamaguchi kenshi kenkyū*, no. 22 (3.2014), p. 11. See also p. 7 for how decisions were first made in Kyoto and then conveyed to local administrators in Yoshihiro's time as well.

shugo of Nagato, became its most prominent member.[143] His skills in nego-
tiation, evidenced by his experience with officials from Tōji early in 1406,
caused Moriakira to grant him plenipotentiary powers as the Kyoto representative for the Ōuchi.[144]

Little continuity existed among this administrative body of Kyoto representatives, for most who had accompanied Yoshihiro later sided with the hapless Hiroshige. The Mori and the Sueyama, who had both been prominent
supporters of Yoshihiro, lost favor under Moriakira. Hirai Dōjo, who engineered
the "succession" of Hiroshige, so alienated Moriakira that his descendants lost influence.[145] The only two notable figures that prominently served both Yoshihiro
and Moriakira were Sugi Shigesada and Toida Sadayo.[146]

Moriakira was deeply concerned with the maintenance of shrines and temples,
and the ongoing performance of rites. More effective tax levies enabled the
Ōuchi to institute regular taxes rather than attempt ad hoc measures. Moriakira
restored temples thanks to provincial labor taxes, assessed from districts within
provinces, and he directed these efforts even when he was in Kyoto.[147]

A document concerned with Tripiṭaka rites dating from 1427 provides clear
evidence of this process. In this case, a province-wide land tax (*tansen*), was
levied on Abu district in Nagato,[148] as well as regions in Suō, and these funds,
more than donations, provided most of the revenue for these ceremonies.[149]

In other cases, *tansen* served to bolster local authority, most prominently
with respect to the ability of Kokushōji to administer the mines. In 1418,

---

[143] Wada Shūsaku, "Ōuchi shi no ryōgoku shihai soshiki to jinzai tōyō," p. 208 for a brief biog-
raphy of Chitoku and assessment of his significance. For Chitoku's appointment as deputy *shugo* of
Nagato, see "Nagato no kuni shugo shiki shidai," *Yamaguchi kenshi shiryōhen chūsei*, vol. 1, p. 603.
The Naitō were originally a family of *gokenin* during the Kamakura era, who were early supporters of
the Washizu.

[144] For an important study of the importance of mediation in medieval Japan, see Megan Gilbert,
"Conciliators and Fixed Points: Dispute Resolution in Fifteenth Century Japan," PhD dissertation,
Princeton University, 2022.

[145] Okamoto, "Nanbokuchō Muromachi shōki Ōuchi shi no shihai kōzō," p. 10, and Tamura
Masataka, "Ōuchi shi Hirai kashin Hirai Dōjo kō," *Nanakuma shigaku* 17 (3.2015), pp. 23–40.

[146] Okamoto, "Nanbokuchō Muromachi shōki Ōuchi shi no shihai kōzō," p. 10. Toida Sadayo's
particulars were not clear, but Sugi Shigesada sided with Moriakira because he had been divested of
lands in the aftermath of 1399.

[147] *Yamaguchi kenshi shiryōhen chūsei*, vol. 2, Amidaji monjo, doc. 71, 11.10.1416 (Ōei 23) Ōuchi
shi *bugyōnin rensho hōsho an*, p. 374, and doc. 64, 1.22 [Ōei 25 (1418)] Ōuchi shi *bugyōnin rensho
hōsho an*, p. 372.

[148] *Yamaguchi kenshi shiryōhen chūsei*, vol. 3, Kōryūji monjo, doc. 154, 4.9.1427 (Ōei 34) Kōryūji
issaikyō ryōsoku chūmon, pp. 294–96. See also Maki Takayuki, "Suō Ōuchi shi to sono ujidera
Kōryūji," pp. 126–27.

[149] Maki, "Suō Ōuchi shi to sono ujidera Kōryūji," p. 126, and Matsuoka, "Muromachi Sengokuki
no Suō no kuni kokuga to Ōuchi shi," *Ōuchi shi no kenkyū*, pp. 155–58.

Moriakira granted Kokushōji the office of *kumon shiki*, which implied local administrative authority over the Mine region, where the mines were located.[150] Kokushōji was in turn supported with revenue from *tansen* in 1421.[151] Later, in 1424, Kokushōji was granted rights to Nima, the important port located a four-hour walk from the silver and copper mines of Iwami.[152] Kokushōji would long have links to mining interests in Naganobori, and at some time these interests would be extended to the silver mines near Nima. This would continue through the 1580s, even after Ōuchi rule had collapsed.[153]

The Localization of a National Shrine (Usa)

Moriakira cemented Ōuchi control of Kyushu's Buzen province, across the sea south of Suō, by rebuilding the massive Usa shrine for the first time in decades. His funding made the shrine local in character, designed to legitimate Ōuchi interests, rather than national interests as before.[154] To be sure, Moriakira's predecessor Yoshihiro had, shortly before his demise, gained authority over Usa in 1397, but he was unable to oversee any major repairs to the shrine complex during the last two years of his life.

By 1416, Moriakira would levy *tansen* taxes for Usa, revealing his complete control over the shrine.[155] However, even these taxes proved insufficient to repair the many buildings in the Usa complex. Moriakira also commissioned scrolls illustrating the miracles of the shrine. The head of the shrine traveled to Kyoto, where he showed Ashikaga Yoshimochi the images, explained old shrine records, and convinced Yoshimochi to help rebuild the complex.[156] With Yoshimochi's support, other *shugo*, too, were forced to pay for these

---

[150] *Yamaguchi kenshi shiryōhen chūsei*, vol. 3, Jōeiji monjo, doc. 49, 2.29.1418 (Ōei 25) Ōuchi Tokuyu (Moriakira) *kishinjō utsushi*, pp. 349–50. See also *Hagi han batsu etsu roku*, vol. 4, Bōchō jisha shōmon, Kōzan Jōeiji ge, doc. 67, 2.29.1418 (Ōei 25) Ōuchi Moriakiara *kishinjō*, p. 229 for a grant of the Mine *kumon shiki* for prosperity of house and peace in the realm.

[151] A 11.6.1421 (Ōei 28) Ōuchi shi *bugyōnin rensho shojō utsushi*, *Yamaguchi kenshi shiryōhen chūsei*, vol. 3, Jōeiji monjo doc. 74, p. 356, and *Hagi han batsu etsu roku* 4 Kōzan Jōeiji ge, doc. 69, p. 230, also mentions *tansen* being applied to Ōta in Yoshiki district.

[152] *Hagi han batsu etsu roku* 4 Kōzan Jōeiji ge, doc. 74, 6.2.1425 (Ōei 32) Ōuchi Moriakira *chigyō ategaijō*, p. 231 for the grant of Nima district and Tamura to Kokushōji, see *Hagi han batsu etsu roku* 4, Kōzan Jōeiji ge, p. 231.

[153] *Bōchō fūdo chūshin an*, vol. 13, p. 139 for links to the silver mines during the sixteenth century. Copies of the earlier documents appear through pp. 130–39.

[154] For this insight, I would like to thank Maki Takayuki. Conversation, 6.2018.

[155] Matsuoka "Ōuchi Buzen shihai," in *Ōuchi shi no kenkyū*, pp. 187–89. See also Fujii, *Muromachiki daimyō kenryokuron*, pp. 69–70.

[156] On 1.16.1418 (Ōei 25) Masanaga, the head of the shrine (*kengyō*) brought sixteen volumes of Usa scrolls to Kyoto. They stayed in Kyoto from 2.13 through 3.18 of that year. *Usa jingūshi shiryōhen*,

repairs. The Shimazu, for example, collected funds from the three provinces of Ōsumi, Satsuma, and Hyūga for the repair of Mirokuji, a temple in the Usa compound, in the ninth month of 1417.[157] Repairs to the shrine began in 1418. They continued for fourteen years and were completed in 1432.

Moriakira directed the reconstruction from Kyoto. Ōuchi administrators such as Sugi Shigetsuna left for Usa, where Shigetsuna supervised the harvesting of trees.[158] He also oversaw thousands of purification rites and made laws prohibiting the killing of animals within shrine precincts or using trees for anything but shrine purposes.[159] Administrators were integrally involved in these affairs, but no one individual predominated. Although Shigetsuna frequently traveled to Usa in the early years, later the Hironaka and Yasutomi took a leading role as well.[160] A detailed account of the rebuilding of the shrine survives.[161] Moriakira's repairs were substantial. They included the reconstruction of Mirokuji, the erection of a three-story pagoda, a lecture hall, and a rotating sutra library (rinzō) for the housing of the Tripiṭaka.[162]

The deities' mikoshi palanquins, which still survive, were completed on 11.17.1423. They were destined for use during major rites that Moriakira planned to have performed at the shrine in 1424.[163] The elaborate paintings inside them had been done by Kyoto artists, using high-quality pigment.[164]

---

vol. 9, pp. 215, 220. For Yoshimochi's prayers to Usa and his offering of a divine horse to celebrate the reconstruction of Mirokuji in 1421, see Usa jingūshi shiryōhen, vol. 9, p. 239, and 6.11.1421 (Ōei 28), p. 318.

[157] Usa jingūshi shiryōhen, vol. 9, 9.12.1417 (Ōei 24) Ashikaga Yoshimochi kudashibumi, pp. 212–13.

[158] Usa jingūshi shiryōhen, vol. 9, 9.10.1418 (Ōei 25), p. 223.

[159] Usa jingūshi shiryōhen, vol. 9, pp. 223–24 and 226–27 for the events of 11.10 and 12.17.

[160] Usa jingūshi shiryōhen, vol. 9, 2.25.1419 (Ōei 26), p. 244; 5.17.1419 (Ōei 26), p. 247. Sugi Shigetsuna, received a document (hōsho) from Kyoto. See also p. 286 for Shigetsuna managing the construction of a shrine gate (torii) on 7.4.1420 (Ōei 27). For the Yasutomi and Hironaka, see Usa jingūshi shiryōhen, vol. 9, 3.21–28.1422 (Ōei 29), pp. 329–31.

[161] Multiple printed editions survive. An accurate albeit abbreviated version appears in Yamaguchi kenshi shiryōhen chūsei, vol. 1, pp. 515–24. Next, this source has been divided accurately in the chronological format, Usa jingūshi shiryōhen, vol. 9. See also Itō Isato, Usagūki no kenkyū (Kōgakkan daigaku shuppan, 2011), pp. 220–27. Itō argues that Moriakira accomplished this as part of his role of being shugo of Buzen province.

[162] Matsumoto Takuya. "Chūsei Usagū no zōei shisutemu to Ōuchi shi," Kamakura ibun kenkyū, no. 31 (4.2013), p. 70.

[163] Usa jingūshi shiryōhen, vol. 9, 11.3.1423 (Ōei 30), p. 396 for Moriakira's request that the major rites be performed in the second and eleventh months of 1424 (Ōei 31). For the arrival of the mikoshi, see 11.17.1423 (Ōei 30), p. 398. See also p. 5 for analysis that the major repairs for the shrine that were completed in 1423.

[164] Allan Grapard, Mountain Mandalas: Shugendō in Kyushu (New York: Bloomsbury, 2016), p. 93, and, for the original report, Ōita kenritsu rekishi hakubutsukan kenkyū kiyō 12 (2011). See Ōuchi bunka to Kita Kyūshū, pp. 6–7 for photos of the interior images.

Moriakira's restoration of Usa, largely funded by other *shugo* and the Ashikaga, garnered praise from the court and Ashikaga themselves.[165]

Why the Ashikaga and the *shugo* invested so much in the reconstruction of Usa and its *mikoshi* is never specifically mentioned, but the destruction of the shrine in the fourteenth century coincided with the lapse of Usa's most significant rite, the "Stately Progress" (*gyōkō-e no junkō*). First performed in 811, the *gyōkō-e no junkō* involved sending elaborately clothed statues of the Hachiman triad of Usa to Iwashimizu Hachiman, south of Kyoto, once every six years, in a procession involving thousands of people.[166] Yoshimochi and others would have assumed that with the reconstruction of Usa, these rites would be re-established. Moriakira made no effort to reinstate them.

The focus of the Usa rituals thus became localized. Usa's gods would no longer travel to the capital, but instead would circulate within the Usa precincts.[167] Ultimately a shrine that had ritually and politically upheld the realm served the interests of Moriakira as much, if not more, than those of the central state.

The Departure

In 1425 an uprising in the nearby provinces of Bungo and Chikuzen led Moriakira to return to his domains after an absence of sixteen years. Shortly thereafter the Usa shrine emitted ill-omened sounds that were understood to express displeasure over the Kyushu uprising and to signify divine support.[168] Later that year, Moriakira made repeated, generous donations to the shrine, which he also took the trouble to visit.[169] Moriakira had auspicious Noh plays performed at Usa, although this practice would end with the turmoil rapidly engulfing northern Kyushu.[170]

In 1425 the Shōni rebelled and quickly defeated the bakufu's representative in Kyushu, Shibukawa Yoshitoshi. Without Ōuchi support, northern Kyushu

---

[165] *Usa jingūshi shiryōhen*, vol. 9, pp. 405–6 for a memorialization of Moriakira's merit from 2.1466 (Kanshō 7). For how Usa proved influential as far afield as Okinawa, see Smits, *Maritime Ryūkyū*, pp. 42–46, 200–201.

[156] Grapard, *Mountain Mandalas*, "Hachiman's traveling icons," pp. 85–93.

[167] Grapard, *Mountain Mandalas*, pp. 90–93.

[168] *Usa jingūshi shiryōhen*, vol. 9, 9.2.1425 (Ōei 32), p. 414 for this visit and pp. 415–16 for an earthquake at the shrine.

[169] *Usa jingūshi shiryōhen*, vol. 9, 11.6.1425 (Ōei 32), pp. 416–17 and 12.3.1426 (Ōei 33), p. 424.

[170] *Usa jingūshi shiryōhen*, vol. 9, pp. 476–77 for reference to Moriakira sponsoring these Noh plays in the Ōei era (1394–1428), which based on the context, would have to date from the mid-1420s.

remained largely ungovernable. Yoshimochi endured several problems, for the Shōkō emperor (1401–28, r. 1412–28) was ill and had no heir, and Yoshimochi's son Yoshikazu (1407–25), who had become shogun in 1423, had died in 1425.

Both Emperor Shōkō and Yoshimochi died in 1428, and the next shogun, Yoshinori, was determined by lot.[171] During this time of political change, Naitō Chitoku transmitted messages, kept Moriakira informed of developments, and encouraged him to abandon his campaign and return to Kyoto.[172] Moriakira did so because Yoshinori feared an attack from the disgruntled Kantō *kubō* (Protector of the East) Ashikaga Mochiuji (1409–39), who governed eastern Japan and thought that he had a better claim to Ashikaga succession.[173] The Kyushu campaign was not going well, however, and in the summer of 1429 Ōuchi Hirotane, the protector of Usa, was killed at Buzen's Umagatake.[174]

Moriakira returned to Kyoto on 10.7.1429.[175] After a month's sojourn, he once again returned to Kyushu. When he did, Ashikaga Yoshinori gave him a new image of Totō Tenjin, a suit of the shogun's armor, and a gold-encrusted sword.[176] In order to better prosecute the campaign, Moriakira was invested with the position of *shugo* of Chikuzen, too, for the first time. Contemporaries recognized this as a great honor.[177]

Chikuzen was a prize, for with control over Iwami's Nima, Nagato, and now Chikuzen, Moriakira could dominate trade with Korea. He extracted two thousand *kan* from Chikuzen, a significant sum, although whether this stemmed from a *tansen* tax or trade is not clear.[178]

---

[171] Conlan, *From Sovereign to Symbol*, p. 189. See also *Kennaiki*, vol. 1 (Iwanami shoten, 1963), 1.17.1428 (Ōei 35), pp. 40–46, and *Manzei jugō nikki*, vol. 1, 1.17.1428 (Ōei 35), pp. 476–78.

[172] *Yamaguchi kenshi tsūshihen chūsei*, pp. 379–80.

[173] *Ninagawa ke monjo*, vol. 1 (Tōkyō daigaku shuppankai, 1981), doc. 15, 10.23.1428 (Shōchō 1) Ashikaga Yoshinobu *gonaisho an*, pp. 17–18. See also Mori Shigeaki, *Muromachi bakufu hōkai: Shōgun Yoshinori no yabō to zasetsu* (Kadokawa gakugei shuppan, 2011), p. 141.

[174] For the 1429 (Shōchō 2) death of Hirotane, see *Usa jingūshi shiryōhen*, vol. 9, p. 499; Moriakira commended lands to Usa on 7.25.1429 (Shōchō 2), pp. 508–9, had a *Senbu kyō* performed on 8.3, p. 509, a *hōjō-e* on 8.12, p. 510, and a *Mirokuji issai kyō-e* on 8.16. See p. 510.

[175] *Yamaguchi kenshi shiryōhen chūsei*, vol. 1, Manzei jugō nikki, 10.7.1429 (Eikyō 1), p. 86.

[176] *Yamaguchi kenshi shiryōhen chūsei*, vol. 1, Manzei jugō nikki, 11.12.1429 (Eikyō 1), p. 87.

[177] *Yamaguchi kenshi tsūshihen chūsei*, pp. 379–80, and *Bōchō fūdo chūshin an*, vol. 13, p. 313. For a Kyushu document that seems to refer to this, see *Fukuoka shishi shiryōhen chūsei 1 Shinai shōzai monjo* (Fukuoka-shi, 2010), Aso monjo, doc. 32–27, 2.25.1429 (Shōchō 2) Ashikaga Yoshinori *gonaisho utsushi*, p. 544. See also *Hagi han batsu etsu roku*, vol. 5, p. 232, 12.12 Yamana Tokihiro *shojō* for an explanation of what an honor it was for Moriakira to receive this post. For more analysis of this document, see *Yamaguchi kenshi tsūshihen chūsei*, p. 380.

[178] *Yamaguchi kenshi tsūshihen chūsei*, pp. 380–81. For the reference to two thousand *kan*, see *Yamaguchi kenshi shiryōhen chūsei*, vol. 1, Manzei jugō nikki, 12.14.1430 (Eikyō 2), p. 88.

Moriakira again returned to Usa on 12.13.1429.[179] He worshiped there repeatedly during the following year, first arriving at Usa on 4.17 and staying for seventeen days, and again on 8.11.1430, for thirteen days.[180] He also rebuilt such other shrines as the Hachiman shrine at Oi, in Abe district, Nagato. Initiated in 1427, the construction progressed so that Moriakira could celebrate its completion in the sixth month of 1430.[181]

Moriakira devoted the last year of his life to again pacifying northern Kyushu, especially defeating the Kikuchi and Shōni, his long-standing rivals who had vexed the Kyushu *tandai* (commander), the Ashikaga, and now Moriakira himself. The campaign proved challenging, for the Ōtomo, who had remained until then an ally of the Ōuchi, took up arms against Moriakira and joined the Kikuchi and Shōni.[182] Moriakira responded by conquering the Ōtomo's "new" Tachibana castle in Chikuzen, located to the northeast of Hakata, and south of Munakata, on 4.29.1431. He then requested an edict from the Ashikaga to destroy the Ōtomo.[183] After this victory Moriakira ignored peace requests from the Ōtomo, being loath to return any captured Ōtomo territory even though the Ashikaga favored peace negotiations.[184]

Moriakira then turned his attention to the Kikuchi. He defeated them repeatedly until midway through 1431, at Haginohara in Chikuzen's Ido district, he was ambushed and killed by the forces of Shōni Mitsusada (d. 1433), Kikuchi Kanetomo (1383–1444), and Ōtomo Mochinao (d. 1445). The area constituted a core Shōni holding. Sugi Shigetsuna, the deputy of Buzen, was forced to flee to Nagato, surrendering these Kyushu lands to the Ōtomo and Shōni.[185] Moriakira also lost the battle flag that Ashikaga Yoshinori had given him in order to chastise the Shōni.[186]

[179] *Usa jingūshi shiryōhen*, vol. 9, 12.13.1429 (Eikyō 1), p. 519.

[180] *Usa jingūshi shiryōhen*, vol. 9, 4.17.1430 (Eikyō 2), p. 525, and 8.11.1430 (Eikyō 2), pp. 530–31.

[181] *Yamaguchi kenshi shiryōhen chūsei*, vol. 3, Ōi Hachimangū monjo, doc. 3, 6.11.1430 (Eikyō 2) Munafuda *meibun geisha utsushi*, and doc. 4, 6.5.1430 (Eikyō 2) Ōi Hachimangū *jōtō hiki uma chūmon*, pp. 948–50. See also Kawamura Kimiaki, *Hagi Abu no chūsei fūdoki*, p. 121.

[182] *Yamaguchi kenshi shiryōhen chūsei*, vol. 1, Manzei jugō nikki, 2.23, 27.1431 (Eikyō 3), p. 88. Ashikaga Yoshinori tried to convince the Ōtomo to ally with the Ōuchi, but this proved unsuccessful. These negotiations are first mentioned on 4.27 and continued through 5.13.1431. See *Yamaguchi kenshi shiryōhen chūsei*, vol. 1, Manzei jugō nikki, 2.27.1431 and 5.13.1431, pp. 88–89.

[183] *Yamaguchi kenshi shiryōhen chūsei*, vol. 1, Manzei jugō nikki, 5.20.1431 (Eikyō 3), p. 90 for the fall of the castle, and 5.24 for Moriakira's request for an edict to smite the Ōtomo (*jibatsu mikyōjo*).

[184] *Yamaguchi kenshi shiryōhen chūsei*, vol. 1, Manzei jugō nikki, 6.8–9.1431 (Eikyō 3), pp. 90–92.

[185] *Usa jingūshi shiryōhen*, vol. 9, 5.3.1418 (Ōei 25), p. 219 for the Usa chronicles, which provide an overview of how Moriakira controlled his territories for thirty-two years and died on 6.28.1430 (Eikyō 2), but this should be the following year. See pp. 545–46 for reference to Moriakira dying and Sugi Shigetsuna, the deputy *shugo* of Buzen fleeing to Nagato. See also *Yamaguchi kenshi shiryōhen chūsei*, vol. 1, Manzei jugō nikki, 8.9.1431 (Eikyō 3), p. 94.

[186] *Ninagawa ke monjo*, vol. 1, doc. 54, Norihiro (Ōuchi Norihiro) *jōsho an*, pp. 111–12. The document, written by Norihiro in the 1460s, states that when Mitsuyo was killed in battle the flag was lost,

This debacle shocked contemporaries. Yoshinori's protector, the monk Manzei (1378–1435), described the defeat as "an unspeakable outrage" and "a crisis for the realm."[187] Prince Sadafusa (1372–1456) recounted how signs, such as the loss of treasures at the Inner and Outer shrines of Ise, the fall of a mighty tree at Iwashimizu Hachiman, or strange sounds emanating from somewhere near Tōji were dire portents of Moriakira's death and the loss of divine favor that this meant.[188]

Sadafusa described the debacle as a "dog's death for a famous general." Although some details were initially incorrect, Sadafusa later confirmed that Moriakira had been struck down on the battlefield and then committed suicide, and he provided a roster of the thirty noted Ōuchi retainers who had been killed. Among them were seven men of the Sugi family; Naitō Morisuke; a Yasutomi; someone affiliated with the Munakata shrine; and the Iwami warrior Masuda Kanemasa.[189] Reports of Moriakira's end were transmitted to Korea as well.[190]

So ended thirty-two years of Moriakira's rule. As a rebel he had fought his enemies to a standstill, then established a symbiotic relationship with the Ashikaga, who in turn bolstered his support by ordering warriors from Aki and Iwami to come to the aid of the Ōuchi.[191] His control over the copper mines allowed him to engage in profitable trade, while his ties with Korea helped him to shift control of trading networks and better link them to his harbors and territories. Likewise, the promotion of varied rituals, and the restoration of major shrines, served to solidify cohesion in the territories. Moriakira established a formidable lordship in control of the western Inland Sea, and was capable of engaging in strong trade with Korea. The Ashikaga needed the Ōuchi, and depended on them, and at the same time were made uneasy by them.

but Mitsuyo did not die in battle, but rather killed himself in Kyoto. This document refers instead to Moriakira's death, a sentiment shared by the editors of this volume.

[187] *Yamaguchi kenshi shiryōhen chūsei*, vol. 1, Manzei jugō nikki, 7.13.1431 (Eikyō 3), p. 92 for Moriakira's defeat of the Kikuchi (and death) and, for more details about the place being Haginohara in Ido, Manzei jugō nikki, 8.9.1431 (Eikyō 3), p. 94. See also *Yamaguchi kenshi tsūshihen chūsei*, p. 382. For the link to the Shōni, conversation Horimoto Kazushige, 11.2011.

[188] *Kanmon gyōki* (Zoku gunsho ruijū kanseikai, hoi, 1930), vol. 1, 7.14.1431 (Eikyō 3), p. 604.

[189] *Kanmon nikki*, vol. 3 (Kunaicho shōryōbu, 2006), pp. 301–3. This appears in the *Gunsho ruijū* version (*Kanmon gyōki*), vol. 1, pp. 604–5, and *Yamaguchi kenshi shiryōhen chūsei*, vol. 1, 7.14, 7.16, 7.23.1431 (Eikyō 3), pp. 123–24. Masuda Kanemasa was not named here, but a retrospective letter from Yoshioki naming him confirms his death.

[190] *Yamaguchi kenshi shiryōhen chūsei*, vol. 1, 8.11.1431 (Sejong 13)/8.10.1431 (Eikyō 1), p. 875. According to this account, twenty-one brave warriors perished. The overall forces are described as comprising 730 men.

[191] *Yamaguchi kenshi shiryōhen chūsei*, vol. 1, Manzei jugō nikki, 7.17.1431 (Eikyō 3), p. 93.

5

Fraternal Succession, Expanding Trade, and Durable Administration

The Ōuchi were eclipsed during the decade following the death of Moriakira (1377–1431) and struggled to respond to a resurgent and more assertive Ashikaga bakufu. In 1432, Yoshinori (1394–1441, shogun 1429–41), the sixth Ashikaga shogun, re-established ties with the Ming. With his reinstated King of Japan title, and its tallies, which allowed for official tributary exchanges, he dispatched flotillas of ships to trade directly to China in 1432–33 and 1435. The Ōuchi continued informally trading with Korea and China, but their position declined vis-à-vis the Ashikaga. At the same time, disputes over Ōuchi succession further forced some factions to rely on Yoshinori, thereby increasing his influence over them as well. Despite conflicts over succession and their weakened economic and political position, Ōuchi improvements in administration allowed them to surmount this period of difficulty, which ended with the death of Ōuchi Mochiyo (1394–1441), a casualty of the 1441 assassination of Ashikaga Yoshinori.

Between 1397 and 1441, eight Ōuchi leaders died violently. All had at one time or another asserted claims to Ōuchi chieftainship. Five—Yoshihiro (d. 1399), Mitsuhiro (d. 1397), Hiroshige (d. 1401), Dōtsū (d. 1403), and Moriakira (d. 1431)—brothers all—perished in battle, with four of this group dying within a span of seven years (1397–1403). Likewise, all three of Yoshihiro's sons (Mochimori, Norisuke, and Mochiyo) were killed within a span of nine years (1433–41).[1] Fraternal inheritance often turned fratricidal, since three—Ōuchi, Hiroshige (d. 1401), Dōtsū (d. 1403), and Mochimori (d. 1433)—died while contesting the rule of their siblings.

---

[1] For relevant genealogies see *Yamaguchi shishi Ōuchi bunka* (hereafter *Ōuchi bunka*), pp. 25–26 for one, from the Mōri archives, that states that Hiroyo had seven sons, and pp. 51–52 for another, found in the Naikaku bunko, that lists nine. Mizono's *Shinsen Ōuchi shi keizu* states that Hiroyo had eight sons. See pp. 64–65. Only sons and grandsons of Hiroyo mentioned in this narrative are included in the Figure 5.1 genealogy.

Kings in All but Name. Thomas D. Conlan, Oxford University Press. © Oxford University Press 2024.
DOI: 10.1093/oso/9780197677339.003.0006

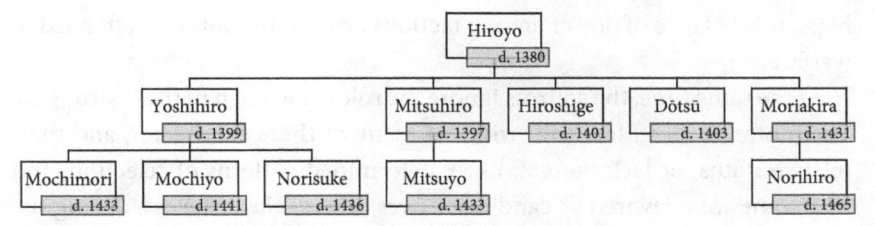

Figure 5.1 Ōuchi Genealogy. Created by Thomas Conlan

During this period the Ashikaga most successfully influenced Ōuchi succession. Through their intervention, a series of candidates became Ōuchi heirs who were beholden to the Ashikaga. This led them to reside for extended periods in Kyoto, and ironically, this resulted in one leader, Mochiyo, becoming unfortunately caught up in the assassination of Ashikaga Yoshinori, and he died as well. With his death ended a period of close Ōuchi cooperation and subservience to the Ashikaga.

This political turmoil should not obscure increasing trade, as at this time, for the first time, Japan proved capable of building extremely large boats as shipwrights, most likely unemployed after the Ming abandoned dispatching armadas under Zheng He (1371–1433). After 1433, one sees large craft sailing from ports such as Moji, and transporting ore, goods, and bringing millions of Ming coins back in return (Figure 5.1).

Naming Patterns and Succession Disputes

Lateral succession proved violent because of the nature of patrimony, since inheritance of an office, rather than of specific lands, underpinned Ōuchi lordship. The Ōuchi governed their core provinces of Suō, Nagato, and Buzen, as well as the recently acquired province of Chikuzen, through the office of *shugo*. Those appointed to this post, of which only sixty-six existed for all of Japan, could collect half of a province's income for military expenditures and thereby mobilize and maintain an army, while those who failed to inherit such an office were denied significant power.

The powers of the office were so great that competition arose for the office among a *shugo*'s heirs. This indivisibility of office exacerbated the intensity of intrafamilial disputes and made compromise difficult. Although on rare occasions a lord's portfolio of *shugo* posts could be divided among his heirs, this balance of power among factions proved unstable and often led to warfare.

At the same time, the sources ignore the roles of women in these struggles. The mothers, daughters, and wives of many of these candidates, and their relative status, or lack thereof, likely determined patterns of selection, and why some were favored as candidates over others. Nevertheless, during the late fourteenth and fifteenth centuries, the only women mentioned were daughters of courtiers, although even their personal names were not known, with the sole exception being the wife of Ōuchi Norihiro (1440–65), whose name (Kuniko) is known only because she was descended from the Yamana, a prominent *shugo* family. She would later play an important role in forming an alliance between the Yamana and Ōuchi, who had been rivals.

During these times of infighting, some contenders for Ōuchi leadership sought the support of the Ashikaga shoguns. The Ashikaga used their position to determine *shugo* inheritance, which left some *shugo* beholden to the Ashikaga for their successful candidacy, while others resented Ashikaga intrusion into their affairs. Ōuchi Mochiyo, the most successful of this cohort, established close ties with them, although this relationship ended with the assassination of Ashikaga Yoshinori in 1441 and the mortal wounding of Mochiyo himself in the same melee.

The high mortality rate of Ōuchi leaders did not, however, fracture their organization. To the contrary, these years witnessed improvements in Ōuchi administration and laws. A growing coterie of Ōuchi retainers, such as the Sue and the Naitō, served as able administrators. In contrast to earlier ages, where the supplanting of a lord led to a bloodletting and the eclipse of his supporters, this time of instability did not lead to disruptions because administration was already becoming uncoupled from the person of the lord. It was at this time, too, that laws were first issued for the Ōuchi domains, and their promulgation became routinized after times of succession. Perhaps unsurprisingly, this same period was one of extensive shipping and trade, which continued without major disruptions. The hitherto overlooked prosperity of the 1430s can be reconstructed through analysis of shipping records, picture scrolls, and hoards of coins.

The decade when Yoshihiro's sons ruled (1431–41) remains obscure, since many traces of their age were erased by subsequent Ōuchi lords. After 1441, Ōuchi succession became lineal, passing uneventfully from fathers to sons. The later Ōuchi also expunged some of Yoshihiro's sons from important memorial rites. Ōuchi Yoshihiro's unusual practice of naming his sons later caused confusion regarding the parentage, relative age, and order of his sons' succession. The discovery of a genealogy dating from the first half of the six-teenth century has helped clarify an admittedly complex picture of succes-sion, and of the social relations among Yoshihiro's sons.[2] Nevertheless, the Ōuchi organization proved capable of governing without too much aware-ness of the individual lords precisely because this turmoil led to greater reli-ance on law and stable ties of administrators.

Since the violent rise of Ōuchi Hiroyo (1325–80), chieftainship to the line was won by force. Hiroyo's son Yoshihiro (1356–99) likewise assured his suc-cession by defeating his brother Mitsuhiro (d. 1397). The rise of Moriakira (1377–1431) was exceptional, however, because his elder brother Yoshihiro entrusted him with authority as a caretaker, to serve until Yoshihiro's sons were ready to rule. Some Ōuchi legends emphasize Moriakira's deference to his brother's line by recounting how he drowned one of his sons to ensure the succession to power of Yoshihiro's sons.[3] Although this story is implau-sible and impossible to verify, Moriakira clearly promoted the candidacy of Yoshihiro's sons rather than his own.

Moriakira's eldest son, Norihiro, became increasingly prominent as Yoshihiro's descendants died off, culminating in his assuming the mantle of Ōuchi chief in 1441. Distinct naming practices reveal the emergence of two lineages of Ōuchi rulership, with one, ultimately less successful, adopting the name Magotarō, associated with Yoshihiro, while others preferred Rokurō, a name linked to Moriakira.

The move toward unitary inheritance led to changes in social and cul-tural practices. The most notable transformation concerned names. In Japan, male progeny were given informal counting names that designated the order of birth. The eldest was called Tarō, the first, followed by Jirō, the second, Saburō, the third, Shirō, the fourth, Gorō, the fifth, Rokurō, the sixth, Shichirō, the seventh, Hachirō, the eighth, Kurō, the ninth, and Jurō, the tenth. Ōuchi Hiroyo followed this practice in naming his eight sons. The only exception was that he named the eldest not Tarō, but rather Magotarō, or the eldest grandson. By naming his eldest son (the future Yoshihiro) Magotarō, Hiroyo emphasized their affinity, since both Yoshihiro and Hiroyo were the

---

[2] Thomas Conlan, "Shiryō shōkai: Yoshida Kanemigi ga utsushita Ōuchi keizu," *Yamaguchi kenshi kenkyū* 21 (3.2013), pp. 65–70.

[3] For the caretaker nature of his rule, see Wada Shūsaku, "Ōuchi shi no sōsho kankei o megutte," in Kage Toshio, ed., *Ōuchi to Ōtomo: Chūsei nishi Nihon no nidai daimyō* (Bensei shuppan, 2013), pp. 36–37. For Moriakira's purported drowning of his son, see p. 36 and p. 56 n. 49.

eldest males of their generation, and accordingly shared the same name.[4] Primogeniture then had no legal meaning in Japan, as the father could select the ultimate heir irrespective of birth order, but the designation of a child as the eldest carried prestige.

This practice of designating heirs through fictive counting names was unique to the Ōuchi. It started from the time of Yoshihiro, who did not name his eldest Magotarō. To the contrary, this child, born in 1394, was granted the counting name of Kurō, the ninth son, which suggested that he was Hiroyo's ninth son.[5] Kurō was, however, conceived fourteen years after Hiroyo's death and could only have been a son of Yoshihiro.[6] Perhaps Kurō's mother had been a younger consort of Hiroyo—this could account for such treatment by Yoshihiro, but the reason for this unusual naming remains unclear. Kurō later adopted the adult name Mochiyo. He shared the latter half ("yo") of his grandfather Hiroyo's name, which suggested further affinity.

By naming the eldest son Mochiyo as if he were his father's ninth child, Yoshihiro demonstrated that he did not favor this son as his potential heir. By contrast, by naming his second son (the future Mochimori) Magotarō, Yoshihiro designated him as a potential and favored heir. This arrangement has caused much confusion. Mochimori was the second son and the first heir, while Mochiyo, the eldest son, was not the initial heir.[7] Other sources reveal that from an early age Mochimori was widely accepted as Yoshihiro's original heir (Figure 5.2).[8]

[4] For evidence of Hiroyo being known as Magotarō, see Matsuoka Hisatō, *Nanbokuchō ibun Chūgoku Shikoku hen*, vol. 3 (Tōkyōdō shuppan, 1990), doc. 2537, 11.18.1353 (Bunwa 2) Ōuchi Sadahiro *chūshinjō utsushi*, pp. 182–83.

[5] See Yamaguchi kenshi hensanshitsu, comp., *Yamaguchi kenshi shiryōhen chūsei*, 4 vols. (Yamaguchi, 1996–2008), vol. 1, Kennaiki, 7.28.1441 (Kakitsu 1), p. 167 for the claim that Mochiyo was forty-eight years old at the time of his death.

[6] This naming has led to confusion, as some genealogists incorrectly assumed that Hiroyo had in fact nine sons. *Ōuchi bunka*, pp. 13, 29, 65–66 for the names of Mochimori and Mochiyo. See also the Naikaku bunko genealogy, p. 52, which lists Mochiyo as Kurō. Kondō Kiyoshi assumed that Mochiyo was the ninth and last son of Hiroyo. See Kondō Kiyoshi, *Ōuchi jitsuroku* (3rd reprint ed., Tokuyama: Matsuno shoten, 1984), p. 53. For confusion regarding Mochimori, see p. 51.

[7] For a reference to Mochiyo as being the elder brother (*shakei*) of Mochimori, see *Yamaguchi kenshi shiryōhen chūsei*, vol. 1, Kanmon gyōki, 2.29.1432 (Eikyō 4), p. 124. For an old, reliable genealogy that portrays Mochiyo as the eldest but Mochimori as the first designated heir, see Conlan, "Shiryō shōkai," pp. 65–70. This does not appear in the 1486 (Bunmei 18) genealogy, a copy of which dates from the eighteenth century. Suda Makiko, *Chūsei Nichō kankei to Ōuchi shi* (Tōkyō daigaku shuppan, 2011), pp. 221–22.

[8] Wada Shūsaku, "Ōuchi shi no sōsho kankei o megutte," pp. 34–35 for Mochimori as being initially designated as the heir. See also *Bōchō fūdo chūshin an*, vol. 14 (Yamaguchi, 1964), p. 96, and Iwakuni shi hensan iinkai, comp., *Iwakuni shishi shiryōhen*, vol. 1 (Iwakuni, 2001), p. 576 for a 1503 reference to Mochimori as being the primary heir.

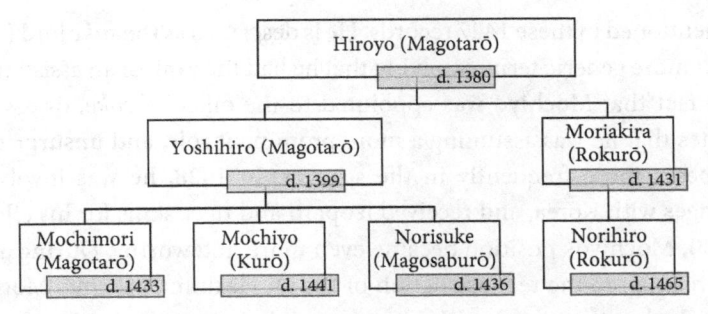

Figure 5.2 Ōuchi Hiroyo's Descendants and their Fictive Counting Names. Created by Thomas Conlan

Yoshihiro's third son was given the name Magosaburō, or third grandson, and by all accounts he was the third of Yoshihiro's children, although much about his life remained obscure. Epitomizing this confusion, some genealogies portray Norisuke as dying in 1397, when that year is more likely the time he was born. In fact, he died in 1436.[9]

In addition to these naming patterns, similarity in the first part of the names of Mochimori and Mochiyo reveals that both came of age during the time of Ashikaga Yoshimochi (1386–1428), who served as their godfather (*eboshi oya*). He in turn bestowed the "mochi" character of his name on both. This practice was not unique since Yoshihiro himself received the name "yoshi" from the shogun Ashikaga Yoshimitsu (1358–1408). To receive such a name was a great honor. As Yoshihiro's youngest son, Magosaburō, came of age after the next shogun, Yoshinori, came to power in 1429, he received the adult name of Norisuke.

Mochimori was the heir apparent of Moriakira for over two decades and as early as 1407 was referred to as *shinsuke*. This office harked back to the Ōuchi's position as deputy governors in the province and marked the holder of this office as the Ōuchi heir.[10] Twenty years later, Mochimori was still listed as the *shinsuke* lord (*shinsuke dono*) during a 1427 celebration of the rebuilding of a gate (*torii*) for the Nagato Ichinomiya shrine. Mochiyo, too, is

---

[9] For the mistaken reference see *Ōuchi bunka*, Mōri keifu, p. 53 for Norisuke's death in 1397. See also p. 66 for another reference to Norisuke as Magosaburō. For proof that Norisuke died in 1436, see Conlan, "Shiryō shōkai," p. 69.

[10] *Yamaguchi kenshi shiryōhen chūsei*, vol. 3, Kōryūji monjo, doc. 237, Kōryūji *issaikyō kanjinchō*, pp. 322–26. I viewed this document thanks to Wada Shūsaku at the Yamaguchi prefectural archives on 6.14.2015. By contrast, another, named Mitsuyo, has the title Baba *dono*, which implied a more subservient role. Itō Kōji, "Ōuchi shi to Hakata," *Shishi kenkyū Fukuoka*, no. 8 (3.2013), pp. 11–12.

first mentioned in these 1427 records. He is described as the *suke* lord (*dono*), a much more generic term, implying that he had the rank of an assistant.[11]

The fact that Mochiyo was appointed to the office of *suke*, or assistant, indicates that he was assuming a more prominent role, and unsurprisingly, he appears more frequently in the sources. In 1428, he was involved in exchanges with Korea, and received leopard and tiger skins for his efforts.[12] By 1430, Mochiyo's position became even more noteworthy. During a ceremony relating to the reconstruction of the Ōi Hachiman shrine, Moriakira is described as the great lord (*Ōdono sama*), but since no one is referred to as *shinsuke*, Mochimori had presumably lost his position as an heir. He was demoted to *sukedomo sama*, or "Mr. Assistant," while Mochiyo, reflective of his new position, is referred to quite simply the new lord (*nii dono*).[13]

Naming practices, established early in life, proved too static to justify inheritance. The position of heir was ritually demonstrated through offerings or participation in ceremonies, which served to enshrine an individual's position as heir. The whole process of inheritance remained rather fluid and murky, since ultimately it was determined by ritual performance rather than by proclamation.

As late as 1430 Mochimori continued to engage in actions suggesting that he remained the primary Ōuchi heir. In 1430, he completed the construction of Kannonji, which later become his mortuary temple, a mark of a major lord.[14] A surviving statue of him may have been originally housed in Kannonji.[15]

During 1430, Mochimori fought in Kyushu, but he was not a particularly successful commander. He lost control of Moji castle and of the Straits of Shimonoseki.[16] If Naitō Chitoku's account is to be believed, on 4.7.1431, Moriakira lost confidence in Mochimori and declared Mochimori

---

[11] Wada, "Ōuchi shi no sōsho kankei o megutte," pp. 34–36. For the relevant documents, see Sumiyoshi jinja monjo, *Yamaguchi kenshi shiryōhen chūsei*, vol. 4, doc. 140, 4.7.1427 (Ōei 34) Nagato no kuni Ichinomiya *zōritsu shūgitō chūmon an*, p. 425.

[12] *Yamaguchi kenshi shiryōhen chūsei*, vol. 1, Richō jitsuroku, 12.7.1428 (Sejong 10)/(Shōchō 1), pp. 873–74 for this reference to Mochiyo in the Korean sources.

[13] *Yamaguchi kenshi shiryōhen chūsei*, vol. 3, Ōi Hachimangū monjo no. 4, 6.5.1430 (Eikyō 2) Ōi Hachimangū *jōtō hiki uma chūmon*, pp. 949–50. See also Kawamura Kimiaki, *Hagi Abu no chūsei fūdoki* (Hagi: Mashiyama insatsu, 2010), p. 121.

[14] See the explanation of the Ōuchi Mochimori statue (*mokuzō*), *Ōuchi bunka to Kita Kyūshū* (Kita Kyūshū shiritsu shizenshi rekishi hakubutsukan, 2012), p. 15. Only one document of Mochimori survives, dating from 12.15 and found in the Zuioji monjo collection.

[15] Kannonji later became renamed as Shō'onji. The main hall of this structure, the Kannondō, was later moved to Tōshunji, where it remains. See *Ōuchi bunka to Kita Kyūshū*, p. 15, and *Ōuchi bunka*, pp. 70–71 for more photos and analysis of this statue.

[16] Kawamura Kimiaki, *Hagi Abu no Chūsei fūdoki*, pp. 122–23.

unqualified to succeed him.[17] Chitoku (d. 1439), the Ōuchi representative in the capital, was esteemed by *shugo* residing there as "a person of deep understanding and unsurpassed abilities." His account therefore carried weight there.[18]

Moriakira's disavowal of Mochimori was apparently known only to Chitoku and, at most, a few others. Prayers dating from 9.24.1431, three months after Moriakira's death, still refer to Mochimori as *shinsuke*, the title that designated the primary Ōuchi heir.[19] His position was enhanced because he had fathered a son in turn styled Magotarō.[20] These naming practices suggested that the main Ōuchi line passed from Yoshihiro to Mochimori and then, in time, to his son. On 7.19.1431 his brother Mochiyo reached out to some of the surviving kin of warriors who had been killed with Moriakira.[21] He may have canvassed them for support.

Chitoku engineered a partible succession, which designated Mochiyo as the main heir, but still gave Mochimori significant powers. During the ninth month of 1431, Mochiyo was made the nominal heir, and gained control of Suō, Buzen, and Chikuzen, having been appointed *shugo* of each of these provinces.[22] By contrast, Mochimori was confirmed as *shugo* of Nagato, and gained control of the vital ports of Tōsai and Nima.[23] The northern district

---

[17] *Yamaguchi kenshi shiryōhen chūsei*, vol. 1, Manzei jugō nikki, pp. 96–97, 9.24.1431 (Eikyō 3) for a conversation of 4.7.1431.

[18] Chitoku was held in such esteem that he was addressed as if he were a *shugo* lord. *Hagi han batsu etsu roku* (Yamaguchi ken monjokan, 1994), vol. 5, p. 232, 12.12 Yamana Tokihiro *shojō*. Early copyists mistakenly assume that the document dates from 1425 (Ōei 32), but the reference to Chikuzen means that the document in fact dates from 1429. *Yamaguchi kenshi tsūshihen chūsei* (Yamaguchi, 2012), p. 380 and p. 383 for the significance of the epistolary format. See also Kuwayama Kōnen, comp., *Muromachi bakufu hikitsuke shiryōshū shūsei*, 2 vols. (Kondō shuppansha, 1980), vol. 1, doc. 49, 8.3 [(Eikyō 3) 1431], pp. 70–71.

[19] *Yamaguchi kenshi tsūshihen furoku* CD-ROM, Tōji hyakugo monjo, Tōji Saishōkō'in *hyōjo hikitsuke* doc. 123, 9.24.1431 (Eikyō 3) Saishō kō'in *hyōjo hikitsuke*, p. 509.

[20] Ōuchi Noriyuki, otherwise known as Dōjun, shared the same counting name (Magotarō) as Mochimori and so logically would have been his son. See *Ōuchi bunka*, p. 66. For more on this possibility of descent, see Suda Makiko, "Ōuchi Noriyuki kō," in *Chūsei Nichō kankei to Ōuchi shi*, p. 249.

[21] Tanaka Hiroki, Nakajima Keiichi, Nakatsukasa Ken'ichi, Nishida Tomohiro, and Watanabe Hiroki eds., "Masuda Saneuji shozō shinshutsu chūsei monjo no shōkai," *Kokuritsu rekishi minzoku hakubutsukan kenkyū hōkoku* 212 (12.2018), doc. 31, 7.19 [(Eikyō 3) 1431] Ōuchi Mochiyo *shojō*, p. 135.

[22] *Yamaguchi kenshi shiryōhen chūsei*, vol. 1, Manzei jugō nikki, 9.3.1431 (Eikyō 3), p. 96. See also p. 94 for a 7.26 reference to Mochimori as *shinsuke*.

[23] *Yamaguchi kenshi shiryōhen chūsei*, vol. 1, Manzei jugō nikki, 10.19.1431 (Eikyō 3), p. 97 for Mochiyo as primary heir (*sōryō*) and 10.23.1431 (Eikyō 3), p. 98 for Mochimori gaining Nagato. See also 4.4.1432 (Eikyō 4), p. 111 for Mochimori's patrimony including, in addition to Nagato, Iwami's Nima district (*gun*) and Aki's Tōsai region (*chō*). *Yamaguchi kenshi tsūshihen chūsei*, pp. 383–84.

of Abu, in Nagato, belonged to neither, however, and was granted to their cousin Mitsuyo, the son of Ōuchi Mitsuhiro.[24]

Naitō Chitoku effectively advanced Ōuchi Mochiyo's interests. Having successfully shepherded Mochiyo's appointment as heir, he secured Ashikaga sanction for an Ōuchi attack on their rivals, as confirmed by the receipt of an Ashikaga battle flag and the expulsion from the capital of representatives of the Ōtomo and Shōni, who sought a pardon for these northern Kyushu warriors for their killing of Ōuchi Moriakira in 1431.[25] He also bolstered Ōuchi support among loosely allied warriors such as the Masuda of Iwami.[26]

Chitoku's successes troubled Mochimori, who resented his brother Mochiyo being made the Ōuchi chieftain (sōryō), and he appealed to the Ashikaga for support.[27] Realizing that it would not be forthcoming, he then turned against the Ashikaga, allied with the Ōtomo, and attacked Mochiyo. Mochiyo had to flee from northern Kyushu to Nagato.[28] Mochimori was supported by many warriors from northern Kyushu. He pursued Mochiyo, defeating him again at the boundary between Nagato and Iwami provinces on the night of 2.10.1432.[29] Mochiyo fled with only fifty horsemen to Iwami, and Mochimori occupied Yamaguchi on 2.13.1432.[30]

Mochimori's victory proved ephemeral. Mochiyo, with the help of Ashikaga communiqués, attracted the support of Iwami province warriors and launched a counterattack.[31] The Ashikaga tacitly allowed Mochiyo to mobilize warriors from Iwami and Aki, even though he was not the shugo of

---

[24] Mitsuhiro had lost to Yoshihiro in a battle for succession and predeceased him in 1397. Yamaguchi kenshi shiryōhen chūsei, vol. 1, Manzei jugō nikki, 9.3.1431 (Eikyō 3), p. 96.

[25] Yamaguchi kenshi tsūshihen chūsei, p. 382, and Yamaguchi kenshi shiryōhen chūsei, vol. 1, Manzei jugō nikki, 8.9.1430, p. 95. For more on Chitoku's role in determining succession, see Suda, "Ōuchi shi no zaikyō katsudō," in Kage Toshio, Ōuchi to Ōtomo, pp. 104–5.

[26] A document in the Masuda collection reveals how Chitoku relied on Ashikaga ties and documents (gonaisho) to help determine alliances and, in this case, secure the important support of the Masuda. Masuda ke monjo, vol. 1 (Tōkyō daigaku shuppankai, 2000), doc. 115, 7.28 [(Eikyō 3) 1431] Chitoku (Naitō shi) shojō kirigami, p. 99.

[27] Yamaguchi kenshi shiryōhen chūsei, vol. 1, Kanmon gyōki, 2.5.1432 (Eikyō 4), p. 124.

[28] Yamaguchi kenshi shiryōhen chūsei, vol. 1, Kanmon gyōki, 2.29.1432 (Eikyō 4), p. 124, and Yamaguchi kenshi shiryōhen chūsei, vol. 1, Manzei jugō nikki, 2.13.1432 (Eikyō 4), pp. 104–5. See also Yamaguchi kenshi tsūshihen chūsei, p. 384.

[29] Yamaguchi kenshi shiryōhen chūsei, vol. 1, Manzei jugō nikki, 2.24–25.1432 (Eikyō 4), p. 106. For analysis of where this castle was located, see Kawamura Kimiaki, Hagi Abu no Chūsei Fūdoki, p. 124.

[30] Yamaguchi kenshi shiryōhen chūsei, vol. 1, Nagato no kuni shugo shiki shidai, p. 604, and Nagato no kuni shugo daiki, p. 607. Other genealogies attribute Mochimori's entry into Yamaguchi at this same time. Agari ke monjo (Nagato shi 1995), Ōuchi ke ryaku keizu 4–8, p. 7, describes Mochimori as entering Yamaguchi on 2.18.1432 (Eikyō 4). See also Yamaguchi kenshi tsūshihen chūsei, p. 384.

[31] Yamaguchi kenshi shiryōhen chūsei, vol. 1, Manzei jugō nikki, 2.29.1432 (Eikyō 4), p. 106 for Mochiyo seeking sanctuary in Misumi castle. See also p. 107 for the Ashikaga encouraging Iwami warriors to support Mochiyo.

either province.[32] This did not prevent him from bestowing rights in Iwami, such as tax exemptions for docking ships in Misumi harbor.[33]

Mochiyo recaptured Yamaguchi on 3.15.1432. He then confiscated lands of Mochimori's supporters and granted them to Kōryūji and Nagato's Ichinomiya shrine, dedicated to Sumiyoshi, thereby rewarding gods of the stars and seas for his success.[34] The defeated Mochimori and Mitsuyo, who threw in his lot with Mochimori, both fled to Kyushu; and since Mochiyo controlled the Straits of Shimonoseki, he prevented Mochimori from crossing back to Nagato or Suō.[35] Mochimori was defeated, and his *shugo* post for Nagato, as well as rights to Nima and Tōsai, were confiscated and granted to Mochiyo.[36]

Mochimori remained allied to the Ōtomo of Bungo province in northern Kyushu.[37] The Ashikaga saw him as a threat and mobilized Aki warriors to attack him.[38] With Ashikaga support, Mochiyo gained the upper hand. As the tide turned, other prominent supporters of Mochimori, such as Sue Morimasa, who had triumphantly entered Yamaguchi with him, defected

[32] *Yamaguchi kenshi shiryōhen chūsei*, vol. 1, Manzei jugō nikki, 3.7.1432 (Eikyō 4), p. 110, and 3.18.1432 (Eikyō 4), p. 110. The Yamana served as the *shugo* for both provinces, but the Ōuchi retained rights in the districts of Nima (Iwami) and Tōsai (Aki). Yoshida Kenji, "Muromachi bakufu no shugo kokujin no rengō gun," *Chūsei shi kenkyū* 34 (2009), p. 30, discusses how the bakufu dispatched edicts of chastisement (*jibatsu rinji*) to Mochiyo for use against the Ōtomo and Shōni. See also pp. 42–43 for their bolstering of Mochiyo's authority.

[33] Nakatsukasa Ken'ichi, "Chūsei kōki Iwami kokujin no dōkō to Muromachi bakufu, daimyō," in *Iwami no Chūsei ryōshu no seisui to Higashi Ajia kai'iki sekai* (Shimane ken kodai bunka sentaa, 3.2018), p. 72 for a transcription of a 3.11.1432 (Eikyō 4) Ōuchi Mochiyo *hanmotsu*. See Ōga ke monjo, in Nakatsukasa Ken'ichi, "Bunken kara mita chūsei no Iwami no minato to ryūtsū," in Iwakuni shi hensan iinkai, comp., *Nihon no kōeki to umi* Chūsei toshi kenkyūkai hen (Yamakawa shuppankai, 2016), doc. 14, 3.11.1432 (Eikyō 4) Ōuchi Mochiyo *hanmotsu* and doc. 15 7.11.1552 (Tenbun 21) Ōuchi Haruhide Yoshinaga *andojō*, p. 103 for a 1552 confirmation of this record.

[34] *Yamaguchi kenshi shiryōhen chūsei*, vol. 1, Nagato no kuni shugo shiki shidai, p. 604, and Nagato no kuni shugo daiki, p. 607, and Manzei jugō nikki, 4.4.1432 (Eikyō 4), pp. 110–11 for Mochiyo entering Yamaguchi. The date, 3.13.1432 (Eikyō 4), is slightly earlier than what appears in other sources and is most likely a copyist's error. For his commendations, see *Yamaguchi kenshi shiryōhen chūsei*, vol. 4, Sumiyoshi jinja monjo doc. 257, 3.17.1432 (Eikyō 4) Ōuchi Mochiyo *kishinjō an*, p. 458. See also *Hagi han batsu etsu roku, Jisha shōmon*, Hikamisan Kōryūji doc. 23, 3.17.1432 (Eikyō 4) Ōuchi shi *bugyōnin rensho hōsho*, p. 162.

[35] *Yamaguchi kenshi shiryōhen chūsei*, vol. 1, Kanmon gyōki, 4.4.1432, pp. 124–25 for Mochimori's defeat and flight. For Manzei's reference to Mochiyo's control of the Straits of Shimonoseki, see Manzei jugō nikki, 4.13.1432 (Eikyō 4), p. 112.

[36] *Yamaguchi kenshi shiryōhen chūsei*, vol. 1, Manzei jugō nikki, 4.14–26.1432 (Eikyō 4), p. 112.

[37] *Yamaguchi kenshi shiryōhen chūsei*, vol. 1, Manzei jugō nikki, 5.9 and 5.19.1432 (Eikyō 4), pp. 112–13.

[38] Tōkyō daigaku shiryōhen sanjo, comp., *Mōri ke monjo*, vol. 4 (Tōkyō daigaku shuppankai, 1924), doc. 1355, 5.12 [(Eikyō 4) 1432] Ashikaga Yoshinori *gonaisho* (*kirigami*), p. 261. See also *Kobayakawa ke monjo* (Tōkyō daigaku shuppankai, 1927), vol. 2, Kobayakawa *shōmon* doc. 319, 5.12 Ashikaga Yoshinori *gonaisho utsushi*, pp. 183–84.

and joined Mochiyo's forces.[39] That administrators such as Sue Morimasa could readily shift sides and still serve on behalf of a rival Ōuchi lord suggests that their administrative skills and knowledge were favored over their allegiance to any individual.

On 4.8.1433 Mochimori was defeated and killed. His compatriot Mitsuyo embarked on a desperate journey, first to Ise where he worshiped, and then to the capital, presumably to seek a pardon, but he was apprehended and killed on 4.20.1433, thus ending the struggle for succession.[40]

With the death of Mochimori and Mitsuyo, Mochiyo became the uncontested leader of the Ōuchi domains. One important aspect of his rule is that he cemented his position as ruler by issuing laws for his lands. He first did this in 1432, while still fighting Mochimori, when he recopied regulations of 1399 and 1408 that Yoshihiro and Moriakira had previously issued.[41]

In 1439, Mochiyo initiated a policy of posting *shoheki*, or laws written on walls.[42] One of his initial regulations served to prohibit cultivators from fleeing their lands, a right that had been tacitly recognized since the Kamakura codes of 1232.[43] Claiming that such actions served as a pretext to avoid paying taxes, Mochiyo ordered these people to be captured, bound, and returned to their lands in all cases when they absconded.[44] By enforcing these edicts irrespective of the situation on estates in his lands, Mochiyo emphasized his transcendent judicial authority over all who resided in his territories. Although Mochiyo initiated these policies, his administrators wrote and copied the laws and determined that these codes would become regularized and well known.

[39] *Yamaguchi kenshi shiryōhen chūsei*, vol. 1, Nagato no kuni shugo shiki shidai, p. 604, and Nagato no kuni shugo daiki, p. 607 for Sue Morimasa. For him later serving Mochiyo, see *Hagi han batsu etsu roku, Jisha shōmon Kōryūji monjo*, doc. 24, 4.23.1432 (Eikyō 4) Ōuchi shi *bugyōnin rensho hōsho*, p. 162.

[40] *Yamaguchi kenshi shiryōhen chūsei*, vol. 1, Manzei jugō nikki, 4.20.1433 (Eikyō 5), p. 117 for Mochimori's death on 4.8.1433. See also the *Kanmon nikki*, 4.21.1433 (Eikyō 5), p. 125 for the death of Mochimori and Baba *dono* (Mitsuyo). Finally, see *Sakkaiki*, vol. 5 (Iwanami shoten, 2013), 4.21.1433 (Eikyō 5), p. 160 for Mochiyo killing his brother, a certain *shinsuke* (*shinsuke no bō*), while Mitsuyo, described here as a son of Mitsuhiro, killed himself in the capital. For references to Mitsuyo's attempt to worship at Ise, see the genealogical reference in *Ōuchi bunka*, p. 64.

[41] *Sengoku ibun Ōuchi shi hen*, vol. 1 (Tōkyōdō shuppan, 2016), doc. 454, 9.21.1479 (Bunmei 11) Ōuchi shi *kokugaryō hatto*, pp. 134–35.

[42] These laws were widely copied and survive in six variants. See Hirase Naoki, "Ōuchi shi sadamegaki (Ōuchi *shoheki*) no denpon rokushū," *Yamaguchi ken monjokan kenkyū kiyō* 18 (3.1991), pp. 65–84.

[43] *Chūsei hōsei shiryōshū*, vol. 1 (Iwanami shoten, 1955), Jōei Code, clause 42, p. 51, which stipulates that commoners (*hyakushō*) could abscond if they had paid their taxes.

[44] *Chūsei hōsei shiryōshū*, vol. 3, *Buke kahō*, vol. 1 (Iwanmi shoten, 1965), no. 4 12.19.1439 (Eikyō 11) Ōuchi shi *shoheki*, p. 35.

Since Mochiyo had no children, the question of succession remained undecided. Mochimori's eldest son survived, but being a rebel, he was ineligible. This led to the selection of Mochiyo's youngest brother as heir. He had previously taken the tonsure, since Yoshihiro's third son was not considered a likely heir, but in 1432, he was laicized, granted the name Norisuke, and given a sword that signified his appointment as the next heir.[45] A genealogy dating from the 1540s confirms this status, but Norisuke's role as heir was later forgotten since he died in an ambush in north Kyushu, not far from where his more illustrious uncle Moriakira perished.[46]

Pacifying Kyushu and Proselytizing Gods

Since Mochiyo owed his success to Ashikaga Yoshinori, both he and his heir, Norisuke, assiduously cultivated ties with the Ashikaga leader. An exchange of picture scrolls pertaining to the conquests of Hachiman highlights the cultural interactions between Mochiyo, Norisuke, and Ashikaga Yoshinori. In 1433, Ashikaga Yoshinori donated two remarkable, still surviving, scrolls to Konda Hachiman shrine, located near Sakai in what is now Ōsaka, just to the south of the tomb of the ancient ruler Ōjin (r. 270–310?). They are entitled the *Jingū kōgō engi emaki* (*Illustrated Legends of Empress Jingū*) and the *Konda sōbyō engi emaki* (*Illustrated Legends of the Konda Mausoleum*). Two sister sets of these scrolls were given to Usa Hachiman and Iwashimizu Hachiman, but these do not survive.[47]

The former scroll depicts Jingū's fictional conquest of Korea. In the narrative, the Straits of Shimonoseki and the harbors of Moji and Akamaseki are featured, and deities under the control of the Ōuchi, such as Sumiyoshi in Nagato, Usa Hachiman in Buzen, and the Kōra of Chikuzen. More remarkably, the Kōra Deity is depicted standing on a turtle, which borrows heavily from the iconography of Myōken.[48] Thus, these scrolls were not only gifts, but also served to glorify Usa Hachiman, Kōra, and Hachiman, as well as to

---

[45] *Yamaguchi kenshi shiryōhen chūsei*, vol. 1, pp. 114–15, Manzei jugō nikki, 6.3.1432 (Eikyō 4).
[46] Conlan, "Shiryō shōkai," pp. 65–70.
[47] *Emakimonoshū Habikinoshishi bunkazaihen bessatsu* (Habikino City, 1991), pp. 135–36 for the fact that three versions of these scrolls were bestowed on Konda Hachiman, Usa Hachiman, and Iwashimizu Hachiman, with only the Konda scrolls surviving.
[48] *Emakimonoshū Habikinoshishi bunkazaihen bessatsu*, pp. 69–71 for departing from Moji Akamaseki, the strategic Straits of Shimonoseki, p. 75 for Kōra shrine's deity resembling Myōken, see pp. 76–77, and pp. 78–79 for Usa and Sumiyoshi.

invoke Myōken, and by doing so emphasized the potency of the deities who resided in the Ōuchi territories.

Relations with the Ashikaga were strong, and the scrolls show how Ōuchi deities and Ashikaga deities were allied to help Jingū's conquest. Norisuke in turn had sixteen volumes of the *Hachiman emaki* copied and donated to the Usa Hachiman shrine in 1435.[49] Exchanges were not confined to these scrolls. Norisuke received an edict legitimating his conquest of Kyushu, along with a battle flag from the Ashikaga, in the third month of 1433.[50] This allowed him to command Buzen warrior families, such as the Sata, who had previously kept their distance from the Ōuchi.[51]

With the aid of families such as the Sata, Norisuke tried to pacify northern Kyushu, where support for Mochimori had been strongest. Mochiyo defeated and killed Shōni Mitsusada (d. 1433) on 8.16.1433 and continued to advance into hostile Ōtomo lands.[52] A grueling siege of the main Ōtomo castle at Himedake lasted nearly a year, from the seventh month of 1435 through the sixth month of 1436. The siege was broken at times, since Norisuke can be documented as tactically retreating from Himedake sometime before the tenth month of 1435.[53] He returned, however, and ultimately the castle fell. Over two thousand of the Ōtomo perished along with one of Ōuchi Mochimori's sons.[54] With this defeat the Ōtomo were weakened and the Ōuchi once again managed to exert control over Chikuzen province, which included much of the important trading city of Hakata.[55]

After the battle of Himedake, Norisuke continued to attack the Shōni in Chikuzen province. The sole surviving document signed by him reveals that he recommended warriors for rewards on 9.12.1436, while still in the

[49] *Usa jingūshi shiryōhen*, vol. 9 (Usa, 1993), p. 237. The source claims that Moriakira had the scroll written in 1418 (Ōei 25), but in this year, Yoshinori was not the shogun, and likewise the third son of Yoshihiro was Norisuke, not Moriakira. The date is miscopied and the document instead most likely dates from 1435.

[50] *Yamaguchi kenshi shiryōhen chūsei*, vol. 1, Manzei jugō nikki, 3.6.1433 (Eikyō 5), p. 116.

[51] Moriakira had exchanged letters with the Sata earlier, but the first sustained interactions are from the time of Mochiyo. See *Kumamoto ken shiryō chūsei hen*, vol. 2 (Kumamoto, 1962), docs. 59–65, pp. 192–96 for the relevant Sata records. For the battles and guard duty near Usa, see doc. 63, 7.16 Ōuchi Mochiyo *shojō*, p. 195. These records also appear in *Usa jingūshi shiryōhen*, vol. 9, pp. 561–63.

[52] *Yamaguchi kenshi shiryōhen chūsei*, vol. 1, Nochikagami, p. 507.

[53] *Daigoji monjo*, vol. 12 (Tōkyō daigaku shuppankai, 2001), doc. 2610, 10.7 [(Eikyō 9) 1437] Chitoku *shojō*, pp. 96–98.

[54] *Yamaguchi kenshi tsūshihen chūsei*, p. 385, and *Yamaguchi kenshi shiryōhen chūsei*, vol. 1, Kanmon gyōki, 6.2 and 6.15.1436 (Eikyō 8), p. 128.

[55] Saeki Kōji, "Ōuchi shi no Chikuzen no kuni shihai Yoshihiro ki kara Masahiro ki made," *Kyūshū chūseishi kenkyū*, vol. 1 (Fukuoka: Bunken shuppan, 1978), pp. 266–69. From 1432 (Eikyō 4) Shōni retainers had issued documents in the region but were supplanted by Ōuchi retainers in the sixth month of 1436 (Eikyō 8).

field.[56] Shortly thereafter, while campaigning in the Shōni heartlands, he was ambushed and killed along with many of his men in an attack that resembled that which had brought Moriakira low five years before.[57] Naitō Chitoku conveyed the shocking news to the capital.[58] Descendants of the dead would in turn recount how early in the tenth month of 1436, "a great number of family members and retainers" died with Norisuke, including members of the Aso and Moji families who had helped the Ōuchi to hold the Straits of Shimonoseki.[59]

With Norisuke's death, the direct descendants of Yoshihiro were all but extinct. Mochiyo, Yoshihiro's only surviving progeny, was forced to designate his nephew Norihiro (1420–65), the eldest son of Moriakira, as his heir. Norisuke's ignominious end ensured that he was mostly forgotten, although monks from his mortuary temple of Hōjuji would play an important role in later Ming trade.[60] In 1486, Norisuke, together with Mochimori, was removed from the rosters of Ōuchi successors.[61] In the 1540s, however, all Ōuchi lords and heirs would be ritually memorialized, and these rites would include Mochimori and Norisuke.[62]

After the debacle of Norisuke's defeat and death, Mochiyo continued to fight in Kyushu for years.[63] The Shōni, defeated, fled to Tsushima late in 1436,

[56] *Munakata shishi shiryōhen chūsei*, vol. 2 (Munakata, 1996), doc. 95, 9.12 [(Eikyō 8) 1436] Bō (Ōuchi ka) Norisuke *shojō*, pp. 78–79. For a photograph of the monogram, see p. 960.

[57] Kuwata Kazuaki, *Chūsei Munakata shi to Munakata sha* (Iwata shoin, 2003).

[58] The most detailed account of battle appears on the 10.14 Chitoku *shojō*. See *Daigoji monjo*, vol. 12, doc. 2643, p. 121. See also doc. 2610, p. 96 for the 10.7 Chitoku *shojō*, written a year after the events, in 1437 (Eikyō 9). Chitoku (Naitō Morisada), who "served Moriakira and Mochiyo," died at the age of eighty-one on 4.15.1438 (Eikyō 10). *Hagi han batsu etsu roku*, vol. 3, maki 99 no 2, Naitō Kogenta genealogy (*keizu*), p. 170.

[59] For Aso records, see *Fukuoka shishi shiryōhen chūsei 1 Shinai shōzai monjo* (Fukuoka-shi, 2010), Aso monjo, doc. 32-30, 12.23.1471 (Bunmei 2) Aso Zenkyō (Iehiro) *okibumi utsushi*, p. 547, and the genealogy on p. 568. See also *Moji monjo*, doc. 29, 2.23.1437 (Eikyō 9) Moji Mochiyo *tsugime andojō*, p. 41 for the death of Moji Chikatada at the battle of Saigō.

[60] Itō Kōji, *Chūsei Nihon no gaikō to zenshū* (Yoshikawa kōbunkan, 2002), pp. 154–56.

[61] *Chūsei hōsei shiryōshū*, vol. 3, *Buke kahō*, vol. 1, Ōuchi *shoheki*, 9.4.1486 (Bunmei 18), p. 73. Only the temples for Shigehiro, Hiroyuki, Hiroyo, Yoshihiro, Moriakira, Mochiyo, and Norihiro were to be included, and those for Mochimori and Norisuke, were to be omitted. See also Itō Kōji and Wada Shūsaku, eds., *Ōuchi shi no sekai o saguru* (Bensei shuppan, 2019), p. 79.

[62] This is evident from the genealogies created to memorialize these men. See Conlan, "Shiryō shōkai."

[63] Evidence stems from recommendations that he offered for warriors who fought under his command or perished with the unlucky Norisuke. See *Fukuoka shishi shiryōhen chūsei 1 shinai shozai monjo* Aso monjo, doc. 32-22, 9.10.1438 (Eikyō 10) Ashikaga Yoshinori *gohan mikyōjo utsushi*, p. 543, doc. 32-23, 9.29 Ashikaga Yoshinori *gonaisho utsushi*, p. 543, and doc. 32-24, 10.26 Ashikaga Yoshinori *gonaisho utsushi*, p. 543.

and by first month of 1437 the situation stabilized, allowing Mochiyo to return to Suō.[64]

After conquering northern Kyushu, Mochiyo concentrated on better ruling the Ōuchi territories. He exempted several Nagato temples from public levies so that they could focus on their rituals, which were important for Ōuchi rule. In doing so, he closely followed the policies of Moriakira.[65] Mochiyo also rebuilt structures for major shrines, such as a Kameyama hall (*den*) for the Nagato Ichinomiya (Sumiyoshi) shrine.[66]

Kōryūji Hikamisan was the focus of Mochiyo's attention. He commended the holdings of ten new subtemples from 1437 through 1440.[67] In all, at least nineteen such structures were built after Moriakira's time.[68] Taken individually, these confirmations may not seem remarkable, but they reveal the size of this monastic complex (*monzen machi*) south of Yamaguchi. It was as large as a small town. The rites performed there continued his predecessors' work. Perhaps unsurprisingly, Mochiyo patronized a subtemple called Kōshakuan, which was affiliated with Yoshihiro's mortuary temple, and he commended lands to it, rather than to Kokushōji, the temple that Moriakira had favored.[69]

[64] *Yamaguchi kenshi shiryōhen chūsei*, vol. 1, Kanmon gyōki 1.23.1437 (Eikyō 9), p. 128. According to the Chosŏn records, the Shōni fled to Tsushima to launch a counterattack. *Dazaifu Dazaifu Tenmangū shiryō*, vol. 13 (Dazaifu Tenmangū, 1986), Sejong Changhŏn Taewang sillok, 12.26.1436 (Sejong 18)/ (Eikyō 8), pp. 192–93. For Mochiyo's confirmation of the rights of oil sellers linked to Hakozaki shrine, see p. 195 for the documents of 5.13 and 6.12.1437 (Eikyō 9).

[65] *Yamaguchi kenshi shiryōhen chūsei*, vol. 3, Agari ke monjo, doc. 10, 2.22.1437 (Eikyō 9) Ōuchi Mochiyo *andojō*, p. 808.

[66] *Yamaguchi kenshi shiryōhen chūsei*, vol. 4, Sumiyoshi jinja zō monjo, doc. 153, 7.13 Ōuchi Mochiyo *shojō an*, p. 429. This letter was addressed to Washizu Hirotada, the deputy *shugo* of Nagato. The date is not specified, but reference to instability in Chikuzen suggests that it was written between 1435 (Eikyō 7) and 1437 (Eikyō 9).

[67] *Yamaguchi kenshi shiryōhen chūsei*, vol. 3, Yamaguchi monjokan shozō Kōryūji monjo, docs. 9–11, 13, 15, 17, 2.12.1437 (Eikyō 9) Ōuchi Mochiyo *kishinjō an*, pp. 233–35. *Yamaguchi kenshi shiryōhen chūsei*, vol. 2, doc. 2, 2.12.1439 (Eikyō 11) Ōuchi Mochiyo *kishinjō*, p. 442, doc. 8 2.12.1437 (Eikyō 9) Ōuchi Mochiyo *kishinjō*, pp. 443–44. See also *Yamaguchi kenshi shiryōhen chūsei*, vol. 2, Kōryūji monjo, doc. 1, 2.25.1437 (Eikyō 9) Ōuchi Mochiyo *andojō*, p. 442, doc. 6, 2.25.1440 (Eikyō 12) Ōuchi Mochiyo *andojō*, p. 443, and *Yamaguchi kenshi shiryōhen chūsei*, vol. 3, doc. 14, 16, 2.12.1439 (Eikyō 11) Ōuchi Mochiyo *kishinjō an*, p. 235.

[68] Maki Takayuki, "Suō Ōuchi shi to sono ujidera Kōryūji," pp. 123–27 for insightful analysis of how the Ōuchi collected funds. For the sources, see *Yamaguchi kenshi shiryōhen chūsei*, vol. 3, Kōryūji monjo, docs. 154, 202–3, pp. 294, 310–11, docs. 237–38, Kōryūji *issaikyō kanjinchō*, pp. 322–26, and *Ōuchi bunka*, pp. 365–68. Suda Makiko analyzes this in her *Chūsei Nichō kankei to Ōuchi shi*, pp. 154–60.

[69] Inoue Minoru, *Hagi Hakubutsukan kitaku Sugi ke monjo*, Hagi hakubutsukan kenkyū hōkoku no. 3 (3.2008), doc. 32, 2.28.1439 (Eikyō 11) Ōuchi Mochiyo *kishinjō* granting lands from Suō to Kōshakuan, p. 6, and doc. 33, 2.28.1439 (Eikyō 11) Ōuchi Mochiyo *kishinjō an*, p. 6 for an explanation to Sue Morimasa of how these holdings were to be administered by a representative (*daikan*). Finally, see doc. 34, 9.29 Ōuchi Mochiyo *azukejō*, p. 6, grants of the legacy of Sugi Jirō, who had supported Mochimori.

Expanding Commerce

Mochiyo was able to expand the temple buildings in part because of his impressive wealth. A hoard of coins found at Kōryūji reveals its extent. During the 1430s, Japan experienced an expansion in the intensity and volume of international commerce. Pottery, coins, and the size of ships indicate a direct and ongoing engagement with East Asia distinctly greater than before.[70] This trade expanded and continued irrespective of the turmoil in Ōuchi leadership and was emblematic of stable infrastructure and administration. The amount of Ming coins imported during the fifteenth century was vast. One mission returned to Japan in 1433 with fifty million coins![71]

Trading ships of unprecedented size possessed complex rigging for their sails.[72] Early evidence of such a large craft appears in a 1437 letter by Naitō Chitoku, which refers to a ship transporting two thousand *koku* of taxable goods from one Kyushu estate to the capital.[73] Since one *koku* equals 85 liters, this cargo would constitute 170,000 liters of rice, or the same volume as 1,069 barrels of oil.

The *Jingū kōgō engi emaki*, scrolls dating from 4.22.1433 that glorify Jingū's conquest of Korea, depict these large ships.[74] The skillfully created scrolls are wonderfully anachronistic, since they represent fifteenth-century contemporary styles of armor and ships rather than anything remotely resembling the fictional third century. The scrolls show large vessels with sails, rigging, and plank-on-keel construction.[75]

Why these dramatically larger craft appeared at this time is a mystery, but perhaps continental shipwrights, based most likely in Fujian, made their way

[70] For the notion of the "Age of Commerce," see Anthony Reid, *Southeast Asia in the Age of Commerce*, 2 vols. (New Haven: Yale University Press, 1988); for the early concept of the "Commercial Revolution" see Robert S. Lopez, *The Commercial Revolution of the Middle Ages* (New York: Cambridge University Press, 1976), pp. 56–147.

[71] Richard von Glahn, "Chinese Coin and Changes in Monetary Preferences in Maritime East Asia in the Fifteenth–Seventeenth Centuries," *Journal of the Economic and Social History of the Orient* 57 (2014), p. 637.

[72] These boats first appeared during the 1430s and are depicted in the contemporaneous *Jingū kōgō engi emaki*. See *Emakimonoshū Habikinoshishi bunkazaihen bessatsu*. For the characterization of these ships as being unprecedented in size, and the "largest vessels unheard of at the times, even in travel to mainland," see Damien, "Late Medieval Japan's Seto Inland Seascape: Shipping, Sailors and Seafaring," PhD dissertation, University of Southern California, 5.2015, p. 59.

[73] *Daigoji monjo*, vol. 12, doc. 2610 10.7 [(Eikyō 9) 1437] Chitoku *shojō*, pp. 96–97.

[74] They were bestowed by the shogun Ashikaga Yoshinori to the Konda Hachiman shrine on 4.22.1433.

[75] *Emakimonoshū Habikinoshishi bunkazaihen bessatsu*, pp. 132–143. At the time that these scrolls were created, Yoshinori welcomed Korean visitors to his Muromachi compound. See *Sakkaiki*, vol. 5, 1.26.1433 (Eikyō 5), p. 120.

to Japan and helped to build these great ships in ports such as Moji. This period was one of great shipbuilding and coincides with the seven great expeditions of the Ming admiral Zheng He. From 1405 through 1433, He commanded a fleet of ships, the largest of which were over two hundred feet long, to destinations in Southeast Asia, the Indian Ocean, and Eastern Africa.[76] These ships would have last been rebuilt and overhauled in 1430,[77] so there could have been a glut of shipbuilders looking for employment in the 1430s.

The Ōuchi were not the only ones in Japan who oversaw such maritime trade, since they were in competition with the Ashikaga. In 1431 Ashikaga Yoshinori asked the *shugo* lords to provide large amounts of sulfur for tributary trade with Ming China, and in 1433 he also rebuilt the docking facilities at the harbor of Hyōgo for these large ships.[78] When Yoshinori dispatched a fleet of five vessels to the Ming in 1432, none sponsored by the Ōuchi was included, but once they had left Hyōgo harbor, one of Mochiyo's tagged along. He notified the Ashikaga, and apparently Yoshinori did not object.[79] Ming representatives also seem to have favored Mochiyo. When the Ming dispatched an ambassador to Japan in 1434, he lodged at Mochiyo's Rokujō residence when visiting Kyoto.[80]

Yoshinori, in contrast to his predecessor Yoshimochi, accepted Ming appointment to the title of "King of Japan" and took a leading role in the China trade. As to Mochiyo, he dabbled in the China trade but focused his attention more on Korea. When communicating with Korea, Mochiyo emphasized his Paekche kingly descent.[81] Under his watch, levies for porters and horses

---

[76] Ming histories have exaggerated the size of the ships of Zheng He. Sally Church, "Zhen He: An Investigation into the Plausibility of 450-ft Treasure Ships," *Monumenta Serica* 53 (2005) (accessed 11.28.2020), http://www.jstor.org/stable/40727457. The very largest ships may have been 200 feet long, but most of the big ships were 150–175 feet long. See pp. 26 and 38. Church also suggests that Fujian, rather than Nanjing, seems to have been the most likely site of shipbuilding. See pp. 24–25. For Japanese innovations in shipbuilding at this time, see William Wayne Farris, "Shipbuilding and Nautical Technology in Japanese Maritime History: Origins to 1600," *The Mariner's Mirror* vol. 95 no. 3 (8.2009), pp. 272–76.

[77] Church, "Zheng He," pp. 20–21.

[78] *Hyōgo kenshi*, vol. 3 (Hyōgo, 1978), pp. 318–24.

[79] *Yamaguchi kenshi shiryōhen chūsei*, vol. 1, Manzei jugō nikki, 9.26.1432 (Eikyō 4), p. 115, and 10.23.1432 (Eikyō 4), p. 116.

[80] Kobata Atsushi first provided an overview of Mochiyo's trading actions in 1432–33 in his *Chūsei Nisshi tsūkō bōekishi no kenkyū* (Tōkōshoin, 1941), p. 69. For this reference to Mochiyo's residence serving as lodging for the Chinese (lit. Tang) ambassador, see *Yamaguchi kenshi shiryōhen chūsei*, vol. 1, Manzei jugō nikki, 1.22.1434 (Eikyō 6), p. 119. Sadly, this residence burned down on 2.14.1434 (Eikyō 6). See *Yamaguchi kenshi shiryōhen chūsei*, vol. 1, Manzei jugō nikki, 1.22.1434 (Eikyō 6), p. 119.

[81] *Yamaguchi kenshi shiryōhen chūsei*, vol. 1, Richō jitsuroku, 6.10.1438 (Sejong 20)/6.9.1438 (Eikyō 10), p. 877.

involved in shipping to Korea continued in 1443, following the 1423 precedent of Moriakira.[82] This Korean trade continued, apparently unabated, and does not seem to have been greatly affected by the turmoil that the Ōuchi experienced.

Wealth accumulated in the burgeoning city of Yamaguchi. Two great hoards of coins provide powerful evidence of Yamaguchi as a commercial center. One, discovered in 1972 at Hikamisan, consists of 89,000 coins, weighing 648 pounds (294 kilograms), while the second, the Shimo Migita hoard, discovered in 2012 at Hōfu (Sabaryō), consists of 13,495 coins and weighs 132 pounds (60 kilograms).[83] Some 17.4 percent (1,527 out of 12,141) of the Hikamisan hoard consists of coins from either the Ming dynasty, or Chosŏn Korea, while the Shimo Migita horde contains 19.6 percent (1,887 out of 13,492) recently minted Korean and Chinese coins.[84]

The increasing number of newly minted coins can be traced to developments during the time of Moriakira and Mochiyo. The newest coins in the Hikamisan hoard are from Chosŏn Korea and date from 1423, which means that they were imported during or after that year. However, there are no Ming coins from 1433. As those Ming coins were commonly imported to Japan, this hoard was buried before any of the 1433 coins reached Japan. In contrast, the Shimo Migita hoard from Hōfu has 178 Ming coins dating from 1433, meaning that it dates from 1433 or later.[85] A remarkable increase in Chosŏn coins is evident as well, with only 13 appearing in the older Hikamisan hoard, but 102 in the newer Shimo Migita one. These numbers may seem small, but Chosŏn coins were not minted in great numbers and were only sent as part of official transactions, thereby revealing an intensification of exchanges.

The discovery of these hoards in Yamaguchi points to another process. Because the great harbor region of Hakata suffered from violence in the 1430s and 1440s, it would have been prudent for merchants and officials to

[82] *Yamaguchi kenshi shiryōhen chūsei*, vol. 4, Inomiya monjo, doc. 224, 8.9.1443 (Kakitsu 3) Ōuchi shi *bugyōnin rensho hōsho*, p. 207.

[83] http://db.yamahaku.pref.yamaguchi.lg.jp/db/kouko/syuzou_ko_06_01.html and http://komiyama.gr.jp/treasure/news2008-2013.html for the Hikamisan hoard (accessed 11.2.2019). For the 2012 discovery, see http://www.ysn21.jp/~eipos/data/01_IM/03_tiikirekisi/IM32_001_216/IM32_077.html. In other cases, smaller amounts of coins, a fragment of a larger hoard, have been uncovered where the Niho (Tairako) lived, but they are not analyzed here. For the Niho coins, see "Maruyama iseki daisen chōsa," *Yamaguchi bunkazai nenpō* 4 (2009) (Yamaguchi kyōiku iinkai, 2011), pp. 71–73.

[84] "Maruyama iseki daisen chōsa," p. 73.

[85] A total of 2,100 Ming coins and 13 Chosŏn coins for a total of 2,113 out of 12,141 for the Hikamisan horde, and 2,647 out of 13,492 coins for the Shimo Migita, with 102 constituting Chosŏn coins. "Maruyama iseki daisen chōsa," p. 73.

store coins in a more stable region than the harbor fought over by the Ōuchi and the Ōtomo.[86] Although evidence for coin usage overall increased during the fifteenth century, archaeologists have noted a pronounced decrease in coins in fifteenth-century Hakata, in contrast to their fourteenth-century abundance.[87] In contrast, trade flourished in Nima, which was under uncontested Ōuchi control.[88] Trade seems to have shifted to harbors like Nima, and coins were shipped to Yamaguchi precisely at the time when such hoards disappear in Hakata.[89]

An Unexpected Death

Mochiyo had unified the Ōuchi under his rule, established encompassing legal jurisdiction, and expanded the size of religious institutions such as Kōryūji. He also pacified northern Kyushu, giving him unfettered access to the port of Hakata, and oversaw expanding trade with Korea. Mochiyo owed his success in part to support from the Ashikaga, but his dependence on the mercurial leader Ashikaga Yoshinori caused him problems. The death of Naitō Chitoku in 1439 left him without a skilled negotiator in the capital, and he suffered for it.

In 1439, Ashikaga Yoshinori notified Mochiyo that he intended to pardon the Shōni. To make matters worse for Mochiyo, Yoshinori also confiscated the port of Tōsai because, in his view, Mochiyo had not traveled to Kyoto as quickly as Yoshinori would have liked.[90] Mochiyo attempted to rectify these

[86] See "Hakata kozu," Ōuchi bunka to Kita Kyūshū, p. 55. for an explanation for how both the Ōuchi and Ōtomo had separate trading headquarters in Hakata in the fifteenth century, with the former at Okinohama and the latter at Hakatahama. For Hakata trade, ties with Tsushima and the evets of the 1430s, see Itō Kōji, Chūsei no Hakata to Ajia (Bensei shuppan 2021), pp. 152–55. According to Itō, Mochiyo gained clear control over Hakata from the fifth month of 1436 (Eikyō 8).

[87] For a helpful overview, see Richard von Glahn, "The Ningbo-Hakata Merchant Network and the Reorientation of East Asian Maritime Trade, 1150–1350," Harvard Journal of Asiatic Studies 74.2 (2014), pp. 260–62.

[88] Ōba Yasutoki, "Hakata to Iwami ginzan: Minato no shiten kara," Iwami ginzan iseki te-ma betsu chosa kenkyū hōkokushō 1 (3.2011), pp. 97–110.

[89] In Iwami, only one harbor had evidence of imported pottery in the fourteenth century, but this expanded to eleven sites during the fifteenth century. Shinkawa Takashi, "Tōjiki kara mita Iwami ginzan shūhen chiiki Nima chō shutsudo shiryō o chūshin ni," Sekai isan Iwami ginzan iseki no chōsa kenkyū 3 (3.2013), p. 13.

[90] Ninagawa ke monjo, vol. 1 (Tōkyō daigaku shuppankai, 1981), doc. 54, Norihiro (Ōuchi Norihiro) jōsho an, pp. 111–12. See also Saeki Kōji, "Muromachi jidai ni okeru Ōuchi shi to Shōni shi-Ninagawa ke monjo Ōuchi Norihiro jōsho an no kentō," Shien 130 (3.1993), pp. 1–26, and Fujii, Muromachiki daimyō kenryokuron (Dōseisha, 2013), p. 192.

unfavorable rulings by issuing a flurry of prayers to Sumiyoshi shrine.[91] He composed *waka* poems with the introductory lines: "The country of the divine winds (*kamikaze*) prospers."[92] Mochiyo also attempted to influence the sea gods with other poetic offerings, but to no avail.[93]

In 1440 the chancellor (*kanrei*) Hosokawa Mochiyuki (1400–1442) informed Mochiyo that the Shōni pardon would not be revoked, and that the confiscation of Tōsai was settled as well.[94] Mochiyo traveled to Kyoto in 1440 in an attempt to restore his ownership of Tōsai and to check the ambitions of the Shōni.[95] He prepared for an extended stay and built a lodging in Kyoto at the intersection of Higashi Tōin and Nakanomikado, a location far more central than Moriakira's.[96] On arrival there he attempted to negotiate the restoration of Tōsai to Ōuchi control and to protest the Shōni pardon.[97]

Mochiyo's sojourn in the capital brought him and his men into close contact with other *shugo*, and this led to bloodshed. During the first month of 1441, one of Mochiyo's retainers was wounded by a follower of Akamatsu Mitsumasa (d. 1445). To secure redress, Mochiyo's forces surrounded the Akamatsu mansion and successfully demanded that the culprit be handed over.[98] This marks the beginning of hostilities between these two lords. While

---

[91] *Yamaguchi kenshi shiryōhen chūsei*, vol. 4, p. 269, Irie monjo, doc. 1, 12.8.1439 (Eikyō 11) Ōuchi Mochiyo *ganmon utsushi*, p. 269. See also Sumiyoshi jinja zō monjo, doc. 248, 12.8.1439 (Eikyō 11), p. 456. For other prayers to Sumiyoshi see doc. 22, 12.8 Ōuchi Mochiyo *shojō*, p. 391.

[92] The precise dating of these documents is not clear, but 1439 is most likely. *Yamaguchi kenshi shiryōhen chūsei*, vol. 4, Sumiyoshi jinja zō monjo, doc. 23, 10.29 Ōuchi Mochiyo *shojō*, pp. 391–92, and doc. 242, 10.29 Ida Hide'ie *shojō an*, pp. 454–55 for details of the dream from Ida Hide'ie, and how it became the basis for a later religious performance (*hōgaku*).

[93] *Yamaguchi kenshi shiryōhen chūsei*, vol. 4, Sumiyoshi jinja zō monjo, doc. 249, 12.13 Ōuchi Mochiyo *hōnō waka narabi ni shojō an*, p. 456, and doc. 250, Ōuchi Mochiyo *hōnō waka an*, pp. 456–57. For Mochiyo's skill as a *waka* poet, see *Ōuchi bunka*, p. 29. Mochiyo had poems included in various anthologies, and one won him promotion to the fourth court rank. For monks later reminiscing about his *waka*, see *Yamaguchi kenshi shiryōhen chūsei*, vol. 1, Gaun Nikken roku batsuyū, of 8.7.1459 (Chōroku 3), p. 175.

[94] *Ninagawa ke monjo*, vol. 1, doc. 28, Ōuchi shi *monjo an*, pp. 43–44 for a 2.25.1440 (Eikyō 12) *Kanrei* Hosokawa Mochiuji *hōsho an*. See also doc. 54, Norihiro (Ōuchi Norihiro) *jōsho an*, p. 112 for confirmation that this was when Shōni Yoshiyori was pardoned. For the view from Kyushu, see *Dazaifu Dazaifu Tenmangū shiryō*, vol. 13, 2.25.1440 (Eikyō 12), pp. 202–4.

[95] *Aso monjo*, vol. 2 (Tōkyō daigaku shuppankai, 1933), Aso monjo *utsushi* no. 8, 4.19.1440 (Eikyō 12) Ōuchi Mochiyo *shojō utsushi*, p. 201. See also Fujii, *Muromachiki daimyō kenrokuron*, pp. 192–93. Fujii postulates that Mochiyo traveled back and forth from Kyoto, but Norihiro refers to Mochiyo's traveling to Kyoto in 1440 (Eikyō 12). *Ninagawa ke monjo*, vol. 1 doc. 54, Norihiro (Ōuchi Norihiro) *jōsho an*, p. 112.

[96] Tasaka Yasuyuki, "Muromachiki Kyōto no kūkan kōzō to shakai," in Momosaki Yūichirō and Yamada Kunikazu, eds., *Muromachi Seiken no shufu kōsō to Kyōto Muromachi Kitayama Higashiyama: Heiankyō Kyōto kenkyū sōsho* (Bunrikaku, 2016), p. 60.

[97] *Yamaguchi kenshi shiryōhen chūsei*, vol. 1, Kennaiki, 6.24.1441 (Kakitsu 1), p. 166.

[98] *Kanmon nikki*, 1.11.1441 (Eikyō 13) *Zoku gunsho ruijū hoi* (Zoku gunsho ruijū kanseikai, 1930), vol. 2, p. 597. This passage was mentioned by Fujii, *Muromachiki daimyō kenryokuron*, p. 193.

in Kyoto, Mochiyo continued to govern his western territories from afar, and his last verifiable document, a confirmation of Kokubunji as a prayer site for the realm, dates from the fourth month of 1441.[99]

Mochiyo accompanied Ashikaga Yoshinori to a Noh (*sarugaku*) performance at the Akamatsu mansion on 6.24.1441. At the climactic moment of the play *Unoha* (*Cormorant Feathers*), when a fisherwoman appeared as the sea goddess Toyotahime, the participants heard something like thunder and a band of warriors leaped from behind a screen. Engrossed in the play, and most likely inebriated, the surprised audience was attacked. Yoshinori could not defend himself from dozens of assassins and died "a dog's death."[100] Yamana Hirotaka and a few other *shugo* died with him, but Hosokawa Mochiyuki, the chancellor (*kanrei*), and most *shugo* present simply fled. Only Mochiyo and Hosokawa Mochiharu (1400–1466) fought back with short swords. They killed none but suffered serious wounds themselves.[101] Accounts of Mochiyo's bravery were later broadcast to Korea. The *Haedong chegukki* of Shin Sukchu describes how Mochiyo fought so hard that he "broke his spear but escaped by climbing over a fence."[102]

Mortally wounded, Mochiyo lingered for over a month. He requested that no burial service be performed but instead demanded that his remains be sent to a temple in Kyushu, with the only funeral service necessary being the slaughter of the Akamatsu plotters.[103] Madenokōji Tokifusa (1394–1457) wrote that rumors of this request were "the work of devils."[104] He perceived Mochiyo's attitude, at least as it was portrayed in these potentially apocryphal rumors, as causing disorder in the realm.

So ended the life of Mochiyo. He gained his position thanks to the support of Ashikaga Yoshinori, and he tirelessly attacked the Ōtomo and Shōni on

---

[99] *Yamaguchi kenshi shiryōhen chūsei*, vol. 2, Kokubunji monjo, doc. 28, 4.28.1441 (Kakitsu 1) Ōuchi Mochiyo *andojō*, p. 409.

[100] *Yamaguchi kenshi shiryōhen chūsei*, vol. 1, Kanmon gyōki, 6.25.1441 (Kakitsu 1), pp. 129–30, translated by Thomas Conlan, *Samurai and the Warrior Culture of Japan, 471–1877: A Sourcebook* (Indianapolis: Hackett, 2022), pp. 178–80. See also the *Kakitsuki, Gunsho ruijū*, vol. 20 (Zoku gunsho ruijū kanseikai, 1959), p. 319. For the play *Unoha*, Royall Tyler, trans., *To Hallow Genji: A Tribute to Noh* (Createspace Independent Publishing, 2013), pp. 227–39.

[101] *Yamaguchi kenshi shiryōhen chūsei*, vol. 1, Kanmon gyōki, 6.25.1441 (Kakitsu 1), pp. 129–30, and Kennaiki, 6.24.1441 (Kakitsu 1), pp. 165–66.

[102] Kenneth Robinson, "Korean Chronicles of Japanese Emperors and Kings: An Annotated Translation from *Haedong chegukki*," *Journal of Northeast Asian History* 8.2 (2011), p. 177.

[103] Paraphrased from *Yamaguchi kenshi shiryōhen chūsei*, vol. 1, Kennaiki, 7.17, 23, 28.1441 (Kakitsu 1), pp. 166–67. Fujii claims that Madenokōji Tokifusa must have been mistaken, and that Mochiyo more likely would have wanted to have been buried in Yamaguchi. See Fujii, *Muromachiki daimyō kenryokuron*, pp. 193–94.

[104] *Yamaguchi kenshi shiryōhen chūsei*, vol. 1, Kennaiki, 7.17.1441 (Kakitsu 1), p. 166.

behalf of the Ashikaga. His brother and heir died in battle, leading to the near extinction of Yoshihiro's line, save for last one surviving son of Mochimori who had become an implacable foe.

Mochiyo unified the Ōuchi domains under his rule, promulgated laws for all these lands, and served as the *shugo* of the four provinces of Suō, Nagato, Buzen, and Chikuzen. But his dependence on Ashikaga Yoshinori proved poisonous, for his failure to pay obeisance in the capital led to a damaging divestment of rights to Tōsai and caused Ashikaga Yoshinori to pardon his enemies, the Shōni. This forced Mochiyo to travel to Kyoto, where he argued his case against an arbitrary and despotic shogun, but found himself an unfortunate bystander to an assassination, and this cost him his life. With his passing ended Yoshihiro's line, the pattern of fraternal succession, and Yoshihiro's custom of relying on Ashikaga support to bolster his cause among the Ōuchi.

Now the Ōuchi had a new enemy, the Akamatsu. They also had a new lord, Norihiro, a son of Moriakira, who realized that reliance on the Ashikaga did not serve Ōuchi interests. Norihiro would not act as an agent of the Ashikaga, for he had seen that a policy of resistance was preferable to an ultimately self-defeating policy of accommodation. Likewise, he benefited from a stable and experienced core of administrators who helped ensure the stability of his rule during a time when new alliances and new vendettas would emerge, as Ōuchi survivors came to perceive the Ashikaga, Akamatsu, and Hosokawa as implacable foes. The work of devils was about to begin.

6

Trader, Shogun, King, and God

During his twenty-four years of rule, Ōuchi Norihiro (1420–65) built on the accomplishments of his forebears, most particularly his father Moriakira. Norihiro could rely upon a stable, able body of administrators in managing his lands and overseeing trade. He even attempted to establish a new warrior government based on the example of the Kamakura bakufu (1185–1333). His actions threatened the Ashikaga shogunate, whose feckless leader Yoshimasa (1436–90) declared war on Norihiro in 1465. Although Norihiro would die shortly thereafter, in 1486 he was posthumously honored with apotheosis as a *daimyōjin* (Radiant Wisdom Deity).

Outbreaks of violence marked the beginning (1441) of Norihiro's rule and its end (1465). The assassination of Ashikaga Yoshinori in 1441 and the death of his uncle Mochiyo led to an upheaval in the west, as old Ōuchi enemies (the Ōtomo and Shōni) strove to wrest northern Kyushu from Ōuchi control. Norihiro vanquished them, and then governed far flung provinces and harbors effectively. He also stabilized Ōuchi succession along the lines of direct generational descent. His successors expressed their debt to him by mimicking his distinctive signature; at times their monograms were all but indistinguishable from his own.[1]

Norihiro has not been well studied, perhaps because of difficulties with the sources on him. Norihiro often relied on undated letters for communication, making even a chronological reconstruction of his life challenging. Compounding the task, some events under his watch, such as the slaughter of over a thousand Washizu and their supporters in Nagato in 1447–48, were almost entirely erased from the historical record.

Norihiro participated in the burgeoning trade of the first half of the fifteenth century. His attention focused on East Asian trade, especially on Korea. His slaughter of the Washizu, who resided in Nagato, was linked to

---

[1] That was particularly true for Norihiro's grandson Yoshioki. For this insight, I am indebted to Wada Shūsaku, conversation 6.11–12.2016.

Kings in All but Name. Thomas D. Conlan, Oxford University Press. © Oxford University Press 2024.
DOI: 10.1093/oso/9780197677339.003.0007

his attempt to control this trade directly, and he established close ties with Chosŏn Korea, profiting mightily.

These trading ties were enhanced with ethnic appeals of shared ancestry. Norihiro explained Ōuchi origins to both Korean and Japanese audiences, and received widespread recognition in both places of his distinct Tatara ethnicity. To Chosŏn officials, he emphasized common ancestry and affinities, highlighting descent from Paekche kings, as well as their imagined ties to Buddhist founders in Japan. Chosŏn recognition of this affinity enhanced mutually beneficial cooperation with the Ōuchi, although these close ties would cause some Ōuchi rivals to emphasize their alien "non-Japanese" nature. The Ashikaga would have been aware of and threatened by Ōuchi power, coupled by their claims of kingly origins, which would have made them the equals, if not superiors, of the shoguns of Japan.

Late in life, Norihiro became the center of an anti-Ashikaga faction, and ruled without regard to official appointment and attempted to establish his own warrior regime. These ambitions would not, however, survive the wars that erupted in Norihiro's waning years. Norihiro gained enough power to oppose the Ashikaga because of his control over the copper trade, and ability to ship this profitable commodity to Korea and China. This meant that the potential loss of a major port was *casus belli*, and with his resources at hand, he believed that he could supplant the Ashikaga.

Early Life

Norihiro was born on 3.20.1420. Some debate exists about his parentage. His mother's identity is not known. Norihiro was styled as Rokurō ("Sixth Son"), a counting name that he shared with Moriakira, which suggested affinity, particularly because Moriakira did not have six sons. At sixteen (1436) Norihiro was adopted by his uncle Mochiyo (1394–1441) and made the Ōuchi heir. This has led many Ōuchi genealogists to assume incorrectly that Norihiro's father was either Mochiyo or Mochimori (d. 1433), his uncles and predecessors as Ōuchi chieftain or heir.[2] A letter from Norihiro's grandson

[2] According to Shin Sukchu's *Haedong chegukki* (J. *Kaitō shokokuki*), written in 1471, Norihiro was the nephew (*oi*) of Mochiyo. Tanaka Takeo et al., eds., *Kaitō shokokuki* (Iwanami bunko, 1991), p. 150. Many later genealogies mistakenly characterize Norihiro as Mochiyo's actual son. See *Yamaguchi shishi Ōuchi bunka* (Yamaguchi, 2010) (hereafter *Ōuchi bunka*), Mōri genealogy, p. 29. Others describe him as a second son of Mochimori. See the Tatara genealogy, *Ōuchi bunka*, p. 13, the *Agari ke*

proves, however, that Moriakira (1377–1431), who would have been forty-four years old at the time, was in fact Norihiro's father.[3]

Little is known about Norihiro during the years of Mochiyo's rule save that Norihiro accompanied Mochiyo to the capital in 1440. The future Ōuchi lord was lucky not to have been invited to the Noh performance in 1441 that led to the assassination of Ashikaga Yoshinori and the mortal wounding of Mochiyo. Norihiro returned to Yamaguchi after Mochiyo's death, now as the Ōuchi leader.[4] There he prepared to attack the Akamatsu, and fulfill Mochiyo's dying request to take their heads, advancing into Aki province at the head of an army on 9.8.1441.[5]

While Norihiro was preoccupied with his campaign against the Akamatsu, Shōni Noriyori (1426–69) and his Ōtomo allies seized Chikuzen province in northern Kyushu, pushing out the Ōuchi entirely.[6] Their supporters included a rival styled Ōuchi Magotarō, also known as Noriyuki, who was a disgruntled cousin of Norihiro, and most likely the son of Ōuchi Mochimori.[7] Noriyori's and Noriyuki's rebellion forced Norihiro to abandon his campaign. With the approval of Hosokawa Mochiyuki (1400–1442), the shogunal chancellor (*kanrei*) and the most prominent surviving bakufu leader, he dispatched his army to the west and attacked the Chikuzen rebels.[8] Hosokawa Mochiyuki,

monjo Ōuchi ke *ryaku keizu*, p. 10, and *Jōeiji shiryō* (Yamaguchi, 1978), doc. 48, Ōuchi *dono gosenzō shidai*, p. 51.

[3] For Norihiro's grandson describing Moriakira as his great-grandfather, see *Sengoku ibun Ōuchi shi hen*, vol. 2 (Tōkyōdō shuppan, 2017), doc. 1167, 10.13 [(Bunki 2) 1502] Ōuchi Yoshioki *shojō*, p. 76.

[4] *Agari ke monjo*, Ōuchi ke *ryaku keizu*, p. 10 for his return there in the eighth month of 1441.

[5] *Ninagawa ke monjo*, vol. 1 (Tōkyō daigaku shuppankai, 1981), doc. 28, Ōuchi shi *monjo an*, 9.27 Iio Sadatsura *renshojō*, p. 43, and doc. 54, Norihiro *jōsho an*, pp. 111–12 for Norihiro's intent to attack the Akamatsu in Harima and his later return to Buzen.

[6] He described his authority there as being nonexistent (*sata ni oyobazu*). *Ninagawa ke monjo*, vol. 1, doc. 54, Norihiro *jōsho an*, pp. 111–12. See also Saeki Kōji, "Muromachi jidai ni okeru Ōuchi shi to Shōni shi-Ninagawa ke monjo 'Ōuchi Norihiro jōsho an' no kentō," *Shien* 130 (3.1993), p. 9.

[7] His name Magotarō suggests that he was a son of Norihiro's uncle Mochimori. *Sengoku ibun Ōuchi shi hen*, vol. 1 (Tōkyōdō shuppan, 2016), doc. 575, 11.27.1484 (Bunmei 16) Sue Hiromori *shōzōsan*, pp. 182–83. Jinson describes him as being an uncle to Norihiro's son Masahiro. See Yamaguchi kenshi hensanshitsu, comp., *Yamaguchi kenshi shiryōhen chūsei*, 4 vols. (Yamaguchi, 1996–2008), vol. 1, Daijōin jisha zōjiki, 5.22.1470 (Bunmei 2), p. 204. For his identity as Mochimori's son, see Suda Makiko, "Ōuchi Noriyuki kō," in *Chūsei Nichō kankei to Ōuchi shi* (Tōkyō daigaku shuppan, 2011), pp. 248–49, and Wada Shūsaku, "Ōuchi shi no sōsho kankei o megutte," in Kage Toshio, ed., *Ōuchi to Ōtomo: Chūsei nishi Nihon no nidai daimyō* (Bensei shuppan, 2013), p. 40. According to the genealogies reproduced in *Yamaguchi shishi*, Magotarō variously appears as the son of Mochimori (p. 14), Mochiyo (p. 29), Moriakira (p. 66), or either of Mochimori or Norihiro (p. 53). Lore found in his mortuary temple describes Noriyuki as Mochimori's son. *Bōchō jisha yurai*, vol. 3 (Yamaguchi, 1933), Kōtakuji, p. 447.

[8] Accordingly, Norihiro received a battle flag and an edict justifying his campaign.

unable adequately to defend Ashikaga interests, delegated authority to Norihiro and encouraged warriors from the provinces of Aki and Iwami, who had no official reason to join Norihiro's forces, to serve under his command.[9] Finally, in what constituted a major concession, Mochiyuki restored the vital port of Tōsai to Norihiro, thereby undoing Ashikaga Yoshinori's confiscation of it.[10]

On 10.5.1441 Norihiro's army landed in northern Kyushu and advanced into Buzen.[11] He first went to Usa, commending statues to Mirokuji so as to secure the support of the Usa Hachiman gods.[12] He then fought in Chikuzen, pacifying that province in half a year.[13] Ultimately Shōni Noriyori was soundly defeated and fled to Tsushima.[14] Norihiro's rival Noriyuki also surrendered and took the tonsure, adopting the name Dōjun.[15] Then Noriyuki waited, hoping for an opportunity for restore his fortunes. This opportunity would come half a dozen years after Norihiro's death, when he would rise against his nephew (Norihiro's son) in 1472. On 2.3.1442 Norihiro was invested as the *Sakyō no daibu*, a prestigious court post with implied authority over the western wards of Kyoto, in commemoration of this success.[16]

[9] See *Masuda ke monjo*, vol. 2 (Tōkyō daigaku shuppankai, 2003), doc. 503, 10.14.1441 (Kakitsu 1) Muromachi *bakufu mikyōjo*, p. 244, and Tōkyō daigaku shiryōhen sanjo, comp., *Mōri ke monjo*, vol. 1 (Tōkyō daigaku shuppankai, 1920), doc. 62, 10.14.1441 (Kakitsu 1) Muromachi shōgun ke (Ashikaga Yoshikatsu) *mikyōjo*, pp. 67–68.

[10] For Norihiro's requests, see the intercalary (*urū*) 9.26.1441 (Kakitsu 1) Muromachi bakufu *kanrei hōsho* in the Sasaki monjo and for the Hosokawa response, *Ninagawa ke monjo*, vol. 1, doc. 28, Ōuchi shi *monjo an*, 10.14.1441 (Kakitsu 1) Muromachi bakufu *kanrei* Hosokawa Mochiyuki *hōsho an*, p. 42, and doc. 54, Norihiro *jōsho an*, pp. 111–13. The Shōni legitimated their actions according to an otherwise unspecified "edict" that was most likely spurious. Yamaguchi Takamasa, "Sasaki monjo-Chūsei Hizen no kuni kankei shiryō jui," *Kyūshū shigaku* 124 (9.1999), doc. 11, p. 55, and Suda Makiko, "Ōuchi Noriyuki kō," pp. 249–52.

[11] *Kumamoto ken shiryō chūsei hen*, vol. 2 (Kumamoto, 1962), Sata monjo doc. 96, 10.5.1441 (Kakitsu 1) shōgun ke *mikyōjo*, p. 198.

[12] *Usa jingūshi shiryōhen*, vol. 9 (Usa, 1993), p. 649 for his grant of Kongō rishi statues to Usa's Mirokuji in 1441.

[13] *Yamaguchi kenshi shiryōhen chūsei*, vol. 3, Atsumo ke monjo, doc. 1, 2.20 Ōuchi Norihiro *shojō*, doc. 2, 2.25 Ōuchi Norihiro *shojō*, and doc. 5, 1.14 Ōuchi Norihiro *shojō*, pp. 98–99 for letters mentioning the Masuda, Yoshimi, and to the Misumi, along with Washizu Hirotada, the deputy *shugo* of Nagato. For the campaign itself, see *Hiraga ke monjo* (Tōkyō daigaku shuppankai, 1937), doc. 35, 3.11.1442 (Kakitsu 2) *Kanrei* Hosokawa Mochiyuki *hōsho*, p. 528, and doc. 36, 3.14.1442 (Kakitsu 2) *Kanrei* Hosokawa Mochiyuki *hōsho*, pp. 528–29.

[14] *Ninagawa ke monjo*, vol. 1, doc. 54, Norihiro *jōsho an*, p. 112 for the Shōni defeat and flight to Tsushima. See also and Itō Kōji, *Chūsei no Hakata to Ajia* (Bensei shuppan, 2021), p. 155.

[15] Wada Shusaku, "Ōuchi shi no sōsho kankei o megutte," pp. 37–38. For more on how Noriyuki renounced the world see *Kumamoto ken shiryō chūsei hen*, vol. 2, Sata ke monjo, doc. 78, 5.16 Ōuchi Norihiro *shojō*, p. 202.

[16] *Yamaguchi kenshi tsūshihen furoku* CD-ROM, *Kuzen rinji inzen mikyōjo an*, doc. 10, 2.3.1442 (Kakitsu 2) Go-Hanazono tennō *kuzen an utsushi*, p. 435. He confirmed Kōryūji rights, signing the document with this title. *Yamaguchi kenshi shiryōhen chūsei*, vol. 2, Kōryūji monjo doc. 4, 3.9.1442 (Kakitsu 2) Ōuchi Norihiro *andojō*, p. 443. For further evidence of the promotion, see *Yamaguchi*

Norihiro built monuments and commissioned Buddhist rites after his victories. In 1442, he oversaw the construction of a beautiful five-story pagoda, in memory of Mochiyo, which survives to this day in Yamaguchi.[17] In 1443 Norihiro also sponsored funeral ceremonies for Mochiyo.[18] He commissioned forty-two monks to pray for the second-month rites in 1443, and later that year he rebuilt the upper shrine at Hikamisan, an extensive effort involving many people, including monks from the subtemples of Kōryūji.[19] In 1444, Norihiro even established a funerary monument for Mochiyo at Seikei-in on Mt. Kōya, a site for graves for important individuals throughout Japan (Figures 6.1 and 6.2).[20]

Norihiro adopted the mantle of lawgiver, and reconfirmed the codes of 1399, 1408, and 1434 as issued by Yoshihiro (1356–99), Moriakira, and Mochiyo.[21] His actions emphasized continuity, as in 1442 he confirmed Suō Kokubunji's position as a prayer site for the realm, a position originally established by Moriakira in 1406 and last confirmed by Mochiyo in 1441.[22] He also aided his supporters, and by allowing many to share the last part of his name (hiro) he established personal bonds of affinity.[23]

kenshi shiryōhen chūsei, vol. 1, "Nagato no kuni shugo shiki shidai," p. 604. In this case, the office was an honorary sinecure, rather than a functioning appointment.

[17] A square weight-bearing block (*makito*) of the pagoda has the year 1442 written on it. I appreciate Wada Shūsaku's explanation of this, email conversation, 6.23.2017. Hirase Naoki, *Ōuchi Yoshihiro* (Minerva shobō, 2017), p. 194, Fujimori Terunobu and Maebashi Shigeji, *Gojūnotō nyūmon* (Shinchōsha, 2012), believe that this pagoda was constructed for the sake of the newly deceased Mochiyo. Histories written under the auspices of the Mōri in 1661 suggest that this five-story pagoda was built for Yoshihiro by Moriakira, but they are incorrect.

[18] *Yamaguchi kenshi shiryōhen chūsei*, vol. 1, Sejong sillok, 10.13.1446 (Sejong 25), pp. 881–82.

[19] *Yamaguchi kenshi shiryōhen chūsei*, vol. 3, Yamaguchi monjokan Kōryūji monjo, doc. 156, 2.1443 (Kakitsu 3) *Nigatsu-e daishū tatsu shihai chūmon*, p. 296, and doc. 80, 2.16.1444 (Kakitsu 4) Hikamisan Myōken Jōgū *hengū chūmon*, pp. 258–60.

[20] Kondō Kiyoshi, *Ōuchi shi jitsuroku* (Yamaguchi, 1885, 3rd reprint ed., Tokuyama: Matsuno shoten, 1984), 2.28.1444 (Bunan 1), p. 58.

[21] *Sengoku ibun Ōuchi shi hen*, vol. 1, doc. 454, 9.21.1479 (Bunmei 11) Ōuchi shi *kokugaryō hatto*, pp. 134–35.

[22] *Yamaguchi kenshi shiryōhen chūsei*, vol. 2, Kokubunji monjo, doc. 29, 8.5.1442 (Kakitsu 2) Ōuchi Norihiro *andojō*, p. 409. For Mochiyo's confirmation, see doc. 28, 4.28.1441 (Kakitsu 1) Ōuchi Mochiyo *andojō*, p. 409, and for the original designation by Moriakira (1377–1431) in 1406, see doc. 30, 3.5.1406 (Ōei 13) Ōuchi Dōyū *andojō*, p. 409.

[23] *Fukuoka shishi shiryōhen chūsei 1 Shinai shōzai monjo* (Fukuoka-shi, 2010), Aso monjo, doc. 32–30, 12.23.1470 (Bunmei 2) Aso Zenkyō (Iehiro) *okibumi utsushi*, p. 547, and the genealogy on p. 568 for Mochiyo confirming Aso Iehiro retroactively as being the Aso heir to allow him to claim family chieftainship from a rival who supported the Shōni. Arikawa Nobuhiro, "Aso Takazane to Aso shi tatekeizu," *Kita kyūshū shiritsu shizenshi rekishi hakubutsukan kenkyū hōkoku* B no. 4 (2007), p. 12. See also Kawazoe Shōji, "Muromachi bakufu hōkōshū Chikuzen Aso shi ni tsuite," *Kyūshū chūseishi no kenkyū* (Yoshikawa kōbunkan, 1983), pp. 196–97. For similar confirmations for Sata Morikaga, see *Usa jingūshi shiryōhen*, vol. 9, 3.8.1444 (Bunan 1) Ōuchi Norihiro *andojō*, p. 666.

Figure 6.1 The Rurikōji (Kōshakuji) Pagoda (1442). Photograph by Thomas Conlan

Marriage ties led to new alliances. In 1443, Norihiro married Yamana Kuniko (1428–95), the sixteen-year-old daughter of Yamana Hirotaka (d. 1441). Hirotaka, like Mochiyo, had fought well against the Akamatsu in 1441, and he too had been killed in the melee. This match proved consequential, for it led to a long and stable bond with the Yamana, thus converting a long-standing rival, and a potential check on Ōuchi power in Aki and

Figure 6.2 The Rurikōji (Kōshakuji) Pagoda (1442). Photograph by Thomas Conlan

Iwami, into an ally.[24] Traces of Kuniko's influence remain evident over the next half century, particularly in the aftermath of Norihiro's death, when she

---

[24] *Yamaguchi kenshi shiryōhen chūsei*, vol. 1, Kennaiki, 6.3.1443 (Kakitsu 3), p. 167. See also *Yamaguchi kenshi tsūshihen chūsei* (Yamaguchi, 2012), p. 395. For how she was most likely named Minamoto Kuniko, see Kurushima Noriko, "Ōnin Bunmei no ran to Masuda shi—Shiryōhen sanjo shozō Masuda ke monjochū no sashidashi fumei kana shojō no kōsatsu," *Daikibo Buke monjogun ni yoru chū kinsei shirōgaku no sōgōteki kenkyū Hagi han karo Masuda ke monjo o sozai ni*, Kagaku kenkyūhi hojokin kiban kenkyū A 5202018 (3.2008), pp. 78–79. Her sister married Hosokawa Katsumoto, who later became an enemy of Norihiro and the Yamana.

stabilized the Ōuchi domain during decades of turmoil and war. Signs of Ōuchi and Yamana cooperation appeared by 1447, when Norihiro supported the Yamana at the battle of Funagoe in Aki.[25] This rapprochement with the Yamana would allow a potent alliance by the lords of western Honshu to become possible.

Urban Development, Commerce, and Trade

Norihiro fully re-established control over northern Kyushu, and by 1443 he governed parts of Hakata, a major harbor.[26] Hakata then prospered under Ōuchi control, in that its merchants had more ready access to valuable commodities, such as copper. Hakata merchants demanded a copper seal with the merchant's name inscribed to gain trading privileges.[27] Norihiro's re-establishment of control over Hakata in 1443 led to a further expansion in commerce and trade.[28]

With enhanced stability and greater wealth, Hakata expanded in size. By the eleventh month of 1456 the Gion festival was held there, thanks to a merchant community large and prosperous enough to sponsor the elaborate festival floats (*yamaboko*) that circulated in the city.[29] A similar process must have taken place in Yamaguchi at this time, as later sources show that this city regularly performed the Gion festival as well.

The rise of these cities of Hakata and Yamaguchi hinged upon trade. Ōuchi Norihiro oversaw an expanded fleet of trading ships. His craft were the largest

---

[25] *Kobayakawa ke monjo*, vol. 2 (Tōkyō daigaku shuppankai, 1927), Shōmon, doc. 382 Yamana Sōhō (Mochitoyo) *kanjō utsushi*, pp. 224–25 for evidence of this cooperation between the Yamana and Norihiro. See also *Yamaguchi kenshi tsūshihen chūsei*, p. 395.

[26] At that time, he exempted Hakozaki shrine officials in Hakata from "oil duties." *Dazaifu Dazaifu Tenmangū shiryō*, vol. 13 (Dazaifu Tenmangū, 1986), 4.3.1443 (Kakitsu 3), pp. 244–45. The monogram of this document is consistent with one of 1443. I am indebted to Wada Shūsaku for this observation, conversation, 6.13.2016. For more on Ōuchi Norihiro and control over Hakata, see Saeki Kōji, "Ōuchi shi no Chikuzen no kuni shihai," *Kyūshū chūseishi kenkyū*, vol. 1 (Bunken shuppan, 1978), pp. 287–93.

[27] For a good overview, see Itō Kōji, "Hakata Merchants and Bogus Embassies in the Fifteenth and Sixteenth Centuries," *Nenpō Mita chūseishi kenkyū* 14 (10.2007), p. 130.

[28] For an overview of the Ōuchi, Hakata, and China trade, see Saeki Kōji, "Chūsei kōki no Hakata to Ōuchi shi," *Shien* 121 (1984), p. 3. Saeki claims that the first China ship departed in 1451 (Hōtoku 3).

[29] The performance of these rites was, as Kawazoe Shōji suggests, a sign of Norihiro's consolidated authority over Hakata. Kawazoe Shōji, "Sōgi no mita Kyūshū," in *Chūsei bungei no chihōshi* (Heibonsha, 1982), pp. 254–55. For the source, see *Yamaguchi kenshi shiryōhen chūsei*, vol. 1, Masatōki, pp. 328–60, 10.24.1478 (Bunmei 10), p. 354. Finally, for an excellent overview of Gion and the importance of the Kushida and Hakozaki shrines, see Saeki Kōji, "Chūsei toshi Hakata no sōchinju to Hakozakigū," *Shien* 149 (3.2012), pp. 1–20.

plying the Inland Sea, and they possessed toll-barrier immunities (*kasho*), further facilitating trade.[30] The chance survival of one remarkable source, the *Hyōgo kitaseki irifune nōchō* (*Register of Incoming Ships at the Hyogo North Checkpoint*), allows for a detailed reconstruction of trade on the Inland Sea for half of a year in 1445.[31] In 1445, one Ōuchi junk, capable of carrying 2,500 *koku* or bales of rice (roughly equivalent to 212,500 liters, 1,337 barrels, or 375 tons), sailed from the deepwater anchorage of Moji, the northern Kyushu port bordering the Straits of Shimonoseki, and arrived at Hyōgo, the gateway to the capital.[32] Three additional Ōuchi ships traveled from Moji to Hyōgo that same year. One carried a cargo of 1,400 *koku* of rice, 100 *koku* of beans, and 200 *koku* of other boiled sundries (*nikomi*); another carried 900 *koku* of rice; and a third 120 *koku* of rice.[33] Other chronicles refer to two still larger Ōuchi ships arriving at Hyōgo in 1447, each capable of transporting 3,000 *koku*, although one encountered an "evil wind" and sank.[34] In contrast the ships of comparable *shugo*, such as the Yamana and the Hosokawa could carry only 1,000 or 2,000 *koku* each.[35]

Although useful in carrying much cargo, the larger craft had trouble docking in Chinese ports. Those capable of hauling 1,800 *koku* or above were known as "great ships" (*ōfune*). In Japan, all docked at Moji, on the Kyushu side of the Straits of Shimonoseki. Vessels holding 1,800 *koku* such as the *Tera-maru*, managed to dock there with some difficulty, but the *Izumi-maru*, a mighty 2,500 *koku* ship, proved unable to travel to China because of the

[30] Peter Shapinsky, *Lords of the Sea: Pirates, Violence, and Commerce in Late Medieval Japan* (Ann Arbor: University of Michigan Center for Japanese Studies, 2014), pp. 133, 210 characterizes ships a third of this size as being the "largest of medieval Japan." For more on ships, and improvements in their construction, see Wayne Farris, *Japan to 1600: A Social and Economic History* (Honolulu: University of Hawaii Press, 2009), pp. 43, 148, 151. For evidence one of these crafts, most likely the *Toi-maru*, transported its tax cargo to Hyōgo, see *Chūsei bōchō shōen shiryō*, in *Yamaguchi kenshi tsūshihen furoku* CD-ROM, Tōfukuji monjo, doc. 31, 11.12.1459 (Chōroku 3) Hyōgo *Toi-maru* Kagenori *ukejō*, p. 620. For more on these toll-barrier immunities, see Shapinsky, *Lords of the Sea*, p. 99.

[31] For analysis of this shipping see Michelle Damien, "Late Medieval Japan's Seto Inland Seascape: Shipping, Sailors and Seafaring," PhD dissertation, University of Southern California, 5.2015, as well as her "As Estates Faded: Late Medieval Maritime Shipping in the Seto Inland Sea," in Joan Piggott and Janet Goodwin, eds., *Land, Power, and the Sacred* (Honolulu: University of Hawaii Press, 2018), pp. 351–74. See also Sakurai Eiji, "Medieval Japan's Commercial Economy and the Estate System," in Piggott and Goodwin, pp. 46–48.

[32] *Hyōgo kenshi shiryōhen chūsei*, vol. 5 (Kobe, 1990), *Hyōgo kitaseki irifune nōchō*, 4.13.1445 (Bunan 2), p. 695. See also Suda Makiko, *Chūsei Nichō kankei to Ōuchi shi*, pp. 119–20. For estimates of the tonnage, see Hayashiya Tatsusaburō, *Hyōgo kitaseki irifune nōchō* (Chūō kōron bijutsu shuppan, 1981), p. 245, and Damien, "Late Medieval Japan's Seto Inland Seascape," p. 59.

[33] *Hyōgo kenshi shiryōhen chūsei*, vol. 5, *Hyōgo kitaseki irifune nōchō*, 4.9.1445 (Bunan 2), pp. 693–94.

[34] *Kennaiki*, vol. 8 (Tōkyō daigaku shiryōhen sanjo, 1978), 3.28.1447 (Bunan 4), p. 49.

[35] Shinjō Tsunezō, *Chūsei suiunshi no kenkyū* (Hanawa shobō, 1994), p. 730. For detailed analysis of shipping through this port, see pp. 495–557.

difficulty of docking there. Vessels of the size of the *Tera-maru* were thus coveted for the trade between Japan and China. The Ōuchi and the Ashikaga alternated use of this craft for trade missions to China.[36]

A tax register for the harbor at Hyōgo reveals the patterns of this shipping network. Large ships docked less often than smaller craft. For half a year in 1445, for example, four boats capable of hauling 1,000 *koku* or more docked five times, while twelve boats, with storage capabilities ranging from 500 to 1,000 *koku*, appear in the record 23 times.[37] Larger craft were more valuable, had a larger crew, and took more time to load. With their access to the excellent harbor at Moji, the Ōuchi dispatched larger ships. Ōuchi craft docked only 38 times in Inland Sea harbors during half a year in 1445. By contrast, smaller Hosokawa ships docked 1,114 times, and Yamana ships 769 times.[38]

The Ōuchi required large craft because they were most directly and continuously engaged with East Asia and shipped large cargoes of heavy ore. Trading profits were considerable. The monk Jinson (1430–1508), a famed abbot of Kōfukuji, explained that international trade allowed for profits of ten or twenty times that of the value of goods.[39] A single tribute ship can be documented as turning a profit of eighteen hundred *kanmon*.[40] This was the equivalent to the tax revenues of one of Japan's provinces, or nearly twice what it would cost to purchase a lucrative estate outright.[41] A *kanmon* was a worth the price of an ox, or half the price of a horse in the fifteenth century.[42]

[36] *Yamaguchi kenshi shiryōhen chūsei*, vol. 1, Boshi nyūminki, p. 832. For further analysis, and how the Ashikaga decided to rely on the *Tera-maru*, see *Ōuchi bunka to Kita Kyūshū* (Kita Kyūshū shiritsu shizenshi rekishi hakubutsukan, 2012), p. 45. See also Boshi nyūminki, p. 833 for reference to another one-thousand-*koku* boat from Suō.

[37] See the analysis of Mutō Tadashi, "Chūsei no Hyōgo to seto naikai suiun," in Hayashiya Tatsusaburō, ed., *Hyōgo kitaseki irifune nōchō* (Chūō kōron bijutsu shuppan, 1981), p. 233.

[38] Imatani Akira, "Seto naisei kaigen no sui-i to irifune nōchō," in *Hyōgo kitaseki irifune nōchō*, pp. 283–84. Imatani recognizes that the Ōuchi probably had a stronger presence to the west and on the high seas, while the eastern reaches of the Inland Sea were mostly plied with smaller craft.

[39] *Daijōin jisha zōjiki* (Jinson), 12 vols. (Kyoto: Rinsen shoten, 1982), vol. 7, 1.24.1483 (Bunmei 15), p. 491. For this citation, I relied upon Kawaoka Tsutomu, *Yamana Sōzen* (Yoshikawa kōbunkan, 2009), p. 103.

[40] Tanaka Takeo, *Wakō* (Kōdansha, 2012), p. 101. A *kanmon* constituted a thousand *mon*.

[41] A major estate was purchased for one thousand *kanmon* in 1411, while the tax revenue for one of Japan's more prosperous provinces constituted two thousand *kanmon* in 1429. See *Dazaifu shishi chūsei shiryōhen* (Dazaifu, 2002), p. 602 for the 1429 revenue from Chikuzen province. For the sale of a Harima province estate for one thousand *kanmon*, see the Tenryūji tatchū Nanpōin monjo, manuscript copy, Yale Beinecke library, for documents of 1411 (Ōei 18) and 1416 (Ōei 23). I viewed these documents on 10.4.2012. For reference to an Ōuchi shipment dating from 1455, see *Mibu ke monjo*, vol. 2 (Kunaichō. Shoryōbu, 1979), doc. 408, pp. 156–57 and doc. 410, p. 158. For more on a a 1492 (Meiō 1) shipment, see doc. 440, pp. 192–93.

[42] *Umi o koeta chūsei no okane: "Bita ichimon" ni himerareta rekishi* (Bank of Japan, 2009), pp. 19–21, and for the general calculation of worth, as well as the cost of buying horses and cows. For the pioneering analysis of the purchasing power of sums of cash, see Tanaka Kōji, "Nihon chūsei ni

By the 1440s, many transactions were monetized, and prices were consistent throughout the Ōuchi domain. For example, lodging, cost 300 *mon* per day, one peach 3 *mon*, a melon 7 *mon* or a candle 10 *mon*, while the harbor toll for a ship sailing from Yodo in central Japan to Nagato was 775 *mon*, and a cash payment to a captain of the *Yamato Izumi-maru* for his services 500 *mon*.[43]

Copper was the mainstay of trade.[44] In 1453, when Ashikaga Yoshimasa as "King of Japan" dispatched ships to the Ming on a tally trade mission after an eighteen-year hiatus, his cargo was well documented. The ten ships that sailed to China transported 102 tons of copper, 9,500 swords, 417 long swords, fifty-one pikes, and 1,250 fans.[45] In exchange they received rare objects, such as Siberian Roe Deer skins (*Capreolus pygargus*), available only from the continent. Although the Ashikaga were nominally the central authorities in Japan, they possessed inadequate funds to load up a trade ship in 1465 and were forced to borrow Ōuchi copper worth (*yōkyaku*) one hundred thousand *hiki*, or one thousand *kanmon* of cash.[46]

The monk Jinson described the profitability of copper. One packhorse load (*da*) of this commodity (roughly 240 lb. or 110 kg) was worth ten *kanmon* of cash within Japan. However, if traded for silk in China, it was worth for to fifty *kanmon*.[47] In other words, in terms of rough purchasing power, 240 pounds of copper were worth the equivalent of $10,000 when exchanged internally, or $40,000 to $50,000 when exchanged for the much more valuable silk.

The Ōuchi effectively monopolized copper exports.[48] The ore from Ōmoriza in Iwami, a site of copper and silver mining near Nima, and from

okeru seni no shakaiteki kinō o megutte," Nōgaya shutsudo zeni chōsa kai Machida shi kyōiku iinkai, comp., *Nōgaya shutsudo chōsa hōkokusho* (3.1996), section 4, pp. 102–23.

[43] *Umi o koeta chūsei no okane*, "Chūsei no mono no nedan no jirei," p. 21, and for analysis of these informative 1446 Tōji documents, see Fujii Takashi, *Muromachiki daimyō kenryokuron* (Dōseisha, 2013), pp. 254–60.

[44] See Saeki Kōji, "Muromachiki no Hakata shōnin Sōkin to Higashi Ajia," *Shien* 136 (1999), p. 118 for ore as being the dominant export. Saeki does not specify copper, but this ore was in the most demand in the fifteenth century, only to be supplanted by silver in the sixteenth.

[45] *Yamaguchi kenshi shiryōhen chūsei*, vol. 1, 1453 (Kyōtoku 2) Daijōin nikki mokuroku, p. 239. The sources mention 154,500 *kin* of copper being shipped. As one *kin* equals 600 grams, this amount is 92,700 kilograms, 204,369 pounds, or 102 tons. See also Delmer Brown, *Money Economy in Medieval Japan: A Study in the Use of Coins* (Institute of Far Eastern Languages, Yale University, 1951), p. 34.

[46] *Yamaguchi kenshi shiryōhen chūsei*, vol. 1, 5.27 and 6.15.1465 (Kanshō 6), "Ninagawa Chikamoto nikki," pp. 186–87. See also *Yamaguchi kenshi tsūshihen chūsei*, p. 398 for the Ashikaga loan of Ōuchi copper. For a more comprehensive version of this chronicle, see *Kaitei shiseki shūran*, vol. 8 (Kondō Keizō shuppanbu, 1932), 5.8–26, 6.14.1465 (Kanshō 6) pp. 185–86

[47] *Daijōin jisha zōjiki*, vol. 7, 12.21.1480 (Bunmei 12), p. 237.

[48] *Umi o koeta chūsei no okane*, p. 30, "Kinzoku kahei no genzairyō to shite no kin gin dō." In addition to Ōmoriza (Iwami), Naganobori (Nagato), the other major mines of the fourteenth to

Naganobori in Nagato, could easily be exported to the continent. The Ōuchi even de facto controlled the production of mines that they did not actually possess. For example, the copper of Myōkenzan, a major mine in Harima, had to pass through the Straits of Shimonoseki if it were to be exported.[49]

Korean chronicles suggest that Japanese emissaries also brought with them a tin and lead compound, called *rō*, and iron.[50] Sulfur was also exported, and was primarily shipped from southern Kyushu to Moji and Hakata, where it would be loaded on ships and sent to the continent.[51] Thus, the Ōuchi had a quasi monopoly of sulfur exports in East Asia. Finally, some finished goods such as swords, fans, and bells were exported as well.

Reasserting Control over Nagato

Nagato, with its mines and good harbors, was the most strategic province in the Ōuchi domain. Washizu Hirotada, the deputy *shugo* of Nagato, as rapacious as he was ambitious, became a significant threat. Appointed to the post by Ōuchi Mochiyo in 1432, he held it until 1446.[52] During these years his authority in the province expanded, and he illicitly skimmed revenue from it. His base was Fukawa, a region with good water and access to a fine port on the Japan Sea.[53] Hirotada could easily dispatch ships to Korea and to northern Kyushu, where he maintained influence. Indirect evidence of his wealth stems from his founding of the Sōtō Zen temple Taineiji under Sekioku Shinryō, a monk who had studied in China.[54]

fifteenth centuries included Harima's Myōkensan, which would have to pass through the Straits of Shimonoseki to reach Asia, and Etchū's Matsukura kinzan (gold mine) the only one not directly or indirectly linked to the Ōuchi. https://www.imes.boj.or.jp/cm/research/zuroku/mod/2009c_30_ 33.pdf.

[49] *Yamaguchi kenshi shiryōhen chūsei*, vol. 1, Boshi nyūminki, p. 826 for "red copper," an alloy of 3–4 percent gold, 1 percent silver and copper, coming from Tajima, Mimasaka, Bitchū, and Bingo. It was shipped to Onomichi, an Inland Sea port. For other references to Bitchū copper, see p. 827.

[50] *Sejo sillok*, 9.27.1464 (Sejo 10), http://sillok.history.go.kr/id/wga_11009027_004.

[51] *Yamaguchi kenshi shiryōhen chūsei*, vol. 1, Boshi nyūminki, p. 827. See also "Io no seiki," in Kage Toshio, *Sengoku daimyō no kaigai kōeki* (Bensei shuppan, 2019), pp. 213–65, and Itō Kōji, *Chūsei no Hakata to Ajia*, pp. 39–42.

[52] *Yamaguchi kenshi shiryōhen chūsei*, vol. 1, Nagato no kuni shugoshiki shidai, p. 604, and Nagato shugo daiki, p. 608. Hirotada was a scion of the Washizu who had acquiesced to Ōuchi rule.

[53] I visited this region in 6.2015 and learned of the good harbors and water from Wada Shūsaku. For an informative article, see Wada Shūsaku, "Chūsei no Washizu shi ni tsuite, *Kudamatsu chihōshi kenkyū* 50 (4.2014), pp. 8–9.

[54] Wada, "Chūsei no Washizu shi ni tsuite," p. 11. For an earlier letter from Washizu Hirotada concerning Nagato's Sumiyoshi shrine in the period of Mochiyo's rule (Eikyō 11), see *Yamaguchi shishi shiryōhen chūsei* (Yamaguchi, 2016), doc. 162, 8.15 Washizu Hirotada *shojō an*, p. 246.

Hirotada had taxed Nagato's ports so heavily that Agari Sukeyoshi rejoiced in 1446 over his departure, because of the burden of these "unilateral" levies.[55] Further evidence for his greed comes from Kaita estate in northern Kyushu's Chikuzen province, where he had absconded with tax revenues shortly after serving there as administrator in 1433.[56] In 1441, in the aftermath of the Kakitsu disturbance and Mochiyo's death, battles against Shōni Noriyori were fought at Kaita, and Hirotada appropriated all revenue from the estate for his personal military use.[57] He was accused of illicitly using these funds. In 1446 he was therefore dismissed in favor of Naitō Arisada, the son of Naitō Chitoku, the skilled Ōuchi plenipotentiary.[58]

Arisada's appointment represents an important shift in focus, for previously the most skilled administrators were sent to live in the capital, whereas now their expertise was required more for the oversight of harbors and international trade.[59] By 1446, Norihiro had concluded that he needed his best men to oversee trade rather than negotiate with the capital. This policy allowed him to prosper greatly, although it eventually led to troubles with the Ashikaga.

Sometime in 1447, Norihiro attacked and ultimately killed Washizu Hirotada and Hirotada's son Hirosada at Fukawa castle. The exact timing of the campaign is not clear, although turmoil in Nagato can be documented on 12.28.1447.[60] Hirotada's retainer Sasuga Masayori was then besieged at nearby Katada castle. When it fell he was killed along with a thousand followers on 2.17.1448.[61] A memorial head mound remains in Fukawa,

[55] Wada, "Chūsei no Washizu shi ni tsuite," p. 9, and *Yamaguchi kenshi shiryōhen chūsei*, vol. 3, Agari ke monjo doc. 25, Agari Sukeyoshi *mōshijō*, p. 817.

[56] *Kōyasan Kongō sanmaiin monjo* (Wakayama: Kōyasan monjo kankōkai, 1936), doc. 174, Kaita *no shō shōmu* Raijun *chūshinjō an*, pp. 122–26. For the reference to events of 1433 (Eikyō 5) and the confiscation of half of the revenue of the estate, see pp. 124–25. For the Ninnaji connection to these lands, see Wada, "Washizu shi ni tsuite," p. 11.

[57] *Kōyasan Kongō sanmaiin monjo*, doc. 168, 6.1442 (Kakitsu 2) Kongō sanmaiin *zasshō* Yūkai *meyasu gonjōan*, pp. 118–19, and doc. 174, Kaita *no shō shōmu* Raijun *chūshin an*, pp. 122–26, with the history of Hirotada appearing on p. 124. See also Hagihara Daisuke, "Chūsei kōki Ōuchi shi no zaikyō," *Nihon rekishi* 786 (11.2013), pp. 21, 30, and Suda Makiko, "Ōuchi shi no zaikyō katsudō," p. 104.

[58] *Yamaguchi kenshi shiryōhen chūsei*, vol. 1, Nagato shugo daiki, p. 608, and *Kongō sanmaiin monjo*, doc. 174, Kaita *no shō shōmu* Raijun *chūshinjō an*, pp. 124–25. With this appointment, half of the revenue of the estate once again returned to the temple administrators of Kongō sanmaiin.

[59] For this observation, see Hagihara Daisuke, "Chūsei kōki Ōuchi shi no zaikyō," pp. 22–25.

[60] *Yamaguchi kenshi shiryōhen chūsei*, vol. 1, Sejong sillok, 12.29.1447 (Sejong 29), p. 887.

[61] This is the "thousand-person mound of Katada" (*Katada sennintsuka*) that still exists. For more on the Washizu, see Wada, "Chūsei no Washizu shi ni tsuite," pp. 7–9, and Fujii Takashi, *Muromachiki daimyō kenryokuron*, p. 216, who suggests a possible alliance between the Washizu and the Shōni. The only written source detailing these events is the history of Taineiji pt. 1 (*jō*) of the *Bōchō jisha shōmon* section of *Hagi han batsu etsu roku* (Yamaguchi ken monjokan, 1994), vol. 4, p. 15.

and Hirotada's grave exists at Taineiji, but the campaign is only obliquely mentioned in sources such as the *Nagato shugo daiki*, which describes the "sudden opening" of a deputy *shugo* post.[62] Hirotada's holdings, particularly those illicitly garnered when he appropriated them through the "half tax" (*hanzei*) while deputy of Nagato, were in turn given to reliable retainers, such as Sugi Masatada, or to subtemples of Kōryūji Hikamisan.[63] Hirotada's destruction is also absent from Korean sources, which sometimes mention Ōuchi affairs, but it is not clear whether this lacuna stems from ignorance or reticence on their part to describe the turmoil.[64]

Korean Ties and Ethnic Imaginations

The Ōuchi had long had extensive trading ties with Korea. As early as 1423, only the Ōuchi, the Shimazu of southern Kyushu, and the increasingly powerless commander of Kyushu (*tandai*) communicated directly with the Board of Rites of the Chosŏn Dynasty.[65] In 1449, Chosŏn officials ranked how ships would be received by members of the Board of Rites. Ships from the "King of Japan" (the Ashikaga) were ranked first, followed by the Ōuchi, and then those from two shogunal chancellor (*kanrei*) houses, the Shiba and Hatakeyama.[66]

Some Chosŏn officials realized that the Ashikaga were a waning force when compared with the Ōuchi. As early as 1440, when tensions with the Ōuchi and Shōni were mounting, the Korean ambassador Song Hŭigyŏng noted that the writ of the Ashikaga shoguns did not apply in the Inland

---

[62] *Yamaguchi kenshi shiryōhen chūsei*, vol. 1, Nagato no kuni shugo daiki, p. 608. Compare with the Nagato no kuni shugoshiki shidai, p. 604.

[63] For the reference to the half tax applied to Kaita estate, see *Kōyasan Kongō sanmaiin monjo*, doc. 174, Kaita *no shō shōmu Raijun chūshin an*, pp. 124–25. For the commendation to Hikamisan, see *Yamaguchi kenshi shiryōhen chūsei*, vol. 3, Kōryūji monjo, doc. 7, 6.13.1448 (Bunan 5) Ōuchi Norihiro *kishinjō an*, p. 233, doc. 12, 6.13.1448 (Bunan 5) Ōuchi Norihiro *kishinjō an*, p. 234, and doc. 18, 6.13.1448 (Bunan 5) Ōuchi Norihiro *kishinjō an*, p. 236. The three subtemples were Shōenbō, Gyōshōbō, and Kōzenbō.

[64] *Yamaguchi kenshi shiryōhen chūsei*, vol. 1, Sejong sillok, 12.29.1447 (Sejong 29), p. 887.

[65] This office would remain functioning through the sixteenth century, with its officials, the Shibukawa, often allied with the Shōni until 1534, when Ōuchi Yoshitaka appointed his own Kyushu *tandai* after effectively destroying the Shōni.

[66] Kenneth Robinson, "Organizing Japanese and Jurchens in Tribute Systems in Early Chosŏn Korea," *Journal of East Asian Studies* 13.2 (2013), pp. 342–44, and *Sejong sillok*, 124: 19a [6.14.1449 (Sejong 31)]. As Robinson notes, the Ōuchi status would drop a bit in that the King of Japan and the Ryūkyūs would later occupy the first tier in 1472, while the Hatakeyama, Hosokawa, Shiba, Yamana, Shōni, and Ōuchi would all occupy the second tier. For more on the nature of 1423 contacts, see Robinson, p. 344, and *Sejong sillok* 1: 10b [8.21.1418 (T'aejong 18)]; *Sejong sillok* 19: 3b [1.12.1423 (Sejong 5)]; *Sejong sillok* 19: 4a [1.12.1423 (Sejong 5)]; *Sejong sillok* 19: 10a–b [1.28.1423 (Sejong 5)]).

Sea.[67] Likewise, in the aftermath of Ashikaga Yoshinori's 1441 assassination, Chosŏn officials sent an ambassador to pay respects to the late Mochiyo and Ashikaga Yoshinori. It is telling that they singled out Mochiyo this way. Some scholars have argued that their main goal was to mourn the Ōuchi lord. That may explain why the Ashikaga did not adequately provide for the Korean ambassador until the Shiba belatedly covered his expenses.[68]

In 1443 another Chosŏn ambassador landed at Akamaseki and treated Norihiro as equal, if not superior, to the ten-year-old Ashikaga shogun Yoshikatsu (1434–43). He gave clothes and gifts to Norihiro that were, the Ōuchi leader complained, too lavish for one of his status, as he was still subordinate to the nominal Ashikaga "King of Japan." Norihiro guarded the ambassador's four ships as they traveled to Kyoto via the Inland Sea, the last time they would visit Kyoto until 1590.[69]

Norihiro ably protected Korean seafarers and aided Chosŏn officials who suffered from the depredations of "bandits" (zokutō) from Tsushima, Iki, and the Gotō islands. He repatriated abducted people and goods plundered by these islanders to Korea, as well as castaways washed ashore in Japan.[70] Norihiro also cooperated with Chosŏn officials to suppress "bandits" who were most likely Kyushu traders affiliated with the Sō of Tsushima and the Shōni, since Noriyori, one of their leaders, had fled to Tsushima and was plotting his return.[71] Norihiro requisitioned laborers from Chikuzen province and mobilized military forces to guard against a Shōni attack from Tsushima.[72]

Wakō, independent, armed seafarers and traders, commonly resided in the Tsushima region. They could operate beyond the easy reach of authorities in

[67] Shapinsky, Lords of the Sea, pp. 2, 197.

[68] Hashimoto Yū, Chūka gensō-Karamono to gaikō no Muromachi jidaishi (Bensei shuppan, 2011), p. 227, and Itō Kōji, "Ōuchi Norihiro Masahiro to Higashi Ajia," Kyūshū shigaku 161 (7.2012), pp. 2–5.

[69] Sejong sillok, 10.13.1443 (Sejong 25), reproduced most conveniently in Yamaguchi kenshi shiryōhen chūsei, vol. 1, pp. 881–82. See also Dazaifu Dazaifu Tenmangū shiryō, vol. 13, pp. 246–48. Shapinsky briefly mentions this in his Lords of the Sea, p. 196. For the gap in Korean embassies to Kyoto, see Kenneth Robinson, "An Island's Place in History: Tsushima in Japan and Chosŏn, 1392–1592," Korean Studies 30 (2006), p. 50. Their officials would, however, travel to Yamaguchi.

[70] Yamaguchi kenshi shiryōhen chūsei, vol. 1, Sejong sillok, 4.30.1444 (Sejong 26), p. 884. For an inventory of the goods returned, see Sejong sillok, 6.19.1444 (Sejong 26), p. 884. These people are referred to as bandits (zokuto) here, but also at times as wajin. See Sejong sillok, 4.9.1445 (Sejong 27), p. 886. Yamaguchi kenshi shiryōhen chūsei, vol. 1, Munjon sillok, 4.5.1451 (Munjon 1), p. 888, mentions Koreans who had landed in Satsuma and yet were repatriated by Norihiro.

[71] Yamaguchi kenshi shiryōhen chūsei, vol. 1, pp. 882–94, contains repeated references to the interactions between Norihiro and Chosŏn officials in trade, or suppression of "bandits."

[72] Dazaifu Dazaifu Tenmangū shiryō, vol. 13, Tōji monjo, 9.10, 9.18, 9.21 [(Kanshō 3) 1462], Ōuchi shi bugyōnin hōsho, pp. 327–29. See also Yamaguchi kenshi tsūshihen furoku CD-ROM, Tōdaiji monjo, doc. 263ff., which refer to Ōuchi Norihiro soon dispatching funds from Kyushu on 9.10.1462 (Kanshō 3), and doc. 264, 9.18.1462 (Kanshō 3) Ōuchi bugyōnin rensho hōsho, which refers to a

Japan, Korea, or China and therefore disrupt trade. Nevertheless, in 1443, they received access to three Chosŏn settlements at Chep'o (薺浦) (Ungch'ŏn), Pusanp'o (釜山浦) (Tongnae), and Yŏmp'o (塩浦) (Ulsan), and a profitable and peaceful period ensued until the Disturbance of the Three Ports (J. *Sanpo no ran* 三浦の乱 Kr. *Samp'o Waeran* 三浦倭亂) by these Tsushima traders in 1510.[73] Tsushima traders remained competitors to the Ōuchi, and in 1436 and 1465 orders were issued that the harbors of Tsushima were to be guarded when tally fleets traveled to China.[74] They frequently forged tallies to engage in Korean trade nevertheless.[75]

Norihiro's ships sailed throughout the Japan and Inland Seas. He also dispatched vessels to the Ryūkyū Kingdom, relying on the Shimazu of southern Kyushu as intermediaries, as is revealed by surviving letters to these kings.[76] Overall trade and shipping seems to have increased in the 1440s as well, as the Munakata shrine, located strategically on the northern coast of Kyushu, can be documented as sending a ship each year to Korea from 1455 onward.[77] Trade flourished, and coins from as far afield as Byzantium found their way to Katsuren, an Okinawan castle abandoned in 1458.[78]

request for one hundred people in a military encampment, laborers, and horses to cross the ocean. See also doc. 265, 9.21, both on p. 153. Because of Tōdaiji resistance, fewer people were dispatched. For more analysis of this episode, see Hatakeyama Satoshi, "Chūsei kōki ni okeru Suō no kuni kokuga kei'ei," *Nihon rekishi* 627 (8.2000), p. 23.

[73] Hasegawa Hiroshi, *Ōuchi shi no kōbō to nishi Nihon shakai* (Yoshikawa kōbunkan, 2020), pp. 31–34. These ports were established for Tsushima traders by the Treaty of Kyehae in 1443, and they were abandoned after 1544, although Pusan continued the site of a Japanese settlement through 1592. For excavations at the Chep'o (Jepo 薺浦) or Naeip'o (乃而浦) Waegwan (倭館), see "Historic site of Jepo Waegwan Discovered" (accessed 1.14.2021), https://www.donga.com/en/article/all/20190313/1667856/1/Historic-site-of-Jepo-Waegwan-discovered.

[74] *Yamaguchi kenshi shiryōhen chūsei*, vol. 1, Boshi nyūminki, p. 828 for a prohibition dating from 6.20.1465 (Kanshō 6). For an earlier reference, see *Yamaguchi kenshi shiryōhen chūsei*, vol. 1, Manzei jugō nikki, 1.23.1434 (Eikyō 6), p. 119.

[75] Itō Kōji, *Chūsei no Hakata to Ajia*, pp. 170–72.

[76] Itō Kōji, "Ōuchi shi no Ryūkyū kotsū," *Nenpō Chūseishi kenkyū* 28 (2003), pp. 189–90, and Itō Kōji, "Ōuchi shi no kokusai hatten: juyon seiki han juroku seiki han no Yamaguchi chiiki to Higashi Ajia sekai," *Yamaguchi kenritsu daigaku kokusai bunka gakubu kiyo*, no. 11 (2005), p. 76 for how Norihiro desired to gain access to Southeast Asian goods to facilitate his China trade. For the turbulence of the first Shō dynasty of the Ryūkyū Kingdom, see Gregory Smits, *Maritime Ryūkyū, 1050–1650* (Honolulu: University of Hawaii Press, 2018), pp. 113–18. See also Saeki Kōji, "Ōuchi shi to Ryūkyū" (accessed 11.10.2018), http://www.tulips.tsukuba.ac.jp/limedio/dlam/B95/B952214/1/dai-1/mokuji/5113.pdf. Copies of the documents are visible on pp. 66–67 of *Ōuchi jitsuroku dodai* 15, accessible at http://archives.pref.yamaguchi.lg.jp/msearch/search.php?m=esy&op=detail&t=2&id=127483&pg=1&odr=28&c=50. Finally, for more on trade routes from Hakata to Okinawa, see Itō Kōji, *Chūsei no Hakata to Ajia*, pp. 92–139.

[77] See *Munakata shishi shiryōhen chūsei*, vol. 2 (Munakata, 1996), p. 100, doc. 118, for a *Kaitō shokokuki* 1455 reference about Munakata shrine sending one boat per year to Korea.

[78] "Japanese First as Ancient Roman Coins Found in Okinawa Ruins," *Asahi Shimbun*, 9.27.2016 (accessed 9.29.2016). Of course, these coins are not direct evidence of Byzantine trade, as the

Varied exchanges between Chosŏn officials and the Ōuchi continued as well. In 1444, Norihiro received another copy of the Buddhist Tripiṭaka from them.[79] In the ensuing ceremonies red lacquered trays and copper were exchanged for leopard and tiger skins.[80] These pelts from Korea found their way to Japan in greater numbers after officials of the Ming Dynasty prohibited their use in tributary exchanges in 1435.[81]

Once Norihiro became *shugo* of Chikuzen in 1447, he could more readily dispatch ships to China.[82] Many merchants from Hakata, concurrently monks involved in trade with China, could readily communicate with Ming officials.[83] The Ōuchi relied on Zen temples at Akamaseki and Hakata for trade and negotiations with the Ming, although they also relied on officials from the temple of Yōkōji, located at the eastern edge of Suō province.[84]

Norihiro was able to trade directly with China and Korea in the 1450s. One milestone was reached in 1451, when for the first time an Ōuchi vessel was officially selected for inclusion in the fleet of Ashikaga ships that would be dispatched to Ming China in 1453.[85] Norihiro's position was further enhanced because in 1453, as an unprecedented sign of favor, he was granted Chosŏn split tallies (K. *t'ongshin-pu* J. *tsūshinpu*). Ōuchi trade had been

venerable empire fell in 1453. Katsuren castle in Okinawa is also the site where some of the oldest stone bullets were discovered. Toma Shi'ichi, "Hiya ni tsuite," *Nantō kōko*, no. 14 (12.1994), pp. 123–52. The Byzantine coins were exceptional as the vast majority, nearly 99 percent, came from China. Richard von Glahn, "Chinese Coin and Changes in Monetary Preferences in Maritime East Asia in the Fifteenth–Seventeenth Centuries," *Journal of the Economic and Social History of the Orient* 57 (2014), p. 645.

[79] *Yamaguchi kenshi shiryōhen chūsei*, vol. 1, Sejong sillok, 7.15.1444 (Sejong 26), p. 885.

[80] *Yamaguchi kenshi shiryōhen chūsei*, vol. 1, Sejong sillok, 6.18.1446 (Sejong 28), p. 887. Likewise, for another reference to trade in tiger and leopard skins, as well as many other goods, see Sejo sillok, 4.3.1456 (Sejo 2), p. 891, and 8.23.1458 (Sejo 4), pp. 892–93.

[81] David Robinson, *Martial Spectacle of the Ming Court* (Cambridge, MA: Harvard Yenching Monograph Series, 2013), pp. 97–101.

[82] Itō Kōji, *Chūsei Nihon no gaikō to zenshū* (Yoshikawa kōbunkan, 2002), pp. 146–47, describes the onset of Ōuchi trade with China in the Eikyō era (1429–41). For this appointment, see Itō Kōji, "Ōuchi shi no Ryūkyū tsūkō," *Nenpō chūseishi kenkyū*, no. 28 (2003), p. 189. For an informative overview of the trading routes with the Ming, Itō Kōji, see "Nyūminki kara mita Higashi Ajia no kaiiki kōryū," in *Higashi Ajia Kaiiki sōsho*, vol. 2, *Ningpo to Hakata* (Kyūko shoin, 2013), and for an invaluable resource on Japanese Ming trade, see Murai Shōsuke et al., eds., *Ajia no naka no kenminsen Nichimin kankeishi kenkyū nyūmon* (Bensei shuppan, 2015).

[83] Itō Kōji, "Ōuchi shi no Nichimin bōeki to Sakai," in *Chūsei Nihon no gaikō to zenshū*, pp. 213–34, and Hirase, *Ōuchi Yoshihiro*, pp. 182–83.

[84] Itō Kōji, *Chūsei Nihon no gaikō to zenshū*, pp. 86–88 for Shōfukuji in Hakata, p. 147 for Yōkōji, and pp. 179–81 for the Akamaseki temples.

[85] *Yamaguchi kenshi tsūshihen chūsei*, p. 396, and *Yamaguchi kenshi shiryōhen chūsei*, vol. 1, Daijōin jisha zōjiki, 1.24.1483 (Bunmei 15), p. 223.

common with Korea, but informal, but the receipt of these tallies allowed Norihiro to officially trade with Korea in ways that his competitors, such as the Shōni, could not. Only the Ashikaga, the nominal "Kings of Japan," also possessed similar Chosŏn seals, and dispatched ships to trade with Korea from the port of Obama, located on the Japan Sea.[86]

The *Boshi nyūminki* reveals that the Ming granted tallies, officially recognizing three ships that would sail from Moji. One was dispatched by the Ashikaga, the second by the Ōuchi, and the third by the Hosokawa. These ranged in size from 2,500 *koku* (Ashikaga), 1,800 (Ōuchi) and 1,200 (Hosokawa).[87] Miscellaneous goods for sale on the largest vessel included 300 fans (each worth 300 *mon*), 80 fans (worth 200 *mon*), 180 ink stones, 500 swords (*tachi*), 40 pikes, 350 *monme* of gold, 30,000 *kin* of sulfur, and 35 horseloads (*da*) of copper—of which 10 horseloads had been sent by the *shugo* of Bitchū.[88]

Having been granted the honor an official ship to the Ming, Norihiro was also involved in another expedition dating from 1465.[89] His connections to the Ming were strong enough, and his wealth great enough, that the famous painter Sesshū Tōyō (1420–1506), who traveled to the Ming, accepted his patronage over that of Ashikaga Yoshimasa, choosing to live in Yamaguchi instead of the capital.[90]

Recognition of Ōuchi Ethnicity

Norihiro was uniquely favored by the Chosŏn Dynasty. In addition to his unprecedented receipt of official trade tallies, Chosŏn officials recorded Norihiro's genealogical claims in their histories. These legends emphasize both Japanese identity and Korean descent and describe Prince Imsŏng's

[86] Kenneth Robinson, "Treated as Treasures: The Circulation of Sutras in Maritime Northeast Asia from 1388 to the Mid-Sixteenth Century," *East Asian History* 21 (June 2001), pp. 50–51 for this tally and more on Korean Ōuchi ties. See also *Ōuchi shi jitsuroku*, p. 58 for reference to this tally, which still survives. For Ashikaga links to Korea through the port of Obama, see Isao Soranaka, "Obama: The Rise and Decline of a Seaport," *Monumenta Nipponica* 52.1 (Spring 1997), pp. 90–93

[87] *Yamaguchi kenshi shiryōhen chūsei*, vol. 1, Boshi nyūminki, pp. 830–31. For the size of the ships see p. 832.

[88] *Yamaguchi kenshi shiryōhen chūsei*, vol. 1, Boshi nyūminki, p. 832.

[89] *Yamaguchi kenshi shiryōhen chūsei*, vol. 1, Inryōken nichiroku, 7.13.1465 (Kanshō 6), p. 138 for reference to Yoshimasa dispatching the first boat, and Norihiro the third to the Ming.

[90] Kawazoe Shōji, *Chūsei bungei no chihōshi*, p. 238.

career for the first time. The genealogy sent by the Ōuchi to Chosŏn officials reads as follows:

The Tatara family came to Japan, and for this reason we are Japanese. A certain Ōmuraji [the Mononobe] raised an army and sought to destroy the Buddhist law. Prince Shōtoku, the son of our King (*waga kuni no ōji*) revered and respected the Buddhist law and fought them in battle. At this time, the King of Paekche ordered Prince Imsŏng to destroy the Ōmuraji. Imsŏng then became the Ōuchi lord. Prince Shōtoku rewarded Imsŏng for his meritorious deeds and presented him with provinces and counties. From that time, Imsŏng took the name of that area and became the Ōuchi lord. Are there not relatives of the Ōuchi in Chosŏn? . . . Approximately 873 years have passed. Your country must have records of Prince Imsŏng's move to Japan. In the lands governed by the Ōuchi the records have been lost because of the many battles over the generations. That which has been recorded now is lore that has been passed down by our elders.[91]

In constructing this shared cultural identity, the Ōuchi portrayed themselves as the descendants of an international protector of Buddhism and symbol of Korean and Japanese cooperation. Prince Imsŏng was now identified as a commander dispatched by the Paekche court to help Japanese authorities quell enemies of Buddhism.

The view of Imsŏng as an international savior of Buddhism found favor among Chosŏn officials, as they recorded the Ōuchi legend in detail. Claims of shared descent caused Korean emissaries to emphasize their affinity. In 1471, Shin Sukchu (1417–75), a high-ranking Chosŏn official and translator, described the Ōuchi in his *Haedong chegukki* (*Annals of the Lands of the Eastern Seas*, J. *Kaitō Shokokuki*) as having "the most powerful warriors, and none disobey their orders in Kyushu. They are descended from a Paekche prince and so are most close to us."[92]

---

[91] Translation based on Robinson, "Treated as Treasures," pp. 50–51, and, for the original, *Tanjong shillok* 6:46a-b 11453/6/241. See also *Yamaguchi kenshi shiryōhen chūsei*, vol. 1, Tanjon sillok, 6.24.1453 (Tanjon 1), p. 889. For further analysis of this passage, see Suda Makiko, *Chūsei Nichō kankei to Ōuchi shi*, pp. 218–20, Itō Kōji, "Ōuchi no sosen shinwa," *Tōhokugaku* series 2, no. 27 (2011), pp. 99–100, and Itō Kōji, "Chūsei saikoku shoshi no keifu ninshiki," in *Kyokai aidentiti* (Kyūshū shigakukai, 2008), pp. 121–22.

[92] Shin Sukchu, *Haedong chegukki*, p. 150. For more on the notion of ethnicity see Itō, "Ōuchi no sosen shinwa," pp. 99–101. A recent study discusses the maps used in this work and their depiction of Mt. Fuji. See Ronald Toby, *Engaging the Other: "Japan" and Its Alter-Egos, 1550–1850* (Leiden: Brill, 2019), pp. 269–71.

In making these claims, the Ōuchi and their supporters drew parallels with the Ashikaga, who were also portrayed as protectors of Buddhism. Their supporters directly compared Ashikaga policies to those of Prince Shōtoku (574–622).[93] This legend implied that Ōuchi and the Ashikaga, like Imsŏng and Prince Shōtoku, could work together as the protectors of Buddhism. In addition, claims of Korean kingly descent allowed the Ōuchi to claim equality with the Ashikaga, who likewise claimed to be Kings of Japan. A Zen monk praised Ōuchi Norihiro as being "the fiercest general of his generation, and the scion of an ancient kingly house" (*ichidai no moshō senko no ōke* 一 代猛将、千古の王家).[94]

The Ashikaga response to Norihiro's claims of Imsŏng as a protector, and equal to Prince Shōtoku, is not known, but some Japanese courtiers claimed that the Ōuchi were not fully Japanese. In 1472, the monk Jinson commented on Ōuchi ancestry upon seeing a panegyric for a mortuary portrait of Norihiro. He wrote: "The Ōuchi are not originally Japanese (*honrai nihonjin ni arazu*). Rather, they are from the land of the Mongols. Some say that they are Korean (*Kōraijin*)." Jinson explained how Ōuchi ancestors traveled to Suō, where they adopted the name Tatara.[95] Jinson was aware of Tatara, which became a sort of Plymouth Rock or Ellis Island, a foundational site of landing for the immigrants who arrived in Japan. A few years later, in 1475, Jinson more accurately ascribed them as being from Paekche rather than simply Korea or Mongolia.[96] Ōuchi claims of Japanese identity, Korean origins, and the importance of Tatara as the site of their immigration suggest that their ethnic difference was widely known and recognized by people in Korea and Japan.

Delegated and Personalized Authority

Norihiro was unique among the great lords for his widely recognized claims of Tatara ethnicity, but in terms of his relations with the Ashikaga,

---

[93] Royall Tyler, trans., *Fourteenth-Century Voices*, vol. 2, *From Baishōron to Nantaiheiki* (Blue Tongue Books, 2016), pp. 117–20 for Musō Soseki's praise of Ashikaga Takauji and Tadayoshi.

[94] Kawaguchi Kōfū et al. eds., *Chūkun Sōtō shū zengoroku zensho Chūsei hen*, vol. 8 (Shikisha, 2006), pp. 107–8. See also Yonehara Masayoshi, *Ōuchi Yoshitaka* (Jinbutsu ōraisha, 1967), pp. 52–53.

[95] *Yamaguchi kenshi shiryōhen chūsei*, vol. 1, Daijōin jisha zōjiki, 5.27.1472 (Bunmei 4), p. 209. Jinson initially recorded a garbled genealogy that confused Norihiro with Mochiyo, showing how little he knew or cared about the Ōuchi. This would change later.

[96] *Yamaguchi kenshi shiryōhen chūsei*, vol. 1, Daijōin jisha zōjiki, 8.14.1475 (Bunmei 7), p. 217, and Itō Kōji, "Chūsei saikoku shoshi no keifu ninshiki," pp. 122–23.

his behavior was comparable to that of other *shugo* magnates, although he chafed under their rule more than most.

It took some time for the Ashikaga to stabilize their rule after Yoshinori's assassination. Yoshinori's eldest son Yoshikatsu, ten years old, had died after a mere eight months of "rule," and his younger brother Yoshimasa (1436–90) was appointed shogun in 1449. The Ashikaga had enough authority to ensure that *shugo*, including Norihiro, would celebrate this succession in Kyoto. Norihiro returned there in the fourth month of 1449, leading two hundred horsemen.[97] He also gave the Ashikaga a thousand *kanmon* of cash, or the equivalent of over half of a province's yearly tax revenue.[98] For his largesse, Norihiro was promoted to the fourth rank lower, and he remained in Kyoto until 1454–55.[99]

During these six years of residence in Kyoto, Norihiro copied many works of court literature, including the Utsusemi chapter of *The Tale of Genji*, the most famous court novel of the early eleventh century; the *Kokinwakashū*, Ki no Tsurayuki (872–945)'s iconic compilation of Japanese-style poetry, dating from 905; and the *Kikashū*, a ten-volume edition of some 1,622 poems written by Minamoto Toshiyori (1055–1129).[100] Norihiro thus became further aware of iconic court texts and with these copies could ensure that his descendants were as well. Norihiro's activities suggest that he believed it important to function as a courtier and attempted to master a courtier's cultural knowledge.

While in Kyoto, Norihiro successfully delegated administrative and tax authority in western Honshu and northern Kyushu. The parameters of his authority are most evident from his ability to assess *tansen* taxes, taxes assessed on lands in a province, a great source of revenue and a crucial prerogative of *shugo* authority.[101] Norihiro assessed this tax in the core provinces of Suō and Nagato and Buzen "in accordance with precedent."[102] These

[97] *Yamaguchi kenshi tsūshihen furoku* CD-ROM, Tōji hyakugo monjo, doc. 143, Saishōkōin kata *hyōjo hikitsuke*, p. 523. For the two hundred horsemen, see *Yamaguchi kenshi shiryōhen chūsei*, vol. 1, Kyōgaku shiyōshō, 4.24.1449 (Bunan 6), p. 176.

[98] *Yamaguchi kenshi tsūshihen chūsei*, pp. 395–96. See also *Yamaguchi kenshi shiryōhen chūsei*, vol. 4, Yasutomiki, 4.27.1449 (Bunan 6), p. 819.

[99] *Yamaguchi kenshi tsūshihen furoku* CD-ROM, *Kuzen rinji inzen mikyōjo an*, doc. 11, 5.26.1449 (Bunan 6) Go-Hanazono tennō *kuzen an utsushi*, p. 435.

[100] Sasaki Takahiro, "'Ōshimabon Genji monogatari' ni kansuru shoshigakuteki kōsatsu," *Keiō Gijuku daigaku fuzoku kenkyūjō Shidō bunko* 41 (2006), p. 184 for how Norihiro copied this chapter of Genji. For the poetic texts, see *Ōuchi bunka*, p. 618 and plates 10–11. The *Kokinwakashū* was attributed to Masahiro, but the monogram is clearly Norihiro's. See pp. 620–21.

[101] Saeki Kōji, "Ōuchi shi no Chikuzen no kuni shihai," pp. 283–85.

[102] *Usa jingūshi shiryōhen*, vol. 10 (Usa, 1993), 10.16.1453 (Kyōtoku 2), Ōuchi Norihiro *mikyōjo*, pp. 36–37 for the precedent of levying *tansen* in Buzen. See *Yamaguchi kenshi shiryōhen chūsei*, vol. 1,

provinces had long been under Ōuchi control, and their revenue was considerable. Suō *tansen* taxes collected on 5.24.1454 constituted at least 169,890 *kanmon*.[103] In 1456, Norihiro was able to levy these *tansen* for Suō, Iwami, Nagato, Bungo, Buzen, and Chikuzen, which included provinces where he was not recognized as *shugo*.[104] These levies were more encompassing than before, as Norihiro canceled shrine exemptions from them.[105]

Norihiro continued to govern some core districts in provinces where he was not appointed as a *shugo* and, in many cases, to link their taxes to specific rites, most notably those devoted to Myōken at Hikamisan performed every second month of the year.[106] He set up a twenty-year schedule, starting in 1450, that demarcated district revenues for such rites. These districts included ones as distant as Nima, which fell under Ōuchi authority, even though the Ōuchi did not technically control Iwami as its *shugo*.[107]

Norihiro set prices for tolls and ferries in his domains, and in 1461 he stipulated how many days were required to travel to Yamaguchi from places within Ōuchi territory. The lands where these codes applied ranged from the islands of the Inland Sea, to Chikuzen, Hizen, and Buzen in Kyushu, to districts in Aki, Iwami, and Hizen that were not directly under Ōuchi *shugo* control.[108] Iwami's Nima and Hizen's Kanzaki districts were described as part of Norihiro's domain (*bunkoku*) by the Ashikaga although he governed neither province as its *shugo*.[109] In contrast to Suō, Buzen, and Nagato, which were fully under his authority, Norihiro only controlled eleven of the fifteen districts of Chikuzen, with the remaining four districts under the administration of his Shōni rivals.[110]

Kennaiki, 10.26.1447 (Bunan 4), p. 169 for Suō and, Yasutomiki, 10.20.1450 (Hōtoku 2), p. 173 for Nagato.

[103] *Yamaguchi kenshi tsūshihen furoku* CD-ROM, Tōfukuji monjo, doc. 28, 5.24.1454 (Kyōtoku 3) Suō no kuni Sabaryō *gun ta fuse tansen nokachō an*, pp. 618–19.

[104] *Yamaguchi kenshi shiryōhen chūsei*, vol. 1, 1456 (Kyōtoku 5) Chūgoku Kyūshū *oharai kubarichō*, pp. 539–45.

[105] This happened for the Ninomiya shrine of Suō. *Sengoku ibun Ōuchi shi hen*, vol. 1, doc. 514, 8.13.1481 (Bunmei 13) Ōuchi Masahiro *kishinjō*, p. 163. For more analysis see Matsuoka Hisatō, "Muromachi sengokuki no Suō kokugaryō to Ōuchi shi," in *Ōuchi shi no kenkyū* (Seibundō, 2011), p. 164.

[106] This is otherwise known as the Hikamisan *nigatsu-e*.

[107] *Yamaguchi kenshi shiryōhen chūsei*, vol. 3, Yamaguchi monjokan Kōryūji monjo, doc. 76, 2.13.1450 (Hōtoku 2) Kōryūji *nigatsu-e wakizu sanzu yaku shidai chūmon*, pp. 253–54.

[108] Iwasaki Toshihiko, *Ōuchi shi kabegaki o yomu* (Yamaguchi, 1997), pp. 36–38, and *Chūsei hōsei shiryōshū* vol. 3, *Bukehō*, vol. 1 (Iwanami shoten, 1965), pp. 38–42.

[109] *Yamaguchi kenshi shiryōhen chūsei*, vol. 1, Ninagawa Chikamoto nikki, 6.5.1465 (Kanshō 6), pp. 186–87.

[110] See the commentary by Kawazoe Shōji, pp. 672–73 of *Dazaifu shishi chūsei shiryōhen*, pp. 672–73 for analysis of Norihiro's 1461 laws. These districts were Munakata, which had a strong tradition

While stationed in the capital, Norihiro also expanded his control over northern Kyushu, receiving in the 1450s the district of Kanzaki, in Hizen province, to the west of Hakata.[111] Norihiro's authority over most of the other districts of Chikuzen province would not, however, become firmly entrenched until 1461.[112] With his political position secure, Norihiro delegated the affairs of the Dazaifu and Hakata to his administrators, the Sugi, Sue, and Niho, each of whom served as a check on the others.[113]

The 1450s witnessed rising tension and turmoil in central Japan. Several succession disputes in the 1450s, among the Shiba and the Hatakeyama, two of three chancellor (kanrei) families, paralyzed the Ashikaga regime. Two members of the Hatakeyama fought pitched battles over succession in 1454.[114] Ashikaga Yoshimasa became embroiled in a dispute with Yamana Sōzen (1404–73), a shugo of provinces to the east of the Ōuchi, and sent out missives encouraging warriors to attack him.[115] None did and Sōzen returned from Kyoto to his stronghold in Tanba. Yoshimasa refused to deal with him and, to save face, appointed Sōzen's son as shugo in his stead. Shortly thereafter, Norihiro, like Sōzen, fell afoul of Yoshimasa and was divested of his post of shugo of Nagato, and presumably other provinces as well.[116]

Ashikaga Yoshimasa has long had a reputation for being Japan's most incompetent shogun.[117] His actions suggest an impressive degree of political maladroitness. Yoshimasa apparently believed that he would harm Sōzen

of autonomy, Shima, Sawara, and Yasu. In 1450, only Munakata and Shima, the location of major shrines, were not included in rosters, suggesting that the loss of Sawara and Yasu happened between 1450 and 1461. For reference to these districts being under Norihiro's control in 1450, see Yamaguchi kenshi shiryōhen chūsei, vol. 3, Yamaguchi monjokan Kōryūji monjo, doc. 76, 2.13.1450 (Hōtoku 2) Kōryūji nigatsu-e wakizu sanzu yaku shidai chūmon, pp. 253–54. Finally, see Saeki Kōji, "Ōuchi shi no Chikuzen no kuni shihai," pp. 274–93.

[111] Seno Sei'ichirō, comp., Hizen no kuni Kanzaki shōen shiryō (Yoshikawa kōbunkan, 1975), doc. 271, 12.2.1455 (Kōshō 1) Ōuchi Norihiro kakikudashi, p. 197, revealing Norihiro's authority over Kanzaki. Likewise, see doc. 272, 12.25.1459 (Chōroku 3) Shibukawa Noritada kakikudashi, p. 197 for an exemption of the tansen for this district that suggests that Norihiro had the ability to levy this tax or this district.

[112] Saeki Kōji, "Ōuchi shi no Chikuzen no kuni shihai," p. 293.

[113] Dazaifu Dazaifu Tenmangū shiryō, vol. 13, 1456 (Kōshō 2) Ōuchi Norihiro gechijō, pp. 311–12.

[114] Kōya shunshū hennen shūroku, in Dainihon Bukkyō zensho, 161 vols. (Bussho kankōkai, 1912–22), vol. 131 (1912), maki 11, p. 240.

[115] Yamaguchi kenshi tsūshihen chūsei, p. 397. For the document, see Kinoshita Satoshi, ed., Ashikaga Yoshimasa hakkyū monjo, vol. 1 (Sengokushi kenkyūkai shiryōshu 1, 2015), doc. 8, 11.3 [(Kyōtoku 3) 1454] Ashikaga Yoshimasa gonaisho, p. 23.

[116] Yamaguchi kenshi tsūshihen chūsei, p. 397, and Shimonoseki shishi shiryōhen, vol. 6 (Shimonoseki, 2001), Chōfu Mōri ke monjo tekagami, doc. 43, 8.9 Ōuchi Norihiro shojō, p. 17.

[117] For the characterization of him as Japan's worst shogun, see Donald Keene, Yoshimasa and the Silver Pavilion: The Creation of the Soul of Japan (New York: Columbia University Press, 2003), p. 166.

and Norihiro by divesting them of their *shugo* offices, but his actions only served to enhance their personal authority at the expense of institutional prerogative. Yoshimasa may have thought that the selection of the young sons of Sōzen and Norihiro as *shugo* replacements would make them malleable to his will, but because they resided near their fathers, they served as mere figureheads for the continued rule of both. Yoshimasa also did Sōzen and Norihiro a favor by appointing their sons to office, as he ensured that they would be the undisputed heirs. This prevented the families from fracturing their allegiances, as commonly happened at times of succession. As the new *shugo*, Norihiro's young son Kidō, the future Masahiro (1446–95), performed ritual functions, such as worshiping the sea gods at the Nagato Ichinomiya (Sumiyoshi) shrine in 1455.[118]

Norihiro returned to Yamaguchi late in 1454 and, although not officially a *shugo*, confirmed tax immunities for shrines in his lands. He did so by relying on his personal authority, rather than on appointment to the office per se.[119] Norihiro emphasized his position as head of the Ōuchi by continuing to worship at the same shrines where his young son worshiped as *shugo*, thus by ritual performance demonstrating his supremacy and potentially erasing any perceived pro-Ashikaga ritual activities by his son Kidō.[120]

Norihiro shored up the ritual activities of Yamaguchi, and enhanced its laws, irrespective of his appointed position. His administrators reformed practices at Usa Hachiman shrine, in his name prohibiting cows, horses, and children from fouling the waters.[121] Divestments of the post of *shugo* were less debilitating than they would have been for other families because the Ōuchi had long controlled districts that were outside *shugo* authority. Authority remained personalized, rather than institutional, although the prerogatives latent in the position of *shugo* remained valuable.

[118] *Yamaguchi kenshi tsūshihen chūsei*, p. 396, and the Nagato no kuni shugoshiki shidai, *Yamaguchi kenshi shiryōhen chūsei*, vol. 1, pp. 604–5. For evidence of Norihiro's son Kidō being invested with the position of Chikuzen *shugo*, and exempting Kaita estate from the *hanzei*, see *Kōyasan Kongō sanmaiin monjo*, doc. 171, 9.28.1459 (Chōroku 3) *Kanrei* Hosokawa Katsumoto *shigyōjō utsushi*, p. 121.

[119] For later reference to his confirmation of temple and shrine immunities on 12.21.1454 (Kyōtoku 3), see *Sengoku ibun Ōuchi shi hen*, vol. 1, doc. 681, 8.22.1488 (Chōkyō 2) Shinjōbō Suiki *mōshijō utsushi*, pp. 220–21.

[120] On 4.22.1455 (Kyōtoku 4), he worshiped at the same Nagato Ichinomiya shrine as his son. *Yamaguchi kenshi tsūshihen chūsei*, p. 396, and *Yamaguchi kenshi shiryōhen chūsei*, vol. 1, Nagato no kuni shugoshiki shidai, p. 605.

[121] *Usa jingūshi shiryōhen*, vol. 10, 8.27, 9.29.1455 (Kyōtoku 4) Ōuchi shi *bugyōnin hōsho*, pp. 146–47, 154–55. See also documents dated 11.25.1455 (Kyōtoku 4), p. 157, and 12.25.1455 (Kyōtoku 4), p. 163.

Sometime between 3.1457 and 8.1463 Ashikaga Yoshimasa, realizing the inefficacy of his *shugo* confiscations, arbitrarily endeavored to undermine Norihiro by divesting him of his position as Ōuchi chieftain.[122] Yoshimasa attempted to make Norihiro's son and heir Kidō his pawn and sent to the young boy all his official correspondence.[123] Norihiro chose not to dispute his nominal divestment as the head of the Ōuchi, and his actions show how ineffectual Yoshimasa's policy was. Archaeological evidence suggests that he moved out of the Ōuchi mansion and set up a new abode just north of it, at a place called Tsukiyama.[124] From there he watched over his son.

Although neither a chieftain nor a *shugo*, Norihiro continued to govern Ōuchi affairs and maintained support among his followers, since he confirmed lands to the Kurihara on 12.25.1453.[125] He also broadened support by delegating authority over the strategic Abu district of Nagato to a relative named Ōuchi Takeharu.[126] Ōuchi cohesion remained strong despite Ashikaga attempts to foment disunion. Norihiro relied on his personal authority to confirm the rank of followers or that of religious institutions, since he continued to grant lands to Usa shrine in 1456 and 1458.[127]

Not having to rely on Ashikaga legitimacy or titles for his rule, Norihiro openly attacked Ashikaga allies and undermined their interests. In 1457 he fought the Takeda, the *shugo* of Aki province, and occupied two of their castles in Tōsai.[128] In these sharp, but limited encounters,

---

[122] This was first recognized by Wada Shūsaku, "Ōuchi Takaharu oyobi sono kankei shiryō," *Yamaguchi monjokan kenkyū kiyō* 30 (2003), p. 11. See also *Yamaguchi kenshi tsūshihen chūsei*, pp. 396–97, and *Yamaguchi kenshi shiryōhen chūsei*, vol. 2, Shoke monjo 2, p. 744. This continued through 1461. See *Kobayakawa ke monjo*, vol. 2, Shomon, doc. 129, 6.9.1461 (Kanshō 2) Aki Tōsai no jō *kotogaki utsushi*, p. 45.

[123] Wada Shūsaku, "Ōuchi shi no sōsho kankei o megutte," p. 38.

[124] Little is known about this dwelling save that it was occupied for only a relatively short period of time. Maruo Kōsuke, "Ōuchi yakata Tsukiyama yakata o horu," Ōuchi shi rekishi bunka kenkyūkai, comp., *Ōuchi shi no sekai o saguru* (Bensei shuppan, 2019), pp. 142–49.

[125] *Yamaguchi kenshi shiryōhen chūsei*, vol. 2, Kurihara ke monjo, doc. 2, 8.19.1450 (Hōtoku 2) Ōuchi Norihiro *kakanjō*, p. 938 for Kurihara Yagorō receiving the name Hirotake. For a photo, see *Ōuchi bunka to Kitakyūshū*, p. 17. For later confirmations, see *Hagi han batsu etsu roku*, vol. 4, Kurihara ke monjo, doc. 17, 12.25.1453 (Kyōtoku 2) Ōuchi Norihiro *andojō*, p. 27. This document no longer apparently survives, for it is absent from the surviving Kurihara ke monjo collection. See *Yamaguchi kenshi shiryōhen chūsei*, vol. 2, pp. 938–40.

[126] Wada Shūsaku, "Ōuchi Takaharu oyobi sono kankei shiryō," p. 11. For Takeharu's control over Abu district (*gun*), see p. 6; for his position as second in line for succession to Masahiro, see p. 8.

[127] *Dazaifu Dazaifu Tenmangū shiryō*, vol. 13, 4.27.1456 (Kōshō 2) Ōuchi Norihiro *andojō*, pp. 310–11, and *Usa jingūshi shiryōhen*, vol. 10, 6.25.1458 (Chōroku 2) Ōuchi Norihiro *andojō*, p. 192.

[128] For an overview, see Kawamura Shōichi, *Aki Takeda shi* (Ebisu kōshō, 2010), pp. 82–84. These battles continued through 1461 and again flared in 1465. See pp. 84–86. For documentary evidence of this campaign, see Wada Shūsaku, "Ōuchi shi kashin Yasutomi shi no kankei shiryō ni tsuite,"

two Takeda retainers were killed by Naitō Moriyo, one of Norihiro's men.[129]

Norihiro started issuing confirmations without delegated authority to do so in lands further afield, where competing *shugo* existed. This first happened in the third month of 1458, when the Fukawa, who fled from Aki province, were granted lands. The Kubo, another warrior family, received similar confirmations.[130] Norihiro gave lands to the Usa shrine, and Usa warriors in 1458.[131] He also confirmed the lands of Chikuzen warriors such as the Ihara, whose ancestors, in 1436, had perished in battle fighting the Shōni under the command of his unlucky uncle Norisuke (1397?–1436).[132]

Norihiro received increasing recognition from Choson officials over the course of the 1450s. Korean sources reveal that as early as 1456 the "Japanese King" Yoshimasa and Ōuchi Norihiro competed for trading prerogatives.[133] In 1458, some Korean accounts merely referred to him as an Ōuchi/Tatara from Japan, without a specific title, but in 1460 and 1463 Norihiro would be addressed by the Koreans as the lord of the four provinces (Suō, Nagato, Chikuzen, and Buzen) even though he technically was not the *shugo* of any of them.[134]

Norihiro harbored others who had fallen afoul of the Ashikaga, such as Shiba Yoshitoshi (1435–1508), who fled to Yamaguchi in 1459.[135] In 1460

Yamaguchi ken monjokan kenkyū kiyō 28 (3.2001), doc. 11, 7.29 [(Kōshō 3) 1457] Ōuchi Masahiro *kanjō utsushi*, p. 75. See also Wada Shūsaku, "Suō Migita shi no sōden monjo," *Yamaguchi ken monjokan kenkyū kiyō* 41 (3.2014), p. 95, and *Kikkawa ke monjo*, vol. 1 (Tōkyō daigaku shuppankai, 1925), doc. 46, 4.26.1462 (Kanshō 3) Bakufu *bugyō rensho hōsho*, p. 28, *Mōri ke monjo*, vol. 1, doc. 88, 5.27.1462 (Kanshō 3) Muromachi shōgun ke *mikyōjo*, p. 91, and doc. 97, 5.23 [(Kanshō 3) 1462] Takeda Kuninobu *shojō*, pp. 97–99.

129 *Hagi han batsu etsu roku*, vol. 3, Naitō Shōgenda monjo, maki 99.2, doc. 58, 1.1 [(Chōroku 1) 1457] Ōuchi Norihiro *shojō*, p. 160 and maki 135, Kushibe monjo, doc. 11, 1.1 Ōuchi Norihiro *shojō*, p. 847. These battles continued through 3.21.1457 (Chōroku 1). *Ōuchi shi jitsuroku*, p. 58.

130 *Munakata shishi shiryōhen chūsei*, vol. 2, doc. 121, 3.11.1458 (Chōroku 2) Ōuchi Norihiro *ategaijō utsushi*, p. 101 for a grant of lands to a Fukawa Tōkurō, who fled from Aki to Suō. See also a 3.11.1458 (Chōroku 2) Ōuchi Norihiro *kudashibumi utsushi*, *Yamaguchi kenshi shiryōhen chūsei*, vol. 3, Kubo ke monjo, p. 851. The format of this copy is anomalous. The 1458 document was either a forgery or copied in accordance with the style of 1461.

131 *Usa jingūshi shiryōhen*, vol. 10, 11.3.1455 (Kōshō 1) Ōuchi Norihiro *gechijō*, pp. 155–56 for grants to Narishige Morishige, and 6.25.1458 (Choroku 2) Ōuchi Norihiro *andojō*, p. 192 for grants of lands to Usa shrine.

132 Moriyama Tsuneyo, "Shiryō shōkai Ihara ke monjo," *Kyūshū Shigaku* 17 (1.1961), Ihara ke monjo, doc. 9, 11.25.1458 (Chōroku 2) Ōuchi Norihiro *chigyō andojō*, p. 56.

133 *Yamaguchi kenshi shiryōhen chūsei*, vol. 1, Sejo sillok, 5.22.1456 (Sejo 2), pp. 891–92.

134 *Yamaguchi kenshi shiryōhen chūsei*, vol. 1, Sejo sillok 8.23.1458 (Sejo 4), p. 892, 12.26.1460 (Sejo 6), p. 893, and 8.6.1463 (Sejo 9), p. 894.

135 *Yamaguchi kenshi tsūshihen chūsei*, p. 397. See also Ienaga Junji, *Muromachi bakufu shōgun kenryoku no kenkyū* (Tokyo daigaku nihon shigaku kenkyūshitsu, 1995), p. 230.

the Ninagawa, Ashikaga administrators, demanded that Norihiro turn over contested lands.[136] At the same time, they criticized Norihiro for not living in the capital, as he had done prior to 1441, and for the years 1449–54/55.[137] Ashikaga Yoshimasa became so upset with Norihiro's protection of Shiba Yoshimasa that he threatened to attack Norihiro early in 1461.[138] Ultimately, Yoshimasa, like his father Yoshinori before him, divested the Ōuchi of Tōsai.

In response, Norihiro did not travel to the capital to beg for their reinstatement as his uncle Mochiyo had done in 1440. Instead, he defended Tōsai by force.[139] Thereupon war erupted between the Ōuchi and the Ashikaga. It would last for the next seventeen years. During this time, Norihiro also laid the foundations for an independent warrior government in the Ōuchi domains of western Honshu and northern Kyushu.[140]

Creating a Western Warrior Government

While in Yamaguchi, Norihiro upheld the legal tradition of the Kamakura bakufu (1185–1333), and he tried to use this code as the basis for common law in his domains. In 1462 he adjudicated a dispute over an incident in which one Ishikawa Sukegorō was killed by a commoner (heimin) named Saburō, who had discovered his wife and Sukegorō in flagrante delicto and killed him but not his wife. Norihiro banished Saburō, his wife, and their

---

[136] Ninagawa ke monjo, vol. 1, doc. 45, 3.18.1460 (Chōroku 4) Bakufu bugyō rensho hōsho an, pp. 102–3.

[137] Kobayakawa ke monjo, vol. 2, doc. 131, 8.11 Ise Sadachika shojō utsushi, p. 46. For a document issued earlier by Yoshimasa, see Ashikaga Yoshimasa hakkyū monjo, vol. 1, urū 9.8 [(Chōroku 4) 1460] Ashikaga Yoshimasa gonaisho an utsushi, p. 83, asking that Norihiro explain why he rebuffed repeated requests to go to the capital.

[138] Yamaguchi kenshi shiryōhen chūsei, vol. 1, Kyōgaku shiyōshō 1.22.1461 (Kanshō 2), p. 176, and Ienaga Junji, Muromachi bakufu shōgun kenryoku no kenkyū, p. 230 for the characterization of this document as an edict of chastisement (jibatsu rinji). For the original, see Kyōgaku shiyōshō, vol. 5 (Iwanami shoten, 1985), p. 18.

[139] See Kawamura Shōichi, Aki Takeda shi, pp. 84–86. This 1461 confiscation resulted in battles here that again flared up in 1465. In 1461, two major Takeda commanders were killed by Naitō Moriyo. See Hagi han batsu etsu roku, vol. 3, maki 99 no. 2, Naitō Kogeneta doc. 58, 1.1 Ōuchi Norihiro shojō, p. 160. This document was mistakenly assumed to date from 1458 (Chōroku 1) by the copyists of Hagi han batsu etsu roku.

[140] Kobayakawa ke monjo, vol. 2, doc. 122, 4.29.1461 (Kanshō 2) Shōgun ke mikyōjo utsushi, p. 41 for a Kyoto messenger joining the Kobayakawa, doc. 123, 6.5 Kotogaki utsushi, p. 41–42 for the bakufu's instructions to forcibly confiscate these lands, and doc. 129, 6.9.1461 (Kanshō 2) Aki Tōsaijō kotogaki utsushi, p. 45 for both messengers notifying Ōuchi Masahiro that the lands would be confiscated and bestowed to Takeda Nobukata.

child to Mishima Island, justifying this decision by appealing to the principles of the 1232 *Goseibai shikimoku*.[141]

In so doing Norihiro relied on Kamakura law to intrude into the internal affairs of the house, where previously the lord's authority had not extended. In some areas of eastern Japan, warrior households would remain outside of the purview of the lord. The *Jinkaishū*, a code created by the Date, warriors who established weak control of regions in the north, would still recognize the legal autonomy of a household in 1536.[142]

On 5.22.1459, Norihiro also set curfews for his domain. Evening activities were prohibited, together with street wrestling, soliciting for prostitution, or, save for some exceptions, visiting the Yuta hot springs at night. The fact that Norihiro attempted to control street wrestling or night visits to hot springs suggests that Yamaguchi's population was expanding. At the same time, Norihiro expressed concern that people from elsewhere might foment dissension and should be employed only with caution. He also set the schedule of his legal councils, stipulating that they would meet regularly on the twentieth of every month.[143] Further legal improvements on 7.8.1461 included regulations covering theft and the pawning of stolen goods.[144] He regularized measurements as well.[145]

Having regulated his territories, Norihiro embarked on an ambitious project to establish a warrior government in the west. These efforts have largely gone unnoticed, but Norihiro's designs are evident because he began issuing edicts known as *kudashibumi*, with his name prominently displayed

---

[141] *Chūsei hōsei shiryōshū*, vol. 3, *Bukehō*, vol. 1, 8.30.1462 (Kanshō 3) Ōuchi shi *hekisho*, clause 14, p. 43. For brief reference to this law (with a mistaken attribution to Norihiro's son) see also Kawamura Kimiaki, *Hagi Abu no chūsei fūdoki*, p. 138. This proved to be a much stronger authority over house law than evident in other regions, such as by the *Jinkaishū* of the north, which dates from the sixteenth century. For analysis see Sugawara Masako, "Sengoku daimyō no bikkaihō to fūfu," *Rekishi hyōron*, no. 679 (11.2006), p. 10. For translations of Norihiro's regulations, see Conlan, *Samurai and the Warrior Culture of Japan, 471–1877: A Sourcebook* (Indianapolis: Hackett, 2022), pp. 193–94, 198–99.

[142] See Kobayashi Hiroshi, "Domain Laws (*Bunkoku-hō*) in the Sengoku Period with Special Emphasis on the Date House Code, the *Jinkaishū*," *Acta Asiatica* 35 (11.1978), pp. 30–45. For a translation of much of this code, see Conlan, *Samurai*, pp. 206–15.

[143] Satō Shin'ichi et al., eds., *Chūsei hōsei shiryōshū* vol. 3, *Bukehō*, vol. 1, section 4, Ōuchi-shi *hekisho*, clauses 2–8, dating 5.22.1459 (Chōroku 3), pp. 36–37. For how long it would take per day to travel from the various regions of the homelands (*bunkoku*) of the Ōuchi, see in the same source, 6.29.1461 (Kanshō 2) Ōuchi-shi *hekisho*, clause 10, pp. 38–42. As we have seen, these regions included districts in provinces not directly controlled by the Ōuchi, most notably Tōsaijō in Aki, Nima, and Iwami and Kanzaki in Hizen.

[144] *Chūsei hōsei shiryōshū*, vol. 3, *Bukehō*, vol. 1, 7.8.1461 (Kanshō 2) Ōuchi shi *hekisho*, clauses 11–13, p. 42.

[145] *Chūsei hōsei shiryōshū*, vol. 3, *Bukehō*, vol. 1, 10.25.1462 (Kanshō 3) Ōuchi shi *hekisho*, clause 15, p. 44. This was done in accordance with the precedent of ancient regulations (*koshiki*).

at the head of the document, suggesting that command was based on his personal authority. This format harked back to Minamoto Yoritomo (1147–99), the founder of the first Japanese warrior government, who used his name to justify edicts while still a rebel with no official standing or office. The *kudashibumi* remained the most prestigious type of document issued by that regime and by its successor, the Ashikaga, until the time of Yoshimochi (1386–1428). The last examples of *kudashibumi* issued by the Ashikaga date from 1426.[146]

In issuing such documents, Norihiro demonstrated that he was the ultimate authority in his domains and required no confirmation or legitimation from the Ashikaga.[147] He was the first regional magnate to take such a bold step, but he could do so because he had been divested of all official positions by the Ashikaga. Norihiro also was one of the first warriors to critique the style of governance of the fifteenth-century Ashikaga shoguns Yoshimitsu (1358–1408), Yoshimochi, Yoshinori (1394–1441), and Yoshimasa (1436–90), who rarely if at all relied on this *kudashibumi* format but preferred a more informal method of rule by communicating through letters (*gonaisho*).

Norihiro started issuing his monogrammed *kudashibumi* edicts in 1461, just after suffering the confiscation of Tōsai, until slightly before his death in 1465, with at least four copies surviving.[148] Some scholars such as Hagihara Daisuke have argued that all are forgeries, but examples have been copied in collections where all of the surviving documents are reliable, such as the

---

[146] Itō Kōji, "Ōuchi shi no potenshiyaru," in Ōuchi shi rekishi bunka kenkyūkai, comp., *Ōuchi shi no sekai o saguru* (Bensei shuppan, 2019), p. 4, argues that these documents were used by the Ashikaga until 1402, but later examples date from 1425/26 albeit in a different format. *Usa* documents suggests that they were used through the time of Ashikaga Yoshimochi in 1417. *Usa jingūshi shiryōhen*, vol. 9, 9.12.1417 (Ōei 24) Ashikaga Yoshimochi *kudashibumi*, pp. 212–13. See too *Shimazu ke monjo*, vol. 1 (Tōkyō daigaku shuppankai, 1952), doc. 72. 8.28.1425 (Ōei 32) Ashikaga Yoshimochi *kudashibumi*, p. 45, which admittedly does not contain the word *kudasu*, while *Rekidai koan* has an Ashikaga Yoshimochi *kudashibumi* dating from 7.14.1426 (Ōei 33). See *Rekidai koan*, vol. 3 (Zoku gunsho ruijū kanseikai, 1998), doc. 682, 7.14.1426 (Ōei 33) Muromachi shōgun ke Ashikaga Yoshimochi *kudashibumi*, pp. 4–5.

[147] For this insight, see Hagihara Daisuke, "Ōuchi shi no sodehan kudashibumi to gokenin sei," *Komonjo kenkyū*, no. 68 (1.2010), pp. 80–102.

[148] *Munakata shishi shiryōhen chūsei*, vol. 2, doc. 132 3.10.1461 (Kanshō 2) Ōuchi Norihiro *andojō utsushi*, p. 106 for a document from the Kawatsu Denki and doc. 136, 6.7.1465 (Kanshō 6) Ōuchi Masahiro (*sic*) *kudashibumi utsushi*, p. 107. The editors of *Munakata shishi* mistakenly attribute this to Masahiro when the copy itself expressly links the document to Norihiro. For another of his *sodehan kudashibumi* issued to Shinohara Shirō [Tadamori] see *Hagi han batsu etsu roku*, vol. 4, maki 150, Usuki saemon monjo doc. 15, 7.20.1461 (Kanshō 2) Ōuchi Norihiro *sodehan hōsho utsushi*. All three of these documents can be classified as *sodehan kudashibumi*. In addition to the three documents, a fourth copy survives for the Ichinomiya shrine of Nagato, dated 4.5.1464. See note 150 below.

Usuki, which includes one dated 7.20.1461.[149] Norihiro's edicts were not confined to warriors, for in 1464, he confirmed the office of a shrine attendant at Ichinomiya shrine in Nagato in a similar *kudashibumi* format.[150] Here too he followed Yoritomo, who likewise often used *kudashibumi* to confirm offices and shrine lands.

Most *kudashibumi* end with a powerful clause demanding obedience. Often such documents were followed up by a separate directive (*bugyōnin hōsho*) from lower-ranking administrators confirming the order.[151] Norihiro issued the *kudashibumi*, but the closing language mirrors that of the administrative directive, showing that he combined both in a single unique format.

Norihiro adopted other approaches that linked him to Minamoto Yoritomo. In laws of 11.25.1460, Norihiro refers to *gokenin*, or housemen, a term used by Minamoto Yoritomo, to describe his warriors in the 1180s and beyond.[152] These laws distinguished *gokenin* from others of lower status and prohibited them from adopting the progeny of non-*gokenin* save for some unspecified exceptions.[153]

Norihiro also promoted Liberation of Living Creatures Rites (*hōjōe*), and *gokenin* were forced to participate in them. These rites involved displays of archery, equestrian skill, and the exchange of gifts. They were performed at Tsurugaoka shrine in Kamakura, as well as Iwashimizu in Kyoto and the Usa

---

[149] *Hagi han batsu etsu roku*, vol. 4, maki 150, Usuki Saemon monjo doc. 15, 7.20.1461 (Kanshō 2) Ōuchi Norihiro *sodehan* Sugi Masayasu *hōsho utsushi* p. 187. Hagihara Daisuke, "Ōuchi shi no sodehan kudashibumi to gokenin sei," pp. 91–93, 98, discounts the veracity of all these documents. Although Hagihara correctly notes that a 1458 confirmation in the Kubo collection is anomalous, and it is not included in analysis here, Wada Shūsaku believes that the later Norihiro documents from 1461, such as the Usuki (Shinohara) records, are reliable. I am indebted to Wada Shūsaku. Conversation 6.13.2016.

[150] *Yamaguchi kenshi shiryōhen chūsei*, vol. 4, Sumiyoshi jinja zō monjo, doc. 258, 4.5.1464 (Kanshō 5) Ōuchi Norihiro *sodehan buninjō an*, p. 458, to Nagato's Ichinomiya shrine, and in the *sodehan kudashibumi* format.

[151] For this insight, I am indebted to Wada Shūsaku. Conversation, 6.2.2017. All later Ōuchi lords would issue documents in this format. For one by Norihiro's grandson Yoshioki dating from 9.23.1511 (Eishō 8), see http://komonjo.princeton.edu/ouchipraise/.

[152] Satō Shin'ichi et al., eds., *Chūsei hōsei shiryōshū*, vol. 3, Bukehō, vol. 1, Ōuchi-shi *hekisho*, clause 9, 11.25.1460 (Chōroku 4), pp. 37–38, and *Yamaguchi kenshi tsūshihen chūsei*, p. 401. This was first noted by Kawaoka Tsutomu, "Ōuchi shi no chigyōsei to gokenin sei," *Nihonshi kenkyū* 254 (10.1983), pp. 1–29.

[153] *Chūsei hōsei shiryōshū* vol. 3, Bukehō, vol. 1, section 4, Ōuchi shi *hekisho*, clause 9, 11.25.1460 (Chōroku 4), pp. 37–38. These regulations have attracted interest among Japanese scholars. Matsuoka, "Ōuchi shi no hatten to sono ryōgoku shihai," in *Ōuchi shi no kenkyū*, pp. 88–94, originally argued for this *gokenin* recognition served as a means of getting Norihiro's retainers to reside in Yamaguchi, while Kawaoka Tsutomu, "Ōuchi shi no chigyōsei to gokenin sei," argues that the *gokenin* system was in fact a means of strengthening the office and authority of *shugo* in general by forcing local warriors to engage in obligatory "public" duties. See pp. 13, 18–20. Fujii Takashi, "Norihiro ki Ōuchi shi no bunkoku shihai to gokenin sei," *Rekishi hyōron* 700 (8.2008), p. 66 supports Matsuoka.

Hachiman shrine in Buzen. Minamoto Yoritomo had prominently overseen them when he first rebelled in 1180.[154] Sometime prior to 1463, Norihiro had Liberation of Living Creatures Rites (*hōjōe*) performed at his important Ichinomiya and Ninomiya shrines at Nagato.[155] These rites too were funded with "public" taxes (*shōbun eki*). Norihiro's *gokenin* householders were obligated to participate in *hōjōe* rites in a manner that resembled what Yoritomo demanded at the Tsurugaoka Hachiman shrine in Kamakura centuries before.[156] He did not confine his attention to shrines, but also built a three-story pagoda for Kōryūji in 1463.[157]

Slouching toward War

While Norihiro was establishing the legal, social, and administrative foundations for rule in the west, he became inexorably drawn into disputes in the capital. During the intercalary ninth month of 1460, Ashikaga Yoshimasa, despairing of a resolution to the Hatakeyama succession dispute, which had festered since 1454, demanded the destruction of Hatakeyama Yoshinari (d. 1491).[158] He mobilized some Iwami warriors, such as the Masuda, to fight in central Japan, and they can be documented as fighting near the capital from 1451 through 1461.[159] Their service proved costly. During the 6.13.1461 battle of Kiriyama, the Masuda helped defeat the Hatakeyama, but suffered severe casualties.[160]

[154] Martin Collcutt, "Religion in the Formation of the Kamakura Bakufu: As Seen through the *Azuma kagami*," *Japan Review* 5 (1994), pp. 75–76. For emphasis on how these *hōjōe* discursively compensated for the violence of Yoritomo's 1180 rebellion, see Vyjayanthi Selinger, *Authorizing the Shogunate Ritual and Material Symbolism in the Literary Construction of Warrior Order* (Leiden: Brill, 2013), pp. 47–48.

[155] They were dedicated to dedicated to the sea god Sumiyoshi, and the emperors Chūai, Ōjin, and Jingū respectively.

[156] Inoue Hiroshi, "Chūsei shokoku Ichinomiyasei no rekishiteki kōzō to toskushitsu: Chūsei kōki Nagato no kuni no jirei o chūshin ni," *Kokuritsu rekishi minzoku hakubutsukan kenkyū hōkoku*, no. 148 (12.2008), p. 214, and *Nihon Chūsei kokka to shokoku Ichinomiyasei* (Iwata shoin, 2009), p. 335. https://rekihaku.repo.nii.ac.jp/?action=pages_view_main&active_action=repository_view_main_item_detail&item_id=1671&item_no=1&page_id=13&block_id=41. See also *Yamaguchi kenshi shiryōhen chūsei*, vol. 4, Iminomiya jinja monjo, doc. 247, 8.1463 (Kanshō 4) Nagato Ninomiya *shobun yaku uketori chūshinjō*, pp. 214–15.

[157] *Ōuchi shi jitsuroku*, p. 58.

[158] *Shiryōshū Masuda Kanetaka to sono jidai* (Masuda 1996), p. 66.

[159] *Shiryōshū Masuda Kanetaka to sono jidai*, pp. 73–74 for doc. 41, 7.4 Nishiyama Myōsei *shojō*. For their aiding Yoshimasa on 5.16.1461, see doc. 36, 5.15 Ashikaga Yoshimiyasei *gonaisho*, pp. 67–68.

[160] *Shiryōshū Masuda Kanetaka to sono jidai*, doc. 38, 6.13 [(Kanshō 2) 1461] Hatakeyama Masanaga *shojō*, p. 69–70. For Yoshinari's defeat, see doc. 45, 5.12 [(Kanshō 4) 1463] Muromachi bakufu *bugyōnin rensho shojō*, pp. 79–80.

As Norihiro strengthened his influence in the west, he endeavored to attract the support of the Masuda, long-standing rivals in Iwami. Norihiro reached out to Masuda Kanetaka while he was fighting in Kii province, expressing concern for Kanetaka's well-being during another Ashikaga campaign against the Hatakeyama in 1463.[161] Through his efforts, Norihiro tried to woo such western warriors away from serving the Ashikaga as guards (hōkōshū) and supporting him instead.

Signs of a rapprochement between Norihiro and the Ashikaga nevertheless appeared during the years 1464–65. For example, Norihiro gave a Chinese bell in memory of Hino Shigeko (1411–63), Yoshimasa's mother, on 8.10.1464.[162] On 5.15.1465 he also gave Yoshimasa a gold sword and five thousand hiki to celebrate the appointment of a new Ashikaga shogunal heir, Yoshimi (1439–91).[163] Norihiro also cooperated with the Ashikaga in shipping copper on tally ships bound for China.[164]

Tally ships sailed for China, with Ashikaga blessing in the midst of these tensions, the first being an Ashikaga vessel, and the third belonging to the Ōuchi.[165] Yoshimasa also gave Norihiro the authority to levy the tansen for all of Kyushu in order to pay for the enthronement Harvest Offerings Ceremony (daijōsai) for Emperor Go-Tsuchimikado (1442–1500, r. 1465–1500) on 7.28.1465.[166] Thus, administrative competence and public tax authority levied in both home provinces and regions not under direct Ōuchi control supplemented the considerable revenue that the Ōuchi received from trade.

A falling-out between Ashikaga Yoshimasa and Kōno Michiharu (1421?–1482), the head of a house in historical rivalry with the Hosokawa, occurred in 1464 and disrupted this warming relationship.[167] Yoshimasa asked Norihiro to attack Michiharu.[168] In order to entice Norihiro to join his offensive, he formalized the return of Tōsai fortifications (jō) to the Ōuchi on

[161] Shimonoseki shishi shiryōhen 6, Chōfu Mōri ke monjo tekagami, doc. 43, 8.9 Ōuchi Norihiro shojō, p. 17, and Shiryōshū Masuda Kanetaka to sono jidai, doc. 46, 10.23 [(Kanshō 4) 1463] Ōuchi Norihiro shojō, p. 80.

[162] Yamaguchi kenshi shiryōhen chūsei, vol. 1, Inryōken nichiroku, 8.10.1464 (Kanshō 5), p. 136. See also 5.26.1464 and 9.8.1464, p. 136 for references of Ōuchi officials notifying the Ashikaga of a Chinese ship arriving.

[163] Yamaguchi kenshi shiryōhen chūsei, vol. 1, Ninagawa Chikamoto nikki, 5.15.1465 (Kanshō 6), pp. 185–86.

[164] Yamaguchi kenshi shiryōhen chūsei, vol. 1, Ninagawa Chikamoto nikki, 5.27–6.2.1465 (Kanshō 6), p. 186.

[165] Yamaguchi kenshi shiryōhen chūsei, vol. 1, Inryōken nichiroku, 7.13.1465 (Kanshō 6), p. 138.

[166] Yamaguchi kenshi shiryōhen chūsei, vol. 1, Ninagawa Chikamoto nikki, 7.25.1465 (Kanshō 6), p. 187.

[167] Yamaguchi kenshi tsūshihen chūsei, p. 398.

[168] Ōuchi shi jitsuroku, p. 58.

6.29.1465.[169] Normally, this would have been enough to secure Norihiro's support, but Yoshimasa's concessions were not in good faith. In fact, the devious Yoshimasa duplicitously ordered Norihiro's cousin Dōjun, who had surrendered in 1443, to attack Norihiro on the very day that he had promised Tōsai to him.[170] Prevaricating further, Yoshimasa then dispatched a doctor to aid Norihiro, who was apparently stricken with illness while shipboard in the Inland Sea.[171]

Dōjun, long eclipsed, had sensed an opportunity, and jumped into action in the fifth month of 1464. Claiming to be the lord of Yamaguchi, Dōjun garnered the support of the Tsushima islanders and Shōni Noriyori, and he intervened in trade with Korea.[172] Dōjun's sudden return to prominence was encouraged by the Ashikaga to thwart Norihiro's ambitions.

Norihiro's alliance with the Yamana and the Kōno coalesced during the eighth month of 1465, when he went to war against the Ashikaga.[173] Hosokawa Katsumoto (1430–73), Yoshimasa's powerful chancellor (*kanrei*), turned against Norihiro on 8.25.1465, when Norihiro's move against the Ashikaga became manifest.[174] Those who ran afoul of Ashikaga Yoshimasa joined Norihiro. For example, Masuda Kanetaka, who had long served in the

---

[169] *Ninagawa ke monjo*, vol. 1, doc. 53, 6.29.1465 (Kanshō 6) Shōgun Ashikaga Yoshimasa *sode han mikyōjo an*, p. 111, and Norihoro *jōsho an*, p. 113 for the return of this harbor. This document also appears in *Ashikaga Yoshimasa hakkyū monjo*, vol. 1, doc. 407, pp. 119–20. See also *Kobayakawa ke monjo*, vol. 2, doc. 136, 6.25.1465 (Kanshō 6) Shōgun ke *mikyōjo utsushi*, p. 51; *Kikkawa ke monjo*, vol. 1, doc. 47, 6.25.1465 (Kanshō 6) Shōgun ke *mikyōjo* p. 29; *Hagi han batsu etsu roku*, vol. 2, Dewa Genpachi monjo, doc. 68, 6.25.1465 (Kanshō 6) *Kanrei* Hatakeyama Masanaga *hōsho*, p. 146; and *Chūsei Masuda Masuda shi kankei shiryōshū* (Masuda, 2016), doc. 413, 6.25.1465 (Kanshō 6) Muromachi shōgun ke *mikyōjo utsushi*, p. 157.

[170] *Ashikaga Yoshimasa hakkyū monjo*, vol. 1, doc. 408, 6.29 Ashikaga Yoshimasa *gonaisho*, p. 120 for a document surviving in the Kikkawa collection.

[171] *Yamaguchi kenshi shiryōhen chūsei*, vol. 1, Ninagawa Chikamoto nikki, 7.28.1465 (Kanshō 6), pp. 187. For a more extended version of this passage see Takeuchi Rizō, ed., *Zōho Zoku shiryō taisei*, vol. 10, *Chikamoto nikki*, vol. 1 (Kyoto: Rinsen shoten, 1967), 7.25-30.1465, pp. 363–72. For Norihiro succumbing to illness while in a boat on his way to Shikoku, and the same Ashikaga doctor being dispatched, see the *Shinsen Chōroku Kanshōki*, in *Gunsho ruijū*, vol. 20 (*Kassen bu*), p. 336. According to Hagihara Daisuke, the person who most likely dispatched this doctor was Ise Sadachika. See "Chūsei kōki Ōuchi shi no zaikyō zasshō," p. 23.

[172] *Yamaguchi kenshi shiryōhen chūsei*, vol. 1, Sejo sillok, 5.10.1464 (Sejo 10), p. 894.

[173] Ienaga Junji, "Gunki Ōninki to Ōnin no ran," in *Rekishi Yūgaku, Shiryō o yomu* (Yamakawa shuppan, 2001), p. 69. He also argues that the key rift with the Yamana happened between the eighth and eleventh months of 1465. See p. 76. See also "Sairon Gunki Ōninki to Ōnin no ran," in *Rekishi Yūgaku, Shiryō o yomu* (Yamakawa shuppan, 2011), p. 62. For more on Norihiro supporting the Kōno in the eighth month of 1465, see *Tsukiyamabon Kōno kefu* in Kawaoka Tsutomu, "Chūsei Iyo no Yamagata Ryōshu to Kōno shi kenryoku," *Ehime daigaku kyōiku gakubu kiyō jinbun shakai kagaku* 36.1 (2003), p. 21, and Kageura Tsutomu, ed., *Kōno ke monjo* (Matsuyama: Iyo shiryō shūsei, 1967), p. 72

[174] *Yamaguchi kenshi shiryōhen chūsei*, vol. 1, Saitō Chikamoto nikki, 8.25.1465 (Kanshō 6), p. 188. For another Hosokawa order demanding that Norihiro not to aid the Kōno, see 9.18.1465, p. 188.

capital, allowed his son to fight for the Kōno and Norihiro. Then, Kanetaka himself fled to Yamaguchi, where he was welcomed by Norihiro.[175]

Ritual curses (*chōbukuhō*) marked the onset of hostilities.[176] On 8.15.1465, Norihiro commissioned five-altar rituals and *Enma tenku* rites. The former were maledictions, thought to weaken enemy resistance, while the latter were longevity rites, suggesting that Norihiro was not in the best of health.[177] Five-altar rites required skilled monks to chant *dhāraṇī* thousands of times. Contemporary documents reveal an Aizen rite, which could be used for maledictions, being performed ten thousand times at the Suō Kokubunji temple.[178] Such rites had been offered for the sake of the realm and had been sponsored by the Ashikaga in the fourteenth and fifteenth centuries, but they declined in the aftermath of Yoshinori's assassination. They were held only eight times in Kyoto between 1452 and 1465, and not at all late in 1465.[179] The Ashikaga were not ritually impotent, as in 1465 they had the Benevolent Kings Sutra performed for peace in Japan.[180] Nevertheless, in contrast to 1399, when the Ashikaga could commission far more extensive rites than the Ōuchi, now the rites commissioned and performed on behalf of the latter were equal, if not superior, to those instigated by the Ashikaga. Ōuchi ability

[175] Nakatsukasa Ken'ichi, "Chūsei kōki Iwami kokujin no dōkō to Muromachi bakufu, daimyō," *Iwami no Chūsei ryōshu no seisui to Higashi Ajia kai'iki sekai* (Shimane ken kodai bunka sentaa, 3.2018), p. 69. For proof of Kanetaka's departure from Kyoto to Yamaguchi, see *Masuda ke monjo*, vol. 1 (Tōkyō daigaku shuppankai, 2000), doc. 203, 10.10 Masuda Munekane *daidai chūsetsu no jō chūmon*, pp. 153–55. He can be documented as being encamped in Kyushu by 1.7.1466 (Kanshō 7). See doc. 113, Masuda Kanetaka *Muromachi dono shōgatsu sanka shusshi*, pp. 96–97.

[176] See Conlan, "Sacred War," in *State of War: The Violent Order of Fourteenth-Century Japan* (Ann Arbor: University of Michigan Center for Japanese Studies, 2003), for maledictions and warfare. For more on these curses and the Ashikaga in the fourteenth century, see Conlan, *From Sovereign to Symbol* (New York: Oxford University Press, 2011).

[177] *Yamaguchi kenshi shiryōhen chūsei*, vol. 2, Kokubunji monjo, doc. 100, 8.15 Ōuchi Masahiro *shojō*, p. 429. The editors estimate that this either occurred in 1465 or 1466. See also Mori Shigeaki, *Chūsei Nihon no Seiji to bunka*, pp. 225–26, 238; "Godanhō no shiteki kenkyū," *Kyūshū bunkashi kenkyū kiyō*, no. 39 (3.1994), pp. 148–49; and "Godanhō shūhō ichiran," *Fukuoka daigaku jinbun ronsō* maki 30 no. 1 (6.1998), p. 847.

[178] *Sengoku ibun Ōuchi shi hen*, vol. 1, doc. 16, 7.25 Ōuchi shi *kashin rensho shojō*, p. 7, and *Yamaguchi kenshi shiryōhen chūsei*, vol. 2, Kokubunji monjo, doc. 98, 7.25 Ōuchi shi *bugyōnin renshojō*, p. 428. This document is not dated and could refer to events of 1465 through 1467. The reference to Masahiro being in Kyoto and being the Ōuchi lord (and described as *Ōyakata-sama*) suggests that it dates from 1467 (Ōnin 1). It also reveals that this rite cost five thousand *hiki* to be performed.

[179] Mori Shigeaki, "Godanhō no shiteki kenkyū," pp. 148–49, and "Godanhō shūhō ichiran," pp. 845–47. The *Chronicle of Ōnin* suggest that the Ashikaga performed this one last time in 1469, which if counted, would bring this number up to nine. See "Godanhō shūhō ichiran," p. 846. For Mori Shigeaki's most recent comments on these rites, see his "Ōuchi Masahiro no seishin sekai," *Sengoku ibun geppō* 1 *Ōuchi shi hen* (7.2016), pp. 1–2.

[180] Steven Carter, *Regent Redux* (Ann Arbor: University of Michigan Center for Japanese Studies, 1996), p. 112.

to sponsor major rituals of state had increased commensurately with their expanding wealth and power.

While preparing to pursue his campaign, Norihiro suddenly died at Gogo island, just off the coast of Shikoku, on 9.3.1465. Hosokawa Katsumoto would claim that Norihiro's death was "the punishment of heaven" because he had aided the Kōno in violation of the shogun's will.[181] On 9.10.1465, the Ashikaga appointed Shōni Noriyori, a thorn in the side of the Ōuchi since 1441, to the *shugo* post of Chikuzen, a core Ōuchi holding.[182] The prospect of warfare caused some, such as Shiba Yoshitoshi, who had earlier fled to Yamaguchi, to cut their ties with the Ōuchi.[183] Others, such as Masuda Kanetaka, remained.

Omens of turmoil appeared shortly after Norihiro's demise, most notably a large comet, known as a sound-emitting Tengu Star (*tengusei*), which was seen as a sign of imminent pestilence and war.[184] For those in the capital, this star was perceived as a sign of impending doom.[185] For a family of star worshipers, the appearance of a shooting star a mere ten days after Norihiro's death seemed profoundly meaningful.[186] It may account for why, after his son won a protracted war against the Ashikaga, Norihiro would be deified as a god.

[181] *Mōri ke monjo*, vol. 1, doc. 118, 10.10 [(Kanshō 6) 1465] Hosokawa Katsumoto *shojō*, p. 111, and *Kōno ke monjo*, p. 74. See also *Yamaguchi kenshi tsūshihen chūsei*, p. 398, and *Ōuchi shi jitsuroku*, p. 58. *Ōuchi shi jitsuroku*, p. 58, also refers to an edict to chastise Norihiro and Norihiro's 9.3 death.

[182] For the negotiations, see *Yamaguchi kenshi shiryōhen chūsei*, vol. 1, Inryōken nichiroku, 9.11.1465 (Kanshō 6), p. 138, and *Kōno ke monjo*, pp. 74–75. Yoshimasa's appointment of the Shōni to Chikuzen can be found in the Ninagawa Motochiki nikki, 9.11.1465. This is transcribed in *Dazaifu shishi chūsei shiryōhen*, pp. 673–74. The Ashikaga also bolstered ties with the Ōtomo, confirming their position as *shugo* of Bungo on 7.30.1465 (Kanshō 6). See *Ōtomo ke monjo hoi*, vol. 2, *Ōita ken shiryō*, vol. 26 (Ōita, 1974), p. 340.

[183] *Yamaguchi kenshi shiryōhen chūsei*, vol. 1, Inryōken nichiroku, 10.14.1465 (Kanshō 6), p. 139.

[184] *Yamaguchi kenshi shiryōhen chūsei*, vol. 1, Inryōken nichiroku, 9.14.1465 (Kanshō 6), p. 138, and Jinson, *Daijōin jisha zōjiki*, vol. 12, 9.13.1465 (Kanshō 6), p. 369. This passage appears in the index (*mokuroku*) but not in Jinson's surviving diary per se. For more on how the designation Tengu Star amounted to political criticism, see Matsubayashi Yasuaki, *Muromachi gunki no kenkyū* (Ōsaka: Izumi shoin, 1995), pp. 100–102.

[185] *Tōdaiji hokkedō yōroku*, *Zoku zoku gunsho ruijū*, vol. 5 (Ichishima Kenkichi, 1909), 8.22.1467 (Ōnin 1), p. 396. For further descriptions of the comet, see 5.26.1467, p. 394. For more on this topic, see Conlan, "The 'Ōnin War' as Fulfillment of Prophecy," *Journal of Japanese Studies* 46.1 (Winter 2020), pp. 31–60.

[186] For Norihiro's death, see *Yamaguchi kenshi shiryōhen chūsei*, vol. 1, Ninagawa Chikamoto nikki, 9.3.1465 (Kanshō 6) and 10.7.1465, p. 188, and Saitō Chikamoto nikki, 9.3.1465 (Kanshō 6), p. 199. See also *Mōri ke monjo*, vol. 1, doc. 118, 10.10 [(Kanshō 6) 1465] Hosokawa Katsumoto *shojō*, p. 111, Conlan. "The 'Ōnin War,'" and Kristina Buhrman, "The Stars and the State: Astronomy, Astrology, and the Politics of Natural Knowledge in Early Medieval Japan," PhD dissertation, University of Southern California, 2012.

Legacies

Norihiro established Yamaguchi as a judicial and administrative center and promulgated laws to ensure that it remained an island of stability in Japan. He also wrote edicts that suggested that he was a great warrior leader, and he modeled his rule after that of the Kamakura shogunate. Norihiro also bolstered his administrative and religious authority over the lands of western Honshu and northern Kyushu by funding rites and rebuilding Hikamisan and Usa and by donating swords and offering invocations at Hakozaki.[187] His authority translated into sacerdotal influence as well. Norihiro professed that he was ultimately responsible for the well-being of all in his provinces, as prayers for rain offered at Hikamisan attest.[188] In addition, his prayers attributed peace and stability, and the pacification of northern Kyushu, to rituals performed at Hikamisan Kōryūji.[189]

Norihiro forged his lands into a cohesive political domain, encompassing far-flung provinces, islands, and districts, including those in Iwami (Nima), Aki (Tōsai), and Hizen (Kanzaki), and the harbors of Hakata, Nagato, and Nima. With his extensive fleet, Norihiro reaped the advantages of trade with Korea, the Ryūkyū Kingdom, and Ming China. Likewise, he promoted a growing sense of Ōuchi ethnicity, recognized by officials in Korea and Japan, which contributed to cohesion among the Ōuchi and their collaterals. These strengths allowed the Ōuchi to survive a long war that lasted years after his death.

---

[187] *Fukuoka shishi shiryōhen chūsei* 1, Tamura monjo, doc. 32, 8.1 Ōuchi Norihiro *kansū henji*, p. 888. This document dates from sometime between 1442 and 1450, or 1462, when Norihiro gained control of Chikuzen province.

[188] *Bōchō fūdo chūshin an*, vol. 12 *Yamaguchi saiban jō* (Yamaguchi, 1960), 6.20 Ōuchi Norihiro *shojō utsushi*, p. 124.

[189] *Bōchō fūdo chūshin an*, vol. 12, 11.27 Ōuchi Norihiro *shojō utsushi*, p. 124.

7

Ōuchi Masahiro and the Rise of Yamaguchi

Ōuchi Masahiro (1446–95) lived two very different lives: a frenetic one of years of warfare, and a quiescent one, where he experienced a long twilight of physical decay. Masahiro was appointed to *shugo* office at the age of ten and performed its ritual and administrative responsibilities under the watchful eye of his father Norihiro (1420–65). When only twenty, Masahiro lost his father, and at twenty-two, he led an armada to the capital. After fighting in a savage conflict for over a decade, he returned to Yamaguchi, thirty-three, his youth exhausted.[1] Peace brought incapacitation, as Masahiro suffered the first of several strokes the year after the war ended (1479). Then, forced to delegate authority to Ōuchi administrators, and aided by his mother Kuniko (1428–95), who had led a spirited defense of Yamaguchi during the war, Masahiro himself turned to more academic pursuits—writing poetry, reorganizing family genealogies, and reordering rites to his ancestors. He also achieved unprecedented posthumous recognition for his father as a god, which served as a template for the apotheosis of powerful leaders in Japan for centuries.

While fighting in Kyoto, Masahiro governed the wards of the capital and their surroundings better in war than the Ashikaga could rule them in peace. He safeguarded the lands and offices of his father, while at the same time abandoning his father's dreams of founding a warrior government. In middle and old age, Masahiro returned to western Honshu, presiding over a stable, well-ordered realm in Yamaguchi, whereby rites were performed and laws administered without his personal intervention. The grizzled warrior died peacefully, an end shared by few Ōuchi lords.

The first years of Masahiro's rule witnessed disruption in trade, particularly after the defection of his uncle Dōjun (Noriyuki) in 1470. His forces

---

[1] For Masahiro's age (twenty-two), see Yamaguchi kenshi hensanshitsu, comp., *Yamaguchi kenshi shiryōhen chūsei*, 4 vols. (Yamaguchi, 1996–2008), vol. 1, Daijōin nikki mokuroku, 7.20.1467 (Ōnin 1), p. 240.

Kings in All but Name. Thomas D. Conlan, Oxford University Press. © Oxford University Press 2024.
DOI: 10.1093/oso/9780197677339.003.0008

lost control of the Hakata region, but they effectively blockaded the Straits of Shimonoseki from all rivals and intercepted Ashikaga tributary ships returning from China. After the war, however, Masahiro asserted his dominance over trade with the continent once again, although his later years were marked with more cooperation with the Ashikaga.

During his long rule, Yamaguchi experienced a burgeoning population and became a thriving entrepôt. The expansion of the town was as much driven by political as by economic factors, as many courtiers and monks traveled from Kyoto to Yamaguchi during both the war and its aftermath, when Kyoto experienced turmoil and upheaval. The immigration of traders, courtiers, and monks allowed Yamaguchi to become a site where important rites of state were performed on scale unmatched in the capital. Masahiro's patronage influenced major intellectual developments of the age and contributed to the establishment of an institutionally independent Shinto, where *kami*-related practices were independent of Buddhism.

Masahiro's stay in the capital resulted in a recalibration of Tatara ethnicity, as he discovered that his ancestry was not that of Paekche kings, but rather an immigrant from Mimana. As a result, he subtly de-emphasized claims of royal descent, favoring instead to describe how even Prince Imsŏng was descended from the stars. Hence, he patronized Myōken worship, revitalizing the shrine at Kudamatsu devoted to this god, and also transferring his Myōken to Kyoto itself, but he also patronized new Shinto practices and oversaw the apotheosis of his father Norihiro as a "Light-Emitting Deity" (*daimyōjin*).

Politically, Masahiro abandoned his father's dream of establishing a warrior government. Over a decade of war taught him that such ambitions were untenable and unnecessary. Having otherwise secured all the rights and privileges that Norihiro had lost, Masahiro was content to support the Ashikaga, going so far as to dispatch forces there, although poor health prevented him from returning there after 1477. The Ōuchi gradually shifted their position from being a rival of the Ashikaga to an upholder of the regime, although their support remained limited and invariably calibrated to their own interests as well.

Although the century after 1467 is generally known as the "Warring States Era" (*Sengoku jidai*), the period from 1477 through 1551 witnessed the increasing political, cultural, and economic significance of Yamaguchi and the Ōuchi domains. Kyoto remained the capital, but Japan's governing and economic center gradually shifted west. The Ōuchi had a disproportionate role in shaping the politics of their time, and they were more closely connected to the imperial court than the increasingly enervated Ashikaga shogunate.

During these years, members of the imperial court (which included the Ashikaga, whose position steadily weakened), increasingly worked in tandem with Ōuchi lords in governing most of Japan and overseeing its trade and economic policies. The period from 1477 through 1551 witnessed the political, cultural, and economic preeminence of this segmented Yamaguchi/ Kyoto polity, and the Japan of this time, and the following chapters, is best characterized as the Age of Yamaguchi (1477–1551).

Birth and Early Years

Masahiro was born sometime in 1446. He was the eldest child of his twenty-six-year-old father, Norihiro, and nineteen-year-old mother, Yamana Kuniko. His childhood name was Kidōmaru, or "Turtle child."[2] This name suggested that Masahiro was an incarnation of Myōken since the iconography of the Buddhist representation of the North Star was a child standing on a turtle.[3] Many other warrior families worshiped Myōken, and some even gave their heirs this same name, but for them, such practices were fleeting.[4] By contrast, all later Ōuchi lords would name their heir Kidōmaru and perform purification rites at Hikamisan each year.

The name Kidō, or Kidōmaru, coincided with a new pattern of succession, as the earlier favored names of Magotarō ("Eldest") or Rokurō ("Sixth Son") were abandoned in favor of a lineal succession by descendants of Norihiro. Masahiro's Kidōmaru name would be shared by his son Yoshioki, grandson Yoshitaka, and great-grandson, also named Yoshitaka.[5] With this practice

---

[2] *Yamaguchi kenshi shiryōhen chūsei*, vol. 3, Yamaguchi ken monjokan Kōryūji monjo doc. 81, Tatara Kidōmaru [Ōuchi Masahiro] Hikamisan Myōken Jōgū *sankei mokuroku*, pp. 260–62, describes Masahiro, styled with his childhood name of Kidō, as being fourteen in 1459 (Chōroku 3), which by the Japanese count would give him a 1446 birth. Wada Shūsaku estimates that his father Norihiro was twenty-seven at the time. "Ōuchi Takeharu oyobi sono kankei shiryō," *Yamaguchi monjokan kenkyū kiyō* 30 (2003), p. 9.

[3] The importance of the name Kidōmaru was first recognized by Ōta Junzō, "Ōuchi shi no Hikamisan nigatsu-e shinji to tokusei," in *Kyūshū chūsei shakai no kenkyū* (Dai-ichi hōki, 1981), p. 219. See also Hirase Naoki, *Ōuchi shi no ryōgoku shihai to shūkyō* (Hanawa shobō, 2017), pp. 278–82, and Kanaya Masato, "Ōuchi shi ni okeru Myōken shinkō no danpen," *Yamaguchi ken monjokan kenkyū kiyō* 19 (1992), pp. 32–33.

[4] The Togashi named one heir, the future Shigeharu, as Kidōmaru. *Himeji shishi*, vol. 2, *Honhen kodai chūsei* (Himeji, 2018), p. 403. The son of Togashi Noriie, Shigeharu died of illness in 1462.

[5] Hirase Naoki, *Ōuchi shi no ryōgoku shihai to shūkyō*, p. 282.

and concomitant rituals of purification at Hikamisan, Ōuchi succession stabilized along generational lines.

Masahiro became the *shugo* of the Ōuchi lands at the age of ten, when his father Norihiro had a falling out with the shogun Ashikaga Yoshimasa (1436–90, shogun 1449–73). Despite holding this title, he was closely watched by his father.[6] He started writing his own official documents in 1459, while only fourteen, and ritually demonstrated his position as heir when he undertook austerities at the upper shrine of Hikamisan in 1459.[7]

The young Ōuchi lord would spend the early days of the new year in seclusion in such areas, for only there could he commune with the gods, from which he was descended.[8] This practice was unique to the son of Norihiro, and not shared with any other warrior families whose heirs adopted the name Kidōmaru. These rites served to make Norihiro and Masahiro exalted, sacerdotal figures among the residents of the Ōuchi domain, as it demonstrated that they were offspring of Myōken who were specially linked to the deity. Only Hikamisan Kōryūji monks, Ōuchi lords, and their designated heirs could ascend this sacred hill, where hunting was banned, as too were women.[9]

The Onset of the Ōnin War

A dozen years of Masahiro's life were bound up with the Ōnin War, a conflict long misunderstood. It has been thought to be a conflict generated by

---

[6] *Yamaguchi kenshi tsūshihen chūsei* (Yamaguchi, 2012), p. 396, and *Yamaguchi kenshi shiryōhen chūsei*, vol. 1, Nagato no kuni shugoshiki shidai, pp. 604–5. For the Hosokawa document see *Yamaguchi shishi shiryōhen chūsei* (Yamaguchi, 2016), doc. 216, 3.24.1456 (Kōshō 2) Muromachi bakufu *kanrei* Hosokawa Katsumoto *hōsho*, p. 272, addressed to "The Hon. Kidō (Kidō *dono*)."

[7] For later laws by Norihiro, see *Yamaguchi shishi shiryōhen chūsei*, doc. 218, Ōuchi Norihiro *sodehan kensei jōjō hekisho utsushi*, p. 272 of 5.22.1459 (Chōroku 3). The oldest document, a 12.1.1459 (Chōroku 3) Ōuchi Kidōmaru *shojō* appears in *Kumamoto kenshi chūsei hen*, vol. 2 (Kumamoto, 1982), Sata ke monjo, doc. 90, p. 207. See also Wada Shūsaku, "Ōuchi Masahiro no hakkyū monjo," *Sengoku ibun geppō* no. 1, Ōuchi shi hen (Tōkyōdō shuppan, 2016), pp. 3–5.

[8] Hirase Naoki, *Ōuchi shi no ryōgoku shihai to shūkyō*, particularly pp. 247–57. Masahiro already prohibited all but specialists (*shūto*) from going to the upper shrine at Hikamisan. See *Sengoku ibun Ōuchi shi hen*, vol. 1 (Tōkyōdō shuppan, 2016), doc. 223, 11.13.1475 (Bunmei 7) Ōuchi Masahiro *hatto jōjō*, p. 73. Nevertheless, Masahiro and his son Yoshioki were excepted from this. See Hirase, p. 249, and for a transcription, pp. 260–61; see also *Yamaguchi kenshi shiryōhen chūsei*, vol. 3, Kōryūji monjo doc. 78, Tatara Kidōmaru [Ōuchi Yoshioki] Hikamisan Myōken *Jōgūsha san[kei] mokuroku*, pp. 255–57.

[9] See Hirase Naoki, *Ōuchi shi no ryōgoku shihai to shūkyō*, pp. 254–56 for a lucid explanation. For prohibitions, see *Sengoku ibun Ōuchi shi hen*, vol. 1, doc. 223, 11.13.1475 (Bunmei 7) Ōuchi Masahiro *hatto jōjō*, pp. 73–74, and vol. 2, docs. 1068–69 of 3.20.1500 (Meiō 9), pp. 41–42.

animosities between Hosokawa Katsumoto (1430–73) and Yamana Sōzen (1404–73), two warrior magnates, which spawned a senseless ten-year conflict that ultimately "signaled a change in Japan's historical experience, but not one that could be apprehended in terms of clear meanings and obvious directions."[10] After the deaths of Katsumoto and Sōzen, according to the narrative, the warriors, exhausted, abandoned the war and returned to their domains, leading to the onset of Japan's Warring States (Sengoku) Era.[11]

This understanding of the war has been unduly influenced by *Chronicle of Ōnin*, which only recounts the events in the capital and treats the war as the culmination of a prophecy, known as the *Yamataishi*, where, among other things, the lower conquered the higher (*gekokujō*) and a dog and monkey fought for hegemony, and these were assumed to be the shogunal chancellor (*kanrei*) Hosokawa Katsumoto, born in the year of the dog, and his rival, Yamana Sōzen, a member of the board of retainers (*samurai dokoro*), born in the year of the monkey. Both commanders died in 1473, and here the chronicle ends; it does not cover the end of the conflict, which lingered for four more years, in any meaningful way.[12] Until recently, scholars have overlooked how prophecies, omitted from later, more popular versions of this tale, influenced the narrative. In addition, they long assumed that *Chronicle of Ōnin* was written by an eyewitness, when in fact someone wrote this work between 1488 and 1521, a time where radically different associations existed from the alliances of Ōnin, and the Ōuchi were no longer implacable enemies to the Ashikaga (see chapter 8).

The following narrative recasts the Ōnin War as a struggle between Ōuchi Masahiro and Ashikaga Yoshimasa, with the Yamana and Hosokawa serving as their respective allies. It does not limit its coverage to the events of Kyoto, as does *Chronicle of Ōnin*, but also shows that battles in western Japan were integrally related to the conflict. Finally, it explains how the war began in 1465, rather than 1467 as is commonly assumed, and that the struggle over the Tōsai region of Aki province, and Chikuzen province in northern

[10] Mary Beth Berry, *The Culture of Civil War in Kyoto* (Berkeley: University of California Press, 1994), p. 14.

[11] For an early characterization of the durable notion of the war as ushering in a Warring States era, see Shigeno Yasuyori (Yasutsugu, 1827–1910) and Hoshino Hisashi (1829–1917) for the Chicago World's Fair, *The History of the Empire of Japan: Compiled and Translated for the Imperial Japanese Commission of the World's Columbian Exposition, Chicago, U. S. A., 1893* (Yokohama: Dai Nippon Tosho Kabushiki Kwaisha, 1893), pp. 254, 274.

[12] For more on how the war has been distorted by later chronicles and notions of prophecy, see Conlan, "The Ōnin War as the Fulfillment of Prophecy," *Journal of Japanese Studies* 46.1 (Winter 2020), pp. 31–60.

Kyushu, were a focal point of that long struggle. Both the harbor of Tōsai and the *shugo* post of Chikuzen were confiscated by Ashikaga Yoshimasa in 1465, and both reverted to uncontested Ōuchi control by 1478.[13]

Masahiro, newly in command of the Ōuchi after the sudden death of his father, seized the harbor of Tōsai and its surrounding castles in 1465, effectively negating Ashikaga Yoshimasa's confiscation. This caused Ashikaga Yoshimasa to formally call for Masahiro's destruction and delegate Hosokawa Katsumoto with the task of defeating him, bestowing on him a sword to symbolize his command on 10.22.1465.[14]

Masahiro countered by blockading the Inland Sea. Masahiro throttled Ashikaga shipping by closing the Straits of Shimonoseki to all hostile traffic late in 1465. One noble noted, thereafter, that "nothing passed from the west" to Ashikaga forces in the capital for the next seven years from the Inland Sea.[15] Of course other sea lanes remained, and the Ashikaga could get supplies from the Japan Sea via Obama, but the disruptions in material were severe.

Masahiro followed his father in issuing *kudashibumi* edicts, which hearkened back to the most illustrious edicts of Japan's previous warrior government, the Kamakura bakufu. Masahiro signed the document with his monogram at the fore (*sodehan*), a sign of higher status and prestige, showing that he emphasized his personal authority as a leader of warriors, and an equal to the Ashikaga.[16]

---

[13] *Dazaifu shishi chūsei shiryōhen* (Dazaifu, 2002), Ninagawa Motochiki nikki, 9.11.1465 (Kanshō 6), pp. 673–74 for the initial confiscations. For a visualization of the conflict from 1465 through 1478, based on where skirmishes can be verified see "The Ōnin War: Visualizing Twelve Years of War in Japan, 1465–1478," http://commons.princeton.edu/onin/.

[14] For evidence of his campaigns see *Hagi han batsu etsu roku*, vol. 3 (Yamaguchi ken monjokan, 1994), maki 99 no. 2, Naitō Kogenda monjo, doc. 55, 9.17 [(Kanshō 6) 1465], Ōuchi Masahiro *shojō*, p. 159 for his fighting before 9.17 of that year in Iyo. For evidence of the 10.3.1465 battle at Tōsai, *Kobayakawa ke monjo*, vol. 2 (Tōkyō daigaku shuppankai, 1927), doc. 139, 10.22 [(Kanshō 6) 1465] Hosokawa Katsumoto *kanjō utsushi*, p. 53. For Yoshimasa's edict of chastisement (*jibatsu*) against Masahiro, see doc. 140, 10.26.1465 (Kanshō 6) Shōgun ke *mikyōjo utsushi*, p. 54, doc. 141, 11.21 Hosokawa Katsumoto *shojō utsushi*, pp. 54–55, *Kikkawa ke monjo*, vol. 1 (Tōkyō daigaku shuppankai, 1925), doc. 48, 10.26.1465 (Kanshō 6) Shōgun ke *mikyōjo*, p. 29, and *Hagi han batsu etsu roku* vol. 2, maki 43 Dewa Genpachi monjo, doc. 69 10.26.1465 (Kanshō 6) *Kanrei* Hatakeyama Masanaga *hōsho*, p. 146. Finally, for Yoshimasa's grant of a sword, see *Yamaguchi kenshi shiryōhen chūsei*, vol. 1, Saitō Chikamoto nikki, 9.3.1465 (Kanshō 6), p. 199.

[15] *Mibu ke monjo*, vol. 1 (Kunaichō shoryōbu, 1979), doc. 152 Mibu Harutomi *shojō an* (*kirigami*), p. 167. Admittedly, some ships slipped through during 1471, but the blockade was re-established and remained in force through 1477.

[16] Masahiro issued the first on 12.7.1465 (Kanshō 6), and the second nearly a year later. These were the first two of 111 such documents that he issued during his lifetime. Wada Shūsaku, "Ōuchi Masahiro no hakkyū monjo," pp. 3–5 for a convenient table of the documents written by Masahiro before 1467. For the 12.7.1465 document, see *Hagi han batsu etsu roku*, vol. 1, maki 18, Enomoto Oga monjo, doc. 54, Ōuchi Masahiro *sodehan kudashibumi utsushi*, p. 513. The 12.23.1466 (Bunshō 1) document appears in *Hagi han furoku Wakehiko Uemon Nobuyuki* (unpublished manuscript).

During the second month of 1466 Masahiro once again fought at Tōsai.[17] Stalemated, the Ashikaga wavered in their opposition to Masahiro. Ise Sadachika (1417–73), the specialist in shogunal finances and Yoshimasa's close and trusted adviser, supported pardoning Masahiro, but the chancellor (*kanrei*) Hosokawa Katsumoto threatened to renounce the world if this happened, as he would "lose honor," and so in the end efforts at pardoning Masahiro came to naught.[18] Even though Hosokawa Katsumoto had blocked Masahiro's pardon, as late as the tenth month of 1466, Masahiro was cooperating with the Ashikaga in preparing to dispatch ships to China. These ships, located on the Kyushu coast, were not hindered by the blockade. Masahiro's forces guarded them at the dock of Ōshima, in Hizen, just under forty miles northwest of what is now Nagasaki.[19]

Cooperation in dispatching tally ships to the Ming notwithstanding, tensions increased early in 1467. Nevertheless, Kyoto remained at peace until the fifth month of 1467. But peace did not mean stability, for as early as the second month of 1467, Hosokawa Katsumoto advised his allies to be vigilant against Masahiro leading an armada to the capital.[20]

Months passed until the next, decisive step, which happened during the fourth month of 1467 when Masahiro advanced into northern Kyushu, defeating Shōni Noriyori (1426–69) there and securing his western flank.[21] Masahiro then prepared to invade the capital at the head of his fleet.[22] In

Mōri ke bunko, furoku wa 8, viewed and photographed, Yamaguchi monjokan, 10.13–14.2011. For his total number of *sodehan kudashibumi*, see Wada, p. 4.

[17] *Kobayakawa ke monjo*, vol. 2, doc. 382, 2.30 Yamana Mochitoyo *kanjō utsushi*, pp. 224–25.

[18] *Daijōin jisha zōjiki*, vol. 4 (Kyoto: Rinsen shoten, 1982), 7.29.1466 (Bunshō 1), pp. 88–89. Sadachika was also the wet-nurse father for Yoshimasa's son Yoshihisa, which meant that he was responsible for raising him.

[19] *Matsuratō kankei shiryōshū*, vol. 4 (Yagi shoten, 2009), doc. 1059, 6.19.1466 (Bunshō 1) Muromachi bakufu *bugyōnin renshō hōsho*, p. 200, and doc. 1060, 10.21 [(Bunshō 1) 1466] Ōuchi Masahiro *shojō*, p. 201. For analysis and how Masahiro's document has to date from 1466, see Saeki Kōji, "Muromachi jidai no kenminsen keigo ni tsuite," *Kodai Chūseishi ronshū* (Yoshikawa kōbunkan, 1990), pp. 473–76. See also Kawazoe Shōji, "Kurushima monjo to Hizen Ōshima shi: Nanbokuchō ikō," *Matsuratō no kenkyū* 8 (1985), p. 23.

[20] Tōkyō daigaku shiryōhen sanjo, comp., *Mōri ke monjo*, vol. 1 (Tōkyō daigaku shuppankai, 1920), doc. 120, 2.16 [(Bunshō 2) 1467] Hosokawa Katsumoto *shojō*, p. 114, and *Kikkawa ke monjo*, vol. 1, doc. 311, 2.16 [(Bunshō 2) 1467] Hosokawa Katsumoto *shojō*, p. 264.

[21] *Sengoku ibun Ōuchi shi hen*, vol. 1, doc. 7, 4.27.1467 (Ōnin 1) Ōuchi Masahiro *kanjō*, pp. 5. See also *Dainihon shiryō* (hereafter DNSR), ser. 8, vol. 1 (Tōkyō daigaku shuppankai, 1913), p. 541, and *Yamaguchi kenshi shiryōhen chūsei*, vol. 4, Matsubara ke monjo, doc. 1, 4.27.1467 (Ōnin 1), Ōuchi Masahiro *kanjō*, pp. 575–76. For a 10.13 letter from Masahiro, while in camp, to the Masuda, which dates from either 1465 or 1466, see *Chūsei Masuda Masuda shi kankei shiryōshū* (Masuda, 2016), doc. 417, 10.13 Ōuchi Masahiro *shojō*, p. 158.

[22] For an animation of Masahiro's advance, see http://commons.princeton.edu/onin/.

attacking, Masahiro most likely desired to establish his own warrior government and supplant the Ashikaga entirely, but other evidence points to an attempt to justify a broader restoration. Some seventeenth-century glosses of the *Yamataishi* prophecy, which proved influential at the time, portray Ōuchi Masahiro as heroically leading an army to Kyoto to defend Buddhism in Japan, following the example of his ancestor Prince Imsŏng, who had helped Prince Shōtoku spread Buddhist teachings in Japan nine hundred years earlier.[23]

On 5.10.1467 Masahiro commanded hundreds of boats, including a force of privateers (*kaizoku*), which departed from harbors near Yamaguchi.[24] This naval muster was possible because Masahiro's administrators adeptly controlled the Inland Sea. They regularized tolls, including fees for shipping cargo such as horses and armor, to ensure an uninterrupted supply while in Kyoto.[25] Ten days after Masahiro departed, Yamana Sōzen fortified his residence, and on 5.26, battles erupted between his forces, styled the Western Army, which Masahiro would later reinforce, and the Eastern Army of Hosokawa Katsumoto and Ashikaga Yoshimasa, with the latter initially having the upper hand.[26]

The Ōuchi so effectively controlled the Inland Sea that news of their departure arrived several weeks after they set off. The monk Jinson (1430–1508), residing in Nara, first knew of Masahiro's advance only on 6.4.1467.[27] Masahiro's fleet arrived at Harima on 6.19.1467.[28] News of the arrival did not become known to Ashikaga Yoshimasa and Hosokawa Katsumoto until 6.25.1467. On that day, Ashikaga Yoshimasa initiated prayers for peace in the

---

[23] Suda Makiko, "Ōuchi Masahiro no "seitō" sōshutsu," *Rekihaku* 217 (11.2019), p. 6, introduces this explanation from the *Kakōshi sanbushō*, a collection of annotations of the *Yamataishi* prophecy published in Kyoto (1669). As we have seen, the Ōuchi promoted the notion of Prince Imsŏng and Prince Shōtoku as protectors of Buddhism. This understanding of the prophecy does not, however, appear in any surviving versions of *Chronicle of Ōnin*.

[24] DNSR, ser. 8, vol. 1, 7.20.1467 (Ōnin 1), p. 334. Some contemporaries estimated that his armada consisted of seven hundred boats, and an army of 250,000 men, the latter an exaggeration of perhaps a hundredfold of what was nevertheless undoubtedly a formidable force of warriors. *Tōdaiji hokkedō yōroku* (Zoku zoku gunsho ruijū, 1909), 7.13.1467 (Ōnin 1), p. 395.

[25] *Sengoku ibun Ōuchi shi hen*, vol. 1, doc. 15, 5.20.1467 (Ōnin 1) Ōuchi shi *hekisho utsushi*, p. 7.

[26] DNSR, ser. 8, vol. 1, Tannowa monjo, 5.26 Hosokawa Tsuneari *kanjō*, pp. 245–46, and https://komonjo.princeton.edu/tannowa/view.html?t=2-16. Jōyū was the *shugo* of Izumi Province, from where the Tannowa hailed. See Imatani Akira, *Shugo ryōgoku shihai kikō no kenkyū* (Hōsei daigaku shuppankai, 1986), pp. 231–33, 237, 241–43 and 494.

[27] *Daijōin jisha zōjiki*, vol. 4, 6.4.1467 (Ōnin 1), p. 196.

[28] DNSR, ser. 8, vol. 1, 6.19.1467 (Ōnin 1), pp. 334–35.

realm at Tōji, while Hosokawa Katsumoto tried to bolster his defenses on the following day.[29]

Masahiro occupied the ports of Hyōgo and Sakai on 7.20, and he advanced to Ōyamazaki, located to the southwest of the capital, two days later.[30] Masahiro's rapid advance was blunted, and one army, which had landed at Hyōgo, was pushed back and had to defend the port itself for weeks.[31] Masahiro was only able to attack Kyoto with his "ferocious force" (*mōsei*) on 8.23.1467, seizing the southern wards of the capital and occupying the most important temple of Tōji, the site of Yoshimasa's prayers a mere two months before. Masahiro advanced north and then made Funaoka his base. This hill was strategically important in northwestern Kyoto, and the site where Myōken had been originally worshiped when the capital was founded in 794.[32] Symbolizing his supremacy over the Ashikaga, Masahiro occupied and fortified Yoshimitsu's (1358–1408, shogun 1368–94) Kinkakuji, located just over a mile to the west of Funaoka. This had a symbolic and military function, as earthworks protecting it and the Kinkakuji garden, which were six feet (two meters) high and designed to defend the region from the southeast, have been discovered.[33]

Stalemate, Supply, and Naval Supremacy

With his army encamped in Kyoto, Masahiro launched attacks on the palace, where Yoshimasa, the emperor, and the shogunal chancellor (*kanrei*)

[29] *Ōnin no ran* (Kyōto fūritsu sōgō rekishi shiryōkan, 1989), p. 1 for photos of a 6.25.1467 (Ōnin 1) Ashikaga Yoshimasa *mikyōjo*. For Hosokawa Katsumoto's missive, see *Kobayakawa ke monjo*, vol. 2, 6.26 Hosokawa Katsumoto *shojō utsushi*, p. 57.

[30] DNSR, ser. 8, vol. 1, 6.8.1467, p. 294, 6.19.1467, pp. 332–35, and p. 343. The harbor of Sakai was not referred to as such in documents issued by the Mikita of Izumi province, but rather was described as Kishiwada Minami estate (*shō*). Iida Toshikuni ed., *Shiryōshū Mikita monjo* (Izumisano no rekishi to ima o shiru kai, Izumi, 2015), doc. 130, pp. 241–42.

[31] DNSR, ser. 8, vol. 1, p. 343.

[32] Wada Hidemichi, "Sonkeikaku bunkozō *Towazu monogatari*," *Atomi gakuen jōshi daigaku kiyō*, no. 16 (3.1983), p. 86 for how it was widely known that western Kyoto was organized in accord with the four directional deities (*shijin sō-ō no chi nari*), including Myōken to the north. For the occupation of Funaoka and the Tōji region in Kyoto, see DNSR, ser. 8, vol. 1, 8.23.1467 (Ōnin 1), pp. 357–64, and 8.29.1467, p. 380. For the characterization of his "ferocious" forces, see *Gohōkō'inki* (Konoe Masaie) (Kyoto: Rinsen shoten, 1978), vol. 1, 8.24.1467 (Ōnin 1), p. 117.

[33] For an inventory of nails, shards of pottery, and ceramics consistent with a military encampment, see *Rokuonji (Kinkakuji) Teien*, Tokubetsu shiseki tokubetsu meishō Rokuonji (Kinkakuji) (Kyoto: Kyōto maizō bunkazai kenkyūjo, 2003), 14, 19. See also Maeda Yoshiaki, "Kitayama tei to Kitayamadono no kokōgaku kenkyū no genjō," in Momosaki Yūichirō and Yamada Kunikazu, eds., *Muromachi Seiken no shufu kōsō to Kyōto Muromachi Kitayama Higashiyama: Heiankyō Kyōto kenkyū sōsho* (Bunrikaku, 2016), 226. Traces of these earthworks were evident on 5.28.2017.

Hosokawa Katsumoto were besieged. They had thought that by harboring the emperor, they would be immune from attack, but Masahiro seems to have been aware of support for the Southern Court as he would later attempt to make one emperor later during the conflict. Early in the tenth month, Masahiro advanced to Shōkokuji in east-central Kyoto, but a defensive wall of the pikemen of the Eastern Army general Hatakeyama Masanaga (1422–93) checked his forces, and a stalemate ensued.[34]

Narratives of the war focus on the battles and subsequent trench warfare in the capital, but control over harbors and control of the seas proved vital. In these naval campaigns, the Ōuchi were supreme. Masahiro blockaded most supplies coming into the capital, while the Hosokawa, who led Ashikaga Yoshimasa's army, tried to cut Masahiro's supplies from the ports of Hyōgo and Sakai.[35] Hyōgo, previously the dominant port, was severely damaged in the ensuing battles, which led to the enervation of trade along the Yodo River for years.[36] Sakai, an inferior, shallow harbor, became strategically vital and essential for Masahiro's survival.[37] Masahiro's control of the roads to Sakai led to new patterns of shipping along the roads from Sakai to Nara and Kyoto.

Masahiro, with his control of the seas, also confiscated Ashikaga Yoshimasa's tribute ships in 1468, which would have included tallies and

[34] DNSR, ser. 8, vol. 1, pp. 343, 388 for the battles of 9.1, and pp. 394, 402, 420–21, 343, 446–48 and 462 for the battles of 9.7, 9.13–14, 9.18–27, 10.2–4.1467. For Masahiro's encampment, see 10.19.1467, p. 479. For later battles through 5.8.1468 (Ōnin 2), see pp. 925–26, 930 and 965–67. Masahiro also camped at Tōfukuji, in southeastern Kyoto, on 8.13.1468. See DNSR, ser. 8, vol. 2, p. 28. For more on the onset of defensive tactics, see Conlan, "Warfare in Japan 1200–1550," in Anne Curry and David A. Graff, eds., *The Cambridge History of War*, vol. 2 (Cambridge: Cambridge University Press, 2020), pp. 542–43.

[35] *Sengoku ibun Ōuchi shi hen*, vol. 1, doc. 19, 12.27.1467 (Ōnin 1) Ōuchi Masahiro *kanjō*, p. 8, and doc. 21, Ōuchi Dōjun *shojō*, p. 9 for the repeated battles at Settsu Nakajima, which was located between Hyōgo and Sakai. For later (1470) discussion of keeping these supply roads open near Miyake castle, see doc. 49, 1.2 [(Bunmei 2) 1470] Ōuchi Masahiro *shojō*, p. 18.

[36] See Nagashima Fukutarō, *Ōnin no ran* (Shibundō, 1968), pp. 148–49 for the destruction of Hyōgo and how it later led to the prosperity of Sakai. For more on Masahiro and the battles in the harbors and their link to Masahiro's supply lines, see pp. 124, 136–37. Documents recounting battles at Hyōgo barrier (*seki*) on 9.12.1468 (Ōnin 2) appear in DNSR, ser. 8, vol. 2, 9.12.1468 (Ōnin 2), p. 96, 11.28.1468 (Ōnin 2), p. 889, and DNSR, ser. 8, vol. 3, 10.16.1469 (Bunmei 1), p. 12; for more battles at the Hyōgo harbor (*tsu*) see *Sengoku ibun Ōuchi shi hen*, vol. 1, docs. 38–39, 11.8 [(Bunmei 1) 1469] Ōuchi Masahiro *shojō*, pp. 14–15. Finally, Shinjō Tsunezō, *Chūsei suiunshi no kenkyū* (Hanawa shobō, 1994), p. 730, recounts the decrease in trade along the Yodo River and the supplanting of Hyōgo by Sakai.

[37] Masahiro wrote of the importance of keeping the road from Sakai open. See Wada Shūsaku, "Ōuchi shi kashin Yasutomi shi no kankei shiryō ni tsuite 1," *Yamaguchi ken monjo kan kenkyū kiyō*, no. 27 (3.2000), doc. 15, 1.2 [(Bunmei 2) 1470] Ōuchi Masahiro *shojō utsushi (an)* p. 67, and *Sengoku ibun Ōuchi shi hen*, vol. 1, doc. 49, 1.2 [(Bunmei 2) 1470] Ōuchi Masahiro *shojō*, p. 18. For more on how the Migita helped secure this castle, see Wada Shūsaku, "Suō Migita shi no sōden monjo," *Yamaguchi ken monjo kan kenkyū kiyō* 41 (3.2014), pp. 93–119, p. 95

seals necessary to dispatch future vessels.[38] Masahiro traded with China and Korea throughout the war and imported coins from the Ryūkyūs.[39] Ōuchi supremacy of the seas remained uncontested as long as their forces were unified. The Ashikaga avoided the Inland Sea and dispatched ships from ports in Wakasa, on the Japan Sea, or directed them along Japan's southern Pacific coast.[40]

Masahiro bolstered his position by welcoming Ashikaga Yoshimi (1439–91), Yoshimasa's younger brother, as the nominal leader of his cause. By making Ashikaga Yoshimi his nominal lord, or *kubō*, Masahiro abandoned his father's dream of establishing an autonomous warrior government, although he would later de-emphasize Yoshimi's position when he accepted a wayward prince who claimed descent from the monarchs of the Southern Court to his cause as well.[41]

Ashikaga Yoshimasa answered the defection of his brother Yoshimi by prodding Masahiro's wavering uncle, Ōuchi Dōjun, to turn against Masahiro. Dōjun launched an attack in the second month of 1470 at the port of Akamaseki, located on the Straits of Shimonoseki.[42] Shortly thereafter, Ōuchi Takeharu, most likely either a cousin, or brother to Masahiro,

---

[38] For an excellent overview, see Itō Kōji, "Ōuchi Norihiro, Masahiro to Higashi Ajia," *Kyūshū shigaku* 161 (7.2012), pp. 9–16. For documents concerning the initial confiscation, see *Sengoku ibun Ōuchi shi hen*, vol. 1, doc. 262, 12.3 Ōuchi Masahiro *shojō utsushi*, pp. 82–83, and docs. 30–31, 3.15.1469 (Ōnin 3) Ōuchi shi *kashin rensho hōsho an*, pp. 12–13.

[39] He delegated the responsibility for the logistics for the China fleets to the first and second shrines of Nagato and exempted them accordingly from taxes. *Sengoku ibun Ōuchi shi hen*, vol. 1, doc. 9, 4.27.1467 (Ōnin 1) Ōuchi Masahiro *andojō an*, p. 5, and docs. 30–31, 3.15.1469 (Ōnin 3) Ōuchi shi *kashin rensho hōsho an*, pp. 12–13. For more on his importation of coins, see Richard von Glahn, "Chinese Coin and Changes in Monetary Preferences in Maritime East Asia in the Fifteenth–Seventeenth Centuries," *Journal of the Economic and Social History of the Orient* 57 (2014), pp. 645–46, and Hashimoto Yū, "Erizeni rei to rettō naigai no senka ryūtsū—'Zeni no michi'ko Ryūkyū o ichizukeru kokoromi." *Shutsudo senka* 9 (1998), pp. 99–100.

[40] For Ashikaga shipping via Wakasa, see *Yamaguchi kenshi shiryōhen chūsei*, vol. 4, Ninagawa Chikamoto nikki, 6.26, 7.3.1478 (Bunmei 10), p. 819. For more on the southern route, see *Yamaguchi kenshi shiryōhen chūsei*, vol. 1, Daijōin jisha zōjiki, 8.13.1469 (Bunmei 1), p. 202. See also Kobata Atsushi, "Nihonkai kaiun ot minato machi," in *Fukui kenshi tsūshihen*, vol. 2, *Chūsei* (Fukui, 1994), p. 843.

[41] *Sengoku ibun Ōuchi shi hen*, vol. 1, doc. 52 1.26 [(Bunmei 2) 1470] Ōuchi Masahiro *shojō*, p. 19, and doc. 62, 3.29 [(Bunmei 2) 1470] Niho Moriyasu *soejō*, p. 22, and Yamada Yasuhiro, *Ashikaga Yoshitane* (Ebisu kōshō, 2016), p. 34. See also DNSR, ser. 8, vol. 2, 4.30.1469 (Bunmei 1), p. 780 for his welcoming of Yoshimi, and pp. 852–53 for Masahiro's receipt of the office of *Sakyō no daibu*, with its implication of governing the western wards of the capital, on 7.9.1469 (Bunmei 1). Finally, for the arrival of a Southern Court prince, see DNSR, ser. 8, vol. 3, p. 499.

[42] *Sengoku ibun Ōuchi shi hen*, vol. 1, docs. 54–55, 2.4 [(Bunmei 2) 1470], Ashikaga Yoshimasa *gonaisho*, p. 19, and *Sengoku ibun Ōuchi shi hen*, vol. 2 (Tōkyōdō shuppan, 2017), doc. 1039, 6.15 [(Meiō 8) 1499] Saigō Ujiie *mōshojō*, pp. 33–34 for reference to this fighting at Akamaseki. See also DNSR, ser. 8, vol. 3, 3.1470 (Bunmei 2), pp. 536–37.

also joined Yoshimasa's cause, and nearly captured the harbor of Sakai.[43] Masahiro stabilized his position once he defeated Takeharu on 5.19.1470.[44] This allowed him to dispatch some forces to reinforce his position in the west.[45]

Yamana Kuniko's Defense of Yamaguchi

Ōuchi wives and mothers are an anonymous lot due to the paucity of sources about them, but in the case of Yamana Kuniko, Masahiro's mother, a few surviving letters reveal her commanding presence in Yamaguchi. Kuniko commanded a group of retainers, the self-styled "garrison" (*rusu-shū*) of Yamaguchi, to defend the town.[46] She did so by directing forces, but also provided advice regarding Hikamisan ritual affairs, such as the process of selecting lots (*omikuji*) for the head (*kashira yaku*) of its ceremonies.[47] Kuniko, and Sue Hiromori (1455–82), the deputy of Suō, managed to reassert control over areas such as Iwami and Aki by having warriors sign repeated oaths of alliance to Masahiro, dedicated to the deities of Hachiman and Myōken.[48] Still, eastern Suō remained vulnerable to Dōjun, who

---

[43] Wada Shūsaku, "Ōuchi Takeharu oyobi sono kankei shiryō," *Yamaguchi monjokan kenkyū kiyō* 30 (2003), pp. 3, 10. The last document that verified Takeharu fighting with Masahiro dates from 12.1469. See *Miura ke monjo* (Tōkyō daigaku shuppankai, 1937), doc. 46, 12.20 [(Bunmei 1) 1469] Ōuchi Masahiro *kanjō* and Wada, doc. 7, p. 19. Often Takeharu was misidentified because he held the same office of censor (*danjō shohitsu*) as Yamana Sōzen.

[44] *Sengoku ibun Ōuchi shi hen*, vol. 1, doc. 72, 5.1470 (Bunmei 2) Ōuchi Masahiro *kanjō*, p. 25, and doc. 74, 6.1.1470 (Bunmei 2) Ōuchi Masahiro *kanjō utsushi*, p. 26.

[45] *Masuda ke monjo*, vol. 1 (Tōkyō daigaku shuppankai, 2000), doc. 112, 5.7 Ōuchi Masahiro *shojō* (*kirigami*), pp. 95–96.

[46] Noshita Toshiki, "Ōuchi Dōjun no hanran to Ōuchi shi 'rusu-shū' Ōnin no ran to Ōuchi shi no ryōgoku shihai," *Shichikuma shigaku* 19 (2017), pp. 49–74 for her supporters; for recognition of her role in defending Yamaguchi, see *Yamaguchi shishi shiryōhen chūsei*, Sengoku zenki doc. 105, Sue Hiromori *zōsan*, p. 340. See also *Sengoku ibun Ōuchi shi hen*, vol. 1, doc. 93, 9.24 [(Bunmei 2) 1470] Ichiki Ietomo *shojō utsushi*, pp. 30–31 for explicit mention of documents being issued by Masahiro's mother (Kuniko). For more on her, see Maki Takayuki, "Ōuchi Masahiro no haha ni kansuru oboegaki," *Yamaguchigaku no kōchiku* 1 (3.2005), pp. 51–60, and Kurushima Noriko, "Ōnin Bunmei no ran to Masuda shi—Shiryōhen sanjo shozō Masuda ke monjochū no sashidashi fumei kana shojō no kōsatsu," *Daikibo Buke monjogun ni yoru chū kinsei shirōgaku no sōgōteki kenkyū Hagi han karo Masuda ke monjo o sozai ni* (Kagaku kenkyūhi hojokin kiban kenkyū A 5202018 (3.2008), pp. 69–91.

[47] *Sengoku ibun Ōuchi shi hen*, vol. 2, doc. 1148, 1.29 Sagara Taketō *jihitsu shojō an*, and 2.3 Sagara Taketō *jihitsu shojō an*, p. 69.

[48] DNSR, ser. 8, vol. 3, 8.6.1470 (Bunmei 2), pp. 688–89, *Sengoku ibun Ōuchi shi hen*, vol. 1, doc. 88, 8.6.1470 (Bunmei 2) Sue Hironori *kishōmon*, p. 29, doc. 89, 8.6 Sue Hironori *shojō*, pp. 29–30 and doc. 107, 1.26 [(Bunmei 3) 1471] Sue Hironori *shojō*, p. 37. These oaths also exhibited hostility to another Iwami family, the Yoshimi. See doc. 148, 11.2.1471 (Bunmei 3) Sue Hiromori *kishōmon*, p. 50, doc. 177, 10.16.1472 (Bunmei 4) Sue Hiromori *kishōmon*, p. 60, and doc. 178, 10.16.1472 (Bunmei 4) Sue Hiromori *kashin rensho kishōmon*, p. 61.

attacked the Suō provincial headquarters (*kokufu*) on 2.4.1472, burning the province's archive of laws, documents, and official record copies.[49] Ultimately, Sue Hiromori dispatched warriors from the recently pacified Buzen to Suō and Nagato, where he crushed the forces of the allied Ōuchi Takeharu on 3.13.1473, capturing thirty and killing 119, including 26 prominent warriors.[50]

Ending the War

The year 1473 (Bunmei 5) was, in the words of a contemporary general Uesugi Fusasada (d. 1493), a year of exhaustion.[51] Both Yamana Sōzen of the Western Army and Hosokawa Katsumoto of the Eastern died within weeks of each other.[52] Here the original *Chronicle of Ōnin* ends its coverage, but the war would continue for another five years. In 1473, Sōzen's son Yamana Masatoyo defected to the Eastern Army. If one were to trust the narrative focusing on the Yamana as the key generals of the Western Army, that would mean that the war would have ended, but in fact his act influenced little, save for demonstrating that the Yamana were not the core Western Army commanders.[53] Masahiro, to the contrary, remained in command and committed to the conflict against Ashikaga Yoshimasa.[54]

Although the wars of Ōnin have been seen as an unmitigated disaster for the capital, the sectors under Masahiro's control prospered, as moneylenders fled to his encampment because the generals of the Eastern Army plundered

[49] *Sengoku ibun Ōuchi shi hen*, vol. 1, doc. 454, 9.21.1479 (Bunmei 11) Ōuchi shi *kokugaryō hatto*, pp. 134–35. Masahiro mentions the destruction of 2.4.1472 (Bunmei 4) in a postscript of laws that he sent to Tōdaiji.

[50] *Sengoku ibun Ōuchi shi hen*, vol. 1, docs. 167–70, 4.14 [(Bumei 4) 1472] Ōuchi Masahiro *shojō* and Ōuchi Masahiro *shojō utsushi*, pp. 57–58, as well as doc. 189, 3.16 [(Bunmei 5) 1473] Sue Hiromori *shojō*, pp. 64–65.

[51] *Rekidai koan*, vol. 2 (Zoku gunsho ruijū kanseikai, 1995), doc. 536, 6.27 Uesugi Fusasada *shojō*, p. 142, and *Rekidai koan*, vol. 3 (Zoku gunsho ruijū kanseikai, 1998), doc. 994, 6.27 Uesugi Fusasada *shojō*, p. 222. See also DNSR, ser. 8, vol. 6, 6.27.1473 (Bunmei 5), p. 655.

[52] DNSR, ser. 8, vol. 6, pp. 427–42 for Sōzen's 3.18 death and pp. 562–621 for Katsumoto's death on 5.11.1473. See also Kinoshita Satoshi, *Ashikaga Yoshimasa hakkyū monjo*, vol. 2 (Sengokushi kenkyūkai, 2016), docs. 659–61, 5.13 Ashikaga Yoshimasa *gonaisho*, pp. 77–78.

[53] For the timing of the Yamana defection, see *Hagi han batsu etsu roku*, vol. 3, maki 117, Kubo 8.19.1474 (Bunmei 6), p. 499. Masahiro had to fortify his defensive perimeter after Masatoyo defected. See DNSR, ser. 8, vol. 7, 8.19.1474 (Bunmei 6), p. 535. For Masahiro describing the difficulty of his position, which had to be reinforced by a contingent from the west, see *Sengoku ibun Ōuchi shi hen*, vol. 1, doc. 202, *urū* 5.27 Ōuchi Masahiro *shojō*, p. 68.

[54] He discussed strategy at his residence, where the nominal leader of their army, Ashikaga Yoshimi, joined him. DNSR, ser. 8, vol. 6, 8.25–26.1473 (Bunmei 5), p. 721.

their parts of the city. The war developed parts of the city while destroying others, mostly located in the more important eastern wards of the capital, where, for years, entrenched armies faced off within a stone's throw of each other. The previously underurbanized west became known as the "Western Encampment" (*nishijin*) from that time onward.[55] Masahiro had levied a half tax (*hanzei*) on temple and shrine lands in his home provinces of Suō and Nagato from 1469 through 1475.[56] Nevertheless, on 1.11.1474 Masahiro disavowed the *hanzei* tax in Yamashiro, and did not rely on this onerous tax to maintain his armies in central Japan.[57] After still another wearing year, Ashikaga Yoshimasa reached out to Masahiro in an attempt to negotiate peace.

Knowing Masahiro's cultural interests, Yoshimasa gave him a copy of "Reference for Viewing Objects of Beauty" (*Kundaikan sōchōki*), a catalog of the Ashikaga art collection, by Nōami (1397–1471), a monk, connoisseur (*dōbōshū*), and manager of the Ashikaga art collection. This work offered commentary on fine artworks in Yoshimasa's collection and served as an early outreach for negotiations to end the war.[58] Presumably as part of these negotiations, Masahiro also received a prized Southern Song celadon from Ashikaga Yoshimasa.[59] On 9.14.1476, Yoshimasa wrote to Masahiro, expressing his desire for peace in the realm.[60] Masahiro responded favorably and dispatched gifts of cash and swords to several Ashikaga officials.[61] After increasingly polite epistolary exchanges over the ensuing months, on 9.10.1477, Ashikaga Yoshimasa visited Kinkakuji, which had long served as an encampment for Masahiro's forces. This could have only occurred with the approval of Masahiro.[62]

---

[55] *Daijōin jisha zōjiki*, vol. 4, 6.2.1467, p. 195.

[56] See Satō et al., eds., *Chūsei hōsei shiryōshū*, vol. 3, *Bukehō*, vol. 1 (Iwanami shoten, 1965), Ōuchi shi *hekisho* clause 22, 4.10.1475 (Bunmei 7), pp. 46–47.

[57] DNSR, ser. 8, vol. 7, 1.11.1474 (Bunmei 6), p. 340.

[58] This copy of *Kundai kansō chōki* appears in *Gunsho ruijū*, vol. 19 *Yūgibu*, p. 678 for the copy of 3.12.1476 (Bunmei 8). See also Sakurai Eiji, *Muromachibito no seishin* (Kōdansha, 2001), p. 334. For more on Nōami, who purchased and mounted paintings, and created this significant catalog of Ashikaga artworks, see Shimao Arata, "The Stewards of Art in Muromachi Japan: Nōami, Geiami, and Sōami," *Chanoyu Quarterly* 84 (1996), pp. 7–8, 15–17, 24–27, 34–35.

[59] *Yamaguchi shishi Ōuchi bunka* (Yamaguchi, 2010) (hereafter *Ōuchi bunka*), pp. 847–48.

[60] *Sengoku ibun Ōuchi shi hen*, vol. 1, doc. 244, 9.14 [(Bunmei 8) 1476] Ashikaga Yoshimasa *gonaisho an*, p. 79.

[61] *Sengoku ibun Ōuchi shi hen*, vol. 1, doc. 248, 9.26 [(Bunmei 8) 1476] Ōuchi Masahiro *ukebumi utsushi*, p. 80, and docs. 249–52, 9.26 Ōuchi Masahiro *shojō utsushi*, p. 81, docs. 253–55, 9.26 Ise Sadamune *shojō utsushi*, pp. 81–82, and doc. 256, 9.26 Ninagawa Chikamoto *shojō utsushi*, p. 82.

[62] Compare *Sengoku ibun Ōuchi shi hen*, vol. 1, doc. 246, 9.14 Ashikaga Yoshimasa *gonaisho utsushi*, p. 80, with doc. 265, 2.3 [(Bunmei 9) 1477] Ashikaga Yoshimasa *gonaisho utsushi*, pp. 84–85 for the increasingly polite exchanges. For Yoshimasa's visit, see DNSR, ser. 8, vol. 9, pp. 740–41.

Ultimately, Yoshimasa restored everything that had been confiscated from Masahiro in 1465: the ports of Nima in Iwami Province, and Tōsai in Aki, and his four *shugo* posts of Suō, Nagato, Buzen, and Chikuzen.[63] All of these regions were in Masahiro's uncontested possession at the time, and *casus belli* since 1465. Masahiro, aware of Yoshimasa's duplicity, prepared for his departure from Kyoto. He first decimated a unit of Yoshimasa's forces at Kozu, thereby clearing the road to Sakai.[64] Ten days after the Kozu forces had been annihilated, Yoshimasa reiterated his desire for peace.[65] Thereupon Masahiro and Yoshimasa exchanged letters, swords, and cash as well as suits of armor, thereby ceasing hostilities.[66]

Masahiro set fire to his camp and departed, leaving behind, of all things, a water buffalo, but he also handed over a China tally ship that he had confiscated in 1468.[67] This was done with tacit recognition that future ships would dock at Masahiro's Akamaseki, located at the Straits of Shimonoseki.[68] In 1478 the shipment of continental goods (*karamono*) arrived in Kyoto after Masahiro had lifted his blockade.[69] As soon as he returned to Tōsai, Masahiro built a new castle there, cementing his control over the very harbor

[63] *Sengoku ibun Ōuchi shi hen*, vol. 1, doc. 274, 10.3.1477 (Bunmei 9) Ashikaga Yoshimasa *gohan mikyōjo utsushi*, p. 87, and DNSR, ser. 8, vol. 9, 10.3.1477 (Bunmei 9), pp. 771.

[64] DNSR, ser. 8, vol. 9, 10.7.1477 (Bunmei 9), pp. 777–78.

[65] *Sengoku ibun Ōuchi shi hen*, docs. 275–76, 10.17 Ashikaga Yoshimasa *gonaisho utsushi*, p. 87.

[66] *Sengoku ibun Ōuchi shi hen*, docs. 277–90, pp. 88–91, dating from 10–12.1477, recount these exchanges well. See also doc. 895, 11.10 Ashikaga Yoshimasa *gonaisho utsushi*, p. 291, and doc. 897, 11.10 Ise Sadamune *shojō utsushi*, p. 291. Yamada Takashi, "Shiryō shōkai Kunaichō shoryōbu zō Sagara Taketō shōsatsu maki no shōkai to honyaku," p. 82 reproduces the 11.10 Ashikaga Yoshimasa *gonaisho utsushi* thanking Masahiro for the simplified armor and the 11.10 Ise Sadamune *shojō utsushi* explaining the Ashikaga gift of "great armor" (*ōyoroi*).

[67] For the ox remaining behind, see *Yamaguchi kenshi shiryōhen chūsei*, vol. 1, Sanetaka kyōki, 11.17.1477 (Bunmei 9), p. 250, and Kaneaki kyōki, 11.11.1477 (Bunmei 9), in *Kanō shiryō Sengoku*, vol. 1 (Ishikawa, 1998) pp. 288–89 for a water buffalo wandering into a camp in the evening (*tasogare*) as Masahiro departed. For the ship, see *Sengoku ibun Ōuchi shi hen*, vol. 1, doc. 262, 12.3 [(Bunmei 8) 1476] Ōuchi Masahiro *shojō utsushi*, pp. 83–84, and doc. 263, 12.3 Ōuchi Masahiro *ukebumi utsushi*, p. 84. See also doc. 285, 11.11 [(Bunmei 9) 1477] Ashikaga Yoshimasa *gonaisho utsushi*, pp. 89–90 and doc. 286, 11.15 [(Bunmei 9) 1477] Ashikaga Yoshimasa *gonaisho utsushi*, p. 90.

[68] *Sengoku ibun Ōuchi shi hen*, vol. 1, doc. 270, 9.3 [(Bunmei 9) 1477] Ashikaga Yoshimasa *gonaisho utsushi*, p. 86, and doc. 272, 9.3 [(Bunmei 9 1477] Ōuchi Masahiro *shojō utsushi*, pp. 86–87.

[69] *Yamaguchi kenshi shiryōhen chūsei*, vol. 4, Ninagawa Chikamoto nikki, 7.25.1478 (Bunmei 10), pp. 820–21, and *Yamaguchi kenshi shiryōhen chūsei*, vol. 1, Kaneaki kyō rekiki, 11.12.1477 (Bunmei 9), p. 250. For an overview, see *Yamaguchi kenshi tsūshihen chūsei*, p. 412. These gifts were transmitted by the *dōbōshū* monk Geiami, who was Nōami's successor as curator of the Ashikaga arts. Shimao Arata, "The Stewards of Art in Muromachi Japan," pp. 14–15. After the blockade was lifted Ashikaga Yoshihisa was briefly able to direct exports of sulfur by the Ōtomo "as before." See *Ashikaga Yoshimasa hakkyū monjo*, vol. 2, Ashikaga Yoshihisa monjo, doc. 5, 6.21 [(Bunmei 13) 1481] Ashikaga Yoshihisa *gonaisho utsushi*, p. 142. For Hakata as a key staging point for sulfur exports, see Itō Kōji, *Chūsei no Hakata to Ajia* (Bensei shuppan, 2021), p. 41.

that Yoshimasa had unsuccessfully confiscated in 1465. The Ōnin War began and ended, for the most part, at the port of Tōsai.[70]

Of course, the war proved so consequential that in some regions, *shugo* were supplanted by their deputies, as in the case of the Asakura, or overthrown altogether, as the case of Honganji sectarians who toppled the *shugo* lord in Kaga province.[71] Nevertheless, the war could only end with the acquiescence, or destruction, of the two dominant protagonists, Ashikaga Yoshimasa and Ōuchi Masahiro. In this case, the war ended, for these two at least, as *status quo ante bellum*.

The war had ended well for Masahiro, at least, for he was able to restore all that had been confiscated in 1465. Ritually the conflict could be conceived as Masahiro's triumph over the Ashikaga, for they prayed for peace in the realm in Ōuchi temples, although Ashikaga Yoshimasa found some solace in that he could claim that he accepted Masahiro's "surrender" as he remained in the capital, unchallenged.[72] Still, much had been sacrificed so that Masahiro could maintain his core holdings in the face of Ashikaga attacks. When he landed at Matsubara, in Suō, in the spring of 1478, he viewed scenery he had last seen with his father in 1464, a time when Norihiro was trying to establish a warrior regime and reminisced on his father's failed attempt to establish a new warrior government. "Undecayed, it remains, the past; the words of the pines were long ago."[73]

During the autumn of 1478, Masahiro took the battle to Kyushu, in what was a final coda for the Ōnin War, and defeated Shōni Masahiro on 9.25.1478. Ōuchi Takeharu surrendered shortly thereafter, commanding only twenty-eight devoted followers in the end, and had all his lands confiscated after meeting Masahiro in Hakata. He was later erased from Ōuchi genealogies

---

[70] DNSR, ser. 8, vol. 10, p. 516, 6.20.1478 (Bunmei 10), pp. 516–17. Masahiro also mopped up resistance in Kyushu later that year. DNSR, ser. 8, vol. 10, 10.1.1478 (Bunmei 10), p. 732.

[71] Morgan Pitelka, *Reading Medieval Ruins: Urban Life and Destruction in Sixteenth-Century Japan* (Cambridge: Cambridge University Press, 2022); David Spafford, *A Sense of Place: The Political Landscape in Late Medieval Japan* (Cambridge, MA: Harvard University Asia Center, 2013); Carol Tsang, *War and Faith: Ikkō Ikki in Late Muromachi Japan* (Cambridge: Harvard East Asia Monographs, 2007); Suzanne Gay, *The Moneylenders of Late Medieval Kyōto* (Honolulu: University of Hawaii Press, 2001); and Hitomi Tonomura, *Community and Commerce in Late Medieval Japan: The Corporate Villages of Tokuchin-ho* (Stanford: Stanford University Press, 1992), provide a sense of the varied impact of this war in other regions.

[72] *Kujō ke monjo*, vol. 6 (Kunaichō shoryōbu, 1976), Kujō Mitsugon'in Chikai *kansu kian*, pp. 218–34, particularly 226–29 for prayers for the realm being performed at Yamaguchi. Conversely for reference to Masahiro as having "surrendered," see Iikura Harutake, ed., *Nagaoki Sukuneki* (Zoku gunsho ruijū, 1998), 11.12.1477 (Bunmei 9), p. 47. This happened six days after Masahiro (as *Sakyō no daibu*) had been "pardoned" and confirmed possession of three Kyushu provinces. See 11.6.1477 (Bunmei 9), p. 46.

[73] *Yamaguchi kenshi shiryōhen chūsei*, vol. 4, Shūjin wakashū, p. 792.

entirely.[74] Of him, or for that matter, Dōjun, nothing more is known.[75] Niho Hirona (d. 1478), who had followed Dōjun to the end, was killed, and his head displayed in front of the Hakata temple of Shōmyōji.[76]

With the restoration of peace, Masahiro demonstrated his authority by sponsoring prayers at the major religious institutions in Hakata.[77] On 10.1.1478, he also met with shrine officials from the Hakozaki, Munakata, and Shika Umi shrines and appointed the head of Usa shrine three days later.[78]

Masahiro privileged rites and in order to ensure that these institutions could function properly, and he revoked the *hanzei* half-tax levies on all lands in the province, returning to them their full rights of income.[79] This led him into direct and violent confrontation with officials such as Sue Hiromori, the deputy governor of Chikuzen, who resigned his post in protest over the loss of this vital tax.[80] Despite Hiromori's violent protest, Masahiro thought that this onerous tax need only be applied in times of war. It would thus be levied once again in 1491, when Masahiro dispatched an army to central Japan.[81] Masahiro reduced other taxes and burdens as well. For example, in addition to exempting the Ninomiya shrine of Nagato from all *tansen* taxes, he prohibited his retainers from seeking lodging in shrines as well.[82]

---

[74] Wada, "Ōuchi Takeharu," pp. 6–7 for analysis of these warriors who came from the provinces of Aki, Suō, Nagato, Buzen, Chikuzen, and quite possibly Iyo.

[75] Wada, "Ōuchi Takeharu," pp. 4–5, and *Yamaguchi kenshi shiryōhen chūsei*, vol. 1, Masatōki, 10.3.1478 (Bunmei 10), p. 331 for Takeharu's arrival and followers, 10.9, pp. 337–38 and 10.10 for the surrender of a sword and horse, and 10.11 for the list of lands, both references appear on p. 340.

[76] *Yamaguchi kenshi shiryōhen chūsei*, vol. 1, Masatōki, 10.4.1478 (Bunmei 10), p. 332, and Kawazoe Shōji, *Chūsei bungei no chihōshi* (Heibonsha, 1982), p. 257.

[77] Kawazoe Shōji, "*Masatōki* ni mieru Ōuchi Masahiro to Hakata jisha," *Seiji Keizai shigaku* 401 (1.2000), pp. 1–15, and Saeki Kōji, "Ōuchi shi no Chikuzen no kuni shihai Yoshihiro ki kara Masahiro ki made," in Kawazoe Shōji, comp., *Kyūshū Chūsei shi kenkyū*, vol. 1 (Bunken shuppan, 1978), pp. 326–57

[78] Kawazoe, "Sōgi no mita Kyūshū," in *Chūsei bungei no chihōshi*, p. 253, and *Yamaguchi kenshi shiryōhen chūsei*, vol. 1, Masatōki, 10.1 and 10.4, pp. 329, 332.

[79] For the best analysis, see Mimura Kōsuke, "Ōuchi shi no hanzeisei," pp. 4–6.

[80] Kawazoe Shōji, "Sōgi no mita Kyūshū," p. 255. Kawazoe believes that the dispute was between Sue Hiromori and the Iida family, and first erupted on 10.17.1478 (Bunmei 10). See *Yamaguchi kenshi shiryōhen chūsei*, vol. 1, Masatōki, 10.17.1478, p. 343. Later Masahiro went to Sue Hiromori's abode to pacify him on 10.23. See 10.4 and 10.23, pp. 332–33 and p. 354. Hiromori would later by killed by Yoshimi Nobuyori. For how this dispute was linked to debates over the *hanzei*, see Fujii Takashi, *Ōuchi Yoshioki* (Ebisu kōshō, 2014), p. 25, and Mimura Kōsuke, "Chūsei kōki ni okeru Ōuchi shi no chokkakuryō," *Kyūshū Shigaku*, no. 136 (9.2003).

[81] Mimura, "Chūsei kōki ni okeru Ōuchi shi no chokkakuryō," pp. 6–7.

[82] *Sengoku ibun Ōuchi shi hen*, vol. 1, doc. 514, 8.15.1481 (Bunmei 13) Ōuchi Masahiro *kishinjō*, p. 163 for the *tansen* exemption and doc. 301, Ōuchi shi *hatto jōjō utsushi*, pp. 95–96 for these lodging prohibitions.

Divinely Sanctioned Authority

The wars of 1465–78 had religious dimensions that stand in continuum with Masahiro's heavy use of rites in the second part of his rule. Masahiro helped restore religious institutions in the capital, many of which had been destroyed in the conflict.

He emphasized that peace in the realm (*kokka anzen*) stemmed from the protection of the gods and buddhas.[83] In his military encampment in western Kyoto during the war, he acted to protect the Rokujō Hachiman shrine, which was one of the Ashikaga's ancestral shrines located in the western wards of the capital, from marauders in the fourth month of 1475.[84] Masahiro linked Hachiman and Myōken worship, patronizing Iwashimizu Hachiman, and providing offerings of horses, an important offering as they were thought to serve as a mount for *kami*. He did so on the same day to that shrine and Hikamisan.[85] He also ensured that Kasuga ceremonies in Nara would be performed and had tens of shrine attendants shoot arrows on horseback, a ritual act designed to please the *kami*. This caused Jinson, a noted scholar monk, abbot of Kōfukuji, with the rank of *sōjō* (sangha prefect), and son of the Regent Ichijō Kaneyoshi (1402–81), to exult that "Shinto has not yet reached the latter age (*Shintō wa matsudai arazaru mono nari. Yorokobu beshi yorokobu beshi*)."[86] Commonly, there existed a sense in the Buddhist world that Japan was in a state of decline, or the latter age, but Jinson felt that for rituals concerning Japan's *kami*, this was not the case.

Masahiro had religious institutions in areas under his control perform prayers for peace in the realm. The monk Chikai, a deputy sangha prefect (*gon daisōjō*) who had managed the temple Kōmyōbuji, founded by Regent Kujō Michiie in 1237, would pray for Masahiro in Kyoto in 1474 before traveling to Yamaguchi, where he would serve on Masahiro's behalf for the next fourteen years.[87] In 1475, a thousand monks could chant the Lotus Sutra for

---

[83] *Sengoku ibun Ōuchi shi hen*, vol. 1, doc. 212, 4.10.1475 (Bunmei 7) Ōuchi Masahiro *hōsho utsushi*, pp. 70–71.

[84] *Sengoku ibun Ōuchi shi hen*, vol. 1, doc. 211, Ōuchi Masahiro *kinzei*, where Masahiro protected the Rokujō Hachiman from harm. See also DNSR, ser. 8, vol. 8, 2.20.1475 (Bunmei 7), p. 103 for reference to Hatakeyama Yoshihiro, one of the antagonists who fought at the Kami Goryō shrine in 1467, praying there as well. For more on the importance of these shrines for the Ashikaga, see Conlan, *From Sovereign to Symbol* (New York: Oxford University Press, 2011), pp. 100–104. They were further renovated by Yoshitaka in the 1540s. See chapter 9.

[85] *Sengoku ibun Ōuchi shi hen*, vol. 1, doc. 227–28, 1.1.1476 (Bunmei 8) Ōuchi Masahiro *kishinjō*, pp. 75–76.

[86] *Daijōin jisha zōjiki*, vol. 6, 7.3.1475 (Bunmei 7), p. 133.

[87] Chikai's role was first noted by Hirase Naoki, "Kōryūji no Tendai mikkyō to ujigami-Myōken no henshitsu," *Yamaguchi kenshi kenkyū* 2 (1994), pp. 111–21. See also DNSR, ser. 8, vol. 7, 6.27.1474

the Second Month rites at Yamaguchi's Kōryūji Hikamisan.[88] This shows that Masahiro could demonstrate power of the very highest magnitude. These Thousandfold Offerings previously had only been performed in the capital and even then only by figures of the first order of political significance, such as the dharma emperor Shirakawa or for that matter, albeit briefly, Taira Kiyomori. They were the largest and most expensive Buddhist rites offered and ones "of a kingly pedigree."[89] It was unprecedented for such rites to be performed outside of the capital; none of Masahiro's competitors had the means or motive to sponsor such extensive rites.

Masahiro ensured that Yamaguchi religious institutions would be well staffed and accordingly prohibited Yamaguchi officials from performing rites in Kyoto in 1475.[90] He did this so that Yamaguchi, rather than Kyoto, could be the site of these greatest rites. Some members of the monastic nobility left Kyoto to worship at Yamaguchi, where they prayed for peace in the realm, acts that were impossible in the war-torn capital.[91] In the sixth month of 1476, the monk Chikai departed for Yamaguchi, where he would remain for years performing rites for the realm at Hikamisan.[92]

Chikai marveled at Ōuchi peace and prosperity. At Yamaguchi's Kōryūji Hikamisan he prayed monthly to Myōken, chanting the Golden Sutra of Victorious Kings (saishō ōkyō) for peace in the realm, fertility of the land, the elimination of starvation and illness, and prosperity for all.[93] These rites

(Bunmei 6), p. 506, and *Daijōin jisha zōjiki*, vol. 5, 6.27.1474 (Bunmei 6), p. 490, for praise of Masahiro by the monk Chikai, who started praying Aizen rites for Masahiro in Kyoto in 1472 (Bunmei 4) and continued to serve Masahiro at Yamaguchi from 1476 through 1486. See also Hirase Naoki, *Ōuchi shi no ryōgoku shihai to shūkyō*, pp. 310–12.

[88] *Sengoku ibun Ōuchi shi hen*, vol. 1, doc. 223, 11.13.1475 (Bunmei 7) Ōuchi Masahiro *hatto jōjō*, pp. 73–74.

[89] Heather Blair, "Rites and Rule: Kiyomori at Itsukushima and Fukuhara," *Harvard Journal of Asiatic Studies* 73.1 (2013), p. 11 for Shirakawa's introduction of these rites; for Kiyomori's offering of them from 1169 through 1177 and their significance, see pp. 27–28. For more on Kiyomori's repeated promotion of these rites, with the support of Go-Shirakawa, see pp. 29–31ff. They were last performed in 1177. See p. 35.

[90] *Sengoku ibun Ōuchi shi hen*, vol. 1, doc. 212, 4.10.1475 (Bunmei 7) Ōuchi Masahiro *hōsho utsushi*, pp. 70–71.

[91] Hirase Naoki, *Ōuchi shi no ryōgoku shihai to shūkyō*, pp. 306–12. Hirase also notes that Chikai's actions were also designed to support his cause and that of allies.

[92] *Kujō ke monjo*, vol. 6, Shoji'in kankei monjo, Kōmyōbuji kankei monjo, Kujō Mitsugon'in Chikai *kansu kian*, pp. 218–34. See also Hirase Naoki, *Ōuchi shi no ryōgoku shihai to shūkyō*, pp. 306–12, and Ōta Junzō, "Ōuchi shi no Hikamisan nigatsu-e shinji to tokusei," *Kyūshū chūsei shakai no kenkyū*, pp. 217–20.

[93] *Kujō ke monjo*, vol. 6, Kujō Mitsugon'in Chikai *kansu kian*, pp. 226–29. Chikai can be documented as later praying for the Ashikaga when Ashikaga Yoshihisa was in a campaign (*dōza*) in Ōmi. See Kyōto furitsu toshokan, ed., *Tōji hyakugo monjo*, vol. 9 hako ni, doc. 83, 9.6.1488 (Chōkyō 1) Muromachi dono *ondōza kitō kechiba kaishō*, pp. 57–58. He also performed rites at Tōji and Chinjufu Hachiman through 1499, before residing at Kono shrine at Amanohashidate, where the

had been the prerogative of the court but were rarely enacted in Kyoto after 1441, but they were performed in Yamaguchi after Chikai took up residence there.[94]

Having established Yamaguchi as a site for major rites greater than anything performed in Kyoto at the time, Ōuchi Masahiro then transferred his Hikamisan Myōken deity to the capital of Kyoto on 2.13.1477.[95] The high-ranking monk (*monzeki*) Dōkō (1430–1527) of Shōgo'in, a son of the Imperial Regent (*kanpaku*) Konoe Fusatsugu (1402–88), wrote the request to move the deity, showing Masahiro's influence with the court while still technically at war with his Ashikaga rivals.[96]

By bringing his god to Kyoto, Masahiro imprinted his ancestral deity on the religious fabric of the capital.[97] He did so near the Ashikaga ancestral shrine of Samegai Wakamiya Hachiman, one of three crucial cultic sites for the Ashikaga regime, which was located near Funaoka. This shrine, not a particularly large structure, had been the historical abode of Minamoto Yoriyoshi (988–1075), Yoshiie (1039–1106), and Minamoto Tameyoshi (1096–1156), progenitors of the Minamoto line, and was venerated by warriors of Minamoto descent. Masahiro protected it during the war.[98]

Masahiro not only patronized star gods; he rebuilt numerous shrines to sea gods, such as a Sumiyoshi shrine in Chikuzen, and a Hachiman shrine in Suō.[99] Finally, he exhibited great deference to the Sumiyoshi Ichinomiya shrine in Nagato, copying seven scrolls of its documents, a sign of how

famous artist Sesshū visited him in 1501, when Chikai became its head administrator. See Nakajima Junji, "Shinkei no shinjitsu: Sesshū hitsu Amanohashidate zu no seiritsu ni tsuite," *Museum* 472 (July 1990), pp. 7–8, 15–16, and *Celebrating the Arts of Japan: The Mary Griggs Burke Collection* (New York: Metropolitan Museum of Art, 2015), p. 29. Sesshū and Chikai would have known each other from shared time in Yamaguchi. I am grateful to Dorinda Neave for this reference.

[94] *Kujō ke monjo*, vol. 6, Kujō Mitsugon'in Chikai *kansu kian*, pp. 226–27.

[95] *Sengoku ibun Ōuchi shi hen*, vol. 1, doc. 266, 2.13.1477 (Bunmei 9) Ōuchi Masahiro *kōbun utsushi*, p. 85. For an earlier transcription, see Kuroita Katsumi, ed., *Shintei zōho Kokushi taikei*, vol. 27 (Yoshikawa kōbunkan, 1965), pp. 144–45.

[96] Suda Makiko, *Chūsei Nichō kankei to Ōuchi shi* (Tōkyō daigaku shuppankai, 2011), p. 233. For further analysis of this document, see Mori Shigeaki, "Ōuchi shi no Kōryū to sosen denju," *Yamaguchi kenshi kenkyū*, no. 11 (3.2003), pp. 93–117. Dōkō had been suspected of communicating with the Western Army in 1476 and was divested of his post that year. He was reinstated as the *monzeki* there in 1479.

[97] Even in the early twentieth century, links to North Star worship lingered. Tanaka Ryōkō, *Kyoto no omogake* (Kyodo shumisha, 1931).

[98] "Wakamiya Hachimangū monjo kiroku," *Gerin* 27.4–5 (8.1978), doc. 11, 3.4.1475 (Bunmei 7) Ōuchi Masahiro *kinzei*, p. 16. See also Conlan, *From Sovereign to Symbol*, pp. 100–102.

[99] DNSR, ser. 8, vol. 10, 4.15, and 9.16.1478 (Bunmei 10), pp. 689–90 for the Suō Hachiman shrine, and *Sengoku ibun Ōuchi shi hen*, vol. 1, doc. 502, 2.13.1481 (Bunmei 13) Yasutomi Fusayuki *buninjō utsushi*, p. 153 for Masahiro rebuilding Chikuzen's Ichinomiya shrine of Sumiyoshi.

important he viewed their records to be, and carefully wrote down the shrine's rites so that they would continue.[100]

Masahiro did much to ensure that rites were performed. He did so by assigning the expenses for these rites to the warriors. At times, he required people of a smaller district, such as Tōsai in Aki to cover the operating expenses for Hikamisan Kōryūji.[101] In addition, he also levied province-wide duties. He had his warriors perform yearly rites at eight shrines in Nagato, a policy that resembled the levies imposed on *gokenin* by Norihiro. In this case, these warriors were described in archaic terminology as the provincial warriors (*zaichō kanjin*) of Nagato.[102]

The Depersonalization of Administrative Practices

Masahiro had been a vigorous and able commander from 1465 through early 1479. He lavished attention on his followers, taking care, for example, to re-confirm the holdings of the Shinohara by documents in the *kudashibumi* format.[103] These personal ties became more remote, however, after Masahiro suffered a stroke in 1479 at the age of thirty-four.[104] He managed to recover for a while, but he wrote shortly before he died that he had relapsed into a condition called a *chūfū*, whereby part of the body is unresponsive.[105]

---

[100] *Sengoku ibun Ōuchi shi hen*, vol. 1, doc. 513, 7.20.1481 (Bunmei 13) Ōuchi Masahiro *gedai ando*, p. 163. See also *Yamaguchi kenshi shiryōhen chūsei*, vol. 4, Sumiyoshi jinja zō monjo, doc. 261, 6.1481 (Bunmei 13) Nagato no kuni Ichinomiya *jinji nenchū kiroku chūshinjō an*, pp. 459–66 for his copying the rites of Sumiyoshi performed throughout the year.

[101] *Sengoku ibun Ōuchi shi hen*, vol. 1, doc. 437, 4.23.1479 (Bunmei 11) Ōuchi *kashin rensho hōsho*, p. 129.

[102] *Yamaguchi kenshi shiryōhen chūsei*, vol. 4, Iminomiya jinja monjo, doc. 249, 4.1481 (Bunmei 13) Nagato Hassha Godō *zaichō kanjinra shusshi shidai*, pp. 215–218, and doc. 250, 6.1481 (Bunmei 13) Nagato Ninomiya *nenjū shinji sokabunmai chūshinjō narabi ni* Ōuchi Masahiro *gedai shōhan*, pp. 218–24. For more analysis, see Inoue Hiroshi, "Chūsei shokoku Ichinomiyasei no rekishiteki kōzō to toskushitsu: Chūsei kōki Nagato no kuni no jirei o chūshin ni," *Kokuritsu rekishi minzoku hakubutsukan kenkyū hōkoku*, no. 148 (12.2008), pp. 206–18.

[103] *Sengoku ibun Ōuchi shi hen*, vol. 1, doc. 448, p. 133, 8.9.1479 (Bunmei 11) Ōuchi Masahiro *sodehan* Shūri *no suke hōsho utsushi*. Compare this with *Hagi han batsu etsu roku*, vol. 4, Usui Heizaemon monjo, doc. 15, 7.20.1461 (Kanshō 2) Ōuchi Norihiro *sodehan* Sugi Masayasu *hōsho utsushi*, p. 187.

[104] The timing of the stroke can be known because Ashikaga Yoshimasa questioned if Masahiro intended to retire in 1479. *Sengoku ibun Ōuchi shi hen*, vol. 1, doc. 461, *urū* 9.20 [(Bunmei 11) 1479] Ashikaga Yoshimasa *gonaisho utsushi*, p. 136, and doc. 462, *urū* 9.28 [(Bunmei 11) 1479] Ise Sadamune *soejō utsushi*, p. 136. This survives from the Naitō collection, located in *Hagi han batsu etsu roku*. See also *Ashikaga Yoshimasa hakkyū monjo*, vol. 2, doc. 744, p. 101.

[105] *Sengoku ibun Ōuchi shi hen*, vol. 1, doc. 796, 5.4 Ōuchi Masahiro *shojō utsushi*, p. 259, which dates from 1495 (Meiō 4).

After 1479, Masahiro relied upon religious specialists to help heal him, such as Kamo Arimune, a yin yang (*onmyōdō*) practitioner who became an important adviser to Masahiro. In 1478–79, a period coinciding with the onset of Masahiro's illness, Arimune prayed for him, relying on star rites that had hitherto been performed in the capital.[106]

On 9.21.1479, Ōuchi law codes were recopied.[107] Previously this had happened at moments of succession, but the copying here was more routinely administrative. Laws were copied to avoid turmoil. As Masahiro was debilitated, laws themselves naturally became a focus of attention, as governance became more regularized and less reliant on the figure of a lord.

Masahiro's physical debilitation led to a depersonalization of administrative practices. After 1478–79, an overlapping system of control was established, in that deputy *shugo* exercised great authority over regions, as too did retainers who were appointed to govern on the district level.[108] These district leaders also concurrently served in Masahiro's council.[109] This meant that those who made policy decisions concurrently exercised authority over specific regions. They were thus aware of the situation on the ground, while those with local authority were so bound in the larger organization that they could not carve out autonomous authority.[110]

Landholding patterns reveal the sophistication of Ōuchi rule, in that warriors had extremely limited and fragmented holdings in provinces such as Chikuzen. No individual could dominate a province or district. Crucial positions such as the district office were invariably staffed by Suō and Nagato warriors. Warriors divorced from their "original" lands were less likely to rebel against the Ōuchi, and this template would underpin successful governance for centuries. However, not all provinces were so governed, for example the earlier conquered districts of Buzen, which were staffed with locals.[111]

---

[106] Mori Shigeaki, "Ōuchi shi to onyōdō- Ōuchi Masahiro to Kamo Akimune to no kankei o chūshin ni," *Nihon rekishi* 583 (12.1996), pp. 9–10.

[107] *Sengoku ibun Ōuchi shi hen*, vol. 1, doc. 454, 9.21.1479 (Bunmei 11) Ōuchi shi *kokugaryō hatto*, pp. 134–35. The original laws were issued in 1399 (Ōei 6) and then again in 1408 (Ōei 15), 1442 (Kakitsu 2) and 1466 (Bunshō 1). As they burned during the turmoil of 1472 (Bunmei 4), Masahiro had them recopied in 1479.

[108] Appointments to district positions at times exhibited extensive turnover. In one case, Niho Moriyasu was executed in 1478, and replaced by Sue Hiromori, who resigned and was replaced by Sue Hiroakira.

[109] Saeki Kōji, "Ōuchi shi no Chikuzen no kuni shugo dai," Kawazoe Shōji, comp., *Kyūshū Chūsei shi kenkyū*, vol. 2 (Bunken shuppan, 1980), pp. 337–39.

[110] Saeki Kōji, "Ōuchi shi no Chikuzen no kuni shihai."

[111] Saeki Kōji, "Ōuchi shi no Chikuzen no kuni gundai," in *Kyūshū daimyō no kenkyū* (Yoshikawa kōbunkan, 1983), pp. 310–46. Analysis of patterns of appointment and contrasting strategies in Buzen and Chikuzen appears on pp. 336–37. For the fragmented nature of holdings in Chikuzen, see Saeki Kōji, "Ōuchi shi no Chikuzen no kuni shihai," pp. 347–53.

Subtle changes in the style and formation of regulations appear in 1485. They ceased to be addressed as direct communiqués with individual followers (*jikijō*) in favor of a more prestigious format known as *gechijō*, which were blanket directives to individuals of varied status.[112] Emblematic of the change, the laws that had been posted were also recorded in a compendium in 1495, the time of Masahiro's death, so that they could serve as a reference in future times.[113]

Ōuchi retainers also established a council that met six times a month. These men of the council required an oath excusing absence in cases of illness. They also were required to circulate written opinions beforehand to prevent meetings from lasting too long.[114] In later years, rosters of officials would be created, and these individuals had to show up before 9 a.m. and would be required to stay at least 100 days in Yamaguchi. By doing so, they imposed an attendance system on their retainers, much like what the Ashikaga had demanded of their *shugo* during their heyday in the first half of the fifteenth century.[115] Thus, the Ōuchi established effective legal institutions and mechanisms for disseminating their laws to retainers and denizens of their territories that did not depend upon the direct commands of Masahiro.

Economic and Cultural Exchanges

When Masahiro conquered Hakata in 1478, he gained access to great wealth. The Hakozaki shrine alone offered Masahiro one thousand *kanmon* of cash.[116] Trade proved profitable, and Masahiro duly established representatives to oversee Hakata who were responsible for people coming overseas from Iki island.[117]

---

[112] Kawato Takashi, "Sengoku daimyō Ōuchi shi no ishi dentatsu shisutemu," *Nihon Rekishi* 713 (10.2007), pp. 66–67.

[113] For an important early study, comparing various texts and showing that the Maeda and Mōri copies of these laws are closest to the original, see Ōmori Mihoko, "Ōuchi shi *hekisho* no jittai o megutte," *Historia*, no. 108 (10.1985), pp. 43–63. For the dating of these laws as around 1495 (Meiō 4), see p. 60.

[114] *Sengoku ibun Ōuchi shi hen*, vol. 1, doc. 505, 3.5.1481 (Bunmei 13) Ōuchi shi *hatto jōjō utsushi*, pp. 154–55.

[115] *Sengoku ibun Ōuchi shi hen*, vol. 1, doc. 596, 11.1485 (Bunmei 17) Ōuchi shi *hatto jōjō*, p. 192 for rosters of officials and mention that they must show up before 9 a.m. (the fifth hour). See also doc. 599, 2.26.1485 (Bunmei 17), Ōuchi shi *hekisho utsushi*, pp. 193–94 for laws demanding that officials must remain in Yamaguchi.

[116] Saeki Kōji, "Ōuchi shi no Chikuzen no kuni shihai," pp. 356–58, 361–62. For the original source, see *Yamaguchi kenshi shiryōhen chūsei*, vol. 1, Masatōki, 10.17.1478 (Bunmei 10), p. 343.

[117] Saeki Kōji, "Ōuchi shi no Chikuzen no kuni shihai," pp. 353–58 for details of Ōuchi control over Hakata and how Yamashika Iki *no kami*, a follower of Iida Hirohide, was granted this authority.

Masahiro's officials also established regulations regarding trade and markets, particularly because they encountered an influx of imported and forged currency. The latter half of the fifteenth century witnessed a dramatic influx of coins from Ming China, Korea, and the Ryūkyū Kingdom (1454–60; 1477–1526). Some coins with no markings that were made in Sakai, or "bird's eyes," were used for exchange as well, and this necessitated a greater regulation of coins.[118] In 1485, Ōuchi administrators established a ratio of acceptable coin usage, requiring that at least 30 percent of coins be Ming fifteenth-century coins (dated 1408 or 1433).[119] The first "assaying" edicts, determining the exchange rates of various imported coins and discouraging the use of low-quality coins, were initiated by the Ōuchi, but they have been relatively underestudied, as scholars implicitly assume that the most sophisticated regulations would be generated by the imperial court or the Ashikaga bakufu. With their extensive trade and access to currency, the Ōuchi experienced disruptions, like the adverse effects of Chinese counterfeit coins, earlier than authorities in the capital.[120] Unsurprisingly, the Ōuchi continued to prohibit privately minted coins in Buzen, where copper was mined.[121]

By 1485, the Ōuchi issued the first assaying (*erizeni*) edicts regulating currency in Japan.[122] Scholars have debated the significance of these edicts, with some suggesting that an inflationary monetary crisis within Ming China led to a similar crisis within Japan, while others have suggested that the widespread adoption of these coins within Japan caused inflationary pressures.[123]

---

[118] For the latter, see the catalog *Yomigaeru akagane: Nanbanfuku to Sumitomo dōfukusho* (Ōsaka: Ōsaka rekishi hakubutsukan, 2003), p. 32 for discovered examples of these unmarked Sakai coins that date from the 1480s. Another type of coin, known as "bird's eyes" (*torime*) were later favored in Okinawa, but the Ōuchi can be documented as using them in 1483. See *Yamaguchi kenshi shiryōhen chūsei*, vol. 1, Ninagawa Chikamoto nikki, 9.2.1481 (Bunmei 13), pp. 194–95.

[119] *Chūsei hōsei shiryōshū*, vol. 3, pp. 58–59, and *Sengoku ibun Ōuchi shi hen*, vol. 1, doc. 582, 4.15.1485 (Bunmei 17), pp. 185–86. See also Kawato Takashi, "Chūsei kōki no ryūtsū kōzō to sensen," *Chūseishi kenkyū*, no. 32 (2007), pp. 191–93. Coin hoards dating from the earlier fifteenth century have a lower percentage of these coins. They constituted 12.6 percent of the Hikamisan hoard (1,527 out of 12,141) and 14 percent (1,887 out of 13,492) of the Shimo Migita hoard.

[120] Kobata Atsushi, *Nihon kahei ryūtsūshi* (1969), pp. 77–78. For recent analysis, see Kuroda Akinobu, *A Global History of Money* (New York: Routledge, 2020), pp. 104–5. Kuroda postulates that "new" counterfeit Ming coins were likely transported to Japan at this time.

[121] *Sengoku ibun Ōuchi shi hen*, vol. 1, doc. 727, 3.1492 Ōuchi shi *kashin rensho hōsho utsushi*, p. 237 for prohibitions of what was undoubtedly illicitly minted "bad coins" (*akusen*) at Buzen.

[122] The scholarly literature on *erizeni* laws is vast. For a brief overview, see Richard von Glahn, *Fountain of Fortune: Money and Monetary Policy in China, 1000–1700* (Berkeley: University of California Press, 1996), pp. 92–97. The classic and still indispensable work is Kobata Atsushi, *Nihon kahei ryūtsū shi* (Tōkō shoin, 1930), particularly pp. 95–109 for the Ashikaga laws and pp. 110–12 for the Ōuchi laws.

[123] Takagi Hisashi, *Nihon Chūsei kahei shiron* (Kōkura shobō, 2010) explains the parameters argument (pp. 135–36), with the scholars Adachi and Honda suggesting that the Chinese crises spread to Japan, while Ōta Yukio argued that it spurred coin usage within Japan.

Regardless of the underlying cause, that the late fifteenth century witnessed an increase in low-quality, privately minted coins is beyond debate.[124]

Decisions regarding the regulation of currency were clearly political, as those in authority had an interest in determining what coins would be accepted and how.[125] In 1485, the Ōuchi established exchange rates for buying and selling of rice and allowed for market rates to dictate the exchange on a daily basis, although they demanded that sale and purchase of rice should be transacted in coins.[126] Ōuchi Masahiro's youngest son, Sonkō (d. 1508?), a monk who managed local estates, decreed that grain taxes should be paid in cash. He established an exchange rate from 1490 onward, which favored the assessors over agriculturalists.[127]

Currency became so widespread in the Ōuchi domains that it was used for a variety of common transactions. For example, tolls costs three *mon* to cross the Straits of Shimonoseki alone, fifteen *mon* for an armor box or a horse, and ten *mon* for a dog.[128] These tolls were enforced by representatives, who posted these prices and would report offenders to Yamaguchi.[129] The demand of cash for service became so widespread that at times the Ōuchi had to remind their followers that they paid for provisions, but not wages of the boatmen for commandeered vessels.[130]

Once coins became widely used as a unit of transaction, the question of what to do with Chinese coins of varying qualities became salient. Here the Ōuchi distinguished between "good" old Chinese coins and inferior specie,

---

[124] Richard von Glahn, "Chinese Coin," p. 650.

[125] See Nakajima Keiichi, "Chūsei kahei no fuhensei to chiikisei," in Amino Yoshihiko, ed., *Kōkogaku to Chūseishi kenkyū* (Meichi shuppan, 1997), p. 188. I am also grateful for insights from Federico Marcon, 2.26.2019, conversation. For studies about coins in Japan, albeit in an earlier era, see Ethan Segal, *Coins, Trade, and the State: Economic Growth in Early Medieval Japan* (Cambridge, MA: Harvard University Asia Center, 2011).

[126] *Chūsei hōsei shiryōshū*, vol. 3, Ōuchi shi *hekisho*, 4.15.1485 (Bunmei 17), pp. 58–59, and *Sengoku ibun Ōuchi shi hen*, vol. 1, doc. 582, 4.15.1485 (Bunmei 17) Ōuchi shi *kashin rensho kinzei utsushi*, pp. 185–86.

[127] *Yamaguchi kenshi tsūshihen furoku CD-ROM*, Tōfukuji monjo (Tōfukuji zō), doc. 36, Suō no kuni Sabaryō gun *tokuchi hō shokata reibutsu sanyōjō*, p. 627 for the new exchange dating from 1490 (Entoku 2). See also *Yamaguchi kenshi tsūshihen chūsei*, p. 162.

[128] *Sengoku ibun Ōuchi shi hen*, vol. 1, doc. 645, 4.20.1487 (Bunmei 19) Ōuchi shi *kashin renshō hatto jōjō*, pp. 210–11. The ferry prices show remarkable consistency, as one can currently take the ferry from Moji to Shimonoseki (Akamagaseki) for 270 yen, or approximately two and a half dollars. Conlan, *Samurai and the Warrior Culture of Japan, 471–1877: A Sourcebook* (Indianapolis: Hackett, 2022), pp. 201–4 translates these codes.

[129] *Sengoku ibun Ōuchi shi hen*, vol. 1, doc. 646, 4.20.1487 (Bunmei 19) Akamagaseki *jigenin rensho oshigaki utsushi*, p. 211.

[130] *Sengoku ibun Ōuchi shi hen*, vol. 1, doc. 662, 1.20.1488 (Chōkyō 2) Ōuchi shi *kashin rensho hōsho utsushi*, p. 216, and doc. 729, 5.2.1492 (Entoku 4) Ōuchi shi *kashin rensho hōsho utsushi* 5.2.1492 (Entoku 4), pp. 238–39.

or "bad" coins (*akusen*), which were broken, of poor quality, forged, or recently minted by the Ming Dynasty in great numbers.

The Ōuchi regulations of 1485 allowed province-wide land tax (*tansen*) payments to include up to 20 percent of *akusen* Ming coins from the Eiraku (Yongle [1402–24]) and Sentoku (Xuande [1425–35]) eras, while transactional expenses, or interest payments (*baibai sen; risen*) could be made up to 30 percent of Eiraku and Sentoku specie. Nevertheless, privately minted "Sakai" coins, hammered coins with no inscriptions (*uchihirame*) and the low-quality Kōbu (Hongwu [1368–98]) Ming coins were prohibited entirely.[131]

The flood of bad coins proved so great that locals rapidly were forced to accept some *akusen*. One sees the first use of *akusen* in 1488 as a means of payment if they constituted 10 percent or less of the total coinage.[132] In 1493, the Sagara, who resided in Ōuchi-controlled territory, tried to establish ratios of good to bad coin usage. They established that otherwise unknown *ji-ōdori* coins would be discounted 60 percent from good coins, while "black coins," poorly made coins with high concentrations of lead or zinc, would be discounted by 50 percent.[133] In 1492, Ōuchi officials in Buzen province criticized the profusion of such prohibited coins and threatened those who used them with imprisonment.[134] Ultimately the Ōuchi provided for some stability in coinage by recognizing some privately minted coins. On 10.7.1497, they allowed the use of *akusen* for purchases, but prohibited the use of Sakai coins (*Sakaisen*), *uchihirame* hammered coins and forged Hongwu coins, also known as rope cutter coins (*nawakiri*). Eiraku (Yongle) and Sentoku (Xuande) coins, considered an inferior specie (*akusen*), were not to be used solely for payments, although they could be interspersed with

131 *Chūsei hōsei shiryōshū*, vol. 3, Ōuchi shi *hekisho*, 4.15.1485 (Bunmei 17), pp. 58–59, and *Sengoku ibun Ōuchi shi hen*, vol. 1, doc. 582, pp. 185–86. See also von Glahn, "Chinese Coin," pp. 651–52. The term *risen* (里銭), more commonly written as *risen* (利銭), describes coins used to pay for profit from interest. For the reading of the term as *risen*, see *Sengoku ibun Ōuchi shi hen*, vol. 2, doc. 984, Ōuchi shi *hatto jōjō utsushi*, 10.7.1497 (Meiō 6), pp. 14–15. See also Iwasaki Toshihiko, *Ōuchi shi kabegaki o yomu*, p. 157.

132 Kanō shiryōhen iinkai, comp., *Kanō shiryō, Sengoku*, vol. 2 (Ishikawa, 2000), Kamowake Ikazuchi monjo, 4.11.1488 (Chōkyō 2) Seni tōrai sanyōjō: 395–413, p. 397.

133 *Chūsei hōsei shiryōshū*, vol. 3, Satara shi *hatto*, 4.22.1493 (Meiō 2), pp. 27–28. For more analysis, see von Glahn, "Chinese Coin," p. 653. See also Nakajima Keiichi, "Chūsei kahei no fuhensei to chiikisei" pp. 176–81 for coinage in Kyushu. See also *Kagoshima kenshiryō kyūki zatsuroku zenhen* (Kagoshima ken ishinshi shiryosanjo, 1979), vol. 2, doc. 1878, 8.26.1516 (Eishō 13) Ishitsuka Tanenobu *kishinjō*, p. 612, referring to nine *kan* of *ji-ōdori* coins being the same as two *kan* of Hongwu coins, and one *to* (slightly over four gallons) of rice.

134 *Sengoku ibun Ōuchi shi hen*, vol. 1, doc. 727, 3.1492 (Entoku 4) Ōuchi shi *kashin rensho hōsho utsushi*, p. 237, and *Chūsei hōsei shiryōshū*, vol. 3, 3.1492 (Entoku 4) Ōuchi shi *hekisho*, p. 93.

higher-quality coins.[135] Tellingly, only in the specie-rich Ōuchi domain were Eiraku (Yongle) and Sentoku (Xuande) coins classified as *akusen*. By contrast, as late as 1499, officials in districts in southern Kyushu defined Eiraku (Yongle) coins as being good ones.[136]

The Ōuchi domains had such an abundance of specie that they did not adopt the long-standing practice in Kyoto and elsewhere to exchange "good" coins at a slightly discounted rate, as strings of cash worth one hundred *mon* contained only ninety-six actual coins. By contrast, from the fourteenth century onward, archaeological evidence reveals that Yamaguchi practice was that one string of cash had in fact one hundred coins.[137]

The Ōuchi regulated other economic affairs as well. They prohibited "forced sales" (*oshiuri*) where people were pressured to purchase items that they did not want or need by well-connected merchants.[138] They also established exchange rates in 1484 in terms that were extremely favorable to their interests. Gold and silver were exchanged on a one-to-one ratio, which benefited their silver-rich domains.

These metals could also be exchanged at a higher rate of 5 *mon* with each other, but only for 4.5 *mon* of cash, which was in line with earlier practices of favoring cash exchanges to those in metals.[139] For centuries after this regulation, gold in Japan would be relatively cheap vis-à-vis silver.

With peace, renewed control over Hakata, and some regularity established in exchanges of coins and metals, Masahiro reached out to the Ryūkyū king and the Shimazu of southern Kyushu.[140] The items exchanged included straw mats (*mushiro*), fans, folding screens, paper, and bowls (*wan*), as well as leopard, seal, and tiger skins.[141] That tiger skins, which could only come from

[135] *Sengoku ibun Ōuchi shi hen*, vol. 2, doc. 984, Ōuchi shi *hatto jōjō utsushi*, 10.7.1497 (Meiō 6), pp. 14–15, and *Chūsei hōsei shiryōshū*, vol. 3, Ōuchi shi *hekisho*, 10.7.1497 (Meiō 6), pp. 100–101.

[136] In southern Kyushu, however, the easily forged and crude Kōbu (Hongwu) coins were classified as being poor-quality "minor coins." See Kawato Takashi, *Sengokuki no kahei to keizai* (Yoshikawa kōbunkan, 2008), particularly pp. 115–18 for the 1499 document, and pp. 119–32 for Ōuchi practices in Kyushu. See also von Glahn, "Chinese Coin," p. 653, and Nakajima Keiichi, "Chūsei kahei no fuhensei to chiikisei."

[137] *Nakatsu kyokan ato*, vols. 1–2 (Iwakuni-shi kyōiku iinkai, 2012–16). See in particular vol. 2, pp. 68–70.

[138] *Sengoku ibun Ōuchi shi hen*, vol. 1, doc. 313, 8.10 [(Bunmei 10) 1478] Ōuchi shi *kashin rensho hōsho*, p. 99.

[139] *Chūsei hōsei shiryōshū*, vol. 3, 5.1484 (Bunmei 16) *Kogane shirogane ryōme hatto no koto*, p. 57, explains how one *ryō* of coins would equal 4.5 *mon* of cash, while for exchanges in gold and silver it would equal 5. See also *Sengoku ibun Ōuchi hen*, vol. 1, doc. 571, 5.1484 (Bunmei 16) Takaishi Shigeyuki *gechijō utsushi*, pp. 181–82.

[140] For a rare example of his correspondence with Okinawan kings, see *Sengoku ibun Ōuchi shi hen*, vol. 1, docs. 663, 665, 2.13 Ōuchi Masahiro *shojō utsushi*, pp. 216–17.

[141] *Sengoku ibun Ōuchi shi hen*, vol. 1, doc. 664, 2.13 Ōuchi Masahiro *tsuikei utsushi*, pp. 216–17. This survives in the *Ōuchi jitsuroku dodai*, vol 15. See also Itō Kōji, "Jugo juroku seiki no Nihon to Ryūkyū,"

Korea, were exchanged reveals that his role as intermediary in facilitating this trade. In 1482 Masahiro imported another Korean Tripiṭaka to a temple that had been damaged in 1469.[142]

Enhanced production in Japan also led to exchanges. Masahiro also oversaw craftsmen who lived in Suō and made large bells. The oldest surviving example dates from 1469, while another, dated thirty years later (1499), was made in Suō by Yamato Sōshū and transported to the Ryūkyū Islands. Some bells were cast with Ming, rather than Japanese, era years.[143] Additional unique, and unusual evidence of his activities is the dissemination of Sago palms (sotetsu Cycas revoluta) in Kyoto. These ferns were unknown in Kyoto, but Masahiro imported some from Korea and planted them in his garden. He then gave some to Ashikaga Yoshimasa in 1488, and since then they have become a mainstay of many gardens in Kyoto.[144] In addition, apparently Masahiro gave Yoshimasa a boulder for his garden, known as the "Ōuchi stone," which to this day appears prominently in the center of the pond.

Masahiro served as an intermediary between the continent and the capital in cultural exchanges. At times he tailored his offering to what he knew were distinct Ashikaga interests and offered these works as gifts. For example, he provided Ashikaga Yoshimasa with a list of ink paintings of a small number of Chinese painters on 7.10.1481.[145] He only included figures from a group of thirty who had already been recorded in the Gomotsu on'e mokuroku, an Ashikaga compendium of their works, ignoring thousands of other Yuan and

Kyūshū Shigaku 144 (5.2006), pp. 4–24, and Saeki Kōji "Ōuchi shi to Ryūkyū," (accessed 11.10.2018), http://www.tulips.tsukuba.ac.jp/limedio/dlam/B95/B952214/1/dai-1/mokuji/5113.pdf. For other items, transported to Kyoto, see Yamaguchi kenshi shiryōhen chūsei, vol. 1, Ninagawa Chikamoto nikki, 1.30.1481 (Bunmei 13), pp. 190–91.

142 Kenneth Robinson, "Treated as Treasures: The Circulation of Sutras in Maritime Northeast Asia from 1388 to the Mid-Sixteenth Century," East Asian History 21 (June 2001), p. 49. For reference to some of a Tripiṭaka being brought to Kyoto, see Yamaguchi kenshi shiryōhen chūsei, vol. 1, Inryōken nichiroku, 2.24.1488 (Chōkyō 2), pp. 150–51.

143 Ōuchi bunka, pp. 852–53 for reference to a surviving Okinawa bell with Ming rather than Japanese era years inscribed. For reference to the Tsushima and Okinawan bells being crafted by Yamato Sōshū of Hōfu, see also Yamaguchi kenshi tsūshi hen chūsei, pp. 915–16.

144 Yamaguchi kenshi shiryōhen chūsei, vol. 1, Inryōken nichiroku, 9.16.1488 (Chōkyō 2), p. 153. The name of the fern was written phonetically, and the plant's Korean origins and links to Masahiro's garden are mentioned. Nevertheless, this very ancient species of cycads is more common in Taiwan and the subtropical coast of China.

145 Yamaguchi kenshi shiryōhen chūsei, vol. 1, Ninagawa Chikamoto nikki, 7.10.1481 (Bunmei 13), p. 193.

Song painters not preferred by the Ashikaga.[146] Likewise, through his trade, he could provide valuable materials for artists under his patronage. Thus, the famed ink painter Sesshū (1420–1506) was provided with highly prized rice paper from China for painting his works.[147]

No mere intermediary only, Masahiro also altered court cultural practices, most notably the creation of *waka* poetic anthologies. He was instrumental in having an imperially sponsored collection of linked renga poetry, at which he excelled, published, while a *waka* anthology, which had been promoted by the late shogun Ashikaga Yoshihisa (1465–89, shogun 1473–89), was abandoned based on his advice.[148] Masahiro did not abandon *waka* altogether, however, as he still took great pains to have monks copy his *waka* and disseminate them at court.[149]

As Masahiro gained higher court offices, his cultural interactions with courtiers became more extensive, and he added works to his library. In 1476, Masahiro seems to have garnered some important texts from the Ichijō, a Fujiwara Imperial Regent family, such as the *Kachō yosei*, their "secret" familial commentary for *The Tale of Genji* written in 1472 by Ichijō Kaneyoshi, and Kaneyoshi's commentaries on the *Ise monogatari* (*Ise monogatari gukenshō*), written between 1460 and 1474.[150] Masahiro had the "At the Pass" (*Sekiya*) chapter of *The Tale of Genji* copied for him by the poet Asukai Masayasu (1436–1509) in 1481, while a complete copy of the tale was copied for Masahiro 1490.[151] Masahiro tried to amass the most important cultural writings of the court, and he also copied poems written by his grandfather Moriakira.[152] Masahiro thus disseminated court writings into the provinces,

---

[146] Shimao Arata, "An East Asian Art History: Chinese Painting and 'Karae,'" Princeton University, 7.16.2019. Comprehensive catalogs of Yuan and Song painters, such as the *Tuhui baojian* (*Zue hōkan*), for example, record over a thousand individuals.

[147] For this insight, I am indebted to Xiaojin Wu, 10.2019.

[148] Okuda Isao, *Sōgi* (Yoshikawa kōbunkan, 1998), pp. 135–36.

[149] For his reputation stemming from that of his renga, see Okuda Isao *Sōgi*, pp. 275. For Masahiro's dispatch of one hundred of his *waka* poems to the capital, see *Kobunsō*, 3.1960 catalog no. 35, p. 30. *Yamaguchi kenshi shiryōhen chūsei*, vol. 1, Daijōin jisha zōjiki, 8.20.1488 (Chōkyō 2), p. 225.

[150] Steven Carter, *Regent Redux* (Ann Arbor: University of Michigan Center for Japanese Studies, 1996), p. 185.

[151] Sasaki Takahiro, "'Ōshimabon Genji monogatari' ni kansuru shoshigakuteki kōsatsu," *Keiō Gijuku daigaku fuzoku kenkyūjō Shidō bunko* 41 (2006), p. 184 for analysis; for the Sekiya colophon, see p. 168. Torii Masayasu copied chapter 16, "At the Pass" (*Sekiya*), for Masahiro in 1481 (Bunmei 13), while the first chapter, "The Paulownia Pavilion" (*Kiritsubo*) and the final "The Floating Bridge of Dreams" (*Yume no ukihashi*) were copied by a high-ranking monk at the Chōfukuji temple in Nagato on 6.19.1490 (Entoku 2). For more on Masahiro's collection, see Shindō Tōru, *Sengoku no toshokan* (Tōkyōdō shuppan, 2020), pp. 38–48.

[152] Tanibayashi Hiroshi, "Ōuchi Morimi [Moriakira] to sonōeisō," *Kokubungaku* 9.1 (1964), pp. 141–45.

served as an intermediary for Chinese ink paintings being imported into Kyoto, and oversaw complex and many-faceted exchanges.

Recalibrating Ōuchi Ethnicity

Ōuchi claims of Korean ethnicity—their Paekche origins and narrative of how Prince Imsŏng, the third son of King Sŏngmyŏng, the founder of Paekche, came to Japan and landed first at Tatara—were known to prominent courtiers such as Ichijō Kaneyoshi and his son Jinson, who, as we have seen in chapter 6, questioned whether the Ōuchi were in fact originally Japanese.

While fighting in Kyoto, Masahiro copied the *Shinsen shōjiroku* (*New Record of Hereditary Titles and Familial Names*), a genealogical encyclopedia that had been written 815 (chapter 1), and, while doing so, made an unsettling discovery. The Tatara, specialists in metallurgy, hailed from Mimana (Kaya), a contested region between the ancient kingdoms of Paekche and Silla, and thus Masahiro was not a descendant of a Paekche king.[153] Masahiro continued his genealogical research in the aftermath of his *Shinsen sōjiroku* discoveries and requested another copy of the Korean national histories (Kr. *guksa*; J. *kokushi*) so that he could gain more detailed awareness of his ancestors.[154]

Masahiro recalibrated his origins, de-emphasizing Imsŏng in favor of making, for the time, the unique claim that he was ultimately descended from the North Star Myōken Great Bodhisattva (*Hokushin Myōken Sonjō-ō daibosatsu*) of Hikamisan Kōryūji, in Suō's Ōuchi district (*agata*). The 1477 prayer commemorating the installation of Hikamisan Myōken in

---

[153] Masahiro had this text copied during the tenth month of 1475 (Bunmei 7). The most accessible version of this text appears in *Gunsho ruijū zatsubu*, vol. 25, pp. 119–209. The colophon showing that it was copied by Masahiro appears on p. 209. Currently the original text is found at the *Kokuritsu rekishi minzoku hakubutsukan*. See Watanabe Shigeru, "Kokuritsu rekishi minzoku hakubutsukan shozō no kodai shiryō ni kansuru shoshiteki kentō," *Kokuritsu rekishi minzoku hakubutsukan kenkyū hōkoku* 153 (2009), p. 227. (The text is numbered H-63-919.) For more analysis of the Tatara, see Saeki Arikiyo, *Shinsen Sōjiroku no kenkyū* (Yoshikawa kōbunkan 2001), *Honbun hen*, vol. 1, p. 311, and *Jūi hen*, vol. 10, p. 264. See also Mori Shigeaki, "Ōuchi shi no kōryū to sosen denju," pp. 106–7; Itō Kōji, "Chūsei saikoku shoshi no keifu ninshiki," in *Kyokai aidentiti* (Kyūshū shigakukai, 2008), pp. 107–39; and Suda Makiko, *Chūsei nichō kankei to Ōuchi shi*, pp. 232–33.

[154] Suda Makiko, *Chūsei nichō kankei to Ōuchi shi*, pp. 221–23, and Hirase Naoki, *Ōuchi shi no ryōgoku shihai to shūkyō*, pp. 283–91, have argued that Masahiro created a genealogy in 1485 with the hope it would be recorded in official Korean histories. See also *Yamaguchi kenshi shiryōhen chūsei*, vol. 1, Richō jitsuroku, 10.7.1485 (Seonjong 16), pp. 914–15. An English explanation appears in Sangnam Lee, "The Joseon Court and the Ōuchi Clan: A Case Study of the Interregional Circulation of Material Culture," *Artibus Asiae* 78.2 (2018), p. 158.

Kyoto was replete with paeans to the deity from Hikamisan Kōryūji.[155] In 1486, Masahiro emphasized not Imsŏng's arrival, but rather how it had been foretold. A new Ōuchi genealogy describes how in 609 a shooting star landed atop a pine tree at Kudamatsu, which "like the light of the full moon" glowed for seven days, before a shaman recounted that within a span of three years, a prince (Imsŏng) would come because the star had landed here, at Kudamatsu, or where the star descended on pine trees. Then all were urged to worship the North Star Myōken Great Bodhisattva, and three years later the prince arrived.[156]

In 1486, the Masahiro oversaw a redefinition of Tatara self-representation. Tatara as a significant place of origin was de-emphasized in favor of Hikamisan. Thus, a panegyric written for Sue Hiromori, who also claimed descent from Hikamisan Myōken, merely described how Prince Imsŏng, the third son of King Sŏngmyŏng of Paekche, came to Japan (raichō) in 611. Although he landed at Tatara, he did not stay there long, and came to live in the Ōuchi district (agata) where Hikamisan was located.[157]

With the focus on descent from Myōken, Masahiro then simplified the Ōuchi genealogy. He expunged people that he wanted to be forgotten, such as his uncle Dōjun and his relative Takeharu, whose precise identity is in fact unknown.[158] He also limited traces of fraternal or contested succession and erased figures whose position as chief was contested, such as Mochimori, or those who were appointed as heirs but never inherited authority, such as Norisuke.[159]

---

[155] Sengoku ibun Ōuchi shi hen, vol. 1, doc. 266, 2.13.1477 (Bunmei 9) Ōuchi Mashahiro kōbun utsushi, p. 85. For another transcription, see Kuroita Katsumi, ed., Shintei zōho Kokushi taikei, vol. 27 (Yoshikawa kōbunkan, 1965), pp. 144–45. See also Hirase Naoki, Ōuchi shi no ryōgoku shihai to shūkyō, pp. 282–92.

[156] Suda Makiko has emphasized the importance of this in her Chūsei nichō kankei to Ōuchi shi, pp. 221–34. For the original records, see http://archives.pref.yamaguchi.lg.jp/msearch/photo.php?t= 2&id=127484&s=2, http://archives.pref.yamaguchi.lg.jp/msearch/photo.php?t=2&id=127484&s=3, and http://archives.pref.yamaguchi.lg.jp/msearch/photo.php?t=2&id=127484&s=4. See also Itō, "Ōuchi no sosen shinwa," (2011), pp. 99–101, and Itō, "Chūsei saikoku shoshi," pp. 121–22. Kudamatsu is described as "Aoyanagi harbor in Washizu estate, Tsuno district of the province of Suō."

[157] Sengoku ibun Ōuchi shi hen, vol. 1, doc. 575, 11.27.1484 (Bunmei 16) Sue Hiromori shōzōsan, pp. 182–83. See also Hirase Naoki, Ōuchi shi no ryōgoku shihai to shūkyō, pp. 287–88. For documents pertaining to the conflict that caused his death, see doc. 524, 6.13 [(Bunmei 14) 1482] Ōuchi shi kashin rensho shojō, p. 166, which also mentions how the Yoshimi and Sue fought at Tsuwano. See also doc. 528, 12.17.1482 (Bunmei 14) Muromachi bakufu bugyōnin rensho hōsho, pp. 167–68. For more on the Yoshimi and their assassination of Hiromori, see Tsuwano chōshi, vol. 1 (Tsuwano, 1970), p. 430.

[158] Wada Shūsaku, "Ōuchi Takeharu oyobi sono kankei shiryō," Yamaguchi monjokan kenkyū kiyō 30 (2003), pp. 4–5. See also Wada Shūsaku, Ōuchi shi no sōsho kankei o megutte," in Kage Toshio, ed., Ōuchi to Ōtomo: Chūsei nishi Nihon no nidai daimyō (Bensei shuppan, 2013), pp. 25–61.

[159] Sengoku ibun Ōuchi shi hen, vol. 1, doc. 626, 9.4.1486 (Bunmei 18) Ōuchi shi hekisho, p. 202.

These prayers and genealogies were designed to emphasize the importance of Hikamisan, where Kōryūji was also located. The 1486 genealogy was in fact appended to an application to the Japanese court to have Kōryūji designated as an imperial prayer temple (*chokuganji*).[160] This endeavor and, implicitly, court recognition of Ōuchi origins was formalized when Kōryūji was made an imperial prayer temple (*chokuganji*). Emperor Go-Tsuchimikado (1442–1500, r. 1464–1500) wrote the name plaque (*hengaku*) for this temple, which heightened the prestige of this institution.[161] This is among the earliest direct contact between Masahiro and Go-Tsuchimikado, whom he slighted and attacked during the Ōnin War.

Concurrent with the transformation of Hikamisan to an imperial prayer temple, and the focus on the North Star, the other *chokuganji*, Jōfukuji, the mortuary temple of Prince Imsŏng, was eclipsed. This building was graced with tiles in a *tekisui* dragon-and-phoenix pattern which had been used for palaces and temples by Korean Koryŏ kings. Although that dynasty collapsed in 1392, the desire to keep the distinctive Korean identity is evident in crude replacement tiles, made by Japanese craftsmen. These were, however, unable to replicate Korean techniques, and so their efforts resulted in the dragons being reversed, and the phoenixes looking more like sad pigeons.[162] Ultimately as the result of a fire, these tiles were discarded entirely, and the Ōuchi muted their most explicit claims of Korean royal ancestry in favor of more general worship of the North Star (Figures 7.1 and 7.2).[163]

160 Suda Makiko, *Chūsei nichō kankei to Ōuchi shi*, pp. 221–23.

161 *Ōuchi bunka*, meibun no. 3, Kōryūji pp. 865–66. See also *Bōchō jisha yurai*, vol. 3, *Yamaguchi mihori*, 10.27.1486 (Bunmei 18) Kōryūji Hokkaimon *hengaku urasumigaki*, pp. 310–11. For contemporary reference to this name plaque, see *Yamaguchi kenshi shiryōhen chūsei*, vol. 1, Sanetaka kōki, 7.20, 8.15 and 8.28.1486 (Bunmei 18), p. 251, and 1.27.1487 (Bunmei 19), p. 252. In addition, a copy of the Hikamisan *Kōryūji engi* was created for Go-Tsuchimikado. Its contents closely resemble that of the 1486 genealogy.

162 *Jōfukuji ato* II (2003), p. 45. See also plate 13 for the reverse dragon, and plate 18 for the pigeon like phoenix, also depicted in Figures 7.1 and 7.2.

163 *Jōfukuji ato* II, p. 29, and *Ōuchi bunka*, pp. 970–71 for debates regarding the dating of this *garanzu*. Likewise, this passage postulates that the tiles were discarded prior to the latter half of the fifteenth century. Jōfukuji burned down in 1520 and was rebuilt in 1531, and a surviving illustration of the compound (*garan*) shows no evidence of Korean tiles, suggesting that they were abandoned well before 1520. See *Jōfukuji ato* I (2001) and *Ōuchi bunka* for color images of this document.

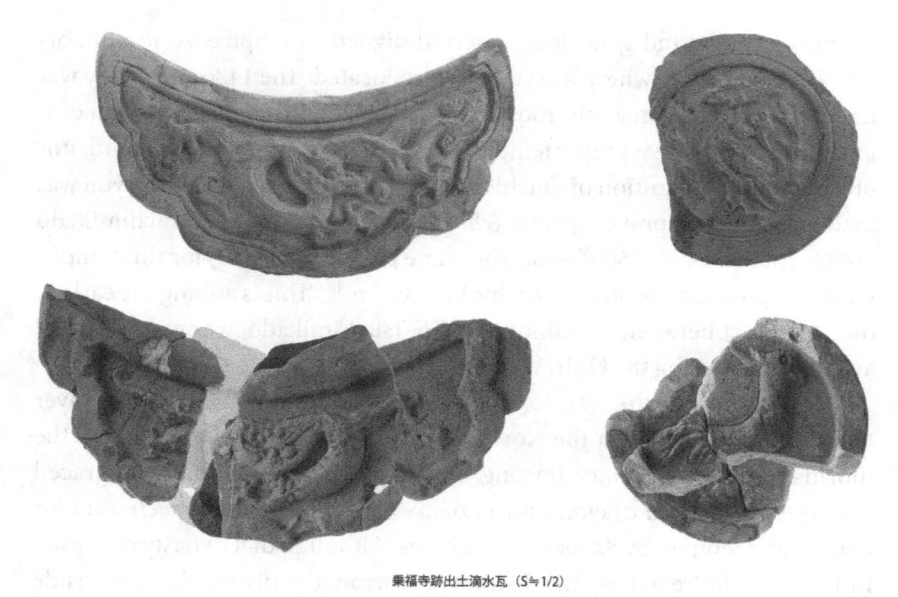

乗福寺跡出土滴水瓦（S≒1/2）

Figure 7.1 Jōfukuji *Tekisui* Roof Tiles (Composite image of original and later Japanese copies). Image and permission provided by Yamaguchi-shi kyōiku iinkai

Forging the Past

At the same time, as the panegyric of Sue Hiromori makes clear, there was an effort to revitalize Myōken worship at Kudamatsu but also subordinate it to Hikamisan. This was a delicate matter, for, as we have seen in chapter 1, Kudamatsu was the original site of Myōken worship for the rival Washizu, the original main line of the Tatara, which was not fully eclipsed until Norihiro wiped out Washizu Hirotada (d. 1448) in Nagato in 1447–48 (chapter 6). Thereafter, Masahiro took it upon himself to protect Kudamatsu and prohibit hunting there in 1467, just before his armada set off to Kyoto.[164] He rebuilt the lower shrine of Kudamatsu sometime prior to 10.6.1478.[165]

---

[164] *Sengoku ibun Ōuchi shi hen*, vol. 1, doc. 3, 4.2.1467 (Ōnin 1) Ōuchi Masahiro *kinzei utsushi*, p. 3, and *Chūsei hōsei shiryōshū*, vol. 3, Ōuchi shi *hekisho* no. 16, 4.2.1467 (Ōnin 1), pp. 44–45. Inspection of the shrine (6.8.2015) revealed some evidence of late medieval pottery, but the site has never been excavated and nothing is known about the earlier era.

[165] *Yamaguchi kenshi shiryōhen chūsei*, vol. 1, Masatōki, 10.6.1478 (Bunmei 10), p. 335. See also Wada, "Chūsei no Washizu shi ni tsuite," *Kudamatsu chihōshi kenkyū*, no. 50 (4.2014), p. 18 for his reconstruction of the lower shrine.

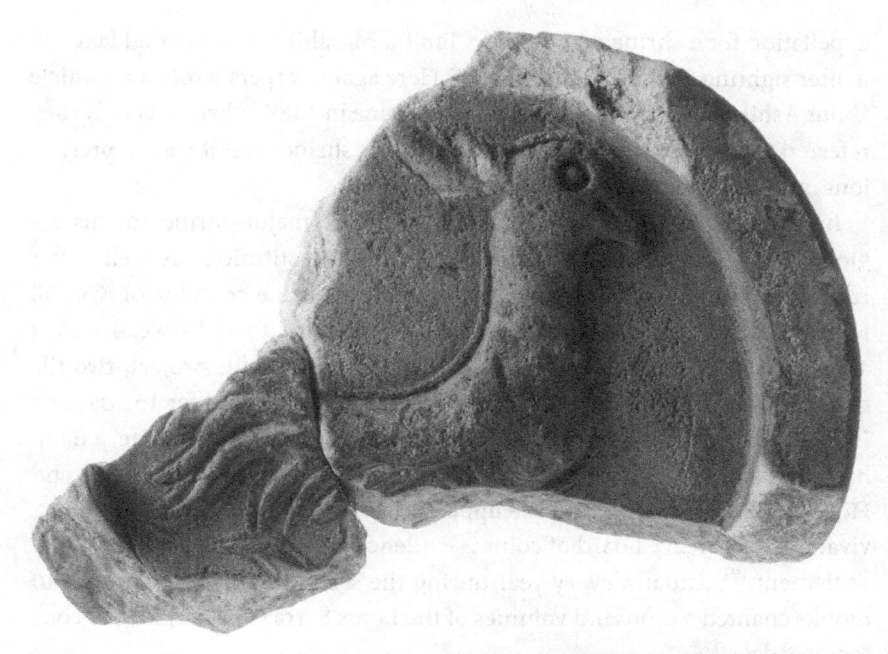

Figure 7.2 Jōfukuji *Tekisui* Roof Tile with Phoenix 乗福寺滴水瓦Ｂ一06. The replacement tile was made by Japanese craftsmen who could not master the earlier Korean techniques. Image and permission provided by Yamaguchi-shi kyōiku iinkai

Kudamatsu, the original site of Myōken's appearance according to Ōuchi lore, was of greater antiquity than Hikamisan, as its oldest surviving document dates from 11.27.1286.[166] During Masahiro's time, the latter half of the fifteenth century, a donation from an otherwise unknown woman of the Tatara lineage was forged, purportedly dating from 6.23.1282. Conveniently for those asserting Hikamisan's primacy, it explicitly described Hikamisan and the official ancestral temple (*ujidera*) of the Tatara (*Hikami tera wa Tatara no uchi tera nari*), thereby making it the oldest and most central temple-shrine complex.[167]

Masahiro also emphasized the importance of the Hōfu shrine in Sabaryō, which received the new name of Tenmangū shrine, the most prestigious

---

[166] *Bōchō fūdo chūshin an*, vol. 13, *Yamaguchi ge* (Yamaguchi, 1961), p. 411.

[167] *Kamakura ibun*, vol. 19, 6.23.1282 (Kōan 5) Tatara *ujime kishinjō*, p. 326. See also Mori Shigeaki, "Ōuchi shi no kōryū to sosen denju," pp. 105–7, and "Ōuchi shi to onyōdō," p. 3 for how this document was forged in the fifteenth century. For more analysis see *Ōuchi bunka*, p. 977, and Wada, "Chūsei no Washizu shi ni tsuite," pp. 16–19.

appellation for a shrine dedicated to Tenjin. Masahiro commended lands to it after sighting a white snake there.[168] Here again, forgers wrote a chronicle about Ashikaga Yoshimitsu's visit to this shrine in 1389, where crucially they referred to it anachronistically as a Tenmangū shrine, as if it was so prestigious in the fourteenth century.[169]

In addition to reshaping the histories of the major shrines of his regions, Masahiro rebuilt the structures of these institutions as well. After rebuilding Kudamatsu, he expanded the temple shrine complex of Kōryūji Hikamisan, as ten new subtemples were constructed there between 2.1478 and 11.13.1479. Emblematic of the efforts involved in this project, two tile makers from Hakata can be verified as staying in Yamaguchi for 152 days.[170] In its heyday, the Hikamisan area was a small town, with a large gate, a main hall, and the subtemples of Anraku'in, Anzen'in, Jōrakubō, Hōjōbō, and Honbō Shinkō'in, along with the upper and lower Myōken shrines. The survival of an extensive hoard of coins is evidence for the wealth and size of the settlement.[171] Ritually, every year during the second month, a team of 110 monks chanted a thousand volumes of the Lotus Sutra (*myōten*) for ten consecutive days.[172]

The Apotheosis of Ōuchi Norihiro

In tandem with bolstering Myōken worship, Masahiro promoted his father's divine ancestry, as it were moving the prestige of his lineage from kings to gods. Masahiro first requested that his father Norihiro receive unprecedentedly high court rank, a request that was facilitated by Ashikaga Yoshimasa and enacted in the sixth month of 1486.[173] Shortly after this,

---

[168] Mori Shigeaki, "Ōuchi shi no kōryū to sosen denju," pp. 99–100, 103. For the commendation, see *Sengoku ibun Ōuchi shi hen*, vol. 1, doc. 465, 10.15.1479 (Bunmei 11) Ōuchi Masahiro *kishinjō*, pp. 137–38. For excellent analysis of this shrine and its significance, see Hirase Naoki, *Ōuchi shi no ryōgoku shihai to shūkyō*, pp. 177–92.

[169] Mori Shigeaki, "Ōuchi shi no kōryū to sosen denju," pp. 99–100, 103.

[170] *Sengoku ibun Ōuchi shi hen*, vol. 1, doc. 469, 11.13.1479 (Bunmei 11) Kōryūji *munafuda mei utsushi*, p. 139, and doc. 309, 7.14 [(Bunmei 10) 1478] Sue Hiromori *shojō*, p. 98 for the building of ten new subtemples. See also doc. 326, 9.13.1478 (Bunmei 10) Ōuchi Masahiro *saikyojō*, p. 102.

[171] Maki Takayuki, "Suō no kuni Hikamisan Kōryūji no kyūkōnai to sono dōsha haichi," *Yamaguchi daigaku bunkakaishi* 65 (3.2015), pp. 41–61, and "Kinsei Hikamisan kyōnai no kōiki sashizu to sono saibu kōsei," *Yamaguchigaku no kōchiku*, no. 7 (2015), pp. 107–45.

[172] *Sengoku ibun Ōuchi shi hen*, vol. 1, doc. 434, 4.13.1479 (Bunmei 11) Ōuchi Masashiro *kishinjō*, p. 128 for the ceremonies involving 110 monks.

[173] *Yamaguchi kenshi shiryōhen chūsei*, vol. 1, Gohōkō'inki, 6.9.1486 (Bunmei 18), p. 242 for the edict being issued on 6.5.1486. For Yoshimasa's role, see *Nagaoki Sukuneki*, 6.27.1486 (Bunmei 18), p. 171. The edict for this promotion was issued on 6.19.

Ōuchi Norihiro was made into the Tsukiyama Radiant Wisdom Deity (Tsukiyama *daimyōjin*), and this apotheosis was sanctioned by Emperor Go-Tsuchimikado in 1486.[174]

This deification, which was formalized some two decades after Norihiro's death, was in and of itself not something unique. Japan's emperors had long been known to have sacerdotal authority, with several sovereigns in the seventh century being referred to as manifest deities (*akitsumigami*), although this term fell out of favor after the eighth century.[175] Other individuals could be deified as well, particularly those thought to hold grudges, and thus in need of pacification.

Japan had since ancient times had the *Jingikan* (Ministry of Divine Affairs), a bureaucratic organ responsible for officially recognizing gods as being significant enough to merit rites emanating from the court, or locality, and at times, bestowing ranks and honors on deities as well. These officials could also recognize that certain angry spirits (*onryō*) in need of pacification were in fact gods, and by doing so, transformed the *onryō* of Sugawara Michizane (845–903), a wronged official for example, into the Tenjin god, but this process took years to accomplish, and only occurred rarely.[176]

Shrines also housed objects, such as swords and mirrors, in which the "divine presence" (*shintai*) dwelled, but some claimed to see gods seeking to find a suitable abode after the destruction of their shrine.[177] Yoshida Kanetomo (1435–1511), an ambitious scion of a family of shrine attendants, solved this crisis by founding the Saijōsho Daigengū on Mt. Yoshida in eastern Kyoto, which was designed to house all of the deities of Japan, particularly those who had been displaced by the destruction of their shrines.[178] Kanetomo founded Yuiitsu Shinto, an attempt at a systematization of *kami*-related teachings and practices independent of Buddhism. He also attempted to establish his

---

[174] See Conlan, "When Men Become Gods: Apotheosis, Sacred Space, and Political Authority in Japan 1486-1599," *Quaestiones Medii Aevi Novae*, no. 21 (2016), pp. 89–106.

[175] Later sovereigns tended to emphasize their cosmic authority with the Buddhist notion of a *kinrin-ō*, or a Universal Golden Wheel Turning monarch (*cakravartin*) who ruled by moral suasion.

[176] For this process, see Robert Borgen, *Sugawara Michizane and the Early Heian Court* (Cambridge, MA: Harvard University Asia Center, 1986), particularly chapter 8, "Michizane as Tenjin," pp. 307–40.

[177] Hagiwara Tatsuo, *Chūsei Saishi soshiki no kenkyū* (Yoshikawa kōbunkan, 1975), pp. 645–46.

[178] See Allan Grapard, "The Shintō of Yoshida Kanetomo," *Monumenta Nipponica* 47.1 (Spring 1992), p. 43; Hagiwara Tatsuo, *Chūsei Saishi soshiki no kenkyū*, pp. 645–46; and David Romney, "Godly Politics: Ise, the Court, and Japanese Religiou 1330-1615," PhD dissertation, Princeton University, 2023, pp. 21–24, 114–46.

Figure 7.3 Yoshida Saijōsho Daigengū. Photograph by Thomas Conlan

lineage and its rites as the sole basis for all rituals for the protection of the state (*chingo kokka*) (Figure 7.3).[179]

By creating the Saijōsho Daigengū, Yoshida Kanetomo initiated a process whereby he asserted overarching authority in all affairs relating to the *kami* of Japan. This in turn served to bolster Kanetomo's claims that he was the ritual guarantor of political legitimacy.[180] Instead of relying on the venerable *Jingikan*, the shrine specialists, Kanetomo secured, with court backing, the position as the arbiter of all Shinto affairs in 1482. This allowed him to issue *sōgensenji*, or edicts that posited him with the full authority of the *Jingikan*.[181] For Masahiro, it was Yoshida Kanetomo, rather than the *Jingikan*, who issued the required paperwork making Norihiro the Tsukiyama *daimyōjin* in 1486.[182]

---

[179] Mark Teeuwen and Bernhard Scheid, "Tracing Shinto in the History of Kami Worship: Editor's Introduction," *Japanese Journal of Religious Studies* 29.3–4 (Fall 2002), p. 205, and Grapard, "Shintō of Yoshida Kanetomo," pp. 46–47.

[180] Grapard, "Shintō of Yoshida Kanetomo," pp. 47–48.

[181] Inoue Tomokatsu, *Kinsei no jinja to chōtei ken'i*, pp. 31–36. For more on *sōgen senji*, see pp. 77–95.

[182] Yamada Takashi, *Chūsei kōki buke kan'i ron* (Ebisu kōshō, 2015), pp. 172–207, and *Sengoku ibun Ōuchi shi hen*, vol. 1, docs. 640–43, 4.3 Ōuchi Masahiro *shojō utsushi*, pp. 209–10 for Masahiro's praise of his father's divine name of Tsukiyama to Emperor Go-Tsuchimikado, through his palace lady Nakahashi (Yotsuji Haruko), as well as his letter of thanks to Yoshida Kanetomo and the head of the *Jinkigan*.

Norihiro's apotheosis has attracted minimal attention from scholars, but the ramifications are profound. The circumstances regarding Norihiro's apotheosis thus profoundly differed from earlier cases. Norihiro was successful, so he had no reason to seek vengeance as an *onryō*. Likewise, the process of his deification differed from that of angry spirits. In contrast to this process, scholars have hitherto associated the deification of political leaders with the establishment of absolutist political authority, a process that was thought to have begun late in the sixteenth century.[183] Nevertheless, Yoshida records reveal that the 1486 deification of Ōuchi Norihiro served as the exact template for the posthumous deification of important figures of the late sixteenth century, such as the hegemon Toyotomi Hideyoshi (d. 1598).[184]

Yoshida Kanetomo had by then profoundly influenced the institutional structure of shrines, regularized previously inchoate beliefs and practices, and influenced the course of politics in the fifteenth and sixteenth centuries. Kanetomo is the first one who established an institutionally independent Shinto, and he was able to achieve this position through Ōuchi patronage. For almost eighty years, this relationship between the Yoshida and Ōuchi proved profitable for both parties, for the Yoshida also moved important gods to Yamaguchi, thereby cementing their primacy as the arbiters of all Shinto affairs, and the authority of the Ōuchi as gods among men.

Kanetomo demonstrated his power over all shrine-related affairs, including deification, and secured a patron independent of the crumbling Ashikaga bakufu. In 1473, Ashikaga Yoshimasa relied upon Yoshida Kanetomo to curse Masahiro's armies, but during the final years of the war, his allegiances shifted.[185] Norihiro went from being an enemy of the court to a god officially recognized by that same court. The following

---

[183] Asao Naohiro first argued that a troika of leaders—Oda Nobunaga (1534–1582), Toyotomi Hideyoshi (d. 1598), and Tokugawa Ieyasu (1543–1616)—had their authority legitimated and sustained by being declared as gods. See Asao Naohiro, "Shōgun and Tennō," in John Whitney Hall, Nagahara Keiji, and Kozo Yamamura, eds., *Japan before Tokugawa: Political Consolidation and Economic Growth, 1500–1650* (Princeton: Princeton University Press, 1981), pp. 248–271. For recent study focusing on this process for Norihiro, see Yamada Takashi, "Chūsei kōki no chiiki kenryoku ni yoru bushi no shinkakuka," *Chūsei kōki buke kan'i ron*, pp. 172–207. Another study briefly mentions Norihiro. See Takano Nobuharu, *Bushi Shinkakuka no kenkyū* (Yoshikawa kōbunkan, 2018), pp. 29–30, 238.

[184] For the role of Yoshida Shinto and the deification of Hideyoshi, see Hagiwara, *Chūsei Saishi soshiki no kenkyū*, p. 613; see pp. 673–77 for listing of the Yoshida Shinto documents (*sōgensenji*) deifying individuals, with Norihiro being the case most analogous to Hideyoshi. The Tsukiyama *daimyōjin* is the fourth record listed here.

[185] Inoue Satoshi, "Bunmei gonen izen no Yoshida Kanetomo Saijōsho: Toku ni sōgen jiki o megutte," *Waseda daigaku daigakuin bungaku kenkyūka kiyō. Tetsugaku, shigaku hen XVII* (1990), p. 48, and Inoue Tomokatsu, *Kinsei no jinja to chōtei ken'i* (Yoshikawa kōbunkan, 2007), p. 29.

year, Masahiro celebrated his father's good fortune and wrote two poems, one for Hikamisan's recognition as an imperial prayer temple and the other for his father's apotheosis. The first read: "With an imperial edict the descendants (*uji*) of the gods flourish," while for his father, he wrote: "With an imperial edict a different light illuminates Tsukiyama—how brilliant the gods!"[186]

The Yamaguchi Polity

Turtle Taboos

Norihiro's apotheosis led to a transformation of the social and geographic identity of western Japan as Yamaguchi, the Ōuchi core city, and the surrounding western provinces, became increasingly defined as a distinct sacred area. The newly recognized Tsukiyama god became the protector of this territory, while soft-shelled turtles and snakes were his messengers, and his descendants had the added prestige of having a god as an immediate ancestor.[187] Masahiro enacted sweeping regulations of Yamaguchi that focused on ritual purity, for prohibitions that had been confined to shrine precincts gradually became applied to much of the city.

The first regulations stem from the period of Yamaguchi's increased ritual prominence during the final years of the Ōnin War. In 1475, Masahiro prohibited the hunting of any animals on Hikamisan, even those that a hunter had wounded and pursued from other regions.[188] In 1478, he demanded that the shrine precincts for the Ima Hachiman shrine be kept clean,[189] but nine years later, Masahiro ordered that Yamaguchi itself had to be cleaned much

---

[186] *Yamaguchi kenshi shiryōhen chūsei*, vol. 4, Shūjin wakashū, p. 793 for poems of 2.11 and 4.3.1487 (Bunmei 19).

[187] *Yamaguchi kan nyūsu* no. 49 (2015), Takamonjo 434 (*Furumatsu Myōkensha engi utsushi*), refers to snakes and turtles as messengers of the gods.

[188] *Chūsei hōsei shiryōshū*, vol. 3, p. 48 for Hikamisan regulations of 11.13.1475 (Bunmei 7). The animals here were referred to as *ryō*. See *Sengoku ibun Ōuchi shi hen*, vol. 1, doc. 223, 11.13.1475 (Bunmei 7) Ōuchi Masahiro *hattō jōjō*, pp. 73–74. For later 1489 prohibitions of killing animals in Ōuchi domains, save for traditional cases where they were sold, fished, or hunted, see doc. 485, 4.26.1489 (Chōkyō 3) Ōuchi Masahiro *hekisho utsushi*, p. 223. Masahiro's laws have been translated by Conlan, *Samurai*, pp. 194–98, 201–4.

[189] *Chūsei hōsei shiryōshū*, vol. 3, p. 49.

in the same manner as these shrines.[190] A cluster of laws issued in this same year served to regulate conduct, prohibiting the playing of instruments in public, or people wandering around Yamaguchi at night.[191]

In 1489, Masahiro forbade the killing of snakes and soft-shelled turtles (*tochigame*)—animals that served as messengers for Myōken—throughout Yamaguchi and prohibited falconers from using them as food for their birds.[192] Masahiro ruthlessly punished those who disobeyed his injunctions, threatening some with imprisonment or death, thereby revealing that the need to purify Yamaguchi and protect its sacred animals transcended concerns of nonviolence per se. These prohibitions occurred in tandem with Hikamisan's increased importance, for similar ones had been issued for Kudamatsu in 1467.[193]

These prohibitions suggest that Yamaguchi became a purified area, and this sentiment can be confirmed in Jesuit writings from 1558, when one Portuguese resident explained that Yamaguchi was a purified area where people would not eat meat—and that he therefore did not so partake for seven years, a sign that these taboos were long lasting and strictly enforced.[194] Thus Yamaguchi became a sacred space, protected by both Tsukiyama and Myōken.[195] Later, Ōuchi retainers such as Sagara Taketō (1498–1551) would swear oaths to the Tsukiyama *daimyōjin*, suggesting that the deified Norihiro mattered as much as, if not more than, Myōken.[196] Tsukiyama served as a

---

[190] Masahiro stipulated that from the Tsukiyama shrine to Matsubara, and another gate, were to be cleaned on the final day (*misoka*) of the month, with laborers assessed at the level of one per one hundred *koku* of revenue. *Chūsei hōsei shiryōshū*, vol. 3, p. 76. The location of Matsubara is unknown but refers to the area south of the Ōuchi mansion, incorporating much of central Yamaguchi. Takahashi Shinichirō, *Bushi no sadame: "Michi" o meguru Kamakura Sengoku bushi no mō hitotsu to tatakai* (Shinjinbutsu ōraisha, 2012), pp. 168–69, 181–82.

[191] *Chūsei hōsei shiryōshū*, vol. 3, pp. 80–81, and Conlan, *Samurai*, pp. 193–97.

[192] *Chūsei hōsei shiryōshū*, vol. 3, pp. 80–81. For an earlier example, limited to temple precincts, Ōuchi Moriakira had prohibited the killing of animals within Kokushōji on 2.10.1404 (Ōei 11). *Chūsei hōsei shiryōshū*, vol. 4, *Bukehō*, vol. 2 (Iwanami shoten, 1998), pp. 96–97, Ōuchi Moriakira Kokushōji *jōsho an*.

[193] *Sengoku ibun Ōuchi shi hen*, vol. 1, doc. 3, 4.2.1467 (Ōnin 1) Ōuchi Masahiro *kinzei utsushi*, p. 3.

[194] *Nihon kankei kaigai shiryō Iezusukai Nihon shokanshū Yakubun hen*, vol. 3 (Tōkyō daigaku shuppankai, 2014), p. 156 for the 1.10.1558 Melchior Barreto letter. For how archaeological evidence shows an upswing in turtle consumption after the Ōuchi collapse, see *Asahi Shinbun*, evening edition 8.15.2006, "Inu ya kame no shokuyō uratsuke? Ōuchi shi yakata no ato shūhen kara setsudan sareta hone Mōri shi jidai to suisoku," p. 35.

[195] *Sengoku ibun Ōuchi shi hen*, vol. 1, doc. 776, 10.16 Sugi Sōgō *shojō an*, p. 253, dating from most likely 1493, describes an oath to Myōken *daibosatsu*.

[196] Tōkyō daigaku shiryōhen sanjo, comp., *Mōri ke monjo*, vol. 4 (Tōkyō daigaku shuppankai, 1924), doc. 1556, 1.5.1551 (Tenbun 20) Sagara Taketō *mōshijō utsushi*, pp. 458–65 for Sagara Taketō's reference to the Tsukiyama *daimyōjin*.

Figure 7.4 Tsukiyama Shrine, Yamaguchi. This structure was originally a Tokugawa era Tōshōgū shrine located near Hikamisan that was transferred to Tsukiyama after 1868. Photograph by Thomas Conlan

deity that enforced oaths by Ōuchi retainers and protected the newly purified Yamaguchi itself (Figure 7.4).[197]

The Age of Yamaguchi

Over the course of his life, Masahiro had triumphed in a war. Rather than attempt to stabilize the center, however, Masahiro abandoned it, preferring instead to consolidate his authority in the western lands. His domanial center Yamaguchi experienced a burgeoning population, a sure sign of which

---

[197] This was epitomized by references to his sword having been buried at Tsukiyama so as to prevent invaders from sacking the town. *Bōchō fūdo chūshin an*, vol. 13, p. 38. See also Yamada Takashi, "Chūsei koki chiiki kenryoku ni yoru bushi no shinkakuka," *Nenpō Chūseishi kenkyū* 33 (2008), pp. 61–84.

was the establishment of public toilets.[198] In the summer, large Gion floats circulated throughout the town of Yamaguchi, and crowds climbed the walls surrounding the earthen walls of Norihiro's Tsukiyama dwelling, and now shrine, located immediately to the north of Masahiro's mansion.[199] When Masahiro was transported in a palanquin, he requested, however, due solemnity, and threatened to punish any porters (*kubushū no genin*) who disturbed him by speaking loudly.[200]

Masahiro chose not to fortify his Yamaguchi dwelling after the wars of the 1470s. He filled in a three-meter-deep moat that surrounded his mansion and made it into a walkway with small stones, so as not to muddy the feet of pedestrians.[201] Masahiro's residence expanded during the late fifteenth and early sixteenth centuries so as to include the garden within its earthen walls.[202] In spite of the increasing size of his garden and abode, and the expanding population of Yamaguchi, Masahiro made no moves to guard his residence. To the contrary, he merely issued prohibitions lamenting that people with only loose ties to the Ōuchi or their retainers were not to wander into his garden or peer into Masahiro's dwelling itself (Figure 7.5).[203]

Yamaguchi experienced, wealth, peace, and prosperity and an increasing population. Hakata, like Yamaguchi, also prospered and experienced an expansion along its waterfront, with settlements extending for the first time beyond the walls that had been built to defend against the Mongols two centuries before.[204] By contrast, the Ashikaga shogunal decline led to destruction and

---

[198] Yamaguchi shi kyōiku iinkai, comp., *Ōuchi shi yakata ato*, vol. 13 (Yamaguchi 2012), pp. 2, 154. The relevant excavation (series 36) is mentioned on pp. 131–66. For archaeological evidence regarding the appearance of toilets, I am indebted to the insight of Kitajima Daisuke, 10.13.2011.

[199] *Sengoku ibun Ōuchi shi hen*, vol. 1. doc. 735, 6.1492 (Entoku 4) Ōuchi shi *hekisho utsushi*, p. 240, which only allowed people to climb on these walls during the Gion festival. For Tsukiyama being rebuilt, see Maruo Kōsuke, "Ōuchi yakata Tsukiyama yakata o horu," Ōuchi shi rekishi bunka kenkyūkai, comp., *Ōuchi shi no sekai o saguru* (Bensei shuppan, 2019), pp. 142–49.

[200] *Sengoku ibun Ōuchi shi hen*, vol. 1, doc. 644, 4.20.1487 (Bunmei 19) Ōuchi shi *hekisho utsushi*, p. 210, and, for further regulations concerning porters, doc. 633, 11.4.1486 (Bunmei 18) Ōuchi shi *hekisho utsushi*, pp. 206–7. See also Peter Arnesen, *The Medieval Japanese Daimyo* (New Haven: Yale University Press, 1979), pp. 205–6.

[201] Conversation with Kitajima Daisuke when visiting Ōuchi *yakata* site, 10.13.2011. See also *Ōuchi shi yakata ato*, vol. 15 (Yamaguchi, 2014), pp. 255–69 for the nature of the gates, moats, and the placing of the stones.

[202] For a pathbreaking study, see Koga Nobuyuki, "Bōshū Yamaguchi ni okeru shiro, tate, tera," in *Toshi no Kyūshin roku* (Shinjinbutsu ōraishia, 2000), pp. 103–6. Koga pointed out how Masahiro's mansion expanded. The most recent surveys reveal that the garden was enclosed within the structure of the mansion, and a simple wall placed around it, a change apparently in response to people wandering through the garden. See *Ōuchi shi yakata ato* 15, pp. 272–76, and for the walls and gates, pp. 255–69.

[203] *Sengoku ibun Ōuchi shi hen*, vol. 1, doc. 694, 12.19.1489 (Entoku 1) Ōuchi shi *hekisho utsushi*, p. 225. See also Conlan, *Samurai*, p. 197.

[204] Ōba Kōji, *Hakata no kōkogaku: Chūsei no bōeki toshi o horu* (Kōshi shoin, 2019), p. 222.

Figure 7.5 Ōuchi Garden. Photograph by Thomas Conlan

turmoil in Kyoto. The Ashikaga palace, rebuilt in 1477, burned again in 1479, and the region fell into ruin.[205] In 1483, Yoshimasa began building a retreat in Kyoto's Eastern Hills (Higashiyama), but it would not be finished before his death in 1490.[206] Making matters worse, Yoshimasa's son died at the age of twenty-five of alcohol poisoning. Yoshimasa, no teetotaler himself, criticized Yoshihisa for his drinking, but, according to the monk Jinson, these entreaties were as useless as preaching to dogs. The Ashikaga were "madmen" who oversaw a Kyoto that was in 1480 far worse than it had been before, when the capital was the site of a battlefield.[207] Epitomizing Ashikaga

[205] For the short-lived reconstruction of the Ashikaga palace, see Sukigara Toshio, *Chūsei Kyōto no kiseki* (Yuzankaku, 2008), p. 137 and *Masuda ke monjo*, vol. 3 (Tōkyō daigaku shuppankai, 2006), docs. 581–82 of *urū* 1.22.1477 (Bunmei 9) and 6.13.1477 (Bunmei 9), pp. 46–49. For its destruction on 7.1.1479 (Bunmei 11), see *Sengoku ibun Ōuchi shi hen*, vol. 1, doc. 447, Mibu Harutomi *shojō an*, pp. 132–33.

[206] Miyakami Shigetaka, "Higashiyama dono no kenchiku to sono haichi," in *Muromachi Seiken no shufu kōsō to Kyōto Muromachi Kitayama* (Kyoto: Bunrikaku, 2016), pp. 273–80 for the initial construction in 1483; building of the Kannondō, which became known as Ginkakuji began in 1489. See DNSR, ser. 8, vol. 28, 9.10.1489 (Entoku 1), p. 323; and 8.33, p. 46.

[207] Carter, *Regent Redux*, p. 189 for the shogun not being able to maintain law and order, pp. 198–99 for criticisms of the drunkard Yoshihisa, p. 199 for the capital being worse in 1480 than before, and finally p. 200 for the Ashikaga as being madmen.

disfunction, the Yoshimitsu's Kinkakuji suffered more damage during the years 1480–85 than it had experienced during the Ōnin War, with half of its trees harvested for wood, including a particular prized tree on an island to its south.[208] Other temples suffered more. Tōji, arguably the most significant temple in Kyoto, which had survived the war intact, was torched by mobs clamoring for debt relief in 1486.[209]

Unable to protect their most vital monuments, areas nominally under Ashikaga control experienced ruin as well. In 1486 and 1487, the Inner and Outer Ise shrines, arguably the most significant cultic sites in Japan, were burned, and would not be rebuilt at Ise for over a century.[210] The year 1486 also witnessed the destruction of the Izumo shrine as well, located just to the east of Iwami and the Ōuchi sphere of control.[211]

The contrast between Kyoto, which suffered under the feckless Ashikaga, and Yamaguchi proved great. Not only did Yamaguchi function well as a political and ritual center, but Kyoto proved to be so derelict and incapable of functioning that Masahiro himself dispatched money for the rebuilding of a bathhouse at Shōkokuji. This caused Ashikaga Yoshimasa to marvel, because the denizens of nearby provinces would not provide adequate funds. Masahiro, newly enriched by a boat returning from the continent, provided ten thousand *hiki* (one hundred *kanmon*).[212] The Mibu family also asked that Masahiro help them repair boxes (*bunko*) where they preserved state records in 1493.[213] Masahiro's aid extended to military matters as well, for in 1487, Ashikaga Yoshihisa attempted to chastise the recalcitrant *daimyō* Rokkaku

---

[208] Twenty-five Buddhist statues were lost at this time as well. *Inryōken nichiroku*, vol. 2, 10.15.1485 (Bunmei 17), pp. 767–69. Yoshimasa visited Kinkakuji in 1477 and 1480 but did not comment on the destruction until 1485. See DNSR, ser. 8, vol. 9, pp. 740–41 for the 1477 visit and *Ninagawa ke monjo*, vol. 1 (Tōkyō daigaku shuppankai, 1981), doc. 109, Ashikaga Yoshimasa *oyako* Kitano Manbu *kyōei sankei sōjusha chūmon*, pp. 187–88 for his 10.15.1480 (Bunmei 12) excursion. See also see Miyakami Shigekata, *Kinkakuji Ginkakuji Nihon meikenchiku shashin senshū* 11 (Shinchōsha, 1992), p. 99.

[209] *Nagaoki Sukuneki*, 9.13.1486 (Bunmei 18), pp. 193–94. See also Kyoto fūritsu sōgō rekishi shiryōkan, comp., *Ōnin no ran* (Kyōto fūritsu sōgo shiryōkan, 1989), p. 3.

[210] See Haga Kōshirō, *Sanjōnishi Sanetaka* (Yoshikawa kōbunkan, 1960), p. 56. The Inner Shrine was not rebuilt from 1462 through 1585, while the Outer Shrine was not rebuilt from 1434 through 1563. See *Ise Matsuki monjo, Kyoto daigaku bungakubu hakubutsukan no komonjo*, no. 12 (6.1994), p. 18.

[211] *Nagaoki Sukuneki*, 10.29.1486 (Bunmei 18), p. 197 for reports of the shrine burning down on 9.1 of that year.

[212] *Yamaguchi kenshi shiryōhen chūsei*, vol. 1, Inryōken nichiroku, 6.13.1486 (Bunmei 18), p. 145. For more analysis of Yoshimasa's attitude regarding Masahiro's largesse, see *Yamaguchi kenshi tsūshihen chūsei*, p. 412.

[213] *Yamaguchi kenshi shiryōhen chūsei*, vol. 1, Harutomi Sukuneki, 8.2.1493 (Meiō 2), p. 323.

Takayori (d. 1520), and Masahiro dispatched Toida Hirotane and Naitō Hironori to support him.[214]

Members of the monastic nobility fled to Yamaguchi. In doing so, some, such as the monk Jiken, the Shingon head (zasu), therefore "gained great authority."[215] Yamaguchi attracted many, ranging from courtiers, such as Sanjō Kinatsu (1439–1507), to the monk Chikai, to artists, such as the renga master Sōgi (1421–1502), and even to itinerant troupes of actors performing sarugaku.[216] Likewise, major artists such Sesshū Tōyō turned down offers of patronage by Ashikaga Yoshimasa to travel to Yamaguchi and reside there, as well as pass from the city to Ming China. He created the masterful *Long Landscape of Mountains and Water*, a magnificent work that extends for fifty feet, which was dedicated to Myōken in the twelfth month of 1486, in commemoration of thirty years of Ōuchi support.[217] This work, classified today as a Japanese National Treasure, served to demonstrate Masahiro's kingship as one who saw the four seasons, and served to cement his authority.[218] Masahiro kept Yamaguchi at peace, regulating the movements of travelers and constraining people wandering around at night so as to prevent violence.[219]

With the death of the alcoholic Ashikaga Yoshihisa, followed by the demise of his father Yoshimasa, Yoshimasa's nephew Yoshitane (1466–1523) became the next Ashikaga lord. Yoshitane was the son of Ashikaga Yoshimi, who had supported the Ōuchi during the Ōnin War and had ambitions

---

[214] *Sengoku ibun Ōuchi shi hen*, doc. 669, 2.1 Ōuchi Masahiro *shojō utsushi*, pp. 217–18, and doc. 670, 2.19 Ōuchi Masahiro *kanjō utsushi*, p. 218. See also doc. 671, 2.19 Ōuchi Masahiro *kanjō utsushi*, p. 218 for more fighting and guard duty in Ōmi.

[215] See the *Genga sōjō onjihitsuki*, unpublished manuscript, part of the *Genjo onenki, Tanaka Yuzuru shi kyūzō tenseki komonjo*, no. 316, currently located in the *Kokuritsu rekishi hakubutsukan*. For brief analysis of this document, see Fujii Masako, "Ōnin Bunmei no rango ni okeru Daigoji no saikō," *Nihon Rekishi* 764 (1.2012), pp. 125–26. A Tendai *zasu*, the head of their order, can also be documented as traveling to Yamaguchi. *Ōuchi bunka*, p. 872.

[216] For Sanjō Kinatsu, see *Yamaguchi kenshi shiryōhen chūsei*, vol. 1, Nagaoki Sukuneki, 4.19.1479 (Bunmei 11), p. 249. For Sōgi in 1480, see his *Tsukushi michinoki*, in *Yamaguchi kenshi shiryōhen chūsei*, vol. 1, p. 677. Sōgi traveled to Yamaguchi twice in his life. See Okuda Isao, *Sōgi*, pp. 77–91 for his 1480 trip and p. 134 for his second journey in 1489 (Chōkyō 3). For the *sarugaku* performers, see Kawazoe Shōji, *Chūsei bungei no chihōshi*, pp. 262–63.

[217] Hata Yasunori, "Bunmei jū-hachinen no Ōuchi shi to Sesshū Tōyō," in *Sesshū Tōyō: Sesshū e no tabi kenkyū zuroku* (Yamaguchi, 2006), p. 250, and Yukio Lippit, *Painting of the Realm* (Seattle: University of Washington Press, 2012), pp. 45–49.

[218] For this insight, I am indebted to Yukio Lippit, conversation 2.27.2016. See also Hata Yasunori, "Bunmei jū-hachinen no Ōuchi shi to Sesshū Tōyō." For the argument that this scroll represents an allegory of Ōuchi control over their lands in accordance with Ming concept of expressing authority, see Steffani Bennett, "The Other Shore: Sesshū Tōyō (1420–ca. 1506) and the Sino-Japanese Cultural Sphere in the Fifteenth Century," PhD dissertation, Harvard University, 2020. For more on Sesshū's travels to China and Yamaguchi, see *Yamaguchi kenshi tsūshihen chūsei*, pp. 458–62.

[219] *Chūsei hōsei shiryōshū*, vol. 3, pp. 80–81.

for restoring Ashikaga rule over recalcitrant rivals. He mobilized an army against the Rokkaku family, and late in 1491 the Ōuchi dispatched a contingent, consisting of fifteen thousand.[220] While the shogun was involved in this campaign, a coup was launched against him by Hosokawa Masamoto (1466–1507), the son of Hosokawa Katsumoto. Yoshitane somehow survived and ultimately fled to Yamaguchi, where he sought the aid and support of Masahiro. Ashikaga Yoshitane worshiped at Hikamisan and Kōryūji, thereby showing his respect for the Ōuchi deities, but Masahiro was in no state to return to Kyoto.[221]

Masahiro was in fact so debilitated by a second stroke that he was confined (*chikkyo*) to his abode.[222] Yin yang specialists marshaled signs, including a hawk eating a dog and a mouse nesting in a horse's tail, to argue that Masahiro could not invade the capital.[223] At Masahiro's request, his mother Kuniko sponsored Yamato Sōshū, who had cast bells for use Okinawa, to make a large bell as an offering.[224] These entreaties were to no avail. Masahiro died peacefully in Yamaguchi in 1495 some months after Kuniko.[225]

While abandoning the notion of a warrior government, and spending most of his able years in Kyoto, Masahiro made Yamaguchi a ritual center, but he could not extract himself from the politics of Kyoto, and his son Yoshioki would in turn forcefully intervene and spend, as he did, over a decade in the capital as well.

---

[220] *Yamaguchi kenshi shiryōhen chūsei*, vol. 1, Daijōin nikki mokuroku, 12.27.1491 (Entoku 3), p. 241.

[221] *Sengoku ibun Ōuchi shi hen*, vol. 1, doc. 789, 4.4 [(Meiō 4) 1494] Ōuchi Masahiro *shojō utsushi*, p. 258.

[222] *Sengoku ibun Ōuchi shi hen*, vol. 1, doc. 772, 8.13 Ōuchi Masahiro *shojō utsushi*, p. 252, and doc. 796, 5.4 Ōuchi Masahiro *shojō utsushi*, p. 259 of 1495 (Meiō 4). His retirement was commented upon by retainers. See doc. 781, 11.27 Naitō Hirokazu *shojō utsushi*, pp. 254–55.

[223] *Kujō ke Rekidai kiroku*, vol. 2 (Kunaichō shoryōbu, 1990), pp. 150–53. Yoshida Kanetomo supported this view.

[224] *Sengoku ibun Ōuchi shi hen*, vol. 1, doc. 770, 1494 (Meiō 3) Kōryūji *kōshōmei utsushi*, p. 251.

[225] For the death of Masahiro's mother see *Yamaguchi kenshi shiryōhen chūsei*, vol. 1, Harutomi Sukuneki, 2.24.1495 (Meiō 4), p. 323; for Masahiro's death on 9.18.1495, see Daijōin jisha zōjiki, 10.14.1495 (Meiō 4), p. 235, and *Sengoku ibun Ōuchi shi hen*, vol. 2, doc. 980, Ōuchi ke kakochō, p. 13.

8

Yoshioki and the Apogee of Ōuchi Rule
(1495–1528)

The affairs of the realm (*tenka no matsurigoto*) shifted to Yamaguchi, where people high and low congregated; and merchant ships from the west came to Hakata, and Yamaguchi. From the time of Masahiro onward the Ōuchi controlled the tally trade between China and Japan (*wakan no kangō*), so people from other lands thought that the Ōuchi were the Kings of Japan (*ihōjin wa Ōuchi dono o motte Nihon kokuō to omoeri*).[1]

Kasai Shigesuke (b. 1632), an early scholar of the Ōuchi, so described their heyday during the rule of Yoshioki (1477–1528). Yoshioki, like his forebears, ably governed his domain and defeated rivals, but his influence expanded to where he became a kingmaker in both Japan and Chosŏn Korea, as coups and countercoups led to the installation of a pro-Ōuchi Japanese shogun (Ashikaga Yoshitane 1466–1523, shogun 1490–93, 1508–21) and a pro-Ōuchi Korean king (Chungjong 1488–1544, r. 1506–44). Robust trade continued under his watch, and silver exports increased dramatically. Yoshioki also regulated exchange rates for precious metals and coins in northern Kyushu, Kyoto, and western Honshu. He patronized shrines and moved Japan's most sacred gods to Yamaguchi. Finally, he formalized his influence

---

[1] Kasai Shigesuke, *Nankai tsūki*, in *Kaitei shiseki shūran*, vol. 7 (Kondō Keizō shuppanbu, 1932), p. 135. The term *matsurigoto* described both governing and ritual affairs. Kasai had access to Ōuchi sources, such as laws that otherwise did not survive, but how he came across them is not known. In this passage Kasai identifies the provinces where the cities of Yamaguchi and Hakata were located (Bōshū or Suō and Chikuzen, respectively) but these province names have been omitted from the translation.

Kings in All but Name. Thomas D. Conlan, Oxford University Press. © Oxford University Press 2024.
DOI: 10.1093/oso/9780197677339.003.0009

by gaining control of the Ashikaga "King of Japan" seal, which allowed him to dominate Japanese trade with China.

In contrast to his father, who had direct contact with the Japanese emperor only during his waning years, Yoshioki maintained close and direct ties with the Japanese court, and these ties were increasingly unmediated by the Ashikaga shoguns. Yoshioki helped to reinstall a shogun, Yoshitane, who had been overthrown in a coup, and became a protector for the regime. For Yoshioki, the Ashikaga were valuable enough to support in Kyoto, at least for a decade, but he ultimately abandoned the capital and, with it, support for Ashikaga interests, and returned to Yamaguchi. Although Yoshioki's connections to the Japanese courts proved deepest, he also oversaw close exchanges with the Chosŏn court as well.

Yoshioki achieved political recognition in both Japan and Korea commensurate with his wealth and authority. His interactions with both states reveal that they were open to outside influences. Ōuchi Yoshioki was aware of the practices of each but was considered a threat by neither. That none of his rivals in Japan or Korea criticized him as being a foreigner, or some sort of fifth column, reveals that nativist notions did not resonate politically, even among Ōuchi rivals. This openness allowed Yoshioki to exercise unparalleled influence without being overly bound by the customs or practices of either state.[2]

Yoshioki abandoned some of the more overt symbols of Korean ethnicity. When Jōfukuji burned in 1520, it was rebuilt without any of the Korean-style tiles, but the depth of engagement with Korea, which included cultural exchanges with Chosŏn emissaries in Yamaguchi, could only be successfully maintained with some in the Ōuchi organization being fluent in Korean, although in the case of Yoshioki, no evidence survives of his proficiency in the language.

Ritually, Yoshioki continued the Ōuchi pattern of relying on state funds to provide for the upkeep of national shrines which he repurposed for Ōuchi interests. He most notably brought the ancestral deities (*kami*) of Japan's imperial line from Ise, Japan's most sacred site, to his burgeoning town of Yamaguchi, thereby making it an important cultic site. Not content to rely solely on the public revenue from the Japanese state, or taxes collected from his domain, he also requested that Chosŏn officials help fund the

---

[2] For these insights I am indebted to Willard Peterson, conversation 2.12.2020, and Jacqueline Stone, 12.14.2020.

reconstruction of a Kameyama Hachiman shrine located near the Straits of Shimonoseki.

In terms of trade, Yoshioki oversaw lucrative copper exports to Korea, and his network extended to the Ryūkyūs and China. Tsushima rivals caused some trouble in Korea, but for much of his rule Yoshioki successfully managed Japanese Korean trade. *Wakō* pirates had few opportunities to exert much influence during the heyday of his control. Receipt of the Ashikaga "King of Japan" seals allowed Yoshioki to take a leading role in tributary/trade relations between China and Japan, although this was disrupted during his last years because of the Ningbo incident of 1523. Internally, Yoshioki's influence over Kyoto affairs for a decade allowed him to oversee coinage exchange rates there, although the ultimate regulations were laxer than in his home domains.

After occupying Kyoto for a decade (1508–18) Yoshioki endeavored to expand the city of Yamaguchi. Yin yang (*onmyōdō*) specialists consecrated it with markers of a capital, and the movement of important shrines to Yamaguchi, coupled with construction projects, made the city larger, more prosperous, and prominent. It fully functioned as a segmented capital, with many courtiers, monks, and shrine specialists residing there.

Yoshioki's powers brought with them the seeds of destruction. His killing of some retainers spawned animosities that would contribute to the coup of 1551; and his military success and political influence led him to gain official appointment over regions that were ungovernable as entire provinces. This was particularly true for Iwami, with its rich silver mines. By trying to administer the whole province, rather than limiting himself to ruling its central district, Yoshioki's authority there became destabilized. The silver mine at Ōmoriza in central Iwami become a target for rivals; and conflicts extended to China itself, where some of Yoshioki's representatives sacked the Ming city of Ningbo. While embroiled in these disputes in China and Japan, Yoshioki suddenly died, leaving pressing affairs to his heir, Yoshitaka (1507–51).

Early Years

Yoshioki was born in Kyoto on 2.15.1477, during the last months of the Ōnin War.[3] His father Masahiro (1446–95) was thirty-two, and his mother, known

---

[3] *Jōeiji shiryō* (Yamaguchi, 1978), doc. 48, Ōuchi *dono gosenzo shidai*. Likewise, the *Masatōki* mentions that the fifteenth was Yoshioki's birthday. See Yamaguchi kenshi hensanshitsu, comp.,

as Imakōji (1455–1512), was twenty-three. She hailed from the Toriōji family of shrine attendants to Kyoto's Kamo Wake-Ikazuchi shrine.[4] Imakōji's match with Masahiro was her second, and she had already borne another a child.[5] She was also the adopted daughter of Hatakeyama Yoshimune (d. 1526), a lord of Noto, who became a lifelong Ōuchi ally.[6] Masahiro too, had fathered another child, named Yoshimasa (1471–1509?), born in 1471 by a nameless consort (*shofuku*).[7] This six-year-old Yoshimasa had accompanied an Ōuchi army to the capital on 12.20.1476, several months before the birth of Yoshioki.[8]

Yoshioki received the coveted name of Kidōmaru. Prayers were offered at Kōryūji in his name confirming the five-year-old's position as heir on 2.13.1481.[9] Befitting his exalted position as a descendant of Myōken, he, rather than his elder brother Yoshimasa, continued the unique Ōuchi practice whereby the designated heir ascended the small hill that constituted the most sacred sanctum of the upper shrine of Hikamisan Kōryūji. This happened when he was ten. There Yoshioki remained, alone, for a week before his father joined him, and then, a week later, a hundred monks performed North Star rites.[10]

Yamaguchi kenshi shiryōhen chūsei, 4 vols. (Yamaguchi, 1996–2008), vol. 1, Masatōki, 10.15.1478 (Bunmei 10), p. 342. See also Fujii, *Ōuchi Yoshioki* (Ebisu kōshō, 2014), p. 33.

[4] Little is known about her, but her mother served the Ichijō Regent family in some fashion.

[5] Jinson provides the most detailed sketch of her life as the mother of Ōuchi *gon no suke* (Yoshioki). See *Yamaguchi kenshi shiryōhen chūsei*, vol. 1, Daijōin jisha zōjiki, 6.1492 (Entoku 4), p. 230. Fujii follows this narrative in his *Ōuchi Yoshioki*, pp. 33–34. For more on her death (on 3.26.1512) and age, see *Yamaguchi kenshi shiryōhen chūsei*, vol. 1, Sanetaka kōki, 4.23.1512 (Eishō 9), p. 287.

[6] Both his biological son and brother would fight for Yoshioki in 1511. Hatakeyama Yoshimune only ruled as *shugo* of Noto from 1497 to 1500, when he lost power to his brother in the turmoil of the Meiō coup. Still, Yoshimune was able to ensure that his biological son Yoshifusa would become heir in 1506, and they fought with Yoshioki at the Battle of Funaoka in 1511. Ōuchi Yoshitaka tried making Yoshifusa's son heir of all the Hatakeyama in 1545. See the 8.19.1545 (Tenbun 14) Yoshida Kanemigi letter to Yoshitaka. Murai Yūki, "Tōkyō daigaku shiryōhen sanjo eishabon 'Tenbun jūyonen nikki,'" *Tōkyō daigaku shiryōhen sanjo kenkyū kiyō* 28 (3.2018), 8.19, p. 145.

[7] See *Yamaguchi kenshi shiryōhen chūsei*, vol. 1, Ōuchi Tatata shi fuchō, p. 743. A Naikaku genealogy does mention a brother Yoshimasa, of the upper fourth rank, who had the title Ōuchi *no suke* but who died on 4.6.1509 (Eishō 6). See *Yamaguchi shishi shiryōhen Ōuchi bunka* (Yamaguchi, 2010) (hereafter *Ōuchi bunka*), p. 53. This person was twenty-one in 1491. *Yamaguchi kenshi shiryōhen chūsei*, vol. 1, Inryōken nichiroku, 12.26.1491 (Entoku 3), p. 161. Yoshimasa was born in Yamaguchi. Masahiro rebuilt a temple (Seiganji) for the mother of the future Yoshimasa, which was famous for aiding women who had difficulty lactating or giving birth. *Bōchō jisha yurai*, vol. 3 (Yamaguchi, 1983), pp. 445–47 for the special properties of the nearby water.

[8] *Yamaguchi kenshi shiryōhen chūsei*, vol. 1, Daijōin nikki mokuroku, 12.20.1476 (Bunmei 8), p. 241.

[9] *Sengoku ibun Ōuchi shi hen*, vol. 1 (Tōkyōdō shuppan, 2016), doc. 469, 11.13.1479 (Bunmei 11) Kōryūji *munafuda mei utsushi*, p. 139.

[10] *Yamaguchi kenshi shiryōhen chūsei*, vol. 3, Yamaguchi ken monjokan Kōryūji monjo doc. 78, Tatara Kidōmaru [Ōuchi Yoshioki] Hikamisan Myōken Jōgūsha *san[kei] mokuroku*, pp. 255–57, and *Sengoku ibun Ōuchi shi hen*, vol. 1, doc. 601, pp. 194–96.

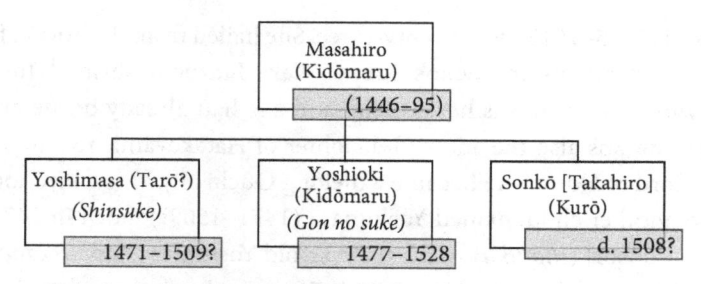

Figure 8.1 Prominent Sons of Ōuchi Masahiro. Created by Thomas Conlan

Kidōmaru's coming-of-age ceremonies occurred in 1488 when he was twelve. Ashikaga Yoshimasa (1436–90, shogun 1449–73) was his godfather (*eboshi oya*) and granted him the character "Yoshi" from his name, a rare honor. His elder brother Yoshimasa was most likely favored by the shogun as well, as he too received the name "Yoshi," suggesting that his rival claims to Ōuchi chieftainship were strong.[11]

Yoshioki was appointed as the acting governor of Suō (Ōuchi *gon no suke*).[12] His brother Yoshimasa received the similar title of the "new governor" (*shinsuke*), which had long designated the Ōuchi heir.[13] Finally, Yoshioki had a younger brother by his mother Imakōji was originally named Kurō, "Ninth Child," a name that he shared with the earlier lord Mochiyo (1394–1441). He became a monk named Sonkō and was later laicized, adopting the name Takahiro (d. 1508?) (Figure 8.1).[14]

Ritually, the siblings were carefully distinguished. Late in 1491 Masahiro, Yoshioki and Sonkō were involved with the reconstruction of Hikamisan's

---

[11] *Yamaguchi kenshi shiryōhen chūsei*, vol. 1, Inryōken nichiroku, 1.30.1488 (Chōkyō 2), pp. 149–50, and Fujii, *Ōuchi Yoshioki*, p. 35. In this diary, Yoshioki was referred to as Jirō, the second eldest, which strongly suggests that his elder brother was known as Tarō, the eldest. By all accounts, he was the older brother of Yoshioki. See the Mōri genealogy, *Ōuchi bunka*, p. 31.

[12] *Sengoku ibun Ōuchi shi hen*, vol. 1, doc. 667, 1488 (Chōkyō 2) 2.13 Go-Tsuchimikado tennō *kuzen an utsushi*, p. 217.

[13] Contemporary sources distinguish Yoshioki (*gon no suke*) from his brother Yoshimasa (*shinsuke*). Daijōin nikki mokuroku, 4.8.1492 (Entoku 4), p. 241, refers to Ōuchi *gon no suke*'s mother Imakōji leaving Kyoto for Yamaguchi, while on 6.9 of that same year, this source mentions a messenger from *shinsuke*, who was not the same person. Yoshioki's title of *gon no suke* as heir was anomalous. Yoshioki's heir Yoshitaka would be known as *shinsuke* as well.

[14] For Takahiro being Yoshioki's younger brother, see *Yamaguchi kenshi shiryōhen chūsei*, vol. 1, Daijōin jisha zōjiki, 6.1497 (Meiō 6), p. 237. He initially had the name Kurō. Mōri genealogy, *Ōuchi bunka*, p. 31. According to this genealogy, after he was laicized, he adopted the name Tarō. Yoshioki also had a fourth brother, Tanehiro, who died at Funaoka in 1511, but he is not included in the Figure 8.1 genealogy.

upper shrine.[15] *Shinsuke* Yoshimasa, by contrast, was sent to Kyoto at the head of an army. Masahiro and Yoshioki commissioned Buddhist statues, but Yoshioki's other siblings did not, showing that these religious actions were a hallmark of Ōuchi leadership and a marker of succession.[16] In addition, Yoshioki alone made offerings of horses to Myōken at Kōryūji Hikamisan and Sumiyoshi at the Nagato Ichinomiya shrine.[17]

Yoshioki's younger brother Sonkō became a Tōdaiji monk but lived in Yamaguchi, where he oversaw Tōdaiji estates in Suō province.[18] Sonkō, an able administrator, realized the difficulty of transmitting tax revenue in kind and advocated payments in cash instead.[19] The Mibu, a court family, praised him for diligently transmitting their absentee tax revenues in 1493.[20] By contrast, Sonkō skimmed Tōdaiji's revenue, which dwindled to almost nothing.[21] As Sonkō was supported by Masahiro, who countersigned his documents, Tōdaiji monks could do little against him.[22] They did, however, curse Yasutomi Hiromasa, a retainer of the Ōuchi who administered Tōdaiji's Fushino estate by "confining" his name (*na o komeru*) for his nonpayment of taxes. This meant that Hiromasa's name was written on a special slip of

---

[15] *Sengoku ibun Ōuchi shi hen*, vol. 1, doc. 710, 2.4.1491 (Entoku 3) Hikamisan Myōkensha *munafuda mei utsushi*, pp. 231–32.

[16] For example, only Masahiro and Yoshioki donated a Zao gongen statue to a temple in Nagato's Abu district. *Sengoku ibun Ōuchi shi hen*, vol. 1, doc. 713, 3.27.1491 (Entoku 3) Zao gongen *gyokuden tobira mei utsushi*, p. 233.

[17] *Sengoku ibun Ōuchi shi hen*, vol. 1, docs. 717–18, 11.3.1491 (Entoku 3) Ōuchi Yoshioki *kishinjō*, p. 234. For Yoshioki's New Year's donation of a horse to Hikamisan, see *Sengoku ibun Ōuchi shi hen*, vol. 1, doc. 721, 1.1.1492 (Entoku 4) Ōuchi Yoshioki *kishinjō*, p. 235.

[18] For Sonkō's appointment in 1491, see 8.28.1491 (Entoku 3), in Shiroishidera *narabi ni* Katsuma *daikan shiki bunin an*, *Tōdaiji monjo*, vol. 15 (Tōkyō daigaku shuppankai, 1992), doc. 671, pp. 66–67. This also appears in *Yamaguchi kenshi tsūshihen furoku* CD-ROM, Tōdaiji monjo, doc. 340, p. 181.

[19] *Yamaguchi kenshi tsūshihen furoku* CD-ROM, Tōfukuji monjo (Tōfukuji *zō*), doc. 36, Suō no kuni Sabaryōgun tokuchi hō *shokata reibutsu sanyōjō*, p. 627. See also *Yamaguchi kenshi hensanshitsu*, comp., *Yamaguchi kenshi tsūshihen chūsei* (Yamaguchi, 2012), p. 162. For one record describing the difficulty of shipping taxes because of bad weather in 1492, see *Sengoku ibun Ōuchi shi hen*, vol. 1, doc. 732, 5.28 [(Entoku 4) 1492] Tōdaiji nigatsudō dōsu Shūhan *shojō an*, p. 239, and doc. 733, 6.22.1492 (Entoku 4) Eguchinabe Hosshi-maru *ukebumi*, p. 240.

[20] *Sengoku ibun Ōuchi shi hen*, vol. 1, doc. 755, 8.13 [(Meiō 2) 1493] Suō no kuni *kokuga kōnin rensho shojō*, pp. 246–47. Hatakeyama Satoshi, "Muromachiki ni okeru jige kanjinryō to shugo daimyō," *Chihōshi kenkyū* 50.2 (4.2000), p. 33.

[21] *Yamaguchi kenshi shiryōhen chūsei*, vol. 1, Suō no kuni *rimu daidai kagen myōchō*, p. 599. See Matsuoka Hisatō, "Muromachi Sengokuki no Suō Kokugaryō to Ōuchi shi," in *Ōuchi shi no kenkyū* (Seibundō, 2011), pp. 163–66. Sonkō was robustly criticized after 1499 once he became persona non grata and rebelled against his brother.

[22] *Sengoku ibun Ōuchi shi hen*, vol. 1, docs. 799–800, 8.20.1495 (Meiō 4) Suō no kuni *rusudokoro kudashibumi*, pp. 260–61. The *mokudai* issuing the documents was Sonkō. See Hatakeyama Satoshi, "Chūsei koki ni okeru Suō no kuni kokuga keiei," *Nihon rekishi*, no. 627 (8.2000), p. 27, and *Yamaguchi kenshi tsūshihen chūsei*, p. 162. Sonkō also gained control of estates that were confiscated from other temples in 1495. *Sengoku ibun Ōuchi shi hen*, vol. 1, doc. 795, 4.29.1495 (Meiō 4) Ōuchi shi *kashin rensho hōsho utsushi*, p. 259.

paper and placed before the altar of Shukongōshin (Kongōshu bodhisattva skr. Vajrapāṇi) in preparation for his being declared an enemy of the temple and becoming a target for maledictions.[23] Shortly after this ritual violence was initiated against Hiromasa, Sonkō resigned his affiliation with Tōdaiji, becoming instead the head (bettō) of Kōryūji Hikamisan in 1497.[24]

The Meiō Coup (1493) and Its Ramifications

Ashikaga Yoshimasa died in 1490, and his cousin Yoshitane (1466–1523, shogun 1490–93, 1508–21) was made the new shogun. In 1491, at the bequest of the energetic and ambitious Yoshitane, who desired to quell nearby rebellious shugo, Yoshioki's elder half-brother Yoshimasa (shinsuke) led an army to Kyoto, consisting of twenty-five high-ranking mounted warriors, three thousand samurai fighters, and a baggage train of fifteen thousand.[25] Supporters of Ōuchi Yoshimasa noted that he, like his father Masahiro, led an army to Kyoto while only twenty-one years of age. By making this comparison of martial prowess, they hinted that Yoshimasa was potentially a worthy heir to Masahiro.[26] Yoshioki, by contrast, first took part in New Year's rites in Yamaguchi before arriving in central Japan slightly before 1.18.1492, when he worshiped at Kyoto's famous Kiyomizudera.[27] Three thousand were in his procession, which was as great a number as the fighting force that Yoshimasa

---

[23] This is explained by Hagihara Daisuke, "Chūsei 'na o komeru' monjo ron," Shirin 93.6 (11.2010), p. 96, (814)-118 (836). For the relevant document, see in this same source doc. 45, 4.26.1496 (Meiō 5), p. 103. The phrase may stem from the fact that the name was placed before the altar in a box. For the earliest verifiable documents pertaining to the Yasutomi, Fushino, and the transportation of taxes to Hyōgo, see Sengoku ibun Ōuchi shi hen, vol. 1, doc. 738, 8.10.1492 (Meiō 1) Yasutomi Hiromasa ukebumi utsushi, pp. 241–42. See also Wada Shūsaku, "Shiryō shōkai: Ōuchi shi kashin Yasutomi shi no kankei shiryō ni tsuite 1," Yamaguchi ken monjo kan kenkyū kiyō 27 (3.2000), doc. 32, 7.13 Yasutomi ukebumi an utsushi, p. 72, and doc. 33, 8.1.1492 (Meiō 1) Fushino no shō Ryōson daikan Yasutomi nengu narabi ni kuji daisen ukebumi an utsushi, pp. 72–73.
[24] Yamaguchi kenshi shiryōhen chūsei, vol. 1, Daijōin jisha zōjiki, 6.1497 (Meiō 6), p. 237 for his Hikamisan appointment.
[25] Yamaguchi kenshi shiryōhen chūsei, vol. 1, Daijōin nikki mokuroku, 12.27.1491 (Entoku 3), p. 241, and Inryōken nichiroku, 12.25.1491 (Entoku 3), p. 161.
[26] Yamaguchi kenshi shiryōhen chūsei, vol. 1, Inryōken nichiroku, 12.25–26.1491 (Entoku 3), p. 161, and Gohōkō'inki, 12.17 and 12.25.1491 (Entoku 3), p. 243.
[27] Sengoku ibun Ōuchi shi hen, vol. 1, doc. 721, 1.1.1492 (Entoku 4) Ōuchi Yoshioki kishinjō, p. 235. This document alone proves that Yoshioki, gon no suke, could not have been the same person as the shinsuke who had already arrived in central Japan on 12.27.1491. For Yoshioki praying at Kiyomizu with his mother Imakōji, see Yamaguchi kenshi shiryōhen chūsei, vol. 1, Inryōken nichiroku, 1.18.1492 (Entoku 4), p. 161.

led.[28] That Yoshimasa (*shinsuke*) helped conquer a castle in Ōmi on 10.2.1492 while Yoshioki was enjoying himself in Nara.[29]

Hosokawa Masamoto (1466–1507), the shogunal chancellor (*kanrei*), disliked Yoshitane's attempt to restore shogunal authority, and plotted to remove Ashikaga Yoshitane from power. When Masamoto was covertly establishing alliances, Yoshioki's younger sister was nearly abducted, or absconded, but this affair came to naught.[30] Shortly after this incident Yoshioki abandoned Ashikaga Yoshitane.[31] On intercalary (*urū*) 4.7.1493, he withdrew most of his troops from Yoshitane's army and left for Sakai, causing Yoshitane's forces to dwindle to a thousand.[32] Yoshioki ordered Aki and Iwami warriors, part of Yoshitane's guard (*hōkōshū*), to depart for Sakai as well. He had technically no authority over these men, but, tellingly, they complied and joined him there.[33]

Hosokawa Masamoto rose against Ashikaga Yoshitane, deposing him on intercalary (*urū*) 4.22.1493.[34] Yoshioki departed from Sakai with his army shortly thereafter, returning to Yamaguchi in the fifth month of 1493.[35] His brother Yoshimasa remained behind, but somehow he ran afoul of Ōuchi Masahiro, who expressly ordered three or four of his followers to commit hara-kiri on 8.4.1493.[36] Yoshimasa remained in the Nara region and warded off a night attack on 12.28 of that year.[37] Nothing more is known about him; he apparently died in 1509.

Over the last few decades Japanese scholars have argued that the 1493 Meiō Coup, in which Hosokawa Masamoto overthrew the reigning shogun,

[28] *Yamaguchi kenshi shiryōhen chūsei*, vol. 1, Daijōin jisha zōjiki, 4.7–8.1492 (Entoku 4), pp. 227–28. For Yoshioki being with her see 4.23.1492 (Entoku 4), p. 229. By contrast, Jinson refers to *shinsuke*'s military movements on 11.21, 11.29, and 12.25.1491 (Entoku 3), p. 226.

[29] *Yamaguchi kenshi shiryōhen chūsei*, vol. 1, Daijōin jisha zōjiki, 10.2.1492 (Meiō 1), p. 230 for *shinsuke* Yoshimasa and 10.17.1492 (Meiō 1) for *gon no suke* Yoshioki.

[30] *Yamaguchi kenshi shiryōhen chūsei*, vol. 1, Harutomi Sukuneki, *urū* 4.1.1493 (Meiō 2), pp. 321–22, and Fujii, *Ōuchi Yoshioki*, pp. 40–41. This sister was linked to the Takeda, historical rivals to the Ōuchi, who at this time were closely allied with Hosokawa Masamoto.

[31] *Yamaguchi kenshi shiryōhen chūsei*, vol. 1, Daijōin jisha zōjiki, *urū* 4.1.1493 (Meiō 2), pp. 231–32. In letters, Naitō Hironori suggested that turmoil in Kyushu was leading Yoshioki to depart for the west. *Sengoku ibun Ōuchi shi hen*, vol. 1, doc. 746, *urū* 4.4 Naitō Hironori *shojō utsushi*, p. 244.

[32] *Yamaguchi kenshi shiryōhen chūsei*, vol. 1, Harutomi Sukuneki, *urū* 4.9.1493 (Meiō 2) and *urū* 4.11 Jishō-in Shōshō *shojō*, pp. 322–23.

[33] *Yamaguchi kenshi tsūshihen chūsei*, p. 414.

[34] *Daijōin jisha zōjiki*, vol. 10, *urū* 4.25–28.1493 (Meiō 2), pp. 386–87, and Takeuchi Rizō, ed., *Gohōkō'inki* (Zoku shiryō taisei. Kyoto: Rinsen shoten, 1967), vol. 3, 4.26.1493 (Meiō 2), p. 90. See also Fujii, *Ōuchi Yoshioki*, p. 42.

[35] See the genealogy appearing in *Agari ke monjo* (Nagato shi shitei bunkazai, 1995), p. 7.

[36] *Yamaguchi kenshi shiryōhen chūsei*, vol. 1, Daijōin jisha zōjiki, 8.4.1493 (Meiō 2), p. 233. Perhaps he was involved in the incident involving Yoshioki's sister.

[37] *Yamaguchi kenshi shiryōhen chūsei*, vol. 1, Daijōin jisha zōjiki, 12.28.1493 (Meiō 2), p. 233.

Yoshitane, in favor of a more pliant leader, Yoshizumi (1481–1511, shogun 1494–1508), irrevocably fractured the power of the Ashikaga bakufu and marked the onset of Japan's *Sengoku* ("Warring States") era.[38] Certainly, Masamoto's coup caused Japan to be divided into two warring camps, as the *shugo* daimyo of central Japan, where the Hosokawa dominated, followed Yoshizumi, while those from Japan's eastern and western regions generally supported Yoshitane.[39] These political fissures put pressure on kinship ties and bonds of lordship and led to turmoil within warrior houses. The Ōuchi were not immune, although Masahiro and Yoshioki navigated the turmoil better than most. As we shall see, Yoshioki and other supporters of Yoshitane were able to establish political stability that would last for decades, and from 1508 through Yoshioki's death in 1528, a dual Kyoto Yamaguchi polity stabilized central and western Japan.

After the coup of 1493, it initially seemed to all that the affair would be rapidly settled. Hosokawa Masamoto captured the deposed shogun Ashikaga Yoshitane and prepared to banish him to a small island in the Inland Sea.[40] Yoshitane's aunt, Hino Tomiko (1440–96), more ruthless than Masamoto, had her agents surreptitiously poison Yoshitane at a banquet. Masamoto, recognizing that Yoshitane had been poisoned, quickly administered an antidote, showing deep knowledge in such matters.[41] Masamoto's compassion backfired, however, as during a storm that arose shortly thereafter, Yoshitane escaped from house arrest and plotted his return to power.[42] The fugitive Yoshitane pleaded with Ōuchi Yoshioki and other lords for support and demanded Masamoto's destruction.[43] War followed and continued through 1511; Masamoto was killed (1507), Yoshizumi died (1511), and most of their troops were decimated by Yoshioki at the Battle of Funaoka (1511).

[38] Yamada Kuniaki, "Sengoku no sōran," in *Iwanami kōza Nihon rekishi*, vol. 4 (Iwanami shoten, 2015), pp. 3–8 for an overview of interpretations of the origins of the Sengoku era and an explanation of the coup. This new interpretation overturns the earlier one, which saw the advent of Sengoku as coinciding with the 1467 onset of the Ōnin War.

[39] Ienaga Junji, "Horigoe kubōfu metsubō no saikentō," *Sengokushi kenkyū* 27 (1994), pp. 1–10.

[40] The Hosokawa planned to banish Yoshitane to Shōdoshima, an island near the coast of Sanuki province, a Hosokawa stronghold, with a mild climate. *Inryōken Nichiroku*, vol. 5, 6.26.1493 (Meiō 2), p. 2557.

[41] Yamada Yasuhiro, *Ashikaga Yoshitane* (Ebisu kōshō, 2016), p. 97, and *Daijōin jisha zōjiki*, vol. 10, 5.22.1493 (Meiō 2), p. 294.

[42] He fled from house arrest on 6.29.1493, during a storm, but left his tasters behind, who were tortured for information. *Daijōin jisha zōjiki*, vol. 10, 7.2.1493 (Meiō 2), p. 303, and *Harutomi Sukuneki* (Meiji shoin, 1971), 7.1.1493 (Meiō 2), pp. 198–99.

[43] *Daijōin jisha zōjiki*, vol. 10, 8.11.1493 (Meiō 2), p. 311. For surviving Yoshitane letters demanding the destruction of the Hosokawa, see Kinoshita Satoshi, ed., *Ashikaga Yoshimi Yoshitane hakkyū monjo* (Sengokushi kenkyūkai shiryōshū 7, 2019), docs. 67–69, 11.2 Ashikaga Yoshiki [Yoshitane] *gonaisho (an)*, pp. 53–54.

Yoshioki's Violent Ascension

Yoshioki, now eighteen years old, did not immediately aid Yoshitane, since he had more pressing concerns. His father Masahiro had another stroke in 1494. Offerings for his recovery at Kōryūji Hikamisan included bells inscribed with the names of Masahiro's mother Kuniko (1428–95), Sonkō, and Yoshioki, but Yoshimasa's name was not included.[44] An offering of a standing drum to Kōryūji described Yoshioki explicitly as Masahiro's heir.[45]

Masahiro's mother Kuniko died in the second month of 1495.[46] Immediately thereafter, several prominent Ōuchi retainers were killed. Sue Takemori (d. 1495), a retainer of the Ōuchi, caused most of the troubles: first he killed his brother Okiaki (1477–95); then he slandered Naitō Hironori (1446–95), a commander who had long fought under Masahiro. Masahiro and Yoshioki then ordered Hironori to be killed at a banquet. Hironori killed several of his would-be assassins, but ultimately died in the melee.[47] After Hironori's death, Takemori's charges were discovered to be baseless, causing both Masahiro and Yoshioki to disavow their support for him. Takemori fled to Mt. Kōya, but this affair was "settled" when he was tracked down and killed.[48]

The assassination of Naitō Hironori clipped the wings of a deputy of the strategic Nagato province. This followed a pattern of nearly fifty years before, when Washizu Hirotada (d. 1447), an earlier Nagato deputy, was exterminated. Even though the charges against Hironori had no merit, Yoshioki did not return his confiscated lands to the Naitō. Rather, he transferred Hironori's properties, which included Mine, site of the Naganobori copper mines, to Zenpukuji, a Nagato province temple, whose monks could readily oversee the mines.[49]

---

[44] *Sengoku ibun Ōuchi shi hen*, vol. 1, doc. 770, Summer 1494 (Meiō 3) Kōryūji *kōshōmei utsushi*, p. 251.

[45] *Sengoku ibun Ōuchi shi hen*, vol. 1, doc. 778, tenth month Kōryūji *gakudaiko dōnai mei utsushi*, p. 254.

[46] *Yamaguchi kenshi shiryōhen chūsei*, vol. 1, Harutomi Sukuneki, 2.24.1495 (Meiō 4), p. 323.

[47] *Yamaguchi kenshi shiryōhen chūsei*, vol. 1, Harutomi Sukuneki, 3.21.1495 (Meiō 4), p. 324. This account was drawn from that remarkable narrative. For another overview, see also Fujii, *Ōuchi Yoshioki*, pp. 44–46. Ironically, Naitō Hironori had been involved in another banquet incident. After Yoshimi Nobuyori killed Sue Hiromori at a gathering on 5.27.1482 (Bunmei 14), Hironori in turn killed Nobuyori there. For analysis see Fujii Takashi, *Muromachiki daimyō kenryokuron* (Dōseisha, 2013), pp. 43–47.

[48] *Yamaguchi kenshi shiryōhen chūsei*, vol. 1, Harutomi Sukuneki, 3.21.1495 (Meiō 4), p. 324, and *Sengoku ibun Ōuchi shi hen*, vol. 1, doc. 797, 6.19 [(Meiō 4) 1495] Ōuchi Yoshioki *shojō*, p. 260 for a letter from Yoshioki to a Tōfukuji monk describing how the affair was "settled," which implies Takemori's death.

[49] *Sengoku ibun Ōuchi shi hen*, vol. 1, doc. 928, 4.15.1496 (Meiō 5), Ōuchi Yoshioki *kishinjō*, p. 300.

Hironori's death roiled the Ōuchi retainers. Yoshioki, lacking the standing to fully command them, had to rely on Masahiro to bolster his authority.[50] Father and son acted in tandem, and documents from this time describe Yoshioki and Masahiro as the "two lords."[51] Early in 1495, even though Masahiro was still alive, Yoshioki began issuing *kudashibumi* edicts, a sign that he was the de facto Ōuchi leader.[52]

Yoshioki did not tolerate dissent. In contrast to Masahiro's earlier policy of not intervening in quarrels among retainers, Yoshioki prohibited all violent altercations and asserted that he alone would determine the right and wrong of all disputes.[53] The dying Masahiro supported Yoshioki and refused to hear entreaties from the dissatisfied because he was physically incapable of leaving his residence.[54] Four short months later Masahiro died, leaving the nineteen-year-old Yoshioki solely in charge.[55] Rumors swirled that Naitō retainers had in fact poisoned Masahiro, but his repeated strokes were most likely the cause.[56]

Yoshioki confronted enemies without and within. His outside enemies included the Hosokawa, while his internal rivals were dissatisfied retainers such as the Naitō. Some Naitō retainers had apparently congregated in Nagato early in 1496 as part of an attempted rebellion.[57] At the same time, because of the Meiō coup, a debilitating conflict erupted in northern Kyushu. There, for decades, the Ōtomo, *shugo* of Bungo, had been on good terms with the Ōuchi. Indeed, their lord Ōtomo Masachika (1444–96) visited Yamaguchi in 1486 to commemorate the apotheosis of Norihiro (1420–65)

[50] *Sengoku ibun Ōuchi shi hen*, vol. 1, doc. 785, 2.3 [(Meiō 4) 1495] Ōuchi Yoshioki *shojō*, p. 256.

[51] *Sengoku ibun Ōuchi shi hen*, vol. 1, doc. 786, 2.29 [(Meiō 4) 1495] Ōuchi shi *kashin rensho hōsho*, pp. 256–57.

[52] *Sengoku ibun Ōuchi shi hen*, vol. 1, docs. 792–93, 4.29.1495 (Meiō 4) Ōuchi Yoshioki *kudashibumi*, pp. 258–59.

[53] *Sengoku ibun Ōuchi shi hen*, vol. 1, doc. 803, 8.1496 (Meiō 4) Ōuchi shi *kashin rensho hekisho utsushi*, p. 262. This has been translated by Conlan, *Samurai and the Warrior Culture of Japan, 471–1877: A Sourcebook* (Indianapolis: Hackett, 2022), p. 200.

[54] *Sengoku ibun Ōuchi shi hen*, vol. 1, doc. 772, 8.13 Ōuchi Masahiro *shojō utsushi*, p. 252, which dates most likely from 1494 (Meiō 3), is a letter by Masahiro where he describes being retired (*inkyō*) and relying on his son. In doc. 796, 5.4 [(Meiō 4) 1495] Ōuchi Masahiro *shojō utsushi*, p. 259, Masahiro also mentions depending on Yoshioki for leadership. Masahiro's retainers commented upon his retirement in doc. 781, 11.27 Naitō Hirokazu *shojō utsushi*, pp. 254–55.

[55] For Masahiro's death, see *Yamaguchi kenshi shiryōhen chūsei*, vol. 1, Daijōin jisha zōjiki, 10.14.1495 (Meiō 4), p. 235, and *Sengoku ibun Ōuchi shi hen*, vol. 2 (Tōkyōdō shuppan, 2017), doc. 980, Ōuchi ke *kakochō*, p. 13.

[56] *Yamaguchi kenshi shiryōhen chūsei*, vol. 1, Daijōin jisha zōjiki, 1.18.1496 (Meiō 5), p. 235.

[57] *Yamaguchi kenshi shiryōhen chūsei*, vol. 1, Daijōin jisha zōjiki, 1.18.1496 (Meiō 5), p. 235.

as the Tsukiyama god.[58] Masachika also married one of Masahiro's daughters, and the child of this match, Yoshisuke (1459–96), was a strong Ōuchi supporter.

These marriage ties between the Ōuchi and the Ōtomo reveals the potential strength of such bonds as well as their weakness, for they allowed for strong personal connections, but at the same time, this very personalization could lead to violence and spawn deep grudges. Yoshisuke was a very active supporter of Ashikaga Yoshitane, copying and transmitting the deposed shogun's missives to other Kyushu warriors such as the Sagara.[59] In 1496, Masachika by contrast decided to support the shogunal chancellor (*kanrei*) Hosokawa Masamoto and the shogun Yoshizumi. In doing so, he broke ties with the Yoshisuke and his Ōuchi allies in the most violent way possible—he killed his son Yoshisuke, who was the cousin of Yoshioki.[60] The Ōuchi soon exacted revenge. Masachika took to the seas to meet some of his important retainers, but unluckily for him, his craft was wrecked, and he washed ashore in Nagato province, where he was captured by waiting Ōuchi forces. They forced him to commit hara-kiri in retribution for the murder of Yoshisuke.[61] Masachika's ignoble end caused the Ōtomo and the Ōuchi to become great enemies.

Yoshioki launched an offensive in Kyushu late in 1496, first attacking Shōni Masasuke (1441–97) of Chikuzen. In this campaign, Yoshioki appointed generals from disgraced families as a way of establishing a new trusted group of Ōuchi retainers. Among those he favored were Naitō Okiyuki, a survivor of the turmoil of 1494, and Niho Morisato (d. 1501), the son of Niho Moriyasu, who had been executed in 1478.[62] Niho Morisato earned Yoshioki's praise in particular for extending control to three contested districts from Hizen province that the Ōuchi had been unable to govern since the end of the Ōnin War.[63]

[58] *Yamaguchi kenshi shiryōhen chūsei*, vol. 1, Shoken nichiroku, 8.26.1486 (Bunmei 18), p. 376, and *Ōuchi Yoshioki*, pp. 55–56.

[59] *Sagara ke monjo*, vol. 1 (Tōkyō daigaku shuppankai, 1917), doc. 237, 11.2 [(Meiō 2) 1493]) Ashikaga Yoshitane *gonaisho utsushi*, p. 274. For the depth of his support of Yoshitane, see doc. 239, 1.11 [(Meiō 3) 1493] Ōtomo Yoshisuke *shojō*, p. 276.

[60] *Yamaguchi kenshi shiryōhen chūsei*, vol. 1, Gohōkō'inki, 7.6.1496 (Meiō 5), p. 243. What happened to Yoshisuke's mother is not known.

[61] *Yamaguchi kenshi shiryōhen chūsei*, vol. 1, Harutomi Sukuneki, 7.3.1496 (Meiō 5), p. 325.

[62] *Sengoku ibun Ōuchi shi hen*, vol. 1, doc. 940, 11.30 [(Meiō 5) 1496] Ōuchi Yoshioki *shojō*, p. 304 for the uprising, doc. 944, 12.26.1496 (Meiō 5) Ōuchi Yoshioki *kanjō*, p. 305 for Okiyuki, and *Sengoku ibun Ōuchi shi hen*, vol. 2, docs. 948–54, pp. 3–5 doc. 959, p. 6, and 961, p. 8 for documents pertaining to Niho Morisato.

[63] *Sengoku ibun Ōuchi shi hen*, vol. 2, doc. 1009, 9.23 Ōuchi Yoshioki *shojō*, pp. 22–23. This letter was addressed to Niho Morisato. For other praise for the campaign, see docs. 1011, 1013, pp. 23–24

While subjugating northern Kyushu, Yoshioki attempted to further consolidate his authority over his retainers. Some Washizu, who had once again rebelled, had their lands confiscated.[64] The Naitō, however, found redemption, as Naitō Hiroharu was made the deputy of Nagato in 1497.[65] At this time Yoshioki married a daughter of Hironori, the assassinated general. She, who is known as Higashi-muki (1470?–1559), would give birth to his heir, the future Yoshitaka, in 1507.

By the ninth month of 1497, Yoshioki defeated Shōni Masasuke and retook most of northern Kyushu.[66] In correspondence with Korean officials, Yoshioki boasted of his authority in northern Kyushu, and stated that he was the lord of the four provinces of Suō, Nagato, Buzen, and Chikuzen.[67] Yoshioki then resolved to fight the Ōtomo of Bungo province.[68] They counterattacked and Ōtomo Chikaharu (1461–1524), the new heir, invaded the Ōuchi lands of Buzen on 10.2.1498.[69]

The shogunal chancellor Hosokawa Masamoto enticed Yoshioki's brother Sonkō to join his cause while Yoshioki was fighting the Ōtomo. Sonkō's plot was discovered, and his main supporter, the Ōuchi retainer Sugi Takeakira (d. 1499), was forced to commit hara-kiri in 1499.[70] Sonkō was laicized after he rebelled. He took the name Takahiro[71] and escaped to Bungo, where he was protected by Ōtomo Chikaharu, but his lands were confiscated

---

for the 9.28 and 11.25 Ōuchi Yoshioki *shojō* to Morisato. See also docs. 1010 and 1012, pp. 23–24. Niho Morisato fought devotedly on behalf of Yoshioki until he died in 1501. Fujii, *Ōuchi Yoshioki*, p. 60.

[64] *Sengoku ibun Ōuchi shi hen*, vol. 2, doc. 988, 11.15.1497 (Meiō 6) Ōuchi Yoshioki *sodehan kudashibumi*, pp. 16–17, and doc. 989, 11.15.1497 (Meiō 6) Ōuchi shi *kashin rensho hōsho*, p. 17 for 11.1497 grants of Washizu lands to the Sugi. See also doc. 965, 6.21.1497 (Meiō 6) Ōuchi Yoshioki *sodehan kudashibumi* for a similar grant to the Kawazu of former Asō lands.

[65] Hiroharu was appointed to this post on 9.5.1497 and entered the province on 9.7 or 9.9.1497 (Meiō 6). See *Yamaguchi kenshi shiryōhen chūsei*, vol. 1, Nagato no kuni shugo shiki shidai, p. 605, Nagato no kuni shugo daiki, p. 608, and *Agari ke monjo*, p. 7. For Naitō Hiroharu's trusted role, see *Sengoku ibun Ōuchi shi hen*, vol. 2, doc. 1038, 6.10 Ōuchi Yoshioki *shojō*, p. 33.

[66] *Sengoku ibun Ōuchi shi hen*, vol. 2, doc. 981, 9.20 Ōuchi Yoshioki *shojō utsushi*, p. 14. Most fighting occurred from 11.1496 through 4.1497. See doc. 982, 9.23.1497 (Meiō 6) Ōuchi shi *kashin rensho hōsho*, p. 14.

[67] *Sengoku ibun Ōuchi shi hen*, vol. 2, doc. 986, 10.1497 (Meiō 6) Ōuchi Yoshioki *shokei utsushi*, pp. 15–16, and doc. 987, 11.3.1497 (Meiō 6) Ōuchi Yoshioki *shokei utsushi*, p. 16.

[68] *Sengoku ibun Ōuchi shi hen*, vol. 2, doc. 1000, 7.13 [(Meiō 6) 1497] Ōuchi Yoshioki *shojō*, p. 20.

[69] *Sengoku ibun Ōuchi shi hen*, vol. 2, doc. 1211, 7.1505 (Eishō 2) Sata Yasukage *gunchūjō*, pp. 90–91.

[70] *Yamaguchi kenshi shiryōhen chūsei*, vol. 1, Daijōin jisha zōjiki, 3.10 1499 (Meiō 8), p. 237 for Sugi Takeaki's death on 2.16 of that year.

[71] Fujii, *Ōuchi Yoshioki*, p. 60. His new name was linked to that of the new shogun, Ashikaga Yoshitaka, who went by this name from 1493 until 1502, later changing his name to Yoshizumi. Takahiro also changed his counting name from Kurō to Tarō. See the Mōri genealogy, *Ōuchi bunka*, p. 31.

and distributed to Hikamisan Kōryūji and to other warriors, effectively neutralizing him as an internal threat.[72]

Yoshioki reinforced Moji, which controlled the Straits of Shimonoseki, and easily thwarted Takahiro's attempted to peel off the support of seafaring privateers (*kaizoku*) such as the Innoshima Murakami.[73] Demonstrating his command of the seas, on 7.25.1499 Yoshioki dispatched Sugi Shigekata and his army to Buzen.[74]

Harboring a Shogun

Ashikaga Yoshitane arrived in Yoshioki's lands on the last day of the year 1500 and entered Yamaguchi two days later. For the next seven years, Yoshitane would live there, making Jōfukuji, the mortuary temple with Korean-style roof tiles, his headquarters.[75] His presence bolstered Yoshioki's authority over warriors of the Ashikaga guard (*hōkōshū*) who sometimes resisted directly serving the Ōuchi.[76]

Yoshioki and Yoshitane garnered support from the imperial court, which turned against the regime of Ashikaga Yoshizumi. The Yoshida shrine specialists also backed the Ōuchi and explained to Yoshizumi that his prospects were dim.[77] The court even went so far as to adopt the era name

[72] *Sengoku ibun Ōuchi shi hen*, vol. 2, doc. 1047, 9.15.1499 (Meiō 8) Ōuchi shi *kashin rensho hōsho*, p. 36 for the initial commendation; doc. 1067, 3.19.1500 (Meiō 9) Ōuchi shi *kashin rensho hōsho*, p. 41 for later dispensation of these lands; and finally doc. 1208, 6.13.1505 (Eishō 2) Ōuchi shi *kashin rensho hōsho*, p. 89.

[73] *Sengoku ibun Ōuchi shi hen*, vol. 2, doc. 1026, 3.27 [(Meiō 8) 1499] Ōuchi Takahiro *shojō*, pp. 29–30 for Takahiro's attempt to gain the support of the Innoshima Murakami. How they responded to his overtures is not clear. For analysis of this document, see http://proto.harisen.jp/hito1/murakami-yosinao.htm. For Yoshioki's response to Takahiro's threat, see *Sengoku ibun Ōuchi shi hen*, vol. 2, doc. 1027, 3.26.1499 (Meiō 8) Ōuchi Yoshioki *kudashibumi*, p. 30, and doc. 1030, 4.13.1499 (Meiō 8) Ōuchi Yoshioki *kudashibumi*, pp. 30–31. The Murakami can be documented as serving Yoshioki in 1501. See doc. 1107, 3.21.1501 (Meiō 10) Ōuchi Yoshioki *shojō*, p. 53.

[74] *Sengoku ibun Ōuchi shi hen*, vol. 2, docs. 1048–52, 9.29.1499 (Meiō 8) Ōuchi Yoshioki *kanjō*, pp. 36–37, and doc. 1211, 7.1505 (Eishō 2) Sata Yasukage *gunchūjō*, pp. 90–91 for a retrospective account from the Sata. See also doc. 1045, 9.8.1499 (Meiō 8) Ashikaga Yoshioki *kanjō*, p. 35 for battles fought there in the eighth month, and docs. 1048–52, 9.29.1499 (Meiō 8) Ōuchi Yoshioki *kanjō*, pp. 36–37 for Yoshioki's documents of praise from the ninth. Battles lingered there through the end of the year. See vol. 2, docs. 1055–56 11.19.1499 (Meiō 8) Ōuchi Yoshioki *kanjo*, p. 38.

[75] *Sengoku ibun Ōuchi shi hen*, vol. 2, doc. 1369, Shirasaki Hachimangū *munafuda mei utsushi*, pp. 141–42.

[76] These families included the Sagara, Masuda, Shibukawa, and Mōri. *Sengoku ibun Ōuchi shi hen*, vol. 2, Ashikaga Yoshitada (Yoshitane) *gonaisho utsushi*, docs. 1071–73, 1075, 4.10.1500 (Meiō 9) *gonaisho*, p. 43. For the Sagara document, see *Sagara ke monjo*, vol. 1, doc. 252, 2.13 [(Meiō 9) 1500] Ashikaga Yoshitane *gonaisho*, p. 290, which asked the Sagara to join with Yoshioki in Suō.

[77] Yoshizumi then asked Kanetomo perform divination to know whether he would be successful against his rivals—the Ōuchi and the deposed shogun Yoshitane. Kanetomo refused. This episode is

Bunki ("cultured turtle") for the years 1501–4. This constituted homage to Myōken, the tutelary Ōuchi deity, because it referred to a turtle, the emissary of this deity. Yoshioki celebrated this honor by donating a sword and a horse to Hikamisan.[78]

The presence of Ashikaga Yoshitane allowed Yoshioki to garner goodwill from Ashikaga officials and retainers, who in turn prayed to his religious institutions. One donated a war banner, dating from 1336, that had belonged to Ashikaga Takauji (1305–58, shogun 1338–58), founder of the Ashikaga regime, to Usa Hachiman shrine.[79] Ashikaga Yoshitane himself also worshiped Myōken at Hikamisan Kōryūji with Yoshioki.[80]

Ashikaga Yoshizumi and Hosokawa Masamoto fought back, and coerced Emperor Go-Kashiwabara (1464–1526, r. 1500–1526) into declaring Yoshioki "an enemy of the court."[81] Yoshioki, fighting in Kyushu, nevertheless crushed his Ōtomo rivals on 2.9.1501, attributing their defeat to the powers of Myōken, and later donated the sword "hawk cutter" to Hikamisan Kōryūji in commemoration of this victory.[82] In another battle against the Ōtomo on 7.23.1501, the carnage was even greater. Documents recount over sixty names of the dead Ōtomo and their allies.[83] The slaughter included over ten enemy generals, and so many rank-and-file soldiers that their heads were piled into a mound.[84] Ōuchi Takahiro survived but lost all power. All his documents were intercepted and handed over to Yoshioki in 1502, which allowed him to identify and act against all of Takahiro's supporters. Ultimately, Takahiro was apparently killed in Suō in 1508.[85] Having

---

discussed in Allan Grapard, "The Shintō of Yoshida Kanetomo," *Monumenta Nipponica* 47.1 (Spring 1992), p. 44.

[78] *Sengoku ibun Ōuchi shi hen*, vol. 2, doc. 1109, 4.13.1501 (Bunki 1), Ōuchi Yoshioki *kishinjō*, p. 54.

[79] *Sengoku ibun Ōuchi shi hen*, vol. 2, doc. 1102, Ima Hachimangū *Hōchō uragaki utsushi*, p. 52.

[80] *Bōchō fūdo chūshin an*, vol. 9, *Mitashiri jō* (Yamaguchi, 1960), pp. 588–94.

[81] *Sengoku ibun Ōuchi shi hen*, vol. 2, doc. 1116, *urū* 6.13. Muromachi bakufu *bugyōnin rensho hōsho*, and doc. 1117, *urū* 6.13. Bō *hōsho utsushi*, p. 56. For how pressure from Ashikaga Yoshizumi caused these documents to have been dispatched, see *Yamaguchi kenshi shiryōhen chūsei*, vol. 1, Sanetaka kōki, *urū* 6.10.1501 (Bunki 1), p. 257.

[82] *Sengoku ibun Ōuchi shi hen*, vol. 2, doc. 1121, 7.4.1501 (Bunki 1) Ōuchi Yoshioki *kishinjō*, p. 57. For the victory over the Ōtomo, see doc. 1100, 2.6.1501 (Meiō 10) Ōuchi Yoshioki *kanjō*, p. 51, and doc. 1101, 2.21 [(Meiō 10) 1501] Ōuchi Yoshioki *shojō*, pp. 51–52. For the best record of the campaign, see doc. 1211, 7.1505 (Eishō 2) Sata Yasukage *gunchūjō*, pp. 90–91.

[83] *Sengoku ibun Ōuchi shi hen*, vol. 2, doc. 1125, 7.23.1501 (Bunki 1) Sugi Hiroyori *kassen tachiuchi buntori teoi chūmon*, pp. 58–60; docs. 1127–41, pp. 61–66 for a sequence of military records for many warriors; and, finally, doc. 1211, 7.1505 (Eishō 2) Sata Yasukage *gunchūjō*, pp. 90–91.

[84] *Agari ke monjo*, Agari ke *keizu*, p. 7.

[85] *Sengoku ibun Ōuchi shi hen*, vol. 2, doc. 1153, 3.26 [1502/Bunki 2] Ōuchi Yoshioki *shojō utsushi*, p. 70. The last reference to him appears in a document dating from 1508, but he was apparently killed

finally defeated his Kyushu rivals, Yoshioki then prepared to conquer the capital.[86]

Conquering Kyoto

Yoshioki relied on taxes and trade to fund his military campaigns.[87] He successfully reinstated the practice, abandoned by Masahiro after the Ōnin War, of appropriating half of a province's revenue for provisions (the *hanzei*). Yoshioki levied the *hanzei* on the provinces of Suō and Nagato by 4.25.1499, and on Buzen and Chikuzen of northern Kyushu by 1503–4.[88] In the case of Chikuzen province, *hanzei* levies remained in force from 1508 through 1515 for some districts, while others did not see relief from them until 1518.[89] Yoshioki was very forward thinking in terms of fiscal policy, as he was one of the first to assess taxes in cash based on a province's yield, a system known as *kandaka*.[90]

Revenue from trade also financed military campaigns. For example, after his escape from the clutches of the Hosokawa, Ashikaga Yoshitane planned to divert three Ming tally ships to the most powerful lords in Kyushu, the Ōuchi, Ōtomo, and Shimazu in 1496 for "military provisions." Each ship had ten thousand *kanmon* of miscellaneous goods, which could be exchanged at

shortly thereafter in Suō. *Sengoku ibun Ōuchi shi hen*, vol. 2, doc. 1266, 2.23 [(Eishō 5) 1508] Ashikaga Yoshizumi *gonaisho an*, p. 111 for Ashikaga Yoshizumi's final edict to Takahiro. For the latter's death in Suō, see *Yamaguchi kenshi shiryōhen chūsei*, vol. 1, Ōuchi Tatara shi *fuchō*, p. 743. A person commonly thought to be his son named Teruhiro was born in 1519, so either Takahiro survived through that time or Teruhiro was his brother or grandson.

[86] *Sengoku ibun Ōuchi shi hen*, vol. 2, doc. 1216, 12.23 [(Eishō 2) 1505] Ashikaga Yoshitada (Yoshitane) *gonaisho utsushi*, p. 92, and doc. 1217, 12.27 [(Eishō 2) 1505], Ōuchi Yoshioki *soejō utsushi*, pp. 92–93.

[87] *Sengoku ibun Ōuchi shi hen*, vol. 2, doc. 1202, 2.29 [(Eishō 2) 1505] Ōuchi shi *kashin rensho hōsho*, p. 87, and doc. 1203, 3.8 Toida Hirotane *jungyōjō*, p. 88.

[88] *Sengoku ibun Ōuchi shi hen*, vol. 2, doc. 1156, 4.10.1502 (Bunki 2) Ōuchi shi *kashin rensho hōsho utsushi*, p. 71, where he revoked "half tax" *hanzei* immunities from the temples and shrines of Suō and Nagato. Disputes would, however, linger about the tax liabilities of these institutions. Buzen and Chikuzen levies took place later. See doc. 1188, 3.5.1504 (Bunki 4) Shiroishi Shigekatsu *hanzei tsubotsuke*, pp. 83–84 for Buzen and doc. 1185, 11.27.1503 (Bunki 3) Sugi Taketsura *hōsho*, p. 82 for Chikuzen. See also Mimura Kōsuke, "Ōuchi shi no hanzeisei," *Komonjo kenkyū*, no. 56 (11.2002), pp. 7–9.

[89] Mimura Kōsuke, "Ōuchi shi no hanzeisei," p. 10. For this happening for the Dazai Tenmangū shrine in 1518, see *Sengoku ibun Ōuchi shi hen*, vol. 2, doc. 1583, 3.23 Ōuchi *kashin rensho hōsho utsushi*, pp. 212–13, and doc. 1609, 12.20.1518 (Eishō 15) Ōuchi shi *kashin rensho hōsho*, p. 221.

[90] Matsuoka Hisatō, "The Sengoku Daimyo of Western Japan: The Case of the Ōuchi," in John Whitney Hall, Nagahara Keiji, and Kozo Yamamura, eds., *Japan before Tokugawa: Political Consolidation and Economic Growth, 1500-1650* (Princeton: Princeton University Press, 1981), pp. 85–86.

roughly three to four times the price. The monk Jinson (1430–1508) surmised that the three returning ships would have goods worth approximately thirty thousand *kanmon*, which would be the approximate equivalent of $30 million in all.[91] Although Yoshitane's plan came to naught, in large part because Ōtomo Masachika turned on and killed Yoshitane's supporters (e.g., his own son), contemporaries still recognized that "treasures from abroad" could cause political change in Japan. This was lamented by the monk Jinson as the decay (*reiraku*) of "the ruler's law" (*ōbō*) in Japan.[92]

Yoshioki advanced to the capital after infighting brought Hosokawa Masamoto low. In 1507, Masamoto himself was killed by two of his retainers. An internecine struggle for succession then erupted among three of his heirs, resulting in the death of Masamoto's designated heir, Sumiyuki (1489–1507) and an ongoing war between two other candidates for the position of chancellor (*kanrei*), Takakuni (1484–1531) and Sumimoto (1489–1520). On 4.16.1508 the noble Konoe Hisamichi (1472–1544) portrayed events as "like the world of the Warring States (*sengoku*) era" of China of old, which was one of the earliest examples of this historical comparison of events within Japan to those of ancient China.[93]

Yoshioki, in letters to fellow warriors dating from 1507, professed his intention to restore prosperity in the realm (*tenka*).[94] He also expressed the desire to establish peace throughout the realm (*tenka kōnei gotansei*) in a prayer to Saidaiji in Nara on 4.30.1508.[95] As these documents and prayer reveal, term *tenka* (the realm), described by the modern historian Asao Naohiro as representing an "all-transcendent political principle" that was first used by the warlord Oda Nobunaga (1534–82) in 1568, had in fact long been in use by warriors such as Yoshioki.[96]

---

[91] *Daijōin jisha zōjiki*, vol. 11, 5.4.28.1496 (Meiō 5), p. 38. See also *Ōuchi Yoshioki*, p. 53.

[92] *Daijōin jisha zōjiki*, vol. 11, 5.4.28.1496 (Meiō 5), p. 38. This term was frequently combined with *buppō*, the teachings of the realm, to symbolize the interdependent rule by the court and Buddhist institutions.

[93] *Gohōjōji kanpakuki*, 4.16.1508 (Eishō 8). For photos of the original, see Atsuta Kō, ed., *Gohōjōji kanpakuki*, vol. 1 (Kyoto: Shibunkaku, 1985), p. 144. For an earlier comparison, Ichijō Kaneyoshi described the *shugo* as being "no different from the seven heroes of Warring States era" in his *Shōdanchiyō*, a textbook written in 1480 for the young shogun Ashikaga Yoshihisa (1465–89, shogun 1473–89). See *Gunsho ruijū*, vol. 27 zatsubu, p. 196.

[94] *Sengoku ibun Ōuchi shi hen*, vol. 2, doc. 1256, 11.23 [(Eishō 4) 1507] Ōuchi Yoshioki *shojō*, p. 108. In this letter, Yoshioki describes his intent for prayers to Sagara Nagatsune, but does not mention the precise format through which these prayers or invocations would be offered.

[95] *Sengoku ibun Ōuchi shi hen*, vol. 2, doc. 1271, 4.30 [(Eishō 5) 1508] Ōuchi Yoshioki *shojō*, p. 113.

[96] Katsumata Shizuo, "The Development of Sengoku Law," pp. 119–23, and Asao Naorhiro "*Shōgun* and *Tennō*," pp. 248–71, in Hall et al., *Japan before Tokugawa*, present this view most clearly. For more on the definition of *tenka*, see Jeffrey P. Mass, *Antiquity and Anachronism*

By 11.25.1507, Yoshioki left Yamaguchi with Ashikaga Yoshitane to re-take the capital.[97] His forces advanced by land and sea. Ōuchi Yoshioki's fleet consisted of 660 boats, included 200 belonging to privateers (*kaizoku*).[98] These boats were not at his permanent beck and call, but had to be mobilized by retainers such as Sue Okifusa (1475–1539).[99] Yoshioki's fleet slowly advanced to the capital, reaching the Tōsai harbor in the third month of 1508.[100] They arrived in Hyōgo approximately a month later 4.23.1508.[101] Six weeks elapsed until 6.8 of that year, when his army occupied the capital. Its size was substantial for the day, with Ashikaga Yoshitane leading five to six thousand troops, while Yoshioki established a camp at Tōfukuji with a force of six to seven thousand, including one thousand of his personal guards (*hashirishū*).[102] Their appearance forced Ashikaga Yoshizumi to flee the capital with his shogunal chancellor (*kanrei*) Hosokawa Sumimoto. In his place, Hosokawa Takakuni, head of a branch line of the Hosokawa, became the new chancellor (*kanrei*) although he co-ruled with Yoshioki.

Yoshioki, together with Hosokawa Takakuni, ultimately destroyed Ashikaga Yoshizumi's battered army in 1511. Yoshizumi suddenly died of illness midway through that year. Then Yoshioki feigned a strategic withdrawal from Kyoto. An army of Hosokawa Sumimoto and Hosokawa Masakata (d. 1511), some five thousand strong, in turn occupied the city. They were surprised by Yoshioki's sudden return to Funaoka. In the ensuing battle, the Hosokawa army was annihilated, with thirty-eight hundred heads taken, including that of Masakata himself, although Sumimoto was able to flee.[103]

(Stanford: Stanford University Press, 1992), p. 62. Mass argues that *tenka* was bound to the sovereignty of the emperor, however, and sees the later use of *tenka* by Nobunaga as being new.

[97] *Sengoku ibun Ōuchi shi hen*, vol. 2, doc. 1369, Shirasaki Hachimangū *munafuda mei utsushi*, pp. 141–42.

[98] *Mibu ke monjo*, vol. 6 (Kunaichō shoryōbu, 1988), doc. 1554, pp. 98–99.

[99] *Sengoku ibun Ōuchi shi hen*, vol. 2, doc. 1468, Spring 1513 (Eishō 10) Sue Okifusa *juzōsan narabi ni jō utsushi*, pp. 172–73 for how Okifusa helped to collect these ships in 1508 (Eishō 5). For a translation of earlier Ōuchi regulations concerning shipping and the commandeering of boats, see Conlan, *Samurai*, pp. 201–4.

[100] *Sengoku ibun Ōuchi shi hen*, vol. 2, doc. 1267, 3.19 Ōuchi Yoshioki *shojō*, p. 111.

[101] *Yamaguchi kenshi shiryōhen chūsei*, vol. 1, Gohōjōji kanpakuki, 4.30.1508 (Eishō 5), p. 399. Yoshioki seems to have arrived at Hyōgo on 4.23. See Chūsei kuge nikki kenkyūkai, ed., *Morimitsu kōki*, vol. 1 (Yagi shoten, 2018), 4.23.1508 (Eishō 5), p. 7.

[102] *Yamaguchi kenshi shiryōhen chūsei*, vol. 1, Gohōjōji kanpakuki, 6.8.1508 (Eishō 5), p. 400. For Yoshioki establishing a camp at Tōfukuji on 6.8, see *Morimitsu kōki*, vol. 1, 6.8. 1508 (Eishō 5), p. 9.

[103] *Yamaguchi kenshi shiryōhen chūsei*, vol. 1, Gohōjōji kanpakuki 8.16.1511 (Eishō 8), p. 402, provides an estimate of two thousand Hosokawa troops and three thousand Yamanaka warriors and comments that the Hosokawa forces were perceived as being weak at the time. Some accounts of the battle suggested that Yoshioki received intelligence about enemy dispositions from a monk who hailed from Yamaguchi. Kasai, *Nankai tsūki*, maki 30, p. 124.

Yoshioki's forces suffered losses as well, including one of his brothers, Tanehiro, the third of his brothers to die in a span of five years, and Toida Hirotane, one of his generals.[104]

Because of his success, he became an effective and popular war leader. After Funaoka, Yoshioki's followers boasted that he had "made his name known throughout the realm" by "defeating the enemies of the shogun."[105] Such sentiments were also expressed by compatriots, such as the *shugo* Asakura Sadakage (1473–1512).[106] The support of the Ashikaga, and his sweeping victory, enabled Yoshioki to expand his command over warriors in Aki and Iwami. Finally, some enemies, recognizing Yoshioki's skill, surrendered to him, most notably the Akamatsu and the Date.[107]

Yoshioki as Commander

Yoshioki's early years of his rule, as well as his last years, were mostly taken up with war. His record as a military commander can be reconstructed from fifty battle rosters that record the wounds of 542 warriors who fought for him between the years 1496 through 1527. They reveal changes in the intensity of conflict, as well as an increasing size of his armies. Yoshioki's initial battles in Kyushu and Kyoto led to many fatalities. In the documents of 1496 through 1515, the ratio of killed to wounded was 40:60; that is, 40 percent of all recorded casualties were deaths and the remaining 60 percent were wounds. The next time that Yoshioki led forces in battles was during the years 1522–27, and here the ratio of fatalities to wounds was 11:89, fatalities consisting of only 11 percent of recorded casualties, suggesting far less intensive fighting.[108] At the same time, the aggregate number of casualties increased

---

[104] *Ōuchi bunka*, Naikaku bunko *keizu*, p. 53 for Tanehiro death. For Toida Hirotane, see *Sengoku ibun Ōuchi shi hen*, vol. 2, doc. 1385 8.27.1511 (Eishō 8) Ryūzaki Michisuke *shojō*, p. 146.

[105] *Agari ke monjo*, p. 7.

[106] Tanaka Hiroki, Nakajima Keiichi, Nakatsukasa Ken'ichi, Nishida Tomohiro, and Watanabe Hiroki, "Masuda Saneuji shozō shinshutsu chūsei monjo no shōkai," *Kokuritsu rekishi minzoku hakubutsukan kenkyū hōkoku* 212 (12.2018), doc. 33, 9.23 [(Eishō 8) 1511] Asakura Sadakage *shojō*, p. 137. Sadakage addressed this letter to Sue Okifusa.

[107] *Sengoku ibun Ōuchi shi hen*, vol. 2, doc. 1456, urū 4.10.1512 (Eishō 9) Ashikaga Yoshitada [Yoshitane] *gonaisho*, p. 167. Other Yoshizumi allies, such as Date Tanemune (1488–1565) of Mutsu province in the far north, allied with Yoshioki shortly after he entered the capital in 1508. See *Date ke monjo*, vol. 1 (Tōkyō daigaku shuppankai, 1908), doc. 54, 3.13 [(Eishō 6) 1509] Ōuchi Yoshioki *shojō*, pp. 73–74.

[108] The earlier period witnessed 192 casualties (114 wounds, caused by arrows [67], swords [17], pikes [27], and three otherwise undescribed weapons) and 78 fatalities, while the latter witnessed 290 casualties (257 wounds, caused by arrows [177], swords [15], pikes [26], rocks (94), and 5 unspecified, and 33 fatalities). These figures were drawn from military documents appearing in *Sengoku ibun*

over time, suggesting somewhat larger armies overall, with 40 percent being listed between 1496–1515 and 60 percent during the years 1522–27.

Most wounds were caused by projectiles. Of all wounds recorded in documents, 80 percent were caused by projectiles and the remaining 20 percent by shock weapons. The percentage of handheld weapons increased markedly during the period of 1496 through 1515, as they caused 41 percent of all wounds. This period also witnessed higher fatalities. In the 1520s, however, such shock weapons caused only 13 percent of all wounds.

The use of handheld weapons remained statistically constant. On average, swords caused 38 percent of wounds caused by such weapons and pikes the remaining 62 percent. By contrast, patterns in projectile wounding shifted greatly, with arrows causing 100 percent of such wounds from 1496 to 1515, but only 65 percent during 1522–27, with the remaining 35 percent caused by rocks. The latter wounds were only inflicted on forces attacking Ono castle in Saeki district, Aki province, a site of extensive rock outcroppings.[109] The prevalence of wounds to the face, head, neck, and shoulder (72 percent) suggests that besiegers were bombarded with boulders, but no evidence exists that these rocks were primitive bullets.

Yoshioki was an effective commander who encouraged warriors to fight for him most intensely from the onset of the 1493 Meiō coup through the 1511 Battle of Funaoka. That time witnessed an upswing in fatalities, linked to hand-to-hand combat. The later battles were more often sieges, resulting in fewer battle deaths, but leading to more casualties overall than the earlier campaigns.

Revisiting Myōken in the Capital

After the Battle of Funaoka, Yoshioki commissioned a commemorative portrait that likened him to Ashikaga Takauji, the founder of the Ashikaga

---

Ōuchi shi hen, vol. 2, docs. 949, 959, 969, 1016, 1025, 1125, 1127, 1133, 1137–38, 1395, 1401, 1403, 1407, 1412, 1421, 1508–9, 1730–31, 1736, 1752–54, 1761, 1787–88, 1790, 1806–8, 1825, 1835, 1892–93, 1906–7, 1909–11, 1917–19, 1925–26, 1936, 1941–42, 1946, 1972–73.

[109] All the examples of prominent rock usage stem from castles located in Aki province. Ono castle in Saeki district is mentioned in *Sengoku ibun Ōuchi shi hen*, vol. 2, docs. 1787–88, pp. 291–92, while other extensive battles on this district are mentioned in docs. 1806–8, pp. 297–300. For battles in other Aki district of Annan, see docs. 1906, 1911, pp. 332–334.

regime.[110] A panegyric written for Yoshioki attributes his victory to Myōken, his lineage deity who had been installed at Funaoka by his father Masahiro in 1477.[111] Yoshioki ascribed the honor of his promotion to third rank, which occurred after this battle, as stemming from aid of Myōken as well. When Yoshioki prayed at Hikamisan Kōryūji, he signed his name with this rank a full month before his promotion was official (Figure 8.2).[112]

This portrait's encomium lauds how Yoshioki restored Ōuchi authority over Kii and Izumi provinces, where Myōken had been installed by Yoshioki's ancestor Yoshihiro (1356–99). Nevertheless, Yoshioki never had official administrative control over these provinces located in central Japan, hundreds of miles from the core Ōuchi domain. Thus, although military and administrative control could be fleeting, political authority linked to the *kami* and the buddhas lingered.

Yoshioki's institutional authority over Izumi was limited, but he could incorporate some local Izumi warriors into his band of retainers. The Numa of Izumi, for example, were followers of the noble Sanjō Kinyasu. During Yoshioki's heyday, they claimed to have ties to the Ōuchi dating back to the time of Yoshihiro. The Numa did not abandon the Sanjō entirely, but took to adopting a dual identity, particularly with regards to epistolary styles, writing documents in the warrior format when communicating with the Ōuchi and the courtly style for the Sanjō.[113] Their ultimate allegiance, however, was to Yoshioki. They readily obeyed him, moving eventually to Yamaguchi, and continued to follow the Ōuchi until 1551, when they were killed in the revolt that brought down Yoshioki's son Yoshitaka.

---

[110] Mori Michihiko, "Muromachiki ni okeru Takauji kachūzō no juyō to shōzōga seisaku: Ōuchi Yoshiokizō no shōkai o kanete," *Suzaku: Kyōto hakubutsukan kenkyū kiyō* 25 (2013), p. 18. I am grateful to Mori Michihiko for his help in securing a copy of this article. For the panegyric, see *Sengoku ibun Ōuchi shi hen*, vol. 2, doc. 1431, Winter 1511 (Eishō 8) Ōuchi Yoshioki *juzōsan utsushi*, pp. 159–60. Although the original portrait does not survive, a high-quality reproduction (Figure 8.2) suggests that it was a product of the Kano school.

[111] *Sengoku ibun Ōuchi shi hen*, vol. 2, doc. 1446, 2.13.1512 (Eishō 9) Kōryūji *shunigatsu-e tōyaku sashibumi*, pp. 146–47.

[112] For his new title, appended to his name before his promotion was official, see *Sengoku ibun Ōuchi shi hen*, vol. 2, doc. 1446, 2.13.1512 (Eishō 9) Kōryūji *shunigatsu-e tōyaku sashibumi*, pp. 146–47.

[113] Discussions with Matsui Naoto, 3.12.2012. For his informative article, see Matsui Naoto, "Yoshioki Yoshitakaki Ōuchi shi kenryoku no kōzōteki tokushitsu: Ōuchi shi hikan Numa shi no dōkō o tegakari ni," *Nihon rekishi* 822 (11.2016), pp. 17–33. For some of the many references to the Numa as appearing in sources, see *Yamaguchi kenshi shiryōhen chūsei*, vol. 1, Gohōjoji kanpakuki, 9.15, 10.4, and 10.8.1516 (Eishō 13), p. 406, and 5.22 and 9.21.1517 (Eishō 14), p. 408. See also *Sanetaka kōki*, 4.11.1512 (Eishō 9), p. 286.

Figure 8.2 Portrait of Ōuchi Yoshioki with Flag (*Ōuchi Yoshioki shōzōga*).
Image and permission provided by Yamaguchi kenritsu Yamaguchi
hakubutsukan

Becoming a Courtier

Although Yoshioki was a successful commander, for much of his life after the
Battle of Funaoka he concentrated his energies on mastering court protocol.
He remained a general to his dying days, but his military successes catapulted
him to the ranks of high nobility, for which he was not fully culturally suited.
Nevertheless, by achieving high court rank, he was about to circumvent

and limit the authority of the Ashikaga and bring stability to Kyoto. With Yamaguchi as his base, Yoshioki tried to stabilize Kyoto as capital, regularize economic affairs, and encourage greater exchanges between both cities.

While in Kyoto, Yoshioki experienced a meteoric rise in court rank, as officials recognized quite early that he was the linchpin of Ashikaga Yoshitane's restoration.[114] In 1508, Yoshioki was promoted to the fourth rank lower. Six weeks later his position was adjusted to fourth rank upper, so that he outranked his ally and rival Hosokawa Takakuni.[115] Five years later, after his triumph at Funaoka, Yoshioki attained the exalted position of junior third rank in 1512, making him a member of the high nobility.[116]

The court made these appointments without conferring with Ashikaga Yoshitane.[117] With his rank, Yoshioki gradually overshadowed the Ashikaga. Yoshioki's promotion to the third rank was only the second time that a warrior of non-Ashikaga blood achieved it.[118] High rank did not, however, mean mastery of court practices, and when the overjoyed Yoshioki became overly

[114] *Yamaguchi kenshi shiryōhen chūsei*, vol. 1, Gohōjōji kanpakuki, 7.23.1511 (Eishō 8), p. 400.

[115] *Sengoku ibun Ōuchi shi hen*, vol. 2, doc. 1281, on 8.1.1508 (Eishō 5) Go-Kashiwabara tennō *kuzen an utsushi*, p. 115, and doc. 1285, 9.14.1508 (Eishō 5) Go-Kashiwabara tennō *kuzen an utsushi*, pp. 116–17. See also *Yamaguchi kenshi shiryōhen chūsei*, vol. 1, Sanetaka kōki, 8.1, 8.7.1508 (Eishō 5), p. 260.

[116] *Sengoku ibun Ōuchi shi hen*, vol. 2, doc. 1453, 3.26.1512 (Eishō 9) Go-Kashiwabara tennō *kuzen an*, p. 166, and doc. 1454, 3.26.1512 (Eishō 9) Kan'iki, pp. 166–67. See also *Yamaguchi kenshi shiryōhen chūsei*, vol. 1, Sanetaka kōki, 4.4 and 4.14.1512 (Eishō 9), p. 286; *Morimitsu kōki*, vol. 1, 4.5.1512 (Eishō 9), p. 62; and Imatani Akira, *Sengoku daimyō to tennō* (Kōdansha gakujutsu bunko, 2001), p. 79. There is some confusion, as another copy of an edict suggests that this happened a month after Yoshioki was appointed to the fourth rank upper in 1508, but this in incorrect. *Kugyō bunin*, vol. 3 (Yoshikawa kōbunkan, 1964), p. 332, mentions how Yoshioki received the appointment of junior third rank on 3.26.1312 because of the merit in winning the Battle of Funaoka during the eighth month of the previous year. See *Sengoku ibun Ōuchi shi hen*, vol. 2, doc. 1288, 10.14.1508 (Eishō 5) Go-Kashiwabara tennō *kuzen an utsushi*, p. 117. This has caused Fujii to mistakenly assume that Yoshioki had the third rank from 1508 onward. See his *Ōuchi Yoshioki*, p. 85.

[117] *Yamaguchi kenshi shiryōhen chūsei*, vol. 1, Sanetaka kōki, 8.1.1508 (Eishō 5), p. 260. For analysis of how this passage reveals that Yoshioki's promotion was decided internally (*nainai*) by the court, which did not confer with Ashikaga Yoshitane, see Imatani Akira, *Sengoku daimyō to tennō*, pp. 66–67.

[118] On *urū* 2.3.1496 (Meiō 5) Akamatsu Masanori received the junior third rank, two months before he died in accordance with Ashikaga precedence. See *Kugyō bunin*, vol. 3 (Yoshikawa kōbunkan, 1964), *urū* 2.3.1496 (Meiō 5), p. 294. Ashikaga shoguns, collaterals such as the Shiba and Hatakeyama, had received this promotion, as well as those with court ties, such as the Kitabatake, but the Hosokawa, including Katsumoto and Masamoto, only achieved the rank of fourth lower. Akamatsu Masanori's promotion was one difficult for the *kanrei* Hosokawa Masamoto, to accept. See *Kazunaga kyōki*, 3.3.1496 (Meiō 5), *Shiryō shūran* series 8, vol. 909, p. 32, searched Tōkyō Shiryōhen sanjo database, 2.28.2019, https://clioimg.hi.u-tokyo.ac.jp/viewer/view/idata/T38/1496/10-5-1/2/0063?m=all&s=0063.

inebriated at the palace, Sanjōnishi Sanetaka (1455–1537), grumbled that Yoshioki behaved like a "bumpkin warrior" (*inaka bushi*).[119]

Sanetaka's disdain for Yoshioki stems from Yoshioki's ignorance of court etiquette. Yoshioki tried to do better, and from 9.3.1509 through 3.7.1514 he frequently consulted with members of the Ise family, who were financial and ritual specialists for the Ashikaga, over matters of etiquette regarding departures, gifts, and processions. Certain queries reveal his outsider status. For example, he questioned the proper placement of tiger and leopard skins on the flooring (*onzashiki*), receiving the answer that it did not matter.[120]

Until recently, the location of Yoshioki's Kyoto residence was unknown, but recent excavations uncovered several pits with rough *haji* ware, manufactured in Yamaguchi, along with discarded pottery, rounded and regular pots (*hagama* and *nabe*). These pits are located to the south of the intersection of Shinmachi and Shimochōjamachi streets, a block west of Muromachi street, where Yoshitane resided, and approximately a mile from the palace.[121] The pottery dates from the late fifteenth and early sixteenth centuries and would be consistent with what Yoshioki would have brought, or had shipped to him, from Yamaguchi.[122] In terms of location, then, Yoshioki could easily communicate with Yoshitane or the palace but remained distant from both.

Cultural Patronage

Yoshioki and his followers took advantage of their wealth, and court presence, to patronize works of art and copy noted texts, thus becoming immersed in Kyoto culture. Two Sue officials, Hiroaki and Okinari, were

---

[119] *Yamaguchi kenshi shiryōhen chūsei*, vol. 1, Sanetaka kōki, 4.14.1512 (Eishō 9), p. 286, and Imatani Akira, *Sengoku daimyō to tennō*, p. 79. For Yoshioki's inebriation, in the same volume, Gohōjōji kanpakuki, 3.14.1512 (Eishō 9), p. 403.

[120] For the most complete and comprehensive compilation of these sources, see Ōuchi bunka, section 6, Yusoku kojitsu doc. 2, Ōuchi Yoshioki *toijō sūhentō*, pp. 585–92. See also doc. 3, *Sōgo ōzōshi*, pp. 592–95, doc. 4, Ise Kaga *no kami* Sadamitsu *hikki*, pp. 595–97, and doc. 5, Ise Sadasuke *zakki*, p. 597. For the dating, see pp. 589, 592; for leopard skins p. 589.

[121] *Kyōtofu iseki chōsa hōkokushū*, no. 176 (Kyōtofu maizō bunkazai chōsa kenkyū sentaa, 2018), p. 143 for the discovery of the Yamaguchi pottery and other artifacts. http://www.kyotofu-maibun. or.jp/data/kankou/mokuzi/gaihou-4.html. For an estimate of the palace location, which according to Google Maps is one mile (1.6 kilometers) from this location, see Okuno, *Sengoku jidai no kyūtei seikatsu*, p. 23.

[122] According to the *Kyōtofu iseki chōsa hōkokushū*, no. 176, this pottery is Ōuchi III style, which would date it to the late fifteenth century, but Kitajima Daisuke, in an email conversation of 5.29. 2019, suggests that it was a mixture of type III and early type IV pottery, which dates from the first half of the sixteenth century.

particularly influential. Sue Hiroaki (d. 1523), a deputy *shugo* of Chikuzen province, managed shipping and trade to the continent.[123]

Hiroaki's son Sue Okinari traveled to Kyoto in 1508. He quickly struck up a relationship with Sanjōnishi Sanetaka and became his poetic disciple. Sanetaka enthusiastically helped Okinari to create a remarkable illustrated book of *The Tale of Genji* in 1510, one of the oldest complete albums.[124] Its calligraphy was written by six skilled writers of the court, who represented distinct schools of writing, and its images were painted in the studio of Tosa Mitsunobu and mounted on excellent quality paper, while the cover was made with imported Chinese silk.[125] After the book was completed, Okinari gave it to his father Hiroaki, who stored it at Myōeiji, a temple located along the route from Yamaguchi to the Nagato ports of Senzaki and Hijū.[126]

Sue Hiroaki also collected and copied the thirteenth-century *Azuma kagami*, a valuable history of twelfth- and thirteenth-century Japan. After twenty years of collecting the scattered volumes of the *Azuma kagami*, Hiroaki came to possess the most accurate and complete version of this chronicle.[127] Ōuchi efforts were not limited to copying older works; they were also instrumental in overseeing the creation of influential chronicles such as *The Tale of Ōnin*, which was finalized while Yoshioki occupied the

---

[123] His brother Sue Okifusa was also an accomplished poet and warrior who fought in northern Kyushu and at the Battle of Funaoka and was involved in commandeering ships.

[124] For an early analysis, see *Tokuyama shishi* (2nd printing, Tokuyama, 1971), vol. 1, p. 165 for Okinari and p. 155 for Okifusa. Much can be known about Sue Okifusa because a short account was written of his life. See *Sengoku ibun Ōuchi shi hen*, vol. 2, doc. 1468, Spring 1513 (Eishō 10) Sue Okifusa *juzō san narabini jo utsushi*, pp. 172–73.

[125] They included Sanjōnishi Sanetaka, Reizei Tamehiro, and the crown prince Kunitaka. This work is now in the Fogg Museum at Harvard. See Anne Rose Kitagawa, "Behind the Scenes of Harvard's *Tale of Genji Album*," *Apollo* 154, no. 477 (November 2001), pp. 28–35. I learned of the imported silk covers from Rachel Sanders, discussion 3.15.2021. See also Melissa McCormick, "Genji Goes West: The 1510 *Genji Album* and the Visualization of Court and Capital," *Art Bulletin* 85.1 (3.2003), pp. 54–85, particularly p. 62 for his skill in selecting representative examples of distinct calligraphic styles. For a full reproduction of this marvelous work, see Melissa McCormick, *The Tale of Genji: A Visual Companion* (Princeton: Princeton University Press, 2018).

[126] This narrative is drawn from McCormick's "Genji Goes West," particularly pp. 59–66, which explains the refinishing of this book in 1516. For documentary evidence of Okinari and Sanetaka's exchanges, see *Yamaguchi kenshi shiryōhen chūsei*, vol. 1, Sanetaka kōki, 8.3.1509 (Eishō 6), *urū* 8.18.1509 (Eishō 6), p. 270, 9.6.1509 (Eishō 6), p. 271, 10.9.1509 (Eishō 6), p. 272, 11.19.1509 (Eishō 6), p. 273, 5.16.1510 (Eishō 7), p. 275. Finally, for Okinari receiving poems from Sanetaka and returning to Yamaguchi, see 9.24 and 9.27.1511 (Eishō 8), p. 283. For reference to a Genji picture book (*ehon*) in the *Mibu* collection, see vol. 7, doc. 1811, p. 57.

[127] *Sengoku ibun Ōuchi shi hen*, vol. 2, doc. 1728, Azuma kagami *tobira ura shikigo*, and doc. 1729, 9.5.[(Daiei 2) 1522] Azuma kagami *okugaki*, pp. 271–72. For a recent study of this text, see Erin Brightwell, *Reflecting the Past: Place, Language, and Principle in Japan's Medieval Mirror Genre* (Cambridge, MA: Harvard University Asia Center, 2020), pp. 203–26.

capital.[128] The survival of many works of literature and art is linked to Ōuchi collection, conservation, and patronage during these peaceful years.

Administering the Capital

Yoshioki ruled as an outsider to the Ashikaga shogunate. He accepted court-based offices that granted him authority over the hinterlands of the capital, as well as its western wards, but did not openly take high position as an Ashikaga official.[129] Although some accounts try to gloss over this by stating that he was a "deputy chancellor" (*kanrei*), a position that does not exist, in fact Yoshioki wielded influence by informally interceding with the government.[130] Examples are rife, with perhaps the most colorful being Yoshioki's intercession to allow the warrior Asakura Takakage (1493–1548) to have the privilege of using a white umbrella and a tiger skin saddle cover (*kuraoi*), both of which marked *shugo* office and status.[131]

During the ten years that Yoshioki, Takakuni, and Ashikaga Yoshitane ruled in the capital, Yoshioki remained in charge of the left, or western wards of the capital as *sakyō no daibu*, while Takakuni governed the right, or eastern wards as *ukyō no daibu*. Their responsibilities were great since the shogun delegated most authority to them.[132]

---

[128] This tale was also crafted in a way to emphasize the Hosokawa role, while the Ōuchi position as enemies of Ashikaga Yoshimasa was deemphasized. Because historically the two families were antagonistic, the role of this period of cooperation has been overlooked. The Akamatsu also wrote an account emphasizing their role as well. For more on the chronicle, see Conlan, "The 'Ōnin War' as Fulfillment of Prophecy," *Journal of Japanese Studies* 46.1 (Winter 2020), pp. 31–60.

[129] Years later, Oda Nobunaga would help Ashikaga Yoshiaki occupy Kyoto and he too carefully refused Ashikaga posts.

[130] *Ōnin kōki* 應仁後記, Kondō Keizō, comp, *Kaitei shiseki shūran*, vol. 3, maki 19, 1–74 (3rd printing, 1932), p. 62 for Yoshioki as deputy *kanrei* (*kanrei dai*). See also Imaoka Norikazu, "Ashikaga Yoshitane seiken to Ōuchi Yoshioki," Uwayokote Masataka, ed., *Chūsei kōbu kenryoku no kōzō to tenkai* (Yoshikawa kōbunkan, 2001), pp. 197–200. For prohibitions regarding intercession (*kunyū*), see *Chūsei hōsei shiryōshū*, vol. 2, Muromachi bakufu *hō*, article 8, p. 5. This has been translated by Kenneth Grossberg, *Laws of the Muromachi Bakufu* (Sophia University Press, 1981), article 8, p. 19.

[131] *Ōnin kōki*, p. 62 for Yoshioki's actions of the sixth month of 1516 (Eishō 13). See also *Ashikaga kiseiki*, *Kaitei shiseki shūran*, vol. 13 (Kondō Keizō shuppanbu, 1902), 6.1516 (Eishō 13), p. 154 for another reference, although the tiger skins are not mentioned. See also other documentary evidence in Imaoka Norikazu, "Ashikaga Yoshitane seiken to Ōuchi Yoshioki," p. 196. Normally only the shogun could grant such prerogatives. Finally, for more on Takakage, see Morgan Pitelka, *Reading Medieval Ruins: Urban Life and Destruction in Sixteenth-Century Japan* (Cambridge: Cambridge University Press, 2022), pp. 53, 115.

[132] *Sengoku ibun Ōuchi shi hen*, vol. 2, doc. 1314, urū 8.18.1309 (Eishō 6) Ashikaga Yoshitada (Yoshitane) *gonaisho* p. 125, and doc. 1312, urū 8.14 Ōuchi Yoshioki *shojō*, p. 124. For further evidence of Yoshitane governing through these men, and their offices, see doc. 1456, urū 4.10.1512 (Eishō 9) Ashikaga Yoshitada [Yoshitane] *gonaisho*, p. 167.

Yoshioki and Takakuni socialized together, attending Noh performances, and later viewing the autumn leaves, but tensions remained.[133] Once, a brawl erupted between the Misumi, retainers of Yoshioki, and the Yanagihara, who followed Takakuni, over possession of a residence, leaving over two dozen of the Misumi men dead. Briefly both lords mobilized armies, but successful mediation by the shogun Yoshitane resulted in the affair being settled amicably.[134] Nevertheless, they generally governed well together, and felt little need to consult with Ashikaga Yoshitane, their nominal leader, who once complained (*onjukkai*) about both and fled, only to return to Kyoto, humiliated, months later.[135]

Yoshioki, like his father Masahiro, exhibited great deference to estate proprietors, such as the major temples of Kyoto. When Ashikaga Yoshitane promised to reward Yoshioki with the Sakai Minami estate, which was the harbor of Sakai, Yoshioki declined, stating that estates should be returned to their original proprietors, in this case Shōkokuji.[136] Yoshioki deemed direct control of the harbor unnecessary, and preferred enlisting agents from the Hibiya family, to manage trade, collect intelligence, and govern the port on his behalf.[137] Thus, for all its "autonomy," Sakai was firmly in the Ōuchi orbit.[138] Yoshioki opted instead to became on 7.13.1508 the protector (*shugo*) of Yamashiro, the central province that surrounded Kyoto.[139]

---

[133] *Yamaguchi kenshi shiryōhen chūsei*, vol. 1, Gohōjōji kanpakuki, 9.5 and 9.25.1508 (Eishō 5), p. 401, and 2.27.1513 (Eishō 10), p. 404 for their viewing Noh performances, 10.14.1508 (Eishō 5), p. 401 for viewing autumn leaves.

[134] *Yamaguchi kenshi shiryōhen chūsei*, vol. 1, Gohōjōji kanpakuki, 1.16.1509 (Eishō 6), p. 401, and Go-Kashiwabara-inki, 1.12–17.1509, p. 419. For a document pertaining to the conflict, see 1.26. 1509 (Eishō 6) Sanetaka kōki shihai monjo, p. 300. See also Yamada Yasuhiro, *Ashikaga Yoshitane*, pp. 146–47.

[135] *Yamaguchi kenshi shiryōhen chūsei*, vol. 1, Gohōjōji kanpakuki. 3.18.1513 (Eishō 10), p. 404. The initial report was that he renounced the world. For Yoshitane's return to the capital see 5.3.1513 (Eishō 10), p. 404. See also Futaki Ken'ichi, "Ashikaga Yoshitane," *Sengoku bushō no tegami o yomu* (Kadokawa shoten, 1991), pp. 32–36 for his 3.7.1513 (Eishō 10) letter to Konoe Hisamichi complaining how his judgments and orders were all ignored, so he had decided to leave.

[136] *Yamaguchi kenshi shiryōhen chūsei*, vol. 1, Bonjoki, 5.9.1508 (Eishō 8), p. 398, and Yamada *Ashikaga Yoshitane*, p. 149.

[137] This was well recognized by the Portuguese when they arrived in Sakai in 1550. They stated that the Hibiya had controlled Sakai since the time of Yoshioki. Alessandro Valignano's 1583 *Sumário de las Cosas de Japón*, ed. Alvarez-Taladriz (Sophia University, 1954), p. 123 n. 73. See also Georg Schurhammer, *Francis Xavier: His Life and Times*, trans. M. Joseph Costelloe, 4 vols. (Rome: Jesuit Historical Institute, 1973–82), vol. 4, p. 180. By contrast, in later years, when confronted with a similar opportunity, Oda Nobunaga requested direct physical control over Sakai. Regarding Sakai, I am grateful to Andrew Watsky and Alexandra Curvelo for their insights.

[138] Sakai forces would defeat Miyoshi Motonaga and force him to kill himself in 1532, while in 1546, Miyoshi Nagayoshi would briefly enter Sakai but withdraw.

[139] *Sengoku ibun Ōuchi shi hen*, vol. 2, docs. 1277–79, 7.13 Ōuchi shi *kashin rensho shojō*, pp. 114–15.

In aiding central proprietors, most notably temples, Yoshioki and his followers were rewarded handsomely. For example, Yoshioki upheld Tōji's rights to the Kuze estate.[140] In exchange, Yoshioki received gratuities of ten *kanmon*, while the two heads of the district, Hironaka Takenaga and Kōjiro Sadafusa, received twenty *kanmon* for their efforts, and a variety of other officials received lesser amounts. The total sum of payments was forty-five *kanmon*, 420 *mon*, which took the residents of the estate over a year to pay, and which required extensive new corvée levies to be assessed on them.[141]

Yamashiro proved to be a challenging province for Yoshioki to govern, as it teemed with hostile supporters of Hosokawa Sumimoto. Yoshioki now was pressured to uphold proprietary rights for courtiers and temples.[142] He also had to adjudicate boundaries between the major temples, such as Daigoji's Sanbōin and Kajuji, and some disputes resulted in battles (*kassen*) between local notables (*myōshu satanin*) and commoners (*hyakushō*).[143]

A mere ten days after his initial appointment, Yoshioki expressed a desire to return to Yamaguchi, and only an imperial command prevented him from leaving.[144] Many of his followers, particularly those that he more loosely controlled from the provinces of Aki and Iwami, agitated to return to their lands, and many left long before Yoshioki was able to do so.[145] Nevertheless, by being the *shugo*, Yoshioki was able to levy the *hanzei* half tax on Yamashiro and gain much income.[146] Yoshioki in effect governed not only the province of Yamashiro, but the capital itself, as he adjudicated more cases than the shogun, showing the extent of his political role.[147] Joint control over Kyoto,

---

[140] *Yamaguchi kenshi tsūshihen furoku* CD-ROM, Tōji monjo, doc. 198, 10.28.1508 (Eishō 5) Muromachi bakufu *bugyōnin hōsho*, p. 559. For confirmation of their identity, see doc. 203, 11.27.1508 (Eishō 5) Chinjū Hachiman Gusō *hyōjō hikitsuke*, pp. 560–61.

[141] *Yamaguchi kenshi tsūshi furoku* CD-ROM, Tōji monjo, doc. 202, 12.21.1508 (Eishō 5) *Reikin ika nyūsoku chūmon*, p. 560, and doc. 204, 5.3.1509 (Eishō 6) Yamashiro no kuni Kami Kuze *no shō onbyakushō shū mōshijō*, p. 561.

[142] *Yamaguchi kenshi tsūshi furoku* CD-ROM, Tōji monjo, docs. 214–15 8.15.1517 (Eishō 14) Muromachi bakufu *bugyōnin rensho hōsho an*, p. 564 for how lands dedicated for court use where to have occupiers removed.

[143] *Sengoku ibun Ōuchi shi hen*, vol. 2, doc. 1489, 8.28.1514 (Eishō 11) Kōjiro Takefusa *shojō utsushi*, p. 180.

[144] *Yamaguchi kenshi shiryōhen chūsei*, vol. 1, Sanetaka kōki, 7.23.1508 (Eishō 5) p. 259, Gohōjōji kanpakuki, 7.23.1508 (Eishō 5), p. 400. For this episode, and the importance of the imperial order, see *Morimitsu kōki*, vol. 1, 7.26.1508 (Eishō 5), p. 17.

[145] For more on the travails of Aki and Iwami warriors, see *Sengoku ibun Ōuchi shi hen*, vol. 2, doc. 1443, 2.2 [(Eishō 9) 1512] Hironaka Takenaga *shojō*, pp. 163–64. For other praise of the Sagara, a Kyushu warrior, long serving in the capital, see doc. 1341 4.30 [(Eishō 7) 1510] Kamishiro Sadafusa *shojō*, p. 132.

[146] *Yamaguchi kenshi shiryōhen chūsei*, vol. 1, Kitano mokudai nikki, 10.1509 (Eishō 6), pp. 411–12.

[147] For recent emphasis on the burdens of the occupation, see Fujii, *Ōuchi Yoshioki*, pp. 85–91. Fujii emphasizes that Yoshioki did not create a local lordship of the province. To the contrary, Imatani Akira focused on how effective his governance was. See Imatani Akira, "Ōuchi Yoshioki

Yamaguchi, and northern Kyushu also gave Yoshioki the authority to oversee currency and exchange rates for much of Japan.

Kyoto Currency Regulations

The Ōuchi had, as we have seen in chapter 7, successfully regulated currency with their assaying edicts, responding to an influx of forged coins by ensuring that some privately minted "bad" (*akusen*) coins would be allowed, although privately minted Sakai coins, hammered coins, forged Hongwu Ming coins, and "rope cutter" coins were prohibited. By contrast, in Kyoto, administrators for Hosokawa Masamoto and Ashikaga Yoshizumi issued coin selection edicts in 1500 that proved to be more lenient regarding *akusen* coins than had been the practice of the Ōuchi domains, or for that matter, southern Kyushu. Disdain for these *akusen* was widespread among the merchants of Kyoto.[148] In 1497, officials of the Kamo shrine in Kyoto criticized their use for tax payments as being outrageous (*gongo dōdan*).[149]

Masamoto's regime nevertheless defined all coins that had been "truly" imported from China including Eiraku, Xuande, and Hongwu coins as being "good" coins, which could be used for all transactions, while all privately made coins from Japan were prohibited.[150] This meant that Chinese coins formerly classified as *akusen* could be used for payments, which de facto devaluated the currency. This caused merchants to withdraw "good" old Chinese coins from the market and hoard them.[151] Compounding this shortage, Masamoto and Yoshizumi, like the Ōuchi, disallowed Sakai coins, but this led to a cash shortage. In 1505 the exasperated administrators for Ashikaga Yoshizumi commanded "everyone" in the capital to accept all Chinese coins at all times "regardless of their quality or minor flaws." The

---

no Yamashiro no kuni shihai," *Yamaguchi ken chihōshi kenkyū*, no. 51 (6.1984), pp. 1–11. Imaoka Norikazu also emphasizes Yoshioki's decisive role in "Ashikaga Yoshitane seiken to Ōuchi Yoshioki," pp. 197–99.

[148] For an excellent overview of Ashikaga currency regulation after the Ōnin War and moneylender attitudes regarding them, see Suzanne Gay, *The Moneylenders of Late Medieval Kyōto* (Honolulu: University of Hawaii Press, 2001), pp. 160–63.

[149] Kanō shiryōhen iinkai, comp., *Kanō shiryō, Sengoku*, vol. 4 (Ishikawa, 2004), 5.10 [(Meiō 6) 1497] *Tōchō shojō*, pp. 339–40.

[150] *Chūsei hōsei shiryōshū*, vol. 2, pp. 105–6. For a translation, which incorrectly portrays these Chinese coins as "bad coins," see Grossberg, *Laws of the Muromachi Bakufu*, p. 126.

[151] Gay, *Moneylenders*, p. 161. This example reveals that even in the sixteenth-century Japanese context, Gresham's Law, "Bad money drives out good," applies.

use of so-called bad coins (*akusen*) was prohibited, but these coins were now only limited to *kinsen* and *uchihirame* (counterfeit coins). The poor-quality Hongwu Ming coins and internally manufactured Sakai coins, which were elsewhere perceived as being *akusen*, were allowed.[152]

Once Ōuchi Yoshioki and Ashikaga Yoshitane supplanted their rivals in Kyoto, they regulated Kyoto currency exchanges again. On 8.7.1508, they criticized earlier Ashikaga practices in coin selection as "exceeding precedent" and being "most improper" but were forced to allow some coins that they had long considered as *akusen*, such as Kōbu (Hongwu), Eiraku (Yongle), Sentoku (Xuande), and broken coins from China *totōsen*, to be used in monetary exchanges. In a concession, they argued that these coins could legitimately constitute up to one-third of the specie used for transactions, but privately minted Chinese *kinsen* and *uchihirame* were prohibited.[153] They too now allowed for some coins minted in Japan (e.g., the Sakai coins) to be used for transactions, albeit only when these coins were fully intact.[154]

This attempt at regulating currency seemed effective, although cash shortages remained. Later regulations became even more flexible, with only *nawakiri*, a name for counterfeit Kōbu (Hongwu) coins, hammered *uchihirame* coins, *kinsen* (京銭) lead coins made in Fujian, and the *ji-ōdori* coins that the Sagara had allowed, albeit at a discounted rate in 1493, being prohibited.[155] The need for coins proved to be so great that in 1526, even

---

[152] *Chūsei hōsei shiryōshū*, vol. 2, clause 334, 10.10.1505 (Eishō 2), p. 109, and Grossberg, *Laws of the Muromachi Bakufu*, article 334, pp. 129–30. In this passage it is difficult to decipher what is meant by *akusen*. Shiba Kentarō argues that it meant buying and selling with bad coins. Nevertheless, Kobata Atsushi believed that it pertained to the denomination of prices in terms of bad coins, which would cause inflation. See Grossberg, p. 130 n. 398, and Kobata, *Nihon kahei ryūtsū shi* (Tōkō shoin, 1969), p. 106. Other clauses are clearer, such as a blanket prohibition of the purchase of *akusen*. *Chūsei hōsei shiryōshū*, vol. 2, clause 361 of *urū* 8.7.1509 (Eishō 6), p. 117, and Grossberg, article 361, p. 136. In 1506, the Ashikaga regime of Yoshizumi backtracked and tried to limit "new" Chinese coins to 32 percent of monetary transactions, while also allowing Sakai coins. See *Chūsei hōsei shiryōshū*, vol. 2, clause 344, 7.22.1506 (Eishō 3), p. 111, and Grossberg, *Laws of the Muromachi Bakufu*, article 344, p. 131.

[153] *Sengoku ibun Ōuchi shi hen*, vol. 2, doc. 1282, 8.7.1508 (Eishō 5) Muromachi bakufu *bugyōnin hōsho utsushi*, pp. 115–16. See also *Chūsei hōsei shiryōshū*, vol. 2, clause 345, 8.7.1508 (Eishō 5), p. 112, clause 348, 8.7.1508 (Eishō 5), pp. 113–14, and clause 360, *urū* 8.7.1509 (Eishō 6), p. 117. For translations, see Grossberg, *Laws of the Muromachi Bakufu*, article 345, p. 131, article 348, 8.7.1508 (Eishō 5), p. 132, and article 360, p. 136. See also Gay, *Moneylenders*, pp. 162–63.

[154] *Chūsei hōsei shiryōshū*, vol. 2, clause 386, 8.30.1512 (Eishō 9), p. 123, and Grossberg, *Laws of the Muromachi Bakufu*, p. 141. For coins manufactured in Japan in the Ishikawa region, see *Ishikawa ken maizō bunka hōkoku*, no. 5 (2000), p. 45 (accessed 2.24.2019), http://www.ishikawa-maibun.jp/wp-content/uploads/2018/03/jouhou_05.pdf http://www.ishikawa-maibun.jp/wp-content/uploads/2018/03/jouhou_05.pdf.

[155] *Sengoku ibun Ōuchi shi hen*, vol. 2, doc. 1600, 10.14.1518 (Eishō 15) Ōuchi shi *kashin rensho gechijō an*, pp. 217–18.

kinsen were permitted, although their use was confined to payments for shipping.[156]

While controlling the capital, the Ōuchi regularized currency exchange rates into a consistent ratio, allowing poorer coins to be used primarily for interest payments and shipping expenses, which prevented the hoarding of cash and allowed new coins to be used in a limited manner. The historian Richard von Glahn correctly argues that "Ōuchi monetary policies should be seen as a balanced effort to maintain a fine coin standard while at the same time accommodating the proliferation of cheap transactional currencies in order to provide sufficient elasticity to the money supply at a time of growing scarcity of fine coin."[157] These effective policies enabled the capital to experience "a period of monetary stability; no new legislation was promulgated between 1514 and 1542."[158]

Although the monetary exchange rates stabilized in the capital, some difficulties arose, as the expansion of specie resulted in inflationary pressures at Yamaguchi. They were ameliorated while Yoshioki and his army long resided in Kyoto, but upon their return to Yamaguchi, Yoshioki once again issued an edict on 10.14.1518 stating that the exchange rate of rice to cash should be as it existed of old.[159]

Trade with Korea, China, and the Ryūkyūs

For over half a century Ōuchi had strong trading ties with Korea, having already been granted Chosŏn tallies for trade.[160] Itō Kōji has shown that they also had created special seals for use with their diplomatic correspondence with Korea or the Ryūkyūs, which had previously only been the prerogative

[156] *Sengoku ibun Ōuchi shi hen*, vol. 2, doc. 1850, 4.5.1526 (Daiei 6), p. 312. For more on *kinsen*, see Richard von Glahn, "Chinese Coin and Changes in Monetary Preferences in Maritime East Asia in the Fifteenth–Seventeenth Centuries," *Journal of the Economic and Social History of the Orient* 57 (2014), p. 652.

[157] von Glahn, "Chinese Coin," p. 657.

[158] von Glahn, "Chinese Coin," p. 658. Although von Glahn treats these two regions, and Kyushu as distinct regions (see pp. 655–59), the fact that the Ōuchi controlled all three allowed for a more consistent exchange policy.

[159] *Chūsei hōsei shiryōshū*, vol. 3, Ōuchi shi *hekisho*, clause 167, 10.14.1518 (Eishō 15), pp. 105–6, and *Sengoku ibun Ōuchi shi hen*, vol. 2, doc. 1600, 10.14.1518 (Eishō 15) Ōuchi shi *kashin rensho gechijō an*, pp. 217–18. See Takagi, *Nihon chūsei shihei shiron*, pp. 140–42.

[160] Kenneth Robinson, "The Printed *Haedong chegukki* and Korean-Japanese Relations in the Early Sixteenth Century," *Ilbon sasang* 9 (10.2005), pp. 101–3.

of the Ashikaga.[161] Yoshioki was well known to Korean officials and was described as a "great lord" of seven provinces of Japan.[162] Korean demand for copper also propelled trade, although debates existed there as to the propriety of importing this commodity. In 1490, the Chosŏn official Yi Kŭk-pae (1422–95) commented that Korea did not produce its own copper, taking a position that favored trade.[163] Nevertheless, the Chosŏn king Yŏnsan'gun (1476–1506, r. 1494–1506), favoring notions of autarky, decided to prohibit trade (*kongyŏk* 公易) in copper and metals (*tongch'ŏlmuyŏk* 銅鐵貿易), and he refused Yoshioki's shipment of these items in 1502.[164] The Chosŏn court was aware that the Ōuchi had a powerful army and so tried to appease Yoshioki by accepting offerings of monkeys, horses, and birds.[165]

Yoshioki's response is not known, but he reached out to Yŏnsan'gun's court and requested funds for the restoration of Kameyama Hachiman shrine, which he claimed was vital for navigation, as it overlooked a treacherous section of the Straits of Shimonoseki. Yoshioki played up Hachiman as a protector of sailors and explained to the Koreans the importance of this shrine in aiding safe passage over the seas.[166] How successful Yoshioki was in restoring the Kameyama Hachiman shrine with Korean funds is not clear. He did rethatch the roof of the shrine in 1527, but by 1551, the shrine was repaired by Yoshioki's son Yoshitaka and was described as being "already largely ruined."[167]

[161] Itō Kōji, "Ōuchi shi no potenshiyaru," in Ōuchi shi rekishi bunka kenkyūkai, comp., *Ōuchi shi no sekai o saguru* (Bensei shuppan, 2019), p. 6.

[162] *Sengoku ibun Ōuchi shi hen*, vol. 2, doc. 1361, Winter 1510 (Eishō 7) Ōuchi Yoshioki *shokei utsushi*, p. 138. This document states that Yoshioki oversaw the seven provinces of Iwami, Aki Chikuzen Buzen Suō, and Nagato. In it, his Korean lineage was emphasized, as too was his animosity to the Sō family, Tsushima people and pirates, who were competitors to the Ōuchi.

[163] *Chosŏn wangjo sillok*, vol. 245, 9.28.1490 (Sŏngjong 21) (accessed 12.3.2019), http://sillok.hist ory.go.kr/id/wia_12109128_001.

[164] Yŏnsan'gun banned the trade in metals (*tongch'ŏlmuyŏkchisa* 銅鐵貿易之事) although the rational for this prohibition is not clear and deserves further research. *Chosŏn wangjo sillok*, 12.14.1502 (Yŏnsan'gun 8) (accessed 12.3.2019), http://sillok.history.go.kr/id/wja_10812014_002, and *Chūgoku Chōsen no shiseki ni okeru Nihon shiryō shūsei. Richō jitsuroku no bu*, vol. 5 (Kokusho kankōkai, 1981), twelfth month (J. *jinshi, mizunoene*, Kr. *Imja* 壬子), pp. 1392–93. I am indebted to Soojung Han for this reference.

[165] *Chosŏn wangjo sillok*, and *Chūgoku Chōsen no shiseki ni okeru Nihon shiryō shūsei. Richō jitsuroku no bu*, vol. 5, twelfth month, p. 1392. The Ōuchi were contrasted with the *wakō* pirates who emanated from Tsushima. See p. 1393.

[166] *Sengoku ibun Ōuchi shi hen*, vol. 2, doc. 1219, Ōuchi Yoshioki *shokei utsushi*, 2.10.1506 (Eishō 3), pp. 93–94.

[167] *Hagi han batsu etsu roku*, vol. 4 (Yamaguchi ken monjokan, 1994), "Kameyama Hachimangū," in Bōchō jisha shōmon, p. 46.

In 1506, Yŏnsan'gun was deposed by his half brother Chungjong, and by 1508 trade resumed between Korea and Japan in copper and metals.[168] Relations with the Ōuchi improved during most of Chungjong's reign. Yoshioki imported a copy of the Tripiṭaka from Korea and donated it to the Jūzenji shrine, one of seven upper shrines of the Hie shrine complex, which symbolized the Big Dipper, in 1510.[169] Yoshioki remained deeply involved in tally trade (*kangō bōeki*) with Korea, and his privileges were duly confirmed by the shogun Ashikaga Yoshitane.[170]

Yoshioki frequently threatened to leave the capital, which became an effective strategy for extracting concessions from the Ashikaga. Sue Okifusa, for example, expected that Yoshioki would return to Yamaguchi sometime in 1516.[171] In the end, by delaying his departure, Yoshioki was able to get Ashikaga Yoshitane to recognize his central role in the China trade.[172] In order to ensure its "safe-keeping," Yoshioki gained control of the coveted Ashikaga "King of Japan" trade (*kangō*) seal in 1516, which was essential for trade with the Ryūkyūs and China.[173] By being entrusted with the Ashikaga "King of Japan" seal, Yoshioki could directly manage international trade with China as King of Japan.

Yoshioki could also manage compatriots in Japan and encourage them to act to enhance the China trade. Using Sue Hiroaki as an intermediary, he gained the support of Shimazu Tadatomo (1466–1540), the *shugo* of the southern province of Satsuma, and a key staging point for travel to the Ryūkyūs and China, to build a dock at their harbor at Kagoshima in 1519,

---

[168] *Chūgoku Chōsen no shiseki ni okeru Nihon shiryō shūsei. Richō jitsuroku no bu*, vol. 5, 8[(Chungjong 3) 1508] (J. *hinoene, heishi*, Kr. *Pyŏngcha* 丙子), p. 1418.

[169] *Yamaguchi kenshi shiryōhen chūsei*, vol. 1, Sanetaka kōki, 7.11.1510 (Eishō 7), p. 277 for Yoshioki's gift of a Tripiṭaka to the Jūzenjisha (Juge shrine). The volumes themselves were presumably stored at the Hie shrine temple (Jingūji), which was located, unsurprisingly, next to a Myōken shrine. See the *Hiesha shintō himitsuki, Gunsho ruijū*, vol. 2 *Jingibu* (3rd revised ed., Zoku gunsho ruijū kanseikai, 1983), pp. 99–100 for references to a shrine near Jingūji devoted to Myōken, and p. 122 for a Myōken hermitage (accessed JapanKnowledge, 1.5.2021). For more on star worship and Hie shrine, see Meri Arichi, "Seven Stars of Heaven and Seven Shrines on Earth: The Big Dipper and the Hie Shrine in the Medieval Period," *Culture and Cosmos* 10, no. 1 (2006), pp. 195–216.

[170] *Sengoku ibun Ōuchi shi hen*, vol. 3 (Tōkyōdō shuppan, 2019), doc. 2078, 3.17 Ōuchi Yoshioki *shojō utsushi*, p. 29, and doc. 2265, Ōuchi shi *kashin mōshijō utsushi*, p. 94. The copy of the latter document purportedly dates from 9.11.1514 (Eishō 11), but this cannot be confirmed.

[171] *Sengoku ibun Ōuchi shi hen*, vol. 2, doc. 1517, 10.23 [(Eishō 12) 1515] Sue Okifusa *shojō*, p. 188, and Fujii, *Ōuchi Yoshioki*, p. 124.

[172] *Sengoku ibun Ōuchi shi hen*, vol. 2, doc. 1530, 4.13.1516 (Eishō 13) Ashikaga Yoshitane *gonaisho an*, p. 192, and doc. 1531, 4.19.1516 (Eishō 13) Muromachi bakufu *bugyōnin rensho hōsho an*, p. 192. For how this entailed control over overseas trade, see Hashimoto Yū, "Muromachi sengokuki no shōgun kenryoku to gaikōken," *Rekishigaku kenkyū* 708 (3.1998), pp. 10, 15.

[173] *Ōuchi bunka*, Yūsoku kojitsu, doc. 5, Ise Sadasuke *zakki*, p. 597.

to allow increased shipment of sulfur to China.[174] He also encouraged the Shimazu to build new boats for the trip to China.[175] Kagoshima became a more prominent port, and their ships transported Ōuchi emissaries.[176] Finally, the islanders of Tsushima, long rivals, abandoned the Shōni after the death of their leader Masasuke in 1497. Sō Yoshimori (1476–1521), the leader of the island, decided to ally himself with the Ōuchi instead. The outbreak of the "Disturbance of the Three Ports" (J. *Sanpo no ran* Kr. *Sampo Waeran*) by Tsushima islanders in 1510 caused the Korean king Chungjong to limit exchanges with them in the 1512 Treaty of Imshin (J. *Jinshin*). The island suffered economically and descended into turmoil after Yoshimori's death. The islanders became more dependent on the Ōuchi to facilitate their trade with Korea.[177]

Yoshioki also had links to the Ryūkyū Kingdom and corresponded with a newly enthroned Ryūkyū king late in 1527, explaining that all matters of Ming Japan relations were to be handled by the Ōuchi. Thus, he opened an important avenue of communication with the Ming bypassing Hosokawa and Ashikaga rivals.[178] Yoshioki's control of the King of Japan seal naturally led "people from other lands" to believe "that the Ōuchi were the Kings of Japan."[179]

---

[174] *Sengoku ibun Ōuchi shi hen*, vol. 2, doc. 1635, 10.10 [(Eishō 16) 1519] Ōuchi Yoshioki *shojō utsushi*, p. 232, doc. 1636, 10.10 Sue Hiroaki *soejō utsushi*, p. 232, and docs. 1639–40, 11.4 [(Eishō 16) 1519] Shimazu Tadatomo *shojō utsushi*, pp. 232–33.

[175] *Sengoku ibun Ōuchi shi hen*, vol. 2, doc. 1665, 11.2 [(Eishō 17) 1520] Ōuchi Yoshioki *shojō utsushi*, p. 247, and 1666, 11.2 [(Eishō 17) 1520] Sue Hiroaki *soejō utsushi*, p. 247. For Tadatomo's response, which was delivered to Hiroaki, who served as a messenger, see docs. 1677–78, 2.11 [(Eishō 18) 1521] Shimazu Tadatomo *shojō utsushi*, pp. 251–52. For more on later construction efforts, see doc. 1683, 3.11 [(Eishō 18) 1521] Ōuchi Yoshioki *shojō utsushi*, p. 253, and doc. 1684, 3.11 [(Eishō 18) 1521] Sue Hiroaki *soejō utsushi*, p. 253.

[176] Miyoshi Yukitaka, "Chūsei Kagoshima no minato to Sengoku jōkamachi no keisei," *Shirin* 101.5 (9.2018), p. 96 for Kagoshima as being a strategic harbor for sulfur shipments, and p. 108 for Zen temples in the harbor having an Ōuchi connection. See also Itō Kōji, *Chūsei Nihon no gaikō to zenshū* (Yoshikawa kōbunkan, 2002), pp. 199–200.

[177] Hasegawa Hiroshi, *Ōuchi shi no kōbō to Nishi Nihon shakai* (Yoshikawa kōbunkan, 2020), pp. 31–34. For more on Sō Yoshimori and his allegiances, see JapanKnowledge, *Kokushi daijiten*, and the *Nihonjinmei daijiten*, accessed 1.14.2021.

[178] *Sengoku ibun Ōuchi shi hen*, vol. 2, doc. 1947, 9.11.1527 (Daiei 7) Ōuchi Yoshioki *shojō utsushi*, p. 345. For analysis, Itō Kōji, "Studies of Medieval Ryūkyū within Asia's Maritime Network," *Acta Asiatica* 95 (2008), pp. 87–90, and Hashimoto Yū, *Chūsei Nihon no kokusai kankei—Higashi Ajia tsūkōken to gishi mondai* (Yoshikawa kōbunkan, 2005), pp. 220–27. Gregory Smits, *Maritime Ryūkyū, 1050–1650* (Honolulu: University of Hawaii Press, 2018), pp. 178–92, has characterized the Ryūkyūs of this time as being a maritime empire in the 1520s, but evidence for Ōuchi connections is limited until the rise to power of Sō Morikata in 1528 (see chapter 9).

[179] Kasai Shigesuke, *Nankai tsūki*, 135.

Return to Yamaguchi

Having received his King of Japan seals, Yoshioki prepared to return to Yamaguchi, particularly because control over the resource-rich provinces of Aki and Iwami once again became contested.[180] Ashikaga Yoshitane's limitations were becoming evident to all. For example, he could not oversee the enthronement ceremonies for Emperor Go-Kashiwabara. Even though taxes for this purpose had been levied in 1501, the rites were not performed until 1520.[181]

One of Yoshioki's letters from late in 1517 reveals his resolution to return to Yamaguchi now that central Japan was at peace.[182] He could not easily do so under Yoshitane's watchful eye, but in the absence of the shogun, he felt free to leave. Emperor Go-Kashiwabara, aware of Yoshioki's plans to depart, warned Yoshitane not to take a vacation to the Arimitsu hot springs in the fall of 1517, but the headstrong shogun ignored him, giving Yoshioki the chance to evacuate to Sakai.[183] Ashikaga Yoshitane belatedly sent emissaries such as Ise Sadamichi (1463–1521) to Yoshioki as part of a last-ditch effort to convince him to remain.[184] His departure from Kyoto would also lead to an estrangement with Hosokawa Takakuni.

Yoshioki remained in Sakai for months, ultimately leaving for Yamaguchi on 8.22 1518.[185] After his fleet had sailed, Ashikaga Yoshitane ex post facto gave Yoshioki permission to leave so that he could "rest his horses" before coming back to the capital.[186] That never happened; after 1518, no Ōuchi lord would ever return to Kyoto.

---

[180] Sengoku ibun Ōuchi shi hen, vol. 2, doc.1569, 9.15 [(Eishō 14) 1517] Ōuchi Yoshioki shojō, p. 208 for Yoshioki's letter to the Hiraga where he discussed an uprising by the Takeda. See also doc. 1573, 10.13 [(Eishō 14) 1517] Ōuchi Yoshioki shojō, p. 209. For an overview of the campaign, which continued through 1528, see Kawamura Shō'ichi, Aki Takeda shi (Ebisu kōshō, 2010), pp. 110–22.

[181] Mizuno Tomoyuki, Muromachi jidai Kōbu kankei no kenkyū (Yoshikawa kōbunkan, 2005), p. 247. This caused Hosokawa Takakuni to get upset with Yoshitane as well.

[182] Sengoku ibun Ōuchi shi hen, vol. 2, doc. 1577, 12.26 [(Eishō 14) 1517] Ōuchi Yoshioki shojō utsushi, p. 210. See also doc. 1578, 12.26 Sugi Okinobu soejō utsushi, p. 211.

[183] Yamaguchi kenshi shiryōhen chūsei, vol. 1, Gohōjōji kanpakuki, uru 10.4.1517 (Eishō 14), p. 408, Morimitsu kyōki, uru 10.1.1517 (Eishō 14), Dainihon shiryō, ser. 9, vol. 7 (Tōkyōdō daigaku shuppankai, 1971), p. 208, and Yamada, Ashikaga Yoshitane, p. 191.

[184] Yamaguchi kenshi shiryōhen chūsei, vol. 1, Nobutane kyōki, 1.22.1518 (Eishō 15), p. 362. See also Fujii, Ōuchi Yoshioki, p. 125.

[185] Yamaguchi kenshi shiryōhen chūsei, vol. 1, Genjo daisōjōki, 8.1518 (Eishō 15), p. 395 for his departure in the eighth month. The Kugyō bunin suggests that Yoshioki returned either on 8.2 or 8.22.1518. See Kugyō bunin, vol. 3 (Yoshikawa kōbunkan, 1964), p. 348. The latter date is correct. See Sengoku ibun Ōuchi shi hen, vol. 2, doc. 1595, 8.24 Toida Okiyuki shojō, p. 216 for Yoshioki's 8.22 departure.

[186] Sengoku ibun Ōuchi shi hen, vol. 2, doc. 1596, 8.27 [(Eishō 15) 1518] Ashikaga Yoshitane gonaisho an, p. 216. The document is a copy of the record written to Ōuchi Yoshioki. See also Fujii, Ōuchi Yoshioki, p. 125.

Once Yoshioki returned to Yamaguchi, he tried to make this town a functioning ritual capital. He had yin yang specialists confirm how the city fit the topographical requirements of the four directional deities (*shijin sō-ō*) that, according to traditional Chinese geomancy, were necessary for a capital.[187] Yoshioki changed Yamaguchi in a variety of ways. Sometime during the early sixteenth century, he built a large garden next to his mansion.[188] Likewise, the mortuary temple of Jōfukuji apparently burned down around the year 1520, and the Korean royal roof tiles were replaced at this time with standard tiles in the Japanese mode.[189] Other sources reveal that numerous courtiers chose to live in Yamaguchi (Figure 8.3).[190]

Broad networks allowed for cultural exchanges and creation of ties between Koreans, Chinese, and Kyoto courtiers who congregated in Yamaguchi. For example, the Tōfukuji monk Ryōan Keigo, while waiting with Sanjōnishi Sanetaka's son Keiyō to travel to China, wrote the inscription for Sesshū paintings in Yamaguchi, as too did two Chosŏn emissaries, Pak Hyeongmun and Yi Ye.[191]

Possessing the Ise Gods

Yoshioki attempted to highlight Yamaguchi as a cultic center. Whereas his father Masahiro had sponsored impressive rituals of state to be

---

[187] *Yamaguchi kenshi shiryōhen chūsei*, vol. 3, Kōryūji monjo doc. 242, 11.1521 (Daiei 1) Ōuchi Yoshioki *keihaku utsushi*, pp. 327–28 for reference to Yamaguchi as being hallowed land befitting the four directions (*shijin sō-ō no rei chi nari*). See also *Bōchō fūdo chūshin an*, vol. 13, *Yamaguchi saiban ge* (Yamaguchi, 1961), p. 373.

[188] Wada Shūsaku, "Yamaguchi de kurashita Ashikaga shōgun," in Kishida, ed., *Mōri Motonari to chiiki shakai* (Hiroshima: Chūgoku shinbunsha, 2007), pp. 222–23. It may have been created after Ashikaga Yoshitane first visited Yamaguchi.

[189] For a convenient overview and explanation of how the temple burned during the end of the Eishō era (1504–21) and was later rebuilt, *Ōuchi bunka*, pp. 970–71, and for the dating of the Jōfukuji *garanzu*, an image of the temple, p. 365. See also Kimura Tadao, "Shihon bokuga tansai Jōfukuji garanzu kaisetsu," in *Yamaguchi kenshi shiryōhen chūsei*, vol. 2 *furoku*. Kimura suggests that this image was designed to solicit funds for the rebuilding of the temple between 1520 and 1531. For the archaeological reports, and images of tiles made by Korean specialists, and poor fifteenth-century copies made in Japan, see *Jōfukuji ato*, 3 vols. (Yamaguchi, 2001–4).

[190] *Bōchō fūdo chūshin an*, vol. 12, *Yamaguchi saiban jō* (Yamaguchi, 1960), pp. 16–18, 42.

[191] McCormick, "Genji Goes West," pp. 63–64 for the famous Sesshū landscape image. See also *Muromachi jidai no naka ni miru Ōuchi bunka ihōten* (Yamaguchi, Yamaguchi kenritsu bijutsukan, 1989), plate 47, pp. 42, 148. For a similar landscape, drawn by Korean emissaries, see plate 49, pp. 42, 148. For this insight, I am indebted to Gina Choi. For some analysis of these emissaries, see Sangnam Lee, "Traces of a Lost Landscape Tradition and Cross-Cultural Relationships between Korea, China and Japan in the Joseon Period (1392–1550)," PhD dissertation, University of Kansas, 2014, particularly pp. 190–91, 203.

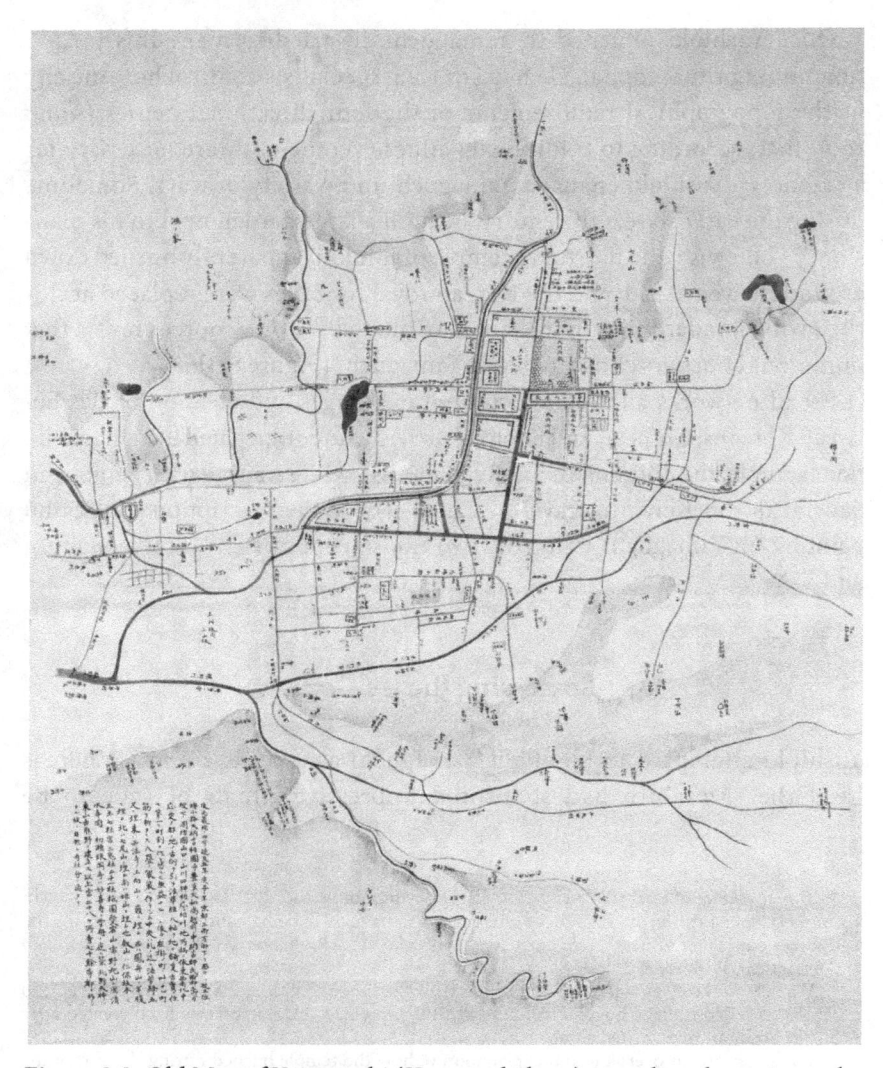

Figure 8.3 Old Map of Yamaguchi (*Yamaguchi kozu*), revealing the main roads and buildings of Yamaguchi during its mid-sixteenth century heyday. Image and permission provided by Yamaguchi monjokan

performed at Yamaguchi, Yoshioki took things further by bringing gods to Yamaguchi itself. He oversaw the transfer of Amaterasu, the sun goddess and progenitor of the imperial line, and Toyo-uke, a deity normally associated with abundance and increase, to Yamaguchi. Toyo-uke had appeal because in medieval period it was also conceived as being linked to Myōken.[192]

The former was housed in the Inner Shrine of Ise, and the latter in the Outer Shrine. Thanks to the goodwill of the court, and in particular the support of the Yoshida, this request was granted and Yoshioki was able to build the Inner and Outer Ise Shrines at a place in Yamaguchi called Kōnomine. Yoshioki was able to request the transfer of the gods right before he departed from Sakai.[193] Doing this was a uniquely powerful form of legitimation for Yoshioki and aligned Japan's most prominent deity with his family.[194] Highlighting this, decorations for the shrines included crests where delicate tendrils intertwined with the Ōuchi *hishi* crest (Figure 8.4).[195]

No other lord could have succeeded in moving the most important gods of Japan, nor could Yoshioki have done so without the aid of the Yoshida and the court. Although the Yoshida worshiped the Ise deities along with all the other gods of Japan at their Saijōsho Daigengū, these new Ise shrines at Kōnomine constituted the only imperially sanctioned sites (Daijingū) that solely housed Amaterasu and Toyo-uke. In Ise, by contrast, both shrines were never rebuilt between 1486 and 1585, although Yoshioki's sometimes ally Hosokawa Takakuni built provisional shrines there in 1521.[196] The ability to

---

[192] Toyo-uke's role as a deity of food and fecundity is widely known; its association with the stars is less known, but it would have been so understood in medieval times. Mark Teeuwen recounts links to Myōken as well as the "Ritual manual of Amaterasu," which dates from the Heian period and links Buddhist North Star rites (*hokuto hō* and Northern Dipper *sonjōō hō*) to these shrines in his "The Creation of a Honji Suijaku Deity: Amaterasu as the Judge of the Dead," in *Buddhas and Kami in Japan: Honji Suijaku as Combinatory Paradigm* (New York: Routledge, 2003), and "The Imperial Shrines of Ise: An Ancient Star Cult?," in "The Worship of Stars in Japanese Religious Practice," *Cultural and Cosmos* 10.1–2 (2006), pp. 91–92. Yoshino Hiroko, to the contrary, argues that the Pole Star is linked to the Inner Shrine and the Outer Shrine was linked to the Big Dipper. See her *Tennō no matsuri* (Kōdansha, 2000). Teeuwen is skeptical of Yoshino's assertion of Amaterasu as being the Pole Star but believes that the identification of the Outer Shrine with the North Star "was not conjured up out of thin air, but actually did have some ancient precedent." See Teeuwen, "Imperial Shrines of Ise," p. 92. For more analysis of ritual links of the Outer Shrine and the North Star see Yamamoto, "Kokoro no mihashira to chūseiteki sekai," *Shunjū*, nos. 302–39 (10.1988–6.1992), *Chūsei shinwa* (Iwanami shoten, 1998), pp. 53–55, and *Ishin Chūsei Nihon no hikyōteki sekai* (Heibonsha, 1998). Bernard Faure, *The Fluid Pantheon: Gods of Medieval Japan*, vol. 1 (Honolulu: University of Hawaii Press, 2016), pp. 101, 349, posits a link to the star Taiyi, part of the Big Dipper.

[193] *Yamaguchi kenshi shiryōhen chūsei*, vol. 2, Yamaguchi Daijingū monjo, doc. 14, 12.26.1551 (Tenbun 20) Sue shi *bugyō rensho hōsho*, pp. 916–17 for reference to how Yoshioki dispatched Matsuda Sadashige to request the movement of the gods on 10.5.1518 (Eishō 15). The gods nevertheless remained in Ise as well, although there they were only worshiped in provisional structures.

[194] For this observation, and other insights, I am indebted to Jacqueline Stone.

[195] For a convenient depiction, see *Ōuchi shi yakata ato*, vol. 15 (Yamaguchi, 2014), p. 238.

[196] The Outer and Inner Shrines were destroyed at Ise in 1486–87. The Outer Shrine was not rebuilt until 1563, and the Inner Shrine was not restored until 1585. Shortly after the new structures were consecrated in Yamaguchi, Hosokawa Takakuni paid to have a provisional structure rebuilt at Ise. Fukuyama Toshio, *Jinja kenchiku no kenkyū* (Chūō kōron bijutsu shuppan, 1984), p. 92. For a recent

Figure 8.4 The Ōuchi Crest and Decoration for the Kōnomine (Ise) Shrines. Image based on an illustration from *Yamaguchi shishi shiryōhen Ōuchi bunka.* p. 884

transfer Amaterasu and Toyo-uke further strengthened Yoshida power vis-à-vis the Ise shrine attendants and made the Yoshida the ultimate arbiter of all shrine affairs.

At the same time, by sanctioning this move, the Yoshida undercut the importance of their Saijōsho Daigengū, which served as a structure for the various gods whose shrines had been destroyed during the Ōnin War.[197] The continued destruction of Kyoto in the aftermath of Ōnin led the Yoshida, with the support of Emperor Go-Kashiwabara, to sanction the movement of the Ise gods to Yamaguchi. This precedent justified later transfers to Yamaguchi and explains too why the Yoshida would later spend so much time there.[198]

---

excellent study of Ise, see David Romney, "Godly Politics: Ise, the Court, and Japanese Religion 1330–1615," PhD dissertation, Princeton University, 2023.

[197] Thomas D. Conlan, "When Men Become Gods: Apotheosis, Sacred Space, and Political Authority in Japan 1486–1599," *Quaestiones Medii Aevi Novae*, no. 21 (2016), pp. 89–106.

[198] The loss of most sources documenting this transfer has caused this process to receive less attention than it deserves.

The process of transferring gods in 1518 proved more significant than the ordinary process of enshrining deities in branch shrines, such as when Hachiman was "moved" from Usa to Iwashimizu (see "Turmoil in Iwami and Aki" below). Here the transfer, the only time that it was sanctioned, meant that for Emperor Go-Kashiwabara, the Yoshida, and their allies, their main site of worship had moved to Yamaguchi. This was where the gods Amaterasu and Toyo-uke were officially housed and worshiped. After their move, the gods were thought to have retained at least a residual presence in Ise, as temporary structures were built for them, but the provisional Ise shrines there, in contrast to those in Yamaguchi, did not ritually function as crucial cultic sites, to be rebuilt every twenty years, that were directly linked to court rites.

The movement of the Ise shrines was for peace in the realm (*kokka anzen*) and for the sake of lasting victory (*buun chōkyū*).[199] The rationale was not merely to bolster Yoshioki's rule, as indicated by the fact that Emperor Go-Kashiwabara inscribed the name plaque (*hengaku*) of the Kōnomine shrine "Kōnomine Daijingū," a sign of his support for the endeavor.[200] In addition, following the construction of the Kōnomine shrines dedicated to Amaterasu and Toyo-uke, Kadenokōji Ariyasu, a courtier and yin yang specialist of the Kamo lineage, wrote the report (*kanmon*) sanctifying the construction of a Gion shrine to a new location in Yamaguchi.[201]

No court or Yoshida records survive that describe the move, but the *Kōnomine Daijingū onchinza denki an*, a narrative written in 1520 by Hironaka Takenaga, the administrator (*sōbugyō*) in charge of the move of the Ise deities, remains.[202] The document, as well as the catalog of yearly rituals, was made into a scroll that was stored in the second floor of the Ōuchi lord's dwelling (*denchū*).[203] Those records were lost in

[199] *Sengoku ibun Ōuchi shi hen*, vol. 2, doc. 1657, 6.1520 (Eishō 17) Kōnomine Daijingū *chinza denki an*, p. 242.

[200] *Bōchō fūdo chūshin an*, vol. 13, p. 40 for a tracing of the no longer extant name plaque. For reference to Go-Yōzei's document referring to it as "Ise," see Yamaguchi shishi hensan iinkai, comp., *Yamaguchi shishi* (Yamaguchi, 1982), p. 168, and the *Yamaguchi Daijingūshi*, http://www.yamaguchi-daijingu.or.jp/history/. Go-Tsuchimikado, who supported Norihiro's apotheosis, likewise wrote name plaques for Kōryūji in 1486. See chapter 7, note 161.

[201] *Sengoku ibun Ōuchi shi hen*, vol. 2, doc. 1657, 6.1520 (Eishō 17) Kōnomine Daijingū *chinza denki an*, p. 243. Ariyasu was a high-ranking courtier, of the junior third rank, descended from the Kamo family.

[202] Takahashi Fumio, *Zoku Yamaguchi ken chimeikō* (Yamaguchi: Yamaguchi ken chimei kenkyūjo, 1979), p. 159, suggests that although this source is reliable, some street names were written in error. For a recent reconstruction of the places mentioned in this source, see *Yamaguchi kenshi tsūshihen chūsei*, pp. 845–46.

[203] *Sengoku ibun Ōuchi shi hen*, vol. 2, doc. 1657, 6.1520 (Eishō 17) Kōnomine Daijingū *onchinza denki an*, p. 244. For a brief overview of the Ōuchi archives, see Wada Shūsaku, "Yamaguchi denchū

1551, but a second copy, written and signed by Takenaga, was preserved elsewhere.[204]

On 4.26.1520, the head of the Yoshida, who would have been Yoshida Kanetomo's grandson Kanemitsu, helped to transmit the *kami* Amaterasu and Toyo-uke to Yamaguchi.[205] Nitō Mitsusada, who was affiliated with the Outer Shrine, but not a descendant of one of the major shrine families, and who hailed from the Yōda region of Ise, participated in these ceremonies as well.[206]

The Hironaka Takenaga document recounts that Yoshioki had long wished for the transfer (*sento*) of the shrines. The site for the shrine complex was determined on 10.26, and slightly over a year later, on 11.4.1519, the Outer Shrine was completed. Construction for the Inner Shrine started on 2.26.1520, and it was finished on 4.8.1520. Tellingly, these "Ise" shrines were built in the style of Yoshida shrine structures, for both were to have thatched roofs, which is consistent with Yoshida practice, but not typical for Ise itself.[207]

Transforming Yamaguchi and the Ōuchi Realm

This construction altered the urban geography of Yamaguchi. Around this time, Gion shrine, which was initially located near Kōshakuji, the mortuary temple for Yoshihiro, was moved, as the area was "defiled" due to the

---

bunko," in Kishida Hiroshi, ed., *Mōri Motonari to chiiki shakai* (Hiroshima: Chūgoku shinbunsha, 2007), pp. 220–21, and his "Ōuchi shi no monjo kanri ni tsuite," *Yamaguchi monjokan kenkyū kiyō* no. 37 (3.2010), pp. 69–83. Most of the documents stored were poems, works of literature, or artifacts relating to religion, like this record.

[204] *Sengoku ibun Ōuchi shi hen*, vol. 2, doc. 1657, 6.1520 (Eishō 17) Kōnomine Daijingū *onchinza denki an*. See also *Ōuchi bunka*, pp. 340–45 for the document, its reliability, and designation as a municipal cultural treasure.

[205] The person involved would have been Yoshida Kanemitsu (1485–1528), the grandson of Kanetomo, who fled the capital in disgrace on 3.18.1525 (Daiei 5). For an overview of his life, see Okuno, *Sengokujidai no kyūtei seikatsu* (2004), p. 318. See also *Sengoku ibun Ōuchi shi hen*, vol. 2, doc. 1657, 6.1520 (Eishō 17) Kōnomine Daijingū *chinza denki* an, p. 242, and, for his flight, *Shiryō shūran* vol. 9, maki 909, p. 469 (accessed 6.12.2020), https://clioimg.hi.u-tokyo.ac.jp/viewer/view/idata/T38/1525/11-4-2/2/0012?m=all&s=0012. For a useful overview of the Yamaguchi shrine, see Hagiwara Tatsuo, *Chūsei Saishi soshiki no kenkyū* (Yoshikawa kobunkan, 1975), p. 68.

[206] Era Hiroshi explained in his Beppu University thesis, "Ise oshi to Usa no miya," *Ōita ken chihōshi* 130 (6.1988), p. 3, how Mitsusada can be traced in sources from 1495 through 1522. For Yōda's tensions with the Ise shrines, I am indebted to David Romney, discussion 3.2019.

[207] *Sengoku ibun Ōuchi shi hen*, vol. 2, doc. 1657, 6.1520 (Eishō 17) Kōnomine Daijingū *chinza denki an*, p. 241. Maki Takayuki, personal conversation 6.2016, believes that the shrine was in the style of the Yoshida Ise shrines.

increasing numbers of residences in the area. On 4.12.1520, the old Gion shrine in Yamaguchi, dating from the time of Ōuchi Hiroyo (1325–80), was torn down and rebuilt near the newly completed Kōnomine Ise shrines in the sixth month of 1520.[208]

The sums involved in the creation of the Kōnomine Ise shrines were considerable. Yoshioki can be documented as spending 556 *kanmon*, 804 *mon*, an amount that surpassed the 500 *kanmon* that Hosokawa Takakuni provided in 1521 to build a temporary shrine for the neglected deities in Ise.[209]

The rebuilding of Yamaguchi served to carefully delineate sacred spaces from residences, with the Ōuchi dwelling now located near Tsukiyama, a temple where Yoshioki's grandfather Norihiro was enshrined as a protector deity. Likewise, Gion, located nearby, served to purify the town and give cohesiveness to its wards.[210] Gion festival floats (*yamaboko*) circulated throughout Yamaguchi, and crane dances, ancillary rites for the Gion festival, were performed in Yamaguchi, but not Kyoto.[211]

The movement of shrines away from inhabited areas, and the concentration of religious sites, seems to have been a response to the expanding size and population of the city.[212] The Kōnomine Ise shrines are located about a mile to the west of the main Ōuchi mansion. The *Denzaki* states that the house gods of the Ōuchi were moved to Kōnomine Ise. There they coexisted with the most powerful gods of Japan.[213] According to Maki Takayuki, the

---

[208] This was drawn from *Sengoku ibun Ōuchi shi hen*, vol. 2, doc. 1657, 6.1520 (Eishō 17) Kōnomine Daijingū *chinza denki an*, pp. 239–45. For more on the movement, dating, and structure of the Yasaka (Gion) shrine, see *Ōuchi bunka*, pp. 650–51.

[209] *Sengoku ibun Ōuchi shi hen*, vol. 2, doc. 1657, 6.1520 (Eishō 17) Kōnomine Daijingū *chinza denki an*, pp. 239–45. For Takakuni funds, see Fukuyama Toshio, *Jinja kenchiku no kenkyū*, p. 92.

[210] The importance of this urbanization and the creation of wards is explained by Mary Elizabeth Berry, *The Culture of Civil War in Kyoto* (Berkeley: University of California Press, 1994).

[211] See *Yamaguchi ken shitei mukei minzoku bunkazai Sagi no mai* (Yamaguchi, 1981), for more on the heron dances, and the *yamaboko*, which survived into the early twentieth century. For references to Gion and crowds of bystanders climbing walls to view the festival, *Sengoku ibun Ōuchi shi hen*, vol. 1, doc. 735 6.1492 (Entoku 4), Ōuchi shi *hekisho utsushi*, p. 240; for the floats (*yamaboko*) *Sengoku ibun Ōuchi shi hen*, vol. 2, doc. 1657, 6.1520 (Eishō 17) Kōnomine Daijingū *chinza denki an*, p. 243, and *Bōchō fūdo chūshin an*, vol. 13, pp. 49–53ff. For evidence of the rebuilding of the Yamaguchi Gion shrine, see *Sengoku ibun Ōuchi shi hen*, vol. 2, doc. 1652, 6.13.1520 (Eishō 17), Yamaguchi Gionsha *munafuda mei utsushi*, pp. 237–38, and *Yamaguchi kenshi tsūshihen chūsei*, pp. 845–47.

[212] Mashino Shinji, "Chūsei no Yamaguchi," in Kage Toshio, ed., *Ōuchi to Ōtomo* (Bensei shuppan, 2013), pp. 277–79. For detailed geographic analysis, see Machinaka daigaku jikō iinkai Ōuchi bunka kaidō machinami kyōgikai, comp., *Chizu no nenpyō de tadoru Ōdono kaiwai* (Yamaguchi, 3.2018).

[213] Kan Takako, "Sengokuki Yamaguchi jōka ni okeru jōkan to yashiki kami," *Yamaguchi ken chihōshi kenkyū*, no. 74 (10.1995), p. 4, and Koga Nobuyuki, "Suō no kuni Yamaguchi no sengokuki shugosho," in Niki Hiroshi et al., eds., *Shugosho to Sengoku jōkamachi* (Takashi shoin, 2006), pp. 381–82. For the source for this movement, see *Sengoku ibun Ōuchi shi hen*, vol. 2, doc. 1657, 6.1520 (Eishō 17) Kōnomine Daijingū *chinza denki an*, p. 244. This period coincided with an expansion of Yoshioki's residence.

Ōuchi could have directly seen the shrine at dawn from their residence,[214] and this blurring of house gods with Ise could lead to a fusing of these mighty gods as protectors of the Ōuchi house as well. Thus, Ōuchi possessiveness of deities, first evident with Moriakira's control of Usa shrine in the early fifteenth century, lived on in the sixteenth. Yoshioki surpassed Moriakira, for he had succeeded in privatizing, or possessing, even the divine imperial ancestor *kami*.

Rites at the Kōnomine Ise shrines were held thrice each month, and in addition provisional levies and other rites associated with the shrine occurred.[215] The audience for these rites was not, however, limited to the populace at Yamaguchi. Yoshioki stipulated that everyone in Nagato, Suō, Buzen, and Chikuzen was to be notified of them as well.[216] At Kōnomine Ise, the same protocols adopted at Ise regarding the limitation of Buddhism were adopted. Monks or people who had renounced the world were prohibited from worshiping there, although scholars note that this does not represent an attempt to establish the primacy of Shinto over Buddhism per se.[217]

Yoshioki continued to patronize Buddhist institutions and constructed what would later become his mortuary temple. Called Ryōunji, it was built slightly under two miles to the west of the Kōnomine Ise shrines and overlooked the crucial route leading to the copper mines of Naganobori and to the ports of Senzaki and Hijū.[218] The walls are extremely well made of fitted granite stones, a more laborious process than cutting stones as would be typical for the castles of the latter sixteenth century.[219] The temple represents an

---

[214] Conversation Maki Takayuki, 6.7.2018.

[215] *Sengoku ibun Ōuchi shi hen*, vol. 2, doc. 1657, 6.1520 (Eishō 17) Kōnomine Daijingū *chinza denki an*, p. 244.

[216] *Sengoku ibun Ōuchi shi hen*, vol. 2, doc. 1657, 6.1520 (Eishō 17) Kōnomine Daijingū *chinza denki an*, p. 244.

[217] They could only come as far as a large rock (*tatsu ishi*) midway up the stairs to the shrine. *Sengoku ibun Ōuchi shi hen*, vol. 2, doc. 1657, 6.1520 (Eishō 17) Kōnomine Daijingū *chinza denki an*, p. 244. That boulder remains. For Ise and Buddhist prohibitions, see Kuroda Toshio, "Discourse on the 'Land of Kami' (Shinkoku) in Medieval Japan," *Japanese Journal of Religious Studies* 23.3–4 (1996), pp. 366–71, and Anna Andreeva, *Assembling Shinto: Buddhist Approaches to Kami Worship in Medieval Japan* (Cambridge, MA: Harvard University Asian Center, 2017), pp. 29, 31–32, 179. I am indebted to Jacqueline Stone for these references. Finally, for the temple Hōrakuji, built in the fourteenth century, which overlooked the Ise shrines, see Conlan, *From Sovereign to Symbol: An Age of Ritual Determinism in Fourteenth-Century Japan* (New York: Oxford University Press, 2011), pp. 108, 172.

[218] Ōuchi Yoshitaka fled on this route after the 1551 coup. Yamaguchi kyōiku iinkai, comp., *Yamaguchi shi maizō bunkazai chōsha hōkokusho*, no. 121, *Ryōunji ato*, vol. 2 (Yamaguchi: Yamaguchi kyōiku iinkai, 2019), pp. 206–8.

[219] For the best overview, with recent archaeological data, showing that the site was only used during the first half of the sixteenth century, see Yamaguchi kyōiku iinkai, comp., *Yamaguchi shi maizō bunkazai chōsha hōkokusho*, no. 115, *Ryōunji ato*, vol. 1 (Yamaguchi: Yamaguchi kyōiku iinkai, 2015).

Figure 8.5 The Walls of Ryōunji are a rare early sixteenth-century example of stone walls. In contrast to later practice, where stones were cut, these walls were made by the more time-consuming process of fitting uncut granite stones, drawn from a nearby stream, and filling the gaps with schist. Photograph by Thomas Conlan

early example of a lord having roof tiles created with his familial crest on it, which is something that the Ōuchi did throughout their realm, including the city of Hakata.[220] Its main hall was large and impressive enough to match the main hall (Kondō) of a major temple. This very structure may, in fact, have been transported to Miidera near Kyoto, in the year 1599 (see the epilogue) (Figure 8.5).[221]

---

[220] *Ryōunji ato*, vol. 2, pp. 62, 224–33 for the roof tiles. They have been discovered in Hakata as well. See Koga Nobuyuki, "Ōuchi shi to Hakata," in *Chūsei toshi Hakata o horu* (Fukuoka, Kaichōsha, 2008), pp. 61–64, and for the imposing nature of the structure that was decorated with these tiles, see *Ryōunji ato*, vol. 2, plate 7. These tiles were discovered with other pottery and roof tiles in the Yamaguchi style, amply demonstrating an Ōuchi connection, and they likewise are in the same style of those of the temple of Ryōunji. For this I am grateful to the insights provided by Kitajima Daisuke, 7.6.2022.

[221] *Ryōunji ato*, vol. 2, p. 230. For this assertion regarding Miidera, see Kinoshita Meiki, *Zusetsu Yamaguchi Hōfu no rekishi* (Yamaguchi: Kyōdo shuppansha, 2005), pp. 96–97. The possibility of the transfer of this temple from Yamauguchi is not mentioned in the most recent report concerning this temple. See Shiga ken kyōiku iinkai, comp., *Kokuhō Onjōji Kondō hozon shūri kōji hōkokusho* (Shiga, 2009).

Figure 8.6 Shakadō of Kōryūji, Yamaguchi. Built in 1521, and located at Hikamisan, it was later moved to the site of the Ōuchi mansion after that building was destroyed in 1551. It was then renamed as Ryūfukuji. Photograph by Thomas Conlan

It is not the only structure created by Yoshioki, as a Shakadō for Kōryūji, was built in 1521. With its *irimoya* hip-and-gabled cedar bark roofing, it represents a typical example of the graceful, simple, Ōuchi architecture (Figure 8.6).

Yoshioki's sudden interest in Ise did not cause Myōken worship to diminish in fervor. Yoshioki relied on oaths to Myōken to bolster important alliances with families such as the Masuda.[222] These vows emphasize the majesty of Hikamisan Myōken and Hachiman bodhisattva and suggest that both watched over the signatories.[223] The Ise shrines also were linked to North Star rites. Rituals associated with the Outer Shrine of Ise, dedicated to Toyo-uke, a god who provided food to Amaterasu, were ritually linked to the North Star, while its iconography shows the cart-like representation of the

---

[222] *Sengoku ibun Ōuchi shi hen*, vol. 1, doc. 938, 10.27 [(Meiō 5) 1496] Ōuchi Yoshioki *shojō*, p. 304.
[223] *Sengoku ibun Ōuchi shi hen*, vol. 1, doc. 775, 10.16 [(Meiō 3) 1494] Sugi Takeaki *shojō an*, p. 253.

Big Dipper constellation.[224] Yoshioki thus enhanced his North Star worship, and the centrality of Yamaguchi, by adding the Outer Shrine, with ritual links to Myōken worship.

Yoshioki also patronized gods of the seas. A battle flag survives from his time (Figure 8.7), listing the names of five deities. Amaterasu, the Sun Goddess, linked to the Inner Ise shrine, appears centrally. The other deities listed on this flag included Kōryūji's Myōken bodhisattva followed by Usa Hachiman, the Kyushu shrine located directly south of Kōryūji across the Inland Sea. To the west, Sumiyoshi, of Nagato, was mentioned, and Shika Umi shrine, located near Hakata, which the Ōuchi had controlled since 1480, was included as well.[225] The shrines, the most important sites during Yoshioki's age, possess an interesting feature, for when mapped out, the sea itself appears as center of the Ōuchi domain. It is the midpoint between Yamaguchi and Usa, and the best way to link Shika Umi shrine in the west. The flag, in other words, represents a geographic mandala of major shrines, linking the scattered Ōuchi holdings and highlighting their dominion of the seas. (See Figures I.1 and I.2, maps of major cities and shrines.)

Turmoil in Iwami and Aki

Yoshioki's ability to make Yamaguchi a political, ritual, and cultic center, and his great wealth, did not mean that he would spend his last years in peace. Much of this stemmed from the fact that during these final years, the mines near Nima witnessed a vast increase in silver production. Yoshioki was rich beyond imagining, but such wealth attracted rivals.

Yoshioki secured the post of *shugo* of Iwami in 1517 and attempted to expand his influence from the central district of Nima, long controlled by the Ōuchi, to all the province.[226] Shortly after his appointment as *shugo*, Yoshioki attempted to bolster his authority and founded an Iwami Hachiman shrine in Nima. In this case, he had the Iwashimizu Hachiman *kami*, located near

[224] Yoshino Hiroko, *Kakusareta kamigami: kodai shinkō to inyō gogyō* (Jinbun shoin, 1992), pp. 120–51; Bernard Frank, *Nihon bukkyō mandala* (Fujiwara shoten, 2002) p. 194; Yamamoto Hiroko, *Chūsei shinwa*, pp. 146–48; and Faure, *The Fluid Pantheon*, p. 101 for how the star Taiyi, which was linked with Myōken (p. 94), was also associated with Toyo-uke of the Outer Shrine.

[225] For the battle flag, see *Ōuchi bunka*, plate 33 and pp. 839–40. Masahiro exercised authority over the shrine from 1480. *Sengoku ibun Ōuchi shi hen*, vol. 1, doc. 490, 7.25.1480 (Bunmei 12) Ōuchi Masahiro *kinzei*, p. 148. For Yoshioki's earliest offerings at Shika Umi, see *Sengoku ibun Ōuchi shi hen*, vol. 2, doc. 955, 3.28.1497 (Meiō 6) Ōuchi Yoshioki *kishinjō*, p. 5.

[226] Fukuo Takeichirō, *Ōuchi Yoshitaka* (Yoshikawa kōbunkan, 1959), p. 23.

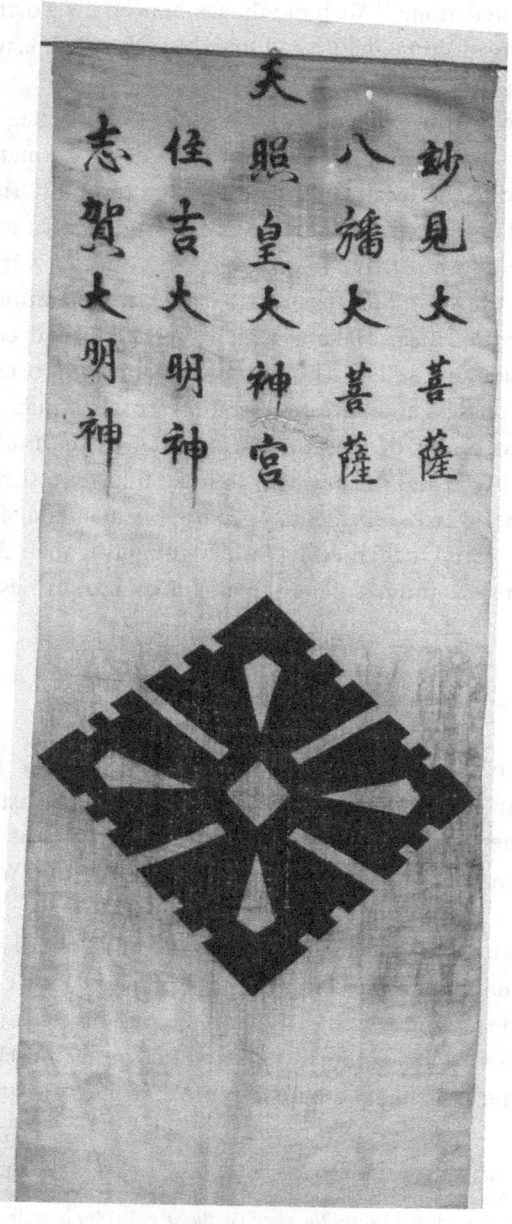

Figure 8.7 The Battle Flag of Ōuchi Yoshioki (*Ōuchi shi gunki*). Possession of Yamaguchi-shi Toyosaka shrine. The deities listed are: Shikaumi (Chikuzen province), Sumiyoshi (Nagato province), Hachiman (Usa in Buzen and Ima Hachiman in Yamaguchi), Myōken (Hikamisan in Yamaguchi) and Amaterasu (Kōnomine shrine, Yamaguchi). Permission by Toyosaka shrine. Image provided by Yamaguchi-shi kyōiku iinkai

Kyoto, installed in this new Iwami Hachiman shrine for "peace in the realm and tranquility throughout the state" (*tenka taihei kokka annei*). This act made Iwami Hachiman a branch shrine of Iwashimizu Hachiman, which was described in the document as being the "main shrine" (*honsha*). This was a different and more typical process than the movement of the Ise gods that Yoshioki supervised in 1518.[227]

This Hachiman could be considered a sea deity, one thought to be able to ensure the safe shipment of silver. Yoshioki also needed the help of all the deities because his great-great-grandfather Ōuchi Hiroyo (1325–80) had largely made Iwami ungovernable by his delegation of *shugo* authority. Compounding these difficulties, the Yamana, the deposed *shugo* of Iwami, now opposed Yoshioki.[228]

These problems first came to a head in nearby Aki province, where the Takeda, *shugo* of Aki, attempted to seize the port of Tōsai.[229] In 1522 Yoshioki dispatched the battle-hardened Sue Okifusa to Aki, where he occupied Niho castle, on the eastern portion of the larger Hiroshima harbor, and guarded it, with members of his forces capturing enemy ships.[230] In 1523, the vital castle of Kagamiyama, guarding Tōsai from the north, fell to the Takeda, thereby forcing Yoshioki and his son Yoshitaka to leave Yamaguchi for Aki in 1524.[231]

[227] *Shimotsuki* (11).3.1517 (Eishō 14) [Ōuchi [Yoshioki] Hachimangū *shinkenritsu* [*munafuda*] transcribed in *Iwami ginzan iseki sōgō chōsa hōkokusho*, vol. 6 (Shimane ken kyōiku iinkai, 1999), Iwami Hachimangū (*munafuda*) no. 1, p. 84. Yoshioki founded this shrine after his appointment as *shugo* of Iwami. See p. 81. Nakano Yoshifumi, personal conversation, argues that this founding commemorated this appointment. See also *Iwami ginzan kaidō: Tomogaura, Yunotsu, Okinohamadō chōsa hōkokusho* (Shimane ken kyōiku iinkai, 2004), p. 144; *Iwami ginzan kaidō: Tomogaura, Okinohama shūraku chōsa hōkokusho* (Shimane kyōiku iinkai, 2005); and "Iwami jōseki: tenzen no yōgai ni kyoten kizuku," *Online News Sanin Chūō Shinpō*, 2.7.2006 (accessed 4.23.2019), https://www.sanin-chuo.co.jp/www/contents/1493222555197/index.html.

[228] Saeki Noriya, *Izumo no chūsei: chiiki to kokka no hazama* (Yoshikawa kōbunkan, 2017), p. 249.

[229] For more on Yoshioki's failed efforts through marriage politics to ally with the Takeda, see Tōkyō daigaku shiryōhen sanjo, comp., *Mōri ke monjo*, vol. 1 (Tōkyō daigaku shuppankai, 1920), doc. 251, Mōri Motonari *chigyō chūmon an*, pp. 222–26, p. 222. The Takeda also allied with the Amako, deputy *shugo* of the province of Izumo. See Fujii, *Ōuchi Yoshioki*, pp. 136–37.

[230] *Sengoku ibun Ōuchi shi hen*, vol. 2, doc. 1710, 3.29 [(Daiei 2) 1522] Ōuchi shi *kashin rensho hōsho*, p. 264 for the capture of an enemy boat. See also doc. 1711, Ōuchi shi *kashin rensho hōsho*, p. 265; doc. 1730, 9.23.1522 (Daiei 2) Ōuchi Yoshioki *kanjō*, p. 272 for guard duty at Nihoshima; and doc. 1744, *urū* 3.20 [(Daiei 3) 1523] Sue Okifusa *shojō utsushi*, pp. 275–76.

[231] *Sengoku ibun Ōuchi shi hen*, vol. 2, p. 3, provides an excellent overview. For the most comprehensive narrative see Kawamura Shō'ichi, *Aki Takeda shi*, pp. 113–22. For a convenient transcription of the *Fusaaki oboegaki*, a crucial source for this narrative, written in the late sixteenth century, see *Ōuchi bunka*, pp. 222–30.

The Ningbo Incident

While Yoshioki was fighting in Aki, tensions increased between him and Hosokawa Takakuni. Yoshioki's unfettered use of "King of Japan" tallies on his missions caused a conflict between him and Takakuni, who tried to use the old Ashikaga tallies for trade.[232]

This competition culminated in a clash in 1523 at the Ming port of Ningbo, located near modern-day Shanghai. Yoshioki's delegation, led by Kendō Sōsetsu, had the most recent tallies of the Zhengde emperor (1491–1521, r. 1505–21), while the Hosokawa, led by Rankō Zuisa, had the badly out of date tallies of the previous Honzhi emperor (1470–1505, r. 1487–1505). Despite having the old tallies, the Hosokawa were given preferential treatment. The outraged Kendō Sōsetsu killed Rankō Zuisa, burned his ships, kidnapped Ming commanders, and plundered Ningbo. As Kendō Sōsetsu's fleet set out to return to Japan, they encountered and defeated a Ming naval force. The only damages suffered by the Ōuchi fleet were the capture of one disabled ship, with the execution of thirty of its crew by Chosŏn officials, who sided with their Ming allies over the Ōuchi.[233] With that, these official exchanges with China would cease for the next seventeen years. This incident represents the last attempt by the Ashikaga and the Hosokawa to engage in this tally trade, which the Ōuchi would resume and monopolize in 1540 and 1549.

Last Battles

During the last years of his life, Yoshioki directed campaigns from the Tōsai region of Aki. He maintained control of the Inland Sea, mobilizing important *kaizoku* privateers, such as Murakami Takakatsu (d. 1532?) of the Noshima Murakami, and relying on ships so large that they had five sails.[234] Takakatsu operated under Yoshioki's command, taking an enemy castle at Kokubunyama in Shikoku, in 1527, for which he received praise and

---

[232] Hashimoto Yū, "Muromachi sengokuki no shōgun kenryoku to gaikōken," pp. 10, 15.

[233] The best overview of this incident remains Kobata Atsushi, *Chūsei Nisshi tsūkō bōekishi no kenkyū* (Tōkō shoin, 1941), pp. 134–46.

[234] *Sengoku ibun Ōuchi shi hen*, vol. 2, doc. 1759, 9.17.1523 (Daiei 3) Ōuchi shi *kashin rensho hōsho*, p. 279 for the capture of some boats and doc. 1825, 3.23.1525 (Daiei 5) Kutsunoya Katsunori *gunchūjō utsushi*, p. 305 for Yoshioki supporters boasting about sailing against enemies in ships with five sails.

confirmation of his chieftainship of the Murakami family over its Kurushima and Innoshima branches.[235] In 1527, battles extended all the way to Bingo, located to the northeast of the areas being fought over in Aki, as Yoshioki tried to block the Amako, a rising power in Izumo, from aiding the Takeda, *shugo* of Aki.[236]

Yoshioki industriously recommended followers for promotion, commissioned prayers while at camp, granted rewards via *kudashibumi* edicts, and communicated with the Shimazu during the eighth and ninth months of 1528. The last of his documents date from 9.15.1528.[237] Shortly thereafter, in his fifty-third year, Yoshioki became seriously ill. He was close to annihilating the Takeda of Aki, but his illness interrupted the campaign. He returned to Yamaguchi, where he died on 12.20, bringing an eventful life to a close.[238] He left unfinished tasks, such as the final pacification of Aki, to his son Yoshitaka.[239] But during the decades of his stewardship, he oversaw prosperity and urban development in Yamaguchi, linked to Kyoto and continental Asia, and made the Ōuchi kings in all but name.

---

[235] *Sengoku ibun Ōuchi shi hen*, vol. 2, doc. 1976, 11.29 [(Daiei 7) 1527] Ōuchi Yoshioki *shojō*, p. 354, and for a more detailed explanation of this letter, https://komonjo.princeton.edu/kono_ouchi/.

[236] For fighting in Bingo, see *Sengoku ibun Ōuchi shi hen*, vol. 2, docs. 1932, 1936, and 1938, dating the 8.5, 8.13, and 8.18 [(Daiei 7) 1527] Ōuchi Yoshioki *shojō utsushi*, pp. 340–42. The link between these battles and the road linking Aki Iwami is evident in the informative doc. 1946, 9.10.1527 (Daei 7) Ōuchi Yoshioki *kanjō utsushi*, p. 345. Something of this conflict can be ascertained in docs. 1972–73 of 11.27–28.1527 (Daiei 7), pp. 352–53.

[237] *Sengoku ibun Ōuchi shi hen*, vol. 3, docs. 2015–19, pp. 11–12 for these last prayers, letters, commendations, and edicts, which all date from 8.1528. For his last letter, see doc. 2021, 9.15 [(Daiei 8) 1528], Ōuchi Yoshioki *shojō*, p. 12.

[238] Kondō Kiyoshi, *Ōuchi shi jitsuroku* (Yamaguchi, 1885, 3rd reprint ed., Tokuyama: Matsuno shoten, 1984), pp. 83–84. See also Fujii, *Ōuchi Yoshioki*, p. 154, and *Ōuchi bunka*, Fusaaki oboegaki, p. 225.

[239] For the abandonment of the Aki campaign after Yoshioki's death, see *Sengoku ibun Ōuchi shi hen*, vol. 3, doc. 2311, 5.23 Sue Okifusa *shojō utsushi*, p. 106, and doc. 2324, 7.23 Ōuchi Yoshitaka *shojō*, p. 111.

9

The Triumphs and Tragedy of Ōuchi Yoshitaka (1528–51)

Yoshitaka (1507–51), the son and heir to Ōuchi Yoshioki (1477–1528), was the last great Ōuchi lord. He was initially very successful, destroying two competitors, the Takeda, of Aki to the east, and the Shōni, of Chikuzen to the west, and exercising uncontested authority over the ports of Tōsai (Aki) and Hakata (Chikuzen). Ōuchi silver trade came into its own, and proved lucrative beyond imagination, although this led to rivals attempting, unsuccessfully, to seize the mines.

Yoshitaka oversaw this trade from Yamaguchi, but he never set foot in Kyoto. Nevertheless, he relied on his appointment to a prestigious court office, the *Dazai Daini*, the Dazaifu Governor General, to justify his rule, and used the King of Japan seal to engage in foreign trade, even though he was never actually appointed to this latter post. Because these offices were so important to him, he consistently upheld court authority. Initially, this policy redounded to his benefit, as he could use his role as *Dazai Daini* to control Kyushu and Tsushima and to crush his Shōni rivals, but at other times, the policy proved disastrous, as his support for absentee rights over local authority led to large-scale defections and defeat during his 1543 campaign against another powerful rival, the Amako.

Instead of modulating his support for the court and its absentee authority, Yoshitaka doubled down, relying more heavily on court authority to enact profound changes. Working in tandem with Emperor Go-Nara (1495–1557, r. 1526–57), he oversaw the search for new sources of precious metal, an arduous process that also led to local resistance. His innovations proved unsettling, particularly among officials and experts from the Iwami mines, who were called upon to analyze samples from other newly opened mines, and by doing so became agents of their own relative marginalization.[1]

---

[1] For this insight and crystallization of my understanding of this process I am indebted to Megan Gilbert, discussion 7.14.2020.

Kings in All but Name. Thomas D. Conlan, Oxford University Press. © Oxford University Press 2024.
DOI: 10.1093/oso/9780197677339.003.0010

Exacerbating this trend, his most trusted followers were, much like Yoshitaka himself, learned but arrogant men who were not afraid to upset the status quo. After briefly attempting to rely on the Ashikaga for prestige, he abandoned them, favoring instead the imperial court. Yoshitaka's reliance on court was not conservative or reactionary; rather it allowed him to govern his widespread domains, enhance his mining efforts, and bypass the dysfunctional Ashikaga entirely. Yoshitaka confronted a world of unprecedented change, however, and the levers of court authority that he so assiduously grasped came to function less effectively.

Yoshitaka did not merely rely on institutional authority to govern; in aiding cohesion among his followers, he also emphasized a distinct Tatara ethnicity. He bestowed the Tatara surname on others and promoted a distinct culture epitomized by the creation of a hybrid style of bells, an intermediary style neither Korean nor Japanese. Korea at the time was experiencing intense intellectual change: Buddhism had been eclipsed by Neo-Confucianism, and Yoshitaka would bring these texts to Japan and abandon further attempts to import Korean Tripiṭaka. Some of the texts he imported were written with phonetic Korean *hangul* (Figure 9.2), suggesting that he was proficient in reading and speaking the language, and he was aware of these new intellectual trends.

He also used the *Dazai Daini* and King of Japan seals to influence Korea, and, in the case of the latter, directly trade with the Ming. These seals gave Yoshitaka the authority to oversee Chinese and Korean trade. Japanese silver, which came from Ōuchi mines in Iwami, flowed to China, making Yoshitaka wealthy beyond measure, and with enough influence to have Ming artisans custom-build writing desks, to Japanese specifications. Likewise, *wakō* piracy was limited as Yoshitaka gained unparalleled influence over Tsushima, one of their bastions, which became a way station for his ships to travel to Korea.

But central Japan, in contrast to the west, was becoming increasingly ungovernable. Whereas many shrines and temples were destroyed in the center, Yoshitaka oversaw the reconstruction of many important institutions (Itsukushima, Usa, Hakozaki) in the west. Yoshitaka's wealth, magnified by favorable internal exchange rates for gold and silver, gave him the resources to contemplate a remarkable and risky move. Not content to have his officials in Yamaguchi oversee trade and bankroll palace centered rites in Kyoto, he favored moving Go-Nara to Yamaguchi, thereby making it the sole capital of Japan.

This endeavor was supported by Emperor Go-Nara and some factions of courtiers (the Nijō) but was opposed by others (the Kujō). The move threatened those with a vested interest in governing from central Japan, who allied with Ōuchi rivals in opposing the move. Internally, disgruntled Ōuchi retainers banded together to overthrow Yoshitaka; they were not hostile to Ōuchi rule but felt that Yoshitaka broke the boundaries of what had been considered acceptable. Governing through court institutions ultimately gave courtiers power over Ōuchi warrior retainers, while the move itself and its constituent ceremonies taxed the resources of the Ōuchi. Ultimately, Yoshitaka's uncle Naitō Okimori (1495–1555) and Sue Takafusa (1521–55) launched a successful coup. They killed Yoshitaka, his heir, many supporters, and court officials in Yamaguchi. Much of the city of Yamaguchi would burn, and this settlement would not fully recover. Ōuchi authority, the idea of governing through the court, and their elaborate trading network would also not long survive Yoshitaka's passing.

Birth and Early Years

Ōuchi Yoshitaka was born in 1507. His mother, Higashi-muki (1470?–1559), was the daughter of Naitō Hironori (1446–95), who had been assassinated at a banquet in 1495 by Ōuchi Yoshioki.[2] Like his father and grandfather, Yoshitaka was named Kidōmaru, but unlike Masahiro and Yoshioki, he spent little time with his father as a youth. Late in 1507, Yoshioki embarked on a campaign to conquer Kyoto. Yoshitaka would not see him again until he returned to Yamaguchi in 1518, when Yoshitaka was eleven.

Yoshitaka was initiated into matters of court hierarchy and ritual from early in life. He received fifth rank lower at the age of twelve. Donations of swords and horses to the Tamanooya Ichinomiya shrine of Suō and to the Sumiyoshi Ichinomiya shrine of Nagato served as affirmations of his standing.[3] He worshiped at the Kōnomine Ise shrines in Yamaguchi, and in 1517 climbed

---

[2] This woman had been previously married and had a child by another man whose identity is unknown. Wada Shūsaku, "Yoshida Kanemigi 'Bōshū gekōki' ni mieru Ōuchi shi kankei kiji," *Yamaguchi ken chihōshi kenkyū* 123 (6.2020), p. 106. This hitherto unknown older half brother to Yoshitaka became a monk.

[3] *Sengoku ibun Ōuchi shi hen*, vol. 2 (Tōkyōdō shuppan, 2017), doc. 1604, 12.2.1518 (Eishō 15) Ōuchi Yoshitaka *kishinjō utsushi*, p. 220, and doc. 1632, 8.29.1519 (Eishō 16) Ōuchi Yoshitaka *kishinjō*, p. 231.

the mountain behind Hikamisan, leaving there incense from Kyoto.[4] These gestures were consistent with his standing as Kidōmaru, the Ōuchi heir and descendant of Myōken.[5] Yoshitaka gained the title of *shinsuke*, institutionally signifying that he was the Ōuchi successor, sometime before 9.27.1521, an honor that his father Yoshioki had not held. Little is known about the relationship between Yoshitaka and his father. They spent time together, and on one occasion searched for prized *matsutake* mushrooms, but overall Yoshitaka's interactions with Yoshoki were limited.[6] Yoshitaka was eighteen when he first campaigned with his father in Aki province, fighting near Tōsai and later Bingo, in the east, in 1524.[7]

When Yoshitaka was twenty, Yoshioki designated a three-year-old boy, Yoshitaka's maternal cousin, as Yoshitaka's heir. The child was the son of Yoshioki's daughter, who had married Ichijō Fusafuyu (1498–1541), a Kyoto noble of the Fujiwara regent line, who resided in Tosa, a province of southern Shikoku.[8] Yoshioki's rationale for making this child an heir is not clear—it may have been an attempt to secure a valued alliance, or he may have known that Yoshitaka was attracted to men and had little apparent interest in fathering children.[9]

During Ōuchi Yoshitaka's youth, Ashikaga authority weakened. Ashikaga Yoshitane (1466–1523, shogun 1490–93, 1508–21) was deposed in 1521 because he could not fund the enthronement ceremonies for Emperor Go-Kashiwabara (1464–1526, r. 1500–1526). Taxes for these rites had been levied in 1501, but the rituals were not performed until 1520, when, after nearly two decades of waiting, the exasperated Hosokawa Takakuni (1484–1531) had

[4] *Sengoku ibun Ōuchi shi hen*, vol. 2, doc. 1657, 6.1520 (Eishō 17) Kōnomine Daijingū *onchinza denki an*, p. 242.

[5] *Sengoku ibun Ōuchi shi hen*, vol. 2, doc. 1706, Ōuchi Yoshioki *kishinbutsu kiroku*, pp. 262–63.

[6] *Sengoku ibun Ōuchi shi hen*, vol. 2, doc. 1699, Oyakatasama *gyoshutsu no gi ni tsuki no mokuroku*, pp. 258–59.

[7] *Fusaaki oboegaki, Hiroshima kenshi kodai chūsei shiryōhen*, vol. 3 (Hiroshima, 1978), pp. 1111–15.

[8] Nomura Shinjō, "Sengoku ki ni okeru shōen yori toshi e no hatten," *Shakai keizai shigaku* 4.11 (1935), pp. 95–97, and Ichimura Takao, "Kaiun ryūtsū kara mita Tosa no Ichijō shi," in Ichimura Takao, ed., *Chūsei Tosa no sekai to Ichijō shi* (Kōshi shoin, 2010), pp. 41–44 for the importance of the Tosa Ichijō. They would have been able to intercept Ashikaga or Hosokawa ships trying to sail to China by avoiding the Inland Sea.

[9] Alexander Reyes, "Flowers on the Battlefield: Intimacy and Hierarchy in the Construction of Japanese Warrior Masculinities, 1507–1636," PhD dissertation, Columbia University, 2022, pp. 34–61, discusses Yoshitaka, who later wrote love poems to a retainer, Sue Takafusa, and showed displeasure when the visiting Portuguese missionary Francis Xavier castigated sodomy as a sin. *Yoshitakaki*, in *Shinkō Gunsho ruijū* 21 *kassen bu*, vol. 2 (3rd revised printing, Zoku gunsho ruijū kanseikai, 1994), p. 410, and *The Letters and Instructions of Francis Xavier* (St. Louis, MO: Institute of Jesuit Sources, 1992), Letter 96, paragraph 14.

to take charge.[10] Takakuni ousted Yoshitane and oversaw the succession of a new shogun, Ashikaga Yoshiharu (1511–50, shogun 1521–46), in 1521.[11]

In 1527, Ashikaga Yoshiharu and Hosokawa Takakuni were defeated by the Miyoshi, a rebellious group of Awa province warriors.[12] Miyoshi Yukinaga (1458–1520), a deputy to the Hosokawa of Awa province, gained power after three of his Hosokawa lords died in short succession.[13] Yukinaga, the nominal deputy *shugo*, became the de facto lord of the province. He was thought to be both "strong in battle" and the "source of great evil."[14] His successor, Miyoshi Motonaga (1501–32), defeated Hosokawa Takakuni, forcing him to flee Kyoto with Yoshiharu, where they found refuge in Kutsuki, a remote, heavily forested mountainous region to the northeast of Kyoto. From 1527 until 1532, Motonaga fought Yoshiharu and his confederates. He even set up Ashikaga Yoshitsuna (1509–73) as a rival shogun in Sakai. Ashikaga Yoshiharu remained in Kutsuki and was further weakened after Motonaga killed Hosokawa Takakuni in battle near Sakai in 1531.[15] Ashikaga authority would never be fully reconstituted, as rival shoguns battled for influence, but lacked the authority or resources to occupy or govern Kyoto.

Succession

Despite the long designation of an heir, authority to wage war and select heirs remained firmly vested with Ōuchi Yoshioki until the sudden onset of illness late in 1527 forced him to abandon his campaign, and he died the following year.[16] It took two years for Yoshitaka to catch up with the paperwork

---

[10] Mizuno Tomoyuki, *Muromachi jidai Kōbu kankei no kenkyū* (Yoshikawa kōbunkan, 2005), p. 247. The delay was most likely due to Yoshitane's desire to snub the court. Yoshitane ultimately fled the capital, dying in 1523.

[11] Yoshiharu was son of the former rival shogun (Yoshizumi) who had been installed in 1495 but deposed in 1508.

[12] For the significance of the Miyoshi, see Amano Tadayuki, *Miyoshi ichizoku-Sengoku saisho no "tenkajin"* (Chūkō shinsho, 2021).

[13] They were Hosokawa Masayuki (1455–88), Yoshiharu (1468–95), and Yukimochi (1486–1512).

[14] *Rōmōki* (Nakarai Yasufusa), *Zoku shiryō taisei*, vol. 18 (Kyoto: Rinsen shoten, 1967), 5.11.1520 (Eishō 17), pp. 123–24. Miyoshi Yukinaga led a revolt (*do-ikki*) against Masayuki, the Hosokawa *shugo* of Awa province, in 1487. Remarkably, he was then appointed as the deputy *shugo* of Sesshū province. See *Shōzui jidai Miyoshi Nagayoshi Tenka o seisu* (Shōzuijōkanseki Kokushiseki shitei kinen tokubetsu ten, Tokushimajō hakubutsukan, 10.2001), and Nagae Shō'ichi, *Miyoshi Nagayoshi* (Yoshikawa kōbunkan, 1968).

[15] Yamada Yasuhiro, *Ashikaga Yoshitane* (Ebisu kōshō, 2016), pp. 200–209.

[16] *Sengoku ibun Ōuchi shi hen*, vol. 3, doc. 2311, 5.23 Sue Okifusa *shojō utsushi*, p. 106, and doc. 2324, 7.23 Ōuchi Yoshitaka *shojō*, p. 111.

concerning his father's last battles in Aki.[17] In 1530, however, Yoshitaka seems to have established firm command. For example, he completed a major reconstruction of the Hōfu Tenmangū in Suō. It became recognized as an imperial prayer temple, offering prayers for the sake of the realm, and enhanced the prestige of the Sabaryō region.[18]

The new lord Yoshitaka had some important successes. Most notably, as he forged a strong alliance with Sō Morikata (1509–73), the lord of Tsushima, an island where *wakō* pirate rivals to the Ōuchi had long resided. Sō Morikata gained power in Tsushima in 1528 and remained an Ōuchi ally through the period of his chieftainship (1528–39). He routinely gave valuable intelligence to Yoshitaka and his generals.[19] The Sō had been staunch Shōni supporters, long-standing rivals to the Ōuchi, and Tsushima had been their sanctuary in times of need, so Morikata's alliance with Yoshitaka greatly undermined Shōni power.

New problems arose for Yoshitaka in 1530, however, as the Amako in the east and the Ōtomo in the west became his implacable foes. The Amako, deputy *shugo* and de facto leaders of the iron-rich province of Izumo, located to the east of Iwami, had been on good terms with the Ōuchi, but after a struggle over succession, the victorious Amako Tsunehisa (1458–1541) became hostile to Yoshitaka in 1531, setting the stage for a debilitating war.[20]

In the west, Ōtomo Yoshiaki (1502–50) challenged Yoshitaka's authority in Hakata by seizing Ikinohama, the Ōuchi dock there, and levied taxes on

[17] Noda Okikata submitted a petition for reward on 7.18.1527 (Daiei 7). *Sengoku ibun Ōuchi shi hen*, vol. 2, doc. 1926, 7.18.1527 (Daiei 7) Noda Okikata *kassen teoi chūmon*, p. 339. Yoshitaka's monogram (*kao*) confirming the document dates from 1530 (Kyōroku 3). For other documents of praise issued late 1529 for the events of 1527, see *Sengoku ibun Ōuchi shi hen*, vol. 3, docs. 2374–75 12.13.1529 (Kyōroku 2) Ōuchi Yoshitaka *kanjō utsushi*, p. 125.

[18] *Sengoku ibun Ōuchi shi hen*, vol. 3, doc. 2381, 1.20.1530 (Kyōroku 3) Sanjō Gyōkū (Sanetaku) *shojō an*, p. 127; doc. 2388, 2.2.1530 Hironaka Masanaga *hōsho utsushi*, p. 129; and doc. 2395, 4.13.1530 (Kyōroku 3) Ōuchi Yoshitaka *kishinjō an*, p. 131; and doc. 2420, 10.14.1530 (Kyōroku 3) Matsuzaki Tenmangū *munafuda mei utsushi*, pp. 141–42.

[19] Morikata was the original name of the fifteenth lord of the Sō family. He confronted numerous rebellions in his early years of rule. In 1534, he changed his name to Masamori and was ousted from power in 1539. His descendants would rule Tsushima in the seventeenth century. For Morikata giving valuable information to the Ōuchi, see *Dazaifu Dazaifu Tenmangū shiryō*, vol. 14 (Dazaifu, 1993), 12.6 [(Tenbun 1) 1532] Sō Morikata *shojō*, pp. 328–29, and *Sengoku ibun Ōuchi shi hen*, vol. 3 (Tōkyōdō shuppan, 2019), docs. 2522–27, 11.13 [(Tenbun 1) 1532] Sō Morikata *shojō an*, pp. 180–81.

[20] *Sengoku ibun Ōuchi shi hen*, vol. 3, doc. 2401, 5.28 Sue Okifusa *shojō utsushi*, pp. 233–34 for battles in Izumo between the Amako and Enya. By 1531, peace was restored between the Amako factions. See doc. 2416, 9.7 Kan Takesuke *shojō*, pp. 139–40. For the formerly cordial relations, Tanaka Hiroki, Nakajima Keiichi, Nakatsukasa Ken'ichi, Nishida Tomohiro, and Watanabe Hiroki, eds., "Masuda Saneuji shozō shinshutsu chūsei monjo no shōkai," in *Kokuritsu rekishi minzoku hakubutsukan kenkyū hōkoku* 212 (12.2018), doc. 27, p. 131, and doc. 64, p. 156. See also Saeki Noriya, *Izumo no chūsei: chiiki to kokka no hazama* (Yoshikawa kōbunkan, 2017), pp. 236–56.

incoming ships.[21] Yoshitaka attempted to rely on Ashikaga Yoshiharu to bolster his authority, and the beleaguered shogun recognized Yoshitaka's monopoly over the Ming tally trade, and by extension, Ikinohama.[22] Ashikaga Yoshiharu's 1530 recognition of preeminent Ōuchi role in the China trade roiled Kyushu and left the Shōni and Ōtomo, long-standing Ōuchi rivals, thirsty for revenge. Later that year, Shōni Sukemoto (1489–1536) of Hizen dispatched his best general, Ryūzōji Iekane (1454–1546), to attack the Ōuchi. He defeated an Ōuchi general named Sugi Okikazu (Okiyuki?, d. 1551) and then marched to the outskirts of the Dazaifu, but he had a falling-out with Sukemoto in the third month of 1532 and withdrew his forces.[23]

Yoshitaka seems to have realized that Yoshiharu's confirmations were not helpful, and he turned against the Ashikaga shogun, refusing to aid him in his attempt to reoccupy Kyoto, even though Yoshiharu sent out many missives requesting aid from various warriors.[24] Ōuchi Yoshitaka would not even allow the Ōtomo and other warriors to pass through his lands and waters to help Yoshiharu. Because of this, Ōtomo Yoshiaki came to detest Yoshitaka for his "evil deeds" and plotted to attack him.[25] Nevertheless, the warriors of northern Kyushu supported Yoshitaka and even tipped him off about Yoshiaki's plans, with only the Shōni allying with the Ōtomo.[26]

[21] Saeki Kōji, "Chūsei kōki no Hakata to Ōuchi shi," Shien 121 (1984), pp. 20–21. See also his "Chūsei toshi Hakata no hatten to Ikinohama," in Nihon Chūsei ronkō (Bunken shuppan, 1987), pp. 435–36.

[22] Kaitei shiseki shūran, 33 vols. (Kondō shuppan 1900–1903), vol. 27, Muromachi ke gonaisho an jō, 3.9.1530 (Kyōroku 3) Ashikaga Yoshiharu gonaisho an, p. 655; Itō Kōji, "Studies of Medieval Ryukyu within Asia's Maritime Network," Acta Asiatica 95 (2008), p. 89; and Hashimoto Yū, Chūsei Nihon no kokusai kankei—Higashi Ajia tsūkōken to gishi mondai (Yoshikawa kōbunkan, 2005), pp. 220–27.

[23] Dazaifu Dazaifu Tenmangū shiryō, vol. 14, 8.15.1530 (Kyōroku 3), pp. 306–18, and 10.15.1531 (Kyōroku 4), pp. 321–23. For the falling out of the Iekane and Suketomo, see 3.17 [(Kyōroku 5) 1532] Sō Morikata shojō, pp. 327–28, and Saeki Kōji, "Sengoku jidai no Dazaifu," in Dazaifu shishi tsūshi hen, vol. 2 (Dazaifu, 2004), p. 280.

[24] Yamaguchi kenshi hensanshitsu, comp., Yamaguchi kenshi shiryōhen chūsei, 4 vols. (Yamaguchi, 1996–2008), vol. 1, Tokitsugu kyōki, 7.5.1532 (Kyōroku 5), pp. 445–46. For an overview of the political context, see Kira Kunimitsu, "Tenbun nenkan Ōuchi shi to Ōtomo," Kyūshū shigaku 162 (2012), p. 5.

[25] Horimoto Kazushige, "Sengoku jidai no Ogori," in Ogori shishi, vol. 2, Tsūshihen chūsei kinsei kindai (Ogori, 2003), particularly pp. 172–80. See also Kira Kunimitsu, "Tenbun nenkan Ōuchi shi to Ōtomo," Kyūshū shigaku 162 (2012), pp. 4–29, and Yamada Takashi, Chūsei kōki buke kan'i ron (Ebisu kōshō, 2015), pp. 213–19. Yoshiaki's comment comes from Kumagai ke monjo (Tōkyō daigaku shuppankai, 1937), doc. 118, 7.20 Ōtomo Yoshiaki shojō, pp. 126–27.

[26] Sengoku ibun Ōuchi shi hen, vol. 3, doc. 2508, 9.24.1532 ([Tenbun 1] Kyōroku 5 [sic]) Ōuchi Yoshitaka kanjō, p. 176 for the Sata (Utsunomiya) notifying Yoshitaka. See also Dazaifu Dazaifu Tenmangū shiryō, vol. 14, 8.25.1532 (Tenbun 1), pp. 329–33, and Saeki, "Sengoku jidai no Dazaifu," p. 280.

When Ōtomo Yoshiaki invaded Buzen in the eleventh month of 1532, Yoshitaka easily checked him by fortifying his Myōgendake castle in Buzen.[27] Yoshitaka's armies then advanced into Hizen province, where they captured the Shōni stronghold of Tachibana castle.[28] In 1533, Ōuchi forces invaded the Ōtomo home province of Bungo and killed several Ōtomo commanders in the process.[29] They remained in the field for years, which proved to be burdensome for members of Yoshitaka's armies hailing from Iwami and Aki provinces.[30] Ultimately, weary with conflict, Yoshitaka reached out to Ryūzōji Iekane to negotiate the surrender of the Shōni in the tenth month of 1534.[31]

Whereas in 1530 Yoshitaka had relied upon the authority of Ashikaga Yoshiharu to assert Ming trading privileges, his falling-out with Yoshiharu in 1532 caused him to reach out directly to the Japanese court for support instead. During the seventh month of 1533, Yoshitaka prayed at Usa shrine, and implored Hachiman to aid him in his pacification of Kyushu. Yoshitaka explained how Hachiman had aided him, and paid homage to the bravery of his princely image, but he also referred to the righteousness of his forces, the mandate of heaven, and the importance of upholding court rule.

Since the autumn of last year in 1532, enemy forces have been attacking on the borders of Buzen and Chikuzen. Yoshitaka gathered righteous armies

---

[27] *Sengoku ibun Ōuchi shi hen*, vol. 3, doc. 2518, 11.3 Ōuchi Yoshitaka *shojō an*, p. 179; doc. 2521, 11.13 Yasutomi shi *dai* Yamazoe Nobutsugu *kassen teoi chūmon*, p. 180; doc. 2513, 10.9 Sugi Okishige *hōsho*, p. 177; doc. 2528, 11.14.1532 (Tenbun 1) Sata Tomokage *kassen teoi chūmon*, pp. 181–83; doc. 2529, 11.14.1532 (Tenbun 1) Sata Tomokage *kanjō*, p. 183; and doc. 2533, 11.15 Sata Tomokage *gunchūjō*, pp. 183–84. For Yoshitaka's praise to the castle defenders, see doc. 2535, 11.21 [(Tenbun 1) 1532] Ōuchi Yoshitaka *shojō utsushi*, p. 184; doc. 2534, 11.19 Sue Dōrin *shojō*, p. 184; and doc. 2536, 11.22 Sugi Okishige *shojō*, p. 184.

[28] *Dazaifu Dazaifu Tenmangū shiryō*, vol. 14, p. 342 for the 3.13 Uno Yoichi Uemon document. See also pp. 342–48 and Saeki, "Sengoku jidai no Dazaifu," p. 280. For the continued investiture of Tachibana, see the 3.6 [(Tenbun 2) 1533] Kurokawa Takahisa *kanjō utushi*, pp. 192–93. See also *Sengoku ibun Ōuchi shi hen*, vol. 3, doc. 2575, 4.11 [(Tenbun 2) 1533] Sō Morikata *shojō an*, pp. 194–95, and *Dazaifu Dazaifu Tenmangū shiryō*, vol. 14, p. 357.

[29] This occurred in the third month of 1534. *Sengoku ibun Ōuchi shi hen*, vol. 3, doc. 2668, 6.14.1534 (Tenbun 3) Ōuchi Yoshitaka *kanjō*, p. 222; docs. 2669–71, 6.14.1534 (Tenbun 3) Ōuchi Yoshitaka *kanjō utushi*, p. 222; and docs. 2689–90, 7.25.1534 (Tenbun 3) Moji Yorichika/Yorifusa *gunchūjō*, pp. 227–28. For the death of enemy commanders, see "Sengoku jidai no Ogori," *Ogori shishi*, vol. 2, p. 173.

[30] *Kikkawa ke monjo*, vol. 3, *besshū furoku Iwami Kikkawa ke monjo* (Tōkyō daigaku shuppankai, 1931) (hereafter *Iwami Kikkawa*), doc. 25, Kikkawa Tsunenori *yuzurijō narabi ni okibumi eisha*, pp. 15–16 for Kikkawa Tsunenori of Nima (Iwami) fighting there for years. Kobayakawa Matarō of Aki also fought in Kyushu for years. *Kobayakawa ke monjo*, vol. 1 (Tōkyō daigaku shuppankai, 1927), 3.23 Kobayakawa Matatarō *shojō*, pp. 136–37.

[31] *Dazaifu Dazaifu Tenmangū shiryō*, vol. 14, 10.30 [(Tenbun 3) 1534], pp. 372–73. For their surrender, see *Yoshitakaki*, p. 416.

(*gihei*) and fought them. The outcome was swiftly decided in what was certainly heavenly fortune with the aid of the gods (*shinmyō eijo nari*). The country [Chikuzen] was returned to peace, the harvests of the people were good, and beginning with my ancestor, Prince Imsŏng, down through the generations we have been blessed with bravery, I have risen to high rank, I am the military governor of seven provinces, and I know the importance of heaven's mandate. I have received wealth and fortune, and like a cloud wandering the sky, I recognize that I ought to be in awe of heaven. There is no one who can challenge me as an enemy, and I could not gain victory in battle without the protection of the deity. Mobilizing forces is not for the protection of my office, but to save the people from fire and ash. I implore you to use your supernatural powers on my behalf. If you do that, then I can bring peace to Kyushu, I can govern the three territories, and I can put away the spear and shield. May the imperial office survive a long time, the gods of the earth and the five grains bestow blessings upon them, and the emperor live long. I humbly offer up this prayer.[32]

Yoshitaka chose to govern, and legitimate his conquest, through the court, and not the shogunate. This did not mean that he ignored the Ashikaga entirely. On 6.24.1535, Yoshitaka accepted a truce with Ōtomo Yoshiaki through the mediation of Ashikaga Yoshiharu.[33] The war between him and the Ōtomo had ended in stalemate, but Yoshitaka was able to extend his powers in Kyushu, and destroy the Shōni, thanks to his appointment to an old office.

Ruling as Governor General of Kyushu (*Dazai Daini*)

After his victory, Yoshitaka desired to be appointed as the *Dazai Daini*, the Dazaifu Governor General, who ruled Kyushu. The position would make

[32] Translated by Chrsitopher Mayo, reproduced here with slight editorial changes. See his "Mobilizing Deities: Deus, Gods, Buddhas, and the Warrior Band in Sixteenth-Century Japan," PhD dissertation, Princeton University, 2013, pp. 142–46, and "The Ōtomo and Competition in the Ritual Marketplace," in Kage Toshio, ed., *Ōuchi to Ōtomo: Chūsei nishi Nihon no nidai daimyō* (Bensei shuppan, 2013), pp. 8–11. For more analysis of this oath, see Alan Strathern, "The Many Meanings of Iconoclasm: Warrior and Christian Temple-Shrine Destruction in Late Sixteenth Century Japan," *Journal of Early Modern History* (2020), pp. 24–25. For a transcription of the original, see *Sengoku ibun Ōuchi shi hen*, vol. 3, doc. 2593, 7.23.1533 (Tenbun 2) Ōuchi Yoshitaka *ganmon an*, p. 199.

[33] *Sengoku ibun Ōuchi shi hen*, vol. 3, doc. 2782, 6.24 [(Tenbun 4) 1535], Ōuchi Yoshitaka *ukebumi utsushi*, pp. 255–56.

him the direct superior of the Shōni, the hereditary deputies to this long-vacated court post.[34] The Shōni surname itself meant "Deputy to the *Dazai Daini*." Thus, by using the nominal name of his office he could assert almost total authority over the surviving Shōni.[35]

The court had leverage over Yoshitaka because no appointment to the *Dazai Daini* had been made for centuries, and it could only be made with court approval. Yoshitaka funded a variety of projects to increase his standing at the court, and by doing so, took over the Ashikaga role as the court's provider. He paid for reconstruction of the palace and contributed two thousand *kanmon* for Go-Nara's enthronement ceremonies on 1.3.1534. He also dispatched one hundred *kanmon* to repair or rebuild one of the palace gates on 9.3.1535.[36] In what seems to have been a condition for his appointment, Yoshitaka also acted as the guardian of public lands (*kokugaryō*) that accrued to old proprietors, and in this case confirmed Tōdaiji's holdings. In this way he established his position as the upholder of absentee rights in Kyushu.[37] This upset some retainers, such as the Sue, but seems to have been a prerequisite for his appointment to this illustrious office.[38]

Yoshitaka was appointed as the *Dazai Daini* in the twelfth month of 1535.[39] This allowed him to control the Dazaifu, the administrative center for all of Kyushu, and to justify his ability to inspect and confiscate lands. As the Ōuchi had long governed Buzen and Chikuzen, this meant most immediately that they could gain control over all the strategic province of Hizen in north-western Kyushu for the first time. In short order, Yoshitaka had his general

---

[34] *Dazaifu shishi Chūsei shiryōhen* (Dazaifu-shi, 2002), pp. 777, 779. For how Yoshitaka communicated with the court independently of the Ashikaga, see Yamada Takashi, *Chūsei kōki buke kan'i ron*, pp. 222–23.

[35] In this sense, the politics of his time was one where *omote*, or surface justification, proved influential, and varied from the later practices described by Luke Roberts in *Performing the Great Peace: Political Space and Open Secrets in Tokugawa Japan* (Honolulu: University of Hawaii Press, 2012).

[36] *Go-Nara tennō jitsuroku*, 3 vols. (Yumani shobō, 2010), vol. 1, 1.3.1535 (Tenbun 4), p. 435. See also pp. 414–7, 432–37, and 476–77, and *Yamaguchi kenshi shiryōhen chūsei*, vol. 1, pp. 428–30, and *Tokitsugu kyōki*, 4.28.1534 (Tenbun 3), p. 446.

[37] *Sengoku ibun Ōuchi shi hen*, vol. 3, doc. 2829, 12.22.1535 (Tenbun 4) Ōuchi Yoshitaka *andojō*, p. 270. See also Matsuoka Hisatō, "The Sengoku Daimyo of Western Japan: The Case of the Ōuchi," in John Whitney Hall, Nagahara Keiji, and Kozo Yamamura, eds., *Japan before Tokugawa* (Princeton: Princeton University Press, 1981), p. 74, and Peter Judd Arnesen, *The Medieval Japanese Daimyo: The Ouchi Family's Rule of Suō and Nagato* (New Haven: Yale University Press, 1979), pp. 93–131, particularly pp. 126–29.

[38] See Ōuchi shi no bodaiji," in Itō Kōji and Wada Shūsaku, eds., *Ōuchi shi no sekai o saguru* (Bensei shuppan, 2019), p. 63.

[39] *Yamaguchi kenshi shiryōhen chūsei*, vol. 1; Go-Nara tennō jitsuroku 12.22, 12.27–28.1535 (Tenbun 4), p. 429, *Sengoku ibun Ōuchi shi hen*, vol. 3, 2830, 12.28 [(Tenbun 4) 1535] *Kuzen shigyōjō an*, p. 270.

Sue Okifusa (1475–1539) survey and appropriate the core holdings of Shōni Sukemoto.[40] One faction of the Tsukushi, Shōni supporters, joined the Ōuchi and were rewarded with a favorable survey of their lands.[41] More decisively, Ryūzōji Iekane joined Yoshitaka as well, effectively destroying the Shōni as a viable regional force.[42] Sue Okifusa continued the campaign against Shōni Sukemoto, forcing him to commit suicide as his castle fell on 9.4.1536.[43]

Yoshitaka's position as *Dazai Daini* made it easy for him to discredit the surviving Shōni. When Fuyuhisa (d. 1559), the last Shōni head, rebelled in 1539, Yoshitaka claimed that he was an impostor, and demanded that he be chastised.[44] Fuyuhisa and his allies ousted Sō Morikata and attempted to more aggressively assert Tsushima interest in Korea, culminating in a 1544 disturbance that led to the closing of Tsushima ports in Korea, and limited the islanders' ability to trade there, but it did not adversely affect the Ōuchi, except that they could not dock so readily in Tsushima.[45] Yoshitaka granted the office of Dazai Deputy (*shōni*) to Sugi Okikazu, a deputy of Chikuzen province, and one of his generals.[46] By doing so he undermined the rationale for their very name.

The appointment to this post of *Dazai Daini* enabled Yoshitaka to grant more exalted titles to his followers than had been customary.[47] He also could issue documents in a prestigious style, and many records demonstrate that *Dazai Daini* edicts were the mechanism for him to control the provinces of Buzen and Chikuzen from 10.6.1536 through 1551.[48] As *Dazai Daini*, Yoshitaka commissioned prayers for the peace and stability

---

[40] For how these surveys and confiscations fatally undermined the Shōni, see *Dazaifu Dazaifu Tenmangū shiryō*, vol. 14, 12.1535 (Tenbun 4), pp. 407–8.

[41] By 8.28.1534 (Tenbun 3), Okifusa oversaw a detailed survey of Hizen's for the Tsukushi, who were a branch family of the Shōni. *Sengoku ibun Ōuchi shi hen*, vol. 3, doc. 2695, 8.28.1534 (Tenbun 3) Tsukushi shi *shoryō chūshin an*. This survey included lands in the Mine district of Hizen, site of the core Shōni holdings. "Sengoku jidai no Ogori," pp. 175–76.

[42] *Yoshitakaki*, p. 416.

[43] *Dazaifu Dazaifu Tenmangū shiryō*, vol. 14, 9.4.1536 (Tenbun 5), pp. 411–17. This was one of the last of the notable acts of this skilled general, who died on 4.18.1539. *Sengoku ibun Ōuchi shi hen*, vol. 3, docs. 3078–79, 4.18.1539 (Tenbun 8) Sue Okifusa *kuyōtō mei*, p. 342.

[44] *Sengoku ibun Ōuchi shi hen*, vol. 3, doc. 3148, 11.17.1539 (Tenbun 8) Ōuchi Yoshitaka *kishinjō*, p. 366.

[45] *Chūgoku Chōsen no shiseki ni okeru Nihon shiryō shūsei. Richō jitsuroku no bu*, vol. 7 (Kokusho kankōkai, 1984), pp. 1964–65 for references to Shōni and Ōuchi emissaries. See also the third, fourth months of 1544, pp. 1961, 1964, 1972, and the seventh month of 1544, p. 1988. Sō Morikata lost power in 1539, and Tsushima became embroiled in the 1544 Saryangjin disturbances, which caused the closure of their outposts in Korea.

[46] *Dazaifu shishi Chūsei shiryōhen* for 7.21.1550 (Tenbun 19), pp. 824–25. Shōni Fuyuhisa would linger in the 1550s, but of him, and other people claming to be Shōni, little is known. The final Shōni document dates from 1576 (Tenshō 4). Saeki, "Sengoku jidai no Dazaifu," pp. 281–83.

[47] Yamada Takashi, *Chūsei kōki buke kan'i ron*, pp. 224–30.

[48] Yamada, *Chūsei kōki buke kan'i ron*, pp. 226–29. The oldest mentioned record dates from 10.6.1536 (Tenbun 5), while his final document was issued on 8.12.1551 (Tenbun 20). See *Dazaifu*

of all nine provinces of Kyushu, and not just regions that he controlled.[49] Yoshitaka used this title for prayers dedicated to temples and shrines outside of Kyushu, such as Hikamisan and Kameyama Hachiman, and for dedications of texts, such as a rhyming dictionary of Chinese.[50] Even the Ashikaga had to write to Yoshitaka concerning all Kyushu affairs, such as the status of some lands there.[51] Finally, as *Dazai Daini*, Yoshitaka could communicate directly with Emperor Go-Nara without any need for Ashikaga intercession.[52]

Yoshitaka governed as a courtier and acted accordingly in terms of language, modes of address and even styles of robes. He used archaic court terms to address the emperor when requesting promotions for his followers.[53] Yoshitaka took court affairs seriously. He even discussed the display of weave (*nuimono*) and crests for a belt, the *hirao*, used for formal court attire.[54] By doing so, he upheld the notion that it was nobles who governed, not warriors, and that he himself was a noble par excellence.

Unlike his father Yoshioki, who was derided as a country bumpkin even though he had long lived in Kyoto, Yoshitaka was, by all accounts, extremely well versed in court affairs. Perhaps his sister's marriage with the Ichijō and the selection of her son as Tsunemochi as heir gave him access to court knowledge unavailable to his father and other Ōuchi.

As his power increased, Yoshitaka's signed documents in a manner that, according to epistolary etiquette, was increasingly arrogant. Yoshitaka's oldest documents from 1529 show that his signed monogram (*kaō*) closely

---

Dazaifu Tenmangū shiryō, vol. 14, 10.6.1536 (Tenbun 5), pp. 420–21 for the former and 8.12.1551 (Tenbun 20), p. 735 for the latter.

[49] *Dazaifu Dazaifu Tenmangū shiryō*, vol. 14, 5.3.1539 (Tenbun 8), pp. 510–11 and 11.17.1539 (Tenbun 8), pp. 530–31. See also Yamada, *Chūsei kōki buke kan'i ron*, p. 233, and *Sengoku bushō no hokori to inori: Kyūshū no haken to yukue* (Kyūshū rekishi shiryōkan, 2013), p. 24.

[50] For Yoshitaka's prayers to Kōryūji, Kameyama Hachiman, and Hakozaki, with most shrines located in Honshu, see *Sengoku ibun Ōuchi shi hen*, vol. 3, docs. 2934–36, 3.15.1537 (Tenbun 6) Ōuchi Yoshitaka *kishinjō*, pp. 302–3. For his writing the dedication for a printed version of the *Shūbun Inryaku*, the first rhyming Chinese dictionary written in Japan, see doc. 3073, *Shūbun Inryaku batsubun*, p. 340.

[51] *Sengoku ibun Ōuchi shi hen*, vol. 3, doc. 3111, 6.21 [(Tenbun 8) 1539] Ashikaga Yoshiharu *gonaisho an*, p. 351.

[52] Yamada Takashi, *Chūsei kōki buke kan'i ron*, pp. 222–24. Epitomizing this, see the Go-Nara document directly dispatched to Yoshitaka in 1539. *Sengoku ibun Ōuchi shi hen*, vol. 3, doc. 3093, 6.3 [(Tenbun 8) 1539] Go-Nara tennō *rinji an*, pp. 346–47.

[53] *Waseda daigkau shozō Ogino kenkyūshitsu monjo gekan* (Yoshikawa kōbunkan, 1980), doc. 1064, 3.17.1543 (Tenbun 13) Ōuchi Yoshitaka *mōshijō*, pp. 213–14.

[54] *Waseda daigkau shozō Ogino kenkyūshitsu monjo gekan*, doc. 1065, 3.9 Ōuchi Yoshitaka *jihitsu shojō*, p. 214.

Figure 9.1 Ōuchi Yoshitaka Name Grant to Follower (*Ichiji no kakidashi*). The signature is larger than the name of the addressee. Image and permission provided by Yamaguchi monjokan

resembles those of his father Yoshioki and great-grandfather Norihiro.[55] This style would quickly change. By the time he issued a 1539 document to the Dazai Tenmangū shrine his signature had steadily become rounder and larger. In documents written in 1550, his monogram had expanded again by a third.[56] Indeed, his signatures are among the largest known in Japanese history (Figure 9.1).[57]

[55] See *Hōfu shishi tsūshi* 1 *genshi kodai chūsei* (Hōfu, 2005), pp. 296 for a photograph of a 5.3.1529 (Kyōroku 2) Ōuchi Yoshitaka *kinzei*. For comparison with other monograms of his father, see p. 288, and for Norihiro, p. 285.

[56] *Sengoku bushō no hokori to inori*, pp. 23–25, for photographs that allow for comparison of *Dazai Daini* documents dating from 11.17.1539 (Tenbun 8), 8.7.1544 (Tenbun 13), and 5.13.1550 (Tenbun 19).

[57] *Yamaguchi kenshi tsūshihen chūsei* (Yamaguchi, 2012), pp. 495–97. For one of the most extreme examples, see Suekane ke monjo, 4.10.1549 (Tenbun 18) Ōuchi Yoshitaka *ichiji kakidashi*, unpublished document, Yamaguchi monjokan dated 4.10.1549 (Tenbun 18). Yoshitaka's name is larger than that of the whole name of Yamagata *Hyōbu no jō* Takamune. Accessed 6.17.2020 (reproduced as Figure 9.1).

Yoshitaka, building on his position as *Dazai Daini*, was able to establish uncontested authority over the Genkai Sea, the southwestern tip of the Japan Sea, including the seas of northern Kyushu, to the west of Honshu. This is because the Dazaifu had administrative authority over the two islands Iki and Tsushima along with the nine provinces of Kyushu. Tsushima was a particularly important prize since seafarers had often been hostile to the Ōuchi and their interests.[58] When Sō Morikata allied with Yoshitaka, it meant that the *wakō* based in Tsushima de facto became incorporated into Ōuchi expeditions. They would not disrupt trade or act against Ōuchi interests. In fact, Ōuchi Yoshitaka used Tsushima as a staging point to send fleets to Korea, particularly during the time of Sō Morikata's ascendancy. A diary of the monk Sonkai (d. 1549) reveals how a 1537 mission bound for Korea entailed the movement of people from Yamaguchi and Hakata to Tsushima. For one fleet, two captains were selected, one hailing from Yamaguchi and the other from Tsushima.[59]

The Munakata, whose priestly lineages headed the three Munakata shrines, including one on Okinoshima in the Genkai Sea, became even more tightly bound to the Ōuchi, as their political allegiance was transformed into an ethnic one. Even though they had no biological links to the Ōuchi, they were granted the lineage name of Tatara and made, by extension, kin of Yoshitaka.[60] These expanding ethnic ties strengthened Ōuchi trading networks between Japan and Korea.

Trade with Korea

With the Sō and the Munakata on friendly terms, and the Genkai Sea at peace, Ōuchi Yoshitaka dispatched massive shipments to the court of the Chosŏn king Chungjong (1488–1544, r. 1506–44) with little fear for disruptions. When the monk Sonkai led a trading party to Pusan in 1539, he unloaded six

[58] For an overview of the Genkai sea and Dazaifu authority, see Bruce Batten, *Gateway to Japan: Hakata in War and Peace, 500–1300* (Honolulu: University of Hawaii Press, 2006), p. 38.

[59] In fact, this fleet did not sail, but Sonkai still made his way to Pusan. *Hiroshima kenshi kodai chūsei shiryōhen*, vol. 3, Daiganji monjo, doc. *hoi* 2, 9.10.1541 (Tenbun 10) Daiganji Sonkai tokai nikki, pp. 1462–63. I am grateful to Gina Choi for her help in clarifying this record. For more analysis, see Sangnam Lee, "The Joseon Court and the Ōuchi Clan: A Case Study of the Interregional Circulation of Material Culture," *Artibus Asiae* 78.2 (2018), pp. 160–73.

[60] *Munakata shishi shiryōhen chūsei*, vol. 2 (Munakata 1996), doc. 330, p. 257 for the genealogies of Munakata Ujio, who received initiation into the Tatara lineage, and was granted the "taka" of Yoshitaka and changed his name to Takamune. He died with Yoshitaka at Taineiji in 1551.

tons (ninety-three *da* [Kr. *tae*]) of materials from a flotilla of ships.[61] The unspecified contents of Sonkai's baggage undoubtedly consisted of copper and silver. On his return, Sonkai brought back leopard and sable skins, Buddhist sculptures, Buddhist and Confucian texts, silk, linen, cotton cloth, ginseng, and honey. Korean objects surviving from the Ōuchi collection in Japan include many statues, paintings, bells, lacquerware, and porcelains.[62] One of the most remarkable surviving artifacts is an eight-panel screen with a popular motif, the *Eight Views of Xiao and Xiang Rivers* (瀟湘八景 J. *Shōshō hakkei* Ch. Xiao-Xiang ba jing).[63]

In his communiqués with Korea, Yoshitaka styled himself the *Dazai Daini*. He even had a special *Dazai Daini* seal created for his documents, which supplanted the earlier Tatara seal used by his predecessors.[64] With this title, Yoshitaka proved directly able to negotiate with the Korean Minister of the Board of Rites (J. *Reisō sanpan*, Kr. *Yejo champan*), who readily accepted missives from what the Board recognized as an important office.[65] Thus Yoshitaka used his seal with the title of *Dazai Daini* to demonstrate his authority over official Japanese and Korean exchanges both within Japan (Tsushima) and with Korea (Figure 9.2).

Yoshitaka encountered a Korea that was radically changing and turning away from Buddhism. He requested a new copy of the Tripiṭaka, to replace one that was in poor condition, explaining how it would help preserve peace in the realm, and make up for the incomplete Tripiṭaka that had been housed at Itsukushima shrine.[66] However, his request was not granted. Officials

---

[61] Sonkai, who was born at Hera estate in Aki province, was affiliated with Daiganji, a temple linked to the Itsukushima shrine there. For his origins, see *Hiroshima kenshi kodai chūsei shiryōhen*, vol. 3, Daiganji monjo, doc. *hoi* 2, pp. 1462–63.

[62] For the amount of baggage in Korea (93 *da* 駄), see Daiganji Sonkai tokai nikki, 6.15, p. 1463. Lee, "Joseon Court," pp. 160–73, analyzes this and the letter from the King of Korea. See also *Muromachi bunka no naka ni miru Ōuchi bunka no ihōten* (Yamaguchi kenritsu bijutsukan, 1989), pp. 147–48. Lee, "Joseon Court," pp. 174–77, lists many of these objects, which are illustrated, along with the diplomatic correspondence, on pp. 61–72.

[63] Sangnam Lee and Jaewon Ahn, "Mōri hakubutsukan shozō no Kankoku ibutsu o tsūshite mita Kankoku ōchō shoki busshitsu bunka no kōryū- Ōuchi shi to Mōri shi o chūshin ni," *Bijutsu kenkyū* 415 (3.2015), pp. 1–20.

[64] *Sengoku bushō no hokori to inori*, p. 18.

[65] *Sengoku ibun Ōuchi shi hen*, vol. 3, doc. 2839, 2.1536 (Tenbun 5) Ōuchi Yoshitaka *shokei utsushi*, pp. 274–75. For how Yoshitaka could directly communicate with Korea see Suda Makiko, *Chūsei nitchō kankei to Ōuchi shi* (Tōkyō daigaku shuppankai, 2011), p. 71. For treatment in English, see Kenneth Robinson, "A Japanese Trade Mission to Chosŏn Korea, 1537–1540: The Sonkai tokai nikki and the Korean Tribute System," in Andrew Goble, Kenneth R. Robinson, and Haruko Nishioka Wakabayashi, eds., *Tools of Culture: Japan's Cultural, Intellectual, Medical, and Technological Contacts in East Asia, 1000–1500s* (Ann Arbor, MI: Association for Asian Studies, 2009), pp. 71–101.

[66] *Sengoku ibun Ōuchi shi hen*, vol. 3, doc. 2839, 2.1536 (Tenbun 5) Ōuchi Yoshitaka *shokei utsushi*, pp. 274–75.

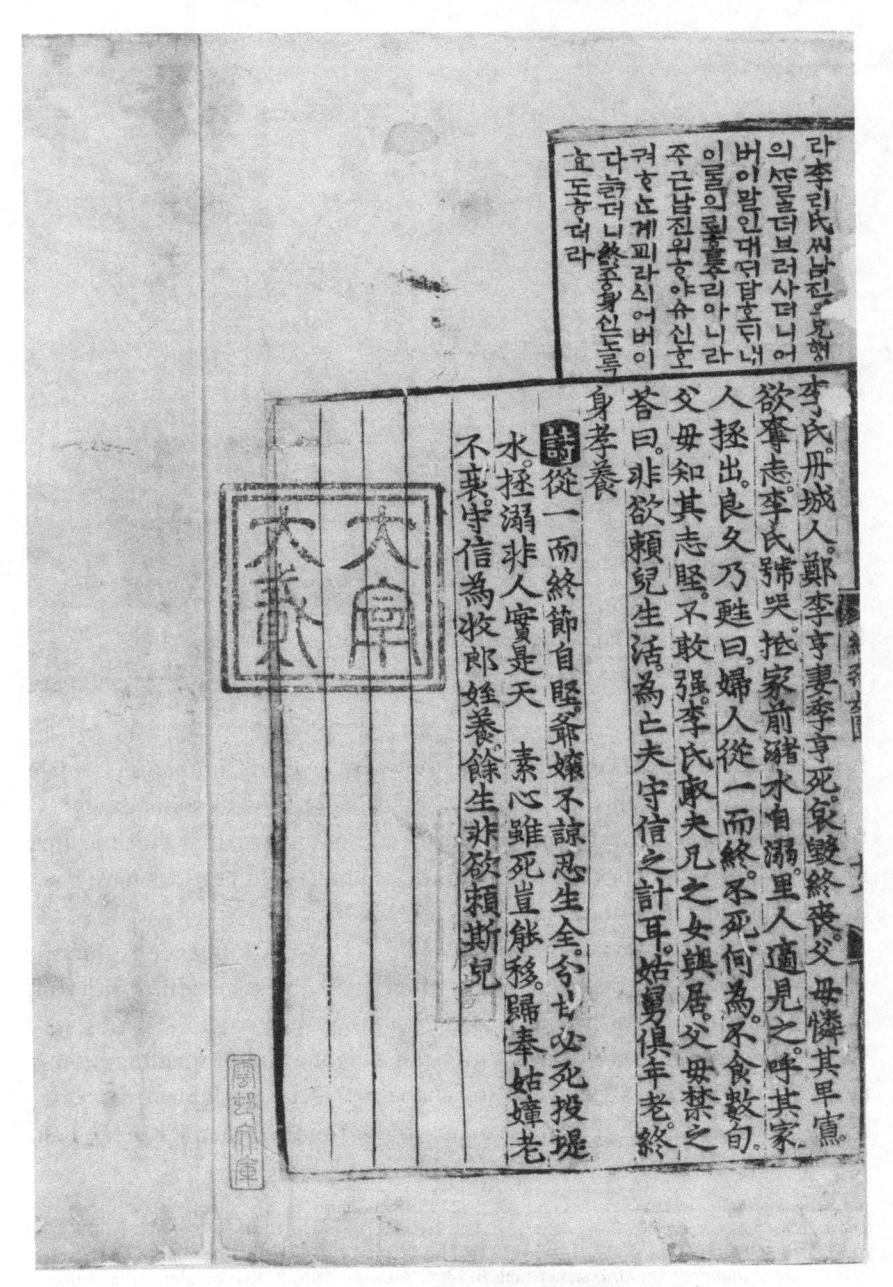

Figure 9.2 *Sok Samgang Haengsil-to* (Illustrated Guide to the Three Relationships), End of section 28 with Yoshitaka's *Dazai Daini* Seal. Image and permission provide by Tōyō bunko (The Oriental Library)

(a)

(b)

Figure 9.3 (a) Kōryūji Hikamisan Bell and (b) Mishima island Kichijōji. Photographs by Thomas Conlan

from the Board of Rites explained that they now revered Confucius (J. *Shūkō* K. *Jukong*) rather than the Buddha. They continued, with some exaggeration because the Ōuchi still imported Korean Buddhist texts at the time, that in Korea "we no longer revere the Buddha; temples and pagodas have been burned and no copies of the scriptures remain."[67]

The Korean repudiation of Buddhism did not unduly influence Yoshitaka. In 1532 he oversaw the casting of a remarkable, massive bell at Kōryūji, over six feet in height, that fuses Korean and Japanese styles (Figures 9.3–9.4).[68] The bell has exterior decorations of dragons and protruding bronze knobs in the Korean style, while the shape represents an intermediary between Japanese and Korean dimensions, more rounded than a Korean bell,

[67] *Sengoku ibun Ōuchi shi hen*, vol. 3, doc. 3132, 9.1539 (Gajŏng 18) ([Chungjong 34/Tenbun 8]) *Chōsen Reisō sanpan Kyōken shokei utsushi*, p. 358. See also *Hiroshima kenshi kodai chūsei shiryōhen*, vol. 3, Daiganji monjo, doc. *hoi* 2, 9.10.1541 (Tenbun 10), p. 1463. Chosŏn Korea last relied on esoteric Buddhist *munduru* (*mudrā*) state rituals in 1400. Youn-mi Kim, "(Dis)assembling the National Canon: Seventh-Century 'Esoteric' Buddhist Ritual, the Samguk yusa, and Sach'onwang-sa," *New Perspectives on Early Korean Art: From Silla to Koryŏ* (Cambridge, MA: Korea Institute, Harvard University, 2013), p. 133.

[68] *Yamaguchi shishi shiryōhen Ōuchi bunka* (Yamaguchi, 2010) (hereafter *Ōuchi bunka*), color plate 37 and p. 851.

(a) (b)

Figure 9.4 (a) Tōdaiji Japanese-style Bell and (b) Kōryūji Hikamisan Bell. Note how it exhibits both Japanese and Korean traits. Photographs by Thomas Conlan

but less than a Japanese one. A large (thirty-three-inch diameter) gong (*waniguchi*) for the Ima Hachiman shrine, created in 1534, exhibits similar characteristics.[69]

Yoshitaka retained his interest in Buddhism and ultimately made up for the insufficiencies of the Itsukushima Tripiṭaka with other copies that he held. However, he also exhibited an interest in Confucian texts from Korea, such as the standard *Book of Odes* and *Book of History* as well as the Neo-Confucian Four Books and Five Classics.[70] Neo-Confucianism would become an important and influential intellectual current in Japan during the ensuing centuries, and Yoshitaka was one of the first to oversee the transmission of these texts to Japan.

[69] *Ōuchi bunka*, pp. 851, 853. A similar gong was made in 1533 for Kōryūji but was lost.

[70] *Hiroshima kenshi kodai chūsei shiryōhen*, vol. 3, Daiganji monjo, doc. *hoi* 2, doc. 313, p. 1351 for Yoshitaka's request for Neo-Confucian texts. Transcriptions of the Korean sources conveniently appear in *Yamaguchi kenshi shiryōhen chūsei*, vol. 1, Yoshitakaki, pp. 197 for his requesting "old" and "new" Confucian texts, which would refer to Zhu Xi. Likewise, see Jurgis Elisonas, "Christianity and the Daimyo," in John Whitney Hall et al., eds., *The Cambridge History of Japan* (New York: Cambridge University Press, 1991), pp. 313–14 for Yoshitaka's interests in Buddhism, Shinto, Confucianism, and Christianity (although whether he recognized Christianity as being distinct from Buddhism is not clear).

Yoshitaka was thus receptive to new ideas and objects. From Korea he managed to obtain a "water clock." The Korean court had apparently created such clocks in the 1430s. One example (*Porugak chagyŏngnu*) survives from the time of King Chungjong. Created in 1536, the elaborate mechanism allowed for small courtier figurines to strike a bell on the hour.[71] These instruments were the size of a small car, and for Yoshitaka to receive one shows his influence in Chungjong's court. Perhaps he merely enjoyed the automatic hourly chiming of bells, but the clock would also have been useful in experiments regarding metals and ores, where the timing of reactions was crucial.[72]

Tally Trade with China

Yoshitaka successfully resume the Ming trade after the disruptions of the 1523 Ningbo incident.[73] The complex diplomatic overtures involved, among other things, the sending of ambassadors from Tsushima to negotiate.[74] Yoshitaka sought materials that would appeal to the continent, contacting Ishiyama Honganji in 1536 because that temple controlled Kaga's Iōzen, a source of agate (*menō*).[75] He also printed books. Copies of *The Analects* (*Rongo*) dating from 1539 survive, although it is not clear whether these volumes were for internal consumption or export.[76]

---

[71] This clepsydra self-striking water clock (*Porugak chagyŏngnu*) is Korean National Treasure no. 229. Older examples exist from Ming China, but the Korean water clocks were well known for their quality.

[72] Fukuo Takeichirō, *Ōuchi Yoshitaka* (Yoshikawa kōbunkan, 1959), pp. 192–93 for a letter to Hirohashi Kanehide, dated 8.17 and the year is most likely before 1549 (Tenbun 18). See *Hiroshima kenshi kodai chūsei shiryōhen*, vol. 3, Daiganji monjo, doc. *hoi* 2, doc. 313, p. 1351. Fukuo argues that this letter, in the Sonkeikaku bunko collection, shows that Yoshitaka received a water clock from Korea, but Lee ("Joseon Court," p. 160) translates this object as a "rain gauge."

[73] For an excellent overview, see Kobata Atsushi, *Chūsei Nisshi tsūkō bōekishi no kenkyū* (Tōkō shoin, 1941), pp. 159–76 for the expedition that Yoshitaka first decided to dispatch in 1536 (Tenbun 5), and pp. 176–95. For more on these expeditions, also see Murai Shōsuke, ed., *Nichimin kankeishi kenkyū nyūmon* (Bensei shuppan, 2015). Itō Kōji provides an excellent overview of the routes taken by these embassies in "Nyūminki kara mita Higashi Ajia no kaiiku kōryū-kōro kōkai gijutsu kōkaishin shinkō funatabi to shi ni tsuite," in Itō Kōji et al., eds., *Higashi Ajia kaiiki sōsho*, vol. 11, *Hakata to Ninpō* (Kyūko shoin, 2013), pp. 191–230.

[74] They were known as "false messengers" because they were not technically from the Ōuchi or the Ashikaga. Itō Kōji, *Chūsei Nihon no gaikō to zenshū* (Yoshikawa kōbunkan, 2002), pp. 89–91. For links to Sakai and Hakata monks, see pp. 224–27.

[75] *Yamaguchi kenshi shiryōhen chūsei*, vol. 1, Ishiyama Honganji nikki, 12.28.1536 (Tenbun 5), p. 431, and for the later shipment of five agates, 12.1.1537 (Tenbun 6), pp. 431–32.

[76] Kawase Kazuma, *Kokatsuji ban no kenkyū* (Antiquarian Booksellers of Japan, 1967), pp. 112–18. See also Fukuo Takeichirō, *Ōuchi Yoshitaka*, pp. 95–101, and Takahashi Satoshi, *Muromachi jidai no koshōhon "Rongo Shūge" no kenkyū* (Kyūko shoin, 2008), pp. 52–54.

Yoshitaka relied on the King of Japan seal for his trade with Ming China (Figure 9.5). That he unilaterally used this seal can be known from surviving imported texts.[77] He oversaw two missions to China, after a hiatus of the Ningbo incident. The first, led by the monk Kōshin Sekitei (1481–1564), departed in 1539 and returned in 1541.[78] The other, led by Sakugen Shūryō (1501–79), left in 1547 and returned in 1549. Yoshitaka's role in dispatching these missions was uncontested, as is evident from a series of letters he wrote to Sakugen Shūryō.[79] No Japanese rivals could successfully compete with Yoshitaka. The Hosokawa attempted a mission to China, but they were rejected by Ming authorities because Ōuchi vessels, relying on the proper, up-to-date tallies, arrived before them.[80] The Hosokawa never tried again.

A law code from 1546 recounts how the Ōuchi regulated ships traveling to China and had them administered by the Murakami privateers (kaizoku).[81] Yoshitaka managed to custom-order items from the Ming empire, such as writing desks designed for Japanese tastes and seating practices.[82] Yoshitaka alone was successful in engaging in such trade, for in 1544, 1545, and 1546, Ōtomo Yoshiaki and the Sagara tried to send separate embassies to Ming China, but they were rebuffed.[83]

[77] Peter Kornicki, "Korean Books in Japan: From the 1590s to the End of the Edo Period," *Journal of the American Oriental Society* 133.1 (2013), pp. 72–73. See also Fujimoto Yukio, "Chōsenban Tō Raku Hinŏ shishū kō," *Chōsen gakuhō* 199–200 (2006), pp. 265–90, and figure 9.5.

[78] Itō Kōji, has provided the first transcription of Kōshin Sekitei's *Ikenroku* in *Chūsei no Hakata to Ajia* (Bensei shuppan 2021), pp. 424–504 and for actions of 1539, pp. 450–52. See also Itō's analysis, pp. 367–374.

[79] *Tenryūji monjo no kenkyū* (Shibunkaku, 2011), Myōchi-in monjo, doc. 1, 6.20 [(Tenbun 15) 1546] Ōuchi Yoshitaka *shojō*; doc. 2, 8.10 Ōuchi Yoshitaka *bugyōnin rensho shojō*; doc. 3, 10.26 [(Tenbun 15) 1546] Ōuchi Yoshitaka *shojō*; and doc. 4, 11.15 Ōuchi Yoshitaka *shojō*, pp. 420–21. Sakugen Shūryō diary recounting the expedition survives. Makita Tairyō, *Sakugen Nyūminki no kenkyū*, 2 vols. (Bukkyō bunka kenkyūjo, 1955), some of which appears in *Yamaguchi kenshi shiryōhen chūsei*, vol. 1, pp. 848–59.

[80] Okamoto Makoto, "'Sakai kentōshi' to Sengokuki no kenminsen hakken," *Shigaku zasshi* 124 (3.2015), pp. 55–56. For reference to this ship, see *Hagi han batsu etsu roku*, vol. 2 (Yamaguchi ken monjokan, 1994), maki 59, Sasaki monjo, doc. 2, p. 442.

[81] Kasai Shigesuke, *Nankai tsūki*, in *Shintei zōho shiseki shūran*, vol. 30 (4th printing, Kondō shuppan, 1931), pp. 456–59. For a more accessible transcription of these laws, *Ōuchi bunka*, pp. 268–70. The editors of *Ehime kenshi shiryōhen kodai*, vol. 2, *chūsei* (Ehime, 1984), p. 658, accept this document as being reliable. See also Peter Shapinsky, *Lords of the Sea: Pirates, Violence, and Commerce in Late Medieval Japan* (Ann Arbor: University of Michigan Center for Japanese Studies, 2014), p. 260.

[82] The *Kachō radenbundai suzuribako* was made by Ming craftsmen to Japanese tastes. See https://webarchives.tnm.jp/imgsearch/show/C0032627. See also *Ōuchi bunka to Kita Kyūshū* (Kita Kyūshū shiritsu shizenshi rekishi hakubutsukan, 2011), p. 60, and *Ōuchi bunka*, p. 841. People in Japan did not sit on chairs and so required lower legs than was typical for Ming examples.

[83] For how Sagara engaged in international trade after 1533, see Itō Kōji, "Higo Sagara shi to Higashi Ajia," in Inaba Tsuguhara et al. eds., *Chūsei Sagara shi no tenkai to chiiki shakai* (Ebisu kōshō, 2020), pp. 268–78. See also Hashimoto Yū, "Muromachi sengokuki no shogun kenroku to gaikōken," *Rekishigaku kenkyū* 708, (3.1998), pp. 4, 13. For further debates about Yoshitaka's monopoly on the China trade, see Okamoto Makoto, "'Sakai kentōshi' to Sengokuki no kenminsen hakken," pp. 38–39.

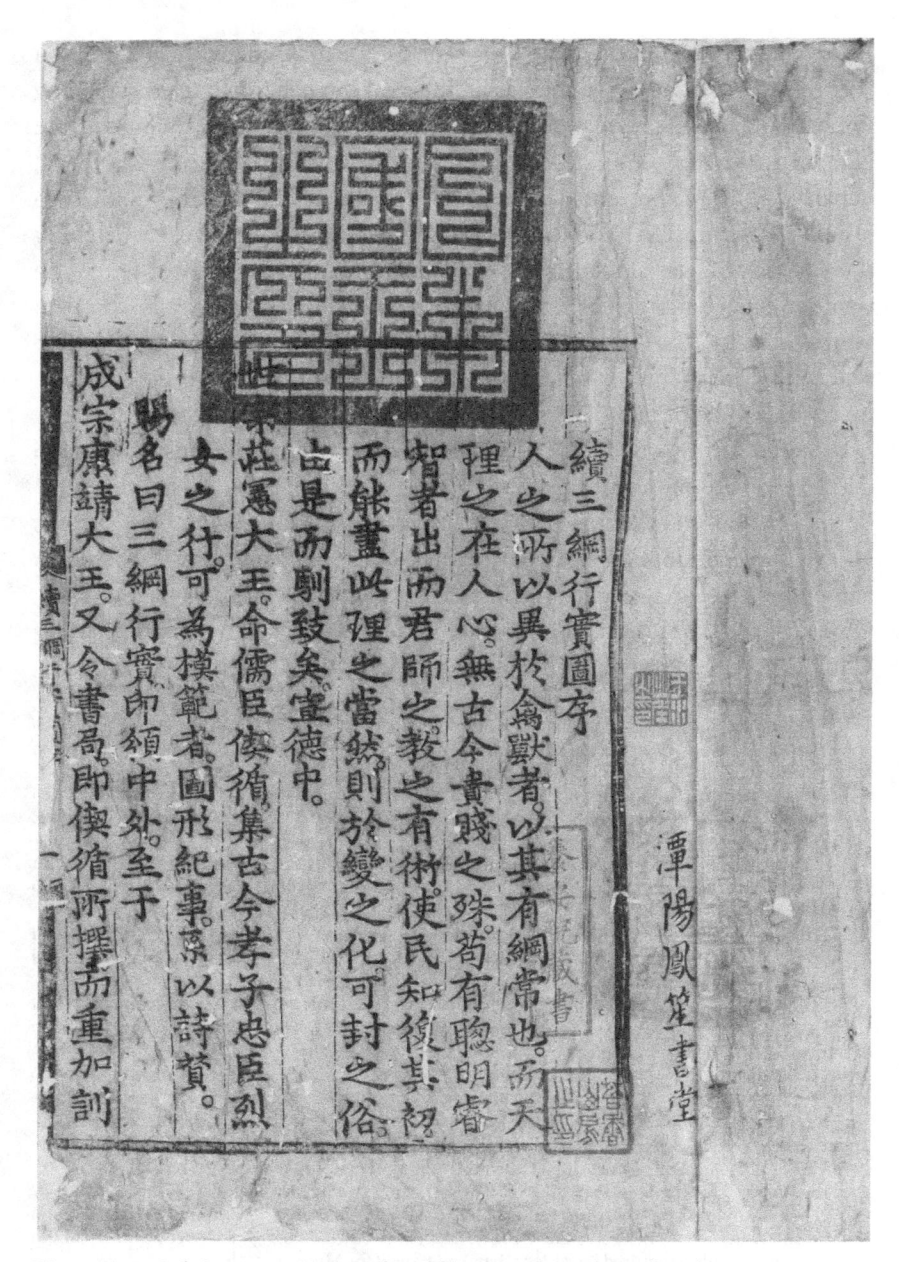

Figure 9.5 *Sok Samgang Haengsil-to* (Illustrated Guide to the Three Relationships), Prologue of Section 1 with Yoshitaka's King of Japan Seal. Image and permission provide by Tōyō bunko (The Oriental Library)

Yoshitaka adopted a variety of strategies in dealing with Ming and Korean officials. As we have seen, at times he affixed to the *Dazai Daini* seal in documents sent to Korea and portrayed himself as a regional official.[84] For other records, he added the stamp of the King of Japan seal, which allowed him to act diplomatically as if he were the King of Japan.[85] It is not clear why he used alternating seals in his interactions with Korea, but in the case of his dealings with the Ming, the King of Japan seal proved essential to oversee this tributary trade that allowed Yoshitaka to ship vast amounts of precious metals to the content.

Increasing Copper and Silver Exports

Yoshitaka oversaw ever-expanding shipments of copper and silver to China and Korea. His vessels exported 197 tons of copper in 1539, nearly doubling the amount carried in such missions from the time of Norihiro (102 tons).[86] In the 1530s and 1540s, silver exports increased dramatically. According to the historian William Atwell, they "not only helped to stimulate rapid economic and urban growth but . . . also made the Japanese a significant force in world economic history for the first time."[87]

Many historians have assumed that this expansion in trade arose because of new smelting techniques. They have relied on a 1533 entry in *Ginzan kyūki*, the only surviving account of silver mining, that suggested that an improved smelting technique called cupellation led to this increase in silver production. However, this assertion is questionable. Cupellation entails heating ore at a temperature high enough to cause impurities to be absorbed into a porous container, known as a cupel; or to be evaporated into the air; or to float at the top of the mixture. Sixth century BCE metallurgists relied on cupellation in China, and this process was used to refine metals in

[84] Seki Shūichi, *Chūsei Nichō kai-iki shi no kenkyū* (Yoshikawa kōbunkan, 2002), pp. 259–60.

[85] Several volumes survive with Yoshitaka's seal on them as King of Japan, including the *Sok samgang haengsil-to* (續三綱行實圖), printed 1514. See Kornicki, "Korean Books in Japan," pp. 72–73. That text with the seal appears in *Tōyō bunko no meihin* (Tōyō bunko, 2007), pp. 240–41 and is illustrated (Figure 9.5) above.

[86] Delmer Brown, *Money Economy in Medieval Japan: A Study in the Use of Coins* (Institute of Far Eastern Languages, Yale University, 1951), p. 34.

[87] William Atwell, "Time, Money, and the Weather: Ming China and the 'Great Depression' of the Mid-Fifteenth Century," *Journal of Asian Studies* 61.1 (2.2002), p. 102.

seventh-century Japan.[88] Cupellation was not a new process, and it therefore seems unlikely that, as the *Ginzan kyūki* suggests, Zongdan (J. Sotan) and Gui Shou (J. Keiju), two Chinese merchants based in Hakata, introduced new techniques to a Japanese merchant named Kamiya Jutei.[89] *Ginzan kyūki* also states that new tunneling techniques allowed extraction of more silver, but in the soft the limestone of Iwami these techniques could only have facilitated removing excess water to prevent flooding, and so this claim too is dubious (Figure 9.6).[90]

Rather, it was better security and improved transportation that contributed to increased exports. Kamiya Jūtei, incorrectly described in *Ginzan kyūki* as having discovered the Ōmori silver mine, founded an Itsukushima shrine at Tomogaura, a harbor that provided vital protection for silver shipments. Tomogaura and a secondary locale called Koryū were hidden harbors, surrounded by high rocks on both sides and reachable only by a single path, were easier to protect than the expansive harbor at Nima. Tomogaura was the better of the two, since it had potable water. Packhorses could travel along the edge of these cliffs. From there, their packs could be dropped to the shore below and placed on boats that took them out to larger ships offshore.

A team of packhorses could carry silver from the mines to Tomogaura in just over four hours.[91] They would travel along a path guarded by numerous castles controlled by Ōuchi officials, including four larger ones on the mountains of Iwami, Yamazaki, Yataki, and Yamabuki. Iwami castle was located near Tomogaura, and the Iwami Hachiman shrine founded by Ōuchi Yoshioki was located at its base. These castles were constructed in the

---

[88] Peter Golas, *Science and Technology in China*, vol. 5, part 13 (New York: Cambridge University Press, 1999), pp. 124–26, and Murakami Ryū, *Kin gin dō no Nihonshi* (Iwanami shinsho, 2007), pp. 73–74.

[89] *Ginzan kyūki*, located most conveniently in *Yamaguchi kenshi shiryōhen chūsei*, vol. 1, pp. 651–58, is riddled with errors and its chronology is unreliable. However, not all its claims are inaccurate. Kamiya Jūtei did hail from Hakata. Saeki Kōji, "Hakata shōnin Kameya Jūtei no jitsuzō," *Kyōkai kara mita uchi to soto "Kyūshū shigaku" sōkan 50 shūnen kinren ronbunshū ge* (Iwata shoin, 2009), pp. 147–65. Nothing is known about Zongdan or Gui Shou, but other Chinese merchants traveled to Yamaguchi and Korea and sailed through the Genkai seas to Munakata, and through the Inland Sea to Suō. *Hagi han batsu etsu roku*, vol. 2, maki 78, Zhao (Chō) Kyūzaemon doc. 15 postscript, pp. 767–69.

[90] Brown, *Money Economy*, p. 34, and Tessa Morris-Suzuki, *The Technological Transformation of Japan: From the Seventeenth to the Twenty-First Century* (Cambridge: University of Cambridge Press, 1994), p. 43. New tunneling techniques would have made a difference for mines like Ikuno, where the silver was encapsulated in hard rock, but not Iwami.

[91] It was slightly more distant than Nima, which could be reached on foot in slightly under four hours.

Figure 9.6 Ōkubo Mine Shaft (Iwami Silver Mine). Photograph by Thomas Conlan

fifteenth and sixteenth centuries, and some sixteen loomed over the paths that led from the mines to the harbors.[92]

Korean sources first mention extensive shipments of silver from Japan in 1538.[93] By 1542, a year before the first European contact with Japan, 3.3 US tons (eighty thousand *ryō*) of silver were exported to Korea. One Korean source called this an unheard-of amount.[94] Around that time, another shipment of silver of roughly the same amount was confiscated by the Ming. Scholars have estimated that total silver shipments for the time consisted of nearly 22 tons per year.[95] The population of the Ōmori silver mines reached thirteen thousand households during this period of its heyday.[96]

These silver exports attracted attention abroad. According to *Yoshitakaki*, "At Ōta in Iwami, a mountain of silver was discovered. News of this mountain of treasure spread to other countries, and ships often arrived from China, India (*tenjiku*), and Korea (Koguryŏ)."[97] The Iberians, when they arrived in Japan, marveled at how plentiful silver was there. The Spanish among them named the archipelago "the Silver Islands," although in the year 1600 they came to prefer the name "Japan" to describe the islands.[98]

Yoshitaka's expansion of mining did not occur in a vacuum; rather he was supported in these endeavors by the court. Between 1528 and 1551 Emperor Go-Nara mobilized metal casters (*imoji*) throughout Japan, although this process has been overlooked because most of the sources pertaining to casters have been thought to be unreliable.[99] Amino Yoshihiko has studied

---

[92] These castles were created during the fifteenth or sixteenth century, although when they were founded remains unknown because they have not been carefully excavated. Discussion Shinkawa Takashi, 6.11.2015.

[93] *Chosŏn wangjo sillok*, 10.29.1538 (Chungjong 33) for reference to the Ōuchi transporting much silver to Korea (accessed 12.3.2019), http://sillok.history.go.kr/id/wka_13310029_001. In addition they brought tin (*tongnabcheol* 銅鑞鐵) lead (*yeon* 鉛) and iron (*cheol* 鐵).

[94] *Chūgoku Chōsen no shiseki ni okeru Nihon shiryō shūsei*, 4.1542, p. 1913. See also 7.1542, p. 1941 for reference to the "King" bringing a similar amount of silver. In this case, this "King" was most likely Yoshitaka. For an overview, see Seki Shūichi, *Chūsei Nichō kai-iki shi no kenkyū*, p. 240.

[95] William Atwell, "International Bullion Flows and the Chinese Economy, circa 1530–1650," *Past and Present* 95 (5.1982), pp. 69–70 for three tons of silver being confiscated, and the estimate of a year trade in silver of 21.9 US tons (19,875 kilograms).

[96] Kobata Atsushi, *Nihon Kōzanshi no kenkyū* (Iwanami shoten, 1968), p. 120. He draws this from the 6.26 Yamane Jōan *shojō*, which appears most conveniently in Nagoya daigaku bungakubu kokushi kenkyūshitsu, ed., *Chūsei imoji shiryō* (Hōsei daigaku shuppan kyoku, 1982), pp. 91–92.

[97] *Yoshitakaki*, p. 411 for events of 1545 (Tenbun 14). The Portuguese came from India, or *tenjiku*, and were referred to as "Indians" (*tenjikujin*) as such. This account also mentions gifts from the Portuguese that included eyeglasses and a clock. For more on these exchanges, see chapter 10.

[98] M. Joseph Costelloe, S.J., trans., *The Letters and Instructions of Francis Xavier* (St. Louis, MO: Institute of Jesuit Sources, 1992), Letter 108, "To Father Simāo Rodrigues, in Portugal from Goa, 4.8.1552" (EX 355–58; FX IV 549–51), p. 378. The Spanish here are referred to as Castilians.

[99] For examples of forged documents, see *Chūsei imoji shiryō*, doc. 1, 1.1167 (Ninan 2) *Kurōdo dokoro no chō utsushi*, pp. 5–6, and *Himeji shishi*, vol. 9, *shiryōhen chūsei*, vol. 2 (Himeji, 2012),

and published a collection of records pertaining to the Matsugi family, arguing that a mining surge in the 1540s was emblematic of nonagricultural economic activity in Japan.[100] Unbeknownst to him, these activities actually commenced a dozen years earlier, in 1528 by the court of Emperor Go-Nara.

Go-Nara attempted to re-establish court taxing authority over metal workers in 1528. He did so because the enervated Ashikaga, who did not reside in the capital, could no longer govern, and the court required more revenue to effectively function. Go-Nara's oldest edict (*rinji*) regarding this policy as the "restoration" of a tax that had long been abandoned. Otsuki (Ōmiya) Koreharu (1496–1551), of a powerful administrative family that drafted important court documents, took a leading role in restoring these levies in 1528.[101] In 1530 Koreharu possessed rights regarding iron (*tetsu*) and painting implements (*egu*) that meant he could tax metal craftsmen.[102]

On 3.16.1543, Go-Nara issued further edicts to regulate metal casters throughout Japan.[103] These edicts were widely disseminated, and surviving records refer to mining activities from Hakata, Nagato, and Iwami.[104] Some of the edicts may have been altered to emphasize the significance of the Matsugi, a metal caster family, but the changes were confirmed by but two prominent courtiers, Yanagihara Sukesada (1495–1578) and Hirohashi

docs. 1–2, pp. 2–3 for examples of the Akuta of Harima. For this topic, see Paula Curtis, "Forgery in Motion: Cross-Status Networks, Authority, and Documentary Culture in Medieval Japan," PhD dissertation, University of Michigan, 2019.

[100] *Chūsei imoji shiryō*, pp. 247–300 for his overview and analysis of these documents.

[101] *Mibu ke monjo* (Kunaichō shoryōbu, 1979), vol. 1, doc. 136, 10.12.1528 (Kyōroku 1) Go-Nara tennō *rinji* (*shukushi*), p. 124, and doc. 137, 12.11 Ōmiya Koreharu *shojō*, pp. 124–25.

[102] *Egu* seems ambiguous but many of the important pigments for colors, such as green from malachite, blue from copper, and red (and white) from lead, were linked to mining. *Mibu ke monjo*, vol. 1, doc. 137, 12.11 Ōmiya Koreharu *shojō*, pp. 124–25. The 1528 Go-Nara *rinji* was not known to Amino, nor does it appear in his *Chūsei imoji shiryō*. See Yoshitake Masaaki, "Matsugi Hisanao to imojishi soshiki no musubitsuki ni okeru Yanagihara Sukesada to Ōuchi shi no yakuwari," *Ryūkoku kenkyū* 38 (3.2015), p. 42 n. 49.

[103] *Chūsei imoji shiryō*, Matsugi monjo, doc. 44, 3.16.1543 (Tenbun 12) Go-Nara tennō *rinji*, p. 41, and doc. 51, 3.16.1543 (Tenbun 12) Go-Nara tennō *rinji utsushi*, pp. 43–44. See also Seikan monjo, doc. 8, 11.13.1551 (Tenbun 20) Go-Nara tennō *rinji*, p. 183, and doc. 17, 5.5.1546 (Tenbun 15), Go-Nara tennō *nyōbō hōsho*, p. 187. According to Amino Yoshihiko (*kaisetsu*, pp. 274–75), these documents are legitimate, but may have been slightly altered to enhance the authority and role of the Matsugi.

[104] The Hirai in Dazaifu possess a 3.1549 (Tenbun 18) Matsugi Munehiro tax levy (*nengu saisokujō*). The Yasuo of Shimonoseki have a nearly identical record. *Yamaguchi kenshi shiryōhen chūsei*, vol. 4, Yasuo ke monjo, doc. 15, 3.1549 (Tenbun 18) Matsugi Munehiro *nengu saisokujō*, p. 376. A document with identical paper and possessing the same Matsugi monogram exists in the Yamane collection. Sakurae-chō kyōiku iinkai, comp., *Iwami no kuni imoji tōryō Yamane shi shiryō chōsa hōkokusho* (Sakurae-shi, 3.1992), 3.1550 (Tenbun 19) Matsugi Munehiro *andojō*, p. 10. See also Kuratsune Kōichi, "Iwami no kuni ni tsutawatta chūsei imoji shiryō," *Nihon rekishi* 841 (6.2018), pp. 82–84.

Kanehide (1506–67).[105] Nearly all of those officials overseeing mining, including Otsuki Koreharu, Yanagihara Sukesada, and Hirohashi Kanehide, found their way to Yamaguchi because Yoshitaka controlled the most important mines and had reorganized his administration of them, but some of his rivals, such as the Amako, also heeded Go-Nara's edicts.[106]

Yoshitaka's Influential Advisers

Otsuki Koreharu acquired great influence in Yamaguchi. The old, powerful Otsuki family was responsible for drafting most important court documents and monopolized the position of *taifu no sakan*, also known as the secretary (*geki*) of the Council of State. Koreharu was an able family head. His daughter, who had been adopted by the courtier Hirohashi Kanehide, also resided in Yamaguchi, and would become Yoshitaka's second wife. In 1545, she gave birth to his son and new heir. His name, also Yoshitaka, would be written with different characters than his father's.[107]

Yoshitaka had several officials with broad interests, including literary texts and matters of mining. Otsuki Koreharu and Yanagihara Sukesada concerned themselves with metallurgy as well as Neo-Confucianism and gave lectures on the Four Books and Five Classics defined by Zhu Xi (1130–1200).[108]

---

[105] *Chūsei imoji shiryō*, Matsugi monjo, doc. 278, 25 Bō *shojō*, p. 174. Yoshitake Masaaki, "Matsugi Hisanao to imojishi soshiki no musubituski ni okeru Yanagihara Sukesada to Ōuchi shi no yakuwari," pp. 29–34, makes the important and obvious point that, irregularities aside, the edicts were accepted as legitimate because Yanagihara Sukesada added his monogram to the reverse of the document, making it an official copy (*an*). Without this, such a record would not be accepted, but as it was in effect notarized by an official, Hirohashi Kanehide, whom Yoshitaka often worked with, it was accepted as genuine. See pp. 29–34. For more on these records and Yoshitaka, see Paula Curtis, "An Entrepreneurial Aristocrat: Matsugi Hisanao and the Forging of Imperial Service in Late Medieval Japan," *Monumenta Nipponica* 75.2 (2020), pp. 256–61.

[106] Sasamoto Shōji, "Kinsei shoki ni okeru Matsugi ke no imoji shihai," *Nagoya daigaku bungakubu kenkyū ronshū Shigaku* 30 (3.1984), pp. 189–90. Takaharu was close with the other courtiers. One of his daughters, for example, was adopted by Hirohashi Kanehide. *Sonpi bunmyaku*, vol. 2, p. 263. For Amako Haruhisa trying to organize Bingo province metallurgists (*kaji sōdaiku*) in response to Go-Nara's edicts, see *Hiroshima kenshi kodai chūsei shiryōhen*, vol. 5 (Hiroshima, 1980), 8.28 Amako Haruhisa *sodehan bugyōnin rensho hōsho utsushi*, p. 631.

[107] Koreharu departed from Yamaguchi to Kyoto at the time of the birth to notify the court. *Sagara ke monjo*, vol. 1, doc. 377, 10.24 [(Tenbun 14) 1545] Ida Okihide *shojō*, p. 431, and doc. 378, Ankokuji Shinpō *shojō* pp. 432–35. For more on this child, see *Yoshitakaki*, p. 422.

[108] Ichikawa Mototarō, *Nihon jukyōshi 3 Chūsei hen* (Tōa gakujutsu kenkyūkai, 1992), pp. 410–11, and Yonehara Masayoshi, *Sengoku bushi no bungei no kenkyū* (Ōfūsha, 1994), p. 792. See also Yonehara, pp. 726–27, for exchanges between Yoshitaka and Yanagihara Sukesada after a bout of heavy drinking and pp. 660–710 for instruction in Confucianism, poetry, and antiques (*yusoku kojitsu*). Fukuo Takeichirō, *Ōuchi Yoshitaka*, pp. 105–15, 192–96, also is insightful.

Koreharu also copied and annotated the *Goseibai shikimoku*, the 1232 law code of the Kamakura shogunate, a venerated code.[109] He not only served as an imperial messenger, but also helped to analyze the quality of silver ingots (*ginsu*) and had them transported to Yamaguchi and from there to the Ōmori silver mine.[110]

Yoshitaka and his officials were interested in mining and experimented with alloys. Several pottery cupels were found in a residence a few feet from the garden of the Ōuchi mansion. Some were used to melt or test gold and silver, while others were used for copper and copper alloys.[111] The techniques discovered included dulling copper by adding arsenic, thereby giving it an aged appearance, and the creation of brass, which required zinc, a rare metal in Japan that most likely came from China.[112]

Sagara Taketō (1498–1551), a skilled scribe and administrator, praised in the *Yoshitakaki* as being "exceedingly skilled and intelligent," was also involved with the testing and analysis of silver in Yamaguchi and Iwami.[113] He analyzed silver, helped to discover new mines, and remained in close contact with Otsuki Koreharu.[114] An innovator, Taketō was unpopular and not easily understood by compatriots, who complained about him as early as 1545.[115] Memories of his abrasive reputation lingered. In 1579, Bekki

---

[109] Otsuki Koreharu, Kyōroku 2 (1529) printing of the *Goseibai shikimoku*, Keiō Library collection (accessed 8.19.2023), https://www.fl-keio.info/fl_img/course01/detail/L09_110X@506@1_001.html

[110] *Sagara ke monjo*, vol. 1 (Tōkyō daigaku shuppankai, 1917), doc. 395, 12.15 [(Tenbun 14) 1545] Otsuki Koreharu *shojō*, pp. 447–48. See also doc. 417, 7.12 [(Tenbun 15) 1546] Sagara Yoshishige *shojō*, pp. 467–68, for a letter from Sagara Yoshishige concerning analysis of rare silver ore.

[111] Kitajima Daisuke, *Yamaguchi shi maizō bunka chōsa hōkokusho*, vol. 112, *Ōuchi shi kanren machinami iseki*, vol. 8 (Yamaguchi shi kyōiku iinkai, 2014), "Kinzoku seisan kanren ibutsu no bunrui," pp. 141–79. These artifacts date from the Tenbun era (1530–57) and predate the 1551 destruction of Yoshitaka's mansion.

[112] Craftsmen in other places used brass as a gold substitute—it came close to the alchemists' goal of creating gold from copper. For this insight I am indebted to Jennifer Rampling, *Sengoku jidai no kin to garasu-Kirameku Ichijōdani no bunka to gijutsu* (Fukui, 2014) provides evidence of brass manufacturing. Whether zinc was imported as ingots or melted down from poor-quality imported coins merits further research, but it is known that some copper objects were made from melted Chinese coins. See Iinuma Kenji, "Nihon Chūsei ni shiyō sareta Chūgokusen no mayō to idomu," *Daikōkai no Nihon to kinzoku kōeki* (Kyoto: Shibunkaku, 2014), pp. 3–17.

[113] *Yoshitakaki*, p. 413, for his intelligence and his skill as a scribe. For his dispatch of messengers to Iwami, see *Jōeiji shiryō* (Jōeiji, 1978), doc. 60, 12.3 [(Tenbun 19) 1550] Ōuchi ke *bugyōshū renshojō*, pp. 60–61.

[114] *Sagara ke monjo*, vol. 1, doc. 395, 12.15 [(Tenbun 14) 1545] Otsuki Koreharu *shojō*, pp. 447–48.

[115] *Yamaguchi kenshi tsūshihen chūsei*, pp. 540–41. The monk Ankokuji Shinhō complained that he could not understand what Sagara Taketō said and needed Sugi Muneaki to translate for him *Sagara ke monjo*, vol. 1, doc. 378, 10.25 ([Tenbun 14] 1545) Ankokuji Shinhō *shojō*, p. 434, and doc. 379, 10.29 ([Tenbun 14] 1545) Kikuchi Yoshitake *shojō*, pp. 435–36.

Akitsura (1513–85), a follower of Ōtomo Yoshishige (Sōrin), would still describe Taketō as being unreasonable.[116]

Yoshitaka attempted to regularize mining practices in his domains and relied on men like Otsuki Koreharu and Sagara Taketō. He dispatched regulations to the provinces of Aki, Suō, Nagato, Iwami, Buzen, and Chikuzen, where they were put in effect.[117] These policies sometimes led to tensions, particularly in Iwami.[118]

Yoshitaka successfully promoted industry and trade, but the abundance of riches did not allow for any innovations in using debt to fund war, which arose among more cash-strapped regimes in Europe.[119] Relative poverty led to fiscal innovation, and in particular new ways of using debt. For example, the Ashikaga, devised a novel 20 percent tax on debt (*ichibun tokusei*), levied first on creditors and then, if they did not pay, on debtors between the years 1454 and 1480.[120] Yoshitaka, with his great wealth, could readily pay for all his projects without resorting to creative ways of extracting revenue. He had to devote more resources to protecting what he had.

---

[116] *Zōho teisei Hennen Ōtomo shiryō*, vol. 24 (Ōita, 1966), 2.16.1579 (Tenshō 8) Tachibana Dōsetsu *shojō*, p. 218. Akitsuki later changed his name to Tachibana Dōsetsu. I am indebted to Wada Shūsaku for this reference.See also Yamamoto Hiroki, *Saikoku no Sengoku kassen* (Yoshikawa kōbunkan, 2007), p. 73.

[117] The documents from Suō, the core province, were issued on 3.18.1549; those from Nagato and Buzen on 4.21; from Iwami on 10.10 through 10.26; and Aki on 11.23. The delays in promulgating the documents apparently stemmed from difficulties in reorganizing mining interests, but already by 9.3.1549, casters were taxed in Hakata. *Chūsei imoji shiryō*, Matsugi monjo, docs. 73–79, 3.18.1549 (Tenbun 18) Ōuchi shi *bugyōnin rensho hōsho an*, pp. 56–60 for Suō; docs. 80–81, pp. 61–62 for Nagato; docs. 82–91, pp. 61–66 for Buzen; docs. 99–101, pp. 70–71 for Iwami; and docs. 102–6, pp. 72–75 for Aki. For a list of such casters being taxed in Dazaifu, surviving in the original and as official copies (*anmon*), see doc. 98, 9.3.1549 (Tenbun 18) Dazaifu *imoji nengusen chūmon*, pp. 69–70.

[118] *Iwami no kuni imoji tōryō Yamane shi shiryō chōsa hōkokusho*, p. 10 for a 3.1550 (Tenbun 19) Matsugi Munehiro *andojō*, for tensions between the Ogasawara and the Yamane, who hailed from Nima and oversaw the Iwami mines. See also pp. 3–4. The monogram of this document is identical to the Yasuo ke monjo 3.1549 3.1549 (Tenbun 18) Matsugi Munehiro *nengu saisokujō*.

[119] David Parrott, *Business of War: Military Enterprise and Military Revolution in Early Modern Europe* (Cambridge: Cambridge University Press, 2012), emphasizes how debt underpinned these regimes. Earlier studies also emphasize the importance of war and state creation. Charles Tilly, *The Formation of Nation States in Western Europe* (Princeton: Princeton University Press, 1975).

[120] *Chūsei hōsei shiryōshū*, vol. 2 (Iwanami shoten, 1957), 7.13.1481 (Bunmei 13), p. 97, and Grossberg, trans., *Laws of the Muromachi bakufu* (Tokyo: Monumenta Nipponica, 1981), article 283, pp. 116–17. For more on the financial acumen of moneylenders, see Suzanne Gay, *The Moneylenders of Late Medieval Kyoto* (Honolulu: University of Hawaii Press, 2001), pp. 142–43.

Wars in Iwami and Aki

Ōuchi mineral-rich domains were targeted by rivals. Amako Tsunehisa, the lord of Izumo, attempted to seize the mineral-rich areas of Iwami and Aki in 1537. Yoshitaka promised to aid Mōri Motonari (1497–1571), a beleaguered Aki supporter, against the Amako, and dispatched an army under the command of Sue Mochinaga.[121] Iwami's mines, with their castles, were secure, although a small disturbance erupted at Ōmori in 1538.[122] Yoshitaka still intended to set off for Kyoto on 5.6.1538, but this lingering trouble in Iwami and Aki kept him from going.[123] For well over a year he still planned to visit Kyoto, until a new round of disturbances forced him to abandon the trip entirely. Why he wanted to go there is unclear, although he did express interest in Sonten, the deity of the northern Kyoto temple of Kurama.[124]

Mōri Motonari established a castle in northern Aki, some fifty miles south of the mines, and promised Yoshitaka his undivided loyalty through a formal oath in 1539.[125] Motonari resisted the combined forces of Amako Tsunehisa and the Takeda, the enervated *shugo* of Aki province, killing thirty-four enemy in a night attack on 6.16.1540.[126] The Takeda were weak, as their leader Mitsukazu (1503?–40) died shortly after this encounter.[127] The Amako laicized a Hagaiji monk, renamed Takeda Nobuzane (1524–55?), who commanded Aki forces.[128] He was not successful. Yoshitaka attacked

---

[121] Yamamoto Hirofumi et al., eds., *Sengoku daimyō no komonjo Nishinihon hen* (Kashiwa shobō, 2013), 1.27 [(Tenbun 6) 1537]. Ōuchi Yoshitaka *shojō*, pp. 242–43. This document was long mistaken to be written in 1551, but Yoshitaka's monogram dates from 1537. *Yamaguchi kenshi tsūshihen chūsei*, p. 505, for the dispatch of an army, *Sengoku ibun Ōuchi shi hen*, vol. 3, doc. 2907, 1.13 Ōuchi shi *kashin rensho hōsho utsushi*, p. 299, and doc. 2908, 1.23 Ōuchi shi *kashin rensho hōsho utsushi*, p. 299. Sue Mochinaga later changed his name to Takamitsu

[122] *Chūsei Masuda Masuda shi kankei shiryōshū* (Masuda, 2016), doc. 576, 9.19.1538 (Tenbun 7) Ōuchi Yoshitaka *kanjō utsushi*, p. 224.

[123] *Sengoku ibun Ōuchi shi hen*, vol. 3, doc. 3009, 3.28 Sō Morikata *shojō an*, p. 324, and doc. 3014, 5.6 [(Tenbun 7) 1538] Ōuchi Yoshitaka *shojō utsushi*, p. 325. See also Tōkyō daigaku shiryōhen sanjo, comp., *Mōri ke monjo*, vol. 1 (Tōkyō daigaku shuppankai, 1920), doc. 212, 12.21 [(Tenbun 6) 1537] Muromachi bakufu *bugyōshū hōsho*, p. 183.

[124] *Sengoku ibun Ōuchi shi hen*, vol. 3, doc. 3134, 10.3 [(Tenbun 8) 1539] Ōuchi Yoshitaka *shojō*, p. 359. For his ultimate abandonment of the Kyoto trip, see *Yamaguchi kenshi tsūshihen chūsei*, p. 506.

[125] *Sengoku ibun Ōuchi shi hen*, vol. 3, doc. 3120, 7.7 [(Tenbun 8) 1539] Ōuchi Yoshitaka *shojō*, p. 354. For Yoshitaka's oath with Motonari, see doc. 3129, 9.13.1539 (Tenbun 8) Ōuchi Yoshitaka *shojō an*, p. 357, and doc. 3131, 9.28.1539 (Tenbun 8) Mōri Motonari *ukebumi an*, p. 357.

[126] *Mōri ke monjo*, vol. 1, doc. 282, 6.16.1540 (Tenbun 9) Aki no kuni Zōka *kassen kubi chūmon*, pp. 250–52. These Takeda were the forces of the *shugo* of Aki province. For an informative study, see Kawamura Shō'ichi, *Aki Takeda shi* (Ebisu kōshō, 2010).

[127] *Fusaaki oboegaki*, p. 1123. Mitsukazu along with with Tomota Okifuji of Itsukushima shrine fought against the Ōuchi in 1524 (Daiei 4), but both lost. See p. 1114.

[128] *Obama shishi shaji monjo hen* (Obama, 1976) Hagaiji monjo, doc. 24, *Nenchū gyōji*, pp. 402–28, p. 421. A monk from Izumo dispatched this Takeda Nobuzane "because they were allied" to the Amako. See also Kawamura, *Aki Takeda shi*, p. 127.

Aki in the ninth month of 1540, commandeered hundreds of boats, and his forces, led by the Sue and Naitō, landed and occupied Itsukushima shrine, in the Tōsai region.[129] He also occupied strategic islands, such as Kutsuna, quelling Takeda partisans in the Inland Sea.[130]

Meanwhile in Iwami, the situation remained unsettled. The Amako tried advancing to the mines, but were checked at Kōriyama, a fort in Aki located forty-five miles directly to the south of them. There a "great battle" was fought on 9.12.1540. Ōuchi reinforcements, led by Sue Takafusa, the adopted son of Sue Okifusa and lover of Yoshitaka, played a crucial role in defeating them on 12.3.1540.[131] On 1.13.1541, an Amako army was cut to pieces.[132] The Amako turned their attention to the mines to the north, and from 1.16 through 3.7.1541, skirmishes occurred in the Kuri region, near Ōta of the Ano district, site of the Ōmori silver mine, causing a small number of wounds and deaths, but then the Amako withdrew.[133]

Possessing Itsukushima and Rebuilding Shrines

Yoshitaka concentrated his energies on destroying his enemies in southern Aki. On 5.13.1541 the Takeda of Aki, bitter rivals of the Ōuchi, were annihilated when their castle at Kaneyama was taken.[134] Yoshitaka donated

[129] *Fusaaki oboegaki*, pp. 1117–18.
[130] *Ehime kenshi shiryōhen kodai chūsei* (Ehime, 1983), doc. 1705, 8.20 [(Tenbun 9) 1540] Ōuchi shi *bugyōnin rensho hōsho*, p. 935.
[131] *Mōri ke monjo*, vol. 1, doc. 286, 2.16.1541 (Tenbun 10) Mōri Motonari Kōriyama *rōjō nikki*, p. 263. See also *Ōuchi bunka*, Fusaaki oboegaki, p. 225 for more on the Sue campaign and Amako defeat. For more on how Takafusa was descended from the Toida, see Wada Shūsaku, "Yoshida Kanemigi 'Bōshū gekōki' ni mieru Ōuchi shi kankei kiji," pp. 106–7.
[132] For the unusually rich source pertaining to this campaign, see the narratives and rosters written by Motonari as well as a document of praise by Yoshitaka. *Mōri ke monjo*, vol. 1, doc. 286, 2.16.1541 (Tenbun 10) Mōri Motonari Kōriyama *rōjō nikki*, pp. 262–64, doc. 287, 1.13 Kōriyamajō *shokuchi kassen chūmon*, pp. 264–295, and doc. 288 1.13.1541 (Tenbun 10) Amako *jin kirikuzushi kubi chūmon*, pp. 295–300. *Kobayakawa ke monjo*, vol. 2 (Tōkyō daigaku shuppankai, 1927), doc. 429, 1.3.1541 (Tenbun 10) Kobayakawa Okikage *teoi kassen chūmon*, pp. 271–73. According to these records, sixty-three enemy heads were taken.
[133] *Yamaguchi kenshi shiryōhen chūsei*, vol. 4, Kuri ke monjo, doc. 22, 2.22.1541 (Tenbun 10) Ōuchi Yoshitaka *kanjō*, p. 851 for the disturbance of 1.16.1541. *Iwami Kikkawa*, doc. 55, 8.28.1543 (Tenbun 12) Kikkawa Tsunefuyu (Yasutsune) *gunchūjō eisha* pp. 59–60 for reference to three of his followers wounded by arrows, and the killing of one enemy on 3.7.1541. See also doc. 56, 10.9.1543 (Tenbun 12) Ōuchi Yoshitaka *kanjō eisha*, p. 60.
[134] For the defeat of the Takeda at Kaneyama, see *Hiroshima kenshi kodai chūsei shiryōhen*, vol. 5, Shiroi monjo, doc. 9, 6.12.1541 (Tenbun 10) Ōuchi Yoshitaka *kanjō*, p. 23, Yamada Gozaemon Naokata monjo, 6.12.1541 (Tenbun 10) Ōuchi Yoshitaka *kanjō utushi*, p. 371, Asonuma monjo, doc. 39, 5.13.1541 (Tenbun 10) Amano Okisada *kassen chūmon* p. 43, and doc. 40 6.12.1541 (Tenbun 10) Ōuchi Yoshitaka *kanjō*, pp. 43–44. See also *Fusaaki oboegaki*, p. 1124. Belying the intensity of the conflict, one sees more fatalities (six) than wounds (two by pike), which is unusual, as almost

the ancestral armor of the Takeda to Itsukushima, as the defeat of this old rival was total.[135] At the same time, Yoshitaka gained full control of Itsukushima shrine, the First Shrine (Ichinomiya) of Aki, and the province's most important cultic site. Because the Tomoda family of Itsukushima shrine attendants were also destroyed with the Takeda fall, Yoshitaka took advantage of the situation and transformed the internal organization of the shrine.[136] He also gave Daiganji, the shrine temple (Jingūji) of Itsukushima, an important role in up-keep of the shrine, as well as authority over metalworkers (*kaji*), craftsmen (*banshō*), smiths, and other workers.[137] Finally, he had these craftsmen re-build the great *torii* gate in the tidal flats of the Inland Sea, which had previously rotted away.[138] The name plaque (*hengaku*) for the *torii*, which survives, dates from 1547.[139] Emperor Go-Nara wrote the deity's name "Itsukushima *daimyōjin*," and his calligraphy is covered in skillfully cut sheets of copper. At the top of the frame appears a depiction of the esoteric Buddhist wish-fulfilling jewel (*cintāmaṇi*), and originally the whole plaque was covered in black lacquer and gold foil (*shippaku*). Several Ōuchi crests, made of the same sheets of copper, appear on both sides of the name plaque, suggesting that Yoshitaka continued the Ōuchi practice of repurposing major shrines to legitimate their familial interests.

Yoshitaka had the resources to rebuild other major shrines as well. He repaired the First Shrine of Usa in 1536 while campaigning in Kyushu.[140] Sonkai, the monk from Itsukushima who went to Korea with tons of baggage, also helped to rebuild Hakozaki shrine of Hakata. It had burned down in

invariably wounds are more common than deaths in these records. Nevertheless, the last Takeda of Aki, Nobuzane, who had been adopted from the Wakasa province branch of the Takeda, seems to have survived and fled.

[135] For the donation of the armor, see *Fusaaki oboegaki*, p. 1124.

[136] *Fusaaki oboegaki*, p. 1124. For the Tomoda rebellion and destruction, see pp. 1120–23, and for the initial Tomoda rebellion on 1.13.1541, Daiganji monjo, doc. 26, 7.13[(Tenbun 10) 1541] Chō Saga *mōshijō an*, pp. 1186–87.

[137] *Hiroshima kenshi kodai chūsei shiryōhen*, vol. 3, Daiganji monjo, doc. 13, 1.18 [(Tenbun 10) 1541] Ōuchi shi *bugyōnin shojō*, p. 1173, doc. 14, 1.28 [(Tenbun 10) 1541] Ōuchi shi *bugyōnin shojō*, p. 1173, and doc. 15, 1.29 [(Tenbun 10) 1541] Ōuchi shi *bugyōnin rensho shojō*, pp. 1174.

[138] *Hiroshima kenshi kodai chūsei shiryōhen*, vol. 3, Daiganji monjo, doc. 44, 2.23 [(Tenbun 15) 1546] Ōuchi shi *bugyōnin rensho hōsho an*, pp. 1200–1205. These documents make clear that the *torii* had long been rotted away. Later the gate was thatched in cedar bark (*hiwadabuki*). See doc. 52, 9.28 [(Tenbun 17) 1548] Kaji *daiku teiji ukebumi*, p. 1210. Mōri Motonari used the same craftsmen to rebuild this gate in 1561. See *Itsukushima Jinja Kokuhōten-Taifu higai fukō shien* (Itsukushima shrine Hatsukaichi-shi, 2005), p. 84.

[139] The name plaque survives in the Itsukushima shrine treasury. Viewed on 4.23.2023.

[140] *Sengoku ibun Ōuchi shi hen*, vol. 3, doc. 2847, 4.24 [(Tenbun 5) 1536] Ōuchi shi *kashin rensho hōsho*, and 2849, 5.6 [(Tenbun 5) 1536] Ōuchi shi *kashin rensho hōsho*, p. 277.

1492, but its restoration began in 1542.[141] Sonkai proved skilled enough that the year after rethatching Hakozaki in the prestigious cedar bark (*hiwada buki*) style, he had his workmen replace the roof of the second shrine at Usa.[142] Hakozaki was completed in 1545, and the treasure hall of Furukuma shrine in Yamaguchi was rebuilt in 1547.[143] Usa had been largely restored to its earlier grandeur and rethatched, but Yoshitaka, in his capacity of *Dazai Daini*, also attempted to restore at least some of its landholdings in the regions that he controlled.[144]

Yoshitaka's Ritual Supporters

Yoshitaka was strongly supported by powerful monks and shrine priests in Kyoto, who came to Yamaguchi to worship and perform important rites. A steady stream of high-ranking monks and Shinto specialists traveled to Yamaguchi, including members of the monastic nobility from Daigoji, Ninnaji, Miidera, and Enryakuji.[145] Sonkai (1472–1543), a prominent Ninnaji monk, not to be confused with the monk who resided in Itsukushima, is buried near Yamaguchi. Genga of Daigoji left an account of his travels; the Tendai monk Kōnin from Kyoto made a Buddhist statue in Yamaguchi 1549; and in 1532, the highest-ranking Tendai monk (*zasu*), an imperial prince, had his signature cast into the Kōryūji bell, with its interesting mixture of Korean and Japanese elements.[146]

---

[141] *Hiroshima kenshi kodai chūsei shiryōhen*, vol. 3, Daiganji monjo, doc. 30, 3.16 [(Tenbun 11] 1542) Ōuchi shi *bugyōnin rensho shojō*, p. 1189.

[142] *Hiroshima kenshi kodai chūsei shiryōhen*, vol. 3, Daiganji monjo, doc. 35, 5.10 [(Tenbun 12) 1543] Ōuchi shi *bugyōnin rensho shojō*, p. 1192.

[143] *Ōuchi bunka*, pp. 666–67, for Hakozaki and p. 654 for Furukuma. A stage (*haiden*) was built in front of Nagato's Sumiyoshi shrine in 1539. See p. 600.

[144] *Sengoku ibun Ōuchi shi hen*, vol. 3, doc. 3075, 4.12.1539 (Tenbun 8) Dazai *sen*, p. 341. This is not the only format he would rely upon, preferring *sodehan kudashibumi* (edicts) for other grants. See doc. 3076, 4.12.1539 (Tenbun 8) Ōuchi Yoshitaka *sodehan andojō utsushi*, p. 341.

[145] The *Yoshitakaki* recounts that Sonkai, of Ninnaji's Shinkō-in subtemple, visited Yamagachi, as did Genga of Daigoji, a Tendai monk Kōnin as well as representatives from Miidera's Kangaku-in. *Yoshitakaki*, p. 408.

[146] For Sonkai (who was not the same person as the Itsukushima monk), see *Ninnaji shiryō jishihen*, vol. 2 (Nara Kokuritsu bunkazai kenkyūjo shiryō, 1967), pp. 100–101; for Genga, Fujii Masako, "Ōnin Bunmei no rango ni okeru Daigoji no saikō," *Nihon rekishi* 764 (1.2012), pp. 125–26; for Kōnin and a statue made by Kyoto craftsmen dating from 1549 (Tenbun 19), see Iwai Tomoji, "Yamaguchi-shi Manpukuji Jizō bosatsuzō ni tsuite," *Yamaguchi kenritsu bijutsukan kenkyū kiyō* 1 (1996), pp. 1–15. For a Tendai *zasu* (name unknown) visiting Yamaguchi in the eighth month of 1532 (Kyōroku 5), see *Ōuchi bunka*, p. 872, and p. 851 for the bell.

Yoshitaka's interest in star worship remained undimmed. Kyoto's Samegai Wakamiya Hachiman Shrine attracted his attention. This shrine was uniquely prized by the Ashikaga and by all warriors of Minamoto descent. In 1541, Yoshitaka had a Rokujō Myōken shrine established at the site of an old Ōuchi residence, located next to that shrine, meaning that two shrines dedicated to Ashikaga and Ōuchi ancestors coexisted side by side.[147] Yoshitaka and his supporters from the west, including the Kobayakawa and Kikkawa, worshiped only at the Rokujō Myōken shrine, while the Ashikaga shogun Yoshiteru prayed at both.[148] Perhaps unsurprisingly, Myōken gained increasing prominence as a warrior god.[149] In 1550, other warriors commissioned scrolls of Myōken, depicting him as a god of war and Minamoto Yoritomo (1147–99) worshiping him, rather than Hachiman.[150]

As Myōken gained popularity in Kyoto and eastern Japan, Yoshitaka became enamored with Yoshida star worship practices. Yoshida Kanemigi (1516–73), the heir to Yoshida Kanetomo (1435–1511), traveled to Yamaguchi, where he explained Yoshida rites to Yoshitaka, his warriors, and shrine attendants.[151] He taught Ōuchi Yoshitaka a variety of empowerment (*kaji*) and fire offering rites (*goma*) that involved secret initiations and

[147] This is evident in the "Wakamiya Hachimangū monjo kiroku," *Gerin* no. 27 vols. 4–5 (1978), doc. 25, 10.24 [(Tenbun 10) 1541] Ōuchi Yoshitaka *shojō*, p. 20. For his commendation of his ancestral lands to this shrine, see doc. 29, 4.9 [(Tenbun 11) 1542] Ōuchi Yoshitaka *kishinjō*, p. 20. Whether this was Yoshitaka's residence or the site of the ancestral dwelling of Ōuchi Hiroyo is not clear. Ashikaga Yoshiharu merely mentions how a Rokujō Myōken Hachiman shrine was built at the site of an Ōuchi residence. See doc. 35, 5.20.1547 (Tenbun 16) Ashikaga Yoshiteru *mikyōjo*, p. 22. For the concurrent existence of two shrines, and Yoshiteru's prayers to both Rokujō Hachimangū and Myōken Hachimangū, see docs. 34–35, 5.20.1547 (Tenbun 16) Ashikaga Yoshiteru *mikyōjo*, p. 22.

[148] "Wakamiya Hachimangū monjo kiroku," doc. 27, 4.9 [(Tenbun 11) 1542] Kobayakawa Takakage *shojō* and doc. 28, 4.9 [(Tenbun 11) 1542] Kikkawa Motoharu *shojō*, p. 20. For Yoshiteru's documents (nos. 34–35), see the preceeding note.

[149] Epitomizing this, see the 5.20.1547 (Tenbun 16) Ashikaga Yoshiteru *mikyōjo*, where he recognized this shrine as "Myōken Hachiman." "Wakamiya Hachimangū monjo kiroku," doc. 35, p. 22. The document is misidentified, however, in that although called an Ashikaga Yoshiteru *mikyōjo*, it is better conceived as a Muromachi bakufu *bugyōnin hōsho*.

[150] For this remarkable scroll, with a 1550 (Tenbun 19) colophon, see *Chiba Myōken dai engi emaki* (Chiba shiritsu kyōdo hakubutsukan, 1995).

[151] Helen Hardacre, *Shintō: A History* (New York: Oxford University Press, 2016), pp. 229–30. For the pathbreaking study using these sources, see Miyachi Naokazu, "Ōuchi Yoshitaka no Shintōkan," *Jingi shi no kenkyū* (Kokon shoin, 1924), 200–220. These transcriptions originally appeared in Shimai Kiyoshi, "Yoshida Bunko no Kanemigi jihitsu hon ni tsuite 1," *Biblia*, no. 25 (6.1963), pp. 22–33; Yoshida Bunko no Kanemigi jihitsu hon ni tsuite 2," *Biblia*, no. 27 (3.1964): 46–58; and Yoshida Bunko no Kanemigi jihitsu hon ni tsuite 3," *Biblia*, no. 29 (10.1964): 34–45. For a convenient transcription of these texts, see *Dainihon shiryō* (hereafter DNSR), ser. 10, vol. 13 (Tōkyō daigaku shuppankai, 1977), pp. 113–57. Likewise, half of a year of Kanemigi's 1545 (Tenbun 14) diary has been transcribed. Murai Yūki, "Tōkyō daigaku shiryōhen sanjo eishabon 'Tenbun jūyonen nikki,'" *Tōkyō daigaku shiryōhen sanjo kenkyū kiyō*, no. 28 (3.2018), pp. 140–46. For more on Kanemigi, see David Romney, "Godly Politics: Ise, the Court, and Japanese Religion 1330–1615." PhD dissertation, Princeton University, 2023, pp. 162–64.

mudrā spells (*jumon*).[152] Worship at Three Altar Rites (*sandan gyōji*) entailed Shinto mudrā rites directed to the Seven Stars of the Big Dipper.[153] Kanemigi performed special rites to aid Yoshitaka, including yin yang rites to protect Yoshitaka's person and special purification rites for horses in battle.[154] Kanemigi attributed the surrender of many Izumo warriors to Yoshitaka as a sign of divine favor, and on 8.28.1543, while Yoshitaka was on his campaign, Kanemigi he worshiped at the seven shrines of Hikamisan, which symbolized the Big Dipper.[155]

Consequences of Upholding Court Authority

Yoshitaka required the ritual support of the Yoshida because he had decided to attack the Amako, his rivals to the east. Yoshitaka first advanced to Izumo, the homelands of the Amako, in the third month of 1542, when he captured Akana castle in Iwami and entered Izumo despite difficulties in keeping his armies supplied. During the fourth month of 1542 Yoshitaka's allies dispatched forces to maintain control over the Inland Sea.[156]

Yoshitaka's offensive reached its high-water mark in the autumn of 1542. To commemorate the immanent triumph, or so he thought, the courtier Nakayama Takachika (1514–78) sent Yoshitaka a sword and Yoshitaka sent one back in exchange.[157] Yoshitaka's support for the court proved to be his undoing in a place he only tenuously controlled, a process most evident after he restored Gakuenji rights in Izumo.[158] Yoshitaka demanded that local warriors abandon rights to imperial lands and return these regions to court control. This did not endear him to them. Yoshitaka's insistence on upholding court rights and central authority led to his defeat.

---

[152] DNSR, ser. 10, vol. 13, pp. 114–16. The curses included *jinku jumon* (spells on altars), *hōhei jumon* (spells with offerings), and *Miki jumon* (spells with offerings of sake).

[153] Hardacre, *Shintō*, pp. 221–25 for a good overview of these practices and p. 224 for a photograph of the octagonal altar.

[154] DNSR, ser. 10, vol. 13, p. 129 for the 2.2.1543 (Tenbun 12) rites to protect Yoshitaka and p. 119 for the 2.19.1542 (Tenbun 12) transmission of the three articles of the *jinme oharae*, which Yoshitaka would lose after his Izumo defeat.

[155] Shimai, "Yoshida bunko 1," pp. 27–30 for Kanemigi's diary for the 8.23.1543 (Tenbun 12).

[156] *Ehime kenshi shiryōhen kodai chūsei*, doc. 1720, 4.6 [(Tenbun 11) 1542] Ōuchi shi *bugyōnin rensho shojō*, p. 940.

[157] *Mibu ke monjo*, vol. 1 doc. 1926, 10.13 Ōuchi Yoshitaka *shojō*, p. 146. The editors estimate this document as dating from 1540 (Tenbun 9), but at that time, Yoshitaka's allies in Aki were besieged.

[158] See Gakuenji monjo kenkyūkai, ed., *Gakuenji monjo* (Hōzōkan, 2015), doc. 145, 10.13.1542 (Tenbun 11) Ōuchi Yoshitaka *kakukudashi*, p. 124.

Victory seemed at hand for Yoshitaka in the autumn of 1542.[159] While besieging the primary Amako castle, Yoshitaka conquered nearby Mt. Uneji. As the campaign continued, however, many of the local warriors grew unhappy with Yoshitaka's undermining of their authority in favor of the court and "changed their mind" and rejoined the Amako.[160] Yoshitaka had to pull back. Once the Amako restored control to nearby regions on 3.5.1543, they voided the absentee rights of Gakuenji, which Yoshitaka had confirmed.[161]

On 5.7.1543 Yoshitaka ended his campaign and retreated, but this became a rout. Many in his army, included warriors of the Masuda family, died.[162] Yoshitaka had difficulty securing adequate ships for his forces, and in one instance promised local seafarers great concessions. He granted the Ōga of Misumi, who controlled one of the best harbors in Iwami, a blanket tax exemption on all their ships, which had previously been limited to three ships.[163] There were simply not enough ships for the defeated army, and when Tsunemochi (Harumochi), Yoshitaka's adopted son and heir, tried to pick up some stragglers during the 1543 retreat, his craft capsized, and he died.[164] Locals feared that Tsunemochi would become a vengeful ghost, so they built an Ōuchi shrine to pacify his spirit in Matsue (Figure 9.7).[165]

[159] For this tumultuous period from the Amako perspective, Hasegawa Hiroshi, *Sengoku Daimyō Amako shi no kenkyū* (Yoshikawa kōbunkan, 2000), pp. 91–93.

[160] *Yamaguchi kenshi shiryōhen chūsei*, vol. 1, Tatara jōsuiki, p. 798. For an overview, see also Fukuo Takeichirō, *Ōuchi Yoshitaka*, p. 88, and Yonehara Masayoshi, *Ōuchi Yoshitaka* (Jinbutsu Ōraisha, 1967), pp. 161–75 for the Izumo campaign and defeat.

[161] *Gakuenji monjo*, doc. 145, 10.13.1542 (Tenbun 11) Ōuchi Yoshitaka *kakukudashi*, p. 124, docs. 146–47, 10.13 [(Tenbun 11) 1542] Ōuchi shi *bugyōnin rensho hōsho*, pp. 124–125, and doc. 148, 2.17 [(Tenbun 12) 1543] Ōuchi shi *bugyōnin hōsho*, p. 125. By contrast, see the 3.5.1543 (Tenbun 12) Amako shi Gakuenji Konpondō *zōei sadamegaki utsushi*, p. 126.

[162] *Chūsei Masuda Masuda shi kankei shiryōshū*, 1.10.1544 (Tenbun 13), p. 223. For an informative narrative of this campaign, and evidence of Masuda participation, see *Kikkawa ke monjo*, vol. 3 besshū, doc. 561, Ninomiya Shunjitsu *oboekagi*, pp. 388–405. For the Izumo campaigns against the Amako, see pp. 388–92.

[163] Yoshitaka originally only exempted three boats from harbor taxes on 6.7.1537 (Tenbun 6), but he offered a more blanket exemption on 5.19.1543 (Tenbun 12), which was modeled after one issued by Ōuchi Mochiyo on 3.11.1432 (Eikyō 4). Neither of Yoshitaka's documents survives. Yoshitaka's 1543 order was reconfirmed in 1552. Nakatsukasa Ken'ichi, "Bunken kara mita chūsei no Iwami no minato to ryūtsū," in *Nihon no kōeki to umi* (Yamakawa shuppankai, 2016), Ōga ke monjo, doc. 15 7.11.1552 (Tenbun 21) Ōuchi Haruhide Yoshinaga *andojō*, p. 103. Likewise, for reference to his 1537 judgment, see doc. 16, 7.11 [(Tenbun 21) 1552] Ōuchi shi *bugyōnin rensho hōsho*, p. 103.

[164] *Yamaguchi kenshi shiryōhen chūsei*, vol. 1, Tatara jōsuiki, p. 798.

[165] *Chūgoku chiranki, Shinkō Gunsho ruijū kassenbu*, vol. 2 (Naigai shoseki kabushiki kaisha, 1930), p. 435.

Figure 9.7 Ōuchi Shrine, Matsue. Photograph by Thomas Conlan

Selecting a New Heir

After returning to Yamaguchi Yoshitaka relied on Yoshida Kanemigi to ritually restore his forces, and he duly recopied horse purifications and curses (*jinku jumon*) on 6.5.1543. He also performed seven-day star rites at Hikamisan, presumed preparations for selecting a new heir.[166]

A fragmentary genealogy survives, a shorthand for Kanemigi's ritual practices when he worshiped Ōuchi ancestors. It was created sometime between the twelfth month of 1541 and the first month of 1545. As it is interspersed with Kanemigi's texts, it most likely constituted notes for him to properly name Ōuchi ancestors while conducting seventeen-day mudrā rites after Tsunemochi's 1543 death.[167] This genealogy focuses more on the appointment to the position of Ōuchi lord, or heir, and even those with no biological offspring such as Ōuchi Norisuke (d. 1437) were included, highlighting an institutional, rather than a biological, approach to succession.

To select a new heir, Yoshitaka engaged in a series of rituals with Yoshida Kanemigi, where he was transmitted special mudrās for seventeen days. These rites occurred twice at Tsukiyama, with the first starting on 5.17 and the second beginning on 8.26.1544.[168] This was the last major contact between Kanemigi and Yoshitaka, as the former returned to Kyoto late in 1544.[169] Ultimately Yoshitaka designated Ōtomo Haruhide (1534?–57), a nephew by a different sister and Ōtomo Yoshiaki, as his heir.[170] Yoshiaki had been a bitter rival of Yoshitaka from 1532 to 1535, but nevertheless his second eldest was selected as heir from 1543 through 1545.

Yoshitaka came to prefer patrilineal descent, and he apparently fathered a son in 1545 with a daughter of Otsuki Koreharu. News of the birth caused a sensation. The monk Ankokuji Shinpō admitted that this would cause trouble

---

[166] *Jinpō shoji kongen gyōji danzu*, Yoshida 65–306 for the copy in Kanemigi's hand, which is badly damaged, and a later, more legible copy, Yoshida 65–361. It states that the rites went on for seventeen days, but also suggests that the rites ended after seven, so perhaps Kanemigi wrote in error.

[167] Conlan, "Shiryō shōkai: Yoshida Kanemigi ga utsushita Ōuchi keizu," *Yamaguchi kenshi kenkyū* 21 (3.2013), pp. 65–70.

[168] DNSR, ser. 10, vol. 13, p. 123 for the 8.6.1544 (Tenbun 13) transmission to Yoshitaka. See also *Yoshida bunko Shintōsho mokuroku*, pp. 126–27 for the Tsukiyama ritual roster (*Tsukiyama sha sairei shidai*), which also appears in Kanemigi's hand in Yoshida 65–306. Unpublished manuscript, Tenri University Library. See also the more legible copy in Yoshida 65–361 and Yoshida 42–383.

[169] *Oyudono no ue no nikki*, vol. 4 (3rd revised printing, Zoku gunsho ruijū kanseikai, 1995), 12.8.1544 (Tenbun 13), pp. 521–22 for Kanemigi returning to Kyoto from Kyushu. Yoshitaka's last direct contact with Kanemigi dates from 1547, when he earnestly requested to receive initiation into Yoshida North Star rites. *Yoshida bunko Shintōsho mokuroku*, Yoshida 42–396, p. 139 for the 3.9.1547 (Tenbun 16) copy of the *Yuiitsu Shintō Hokuto Shichigen[sei] shinpō shidai*.

[170] *Ōuchi bunka*, Shinsen Ōuchi shi keizu, p. 67.

with the "Buzen heir" Haruhide.[171] Yoshitaka had reasons for favoring his own son, as such succession was consistent with Ōuchi inheritance practices, and allowed him to name his son Kidōmaru, as was customary, but this episode did not endear him to the Ōtomo and left them in control of a potential and once-recognized Ōuchi heir.[172]

Defending Iwami

Taking advantage of Yoshitaka's defeat, Amako Haruhisa (1514–61), the grandson of Tsunehisa, tried to once again capture the Iwami silver mines. He fought at Kuri in Nima district during the ninth month of 1543.[173] The Amako were ultimately defeated by forces under the command of Toida Okikuni (Okiyuki) the deputy *shugo* of Iwami, and Numa Takamori.[174]

Having defended the strategic mines of Iwami, Yoshitaka consolidated his control over all of Aki, particularly the southern reaches of the province and the Inland Sea. Succession disputes among the Kōno led to some of their Murakami privateer (*kaizoku*) allies turning against the Ōuchi, but Yoshitaka attacked one of their harbors, destroying some Murakami craft late in 1543.[175] Demonstrating his authority, on 9.23.1545 he worshiped at Ōyamazumi shrine, the Ichinomiya of Ehime province, located on Ōmi

---

[171] Wada Shūsaku, "Ōuchi shi no sōsho kankei o megutte," in Kage, *Ōuchi to Ōtomo*, pp. 46–47, and Fukuo Takeichirō, *Ōuchi Yoshitaka*, pp. 67–68. For the sensational impact of news of the birth, the 10.25 [(Tenbun 14) 1545] Ankokuji Shinpō letter is revealing. *Sagara ke monjo*, vol. 1, doc. 378, Ankokuji Shinpō *shojō*, pp. 432–35. For an overview of this child's life, see Kondō Kiyoshi, *Ōuchi shi jitsuroku* (Yamaguchi, 1885, 3rd reprint ed., Tokuyama: Matsuno shoten, 1984), pp. 220–21. Confusingly, his name was also pronounced "Yoshitaka" although it was written with different characters.

[172] In addition, doubts about Yoshitaka's paternity persisted. *Yoshitakaki*, p. 422.

[173] *Iwami Kikkawa*, doc. 57, 10.7.1543 (Tenbun 12) Kikkawa Tsunefuyu (Yasutsune) *gunchūjō eisha*, pp. 61–62, and *Yamaguchi kenshi shiryōhen chūsei*, vol. 4, Kuri ke monjo, doc. 24, 10.11.1543 (Tenbun 12) Kuri Tarō Hosshi-maru *gunchūjō*, pp. 851–52.

[174] *Iwami Kikkawa*, doc. 58, 9.17 Ōuchi Yoshitaka *kanjō eisha*, p. 62. This document seems closely related to doc. 57 and is likely from the same year. According to doc. 25, Kikkawa Tsunenori *yuzurijō narabi ni okibumi eisha*, p. 18, Numa Takamori can be documented as confirming a will on 12.13.1541 (Tenbun 10). The Numa were followers based in Izumi Province who were transferred to Iwami around this time.

[175] *Ehime kenshi shiryōhen kodai chūsei*, doc. 1764, 5.21.1550 (Tenbun 19) Ōuchi Yoshitaka *kanjō*, p. 952 for praise of battle service, and the capture of a boat, on 12.23.1543 (Tenbun 12). For a later skirmish on 8.6.1546 (Tenbun 15) see doc. 1755, 9.13 [(Tenbun 15) 1546] Ōuchi shi *bugyōnin rensho hōsho*, p. 950, and doc. 1761, 5.9.1547 (Tenbun 16) Shiroi Fusatane *teoi chūmon narabi ni* Ōuchi Yoshitaka *shōhan*, pp. 951–52.

Island in the Inland Sea.[176] Although some trouble with the Murakami lingered in 1546, they were securely enough in Yoshitaka's orbit that some served on Ōuchi ships bound for Ming China in 1547.[177]

Yoshitaka's control over central Aki and Iwami, closer to the Amako, remained more tenuous. Nomi, in central Aki, was vulnerable to Amako incursions, and from the fourth month of 1545 onward battles were fought there intermittently.[178] On 10.24.1549, armed forces, presumably allied with the Amako, attacked Ōta, in Ano district, the site of the mines, and Kikkawa Tsunefuyu and three of his followers were injured.[179] Toida Takamori ably defended this vital area. He was the deputy *shugo* of Iwami during these years, and he supervised the Ogasawara, who managed the mines.[180] To pressure the Amako, Yoshitaka attacked Murao (Kannabe) in Bingo in 1549 and reduced an important castle held by Yamana Tadaoki (d. 1557).[181] Battles in Bingo lingered through 1550.[182]

The Prosperity of Yamaguchi

During the period of Yoshitaka's heyday, Yamaguchi was a prosperous urban center. Portuguese visitors to Yamaguchi described it as "a leading city in Japan" in 1550.[183] In 1552, Francis Xavier (1506–52) wrote that Yamaguchi

---

[176] *Ehime kenshi shiryōhen kodai chūsei*, doc.1741, 7.3.1544 (Tenbun 13) Ōuchi Yoshitaka *kudashibumi*, p. 946 for his confirmation of Innoshima Murakami holdings, and doc. 1744, 9.23.1544 (Tenbun 13) Ōuchi Yoshitaka *kishinjō*, p. 947 for his prayers at Ōyamazumi shrine.

[177] For his lingering conflict with the Noshima Murakami, who were close to the Kōno of Ehime, see doc. 1752, 3.7 [(Tenbun 15) 1546] Ōuchi shi *bugyōnin rensho hōsho*, p. 948, docs. 1755–56, 9.13 [(Tenbun 15) 1546] Ōuchi shi *bugyōnin rensho hōsho*, p. 950, *Yamaguchi kenshi tsūshihen chūsei*, pp. 508–9, and Kasai Shigesuke, *Nankai Tsūki*, pp. 456–59.

[178] *Kobayakawa ke monjo*, vol. 2, *furoku, Ura ke monjo*, doc. 8, 12.22 [(Tenbun 15) 1546] Ōuchi Yoshitaka *shojō*, pp. 5–6. A similar monogram for Yoshitaka appears on *Kobayakawa ke monjo*, vol. 1, doc. 120, 10.16 Ōuchi Yoshitaka *shojō*, pp. 102–3, which dates from either 1545 (Tenbun 14) or 1546 (Tenbun 15).

[179] *Iwami Kikkawa*, doc. 63, 11.27.1549 (Tenbun 18) Kikkawa Tsunefuyu (Yasutsune) *gunchūjō eisha*, pp. 64–65 for a disturbance at Ōta, in Ano district, at the site of the silver mines, although they are not mentioned directly.

[180] *Chūsei imoji shiryō*, doc. 99, 10.10 [(Tenbun 18) 1549] Iwami no kuni *shugodai* Toida Takamori *shigyōjō*, p. 70, and docs. 100–101, 10.26 [(Tenbun 18) 1549] Ogasawara Nagao *shojō*, pp. 70–71.

[181] *Kobayakawa ke monjo* vol. 2, doc. 267, 3.10.1549 (Tenbun 18) Ōuchi Yoshitaka *kanjō utsushi*, p. 151 for a 2.26 battle at Murao in Bingo. Murao, or Kannabe, was an important castle astride the San'indō. It was held by the Yamana, former allies and now rivals to Yoshitaka.

[182] *Munakata shishi shiryōhen chūsei*, vol. 2, doc. 335.1 9.17.1550 (Tenbun 19) Ōuchi Yoshitaka *kanjō*, p. 255. Yoshitaka recommended this warrior, Ihara Nagayori, for the title of governor of Oki on 7.3.1551 (Tenbun 20). This, doc. 338, 7.3.1551 (Tenbun 20) Ōuchi Yoshitaka *kanto suikyojō*, p. 256, is one of his last surviving documents.

[183] Costelloe, *Letters and Instructions*, p. 384.

was "a city of more than ten thousand inhabitants and all its houses are made of wood."[184] Melchior Nuñez Barreto (1520–71) compared Yamaguchi to Lisbon in size, while a Portuguese translation of a 1552 document refers to "Yamaguchi the great city."[185] By 1551, some monks departing from Yamaguchi described Kyoto as the Eastern Capital (*Tōkyō*), and thus implicitly characterized Yamaguchi as the Western Capital.[186]

Ōuchi Yoshitaka had untrammeled wealth. He oversaw a prosperous settlement and, as we have seen, rebuilt many shrines and paid for court ceremonies. Gold was cheap, as it was exchanged equally with silver, and archaeologists have discovered gold-plated pottery that was simply discarded in his mansion's well.[187] In fact, Ōuchi banquets were spectacular affairs, involving over twenty courses. One, which likely occurred on 5.17.1549, has been reconstructed based on archaeological evidence. It was comparable to the finest Japanese fare (*kaiseki ryōri*) today.[188] Fittingly, a law dating from 1545 stipulated that frugality should be encouraged "except when guests are present."[189] And during the last years of Yoshitaka's rule, many guests resided in Yamaguchi.

The court was the repeated beneficiary of Yoshitaka's largesse. At times, he would pay for palace repairs, but the expenses tended to become associated with ongoing rites, such as when he funded sacred dances (*mikagura*) in 1548. In 1549, he provided two hundred *kanmon* yearly to finance all major court ceremonies, and in 1550 Yoshitaka increased the sum to three hundred

---

[184] Costelloe, *Letters and Instructions*, p. 331. The translations found of *Nihon kankei kaigai shiryō yakubun hen* 1.1 (Tōkyō daigaku shuppankai, 1990), 77–117, particularly p. 87, were also consulted.

[185] See *Yamaguchi kenshi shiryōhen chūsei*, vol. 1, 1025, for the 1.10.1558 letter from Cochin by Padre Melchior Nuñez Barreto. See also Donald Lach, *Japan in the Eyes of Europe* (Chicago: University of Chicago Press, 1968), p. 677, and Urs App, "St. Francis Xavier's Discovery of Japanese Buddhism: A Chapter in the European Discovery of Buddhism (Part 2: From Kagoshima to Yamaguchi, 1549–1551)," *Eastern Buddhist*, new series, 30.2 (1997), p. 235.

[186] See the 2.1551 (Tenbun 20) *Rokuon Nichiroku* documents in *Yamaguchi kenshi shiryōhen chūsei*, vol. 1, p. 386.

[187] See the *Ōuchi shi kanseki chisen teien* pamphlet for the discovery of gold-plated dishes that had been discarded in a well (accessed 11.24.2019), https://www.city.yamaguchi.lg.jp/uploaded/attachm ent/35940.pdf.

[188] *Yamaguchi kenshi shiryōhen chūsei*, vol. 1, pp. 458–67 for the 5.17.1549 (Tenbun 18) Motonari kō Yamaguchi gogekō no setsukyō ōshidai, or record by Motonari of his banquet. For a convenient record of this and an earlier banquet, dating from 1500 (Meiō 9), see *Ōuchi bunka*, pp. 206–10, and for the later Motonari banquet, pp. 213–16. These banquets have been reconstructed from waste scraped off the plates. It closely resembles that of what Motonari described. See *Ōuchi shi yakata ato* 13 (2012), "Ōuchi shi no en o saigen suru," pp. 207–34. For a pamphlet recounting the 2010 reconstruction of a banquet, with the assumption that it dated from 1500, see *Meiō kyūnen sangatsu itsuka Shōgun onnari kenritsu* (Yamaguchi meibutsu ryōri soshutsu suishin kaigi, 2017), https://yamagu chi-city.jp/informations/Download/110303_ooutigozen.pdf.

[189] This law appears in *Yoshitakaki*, pp. 410–11.

kanmon.[190] Here he was fully assuming the responsibility of the Ashikaga shoguns in paying for court rites, as they had failed to do so for over half a century. In recognition of his service to the court, he achieved the extremely high Second Rank, a virtually unprecedented appointment, which made him the equivalent of Grand Minister of State and superior to the Ashikaga shoguns of his day.[191] Ōuchi payments allowed emperor-centered rites to continue in Kyoto, but turmoil in the central provinces in 1550 delayed the transmission of these funds by over half a year.

Turmoil in Kyoto

Miyoshi Nagayoshi (1522–64), eldest son and heir to Miyoshi Motonaga, greatly disrupted Kyoto politics and court rites. In 1548, Nagayoshi attacked Hosokawa Harumoto (1514–63) and subsequently forced the shogun Ashikaga Yoshiharu, who had only just returned to Kyoto in 1546, to once again flee.[192] Many courtiers, including the Regent Konoe Taneie (1503–66), and Koga Harumichi (1519–75), fled with Ashikaga Yoshiharu to Sakamoto in Ōmi province to the east.[193] Nagoyoshi occupied Kyoto on 3.8.1551,[194] and he was so reviled in some quarters that assassins struck five days later, stabbing him twice at a banquet, but somehow he escaped with minor injuries.[195]

---

[190] The *Nakahara Yasuoki*, an unpublished manuscript that survives for the years 1549 (Tenbun 18), 1550 (Tenbun 19) and early 1551 (Tenbun 20) mentions these yearly payments of 200 *kanmon*. For the 1550 payments, see *Oyudono no ue no nikki*, vol. 5, 7.12.1550 (Tenbun 19), p. 140, and Lee Butler, *Emperor and Aristocracy in Japan 1467–1680* (Cambridge, MA: Harvard University Asia Center, 2002), p. 85. See also *Go-Nara tennō jitsuroku*, vol. 2, pp. 686, 948, 1022–23, 1036–37, 1056–59, 1088–89, 1092–94 for how Yoshitaka paid for ceremonies in 1550–51.

[191] *Kugyō bunin*, vol. 3 (Yoshikawa kōbunkan, 1936), p. 425 for Yoshitaka's appointment to the junior second rank in 1549 (Tenbun 18). By contrast, Ashikaga Yoshiharu, was only of the third rank that same year. See p. 424. Most Ashikaga shoguns—Takauji, Yoshiakira, Yoshimitsu, Yoshimochi, Yoshinori, Yoshimasa, Yoshihisa, and Yoshitane—all received appointment to the second or first court rank in their lifetime, with the exceptions being Yoshizumi, and Yoshiharu, who died while still at the third rank.

[192] For more on Nagayoshi, see Imatani et al., eds., *Miyoshi Nagayoshi* (Kyoto: Miyaobi shoten, 2013).

[193] Yugawa Toshiharu, "Ashikaga Yoshiharu shōgun ki," *Nihon rekishi* 604 (9.1998), p. 72. Yoshiharu died in 1550 and was succeeded by his son, Yoshiteru, who remained in Sakamoto along with Taneie and Harumichi. He was killed by the Miyoshi in 1565.

[194] *Tokitsugu kyōki*, vol. 3 (Zoku gunsho ruijū kanseikai, 1998), 3.8.1551 (Tenbun 20), p. 135. See also Amano Tadayuki, "Sengokuki no shūkyō jitsujō no henyō to Miyoshi shi," *Shokuhōki kenkyū* 12 (10.2010), p. 28.

[195] Nagae Shō'ichi, *Miyoshi Nagayoshi*, pp. 116–20. See also *Tokitsugu kyōki*, vol. 3, 3.14–16.1551 (Tenbun 20), pp. 137–38, and *Genjo daisōjōki ge*, in *Zoku gunsho ruijū* vol. 30 Zatsubu 1 (Zoku gunsho ruijū kanseikai, 1957), 3.14.1551 (Tenbun 20), p. 54.

Nagayoshi seized imperial lands and constricted the flow of revenue to the court. Reliant on force to achieve his political objectives, he favored military might above all and made little effort to obtain imperial sanction or support. Rather, he devoted his energies to constructing fortifications. Miyoshi Nagayoshi initiated a new style of castle walls, relying heavily on stone rather than earthworks, most likely an early reaction to cannon.[196] He also ignored hoary taboos and used an ancient tomb as a castle. These tombs had often been plundered, but people had generally refrained from incorporating them into a castle's structure.[197]

Weeks after Nagayoshi occupied the capital, Emperor Go-Nara appointed Ōuchi Yoshitaka as the acting governor of Yamashiro (Yamashiro *gon no kami*) on 3.27.1551.[198] Yoshitaka's appointment in absentia meant that the court relied on him as its protector.[199] Yoshitaka could not, however, bring stability to central Japan, although scholars have suggested that Yoshitaka may have been planning a military campaign to occupy Kyoto.[200] Miyoshi and Hosokawa soldiers continued to fight there during the summer of 1551.[201] Yoshitaka, in his role as protector of the court, decided that the best way to ensure the safety of the emperor and palace officials would be to move them to Yamaguchi.[202] Obviously this would also enhance his prestige as the dominant authority in Japan. He justified this by planning to have *sechie* rites performed there on New Year's Day in 1552, which required the emperor's presence.

---

[196] For discoveries concerning Miyoshi Nagayoshi's innovative use of stone fortification for his castles, see "Miyoshi Nagayoshi, Nobunaga yori saki ishigaki dōnyū ka? Imorijō de tairyō ni hakken," *Asahi News*, 6.26.2019 (accessed 8.21.2019), https://www.asahi.com/articles/ASM6T5TH8M6T PPTB00G.html.

[197] Endō Keisuke, "Kofun no jōkaku riyō ni kan suru ikkōsatsu," in *Jōkan shiryō gaku*, vol. 3 (Jōkan shiryō gakkai, 7.2005), pp. 1–22.

[198] His title was that of acting governor of Yamashiro (Yamashiro *gon no kami*). See *Ōmagaki*, in *Zoku gunsho ruijū Kuji bu*, vol. 10, no. 2 (Zoku gunsho ruijū kanseikai, 1981), p. 720. His appointment was recorded in an official record of promotions, the *Ōmagaki*, which refers to his surname, Tatara, rank (second) and office of the *Dazai Daini*. When deciphering calligraphy, the name Yoshizumi (義澄) can easily be mistaken for Yoshitaka (義隆), but Ashikaga Yoshizumi died in 1508, and had only attained the third court rank.

[199] Conlan, "The Failed Attempt to Move the Emperor to Yamaguchi and the Fall of the Ōuchi," *Japanese Studies* 35.2 (9.2015), pp. 5–6, and "Ōuchi Yoshitaka no sento keikaku," *Yamaguchi ken chihōshi kenkyū* 123 (6.2020), p. 17.

[200] Fujii Manabu, *Ōuchi Yoshitaka* (Minerva shobō, 2019), pp. 288–89 for possible military actions after the death of Ashikaga Yoshiharu in 5.1550.

[201] *Eikanshi danki nenroku* (Tokushima, 2001), a reliable chronicle pertaining to the Izumi branch family of the Hosokawa, mentions a battle between the Hosokawa and Miyoshi on p. 75.

[202] For an overview of this discovery, see Conlan, "Failed Attempt," and "Ōuchi Yoshitaka no sento keikaku."

All the courtiers necessary to perform important *sechie* rites had traveled to Yamaguchi midway through 1551. They included Nijō Tadafusa (1496–1551), a Retired Regent (*taikō*); Sanjō Kin'yori (1495–1551), a retired Grand Minister, Jimyōin Motonori (1492–1551) and Tadafusa's son Yoshitoyo (1536–51). Kin'yori, for example, had written a treatise on New Year *sechie* rites in 1537, and worked closely with Jimyōin Motonori, a Counselor (*chūnagon*) who wrote drafts of documents and participated in New Year's ceremonies in 1535 and 1539.[203]

Nijō Tadafusa even summoned low-ranking functionaries, such as Kushida Munetsugu (d. 1551) for these rites. Munetsugu constructed small buildings (the *jin no za*) used for the *sechie* rites (Figure 9.8).[204] Thus, both high- and low-ranking officials had to be housed, materials transported, and preparations made for the performance of these complex rites. Unfortunately for Yoshitaka, however, his ambitious scheme triggered a violent backlash that resulted in his death and the ultimate collapse of the Ōuchi organization, and the death of most of the participants in the efforts to bring the emperor to Yamaguchi and, by extension, make it Japan's capital.

The Revolt

Although the coup against Yoshitaka was successful, a basic chronology of the plot itself remains obscure, as well as the motives of many involved. Most of the court, including Go-Nara, who had appointed Yoshitaka as a protector, supported the move, with the Nijō faction, headed by the Retired Regent Tadafusa, being most active in these preparations. The Ashikaga would have been opposed, as too presumably the Konoe line of regents, who had fled

---

[203] Kinyori's *Ganjitsu sechie ki* of 1537 recounts this rite and reveals Kinyori's connections to Motonori. *Kosechiryo gyoki*, another manuscript in the Kujō family archives, reveals Motonori's expertise and participation in these rites in 1535 and 1539. For these sources, see Tajima, *Kinri kuge bunko kenkyū*, 4 vols. (Kyoto: Shibunkaku, 2003–12), vol. 2, p. 337 (58) (*Kosechiryo gyoki*), and vol. 4, p. 343 (*Ganjitsu sechie ki*). See also Tomita Masahiro, "Sengokuki no kugeshū," *Ritsumeikan bungaku* 509 (1988), pp. 257–60, 278–79. Another noble, Minase Chikayo, of the third rank (*hisangi*) can also be documented as being in Yamaguchi. See Tomita, p. 288, and *Kugyō bunin*, vol. 3, p. 429.

[204] Tadafusa wanted to consult with Kushida Munetsugu regarding *jin* [*no za*] affairs (*jingi*) and headgear. Munetsugu's heirs correctly characterized his travel, and subsequent demise, as constituting service (*chūsetsu*) that required compensation, but this was disputed by nameless others who argued that Munetsugu's travel merely constituted a "private affair." See *Jige monjo* (Yagi shoten, 2009), doc. 106, 11.4 Hōseiji Chika-o *shojō*, doc. 107, 11.20 Tojima Shigesada *shotojō*, doc. 108, 2.1558 (Kōji 4) Hōseiji Chika-o *nimonto*, and doc. 109, 2.27.1558 (Kōji 4). Tojima Shigesada *nitojō*, pp. 146–53. Kushida Munetsugu's actions were later recognized by the Kajūji as constituting official court business. See *Jige monjo* doc. 110, 3.4.1558 (Eiroku 1) Hōseiji Chika-o *sanmonjō*, pp. 154–56.

Figure 9.8 Note the *jin no za* in the foreground of this sixteenth-century illustration of the *sechie*, "*Uesugi-bon Rakuchū rakugai zubyōbu.*" Image and permission provided by Yonezawa-shi Uesugi hakubutsukan

Kyoto with the shogun Yoshiharu. Finally, Kujō Tanemichi (1507–94) of the Kujō regent family was strongly opposed and emphasized that Kyoto should not be moved. Tanemichi was, however, ousted from court politics, and traveled widely, where he had interactions with two of Yoshitaka's great rivals, the Amako and the Miyoshi.

The Amako remembered their major war with Yoshitaka and desired to control the nearby silver mines, so they would naturally gravitate to an anti-Yoshitaka alliance. Miyoshi Nagayoshi, the brutal conqueror of Kyoto, was violently opposed to many at the court, but if the emperor were to flee, his position would be undermined, so Nagayoshi had an active interest in preventing this from happening. The final outside lord, and the one most directly involved in the coup, was Ōtomo Yoshishige (Sōrin, 1530–87), who had recently gained power by killing his father Yoshiaki and Yoshiaki's favored heir.

The Ōuchi had withstood more powerful external enemies without collapsing and without serious internal divisions, but this potential alliance was potent. Exacerbating the situation, internal divisions ultimately brought Yoshitaka down. The disgruntled Sue Takafusa allied with Naitō Okimori and found broad support among three families of Ōuchi retainers—the Toida, Naitō, and Masuda—and scattered support from the Sugi and the Mōri families.

A combination of personal and policy disputes led to the divisions. In the case of the Naitō, they never seem to have forgotten the injustice when Yoshitaka's father Yoshioki killed Yoshitaka's maternal grandfather Naitō Hironori in 1495. Naitō Okimori, one of the key plotters, was Yoshitaka's uncle.[205] He also communicated with the Ōtomo and was close to another core plotter, Sue Takafusa.

Sue Takafusa resented Yoshitaka; he was Yoshitaka's lover, although whether that relationship contributed to the animosity is not clear. Takafusa was the heir of the Sue family, but critically, many other Sue did not support his rebellion. Takafusa's ties through his mother to his half brother, Toida Takamori, the deputy *shugo* of Iwami and overseer of the mines, were more enduring, as they did ally during the coup.[206] Takamori controlled the mines and favored a more robust response against the Amako, who were a nearby threat. In addition, Takamori and Takafusa despised Yoshitaka's helpers, such as Sagara Taketō, who was most deeply involved with innovations in mining and smelting. These officials of the Iwami mines must have resented the spread of their knowledge of smelting techniques, as well as authorizing new mines based on samples that were sent to them. Finally, Yoshitaka's plan to move the capital to Yamaguchi involved considerable preparation and great expense, and so preoccupied him that the coup plotters had ample opportunity to strike.

One Ōuchi adviser, the abrasive Sagara Taketō, became a particular target for the plotters. The *Yoshitakaki*, for example, argues that his slander was the cause for the disorder, and describes Taketō as being both skilled and intelligent but also a bitter rival to Sue Takafusa.[207] Some personal animosities may

---

[205] He was married to the sister of Yoshitaka's mother. She was the daughter of Hironori, who had been killed at a banquet on the orders of Masahiro and Yoshioki. This incident was well remembered and is explicitly mentioned in the *Yoshitakaki*. See p. 418.

[206] Takafusa's mother first gave birth to Toida Takamori, but she later married into the Sue, giving birth to Takafusa. Wada Shūsaku, "Yoshida Kanemigi 'Bōshū gekōki' ni mieru Ōuchi shi kankei kiji," pp. 106–7. His father may have been Toida "Kii *no kami*" (governor of Kii), who fought in Iwami early in 1541.

[207] *Yoshitakaki*, p. 413 for Taketō's intelligence and pp. 416–17 for his bad relations with others.

also have come to the fore, as Taketō apparently turned down the chance to have Sue Takafusa adopt one of his sons.[208]

Differences in policy also played a role in fostering these divisions. Bekki Akitsura later criticized Yoshitaka for favoring Sagara Taketō over Sue Takafusa.[209] Taketō, an innovator interested in metallurgy, was not popular with administrators of the silver mines such as Toida Takamori, the deputy *shugo* of Iwami, as disputes arose between them regarding the use of resources and laborers for these mines.[210] A plot may have existed to assassinate Taketō on 9.15.1550.[211] For all of his knowledge, Taketō had an opportunity to foil a coup against Yoshitaka, but in these endeavors he failed.

Sugi Shigenori (d. 1553), the deputy *shugo* of Buzen province, learned of a plot by Sue Takafusa several years before 1551. He notified Yoshitaka, but the Ōuchi lord remained skeptical, in part because Shigenori was a rival of Takafusa. In 1549, a suspicious death piqued Yoshitaka's suspicions, and he sent the trusted Sagara Taketō to Kyushu, where Shigenori informed him of a grave plot that, in his view, threatened the Ōuchi. Taketō discounted Shigenori's story as slander. He found it inconceivable that Naitō Okimori, one of the purported co-plotters who had close ties to Yoshitaka's mother, could be involved.[212] Yoshitaka concurred with Taketō's assessment and did not act. Later, Shigenori later reluctantly joined the plotters.

Sue Takafusa apparently decided to try to overthrow Yoshitaka sometime before the fifth month of 1550, but it was at that time that he reached out to the Ōtomo to have Ōtomo Haruhide, the nephew of Yoshitaka who had briefly

---

[208] *Yoshitakaki*, p. 413 for how he promised to allow Sue Takafusa to adopt one of his sons but later reneged on the agreement.

[209] *Zōho teisei Hennen Ōtomo shiryō*, vol. 24, 2.16.1579 (Tenshō 8) Tachibana Dōsetsu *shojō*, 213–220, p. 218 for how Yoshitaka lacked deep thought and supported Sagara Taketō, who planned unprincipled things, instead of the reasonable Sue Takafusa (*shiryo o kaita Yoshitaka ga dōri o toiteiru Sue Takafusa yori mudō o kuwadateta Sagara Taketō o hiiki shita*).

[210] Sue Takafusa (Harukata) complained about requisitions of laborers and the silver mines of Iwami. *Jōeiji shiryō*, doc. 61, 11.28 Sue Harukata *bugyōshū renshojō*, p. 62, which dates presumably from 1552. For Taketō's earlier mobilization of of such laborers, see doc. 60, 12.3 [(Tenbun 19) 1550] Ōuchi ke *bugyō shū renshojō*, pp. 60–61.

[211] *Yoshitakaki*, pp. 413–14.

[212] This narrative was drawn from Sagara Taketō letter in the Mōri house records, which recounts these events in detail. Tōkyō daigaku shiryōhen sanjo, comp., *Mōri ke monjo*, vol. 4 (Tōkyō daigaku shuppankai, 1924), doc. 1556, 1.5.1551 (Tenbun 20) Sagara Taketō *mōshijō utsushi*, 458–65. For other documents suggesting an alliance between Takafusa and Okimori, see *Hagi han batsu etsu roku*, vol. 3, doc. 62, 9.19 [(Tenbun 19) 1550] Naitō Okimori *kishōmon* and 9.14 [(Tenbun 19) 1550] Sue Takafusa *shojō*, pp. 160–61. For analysis of this document, see Yonehara Masao, ed., *Chūgoku shiryōshū* (Jinbutsu ōraisha, 1966), pp. 129–36. See also his *Ōuchi Yoshitaka* (Jinbutsu ōraisha, 1967), pp. 227–32.

been selected as an heir in 1543 or 1544, installed as the next Ōuchi lord.[213] Sue Takafusa, Naitō Okimori, and Sugi Shigenori were coconspirators.[214] Takafusa in turn contacted Mōri Motonari in Aki, and the Kikkawa, in order to attract support for a plan to remove Yoshitaka in favor of Yoshitaka's young son Yoshitaka (1545–51), a name pronounced like his father's but written with different characters.[215]

Yoshitaka was aware of Sue Takafusa's discontent and ordered that curses be performed against Takafusa, who had an "evil heart," during the eleventh month of 1550.[216] Also, he ritually tried to protect his own life and had a Kyoto craftsman construct a statue of Jizō (Skr. Kṣitigarbha) for longevity rites in 1550.[217] On 8.10.1551, mere weeks before the rebellion began, Yoshitaka dispatched Sagara Taketō as a trusted messenger to his brother-in-law Yoshimi Masayori (1513–88) of Iwami.[218] Masayori's mission was unclear, but he was married to Yoshitaka's sister and thus a highly trusted figure. It seems that Yoshitaka was at last preparing to act against the plotters.

Yoshitaka must have been surprised, however, for they struck first when he was attending a banquet. Not knowing who was allied or hostile, Yoshitaka sent messengers to the Naitō, as they included his mother and brother-in-law, and he was confident that they and the Sugi would remain

[213] *Yamaguchi kenshi shiryōhen chūsei*, vol. 1, Tatara jōsuiki, p. 802. For the inference regarding Haruhide, I am indebted to the insightful analysis of Wada Shūsaku, 8.9.2019.

[214] Although Toida Takamori (d. 1557) was not directly mentioned in documents concerning the coup, later events would show him to be closely allied with Sue Takafusa.

[215] For plans to make this son Yoshitaka heir, and discussions between Sugi Shigemasa and Naitō Okimori, see *Kikkawa ke monjo*, 2 vols. (Tōkyō daigaku shuppankai, 1925), vol. 1, doc. 609, 8.24 Sue Takafusa *shojō*, pp. 543–44, and vol. 2, doc. 1253, 8.24 Sue Takafusa *shojō*, p. 458. See also *Yamaguchi kenshi chūsei shiryō*, vol. 3 (Yamaguchi, 2004), Migita Mōri ke monjo, docs. 92–93, 8.24 Sue Takafusa *shojō*, p. 462, which refers to Yoshitaka's heir (*wakagimi*), and Wada, "Ōuchi shi no sōsho kankei o megutte," p. 47. For further support of these documents, see Ōuchi shi metsubō shidai, otherwise known as the Kotonobu oboegaki, *Yamaguchi kenshi shiryōhen chūsei*, vol. 1, p. 744. There is a slight chance that Takafusa released these letters on 8.24.1551, four days before his uprising, which meant that he started his coup before waiting for a reply. The earlier date for these letters is more plausible, but it is impossible to definitively know if they dated from 8.24.1550 or 8.24.1551. Finally, for analysis of the Mōri Sue alliance, see Yamamoto Hiroki, *Saikoku no sengoku kassen*, pp. 72–73.

[216] For crucial documentary reference to prayers for Yoshitaka's health, and for Sue Takafusa's "evil heart" to be quelled (*onshin kifuku*), see the *Yamaguchi kenshi tsūshihen furoku* CD-ROM, doc. 387, 1550 (Tenbun 19).11 Aizen myō-ō hō *senza kigan kotogaki*, 207. Chronicles suggest that these maledictions began much later, during the eighth month of 1551. See *Yoshitakaki*, p. 184. The *Rokuji no hō* maledictions themselves were, according to a variant of the *Yoshitakaki*, the reason that Sue Takafusa rebelled. See *Ōuchi bunka*, p. 104. Ichnographically, the Rokuji Myōō deity resembles Myōken, but no direct connection existed. Bernard Faure, *The Fluid Pantheon: Gods of Medieval Japan*, vol. 1 (Honolulu: University of Hawaii Press, 2016), p. 86.

[217] Iwai Tomoji, "Yamaguchi-shi Manpukuji Jizō bosatsu ni tsuite," *Yamaguchi kenritsu bijutsukan kenkyū kiyō* 1 (1996), pp. 1–14.

[218] *Yamaguchi kenshi shiryōhen chūsei*, vol. 1, Ōuchi shi metsubō shidai, p. 745 for Taketō transmitting messages to Yoshimi Masayori.

loyal, but they did not respond. Yoshitaka's mansion was not fortified, so he was forced to flee, first to Hōsenji, where escape from Yamaguchi was easy via the road leading to Hijū. The rebels, led by the Sugi, the Sue, and the Naitō, entered Yamaguchi; they first destroyed Sagara Taketō's residence, as he was a major target. The invaders then piled up treasures and slaughtered the birds in Yoshitaka's garden. Yoshitaka left his archive of documents and genealogies behind, entrusting them to the head of the Ima Hachiman shrine, but that man, fearing that he would be killed, burned them all.[219] Thus save for a few copies surviving by chance, the core Ōuchi archives were lost in 1551.

Yoshitaka fled, along with his aged mother and followers ranging from nobles to maids.[220] They would have taken the route past Ryōunji, the grand mortuary temple of his father, passing to the south of the Naganobori mines, and then at Mine, instead of continuing to Hijū, would have turned north to the harbor at Senzaki. The Agari, a warrior family who lived near Senzaki, wrote that Yoshitaka left that harbor and attempted to sail for Kyushu, an assertion all the more plausible because the former head of Munakata shrine was a member of this party, and other documents show that ships sailed easily from Iwami and Nagato to Kyushu.[221] Strong winds prevented them from heading out to sea, and they skirted from nearby harbor to harbor, before turning back to Senzaki, where they then traveled inland to Taineiji and met their end.[222] According to Taineiji lore, Yoshitaka looked into a well whose waters would not reflect the image of those about to die. He saw nothing and realized the end was near.

---

[219] The previous narrative is drawn from *Yoshitakaki*, pp. 418–20.

[220] *Yoshitakaki*, p. 419 for the composition of the fleeing party and Ōuchi shi metsubō shidai, *Yamaguchi kenshi shiryōhen chūsei*, vol. 1, p. 744. His frail mother Higashi-muki remained behind and she was spared by the plotters. *Yoshitakaki*, p. 423.

[221] Nakatsukasa, "Bunken kara mita chūsei no Iwami no minato to ryūtsū," *Ōga ke monjo*, doc. 21, 8.20 Matsura Takanobu *shojō utsushi*, p. 105 for how ships sailed from Misumi harbor in Iwami to Abu district in Nagato and the Matsura region of Hizen.

[222] See Yamaguchi kyōiku iinkai, comp., *Yamaguchi shi maizō bunkazai chōsha hōkokusho*, no. 121, *Ryōunji ato*, vol. 2 (Yamaguchi: Yamaguchi kyōiku iinkai, 2019), pp. 206–7 for how the route that Yoshitaka took was linked to Nagato ports and mines. Ōuchi shi metsubō shidai, *Yamaguchi kenshi shiryōhen chūsei*, vol. 1, p. 744, and the *Yoshitakaki*, p. 427, suggests that they wanted to flee by boat, but bad winds drove them back to Taineiji. For another account stating that they briefly launched ships, only to return, see the *Bōshū Yamaguchi Tsukiyama yakata jōsui* (Yamaguchi, Ryūfukuji, 1993), pp. 26–27. The most detailed narrative, describing their attempted destination and details of how they tried to set forth from Senzaki can be found it the summary of the Ōuchi genealogy (Ōuchi ke ryaku keizu), in *Agari ke monjo* (Nagato shi shitei bunkazai, 1995), doc. 13, pp. 7–8, 11–12. For their flight and a list of the dead, see also doc. 15, p. 13. For the presence of Munakata supporters with Yoshitaka until the very end, see *Munakata shishi shiryōhen chūsei*, vol. 2, doc. 330, p. 257.

Yoshitaka, seeing that all was lost, tried to get his son to flee, but decided to kill himself.[223] His purported last poem, based on the Diamond Wisdom Sutra (*Kongō hannyakyō*), reads: "Those who strike and those struck down are both, like dew or lightning, gone in a flash" (*utsu mono mo utaruru mono mo morotomo ni nyoro yaku nyoden ōsa nyozekan*).[224] The *Yoshitakaki*, the most reliable account of his end, states that Yoshitaka's death poem was lost, making this seemingly prophetic poem a later creation. It does, however, record the last poem of Reizen Takatoyo, one of Yoshitaka's followers, which survived because he wrote it in blood on the cover of the Taineiji copy of the Tripiṭaka. "Even the sound of wind that invited both the smoke to rise and the clouds to descend to meet halfway is no more" (*miyo ya tatsu kemuri mo kumo mo hanten ni sasoishi kaze no oto mo nokorazu*). Takatoyo, by writing his poem of resignation in blood on a sutra, more likely possessed a consuming desire for vengeance than a sense of resignation from the world.[225]

After Yoshitaka's death, Nijō Tadafusa tried to negotiate a surrender but was mercilessly cut down by the Naitō, along with his son.[226] Yoshitaka's son was later captured and killed along with his nurse and his sisters.[227] Sagara Taketō, not part of the party, was hunted down and killed shortly thereafter as well.[228] Not content with Taketō's death, as well as that of Taketō's son, Sue Takafusa ordered that Taketō's wife and daughters also be killed.[229] Sue Takafusa, upon hearing of the death of Yoshitaka at Taineiji, expressed satisfaction to his Iwami allies, the Masuda.[230]

The spasm of violence affected many, of status both humble and exalted. Tōgi Kaneyasu, a musician specializing in court music (*gagaku*), perished at Taineiji, and his grave is located near that of Yoshitaka and the other

---

[223] *Yoshitakaki*, pp. 421–22. Yoshitaka encouraged his nurses, maids, and his son to flee.

[224] This has been translated by Yoel Hoffmann, *Japanese Death Poems: Written by Zen Monks and Haiku Poets on the Verge of Death* (Rutland, VT: Tuttle 1998), p. 53.

[225] *Yoshitakaki*, p. 427.

[226] *Yoshitakaki*, p. 424. For how other nobles were beaten to death, see p. 425.

[227] *Yoshitakaki*, pp. 428–29. For his nurse and Yoshitaka's daughters being killed, see *Hagi han batsu etsu roku*, vol. 4, Bōchō jisha shōmon, Taineiji pt. 1 (*jō*), p. 19.

[228] *Yoshitakaki*, p. 429, and Ōuchi shi metsubō shidai, p. 745.

[229] *Chūsei Masuda Masuda shi kankei shiryōshū*, 10.13 [(Tenbun 20) 1551] Sue Takamitsu *shojō*, p. 244. Sue Takamitsu was one of Sue Takafusa's confederates.

[230] *Chūsei Masuda Masuda shi kankei shiryōshū*, doc. 601, 9.6 [(Tenbun 20) 1551] Sue Takafusa *shojō*, pp. 240–41. The letter is addressed to a member of the Sufu family and states that the Sufu should discuss the details of what happened with Masuda Tōkane, who was knowledgeable about them. See also doc. 602, 9.15 [(Tenbun 20) 1551] Sue Takafusa *shojō*, p. 241. For more on these documents, see Wada Shūsaku, "'Sue shi no coup d'état to Iwami kokujin Sufu shi no dōkō' Sufu ke monjo no shōkai," *Yamaguchi ken chihōshi kenkyū* 70 (10.1993), pp. 63–72.

nobles.[231] Although not mentioned in the chronicles, devoted followers such as the Numa, who had originated in Izumi but later moved to the west, perished, and that line went extinct.[232] Much was lost with the passing of Yoshitaka and his supporters, although the magnitude of the loss may not have been fully apparent at the time.

Conclusion

Yoshitaka has been remembered as a failure or a passive practitioner of court culture, but he encountered many successes, extinguishing two rivals, the Takeda and the Shōni, and overshadowed the Ashikaga entirely. He promoted improvements in mining, fostered trade, rebuilt religious institutions in his territories, and encountered European missionaries. Espousing the notion that court rights needed to be upheld, and the idea that the court was the vehicle for governance, Yoshitaka oversaw a dramatic expansion of mining. However, he failed to realize that by upholding court rites and policies, many warriors came to despise him.

When confronted with unprecedented turmoil in central Japan, Yoshitaka gambled by attempting to make Yamaguchi Japan's capital. While engrossed in these preparations, he was attacked, and his plans ended in spectacular failure. Most of the Ōuchi retainers sided with Sue Takafusa and Naitō Okimori and overthrew Yoshitaka because they opposed moving the court to Yamaguchi. The merciless way in which Yoshitaka, his family, followers, and supporters were killed reveals how much they were hated.

The plotters must have assumed that they could easily govern in Yoshitaka's stead. It is doubtful that they realized that their actions would destroy this trading network and the prosperity of Yamaguchi and plunge Japan into a civil war. Ripples would spread throughout East Asia, as China and Korean trade would be disrupted; the Ming emperor would send emissaries to Japan, while the Portuguese reported these events to Europe.

---

[231] Viewed at Taineiji, 6.15.2015. Of Kaneyasu nothing else is known, but the Tōgi were a noted family of court musicians. For the death of the other nobles, see *Kugyō bunin*, vol. 3, pp. 428–29. See also *Rekimei dodai* (Zoku gunsho ruijū kanseikai, 1996), pp. 272–74. For another list, see *Hagi han batsu etsu roku*, vol. 4, Bōchō jisha shōmon, Taineiji pt. 1 (*jō*), p. 19. Finally, for some of the dead, and their death poems, see Taineiji, in *Bōchō fūdo chūshin an*, vol. 19, *Zen Ōtsu saiban* (Yamaguchi, 1962), pp. 272–74.

[232] Matsui Naoto, "Yoshioki Yoshitakaki Ōuchi shi kenryoku no kōzōteki tokushitsu: Ōuchi shi hikan Numa shi no dōkō o tegakari ni," *Nihon rekishi* 822 (11.2016), p. 27 for how they joined Sanjō Kinyori to Yamaguchi and disappeared from the historical record in 1551.

The Ōuchi organization survived Yoshitaka's death for six more years. After destroying Yoshitaka, murdering courtiers and his compatriots, and burning parts of Yamaguchi, Sue Takafusa and Naitō Okimori attempt to rule in Yoshitaka's stead, but they failed abjectly and would die, along with nearly all who had been involved in the coup, including the final Ōuchi lord, Ōtomo Haruhide, who is known to posterity as Ōuchi Yoshinaga. Haruhide witnessed violence, the destruction of Yamaguchi, and oversaw the long unwinding of Ōuchi rule.

10

The Collapse

The Ōuchi organization initially survived the death of Yoshitaka (1507–51) and many of his supporters. Its laws continued to be followed, taxes were collected, and diplomatic relations were maintained. Despite the turmoil of the coup, tributary trade continued, culminating in the receipt of an official trade tally from the Ming in 1556.

The new lord Ōtomo Haruhide (1534?–57), who later adopted the name of Ōuchi Yoshinaga, compensated for his violent rise by appealing to his Tatara ethnicity. He re-enacted the landing of the imaginary Prince Imsŏng at Tatara to demonstrate how he was restoring Ōuchi rule. He continued Second Month rites at Hikamisan Kōryūji and allowed newcomers from Goa, India, presumed practitioners of a reformist sect of Shingon Buddhism, to build Daidōji, the "Temple of the Great Way," in Yamaguchi. It was the first Christian church in Japan.

Being raised by the Ōtomo, he adopted their norms concerning the Ashikaga shogunate and accepted a position that was inferior to them in terms of office and rank. Unlike Yoshitaka, he had no discernible ties to the court, which was reeling from the deaths of so many courtiers and the sudden loss of Ōuchi revenue.

Haruhide ruled over a fractured domain. The overthrow of Yoshitaka spawned multiple factions. The first were the core plotters who detested Yoshitaka, his allies, and his style of governance. The second, Yoshimi Masayori (1513–88) and his confederates, supported the memory of Yoshitaka and strove to exact revenge. A third consisted of peripheral members of the coup, men such as Sugi Shigenori (?–1553) and Mōri Motonari (1497–1571), who were not fully aware of the core plotters' aims and came to abhor their methods. Finally, some tried to maintain the regular administration of Ōuchi rule. These men were swept up into the seething emotions of the plotters and their enemies. Once their position became

Kings in All but Name. Thomas D. Conlan, Oxford University Press. © Oxford University Press 2024.
DOI: 10.1093/oso/9780197677339.003.0011

untenable, they joined either the Mōri or the Ōtomo, and administered on behalf of these new lords. Ōuchi governance disintegrated.

With the Ōuchi collapse, trade networks were disrupted. Some merchants would be killed, while others would flee. Those without Ōuchi ties, the *wakō*, would venture into core Ōuchi seas. Likewise, the city of Yamaguchi, already damaged in the 1551 coup, would suffer greatly from war and fire.

Like most last rulers, Haruhide has not been treated well by posterity. Sources ranging from a genealogy written by the Agari of Nagato, who witnessed Yoshiaka's doomed attempt to escape, to the *Ōuchi shi jitsuroku*, compiled by the historian Kondō Kiyoshi (1833–1916), do not even include him in the rosters of Ōuchi rulers.[1] Kondō's omission leaves the false impression that the Ōuchi organization collapsed with the death of Yoshitaka when six more years were required to bring it to ruin.

Haruhide does not appear to have been a bad man; unlike many of his compatriots, he was not ruthless, and he repeatedly expressed sympathy for those who died for him, but he could not cope with the demands of leadership. The institutions of Ōuchi governance could not survive incompetent leaders, factional disputes, and attacks from without and within. In the end, powerless, he witnessed the collapse of Ōuchi rule and died.

Ōtomo Hachirō

The man who became the final Ōuchi lord was the second son of Ōtomo Yoshiaki (1502–50). For whatever reason he was known colloquially as Hachirō, the eighth son.[2] His mother, Yoshiaki's primary wife, was the daughter of Ōuchi Yoshioki (1477–1528). Yoshiaki also had a second wife, a woman of the Bōjō court family, who gave birth to his

---

[1] The oldest example, *Agari ke monjo monjo* (Nagato shi shitei bunkazai, 1995), doc. 13, Ōuchi ke *ryaku keizu*, p. 8, pp. 12–13, records Yoshinaga (Haruhide) as a postscript, in contrast to the earlier lords, who are numbered and identified. Other genealogies, such as the 1685 Ōuchi Tatara shi *fuchō*, likewise list Yoshitaka as the last lord. Yamaguchi kenshi hensanshitsu, comp., *Yamaguchi kenshi shiryōhen chūsei*, 4 vols. (Yamaguchi, 1996–2008), vol. 1, pp. 740–43. Kondō Kiyoshi, *Ōuchi shi jitsuroku* (Yamaguchi, 1885, 3rd reprint ed., Tokuyama: Matsuno shoten, 1984), pp. 276–83, insets his coverage in his "treason" (*hangyaku*) chapter, rather than with the biographies of the other Ōuchi leaders.

[2] For his name as being Hachirō, see *Yamaguchi kenshi shiryōhen chūsei*, vol. 3, Hagi shi kyōdo hakubutsukan zō monjo, Yuasa ke monjo, doc. 114, 10.6 [(Tenbun 20) 1551] Ōuchi shi *toshiyori rensho shojō*, pp. 1029–30.

eldest son and heir, Yoshishige (Sōrin 1530–87).[3] According to one genealogy Haruhide was eighteen in 1551, which would indicate a 1534
birth.[4]

Haruhide became Yoshitaka's heir in 1543 at the age of ten after the
drowning of his maternal cousin, Tsunemochi (Harumochi, 1524–43). Like
his cousin, Haruhide received part of his name, "haru" from the Ashikaga
shogun Yoshiharu (1511–50, shogun 1521–46).[5] When Yoshitaka presumably fathered a son in 1545, Haruhide lost his position as the designated
Ōuchi heir.[6]

In 1550, Ōtomo Yoshiaki designated Shio-ichi-maru, his son by a third
consort, as his official heir to Ōtomo chieftainship. Yoshiaki's eldest son,
Yoshishige took matters into his hands, and his confederates killed Shio-
ichi-maru and his immediate family—mother and two sisters—on 2.10.1550
and mortally wounded Yoshiaki, who died two days later.[7] Yoshishige, more
commonly known to posterity as Sōrin, assumed the mantle of Ōtomo leadership.[8] He then set out to find a way through similar bloodshed to have his
younger brother installed as the next Ōuchi heir.

Heirs mattered, for claims to rule were tethered to hereditary succession. When Sue Takafusa (aka Harukata 1521–55) first planned to overthrow Yoshitaka in 1550, he hoped to force Yoshitaka to abdicate in favor
of Yoshitaka's son, the "young lord" who was also named Yoshitaka (1545–
51).[9] Realizing that the younger Yoshitaka could not be used so readily to
overthrow his father, Takafusa reached out to the Ōtomo, as they controlled

---

[3] One genealogy compiled by the Mōri portrays Hachirō as also having the Bōjō woman as his
mother, but this may have merely been an attempt to emphasize his position as a pretender. Ōtomo
keizu, in *Zoku gunsho ruijū*, vol., 3rd ed., 6.1 (Zoku gunsho ruijū kanseikai, 1990), p. 354. The Bōjō
were an administrative family (*meike*) of the Fujiwara lineage.

[4] *Yamaguchi shishi shiryōhen Ōuchi bunka* (Yamaguchi, 2010) (hereafter *Ōuchi bunka*), Mōri ke
bunko Ōuchi *kakei*, p. 32.

[5] Tsunemochi changed his name to Harumochi, having received the character "haru" from
Ashikaga Yoshiharu in 1542; see *Chūgoku chiranki, Shinkō Gunsho ruijū kassenbu*, vol. 2 (Naigai
shoseki kabushiki kaisha, 1930), p. 435.

[6] *Sagara ke monjo*, vol. 1 (Tōkyō daigaku shuppankai, 1917), doc. 378, Ankokuji Shinpō *shojō*,
pp. 432–35. For questions regarding Yoshitaka's paternity of his son Yoshitaka (1545–1551), see
Yoshitakaki, Shinkō Gunsho ruijū, vol. 21, *kassen bu*, vol. 2 (3rd revised printing, Zoku gunsho ruijū
kanseikai, 1994), p. 422.

[7] *Ōtomoki, Gunsho ruijū*, vol. 21, *kassen-bu*, 3rd ed. (Zoku gunsho ruijū kanseikai, 1994), pp.
557–59.

[8] As he is widely known as Ōtomo Sōrin, he will be referred to as such, even though he did not
adopt this name until later.

[9] *Kikkawa ke monjo*, vol. 1 (Tōkyō daigaku shuppankai, 1925), doc. 609, 8.24 Sue Takafusa
(Harukata) *shojō*, pp. 543–44, and vol. 2 (1925), doc. 1253, 8.24 Sue Takafusa (Harukata) *shojō*,
p. 458. See also *Yamaguchi kenshi shiryōhen chūsei*, vol. 3, Migita Mōri ke monjo, docs. 92–93, 8.24
Sue Takafusa (Harukata) *shojō*, p. 462.

a former Ōuchi heir. The new Ōtomo lord (Yoshishige/Sōrin) realized Haruhide's value, and had retainers escort him to a place of safety in Chikugo province, where he remained hidden.[10] After all, for their coup to succeed, they needed a plausible Ōuchi heir.[11]

Appeals to Ōuchi Ethnicity

Shortly after killing Yoshitaka and his supporters, a commission of four, Sue Takafusa, Naitō Okimori (1495–1555), Sugi Shigenori, and Sue Takamitsu (b. 1497), announced throughout the Ōuchi domains that a new lord would leave for Suō now that "peace was restored."[12] Ōtomo Sōrin would gleefully report Haruhide's travel plans to Suō to his followers as well.[13] The Ōtomo had governed northeastern Kyushu in the shadow of the Ōuchi, but now Sōrin, with his brother installed as the Ōuchi leader, headed an alliance of two formerly hostile domains, making him the dominant power of western Japan.[14]

Haruhide emerged from hiding late in 1551 and was met by Sue Takafusa, Sugi Takasuke (1522–85), and Ida Okihide (1506–57), who escorted him to Funai, the trading city of the Ōtomo, early in 1552.[15] After staying at Sōrin's Funai mansion for little over a month (1.6–2.11) Haruhide set off for Suō.[16]

---

[10] *Ōita ken sentetsu sōsho Ōtomo Sōrin shiryōshū*, vol. 1 (Ōita, 1993), doc. 205, 6.29 [(Tenbun 20) 1551] Ōtomo Sōrin *shojō*, pp. 166–67. Hashizume, the messenger, was granted some six acres (*chō*) of lands for his troubles, but this is insufficient evidence to prove that Haruhide was hiding in Chikugo.

[11] Francis Xavier (1506–52) was aware of these plans. In a letter of January 1552, he wrote: "The lords of the land discovered that it could not be ruled if it did not have a duke. They consequently sent ambassadors to the duke of Bungo [Ōtomo Sōrin] asking him to give them one of his brothers to be the duke of Yamaguchi." This passage continues, "The duke of Bungo is a very great friend of the Portuguese. His people are very warlike, and he is lord over many lands."M. Joseph Costelloe, S.J., *The Letters and Instructions of Francis Xavier* (St. Louis, MO: Institute of Jesuit Sources, 1992), p. 339.

[12] *Yamaguchi kenshi shiryōhen chūsei*, vol. 3, Hagi shi kyōdo hakubutsukan zō monjo, Yuasa ke monjo, doc. 114, 10.6 [(Tenbun 20) 1551] Ōuchi shi *toshiyori rensho shojō*, pp. 1029–30. See also Uoya Shōhei, "Sue Harukata no kaimei jiki ni tsuite," *Yamaguchi ken chihōshi kenkyū* 115 (6.2016), pp. 64–68.

[13] *Ōtomo Sōrin shiryōshū*, vol. 1, doc. 211, 9.11 [(Tenbun 20) 1551] Ōtomo Sōrin *shojō*, p. 170 for his delight about Yoshitaka's destruction, and doc. 213, 11.22 [(Tenbun 20) 1551] Ōtomo ke *kahanshū renshojō*, pp. 171–72, and doc. 296, 1.28 [(Tenbun 21) 1552] Ōtomo Sōrin *shojō*, pp. 225–26 for Haruhide's travels.

[14] Christopher Mayo, *Swearing Oaths and Waging War: People, Place, and Ritual Practice within the Ōtomo Warrior Band in Sixteenth-Century Japan* (Kogakkan University Press, 2019), pp. 69–70.

[15] *Usa jingūshi shiryōhen*, vol. 12 (Usa, 1995), pp. 484–85.

[16] *Yamaguchi kenshi shiryōhen chūsei*, vol. 3, Yuasa ke monjo doc. 2, 2.19 Sue Harukata *shojō*, p. 997. Chronicles for some reason suggest that he departed a week later. See *Ōuchi bunka*, Yatsushiro nikki for Haruhide's departure from Bungo on 2.18.1552 (Tenbun 21), p. 248. For his arrival, see *Kumagai ke monjo*, doc. 127, 3.1 [(Tenbun 21) 1552] Sue Harukata *soejō*, p. 132.

Haruhide had intended to travel overland but was advised by Sōrin that he should appeal to his Ōuchi ancestry and disembark at Tatara, the site where Prince Imsŏng had purportedly landed long ago.[17]

By appealing to his descent from this imaginary Korean prince, Haruhide emphasized his Ōuchi ethnicity. Haruhide tried to "do what was done before," and act as if he were the second coming of Imsŏng.[18] Yoshitaka had prominently mentioned Prince Imsŏng in his prayer to Usa in 1533, but neither he, nor any earlier lord, felt the need to follow in Imsŏng's footsteps.[19] Chroniclers would recount how Haruhide had "landed where the ancestors had landed [in Tatara] thinking that it would be a good precedent," but they questioned the relevance of signs from five centuries past.[20]

Haruhide attempted to project continuity. He accepted a sword and horse from emissaries of Hachiman once he was made the Ōuchi heir in accordance with long-standing rites, albeit ones performed two months later than had been customary.[21] He would diligently perform Hikamisan Kōryūji Second Month (*nigatsu-e*) rites through 1556, and he exempted this temple shrine complex and its branches from province-wide taxes.[22]

The Pliant Ruler

Haruhide spent his life being told by others what to do. He obeyed the orders of his father, Ōtomo Yoshiaki, in agreeing to become an Ōuchi heir in 1543, and then, after the brutal murder of his father, he followed the commands of

---

[17] *Ōita ken sentetsu shiryōkan zō*, 3.27 [(Tenbun 21) 1552] Ōuchi Haruhide *shojō*. A photograph of the document and summary appears in *Yamaguchi kenshi tsūshihen chūsei* (Yamaguchi, 2012), p. 548.

[18] *Yamaguchi kenshi shiryōhen chūsei*, vol. 1, Ōuchi shi metsubō shidai, pp. 745–46.

[19] *Sengoku ibun Ōuchi shi hen*, vol. 3 (Tōkyōdō shuppan, 2019), doc. 2593, 7.23.1533 (Tenbun 2) Ōuchi Yoshitaka *ganmon an*, p. 199.

[20] *Yoshitakaki*, p. 431, and *Chūgoku chiranki*, p. 440, are critical of his actions. The *Ōtomoki*, a pro-Ōtomo record, p. 560, portrays it in a more positive light, as does one genealogy. *Ōuchi bunka*, Naikaku bunko Tatara *ason kabane* Ōuchi [*keizu*], p. 54. See also Suda, *Chūsei Nichō kankei to Ōuchi shi*, p. 235.

[21] *Yamaguchi kenshi tsūshihen furoku* CD-ROM, Iwashimizu Tanaka ke monjo, doc. 72, 3.20 [(Tenbun 21) 1552] Ōuchi Haruhide *shojō*, p. 712, and *Yamaguchi kenshi shiryōhen chūsei*, vol. 3, Yamaguchi monjokan Kōryūji monjo, doc. 164, 4.13.1552 (Tenbun 21) Kōryūji *shunigatsu-e tōyaku sashibumi*, p. 299.

[22] *Yamaguchi kenshi shiryōhen chūsei*, vol. 3, Kōryūji monjo, docs. 165–66 of 2.13.1555 (Tenbun 24) and 2.13.1556 (Kōji 2), p. 299 for the rites. Hikamisan Kōryūji was exempt from province-wide *tansen* levies, but some debate remained concerning the status of its subtemples: doc. 139, 4.19.1553 (Tenbun 22) Ōuchi shi *bugyōnin rensho hōsho*, p. 287, and doc. 223, 5.13.1553 (Tenbun 22) Ōuchi Yoshinaga *hanmotsu*, p. 318.

his older brother Sōrin both in landing at Tatara and in welcoming the Jesuits to Yamaguchi.[23]

In Yamaguchi, Haruhide depended on Sue Takafusa and had no expectations or any desire to govern on his own. The two men demonstrated their close ties by changing their names. Sometime between 11.16 and 12.10.1551 Sue Takafusa abandoned the "taka" character of Yoshitaka, the lord that he killed, in favor of the "haru" of Haruhide, thus becoming known to posterity as Sue Harukata. This name choice is unusual. In most cases, retainers adopted the second character in a lord's personal name. Yoshitaka, for example, liberally bestowed the "taka" on hundreds, but not the "yoshi." Harukata, for his part, took the "haru," of Haruhide, thus implying a closeness between lord and retainer that most lords avoided.[24] In fact, and in contrast to the behavior of most lords, Haruhide made it known that it was Sue Harukata, and not he, who would determining the bestowing of rewards to warriors in Iwami, Nagato, and Buzen provinces.[25]

Haruhide adopted the practice of prominently writing his monogram at the head of each document of commendation (*sodehan andojō*), the prerogative of an Ōuchi leader.[26] He did so in order to affirm continuity with the earlier lords, including Yoshitaka.[27] For example, he upheld Ōga family rights of tax-free passage of ports and harbors while at the same time limiting

[23] *Ōita ken sentetsu shiryōkan zō*, 3.27 [(Tenbun 21) 1552] Ōuchi Haruhide *shojō*. A photograph of the document and summary appears in *Yamaguchi kenshi tsūshihen chūsei*, p. 548.

[24] See Fukuo Takeichirō, *Ōuchi Yoshitaka* (Yoshikawa kōbunkan, 1959), p. 180 for the timing of the change and the unusual nature of Harukata's new name. Fukuo argued that this change happened sometime between the tenth and eleventh months of 1551, but Uoya Shōhei has shown that this happened between 11.16 and 12.10. See his "Sue Harukata no kaimei jiki ni tsuite," p. 65. Although lords did not bestow the first character of their name to followers, sometimes the Ashikaga would give the first character of their name as a particular honor.

[25] *Masuda ke monjo*, vol. 1 (Tōkyō daigaku shuppankai, 2000), doc. 285, 7.1552 (Tenbun 21) Ōuchi Haruhide *andojō*, p. 252 for Iwami, *Yamaguchi kenshi shiryōhen chūsei*, vol. 4 (Yamaguchi, 2008), Miyoshi ke monjo, doc. 3, 11.6 [(Tenbun 21) 1552] Ōuchi Haruhide *shojō utsushi*, p. 367 for Nagato, and *Kumamoto ken shiryō chūsei hen*, vol. 2 (Kumamoto, 1962), Sata ke monjo, doc. 161, 4.2 [(Tenbun 22) 1553] Ōuchi Yoshinaga *shojō*, p. 247 for Buzen.

[26] Wada Shūsaku, "'Furoku' Sasaki Shichibe Sukeyoshi no honyaku to shōkai," *Yamaguchi monjo kan kenkyū kiyō*, no. 39 (3.2012), pp. 121–28, Sasaki monjo, doc. 8, Ōuchi Haruhide (Yoshinaga) *sodehan tsugime andojō utsushi*, p. 126, and *Shimonoseki shishi shiryōhen* 6 (Shimonoseki, 2001), Chōfu Mōri ke monjo tekagami, doc. 36, 9.4.1552 (Tenbun 21) Ōuchi Yoshinaga *sodehan andojō*, p. 15. For a later example with his newly promoted rank, see *Yamaguchi kenshi shiryōhen chūsei*, vol. 4, Iminomiya monjo, doc. 10, urū 1.27.1553 (Tenbun 22) Ōuchi Haruhide *sodehan andojō*, pp. 381–82.

[27] *Fukuoka shishi shiryōhen chūsei*, vol. 1, *Shinai shōzai monjo* (Fukuoka, 2010), Shikaumi jinja monjo, doc. 6, 8.23.1552 (Tenbun 21) Ōuchi Haruhide *andojō*, p. 191 for confirmation of a 6.23.1542 (Tenbun 11) Yoshitaka Dazaifu *daifusen*. That document survives as the fourth document in the Shikaumi collection and is reproduced on p. 190.

the number of ships (three) that were exempt, as had been decided in 1537.[28] Nevertheless, while praising the Ōga for their actions in the coup, Haruhide abolished their autonomy. On the recommendation of Sue Harukata, he made them retainers of the Masuda. This decision showed that the will of Harukata trumped precedent and administrative practice. Such decisions were often unpopular.[29]

Christianity and the Portuguese in Yamaguchi

In 1550, during the last year of Yoshitaka's rule, European missionaries arrived in Yamaguchi for the first time. Francis Xavier (1506–52), a Jesuit Portuguese missionary, came to Yamaguchi twice, first in the eleventh and twelfth months of 1550, and then after his failed mission to Kyoto. To the people of Yamaguchi, including the previous lord Yoshitaka and others, Xavier was one of a reformist group of Buddhist monks. After all, Xavier himself had come from India, and, in a translation error, he commanded that the Japanese should worship Dainichi (Vairocana) (*Dainichi o ogami are*) when he meant to exhort that they pray to Deus, the Christian God.[30] Yoshitaka's officials assumed that these men from India were Shingon monks and accordingly came to assume that Shingon Buddhism still flourished in India.[31]

Yoshitaka, who was interested in new ideas and consulted with a variety of religious and ritual specialists, famously had an audience with Francis Xavier. This alone caused Yoshitaka to be criticized by Yoshida Kanemigi (1516–73), who claimed that Yoshitaka "dabbled in magic," but the meaning of this phrase is unknown.[32] Although the *Yoshitakaki* claims that Yoshitaka was intrigued by the objects that they brought, including clocks, telescopes, and

---

[28] Nakatsukasa Ken'ichi, "Bunken kara mita chūsei no Iwami no minato to ryūtsū," in *Nihon no kōeki to umi* (Yamakawa shuppankai, 2016), Ōga ke monjo (hereafter Ōga ke monjo), doc. 15, 7.11.1552 (Tenbun 21) Ōuchi Haruhide *andojō*, and doc. 16, 7.11 [(Tenbun 21) 1552] Ōuchi shi *bugyōnin rensho hōsho*, p. 103.

[29] Ōga ke monjo, doc. 17, 7.11.1552 (Tenbun 21) Ōuchi Haruhide *andojō*, p. 104.

[30] Jurgis Elisonas, "Christianity and the Daimyo," in John Whitney Hall, et al. eds., *The Cambridge History of Japan* (New York: Cambridge University Press, 1991), pp. 307–10, and Urs App, *The Cult of Emptiness: The Western Discovery of Buddhist Thought and the Invention of Oriental Philosophy* (Kyoto: University Media, 2012), pp. 14–17.

[31] *Yoshitakaki*, p. 425, and App, "St. Francis Xavier's Discovery," part 2, pp. 219–21. For more on Xavier and Yoshitaka, see Elisonas, "Christianity and the Daimyo," pp. 312–15.

[32] Okada Akio, *Kirishitan bateren* (Shibundō, 1955), 160 for a transcription of Kanemigi's diary concerning Yoshitaka. The location of Kanemigi's 1551 diary is currently unknown.

glasses, he did not convert to Christianity. Xavier's criticisms of Yoshitaka for the sin of sodomy did little to endear him to the Ōuchi lord.

However, Xavier and the Portuguese developed close ties to Ōtomo Sōrin, who would ultimately convert to Christianity and assume the name Ōtomo Francisco.[33] Xavier may have had foreknowledge of the 1551 coup, as he fled Yamaguchi a few days before it erupted. He left behind two followers, who were protected in Yamaguchi during the coup by Naitō Okimori, who later converted to Christianity.[34]

The new Ōuchi lord Haruhide supported this new religion. On the advice of his brother Sōrin, Haruhide allowed Christian proselytizing. He granted lands for Daidōji on 8.28.1552.[35] This document was translated into Portuguese in Yamaguchi shortly after having been written out phonetically by them.[36] Two copies of this document exist, with one version in Portugal, and another copy (*anmon*) in Yamaguchi.[37]

The gulf in understanding remained wide. Haruhide believed that the Portuguese were from India and were proponents of a reformist Buddhist sect. He wrote as follows:

Monks from the western regions who came to Japan[38] desiring to revitalize the Buddhist Law, wish to build the Temple of the Great Way (Daidōji) in Yamaguchi county (*agata*) Yoshiki district of Suō Province. In accordance with their request, permission is granted thus (Figure 10.1).

[33] Conlan, *Samurai and the Warrior Culture of Japan, 471–1877: A Sourcebook* (Indianapolis: Hackett, 2022), pp. 225–28.

[34] Costelloe, *Letters and Instructions*, p. 270.

[35] *Nihon kankei kaigai shiryō Iezusukai Nihon shokanshū Yakubun hen*, vol. 2.2 (Tōkyō daigaku shuppankai, 2000), pp. 207–8 for the 8.28.1552 (Tenbun 21) Ōuchi Haruhide *saikyojō*. For a photograph, see *Nihon kankei kaigai shiryō Iezusukai Nihon shokanshū genbun hen*, vol. 2 (Tōkyō daigaku shuppankai, 1996), "Appendix 2," pp. 329–30 and Figure 10.1. Haruhide signed this document as Ōuchi *no suke*. For analysis, see Matsuda Kiichi, "Ōuchi Yoshinaga no Daidōji saikyojō ni tsuite," *Komonjo kenkyū*, no. 4 (1970): 20–36, and Georg Schurhammer, *Francis Xavier: His Life and Times*, trans. M. Joseph Costelloe, 4 vols. (Rome: Jesuit Historical Institute, 1973–82), vol. 4, p. 271.

[36] According to Patrick Schwemmer, email discussion 7.4.2020, this document was originally written in Japan. See also Conlan, *Samurai*, pp. 223–25.

[37] *Ōuchi shi no tobira: Yamaguchi o tsukutta saikoku daimyō* (Yamaguchi shi rekishi minzoku shiryōkan, 10.2019), pp. 26, 73 for illustrations and transcriptions of the Yamaguchi copy. See also Urs App, *The Cult of Emptiness*, pp. 14–18. The 8.28.1552 (Tenbun 21) Ōuchi Haruhide *saikyojō* is stored in the Ministério dos Negócios Estrangeiros Instituto Diplomático Divisão de Arquivo e Biblioteca PT/MNE/DAB/SCF28- C ff348–349 r. This idocument is reproduced as Figure 10.1. A facsimile was also published in 1570 in the *Cartas de Japão* of 1570.

[38] Literally "came to the court" (*raichō*), an alternate way to describe Japan.

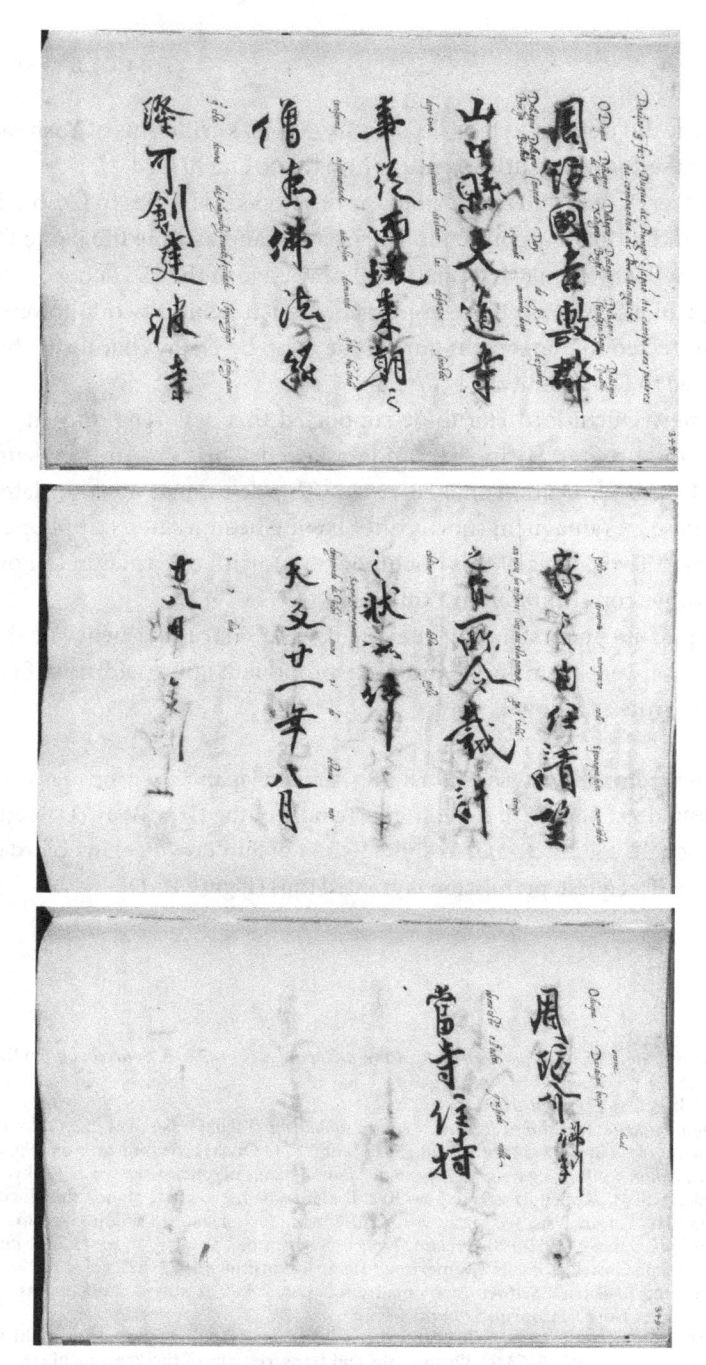

Figure 10.1 Daidōji Commendation (*saikyojō*) with Portuguese Translation. Livro primeiro em que se treladão as cartas que mandão os irmãos da Compa. de Jesu que andão na India das coisas que Nosso Señhor par elles obra e começa do año do nacimento de N. Sñor Iesu Christo de 1544 en diante. [S.I.]:[s.n.], 1602, belonging to the Diplomatic Archive. PT/MNE/DAB/SCF28- C ff348-349 r. Images and permission provided by Ministério dos Negócios Estrangeiros Instituto Diplomático Divisão de Arquivo e Biblioteca.

The Portuguese understanding of this grant was far more encompassing than Haruhide intended. In their translation, they write that Haruhide "concedes Daidōjio to the Priests of the Occident, who have come to preach a law for making Saints, according to his will, until the end of the world, which is a plain which is behind [Y]amaguchi, a great city, with privileges, which no one may be killed nor captured in it, and in order that it may be clear to my successors I give them this patent so that at no time may they be able to take them out of this [temple]."[39] The Portuguese treasured this document, one of the first Japanese records to be reproduced in Europe.

The Portuguese translation not only describes Haruhide as the lord of the western provinces, but also suggests that he wields authority over all of Japan.[40] It also portrays him as a fervent Christian and "a greater lord in lands and vassals than the king of Castile" who "gave us a very large piece of property so that we might build a college upon it."[41]

These early contacts, and Yamaguchi's position as the site of a Christian church, profoundly influenced the earliest European maps of Japan. Starting in the 1550s two Italian cartographers drew up maps that were based on information from Xavier. A 1560 map by the Portuguese cartographer Bartolomeu Velho (d. 1568) depicts Japan with increasing accuracy.[42] This map of Japan shows the regions from southern Kyushu through the Miyako, or capital of Japan. The silver mines appear prominently, and the center of Japan is described in large letters as Maguch.[43] This map reveals what the Portuguese translation only suggests: Yamaguchi was the center of Japan, and its realm was nearly coextensive with the whole archipelago (Figure 10.2).

---

[39] Translation by Patrick Schwemmer, 7.4.2020.
[40] For this interpretation, I am indebted to Patrick Schwemmer.
[41] Quoted in Georg Schurhammer, *Francis Xavier*, vol. 4, p. 270.
[42] Alfredo Pinheiro Marques, "Japan in Early Portuguese Maps," in *The UNESCO Courier: A Window Open on the World* 42.4, *Camões and the Portuguese Voyages of Discovery* (Paris, April 1989), pp. 14–16 (accessed 7.13.2020), https://unesdoc.unesco.org/ark:/48223/pf0000083172.
[43] See the Getty's 1560 *Bartolomeu Velho Portolan Atlas* (accessed 10.2012), http://dpg.lib.berkeley.edu/webdb/dsheh/heh_brf?Description=&CallNumber=HM+44. Other later maps depicting Yamaguchi, Miyako and the silver mines appear in the *Asiae Nova Descripto* of 1567 and Abraham Ortelius, *Theatrum Orbis Terrarum* of 1570.

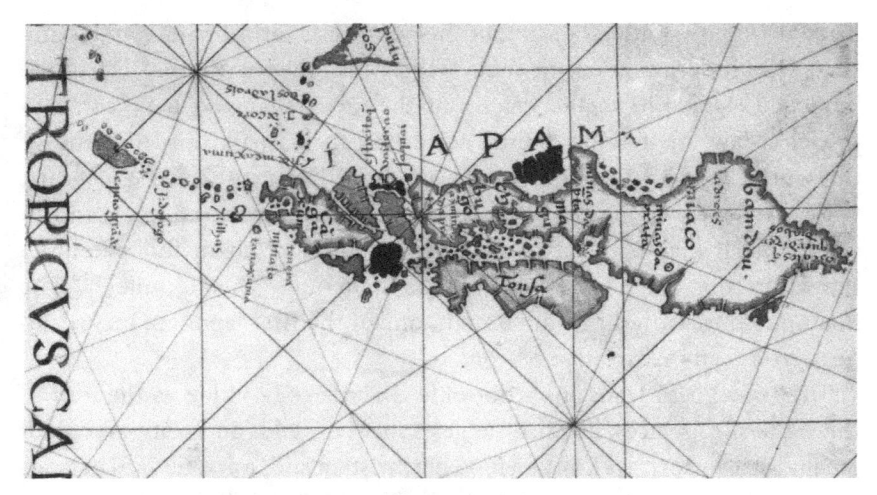

Figure 10.2 Map of Japan by the Portuguese cartographer Bartolomeu Velho, 1560. Image and permission provided by The Huntington Library, San Marino, California, Manuscripts MSS HM 44

Becoming Ōuchi Yoshinaga

Haruhide tried to consolidate his authority by reaffirming his ritual and social position. Through the third month of 1552, he signed his documents quite simply as Haruhide.[44] By 4.13, he broadcast his identity by adding the name Tatara to prayers offered for Second Month Kōryūji Hikamisan rites.[45] As a New Year gift in 1553, Ashikaga Yoshiteru (1536–65, shogun 1546–65) gave Haruhide the right to use the character "yoshi," character of his own personal name, a sign of respect, and appointed him to the office of *Sakyō no daibu*, which had been historically an important Ōuchi title.[46] He also

[44] *Yamaguchi kenshi tsūshihen furoku* CD-ROM, Iwashimizu Tanaka ke monjo, doc. 72, 3.20 [(Tenbun 21) 1552] Ōuchi Haruhide *shojō*, p. 712.

[45] *Yamaguchi kenshi shiryōhen chūsei*, vol. 3, Yamaguchi monjokan Kōryūji monjo, doc. 164, 4.13.1552 (Tenbun 21) Kōryūji *shunigatsu-e tōyaku sashibumi*, p. 299.

[46] *Ninagawa ke monjo*, vol. 3 (Tōkyō daigaku shuppankai, 1987), doc. 663, 1.1 [(Tenbun 22) 1553] Ashikaga Yoshiteru *gonaisho an*, p. 198 for the appointment to the office of *Sakyō no daibu*, and doc. 664, 1.1 [(Tenbun 22) 1553] Ashikaga Yoshiteru *gonaisho an*, pp. 198–99 for bestowing the character "yoshi" for his name. Yoshinaga first used this title in documents dating from early in 1553 (Tenbun 22). See *urū* 1.27.1553 (Tenbun 22) *Yamaguchi kenshi shiryōhen chūsei*, vol. 4, Iminomiya monjo, doc. 10, *urū* 1.27 Ōuchi Haruhide *sodehan andojō*, pp. 381–82.

recognized Haruhide's succession to the Ōuchi chieftainship with the gift of a sword.[47] At this time, Haruhide became known as Ōuchi Yoshinaga.

Yoshinaga relied on the titles of *Sakyō no daibu* and that of Suō *gon no suke*, both of which had been used by Yoshioki (1477–1528), to sign his documents. Unlike Yoshioki, however, he used these two titles simultaneously. This was unorthodox because the former was a prestigious title, which implied authority to govern the western wards of Kyoto, while the latter was merely that of provisional governor of Suō. In a system where court offices were functioning, one would never hold both simultaneously, for they implied vastly different statuses.[48]

Yoshinaga was also appointed to the lower fifth court rank, a common initial status for Ōuchi leaders.[49] Unlike his predecessors, Yoshinaga never advanced in rank. Likewise, Ashikaga Yoshiteru appointed Yoshinaga to the Ashikaga guards (*shōbanshū*), which implied a subservient relationship with the Ashikaga, and something that no Ōuchi lord would have previously countenanced.[50] Ashikaga Yoshiteru also rewarded the key plotters of the coup, including Sue Takafusa, Naitō Okimori, Sugi Shigenori, Ida Okihide, and Toida Hidetane, at the same time that he recognized Yoshinaga's diminished chieftainship.[51]

---

[47] *Ninagawa ke monjo* 3, doc. 665, 1.1 [(Tenbun 22) 1553] Ashikaga Yoshiteru *gonaisho an*, p. 199.

[48] Yoshioki went by the title of Suō *gon no suke* through 9.18.1498 (Meiō 7) and only started using the *Sakyō no daibu* title on 3.20.1499 (Meiō 8). He was not referred to the two offices simultaneously. Compare *Sengoku ibun Ōuchi shi hen*, vol. 2 (Tōkyōdō shuppan, 2017), doc. 1006, Ōuchi Yoshioki *andojō*, pp. 21–22, with doc. 1024, Ōuchi Yoshioki *andojō*, p. 29. By contrast, Yoshinaga was known as Suō *no suke* through 1556, when he combined the *Sakyō no daibu* Suō *no suke* titles. Compare *Yamaguchi kenshi shiryōhen chūsei*, vol. 4, Shuzenji monjo, doc. 2, 11.14.1552 (Tenbun 21) Ōuchi Haruhide *andojō*, p. 551, with *Yamaguchi kenshi shiryōhen chūsei*, vol. 3, Yamaguchi monjokan Kōryūji monjo, doc. 166, 2.13.1556 (Kōji 2) Kōryūji *shunigatsu-e tōyaku sashibumi*, p. 299. In his "King of Japan" seal from the Ming, Yoshinaga is referred to as *Sakyō no daibu* Suō *gon no suke*. *Yamaguchi kenshi shiryōhen chūsei*, vol. 2, Ōuchi shi kangō bōeki kankei shiryō, doc. 2, 11.1556 (Kōji 2) Ōuchi Yoshinaga *shōjō* p. 705.

[49] *Ōuchi bunka*, Naikaku bunko Tatara *ason kabane* Ōuchi [*keizu*], p. 54.

[50] *Ninagawa ke monjo*, vol. 3, doc. 666, 1.1 [(Tenbun 22) 1553] Ashikaga Yoshiteru *gonaisho an*, p. 199.

[51] *Ninagawa ke monjo*, vol. 3, docs. 667–72, 1.1 Ashikaga Yoshiteru *gonaisho an*, pp. 200–202, issued to Toida Hidetane, Sue Takamitsu, Ida Okihide, Sugi Shigenori, Naitō Okimori, and Sue Harukata respectively. Sue Harukata and Naitō Okimori were ringleaders of the coup and Sugi Shigenori joined them. Ida Okihide was one who greeted Ōtomo Haruhide when he was about to depart from Bungo to Suō, but his role is less well known, while Toida Hidetane resided in Iwami in late 1551 and early 1552, but otherwise he is unknown. *Kikkawa ke monjo*, vol. 3, *besshū furoku Iwami Kikkawa ke monjo* (Tōkyō daigaku shuppankai, 1931), docs. 66–68, pp. 66–68.

Turmoil

Yoshinaga relied on the Toida and the Masuda to consolidate authority over the mineral-rich province of Iwami. The Toida erected more castles to defend the silver mines, and in the third month of 1552, they replaced the Ogasawara, who had long managed them, with another family, the Yamane.[52] He also bolstered the authority of the Masuda, and in one case commanded the Ōga, who oversaw the vital harbor of Misumi, to become their retainers.[53]

Nevertheless, significant resistance arose in Iwami. The Ōga of Misumi did not take their loss of autonomy lightly and fought the Masuda on the high seas as far afield as Munakata.[54] Likewise, Yoshimi Masayori, Yoshitaka's brother-in-law, actively and effectively resisted Yoshinaga's rule.[55] He attacked and defeated the Masuda on 10.6.1551, approximately six weeks after Yoshitaka had been killed in the coup.[56]

Yoshinaga did not consolidate his support in Iwami and instead attacked Amako Haruhisa (1514–61) in the provinces of Bingo, east of Iwami, on 7.23.1552. The campaign lasted for over a year, with one major battle being fought on 3.21.1553.[57] Ultimately, with the help of the Mōri,

---

[52] The Yamane would maintain that position at least through 1555. *Iwami no kuni imoji tōryō Yamane shi shiryō chōsa hōkokusho* (Sakurae-shi, 3.1992), p. 11 for 3.1552 (Tenbun 21) and 3.1555 (Tenbun 24) Matsugi Munehiro *nengu saisokujō*. Late in 1551, a certain Watanabe Shūroku also gained control over the mines. *Chūsei imoji shiryō*, doc. 132, 7.16 [(Tenbun 21) 1552] Sue Harukata *bugyōnin rensho hōsho an*, p. 89. For Watanabe's control of the mines, see p. 286. For ongoing evidence of turmoil, see the 6.26 Yamane Jōan *shojō*, pp. 91–92.

[53] *Masuda ke monjo*, vol. 1, doc. 285, 7.1552 (Tenbun 21) Ōuchi Haruhide *andojō*, p. 252. For the Ōga, see *Ōga ke monjo*, doc. 18, 7.11.1552 (Tenbun 21) Ōuchi Haruhide (Yoshinaga) *andojō*, p. 104, doc. 18, 2.13 [(Tenbun 24) 1555] Masuda Fujikane *kanjō utsushi*, p. 104, doc. 19, 8.10 [(Tenbun 24) 1555] Ōuchi shi *bugyōnin rensho hōsho*, p. 105, and doc. 20, 1.29 Masuda Fujikane *kanjō utsushi*, p. 105.

[54] *Ōga ke monjo*, doc. 17, 7.11.1552 (Tenbun 21) Ōuchi Haruhide *andojō*, p. 104. See also docs. 18–20, for their loss of autonomy and docs. 22–23, pp. 104–6 for their battles against the Masuda.

[55] For a good overview, see Nakatsukasa Ken'ichi, "Yoshimi Masayori," in *Shimane ken no kassen* (Iki shuppan, Shimane, 2018), pp. 120–21. See also *Tokubetsu ten Masuda shi vs. Yoshimi shi—Iwami no Sengoku jidai* (Shimane kenritsu Iwami bijutsukan, 9.2019). For more on the closeness of Yoshimi Masayori with Ōuchi Yoshitaka, see *Fusaaki oboegaki*, in *Hiroshima kenshi kodai chūsei shiryōhen*, vol. 3 (Hiroshima, 1978), p. 1133.

[56] *Yamaguchi kenshi shiryōhen chūsei*, vol. 2, Yasutomi monjo, doc. 11, 10.6.1551 (Tenbun 20) Yoshimi Masayori *kanjō utsushi*, p. 220. For the defeat from the Masuda perspective, see *Chūsei Masuda Masuda shi kankei shiryōshū* (Masuda, 2016), doc. 612, 10.12 Masuda Fujikane *kanjō*, pp. 243–44.

[57] *Fukuhara ke monjo* (Ube-shiritsu toshokan, 1983), doc. 192, 7.23.1552 (Tenbun 21) Ōuchi Yoshinaga *kanjō*, pp. 342–43 and docs. 193, 195–99, p. 344 for the early battles. Next, for the battles of Bitchū on 3.21.1553 (Tenbun 22) see docs. 200–202, p. 344. For Yoshinaga mobilizing Mōri Motonari to fight the Amako in Izumo in the fourth month of that year, see also *Ōita ken shiryō* 32 *dai* 2 *bu hoi* 4 *Ōtomo ke monjoroku* 2 (Ōita, 1980), doc. 1299, 11.28 [(Tenbun 22) 1553] Ōtomo shi *nenrō rensho hōsho*, pp. 235–36.

Yoshinaga captured a strategic Amako castle in the tenth month of 1553.[58]

Success, or at least a stalemate against the Amako, did not lead to stability. Sue Harukata killed many whom he suspected of treason. Among them were Munakata Ujitsugu and his son Ujimitsu, attendants of Munakata shrine, and the head of Hakozaki shrine.[59] More notably, Harukata attacked and killed Sugi Shigenori, one of the coconspirators of the 1551 coup, on 8.28.1553, not long after he learned that Shigenori had warned Yoshitaka of the coup attempt years before.[60] Shigenori, a key lieutenant to Yoshinaga, had been rewarded by Ashikaga Yoshiteru and had administered Kyushu effectively.[61] After Shigenori's death, Ōtomo Sōrin moved into Hakata, effortlessly taking over Hakozaki and surrounding regions as Ōuchi and Ōtomo administration increasingly fused there.[62] Ōuchi influence over Hakata ended with the demise of Shigenori, although the last traces of Ōuchi rule would linger in northern Kyushu through 8.1556.[63]

---

[58] See *Ura ke monjo*, in *Kobayakawa ke monjo*, vol. 2 (Tōkyō daigaku shuppankai, 1927), doc. 74, 8.22.1553 (Tenbun 22) Kobayakawa Takakage *kanjō utsushi*, p. 86 for the defeat of the Takasugi at Mitani castle in Bingo in the eighth month. For victory against Amako forces on 10.19.1553 (Tenbun 22), see docs. 208–12, pp. 346–47. See also *Yamaguchi kenshi shiryōhen chūsei*, vol. 3, Yamamoto ke monjo, doc. 121, 12.16 [(Tenbun 22) 1553] Ōuchi shi *bugyōnin rensho shojō*, p. 1031.

[59] *Munakata shishi shiryōhen chūsei*, vol. 2 (Munakata, 1996), doc. 352–1, Munakata shi *jūshin rensho hōsho utsushi*, p. 320. For more on the assassination of Ujitsugu and his son, see pp. 321–29 and Kuwata Kazuyuki, "Ōuchi Yoshitaka no metsubō to Chikuzen Munakata shi," *Kyūshū shigaku*, no. 105 (9.1992), pp. 23–40. Munakata Masauji and his son Masao had died with Yoshitaka in 1551. For Hakozaki experiencing turmoil after an attack (*tsuitō*) on the head (*gohonke*) of the shrine, see *Yamaguchi kenshi tsūshihen furoku* CD-ROM Tanaka ke Iwashimizu monjo, doc. 77, 6.20 [(Tenbun 22) 1553] Mōri Fusahiro *shojō an*, p. 714.

[60] A document written by Sagara Taketō in the possession of the Mōri is quite incriminating. Tōkyō daigaku shiryōhen sanjo, comp., *Mōri ke monjo*, vol. 4 (Tōkyō daigaku shuppankai, 1924), doc. 1556, 1.5.1551 (Tenbun 20). Sagara Taketō *mōshijo utsushi*, 458–65. Yonehara Masayoshi made this connection in his *Ōuchi Yoshitaka* (Jinbutsu ōraisha, 1967), p. 265, but he assumed, incorrectly, that Shigenori was killed in 1552 (Tenbun 21). Documentary evidence of Shigenori's survival into 1553 comes from a 11.15.1553 (Tenbun 22) Sue Harukata *kanjō* addressed to Kuraki Kikō no suke. *Kōbunsō* catalog 44 (1.1973), p. 139.

[61] For his appointment, see *Ninagawa ke monjo*, vol. 3, doc. 670, 1.1 Ashikaga Yoshiteru *gonaisho an*, p. 201; for some administrative records in 1553, see *Usa jingūshi shiryōhen*, vol. 12 (Usa, 1996), 1.23 [(Tenbun 22) 1553] Ōuchi *bugyōnin hōsho an*, p. 509, 3.21 [(Tenbun 22) 1553] Ōuchi *bugyōnin hōsho an*, p. 515, 3.27 [(Tenbun 22) 1553] Ōuchi *bugyōnin hōsho an*, p. 516, and for the final record of 8.19.1553 (Tenbun 22), see pp. 522–24.

[62] *Yamaguchi kenshi tsūshihen furoku* CD-ROM Tanaka ke Iwashimizu monjo, doc. 82, 1.19 [(Tenbun 23) 1554] Seizei *shojō*, p. 716 which recounts the last time a Hakozaki official traveled to Yamaguchi. *Hakozakigū shiryō* (Fukuoka: Hakozakigū, 1970), doc. 144, 3.23.1554 (Tenbun 23) Ōtomo Yoshishige *mikyōjo*, p. 161, shows that the Ōtomo were adjudicating Hakozaki shrine lands at the same time. For more on how the Ōtomo absorbed Ōuchi officials into their instiutions, see Horimoto Kazushige, "1550 nendai ni okeru Ōtomo shi no hokubu Kyūshū shihai no shinten-Ōuchi Yoshinaga no chiseiki o chūshin ni," *Kyūshū shigaku* 162 (8.2012), p. 34.

[63] Horimoto, "1550 nendai ni okeru Ōtomo shi no hokubu Kyūshū shihai no shinten," p. 34.

Not long after Shigenori was killed, Yoshimi Masayori once again rebelled in Nagato and Iwami. He met with limited success and was pushed back to his Sanbonmatsu castle.[64] There he appealed to Mōri Motonari, who still perceived Yoshinaga as his lord, but disliked and distrusted Sue Harukata.[65] In the end, Motonari realized that if he did not attack Sue Harukata, he would be killed like Sugi Shigenori.[66] Motonari's son Takamoto (1523–63) would later recount how they attempted instead to turn Yoshinaga against Sue Harukata, but without success.[67]

Sue Harukata called Motonari's rebellion "treason" (*akugyaku*) and "great and wanton evil" (*mōaku mudō*).[68] Yoshinaga, by contrast, appealed to Myōken for support. In his prayer to Kōryūji, Yoshinaga acknowledged the Iwami (Yoshimi) and Aki (Mōri) uprisings and confessed that the Myōken's aid was necessary to destroy these rebels. In his prayers, Yoshinaga promised that if he were able to return to Yamaguchi victorious, he would rethatch the roof of Myōken's temple.[69] As it happened, Yoshimi Masayori surrendered to Yoshinga on 9.2.1554. He sent a son as a hostage, but his wife, the sister of Yoshitaka, wisely fled.[70]

[64] *Ura ke monjo*, doc. 11, 9.2.1554 (Tenbun 23) Nomi Katakatsu *gunchūjō*, pp. 7–9 for battles on the road to Iwami to Tsuwano's Sanbonmatsu castle. See also *Ōita ken shiryō* 32 *dai* 2 *bu hoi* 4 *Ōtomo ke monjoroku* 2, Ōtomo ke monjoroku 4, 4.1554 (Tenbun 23), p. 237. For an excellent overview of the Sue Yoshimi battles, see Akiyama Nobutaka, "Muromachi Sengokuki ni okeru Aki Iwami kōtsū," *Shigaku kenkyū* 218 (10.1997), p. 12.

[65] Tōkyō daigaku shiryōhen sanjo, comp., *Mōri ke monjo*, vol. 2 (Tōkyō daigaku shuppankai, 1922), doc. 664, 1.2 [(Tenbun 23) 1554] Mōri Motonari *jihitsu shojō*, pp. 398–401, particularly pp. 398–99. See also *Agari ke monjo monjo*, doc. 13, Ōuchi ke *ryaku keizu*, pp. 8, 12–13 for Masayori's role in causing the Mōri to rebel against Yoshinaga.

[66] *Mōri ke monjo*, vol. 2, doc. 665, 4.16 [(Tenbun 23) 1554] Mōri Motonari *jihitsu shojō*, pp. 401–4.

[67] *Mōri ke monjo*, vol. 2, doc. 667, Mōri Takamoto *jihitsu oboegaki*, pp. 407–10 for the attempt to convince Yoshinaga to turn on the Sue, and doc. 671, Mōri Takamoto *jihitsu oboegaki*, pp. 413–14 for the decision to aid Yoshimi Masayori.

[68] *Hagi han batsu etsu roku*, 6 vols. (Yamaguchi ken monjokan, 1994), vol. 4, Kuba Shō-uemon collection, doc. 26, 5.19 [(Tenbun 23) 1554] Sue Harukata *shojō an*, p. 111. This document was analyzed by Yamamoto Hiroki, *Saikoku no Sengoku kassen Sensō no Nihonshi* 12 (Yoshikawa kōbunkan, 2007), pp. 79–80.

[69] *Yamaguchi kenshi shiryōhen chūsei*, vol. 3, Kōryūji monjo, doc. 224, 5.22.1554 (Tenbun 23) Ōuchi Yoshinaga *gammon*, p. 318.

[70] *Hagi han batsu etsu roku*, vol. 4, maki 148, Shimose Shichibei monjo, doc. 1, 8.23 [(Tenbun 23) 1554] Masuda Kenjun *shojō an*, p. 150, and doc. 7, 5.25(15) [(Tenbun 23) 1554] Masuda Fujikane *shojō*, p. 153 for the Yoshimi, Masuda, Amako, and Sue peace negotiations. For the treaty itself and the flight of Masayori's wife (Yoshitaka's sister) see doc. 12, 9.7.1554 (Tenbun 23) Yoshimi Masayori *shitsu shōshō shōsoku*, pp. 154–55, and *Ōita ken shiryō* 32 *dai* 2 *bu hoi* 4, Ōtomo ke monjoroku 2, Ōtomo ke monjoroku 4, 9.1554 (Tenbun 23), p. 244.

The Itsukushima Defeat

Having pacified Iwami, Yoshinaga and Sue Harukata turned against the forces of Mōri Motonari and the "rebels" of Aki. Motonari in turn allied himself with the Kurushima Murakami *kaizoku* privateers of the Inland Sea.[71] He could do so because these privateers were upset with the policies of Sue Harukata, who prohibited them from charging tolls (*dabetsuryo*) or levying protection fees (*keigo mai*) on merchant ships (*kaisen*), which Yoshitaka had previously allowed.[72]

Harukata advanced to Itsukushima shrine in Aki. Although he had the larger army, he inexplicably stationed it in on the island of Itsukushima itself, where the shrine was located. One of his generals, Hironaka Takakane (1521?–55), who hailed from the Tōsai region, wrote to his family complaining of Harukata's poor disposition of forces.[73] He proved prescient, but did not survive the battle.

Taking advantage of bad weather, Mōri Motonari landed on the eastward side of Itsukushima island at Tsutsumigaura. In the middle of the night, he ascended the ridge of Bakuchio to his west and attacked over the crest of these hills. Hironaka and the Sue forces were so surprised that, according to the *Fusaaki oboegaki*, they fired not a shot.[74] The Nomi, who had fought for Yoshinaga, sided now with the Mōri, and their documents show the magnitude of their victory over Harukata's forces.[75] Guns may have played a role in the smashing victory, for although there are no verifiable wounds caused

---

[71] Peter Shapinsky, *Lords of the Sea: Pirates, Violence and Commerce in Late Medieval Japan* (Ann Arbor: University of Michigan, Center for Japanese Studies, 2014), pp. 114–17 for the marriage of Motonari's fourth son Hoida (Mōri) Motokiyo to a daughter of Kurushima Murakami Michiyasu and the establishment of an alliance.

[72] *Hiroshima kenshi kodai chūsei shiryō hen*, vol. 3, Daiganji monjo, doc. 65, 2.28.1552 (Tenbun 21) Sue Harukata (Takafusa) Itsukushima *sadamegaki utsushi*, pp. 1221–22 for reference to levies on cargo ships, and doc. 67, 4.20 Sue Harukata *shojō an* (*kirigami*), p. 1223 for the prohibition of tolls. For Yoshitaka's earlier missives to the Murakami, see *Ehime ken shi shiryōhen kodai chūsei*, docs. 1729–30, 5.21 [(Tenbun 11) 1542] Ōuchi shi *bugyōnin rensho shojō*, and doc. 1731, 5.21 [(Tenbun 11) 1542] Ōuchi shi *bugyōnin rensho shojō an*, pp. 942–43.

[73] *Buzen shishi monjo shiryō* (Buzen shi, 1991), Saigō ke monjo, doc. 12 9.29 [(Tenbun 24) 1555] Hironaka Takakane *shojō*, pp. 97–98. This letter served as a will, as Takakane asked that his daughter succeed him. For analysis of this remarkable document, written on the eve of battle, see Yamamoto Hiroki, *Saikoku no Sengoku kassen*, p. 86. For more on the Hironaka in Kyushu, see Horimoto, "1550 nendai ni okeru Ōtomo shi no hokubu Kyūshū shihai no shinten," pp. 32–33.

[74] *Fusaaki oboegaki*, pp. 1135–36.

[75] *Ura ke monjo*, doc. 76, 10.20.1555 (Tenbun 24) Kobayakawa Takakage *kanjō utsushi*, p. 87 and Fukuhara ke *monjo* doc. 277, p. 360 for the 10.12.1555 (Tenbun 24) Yamada Mitsukane *kanjō utsushi*. See also docs. 274–75, pp. 359–60, and docs. 278–80, pp. 360–61. *Hagi han batsu etsu roku*, vol. 1, maki 15-1 Kokushi Hayato monjo, explains the significance of doc. 25, 2.21.1560 (Eiroku 3) Ashikaga Yoshiteru *sodehan mikyōjo an*, pp. 415–16. *Hagi han batsu etsu roku*, vol. 1, maki 31, Yamada Kichibei monjo, doc. 17, 10.12.1555 (Tenbun 24) Kodama Nariaki onajiku Narikata *rensho kubi chūmon an*, pp. 737–38, recounts the Itsukushima battles. See also *Ōita ken shiryō 32 dai 2 bu hoi 4 Ōtomo ke*

by them at this encounter, participants in the battle do mention the need for lead or potassium nitrate in documents dating from 1557.[76]

After the defeat, Harukata killed himself. His last thoughts are not known, but the death poem attributed to him suggests resignation: "What should I regret? What should I resent? This outcome was decided for me long ago (*nani o oshimi nani o uran moto yori mo kono arisama ni sadamareru mi ni*)."[77] After the Battle of Itsukushima, more turned against Yoshinaga, including most notably Sugi Shigesuke, Shigenori's son.

Prayers, Defeat, and Death

What was Yoshinaga's response to the annihilation of his army? Direct evidence is rare, although compassionate letters that he wrote to the bereaved of Hironaka Takakane survive.[78] He held out hope that Takekane might still be alive.[79] In reality, the defeat proved devastating. The Mōri killed over 4,740, including all the army's commanders, Takakane among them.[80] Yoshinaga could do little but uphold Takakane's testament, which conveyed his holdings to his daughter Ume.[81]

After the debacle, Yoshinaga started fortifying Kōnomine, a steep hill that overlooks Yamaguchi. It was difficult to climb but promised to make an

---

monjoroku 2, Ōtomo ke monjoroku 4, doc. 1328, *urū* 10.18 [(Kōji 1) 1555] Ōtomo shi *nenrō rensho shojō*, pp. 247–48.

[76] *Hagi han batsu etsuroku*, vol. 3, maki 134 Urashirōbei doc. 8, 2.19 [(Kōji 3) 1557] Kobayakawa Takakage *shojō an*, p. 828 for Takakage wanting lead for guns (*teppō*) and vol. 2, maki 84, Kodama Yashichirō doc. 7, 3.1 [(Kōji 3) 1557] Mōri Motonari *shojō an*, p. 857 for Mōri Motonari's request for *enshō* (nitrate) later that year while attacking Susumanuma castle. These documents were first discovered by Yamamoto Hiroki, *Saikoku no Sengoku kassen*. For gunpowder recipies dating from 1559, see https://komonjo.princeton.edu/uesugi/. Nevertheless, the earliest verifiable wound attributed directly from "firearms" dates from 1563. See Conlan, "Instruments of Change: Organizational Technology and the Consolidation of Regional Power in Japan 1333–1600," in *War and State Building in Medieval Japan* (Stanford: Stanford University Press, 2010), p. 147.

[77] Kuwata Tadachika, *Nihon kassen zenshū: Ōnin Muromachi hen* (Akita shoten, 1973), p. 198.

[78] Takakane's wife and daughter were in Buzen province, which remained relatively peaceful.

[79] *Buzen shishi monjo shiryō*, Saigō ke monjo, doc. 13, 10.3 Ōuchi Yoshinaga *shojō*, p. 98.

[80] *Agari ke monjo*, doc. 13, Ōuchi ke *ryaku keizu*, pp. 8, 12–13. For Motonari's and Takamoto's report on their victory, describing how Harukata's encampment collapsed (*kirikuzushi*), see Tōkyō daigaku shiryōhen sanjo, comp., *Mōri ke monjo*, vol. 1 (Tōkyō daigaku shuppankai, 1920), doc. 284, 10.23.1555 (Tenbun 24) Mōri Motonari *onajiku* Takamoto *rensho kanjō an*, pp. 260–61. This copy was written in Takamoto's own hand.

[81] *Buzen shishi monjo shiryō*, Saigō ke monjo, doc. 13, 10.7.1555 (Tenbun 24) Ōuchi Yoshinaga *tsugime andojō*, pp. 98–99. For the death of Hironaka Takakane, his son, and some two or three hundred others at Itsukushima, see *Fusaaki oboegaki*, pp. 1186–87.

effective castle. However, the sharp incline made construction extremely difficult, and the fortress was not finished on Yoshinaga's watch.

Motonari's triumphant army continued their advance to Yamaguchi. The Mōri came to control Suō province for the first time late in 1555.[82] Around this time, Sugi Takasuke, who had escorted Yoshinaga to Yamaguchi in 1552, joined the Mōri. He received a new name, abandoning the "taka" of Yoshitaka in favor of the "moto" of Motonari, and became known thereafter as Sugi Motosuke.[83]

Yoshinaga attempted to maintain Ōuchi rule. During the twelfth month of 1556, he tried unsuccessfully to collect funds for rebuilding the Kōnomine Ise shrines.[84] Yoshinaga also prayed to Hikamisan, lamenting that he could not adequately perform the Second Month (nigatsu-e) rites, which had formed the ritual bedrock of Ōuchi rule. He promised to devote himself to prayers and to stay on the mountain for seventeen days in the following year if he encountered success. This vow went unheeded.[85]

The Jesuits remained in Yamaguchi and built their new church, Daidōji. According to Cosme de Torres (1510–70), the Jesuits were referred to as chensicus or tenjikujin ("Indians"). He stated that many in Yamaguchi blamed them for the bloodshed. "Because they have spoken evilly of the gods, the war broke out. May they be stricken dead and expelled from the land."[86] Torres explained too how in aftermath of the coup, opponents "went constantly about in search of us so that they might slay us, some because of the great hatred they had for us, and others to obtain what we possessed."[87]

As we have seen, Naitō Okimori concealed two of Xavier's followers in Yamaguchi (Torres and Fernandez) during the 1551 coup.[88] The Jesuits described him as "a very important lord who has been of great assistance to us, and especially his wife, by giving us all the help that they could so that the law of God might be increased."[89] Okimori did not immediately convert to

[82] Fukuhara ke monjo, doc. 281, urū 10.1 (sakujitsu) [(Kōji 1) 1555] Mōri Motonari narabi ni Takamoto renshojō, p. 361. See also Fusaaki oboegaki, p. 1187.

[83] Motosuke would play a crucial role in defeating an Ōuchi uprising in 1569 and would also rescue Ashikaga Yoshiaki when he fled the capital. He controlled the important regions of Sawa and Tsuno and died in 1585. Tokuyama shishi (2nd printing, Tokuyama, 1971), pp. 116–18.

[84] Yamaguchi kenshi shiryōhen chūsei, vol. 2, Yamaguchi Daijingū monjo, doc. 18, 12.27.1555 (Kōji 1) Ōuchi Yoshinaga buninjō, p. 918.

[85] Yamaguchi kenshi shiryōhen chūsei, vol. 3 Kōryūji monjo, doc. 226, 2.13.1556 (Kōji 2) Ōuchi Yoshinaga ganmon, pp. 318–19.

[86] Schurhammer, Francis Xavier, vol. 4, p. 272.

[87] Schurhammer, Francis Xavier, vol. 4, p. 274.

[88] Costelloe, Letters and Instructions, p. 270.

[89] Costelloe, Letters and Instructions, p. 337.

Christianity. He worshiped at Hachiman, commending lands there through 7.1.1553 and promised to rethatch the roof if Ōuchi forces triumphed over the Amako.[90] His grandson Takayo (1536–57) also granted a sword and horse to the shrine early in 1554. Okimori's last such offering occurred in the second month of 1555.[91] In 1556, prayers by Naitō Okimori and Takayo ceased, which may support claims from Jesuit sources that Okimori converted to Christianity in 1554 and was followed by his grandson Takayo in 1555.[92] They wrote how Okimori, "a very old man," was baptized. Afterward, he "knelt down with his hands lifted up to heaven and prayed to God that, since he had now attained this age, He should take him to Himself in heaven."[93] The Jesuits accounts mention how two of his sons converted. Their identities are not clear, but one must have been his grandson Takayo.[94] As many as one to two thousand others converted as well.[95]

Of course, not all would convert, even among the Naitō themselves. Naitō Takaharu sided with the Mōri and continued to pray at temples and shrines. Yoshitaka's mother, Higashi-muki (1470?–1559), survived the coup and lived to be ninety, but for her this religion seemed to offer no appeal.[96] Whether they understood Christianity to be a belief profoundly different from Buddhism is not clear. Yoshinaga himself tolerated Christianity, but

---

[90] *Yamaguchi kenshi shiryōhen chūsei*, vol. 2, Kumage jinja monjo, doc. 2, 1.11.1551 (Tenbun 20) Naitō Okimori *andojō*, p. 220–21, for a commendation of lands to the shrine, and 7.1.1553 (Tenbun 22), Naitō Okimori *ganmon*, p. 222, for a promise to rethatch the shrine with victory in Izumo over the Amako.

[91] *Yamaguchi kenshi shiryōhen chūsei*, vol. 2, Kumage jinja monjo, doc. 4, 2.11.1554 (Tenbun 23) Naitō Takayo *kishinjō*, p. 222 and doc. 5, 2.11. Naitō Takayo *shojō*, p. 222 for Takayo's prayers in the following year.

[92] *Yamaguchi kenshi shiryōhen chūsei*, vol. 2, Kumage jinja monjo, doc. 6, 7.24.1556 (Kōji 2), Naitō Takaharu *ganmon*, p. 222. Nevertheless, after Okimori's death, at some time, we see where he was buried at Zenshōji a Pure Land temple where a five-ringed tower (*gorintō*) dedicated to him remains. For information about this *gorintō*, I am indebted to Wada Shūsaku.

[93] Translation from Schurhammer, *Frances Xavier*, vol. 4, p. 157. See also *Nihon kankei kaigai shiryō Iezusukai Nihon shokanshū genbun hen* vol. 3 (2011), letter 101, Letter from Luis Frois, S.J., to the Jesuits in Goa, Malacca, 1.7.1556, p. 9, and *Yamaguchi kenshi shiryōhen chūsei*, vol. 1, p. 1021 for other translations of the conversion letter.

[94] Costelloe, *Letters and Instructions*, p. 270. See also *Nihon kankei kaigai shiryō Iezusukai Nihon shoyushū yakubun hen* 3, p. 13 for the 1.7.1556 Luis Frois letter, and doc. 108, p. 107 for the 11.7.1557 Cosme de Torres letter describing Naitō Okimori's conversion.

[95] *Nihon kankei kaigai shiryō Iezusukai Nihon shoyushū yakubun hen* 3, pp. 156–57 for the 1.10.1558 Melchior Barreto letter that mentioned that Yamaguchi had one thousand converts, some of whom protected Jesuits when monks threw rocks at them, for it was not safe to go out after the fall. Likewise, see p. 164 for his characterization of these converts as being of high social status. See also *Nihon kankei kaigai shiryō Iezusukai Nihon shoyushū yakubun hen* 3, Letter 108, 11.7.1557 by Cosme de Torres, p. 107 for the estimate of two thousand converts.

[96] *Ōuchi Yoshitakaki*, pp. 423–24, and for more on her life and death, Fukuo Takeichirō, *Ōuchi Yoshitaka* (Yoshikawa kōbunkan, 1959), pp. 61–62.

apparently only as a reformist Buddhist sect. Until his end, he remained devoted to Myōken.

Ruin

Sugi Shigesuke (d. 1556), the son of Sugi Shigenori, rebelled in 1556, and in the third month he burned large swathes of Yamaguchi.[97] The fires smoldered in some spots for twenty to thirty days, burning major shrines, such as Gion.[98] A violent clash, resulting in Sugi deaths at the hands of Naitō Takayo, the grandson, and successor to Okimori, may have provoked this disaster.[99] Where Yoshinaga was during these months is unclear. His redistribution of Sugi Shigesuke lands on 8.22.1556, and his reference to Shigesuke's "legacy" lands (ato) suggests that Shigesuke had died by this time, although not before leaving ruin behind.[100]

After Shigesuke's death Ōuchi followers and officials in Kyushu joined the Ōtomo. Sata Takaoki, scion of a long-loyal Buzen warrior family, refrained from traveling to Yamaguchi because of the disturbances, sending paperwork instead on 4.13 of 1556. By the fifth month of 1556, he turned to the Ōtomo to adjudicate his case, and by doing so accepted their authority.[101] This was not seen as a betrayal, since he still fought for Ōuchi Yoshinaga in Chikuzen, against Mōri rebels, as late as 7.3.1556. Yoshinaga indeed praised Takaoki in a document dated 8.10.1556.[102] Ōuchi administrators tried

[97] Nihon kankei kaigai shiryō Iezusukai Nihon shoyushū yakubun hen 3, Letter 112 of 1.10.1558 by Melchior Barreto, p. 158 for how nearly all of Yamaguchi burned at this time.

[98] Nihon kankei kaigai shiryō Iezusukai Nihon shoyushū yakubun hen 3 (2014), Letter 106 (Gaspar Vilela), pp. 107–8, and Yamaguchi ken shitei mukei minzoku bunkazai Sagi no mai (Yamaguchi, 1981), p. 90, for the burning of the town on 3.2.1556 and the loss of records. See also Bōchō fūdo chūshin an, vol. 13, Yamaguchi saiban ge (Yamaguchi, 1961), Kami uno rei no 2, 10.6.1557 (Kōji 3) Mōri Motonari funshitsu andojō, p. 54.

[99] Ōita ken shiryō 32 dai 2 bu hoi 4 Ōtomo ke monjoroku 2, Ōtomo ke monjoroku 4, 3.1556 (Kōji 2), p. 249.

[100] Yamaguchi kenshi shiryōhen chūsei, vol. 4, for the Kunai ke monjo of Tottori. See doc. 4, 8.22.1556 (Kōji 2), Ōuchi Yoshinaga kudashibumi, p. 626 and for the Nagaoka ke monjo of Shimonoseki, see doc. 11, 8.22.1556 (Kōji 2), Ōuchi Yoshinaga sodehan kudashibumi, p. 382 for the confiscation of ex-Sugi Shigesuke lands in Buzen province.

[101] Kumamoto ken shiryō chūsei hen, vol. 2, Sata ke monjo, doc. 165, 4.13 [(Kōji 2) 1556] Ōuchi karyō renshojō, pp. 249–50, and docs. 166–67, 5.5 and 5.7 Ōtomo ke nenrō renshojō, pp. 250–51. See also doc. 168, 5.8 [(Kōji 2) 1556] Ōtomo ke nenrō rensho hōsho, pp. 252–53 for reference to people fleeing the turmoil and Horimoto, "1550 nendai ni okeru Ōtomo shi no hokubu Kyūshū shihai no shinten," pp. 38–39.

[102] Kumamoto ken shiryō chūsei hen, vol. 2, doc. 171, 7.3 Ōuchi Yoshinaga shojō, p. 254, for Akitsuki Fumitane's rebellion. For the Mōri connection, see Usa jingū shi shiryōhen 12, pp. 601–2. The later Sata documents appear in Kumamoto ken shiryō chūsei hen 2, doc. 172, 7.3.1556 (Kōji 2) Sata Takaoki

assessing the half-tax (*hanzei*) throughout their domain, but it is not clear how far afield Yoshinaga's writ was valid.[103] Ōtomo Sōrin would later characterize Yoshinaga's rule as one of unending turmoil from the moment he set foot in Suō,[104] but the real collapse was from 1555.

Ōuchi ruin progressed inexorably, yet the final collapse still took over a year. Yoshinaga lost control of the Iwami silver mines in the eighth month of 1556 when the Amako conquered them. The Amako relied on support from smelters (*Yamafuki shū*) and the Ogasawara, who had been ousted in 1552.[105] Yoshinaga's forces had some success in Chikuzen, but the western reaches of his territory became engulfed in war.[106]

Ming officials were unaware of Yoshinaga's weakness, and in 1556 he received a trade tally (*inkan*) from them as "King of Japan," the last ever to be received in Japan.[107] However, having lost control of the silver mines of Iwami, and lacking erudite officials to help him with the proper protocol to oversee trade, for most died with Yoshitaka, Yoshinaga could not benefit from trade with the Ming.[108] Others tried to supplant the Ōuchi, but they lacked the cultural and diplomatic knowledge and the linguistic skills to do so. In the ensuing turmoil, *wakō* pirates seized their chance, and scrolls show their activity during the year 1557.[109] Ōtomo Sōrin dispatched

---

uchiji teoi chūmon, pp. 254–56, doc. 173, 7.23.1556 (Kōji 2) Sata Takaoki *gunchū chūshinjō*, pp. 256–260, and doc. 174, 8.10.1556 (Kōji 2) Ōuchi Yoshinaga *kanjō*, p. 260.

[103] *Yamaguchi kenshi shiryōhen chūsei*, vol. 4, Jinjōji monjo, doc. 2, 5.10.1556 (Kōji 2) Ōuchi shi *bugyōnin rensho hōsho*, p. 552.

[104] *Ōita ken sentetsu sōsho Ōtomo Sōrin shiryōshū*, vol. 2, doc. 526, 12.9.1557 (Kōji 3) Ōtomo Yoshishige *shojō utsushi*, pp. 165–66.

[105] *Ura ke monjo*, doc. 21, 8.9.1556 (Kōji 2) Mōri Motonari *shojō*, pp. 16–17. This letter names the Ogasawara but does not clearly explain their actions at the time. For more on how they aided the Amako, see Saeki Noriya, *Izumo no chūsei* (Yoshikawa kōbunkan, 2017), pp. 281–83.

[106] *Kumamoto ken shiryō chūsei hen*, vol. 2, Sata ke monjo, doc. 174, 8.10.1556 (Kōji 2) Ōuchi Yoshinaga *kanjō*, p. 260.

[107] *Yamaguchi kenshi shiryōhen chūsei*, vol. 2, Ōuchi shi kangō bōeki kankei shiryō, doc. 2, p. 705 for an 11.1556 (Kōji 2) Yoshinaga seal with the name *Sakyō daibu* Suō *gon no suke* Yoshinaga imprinted above it. This was rescued by Yoshimi Masaharu in 1557. See doc. 3, p. 706 for the 1557 (Kōji 3) Yoshimi Masaharu *oboegaki*.

[108] Kage Toshio, "Ōuchi Ōtomo shi no 'kōji' kenminsen," *Tōkyō daigaku shiryōhen sanjo kenkyū kiyō* 23 (3.2013), pp. 296–307. Yoshinaga's failure to follow basic documentary protocol caused the Ming to not accept these late messengers from the Ōuchi/Ōtomo as being legitimate. The breakdown of this trade, coupled with the great turmoil of 1557, led to the rise of *wakō* incidents. For more recent analysis, see Kage Toshio, "'Kōwa zukan' 'Wakō zukan' to Ōuchi Yoshinaga Ōtomo Sōrin," in *Sengoku daimyō no kaigai kōeki* (Binsei shuppan, 2019), pp. 269–93.

[109] *Egakarata wakō "Wakō zukan" to "Kōwa zukan"* (Yoshikawa kōbunkan, 2014), pp. 76–77, and Suda Makiko, "'Kōwa zukan' no hakken 'Wakō zukan' no saikō," in Suda Makiko, ed., *"Wakō zukan" "Kōwa zukan" o yomu* (Bensei shuppan, 2016), pp. 38–42.

a mighty ship to the Ming (Ningbo) in 1557, but the Ming attacked and sank it.[110]

The disruptions between the years 1551 and 1557 proved costly for many. Major merchant houses, which sold their wares from Shimonoseki in the west to Sakai in the east, sought protection, and some perished outright.[111] Others fled to Sakai.[112] Some valued objects, such as a prized flower container, the property of Sagara Taketō, ended up there as well.[113] Likewise, a skilled doctor named Paolo Eisan fled to Sakai, and he, along with the merchant Hibiya Ryōkei converted to Christianity.[114]

Nothing went well for Yoshinaga during the final months of his rule. Portents of divine displeasure, most notably a baleful shooting star, are prominently mentioned in the *Yatsushiro nikki*, a chronicle of the Sagara.[115] The rites at Hikamisan lapsed, and weeks later Yoshinaga fled, traveling the route to Nagato, through Hōsenji, that Yoshitaka had taken in the fall of 1551.[116]

After Yoshinaga's flight, Mōri Motonari sacked the city, and took great care to destroy Daidōji church, completed just the year before, to ashes, obliterate its texts, and expel resident Catholic priests. Shortly before Yoshinaga's fall, the Catholic priests implored Yoshinaga to protect them. He plaintively responded that he could not since he was unable even to protect himself.[117] Ultimately, nearly all of Yamaguchi, including the "palace of the King," burned down.[118] So great was the damage that the Jesuits believed that the city would never recover.[119]

[110] Kage Toshio, "Kōji" nenki wakōsen to Sengoku daimyō suigun," in Suda Makiko, *"Wakō zukan" "Kōwa zukan" o yomu*, pp. 288–89.

[111] *Hiroshima kenshi kodai chūsei shiryō hen*, vol. 3, Daiganji monjo, doc. 68, 8.26 Daiganji Enkai *shojō*, pp. 1223–24, for a 1552 letter that recounts the disruptions suffered by Kyoto and Sakai merchants. See also *Ōuchi bunka to Kita Kyūshū* (Kita Kyūshū shiritsu shizenshi rekishi hakubutsukan, 2012), p. 38 for a roster in the *Chūgoku Kyūshū oharai kubarichō* indicating that a powerful Shimonoseki merchant named Itō Saburōemon perished with the Ōuchi collapse.

[112] The Hibiya of Sakai were also key agents for the Ōuchi, and one Hibiya Ryōkei would convert to Christianity in 1561. Schurhammer, *Francis Xavier*, vol. 4, p. 180.

[113] Yamada Sōji, *Yamada Sōjiki* (Iwanami bunko, 2006), p. 64. This object, the vase *kaburanashi*, found its way to the Satsumaya merchant house in Sakai.

[114] Matsuda Kiichi and Kawasaki Momota, trans., *Zenyaku Furoisu Nihonshi Shōgun Yoshiteru no saigō oyobi jiyū toshi Sakai: Oda Nobunaga hen*, vol. 1 (Chūō kōron shinsha, 2000), pp. 45–46 for a doctor who adopted the name of Paolo Eisan.

[115] *Ōuchi bunka*, Yatsushiro nikki, p. 248 for the events of 1.20 through the second month of 1557.

[116] *Ōuchi bunka*, Yatsushiro nikki, 3.1–7.1557 (Kōji 3), p. 248.

[117] *Nihon kankei kaigai shiryō Iezusukai Nihon shoyushū yakubun hen*, vol. 3 (Tōkyō daigaku shuppankai, 2014), Letter 106, 10.29.1557 by Gaspar Vilela, p. 67, and doc. 112 for a 1.10.1558 Melchiro Nunez Barretto letter, p. 158.

[118] *Nihon kankei kaigai shiryō Iezusukai Nihon shoyushū yakubun hen*, vol. 3, doc. 108, 11.7.1557 Cosme de Torres, p. 107 for an initial description of the destruction, and doc. 112 for a 1.10 Melchiro Nunez Barretto letter, p. 158, for reference to the burning of the palace.

[119] *Nihon kankei kaigai shiryō Iezusukai Nihon shoyushū yakubun hen*, vol. 3, doc. 112, p. 162.

Figure 10.3 Kōzanji (1329). Site of Ōuchi Yoshinaga's death. Photograph by Thomas Conlan

On 3.28.1557, Yoshinaga, who had fled to Nagato, praised one follower, thanking him for his service in what would be his final surviving document.[120] Days later, Naitō Takayo, his most devoted supporter, killed himself in a misguided attempt to save his lord.[121] Yoshinaga was imprisoned, and ordered by Mōri commanders to commit suicide the next day. He did so on 4.7.1557, but not before expressing regret that Takayo had died a senseless death.[122] Through to the very end, Yoshinaga could not do anything right.

---

[120] *Fukuoka shishi shiryōhen chūsei*, vol 1, Yanagigawa Ōmura monjo, doc. 1, 3.28.1557 (Kōji 3) Ōuchi Yoshinaga *kanjō*, p. 1016. The Ōmura survived and crossed over to Kyushu, where they served the Ōtomo. This original document, which can be verified as being in Yoshinaga's own hand, was exhibited at the *Fukuoka shiritsu hakubutsukan* in 7.2020. I am grateful to Nathan Ledbetter for bringing this to my attention.

[121] *Fukuhara ke monjo*, Mōri ke *kanjō*, doc. 21–23, pp. 367–68 for the 4.3 death of Naitō Takayo.

[122] *Ōita ken shiryō 32 dai 2 bu hoi 4 Ōtomo ke monjoroku 2*, Ōtomo ke monjoroku 4, 2.1557 (Kōji 3), pp. 250–51, *Ōuchi bunka*, Yatsushiro nikki, 4.7.1557 (Kōji 3), p. 248, and *Agari ke monjo*, doc. 13, Ōuchi ke *ryaku keizu*, p. 13.

He lacked the charisma, the fortitude, the knowledge, and skill to rally his supporters, and his attempt to lead an organization he did not fully understand only exacerbated its ruin. His head was sent to Mōri Motonari and Takamoto, who inspected it, and returned it for burial.[123] Thus passed the last lord of the Ōuchi (Figure 10.3).

---

[123] *Ōuchi shi jitsuroku*, pp. 282–83.

Epilogue

Legacies

Survivors of the Ōuchi collapse experienced an impoverished and dislocated world, with Yamaguchi largely ruined and the previously integrated regions of northern Kyushu and western Honshu now distant and remote. In Kyoto, the court, bereft of Ōuchi funds that had underpinned its activities, mostly ceased to function. Epitomizing this decline, Emperor Go-Nara (1495–1557, r. 1526–57) remained unburied in the heat of summer for seventy days after his death in 1557.[1] Miyoshi Nagayoshi (1522–64) and his successors continued their terror, most notably killing Ashikaga Yoshiteru (1536–65, shogun 1546–65) in 1565. Their retainer Matsunaga Hisahide (1510–77) burned the great Tōdaiji in 1567. Oda Nobunaga (1534–82) ousted the Miyoshi and occupied the capital in 1568, briefly upholding the claims of a new shogun, Ashikaga Yoshiaki (1537–97, shogun 1568–73), the last of his line, before ultimately expelling him, thus ending the Ashikaga regime.

Trade suffered because the diplomatic knowledge required to facilitate exchanges with Korea and China had been lost. In addition, many merchants were scattered, their stores plundered and ships lost, while the Straits of Shimonoseki became a contested frontier between the Ōtomo and the Mōri. Funai, the city of the former, had advantages as a deep-water port where Portuguese vessels were welcomed, but it too would be destroyed along with the Ōtomo. For the Mōri, Yamaguchi ceased to matter after the fall of the Ōuchi, and so the settlement would decay. The Mōri ultimately abandoned it in favor of making Hagi, on the Japan Sea, a new castle town, but they could not readily trade with Asia. In this vacuum, a new harbor, at Nagasaki,

---

[1] *Kugyō bunin*, vol. 3 (Yoshikawa kōbunkan, 1936), p. 440 for his death on 9.5.1557 (Kōji 3) and *Oyundo no ue no nikki*, vol. 5, 11.22.1557, p. 364 for his burial. See also Watanabe Daimon, *Sengoku no binbō tennō* (Kashiwa shobō, 2012), p. 237.

Kings in All but Name. Thomas D. Conlan, Oxford University Press. © Oxford University Press 2024.
DOI: 10.1093/oso/9780197677339.003.0012

located on the western shores of Kyushu, would come to the fore and become a thriving settlement.

For *wakō* and others, opportunities existed. The breakdown of the earlier infrastructure of trade allowed for freedom of movement and exchange, but these traders were generally only capable of operating smaller ships. Precious metals, the most prized item of exchange, were hauled by the Spanish and Portuguese, who sailed the largest crafts. But the network of East Asian diplomacy and tribute, which had allowed for extensive exchanges, would never function so well. Trade would continue, of course, but without the institutions that readily fostered extensive intellectual, cultural, and economic exchanges. Japan, Korea, and China became more remote. As that happened, the idea of shared ethnicities that were neither one nor the other, such as the Tatara, became well-nigh inconceivable.

Ōuchi Nostalgia

After the fall of the Ōuchi many, realizing that they had governed better than their successors, lamented their passing. Shortly before his death, Go-Nara commanded the Mōri to build Ryūfukuji, a mortuary temple for Yoshitaka (1507–51), at the site of his mansion.[2] Mōri Takamoto (1523–63) and Terumoto (1553–1625) did so and sponsored Second Month rites (*nigatsu-e*) at Hikamisan Kōryūji from 1559 through 1570.[3]

Other practices lingered. After a delay of a year, Mōri Motonari (1497–1571) secured enough silver to pay for the enthronement rites of Emperor Ōgimachi (1517–93, r. 1557–86), but he could not support the rite as lavishly as the Ōuchi had done.[4] The Mōri also could not rebuild Yamaguchi's Kōnomine Ise shrine in 1560, as they should have done according to stipulated schedule of every twenty-one years. Their successors would

[2] Yamaguchi kenshi hensanshitsu, comp., *Yamaguchi kenshi shiryōhen chūsei*, 4 vols. (Yamaguchi, 1996–2008), vol. 2, Ryūfukuji monjo doc. 1, 7.13.1557 (Kōji 3) Go-Nara tennō *rinji*, p. 927. Go-Nara died on 9.5.1557.

[3] *Yamaguchi kenshi shiryōhen chūsei*, vol. 3, Kōryūji monjo, docs. 102–12, pp. 276–80 for 2.13 Hikamisan rights being performed yearly by Takamoto through 1563 (Eiroku 6) and Terumoto (from 1564 through 1370). Documents from 1567 (Eiroku 10) are missing, but these rites were most likely performed.

[4] *Tsunemoto gyoki*, box 553, *Chokuzai anmon* no 16, 8.15.1558 (Eiroku 1) *Onsokui fu an* for Mōri Motonari paying for the enthronement (*sokui*) ceremonies of Emperor Ōgimachi. Unpublished document, viewed at the Kyoto University Museum on 3.12.2012.

finance this reconstruction sporadically until the turn of the eighteenth century.[5]

The Mōri collected as many surviving Ōuchi artifacts as possible.[6] They also commissioned artworks in the style of their Ōuchi predecessors.[7] Yoshimi Masayori (1513–88) saved the greatest of the Ōuchi treasures. He rushed into Yamaguchi after Yoshinaga (1534?–57) had fled, entering the unguarded Ōuchi mansion to secure Yoshinaga's "King of Japan" seals and several volumes of Ōuchi Masahiro's (1446–95) *Tale of Genji* copy.[8] Masayori knew the location and identity of the most valued objects because his wife Ōmiyahime (d. 1577) was Ōuchi Yoshitaka's sister.

Masayori also rescued Sesshū's (1420–1506) *Long Landscape of Mountains and Water*. He gave it to the Mōri, along with other picture scrolls, and a chicken-shaped incense burner (*niwatori no kōro*).[9] The timing of this transfer is not clear, but Ōmiyahime lived until 5.12.1577. Masayori presumably did not hand over Sesshū's *Long Landscape* until after her death.[10] Still, many great works were lost. Decades after the Ōuchi collapse the tea master Yamada Sōji (1544–90) lamented the destruction in Yamaguchi of the image "Evening Snow over the River" (*kōten no bosetsu*).[11]

Some manuscripts survived because they were not stored in Yamaguchi. The *Genji* picture album of Sue Hiroaki (d. 1523) remained at Myōeiji, but

---

[5] *Bōchō fūdo chūshin an*, vol. 13, *Yamaguchi saiban ge* (Yamaguchi, 1961), p. 18. They last had been rebuilt in 1539 (Tenbun 8); they were rescheduled for reconstruction in 1560 (Eiroku 3). War with Nobunaga in 1579 (Tenshō 8) delayed this project until 1588–89 (Tenshō 16–17). The shrines were again rebuilt in 1608–9 (Keichō 13–14) and continued to be reconstructed every twenty-one years until the Genroku era (1688–1704), when this practice ceased.

[6] *Hiroshima kenshi kodai chūsei shiryōhen* (Hiroshima, 1978), Fusaaki oboegaki, p. 1138.

[7] Yukio Lippit, *Painting of the Realm: The Kanō House Painters in 17th Century Japan* (Seattle: University of Washington Press, 2012), p. 49.

[8] For the seals, see *Yamaguchi kenshi shiryōhen chūsei*, vol. 2, Ōuchi shi kangō bōeki kankei shiryō, doc. 3, 1557 (Kōji 3) Yoshimi Masaharu *oboegaki*, p. 706. For a narrative account of his successful occupation of Yamaguchi after Teruhiro's defeat see Yonehara Masayoshi, *Intoku Taiheiki*, 6 vols. (Tōyō shoin, 1980–84), vol. 3 (1981), maki 44, "Niho kassen tsuke Yamashiro Tokuji ikki hōki no koto," pp. 342–43. See also *Tokubetsu ten Masuda shi vs. Yoshimi shi—Iwami no Sengoku jidai* (Shimane kenritsu Iwami bijutsukan, 9.2019) and Nakatsukasa Ken'ichi, "Yoshimi Masayori," in *Shimane ken no kassen* (Iki shuppan, Shimane, 2018), pp. 120–21. For the Ōshimabon *Tale of Genji*, Sasaki Takahiro, "Shugo daimyō Ōuchi kanren waka tanzaku shūsei (kō)," *Keiō Gijuku daigaku fuzoku kenkyūjō Shidō bunko* 50 (2015), pp. 99–100, and his "'Ōshimabon Genji monogatari' ni kansuru shoshigakuteki kōsatsu," *Keiō Gijuku daigaku fuzoku kenkyūjō Shidō* bunko 41 (2006), p. 184.

[9] Yonehara Masayoshi, *Intoku Taiheiki*, vol. 2 (1981), maki 31, "Ōuchi sakyō no daibu Yamaguchi otsuru no koto" pp. 365–66, and vol. 3, maki 32, "Bōchō ikki hōki no koto," p. 19.

[10] For her death, see Tamura Tetsuo, comp., "Ichimon Ōno Mōri ke," *Kinsei Bōchō shokeizu shūran* (reprint ed., Shōnan-shi: Matsuzono, 1980), p. 91. Mōri Terumoto (1533–1625) gave this scroll to a member of the Unkaku family later in the sixteenth century. Yukio Lippit, *Painting of the Realm*, p. 49. See also *Sesshū e no tabi kenkyū zuroku hen* (Yamaguchi, 2006), pp. 134–36.

[11] Yamada Sōji, *Yamada Sōjiki* (Iwanami bunko, 2006), p. 260.

the temple was seldom visited since the road passing in front of the temple led to the all-but-abandoned port of Hijū. Hiroaki's copy of the *Azuma kagami* was also stored there, but it would be given to Mōri Motonari's son Kikkawa Motoharu (1530–86).

Many documents and items were preserved at Hikamisan Kōryūji, located just to the south of Yamaguchi, but gradually its treasures and records were scattered as the temple compound decayed. One, a portrait of Ōuchi Yoshioki (1477–1528), was taken from one of its subtemples to Kyoto in 1789, where it was copied. The original was ultimately lost, but copies survive (Figure 8.2).[12]

Nostalgia for the Ōuchi could not prevent the disintegration of their domain. After the collapse of Yoshinaga's authority, Mōri Motonari governed the eastern half of the Ōuchi lands in western Honshu, while some northern Kyushu provinces, such as Buzen, came under Ōtomo control. Chikuzen and Hizen were contested by the Mōri, the Ōtomo, and Ryūzōji Takanobu (1529–84), one of Ōuchi Yoshitaka's generals.[13] For those ruled by the Ōtomo in Kyushu, Yamaguchi became "far away and hard to know."[14]

Mōri Motonari (1497–1571) tried to restore Ōuchi rule under the stewardship of Ōuchi Teruhiro (1519–69), an Ōuchi of uncertain parentage.[15] Ōtomo Sōrin (1530–87) refused to recoginze Teruhiro, since as Ōuchi Yoshinaga's half brother he claimed that position himself.[16] Ashikaga

---

[12] The image had belonged to Kōryūji's subtemple of Shinkōin, and is mentioned in a list of old treasures, the *Bōchō kokikō*, that was compiled between 1769 and 1774. Thereafter the original was lost. For more on the Kyoto copy, which was transmitted by members of the Reizen family, see Mori Michihiko, "Muromachiki ni okeru Takauji kachūzō to shōzōga seisaku: 'Ōuchi Yoshioki' 'Kyōto furitsu sōgō shiryōkanzō Kyōto bunka hakubutsukan kanri' no shōkai o kasanete," *Suzaku: Kyōto bunka hakubutsukan kenkyū kiyō* 25 (2013), pp. 4–5.

[13] *Ōita ken sentetsu sōsho Ōtomo Sōrin shiryōshū*, vol. 1 (Ōita, 1993), doc. 178, 4.3 [(Kōji 3) 1557] Ōtomo ke *nenrō rensho hōsho*, pp. 263–64, and for Buzen coming under Ōtomo control, doc. 197, 7.9 [(Kōji 3) 1557] Ōtomo Yoshishige *kanjō*, p. 279. See also Horimoto Kazushige, "Sengokuki Hizen no seiji dōkō to Gotōshi," in *Sengoku no Kyūshū to Takeo* (Takeo shi toshokan rekishi shiryōkan, 2009), pp. 5–9.

[14] *Ōita ken sentetsu sōsho Ōtomo Sōrin shiryōshū*, vol. 2 (Ōita, 1993), doc. 176, 3.13 [(Kōji 3) 1557] Ōtomo ke *nenrō rensho hōsho*, pp. 261–62.

[15] A 10.11.1569 Portuguese letter describes Teruhiro as being fifty, suggesting a 1519 birth. *Yamaguchi kenshi shiryōhen chūsei*, vol. 1, pp. 1028–29. *Yamaguchi shishi shiryōhen Ōuchi bunka* (Yamaguchi, 2010) (hereafter *Ōuchi bunka*), Shinsen Ōuchi shi, p. 67, describes him as being the son of Ōuchi Takahiro, the younger brother to Ōuchi Yoshioki, who had rebelled in 1499 and apparently died in 1508. Either Takahiro lived over a decade longer or Teruhiro was a son of Yoshioki. The Mōri and Naikaku genealogies confuse Teruhiro with Takahiro and portray him as a son of Yoshioki. See *Ōuchi bunka*, pp. 31, 54.

[16] *Ōita ken sentetsu sōsho Ōtomo Sōrin shiryōshū*, vol. 2, doc. 442 4.6 [(Kōji 3) 1557] Ōtomo Yoshishige *shojō*, for discussions over the question of succession. See doc. 449, 5.14 [(Kōji 3) 1557] Ōtomo Yoshishige *shojō utsushi* pp. 104–5 for the Mōri as favoring the succession of an Ōuchi lord.

Yoshiteru recognized Sōrin's claims, appointing him as the heir to the Ōuchi and the commander of Kyushu (Kyūshū *tandai*), an Ashikaga bakufu office that had been dysfunctional for a century.[17]

Sōrin's appointment proved wildly unpopular, with the surviving Naitō leading an uprising (*ikki*) in Suō and Nagato (Bōchō) late in 1557. They failed and thirty-eight were killed when their Myōkenzaki castle in Nagato fell.[18] After this revolt, most Ōuchi supporters in Suō and Nagato supported the Mōri.[19]

Geography determined most patterns of allegiance. In the province of Buzen, the fact that Yoshinaga was both of recognized Ōuchi descent and the brother to the Ōtomo lord meant that Ōuchi retainers such as the Sata could vow allegiance to "both houses" and then, after Yoshinaga's death, easily follow the Ōtomo.[20] A Buzen figure such as Takahashi Akitane (1529?–79), who followed Ōuchi Yoshinaga to Yamaguchi in 1552, found himself serving the Mōri as an administrator (*bugyō*) after Yoshinaga's flight.[21]

Areas of eastern Chikuzen province, nearest Honshu, long resisted the Ōtomo. The Moji, gatekeepers to the strategic straits, and the Munakata, with their easy access to the Genkai Sea, supported the Mōri. Thanks to the efforts of both families, the Mōri maintained a foothold in northern Kyushu for years. Nevertheless, the Ōtomo were able to occupy a strategic castle at Moji on 9.1559.[22] This forced Munakata Ujisada (1545–86), the head of the main

---

[17] *Ōtomo ke monjo, hoi 2, Ōita ken shiryō*, vol. 26 (Ōita, 1974), doc. 424, 11.9 [(Eiroku 2) 1559] Ashikaga Yoshiteru *gonaisho an*, p. 358, and *Ōita ken sentetsu sōsho Ōtomo Sōrin shiryōshū*, vol. 2, doc. 634, 11.9 [(Eiroku 2) 1559] Ashikaga Yoshiteru *gonaisho an*, pp. 246–47.

[18] *Fukuhara ke monjo* (Ube-shiritsu toshokan, 1983), Mōri ke kanjō, doc. 24, 12.2.1557 (Kōji 3) Mōri Motoharu *kanjō*, pp. 368–69. For the name of their uprising, see doc. 25, 12.21 [(Kōji 3) 1557] Mōri Takamoto *shojō*, p. 369. See also *Yamaguchi kenshi tsūshihen chūsei* (Yamaguchi, 2012), pp. 577–79.

[19] *Yamaguchi kenshi shiryōhen chūsei*, vol. 4, Jinjōji monjo, doc. 9, 8.5 Mōri shi *bugyōnin rensho hōsho*, pp. 554–55. *Yamaguchi kenshi tsūshihen chūsei*, pp. 576–77, dates this record to the years 1557–58.

[20] *Kumamoto ken shiryō chūsei hen*, vol. 2 (Kumanoto, 1962), doc. 178, 4.3 [(Kōji 3) 1557] Ōtomo ke *nenrō rensho hōsho*, pp. 263–65, doc. 179, 4.12 [(Kōji 3) 1557] Ōtomo ke *nenrō rensho hōsho*, pp. 265–66; and *Usa jingūshi shiryōhen*, vol. 12 (Usa, 1996), pp. 634–37. See also Horimoto Kazushige, "1550 nendai ni okeru Ōtomo shi no hokubu Kyūshū shihai no shinten-Ōuchi Yoshinaga no chiseiki o chūshin ni," *Kyūshū shigaku* 162 (8.2012), p. 39.

[21] Wada Shūsaku, in Kishida Hiroshi, "Ōuchi shi no ryōgoku shihai soshiki to jinzai tōyō," in *Mōri Motonari to chiiki shakai* (Chūgoku shinbunsha, 2007), pp. 197–217. For Akitane serving as Yoshinaga's administrator from 1553 through 1556, see *Usa jingūshi shiryōhen*, vol. 12, 1.23.1553 (Tenbun 22) Ōuchi *bugyōnin hōsho an*, p. 509; 1.21.1553 (Tenbun 22) Ōuchi *bugyōnin hōsho an*, p. 515; 3.27.1553 (Tenbun 22) Ōuchi *bugyōnin hōsho an*, p. 516; and 3.14.1556 (Kōji 2) Ōuchi *bugyōnin hōsho an*, pp. 587–88.

[22] *Moji monjo* (Kita Kyūshū, 2005), doc. 54, 3.15 Ōtomo Yoshishige *kanjō*, p. 74. See also Yagita Ken, *Moji Kokura no kojōshi* (Kita Kyūshū, 2001), pp. 108–70; *Kita Kyūshū Sengokushi shiryōshū*, vol. 1 (Kita Kyūshū, 2004), pp. 84–414; and *Shiryō ni miru Chūsei no moji*, 2nd ed. (Kita Kyūshū, 2010), pp. 80–193.

Munakata shrine, to flee with his shrine treasures to Ōshima, a secondary shrine located on an island two miles from the mainland.[23] He remained there for years.

Takahashi Akitane caused Ōtomo rule in eastern Chikuzen to collapse in 1562. He left Yamaguchi and returned to Kyushu, where he built a castle at Mt. Homan, near the Daizaifu.[24] The Mōri gained full control of Moji and dispatched their forces to eastern Chikuzen province, where they threatened Hakata and rescued Munakata Ujisada from his island refuge.[25]

After 1566, the Mōri were in an even stronger position because at that time they defeated the forces of the Amako, who never recovered after Amako Haruhisa's (1514–61) death.[26] This victory rid them of a troublesome rival and allowed them to secure uncontested control of Iwami's Ōmori silver mine. There they relied on monks from the temple of Kokushōji to manage their mining interests in Naganobori and Iwami, a relationship that endured through the 1580s.[27]

Ōuchi Teruhiro's Gambit

By early 1569, the Mōri were well on their way to establishing authority over much of northern Kyushu.[28] The Ōtomo position was further weakened because Ryūzōji Takanobu, one of Ōuchi Yoshitaka's generals, conquered most of Chikugo and Hizen provinces in 1570.[29]

---

[23] *Munakata shishi shiryōhen chūsei*, vol. 2 (Munakata, 1996), doc. 395, pp. 401–7.

[24] Allan Grapard, *Mountain Mandalas: Shugendō in Kyushu* (New York: Bloomsbury, 2016), p. 196, for how Takahashi Akitane built fortifications on Mt. Homan's ridges in 1552. The castle stood until its destruction in 1586. *Kita Kyūshū shiritsu rekishi kakubutsukan kenkyū kiyō*, vol. 1, *Tokushū Buzen Shugendō (Kubotesan, Hikoyama)* (Kita Kyūshū shiritsu rekishi hakubutsukan, 1979).

[25] *Ogori shishi*, vol. 5 *shiryōhen* (Ogori, 1999), pp. 298–348. For more on the alliance between the Takahashi and the Munakata, see *Munakata shishi tsūshihen* (Munakata, 1997), p. 527.

[26] For an overview, see Saeki Noriya, *Izumo no chūsei* (Yoshikawa kōbunkan, 2017), pp. 290–92. The Mōri were able to gain control over the Izumo region, evidenced by the confirmation of Gakuenji lands, by 8.16.1562 (Eiroku 5). See Gakuenji monjo kenkyūkai, ed., *Gakuenji monjo* (Kyoto: Hōzōkan, 2015), docs. 232–33, 8.16 [(Eiroku 5) 1562] Mōri Motonari *onajiku* Takamoto *rensho shojō*, pp. 214–15.

[27] This was first mentioned in Kitajima Daisuke, *Ōuchi shi kanren machinami iseki*, vol. 8 (Yamaguchi, 2014), p. 256. *Bōchō fūdo chūshin an*, vol. 13, p. 139, shows that this temple was connected to the silver mines during Mōri rule.

[28] Arikawa Nobuhiro, "Buzen Nagano shi ni tsuite," in *Kita Kyūshū shiritsu rekishi hakubutsukan* (Kita Kyūshū, 1995), p. 48.

[29] An informative map and overview of Ryūzōji Takanobu appears in the *Tokubetsu kikakuten Sengoku Kyūshū to Takeo Gotō Takaaki Ienobu no jidai* (Takeo shi toshokan rekishi shiryōkan, 2009), pp. 21–26.

Ōtomo Sōrin decided to disrupt the Mōri offensive in Kyushu by fomenting a pro-Ōuchi uprising. He dispatched Ōuchi Teruhiro and a few thousand supporters to conquer Yamaguchi.[30] Sōrin wanted Teruhiro to serve as a diversion but did not want him to succeed. He explained to the Jesuits that the restoration of Yamaguchi would damage the prospects of Funai, his trading port.[31] Ōuchi Teruhiro and his followers were not aware that they were pawns to be sacrificed. To them, an Ōuchi restoration was attainable.

After several feints, Teruhiro and his army landed at Aio, at the mouth of the Fushino River.[32] With the support of local guides, he defeated the surprised and scattered Mōri forces, and took a little-known path that brought him into Yamaguchi on 10.11.1569.[33] Teruhiro fortified Tsukiyama, where Norihiro was deified in central Yamaguchi, next to the site of the old Ōuchi mansion.[34] This was not a wise choice, for it was indefensible, being located on the plain just a mile to the east of Kōnomine, a mountain castle that the Mōri had completed after 1557.[35] Mōri supporters, including the widow of a Yamaguchi administrator, townsmen, and monks from Jōfukuji, climbed the steep Kōnomine and remained in the castle, hoping for reinforcements.[36]

Teruhiro's forces could not take this castle, which loomed over them. They skirmished at the base of the mountain, burning the Taga shrine in

---

[30] *Ōita ken sentetsu sōsho Ōtomo Sōrin shiryōshū*, vol. 4 (Ōita, 1994), doc. 1124, 3.18 [(Eiroku 12) 1569] Ōtomo Sōrin *shojō*, pp. 8–9.

[31] Kishida Hiroshi, "Sakaime no dōshu Mōri Motonari no 'kokka' zukuri," in *Mōri Motonari to chiiki shakai* (Hiroshima: Chūgoku shinbunsha, 2007), p. 33 for analysis of a 9.15.1567 (Eiroku 10) Ōtomo Sōrin letter to the Jesuits.

[32] For these earlier attacks, see *Ōita ken sentetsu sōsho Ōtomo Sōrin shiryōshū*, vol. 4, doc. 1209, 8.9 1569 (Eiroku 12) Ōtomo Sōrin *gunchū hikenjō*, pp. 72–73. The wounded included three by guns (*tebiya*). See also docs. 1215–16, 8.16 Ōtomo Sōrin *shojō*, pp. 76–78. For the mobilization of a transportation fleet, see docs. 1223–28, 9.13 [(Eiroku 12) 1569] Ōtomo Sōrin *shojō* (*utsushi*).

[33] *Yamaguchi ken monjokan*, comp., *Hagi han batsu etsu roku*, vol. 3 (Yamaguchi ken monjokan, 1994) maki 126, Inoue Zenbei monjo, doc. 13, 1.23 [(Tenshō 6) 1578] Mōri Terumoto *andojō an*, p. 695.

[34] *Yamaguchi kenshi shiryōhen chūsei*, vol. 4, Nakamaru ke monjo, doc. 20, 12.16 [(Eiroku 12) 1569] Mōri Motonari *onajiku* Termuto *rensho kanjō*, p. 512, doc. 21, 12.16 [(Eiroku 12) 1569] Hoda Motokiyo *kanjō*, p. 512, and *Yamaguchi kenshi shiryōhen chūsei*, vol. 3, Kobijutsu Ube Bijutsu sentaa zō monjo, doc. 1, 11.18 [(Eiroku 12) 1569] Kobayakawa Takakage *shojō*, p. 710.

[35] For Sōrin's advice and gift of a sword and armor to Teruhiro, see *Ōita ken sentetsu sōsho Ōtomo Sōrin shiryōshū*, vol. 4, doc. 1235, 10.18 [(Eiroku 12) 1569] Ōtomo Sōrin *shojō*, p. 91.

[36] *Hagi han batsu etsu roku*, vol. 2 (Yamaguchi ken monjokan, 1994), maki 38, Ichikawa Shichiuemon monjo collection, doc. 2, 7.16 ([Tenshō 5 (1577)] Mōri Terumoto *shōsoku an*, p. 59. Terumoto, writing in phonetic *kana*, praised her actions. See also *Hagi han batsu etsu roku iro*, p. 29; Yamaguchi *chōnin* Kikuya Minzō collection, doc. 1, 1.28 [(Eiroku 13) 1570] Mōri shi *bugyōnin rensho shojō an*, p. 29; *Yamaguchi kenshi shiryōhen chūsei*, vol. 2, Arima ke monjo, doc. 5, 11.10 [(Eiroku 12) 1569] Mōri Terumoto *sodehan* Ichikawa Tsuneyoshi *hōsho*, p. 688; *Yamaguchi kenshi shiryōhen chūsei*, vol. 3, Terado ke monjo 1, 10.21 [(Eiroku 12) 1569] Naitō Takaharu *shojō*, p. 825; and *Yamaguchi kenshi shiryōhen chūsei*, vol. 2, Jōfukuji monjo, doc. 14, 11.24 [(Eiroku 12) 1569] Mōri Terumoto *shojō*, p. 844.

the process, although the nearby Ise shrines survived unscathed.[37] Yoshimi Masayori, leading the first Mōri reinforcements, arrived from the northeast. Scattered gravestones along the roadside mark where his army collided with Teruhiro's defenders; men were later buried and memorialized where they died.[38] Much of Yamaguchi burned again. Ultimately, the Mōri withdrew their forces from Kyushu and dispatched them to Yamaguchi.[39] This effectively ended any hopes of their holding onto territories in Kyushu, thereby fulfilling a strategic objective of Ōtomo Sōrin.

After Teruhiro had occupied Yamaguchi for ten days, his position became untenable. He fled to Aio on the coast, but he could not return to Kyushu because his boats had somehow vanished. Some of his men abandoned their helmets at a barrow mound (*kofun*) overlooking the coast, where Kyushu is faintly visible on a clear day.[40] The Mōri killed many of Teruhiro's cornered men on the banks of the nearby Saba River. Two stelae, one a *nenbutsu-ishi*, dedicated to the Amida Buddha and rebirth in his Pure Land, mark the death of eight hundred.[41] Hōfu Tenmangū burned during these battles, which disrupted its rites for weeks and resulted in the death of many shrine attendants.[42]

Teruhiro and a thousand of his supporters fled east in a desperate bid to find ships. After traveling two miles, they encountered the forces of Sugi

[37] *Bōchō fūdo chūshin an*, vol. 13, p. 71, for Teruhiro's failed attack and the burning of the Taga shrine. See p. 42 for a 11.28 Mōri Motonari *shojō utsushi* that mentioned that the Ise shrines were intact after Teruhiro's rebellion. See also *Hagi han batsu etsu roku iro*, p. 29, Yamaguchi *chōnin* Kikuya Minzō, doc. 1, 1.28 [(Eiroku 13) 1570] Mōri shi *bugyōnin rensho shojō*, p. 29 for evidence of the town suffering damage by fire.

[38] *Hagi han batsu etsu roku*, vol. 4, maki 143, Furuga 4, 11.30 [(Eiroku 12) 1569] Yoshimi Masayori *kanjō an*, p. 79. These graves, and the nearby shrines, which had been destroyed in 1569, were viewed on 6.14.2016.

[39] *Moji monjo*, doc. 33, 11.4.1569 (Eiroku 12) Mōri Terumoto *tsugime andojō*, p. 47, for how Teruhiro's revolt forced the Mōri to leave Kyushu. See also *Fusaaki oboegaki*, pp. 1144–45. For the burning of Yamaguchi, see *Bōchō fūdo chūshin an*, vol. 12, *Yamaguchi saiban jō* (Yamaguchi, 1960), p. 67, 84; *Bōchō fūdo chūshin an*, vol. 13, p. 195.

[40] Much of this evidence comes from a tour of the course of Teruhiro's rebellion with Wada Shūsaku, 6.14.2016. The tomb is now known as Kabuto-yama, or helmet hill, because of this.

[41] For evidence of Teruhiro's fleeing supporters being killed near Hōfu, see *Hagi han batsu etsu roku* vol. 3, maki 126, Kurata Tō-uemon monjo, doc. 3, 2.9 [(Tenshō 20) 1592] Kurata Tsukisada *oboegaki an*, pp. 703–4, and *Hagi han batsu etsu roku*, vol. 1, maki 19, Kodama Shirobei monjo, doc. 15, 10.30 (*misoka*) [(Eiroku 12) 1569] Mōri Terumoto *shojō an*, p. 518.

[42] *Yamaguchi kenshi shiryōhen chūsei*, vol. 2, Hōfu Tenmangū monjo, doc. 102, 11.11.1569 (Eiroku 12) Mōri Terumoto *sodehan jōsho*, p. 512 for the delay of the rites, and doc. 271, 11.26.1569 (Eiroku 12) Tenmangū *jūgatsu shoeki sashifumi*, pp. 630–31 for the burning of the shrine and the death of many shrine officials. See also *Hōfu shishi tsūshi* 1 *Genshi kodai chūsei* (Hōfu, 2004), pp. 345, and Hirase Naoki, "Chūsei Hōfu Tenmangū no shabō ni tsuite," *Yamaguchi monjokan kenkyū kiyō*, no. 15 (3.1988), pp. 55–71.

Motosuke (Takasuke, 1522–85), which were based in eastern Suō.[43] Since Teruhiro was already being pursued from the west already, he could not escape. He and his men climbed nearby Chausuyama. At a secluded spot on its northern slope, where the sea is no longer visible, they all committed hara-kiri.

Mōri Motonari later praised Teruhiro and his men for this final act (*migoto ni hara kirare sōrō*).[44] Most of these men were warriors from Buzen, but some ex-Ōuchi administrators such as Yoshida Okitane (d. 1569) perished there as well.[45] Local lore also refers to a forlorn site where a monk and five villagers who had led Teruhiro's army into Yamaguchi were slaughtered.[46]

After the revolt, the Mōri inspected travelers to ensure that none of Teruhiro's supporters could escape. They set up a station at a place known as "Inspection Grove" (*shirabe no mori*) to try to uncover ex-soldiers in disguise. They did, however, provide provisions for prisoners. This "prisoner's rice" was unheard of, since customarily prisoners were killed. This generous policy blunted the desire of the defeated and their kin to rebel again.[47] Once active resistance was quelled, the Mōri restored the badly damaged Ryūfukuji, the mortuary temple of Yoshitaka, located next to Tsukiyama.[48] They also rewarded their Yamaguchi supporters, who included townsmen who had lost much in the fires, and the wives of warriors who helped defend Kōnomine castle.[49] Kikkawa Motoharu even gave a banner (*hatazao*)

---

[43] Sugi Motosuke, originally known as Takasuke, escorted Ōuchi Yoshinaga from Buzen to Yamaguchi in 1552 but joined the Mōri late in 1555 and changed his name to Motosuke. See chapter 10.

[44] *Yamaguchi kenshi shiryōhen chūsei*, vol. 3, Hagi shi kyōdo hakubutsukan monjo Kohata ke monjo, doc. 6, Mōri Motonaru *shojō*, pp. 961–62. In this document, Motonari refers to the site of the death of Teruhiro as being on the coast at Tonomi. Graves of two followers of Teruhiro can be found at a Kannondō at Tonomi, but Teruhiro himself died inland at Chausuyama. For a detailed narrative of the rebellion Teruhiro's actions in Hōfu, and his end, see *Hōfu shishi tsūshi 1 Genshi kodai chūsei*, pp. 342–45.

[45] For more on Yoshida Okitane, see *Yamaguchi kenshi tsūshihen chūsei*, pp. 584–85, and Kishida Hiroshi, "Ōuchi shi metsubō go no Bōchō kyūshinzō to Mōri shi," *Shigaku kenkyū* 200 (3.1993), 3–25, pp. 4–15. See also *Bōchō fūdo chūshin an*, vol. 13, Kami uno rei no 2, p. 64, for reference to the *ikki* revolt of 1568 (Eiroku 11).

[46] They were executed at a place called Kubitanigaeki. In 1924 a memorial stele was erected there, and Buddhist rites were performed, to pacify their spirits.

[47] *Hōfu shishi tsūshi 1 Genshi kodai chūsei*, pp. 345–46. This was first recognized by Kishida, "Ōuchi shi metsubō go no Bōchō kyūshinzō to Mōri shi," pp. 15–20.

[48] Takahashi Ken, "Sengoku daimyō Mōri shi no Bōchō shihai to genki sannnen Ryūfukuji no 'saikō,'" *Yamaguchi ken chihōshi kenkyū* 99 (6.2008), pp. 19–33. This structure survived until 1883, when it burned down, and was replaced with the main hall of Kōryūji, which remains there to this day. *Ōuchi bunka*, p. 689.

[49] *Hagi han batsu etsu roku iro*, p. 29, Yamaguchi *chōnin* Kikuya Minzō, doc. 1, 1.28 [(Eiroku 13) 1570] Mōri shi *bugyōnin rensho shojō*, p. 29 for the townsman of Yamaguchi who fought against Teruhiro, and *Hagi han batsu etsu roku*, vol. 2, maki 38, Ichikawa Shichiuemon collection, doc. 2, 7.16 [(Tenshō 5) 1577] Mōri Terumoto *shōsoku an*, p. 59 for the woman leading defenses of the castle.

to his twenty-one-year-old son Motonaga (1548–87) for his valor against Teruhiro.[50]

Toida Kametsurumaru, who claimed to be a younger son of Yoshitaka, adopted the name Ōuchi Yoshinori and staged one last revolt. According to some accounts, he was killed in 1570, but a legend remained that he in fact escaped to Iyo, in Shikoku, where he changed his name and lived to the age of ninety-three.[51] According to lore, another son of Yoshitaka by a concubine survived as well, but he remained aloof from politics, becoming the monk Daien Sōgaku at Katamata's Yō-un'in.[52]

Aware that their authority in the Ōuchi homelands remained precarious, the Mōri abandoned attempts to control any territory in Kyushu. Their Kyushu supporters, the Takahashi, Moji, and Munakata, eventually joined the Ōtomo, but stability would not return. In the following decades, Ryūzōji Takanobu was killed after a defeat in 1584, and his forces scattered, while Ōtomo Sōrin was crushed in the battle of Mimigawa in 1578, witnessed the destruction of Funai by the Shimazu in 1587, and died shortly thereafter.

The Mōri, however, remained, and consolidated control of half of what had been the Ōuchi domain. Increasingly, they would have to confront another lord, Oda Nobunaga, who had entered the capital in 1568, bringing an end to the two decades of unrest and setting Japan on another path. But that is another story.

For more on the burning of the town and its widespread destruction, see *Yamaguchi ken shitei mukei minzoku bunkazai Sagi no mai* (Yamaguchi shi kyōiku iinkai, 1981), p. 90, *Bōchō fūdo chūshin an*, vol. 13, Kami Uno rei no. 2, 10.6.1557 (Kōji 3) Mōri Motonari *funshitsu andojō*, p. 54, and docs. on p. 55, p. 64, and *Hagi han batsu etsu roku iro*, p. 29, Yamaguchi chōnin Kikuya Minzō, doc. 1, 1.28 [(Eiroku 13) 1570] Mōri shi *bugyōnin rensho shojō an*, p. 29.

[50] *Kikkawa ke monjo*, vol. 1, doc. 642, 12.24 [(Tenshō 10) 1582] Kikkawa Motoharu *jihitsu shojō*, p. 577.

[51] For a summary of Toida Kametsurumaru, who claimed to be a son of Yoshitaka, see Fukuo Takeichirō, *Ōuchi Yoshitaka*, p. 69. According to legends (*engi*) of Hōzenji, he changed his name to Toyota Kinosuke Motoyoshi and became a sake brewer. This story is most conveniently reproduced at https://honmyouzan.houzenji.nichiren-shu.jp/engi/index.htm, accessed 8.23.2019.

[52] I visited the grave of Daien Sōgaku (大円宗岳) at Katamata, Hagi, on the side of an overgrown hill, on 10.20.2022, with Wada Shūsaku. Three stone pagodas (*hōkyōintō*) survive with the others purportedly dedicated to Yoshitaka and his consort, Daien Sōgaku's mother. *Kadokawa chimei daijiten*, vol. 35 (1978), p. 1111.

Post-Ōuchi Trade Disruptions

None could trade with Korea and China as easily and effectively as the Ōuchi, and so supply lines were disrupted and merchant fleets scattered. Old trading relations had ended, and competitors vied for trading rights and wealth. While some bustling trading ports declined, others prospered as trading networks shifted to new hubs. Exchanges with the continent diminished as the Ōtomo, the Sagara, the Shimazu of Kagoshima, the Sō of Tsushima, and the Portuguese struggled to control the Ōuchi trade.[53]

Members of the Ming court wondered what had happened to the Ōuchi kings of Japan. In 1564–65, their emissary Zheng Shungong (鄭舜功) visited Hakata so as to restore "old friendships" and re-establish licensed trade with the "King of Japan."[54] According to the *Nankai chiranki*

> Because Ōtomo Yoshishige [Sōrin] of Bungo controlled the western provinces at that time, he was seen as the King of Japan, and the imperial letter was delivered to him. He responded as follows: "The so-called King of Japan is in fact the lord of the capital (*miyako ni iru kimi o sashite iu*). I only possess and protect the western domains. I am not a king. Now Japan is a world beset by war, and the great lords of the domains do not heed the King's commands. Thus, there is no need to report this to the court."[55]

Kasai's account cannot be verified with contemporary sources, but Zheng Shungong did travel to the Ōtomo domains and Kyoto. While in Kyushu he wrote his *Riben Yijian*, published in 1565.[56] He was not the only Ming visitor, as Chinese merchants continued to live in Yamaguchi through 1565.[57]

The Ming still looked for kings in Japan but found none after Yoshinaga's passing. None were able to master the intricate diplomacy required for successful tributary trade. The Ōtomo, as we have seen, had a trading vessel sunk

---

[53] Kage Toshio, "Kenminsen to Sagara Ōuchi Ōtomo shi," *Nihonshi kenkyū* 610 (6.2013), pp. 3–28.

[54] Kasai Shigesuke and Ii Haruki eds. and trans., *Nankai chiranki* (Kyōikusha, 1981), vol. 1, pp. 228–29, and Matsuda Wataru, *Japan and China: Mutual Representations in the Modern Era*, trans. Joshua Fogel (Surrey: Curzon, 2000), pp. 170–71.

[55] Translation drawn from Matsuda, *Japan and China*, pp. 170–71. For the original narrative, see *Nankai chiranki*, pp. 228–29.

[56] For this insight, and reference to the maps of Japan that he copied, I am indebted to Peter Shapinsky.

[57] *Hagi han batsu etsu roku*, vol. 2, maki 78 Zhao (Chō) Kyūzaemon collection, doc. 2, 9.14.1565 (Eiroku 8) Mōri Motonari *andojō utsushi* and doc. 3, 9.8.1565 (Eiroku 8) Mōri Terumoto *andojō utsushi*, p. 766. For Mōri Takamoto describing meeting this family in person, see doc. 1, 6.27 Mōri Takamoto *shojō utsushi*, p. 765. This document predates 1564.

by the Ming at Ningbo in 1557. The Mōri still had dreams of trading with the Ming, and even created a trading flag in 1584, but they were not particularly successful.[58]

For the Jesuits the destruction of Ōuchi Yoshinaga forced them to abandon western Honshu in favor of Kyushu. After Yoshinaga's death, no Christians remained in Yamaguchi. To the missionaries, Mōri Motonari was a great enemy.[59] The collapse of Yamaguchi Christianity caused them to subtly revise their histories, replacing Ōuchi Yoshitaka and Yoshinaga with Ōtomo Sōrin, a far more successful lord and Christian convert.[60] Yoshinaga's 1552 edict allowing a church in Yamaguchi would be reproduced, but his title "Lord of Bungo" would be associated with Ōtomo Sōrin rather than the "Lord of Suō," Yoshinaga.[61] (See Figure 10.1.)

Ultimately, the Spanish and Portuguese were among the greatest beneficiaries of the ensuing turmoil. Forced from Yamaguchi, they made the Ōtomo port of Funai a headquarters and a deep-water port. They lived and prospered in Funai, but after its 1587 destruction by the Shimazu, they preferred the new port of Nagasaki. They oversaw vibrant trade between Macao and Kyushu with their great ships, and they served as middlemen for the exchange of Japanese silver and Chinese silk.[62] Likewise, the durable Sō of Tsushima also became crucial figures in the Korean trade.[63]

---

[58] See the 1584 *Nichimin bōeki senki* from the Takasu house collection, located in the Yamaguchi prefectural archives.

[59] *Yamaguchi kenshi shiryōhen chūsei*, vol. 1, p. 1026 for the 10.11.1562 letter for how no one had taught Christian precepts for six to seven years. See p. 1028 of the 10.11.1569 letter for reference to Motoanari as a rebel and great enemy of Christianity. For Motonari's 1564 (Eiroku 7) destruction of churches and confiscation of their lands in Yamaguchi, see Matsuda Kiichi, "Ōuchi Yoshinaga no Daidōji saikyojō ni tsuite," *Komonjo kenkyū* 4 (1970), p. 31. For the persecution of Christians lasting from 1556 through 1571, see Georg Schurhammer, *Francis Xavier: His Life and Times*, trans. M. Joseph Costelloe, 4 vols. (Rome: Jesuit Historical Institute, 1973–82), vol. 4, pp. 235, 280. The Portuguese were expelled from the city of Yamaguchi. Not until 1574 would another enter the town. See Schurhammer, p. 280.

[60] Joan-Pau Rubiés, "Real and Imaginary Dialogues in the Jesuit Mission of Sixteenth-Century Japan," *Journal of the Economic and Social History of the Orient* 55 (2012), p. 458.

[61] See Figure 10.1 and *Nihon kankei kaigai shiryō Iezusukai Nihon shokanshū yakubun hen*, vol. 2.2 (Tōkyō daigaku shuppankai, 2000), pp. 207–8 for the 8.28.1552 (Tenbun 21) Ōuchi Haruhide *saikyojō*. Although Haruhide signed this document as Ōuchi *no suke*, this letter was translated as coming from the "Lord of Bungo" (Bungo *no daishu*).

[62] Charles Boxer, *The Great Ship from Amacon: Annals of Macao and the Old Japan Trade* (Lisbon: Center de Estudos Históricos Ultramarinos, 1963), p. 21. See also Amano Tadayuki, "Sengokuki no shūkyō jitsujō no henyō to Miyoshi shi," *Shokuhōki kenkyū* 12 (10.2000), p. 28 for how the Ōtomo and Portuguese monopolized the China trade after the Ōuchi destruction.

[63] Later scholars would focus on the Sō family of Tsushima as having a dominant role in Japanese-Korean trade. Takeo Tanaka, "Relations with Overseas Countries," in John Whitney Hall and Toyoda Takeshi, eds., *Japan in the Muromachi Age* (Berkeley: University of California Press, 1977), 159–78, mentions the Ōuchi as conducting trade missions (p. 169) but does not explore them in depth, preferring to focus on the Sō (pp. 174–76).

It still took decades for the full realization to sink in that the Ōuchi were no more. As late as 1582–85, one captain named his boat plying the seas to Korea Ōuchi-maru, in homage to Ōuchi (Toida) Kametsurumaru. In fact, this craft was operated by the Sō of Tsushima.[64] In Korea, memories of the Ōuchi patterns remained at least until 1603, in the aftermath of the two Japanese invasions.[65]

After 1615, the Tokugawa shogunate (1603–1867), Japan's next warrior government, encouraged rice production and not foreign trade. They attempted to monopolize trade in ports such as Nagasaki, which cut off the old Ōuchi territories in northern Kyūshū and western Honshu from trade with China or Korea. Exchanges were further limited by prohibiting all boats that could transport more than five hundred koku, a cargo one-sixth what could be hauled by the earlier Ōuchi craft.[66]

Rewriting and Reordering the Past

The Mōri and the other survivors seem to have sensed that 1569 was an ending of sorts. Many recorded their reminiscences (oboegaki) of Yoshinaga's defeat in 1557 and Teruhiro's in 1569. Before his 1563 death, Mōri Motonari's son Takamoto took the time to write an account including the fall of Yoshinaga and how he aided Yoshimi Masayori.[67] Yoshimi Masayori unfortunately wrote little, as his oboegaki merely consists of a list of some items rescued from the Ōuchi mansion in 1557.[68]

The Mōri had an active interest in obfuscating their lukewarm support for the coup in 1551, but this was tempered by their position as being the heirs to

[64] Itō Kōji, "Gi-Ōuchi dono shikō-Ōuchi shi no Chōsen tsūkō to gishi mondai," Nihon rekishi 731 (4.2009), p. 31, and Yonetani Hitoshi, "Jūrokuseiki Nichō kankei ni okeru gishi hakken no kōzō to jittai," Rekishigaku kenkyū 697 (1997), pp. 1–18.

[65] See the Chosŏn wangjo sillok, 1603 (Sŏnjo 36) http://sillok.history.go.kr/id/kna_13608008_005. I am indebted to Gina Choi for bringing this to my attention.

[66] Peter Shapinsky, Lords of the Sea: Pirates, Violence and Commerce in Late Medieval Japan (Ann Arbor: University of Michigan, Center for Japanese Studies, 2014), p. 263 for regulations of 1609.

[67] Tōkyō daigaku shiryōhen sanjo, comp., Mōri ke monjo, vol. 2 (Tōkyō daigaku shuppankai, 1922), doc. 667, Mōri Takamoto jihitsu oboegaki, pp. 407–10 for the attempt to convince Yoshinaga to turn on the Sue, and doc. 671 Mōri Takamoto jihitsu oboegaki, pp. 413–14 for the decision to aid Yoshimi Masayori.

[68] Yamaguchi kenshi shiryōhen chūsei, vol. 2, Ōuchi shi kangō bōeki kankei shiryō, doc. 3, 1557 (Kōji 3) Yoshimi Masaharu oboegaki, p. 706. Unfortunately, the Yoshimi records are scattered. Few survive, although some were copied in the Hagi han batsu etsu roku. Fukuda Ikuo, "Yokohama shiritsu daigaku toshokanzō no monjo ni tsuite, sono san Yoshimi," Yokohama shiritsu daigaku ronsō jinbun kakagu keiretsu 2–3 (3.1979), pp. 313–47.

the Ōuchi. Motonari and his heirs portrayed the Mōri as being loyal to Ōuchi Yoshitaka and, unsurprisingly, obscured traces of their rebellion.[69] They nevertheless criticized Ōuchi Yoshitaka for being too concerned with the court, its rites, and cultural matters, and negligent in military affairs. Mōri Terumoto summed up his family's attitude in 1613 when he commented that Yoshitaka's arrogance caused the Ōuchi downfall.[70] Terumoto did not, however, mention Yoshitaka's plan to make Yamaguchi Japan's capital. Although Ōtomo Sōrin's retrospective view of the Ōuchi is not known, in 1579 his retainer Tachibana Dōsetsu likewise criticized Yoshitaka for his bad judgment.[71]

In the 1580s, the head of the Itsukushima shrine wrote the *Fusaaki oboegaki*, a generally accurate representation of past events from the time of Yoshioki through the rule of Mōri Motonari, although the attempt to move the capital in 1551 and Mōri complicity in the ensuing coup was ignored.[72] As late as 1592, a certain Kurata Tsukisada recounted Teruhiro's 1569 rebellion.[73] Teruhiro's uprising was dramatic and uncomplicated by treachery or ambivalence. In 1569, a brave enemy fought and died well, gaining glory for himself and his adversaries.

While respecting the Ōuchi legacy, the Mōri also subtly undermined it. The Mōri tried to maintain an image of themselves as upholders of Ōuchi rule, but at the same time, they sold or transferred many of the most notable remaining Ōuchi temples. The main hall (Kondō) of Kōshakuji, the mortuary temple of Ōuchi Yoshihiro, was moved to the new castle town of Hiroshima, in Aki, where it was renamed Fudō-in. It would miraculously survive the atomic bombing of 1945. Other Jōfukuji subtemples were moved to Hakata, while the main temple itself would burn in 1669 (Figure E.1).[74]

---

[69] *Hagi han batsu etsu roku*, vol. 4, Bōchō jisha shōmon, for the *Taineiji yuisho*, p. 7, describes how he conquered the rebel Sue Takafusa and avenged Yoshitaka. See also *Zoku Ōnin kōki*, in *Kaitei shiseki shūran*, vol. 3 (Kondō Keizō shuppanbu 1900), maki 6, pp. 108–9. In 1615, Mōri Terumoto commissioned Takahashi Kotonobu, the head of Yamaguchi's Taga shrine, to write a history called the *Ōuchi sama o-ie konponki*, which was completed in 1615. *Ōuchi bunka*, Shiryō kaidai, p. 2. This is otherwise known as the *Ōuchi metsubō shidai* or the *Kotonobu oboegaki*.

[70] Tōkyō daigaku shiryōhen sanjo, comp., *Mōri ke monjo*, vol. 3 (Tōkyō daigaku shuppankai, 1922), doc. 1157, 12.1613 (Keichō 18) Mōri Sōzui *shojō an*, 430–44, p. 442.

[71] *Zōho teisei Hennen Ōtomo shiryō*, vol. 24 (Ōita, 1966), 2.16 [(Tenshō 8) 1579] Tachibana Dōsetsu *shojō*, p. 218. Dōsetsu was previously known as Bekki Akitsuki.

[72] For the reliability of the *Fusaaki oboegaki*, see *Dazaifu shishi chūsei shiryōhen* (Daizaifu, 2002), p. 834.

[73] *Hagi han batsu etsu roku*, vol. 3, maki 126 Kurata Tō-uemon monjo, doc. 3, 2.9 [(Tenshō 20) 1592] Kurata Tsukisada *oboegaki an*, pp. 703–4.

[74] Itō Kōji, ed., *Daigakuteki Yamaguchi gaido* (Yamaguchi: Shōwadō, 2011), pp. 61–67 for the movement of buildings. For the miraculous nature of the pagoda remaining, see p. 64. See also *Ōuchi bunka*, pp. 730–34 for the moving of the mail hall of Kōshakuji to Hiroshima, leaving the pagoda (Rurikōji) as the only structure remaining. For the pagoda, see pp. 684–88. For the moving of

Figure E.1   Fudō-in (formerly Kōshakuji). The Mōri moved this structure to Hiroshima. It survived the 1945 atomic bombing. Photograph by Thomas Conlan

Mōri Terumoto dismantled Ryōunji, the mortuary temple of Yoshioki, leaving behind only its stone foundations, and transported the main hall (Kondō) to central Japan, where it became the main hall of Miidera (Onjōji), located to the east of Kyoto.[75] The fact that Miidera had a deep connection to North Star (Myōken) worship may have led to this Ōuchi structure as being selected to become Miidera's "new" main hall (Figure E.2).[76]

Jōfukuji's Hōjō, Butsuden, and Hōdō to Sūfukuji in Hakata, see pp. 969–70. The Mōri would rebuild Jōfukuji in 1690.

[75] For the possibility of a 1599 moving of Ryōunji to become the main hall at Miidara, see Yamaguchi kyōiku iinkai, comp., *Yamaguchi shi maizō bunkazai chōsha hōkokusho*, no. 121, *Ryōunji ato*, vol. 2 (Yamaguchi: Yamaguchi kyōiku iinkai, 2019), p. 230. For this assertion regarding Miidera, see also Kinoshita Meiki, *Zusetsu Yamaguchi Hōfu no rekishi* (Yamaguchi: Kyōdo shuppansha, 2005), pp. 96–97.

[76] For this connection, as this was the site where springs were throught to have "gushed forth after Myōken came down to earth," see Bernard Faure, *The Fluid Pantheon: Gods of Medieval Japan*, vol. 1 (Honolulu: University of Hawaii Press, 2016), p. 101.

Figure E.2 The size of the Miidera Kondō (formerly Ryōunji) is identical to that of the missing Ryōunji main hall, which was dismantled and moved by the Mōri. Compare with Figures 8.6, 10.3, and E.1. Photograph by Thomas Conlan

In 1599, three hundred workers and four supervisors departed Yamaguchi and (re)built this main hall in only thirteen months.[77] This structure, in a hip-and-gable (*irimoya*) style, with cedar thatching, is consistent with the architectural style of Ōuchi temples and not typical of the colorful and ornate styles favored in 1599 (the Momoyama era 1568–1600). Another structure, a rotating Tripiṭaka library (*rinzōkyō*), including the building and the sutras themselves (see Figure 4.2), was removed from Moriakira's Kokushōji and transported to Miidera in 1602.[78] Kōshakuji, the mortuary temple of Yoshihiro, would be moved to Hagi in 1602 in name, but the five-story pagoda would remain, the last magnificent trace of Ōuchi rule, although in 1690 its name would be changed to Rurikōji.[79]

[77] See Shiga ken kyōiku iinkai, comp., *Kokuhō Onjōji Kondō hozon shūri kōji hōkokusho* (Miidera, 2.2009), particularly p. 111–12 for the history of the reconstruction of the Onjōji Kondō and Terumoto's role as in 3.1598 (Keichō 3). See also the *Onjōji koki*, compiled in 1739, 4.3.1598, 4.5 and 4.13.1599 (Keichō 4), p. 101. For more on the age of the temple, and the thirteenth-month period of its "construction," see pp. 47–48. Transcriptions of the chronicle of the temple's reconstruction appear on pp. 101–6 and transcriptions of writings on the timbers from 3.1599 can be found on pp. 89–97.

[78] *Ōuchi bunka*, pp. 725–29 for the Kokushōji Tripiṭaka and the hall housing it, which was moved in 1602. See also *Kokuhō Onjōji Kondō hozon shūri kōji hōkokusho*, p. 105, for the sources explaining Terumoto's donation of a copy of the Tripiṭaka and a sutra hall on 7.3.1602 (Keichō 7).

[79] This was formerly the name of the mortuary temple of Sue Hirofusa.

Ultimately, the Mōri decided to abandon Yamaguchi and moved to Hagi, an easily defendable location on the Japan Sea. By Tokugawa order, lords could maintain only a single castle in their territories, and these surviving castles became the nucleus of new settlements. Yamaguchi was not a fortified town, and its castle perched on top of a steep mountain made it ill-suited for a lord's residence.

The Mōri did not bring Myōken to their castle town of Hagi. Rather they favored Ikkōshū, or Jōdo Shinshū, originating from Shinran (1173–1263).[80] Ikkōshū, with its worship of Amida, had previously not established much of a presence in the city of Yamaguchi, although these temples are scattered throughout western Japan, but became a mainstay of Mōri belief.[81] The Mōri also continued praying at Hōfu's Manganji, throughout the Tokugawa period, fearful of vengeful spirits. Even today, copies of hundreds of their prayers for protection remain there. Motonari's role in the events of 1551 did not sit well with him and his descendants.

In Yamaguchi, the old beliefs withered. Turtles, thought to be the messenger of Myōken, were consumed in great numbers during the time of Mōri rule. This contrasted to practices of even a few years earlier, as early Jesuit visitors had stated that meat was not eaten in Yamaguchi.[82] Not all areas would, however, abandon Myōken worship. At Kudamatsu shrine, shrine attendants would write accounts attributing Yoshitaka's destruction to his failure to adequately worship Myōken.[83] Turtles were still protected there. Life-releasing ponds, where turtles were protected, can be found throughout East Asia, but turtles carried special significance in the former Ōuchi domains because of their connection with Myōken. As late as the mid-twentieth century, the head priest of Kudamatsu gave candy to the children of the area for rescuing turtles and bringing them to a pond at the top

---

[80] See the website "Bōchō ni okeru Jōdo Shinshū no enkaku," (accessed 10.12.2019), 防長におけ る浄土真宗の沿革, https://www.yamaguchibetsuin.net/.

[81] Shinran's teachings focused on Amida, and so references to Myōken would have been nonexistent. For this insight, I am indebted to James Dobbins, conversation 10.4.2019.

[82] *Asahi Shinbun*, evening edition, 8.15.2006, "Inu ya kame no shokuyō uratsuke? Ōuchi shi yakata no ato shūhen kara setsudan sareta hone Mōri shi jidai to suisoku," p. 35. For the lack of meat consumption in Yamaguchi, see *Yamaguchi kenshi shiryōhen chūsei*, vol. 1, p. 1024, for the letter of 1.10.1558.

[83] Sugihara Takatoshi, *Myōkensama* (Kudamatsu: Myōkengū Washizuji, 1985).

of the mountain near where a small Myōken shrine exists.[84] Many of these creatures still live there.

Yamaguchi's shrines were reordered as well. A Tōshogū shrine, which the Tokugawa had required to be built in all domains to deify Tokugawa Ieyasu, was built at Hikamisan after 1615 and remained there for centuries. After the Tokugawa collapsed, it was moved to Tsukiyama, where it would serve as the shrine for Ōuchi Norihiro (Figure 7.4). In Yamaguchi at least, one of the first deified lords thus outlasted his successor.[85] The Kōnomine Ise shrines were diminished, with their Ise connection obscured when they were renamed as the Great Yamaguchi shrines in the mid-twentieth century.[86]

Officials of the Tokugawa shogunate perceived their regime as the heir to the Ashikaga, and accordingly were not favorably included to pay much attention to the Ōuchi. Their histories emphasized the importance of the Ashikaga regime, enervated as it was, over court-based polities such as the Ōuchi.[87] That court rituals functioned as the vehicle for politics through the mid-sixteenth century was forgotten, as too was the greatness of Yamaguchi and the Ōuchi. The Tokugawa had good reasons for doing so, as they had poor relations with the court and saw it as a potential and ongoing threat, and they had no desire to glorify figures from western Japan, a region more hostile to their interests, particularly in the larger domains. Memories of a Japan as a segmented polity faded, and the death and destruction of the years 1551–68 were read back over a century.

The Tokugawa were hostile to the idea of a politically powerful court, and this influenced their histories of the Ōuchi. For example, the Tokugawa scholar Arai Hakuseki (1657–1725) castigated Yoshitaka for his inadequate military preparations, arguing that "his retainers, both old and young, lamented that he had surrounded himself with useless court nobles and that the warriors of the Ōuchi House had deteriorated."[88] The critique that

---

[84] Kawamura Jōichirō. Kudamatsu, 6.8.2015. This happened during the Occupation period (1945–52).

[85] For more on how the Mōri provided funds for ceremonies for the Tsukiyama shrine throughout the Tokugawa era, including moving a Tōshogū shrine there in the Meiji era, see Yonehara Masayoshi, *Ōuchi Yoshitaka* (Jinbutsu ōraisha, 1967), pp. 274–75. For his explanation of its earlier location at Hikamisan, I am grateful to Maki Takayuki.

[86] Itō Kōji, *Daigakuteki Yamaguchi gaido*, pp. 48–51. The name Kōnomine daijingū was changed in 1928 to the Kōnomine jinja, and once again in 1947 to Yamaguchi daijingū.

[87] For this insight, I am indebted to Nam-lin Hur. Conversation, Vancouver, 9.20.2017.

[88] Muraoka Tsunesugu, ed., *Tokushi yoron* (Arai Hakuseki) (Iwanami shoten, 1995), p. 276. For more on Yoshitaka and the Sue, see p. 279. For a convenient translation, see Joyce Ackroyd, *Lessons from History: The Tokushi Yoron* (St. Lucia: University of Queensland Press, 1982), p. 279. See also pp. 275, 278.

Yoshitaka cared too much for "useless poetry" and too little for governance or war would endure. In his survey of Tokugawa literature, Hirase Naoki has shown that the Ōuchi were not portrayed in a particularly good light, although their "exotic" ancestry was emphasized.[89]

Fading Ōuchi Identity

Over the course of the Tokugawa era, the concept of a distinct Ōuchi identity withered. The death of many who claimed descent from Prince Imsŏng hastened this process. Those families that survived, such as the Reizen, who were Ōuchi retainers, continued to claim descent from the Paekche Prince as late as 1717, although the legends of his arrival were abbreviated.[90]

The 1677 *Go-Taiheiki* of Tatara Nansōan Ichiryū, a presumed descendant of the Ōuchi, covers events of the Ōan (1368–75) through the Tenshō (1573–93) eras.[91] This forty-two-volume account recounts Ōuchi origin myths little changed from those written in 1486, save that the date that the Ōuchi progenitor Imsŏng arrived in Japan is moved from 611 to the year 595.

On the eighth day of the ninth month of 595 (Suiko 3) in the reign of Empress Suiko, a big radiant star suddenly fell from the heavens to Aoyanagi no Ura, Washizu estate (Washizunoshō) Tsuno District, Suō Province, and landed on the top of a pine tree. It was like the light sent out by a full moon, and it glowed for seven days and nights. The various people of the region were very surprised and thought it strange. They immediately engaged a shaman. She spoke. "I am this Hokushin Myōken Sonshō. Three years from now, on the second day of the third month, Prince Imsŏng of

---

[89] Hirase Naoki, "Kinsei no bungaku engeki ni egakareta Ōuchi shi," *Yamaguchi ken chihōshi kenkyū* 112 (10.2014), pp. 1–12.

[90] *Hagi han batsu etsu roku*, vol. 3, maki 102.2 Reizen Gorō collection, for a 1717 (Kyōho 2). postscript appearing immediately after doc. 128, 8.13 Ise Sadataka *shojō an*, pp. 234–36. They adopted the characters of the court Reizei (冷泉) family for their name, but read it as Reizen. For another Ōuchi branch that survived in Kaga, see Suda Makiko, "Kaga no Ōuchi shi ni tsuite," *Yamaguchi ken chihōshi kenkyū* no. 99 (6.2008), pp. 1–18.

[91] For one of the oldest versions, see the Library of Congress Japanese Rare Book Collection. Kōfu [Edo]: Watanabe Zen'emon no Jō kaihan, Enpō 5 [1677]. This passage is most easily accessible in Hayakawa Junsaburō, ed., *Shinkō sōsho* (Kokusho kankōkai, 1915), p. 453.

Paekche should come to this country. I have announced this fact to Prince Shōtoku, and he has agreed that Prince Imsŏng should stay."[92]

The account is otherwise garbled, as later passages describe Ōuchi district (*agata*) incorrectly as being part of Nagato province. Tatara Nansōan Ichiryū knew little of local geography.[93] After the early eighteenth century, references to the elusive Prince Imsŏng would fade, although even as late as 1772 a portrait of Ōuchi Yoshitaka lauding his kingly status and descent from Prince Imsŏng would be created, copied (1800), and stored in Yamaguchi's Taga shrine archive (Figure E.3).

During the centuries after the Ōuchi passing, the division between Japan and Korea became firm, and Ōuchi identities that straddled both became inconceivable. Retrospective accounts of the Iwami silver mines would state, for example, that the Ōuchi aided the Mongol invaders of Japan and thus were not "Japanese."[94] Even modern scholarship mirrors this idea, as some authors suggest that the Ōuchi only "pretended" to have Korean ancestry.[95]

Ōuchi interactions with Ming China and Korea were largely ignored and the magnitude of trade forgotten. Korean goods imported by the Ōuchi, for example, and later housed in the Mōri Museum were sometimes assumed to have been war booty from the 1592–98 invasions of Korea by Toyotomi Hideyoshi (1537?–98).[96] Likewise, shards of pottery discovered in Nagato were assumed to have been made by potters coming from China to set up kilns in Nagato, rather than objects of trade.[97]

[92] Hayakawa Junsaburō, *Shinkō sōsho*, p. 453. Translation drawn from Yoshihiro Nikaidō, "Cultural Interaction: Myōken Bosatsu and the God Zhenwu (真武)," in *Asian Folk Religion and Cultural Interaction* (Göttingen: Vandenhoech & Ruprecht, October 2015), pp. 122–23.

[93] Hayakawa Junsaburō, *Shinkō sōsho*, p. 453.

[94] *Ginzan kyūki*. For the myths, see *Yamaguchi kenshi shiryōhen chūsei*, vol. 1, Ginzan kyūki, p. 651, and Tottori ken kyōiku chō bunka ka zaika sekai isan toroku suishin shitsu, ed., *Iwami Ginzan shiryō kaidai Ginzan kyūki* (Shimane, 2003). I am grateful to Nakagi Sayumi for generously providing me with an informative analysis of the text.

[95] Jurgis Elisonas, "Christianity and the Daimyō," in John Whitney Hall et al., eds., *The Cambridge History of Japan*, vol. 4: *Early Modern Japan* (New York: Cambridge University Press, 1991), particularly "Xavier and Ōuchi Yoshitaka," p. 314, which states: "The Ōuchi family, which itself *pretended* to a royal Korean ancestry, had a long history of diplomatic and economic relations with Korea and a long history of borrowing from overseas."

[96] Sangnam Lee and Jaewon Ahn, "Mōri hakubutsukan shozō no Kankoku ibutsu o tsūshite mita Kankoku ōchō shoki busshitsu bunka no kōryū- Ōuchi shi to Mōri shi o chūshin ni," *Bijutsu kenkyū* 415 (3.2015), pp. 1–20.

[97] For claims of Chinese kilns being created in the Abu region of Nagato see Yamamoto Benya, *Hagi no tōjiki* (Hagi, 1978), p. 17. Yamamoto describes the discovery of such a locally produced shard of porcelain in 1938, but it has unfortunately been lost. Yamamoto nevertheless alludes to references to the Ōuchi exporting Ming porcelain to Korea based on the Korean *Richō jitsuroku*, but he provides no citations. See also Kōno Ryōsuke, "Nagato no yakimono," in Mitsuoka Tadanari, Narasaki Shōichi,

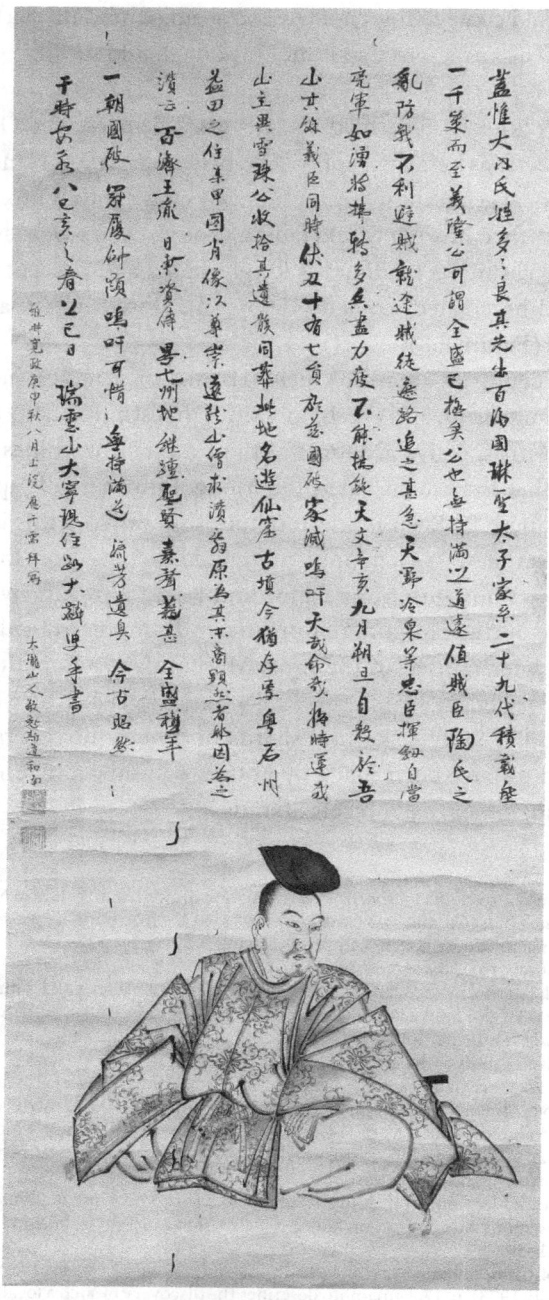

Figure E.3 The portrait of Ōuchi Yoshitaka (1800), from the Yamaguchi Taga shrine, does not resemble him, but the colophon reveals lingering memories of Ōuchi ethnicity. Image and permission provided by Yamaguchi monjokan

As the centuries passed, histories were selectively edited to obscure Yoshitaka's attempt to move the capital in 1551. The most direct evidence of obfuscation of these events appears in the writings of Narushima Chikuzan (1803–54), a Confucian scholar who was employed by the Tokugawa bakufu and compiled the *Nochi kagami*, a chronicle of the Ashikaga regime.[98] Narushima relied on both the *Ashikaga kiseiki* and the *Chūgoku chiranki* to reconstruct the events of 1551. Although he recounted the coup against Yoshitaka in 1551, he nevertheless omitted references from these sources regarding Yoshitaka's attempt to move the emperor to Yamaguchi.[99] Of course, not all Tokugawa-era historians would belittle the role of the Ōuchi. Some prominently mention certain events, such as Ōuchi Yoshioki's occupation of the capital in 1508.[100]

Some scholars would still acknowledge Ōuchi grandeur. *The History of the Empire of Japan: Compiled and Translated for the Imperial Japanese Commission of the World's Columbia Exposition* (1893), describes them as follows:

> In the Western provinces, the Ouchi Family stood at the head of all the great territorial magnates. In the days of Yoshioki that family possessed the six provinces of Suwo, Nagato, Buzen, Chikuzen, Aki and Iwami. They also carried on commerce with China and Korea, and were not only powerful but wealthy.[101]

Takekoshi Yosaburō (1865–1950), writing a generation later, saw the Ōuchi as traders, patrons, and lords of *wakō* pirates, "far richer than any other feudal lord" and with "a great advantage of sea power."[102] Takekoshi also stirringly argued for Ōuchi greatness, explaining that "in the eyes of the

and Hayashiya Seizō, eds., *San'in, Nihon yakimono shūsei*, vol. 8 (Heibonsha, 1981), p. 123. I am indebted to Louise Cort and Kitajima Daisuke for this information.

[98] This work was compiled between the years 1837 and 1853.

[99] See Kuroita Katsumi, comp., *Nochi kagami, Shintei zōho kokushi taikei* 34–37, 4 vols. (Yoshikawa kōbunkan, 1932), vol. 4, pp. 640–42.

[100] *Nihon Gaishi*, vol. 2 (Iwanami shoten, 2016), pp. 116–17. This would influence compendia of historical sources. The *Dainihon shiryō* starts its ninth section with Yoshioki's advance on the capital.

[101] *The History of the Empire of Japan: Compiled and Translated for the Imperial Japanese Commission of the World's Columbia Exposition. Chicago, U.S.A., 1893* (Dai Nippon tosho kabushiki kwaisha, 1893), p. 260.

[102] Takekoshi Yosaburō, *Economic Aspects of the History of the Civilization of Japan*, vol. 1 (London: George Allen & Unwin, 1930), p. 346. This perspective can be found in other works such as Kazuo Miyamoto, *Vikings of the Far East* (New York: Vantage Press, 1975), pp. 29–32.

Ōuchi, the Shogun was a nobody, and in the messages he sent to the King of Korea he used to write his name as if he was really a ruler of an independent country."[103]

So, in the end, the Ōuchi were simply too great to be completely forgotten. Their history was all but lost along with knowledge of their large ships, their mines, their culture, and their identity. But traces, like the Rurikōji pagoda, remain, and for those who look, this lost history can be recovered. The Ōuchi were magnificent, but their fall allowed new opportunities, new regimes, new cultures, and new notions of Japan and its people to arise, although, in the end, it was a narrower and more divided world that came into being after their final and irrevocable passing.

[103] Takekoshi, *Economic Aspects*, p. 347.

Bibliography

Unless otherwise noted, the city of publication is Tokyo.

Archival Sources

Bartolomeu Velho Portolan Atlas. [Portugal] [between 1550 and 1599]. Manuscripts mss HM 44. Huntington Library, San Marino, CA.

Ganjitsu sechie ki (Sanjō Kin'yori). Unpublished manuscript. Kunaichō.

Genga sōjō onjihitsuki, unpublished manuscript, part of the *Genjo onenki*, *Tanaka Yuzuru shi kyūzō tenseki komonjo* no. 316. *Kokuritsu rekishi hakubutsukan*.

Go-Taiheiki (Tatara Nansōan Ichiryū). Kōfu [Edo]: Watanabe Zen'emon no Jō kaihan, Enpō 5 [1677]. Library of Congress Japanese Rare Book Collection.

Ihon Yoshitaka-ki. Unpublished Manuscript. Yamaguchi monjokan. http://ymonjo.ysn21.jp.

Jinpō shoji kongen gyōji danzu. Yoshida bunko. Yoshida 65-306, 65-361. Unpublished manuscript, Yoshida bunko. Tenri University Library.

Kosechiryo gyoki. Unpublished manuscript. Kunaichō.

Mōri ke bunko, furoku wa 8. Unpublished manuscript. Yamaguchi monjokan.

Nakahara Yasuo-ki. Unpublished manuscript. Hirata Archives, Waseda University. http://archive.wul.waseda.ac.jp/kosho/i04/i04_02478/i04_02478_0008/i04_02478_0008_0001/i04_02478_0008_0001.html.

Nichimin bōeki senki. Yamaguchi monjokan.

Tenryūji tatchū Nanpōin monjo. Unpublished manuscript, Yale Beinecke library.

Tsunemoto gyoki. Unpublished manuscript, Kyōto University.

Yoshida bunko. Yoshida 31-6; 31-159. Unpublished manuscripts, Yoshida bunko. Tenri University Library.

Yuiitsu Shintō Hokuto Shichigen[sei] shinpō shidai. Yoshida 42-396. Unpublished manuscript, Yoshida bunko. Tenri University Library.

Reference Works

Gunsho kaidai. 22 vols. Zoku gunsho ruijū kanseikai, 1961–66.

Gunsho ruijū. Compiled by Hanawa Hokinoichi et al. 24 vols. Naigai kabushiki kaisha, 1928–38.

Kadokawa Nihon chimei daijiten. 49 vols. Kadokawa shoten, 1978–90.

Kaitei shiseki shūran. 33 vols. Kondō shuppan 1900–1903.

Koji ruien. Compiled by Kiyonori Konakamura. 60 vols. Yoshikawa kōbunkan, 1967–71.

Kokushi daijiten. 15 vols. Yoshikawa kōbunkan, 1979–97.

Kugyō bunin. 5 vols. Edited by Kuroita Katsumi. Yoshikawa kōbunkan, 1964–66.

Rekimei dodai. Edited by Yukawa Toshiharu. Zoku gunsho ruijū kanseikai, 1996.
Seishi kakei daijiten. Compiled by Ōta Akira. 3 vols. Seishi kakei daijiten kankōkai, 1934.
Zoku gunsho ruijū. Compiled by Hanawa Hokinoichi. 37 vols. Zoku gunsho ruijū kanseikai, 1957–59.
Zoku zoku gunsho ruijū. 16 vols. Kokusho kankōkai, 1906–9.

Primary Sources

Agari ke monjo. Nagato shi shitei bunkazai, 1995.
Ashikaga kiseiki. In *Kaitei shiseki shūran* vol. 13, no. 116, 132–264. Kondō Keizō shuppanbu, 1902.
Ashikaga Yoshimasa hakkyū monjo. 2 vols. Edited by Kinoshita Satoshi. Sengokushi kenkyūkai shiryōshu, 2015–16.
Ashikaga Yoshimi Yoshitane hakkyū monjo. Edited by Kinoshita Satoshi. Sengokushi kenkyūkai shiryōshu, 2019.
Baishōron Gen'ishū. Edited by Yashiro Kazuo and Kami Hiroshi. Gendai shichōsha, 1975.
Bōchō fūdo chūshin an. 23 vols. Compiled by Yamaguchi ken monjokan. Yamaguchi, 1960–65.
Bōchō jisha yurai. 7 vols. Compiled by Yamaguchi ken monjokan. Yamaguchi, 1982–86.
Bōshū Yamaguchi Tsukiyama yakata jōsui. Yamaguchi: Ryūfukuji, 1993.
Buzen Agano Kōkokuji Kyūshū no jisha shirizu 17 *Kyūshū rekishi shiryōkan.* 3.2000.
Buzen shishi monjo shiryō. Buzenshi, 1991.
Chiba Myōken dai engi emaki. Edited by Chiba ken shitei yūkei bunkazai. Chiba shiritsu kyōdo hakubutsukan, 1995.
Chikamoto nikki 1. Zōho Zoku shiryō taisei. Vol. 10. Edited by Takeuchi Rizō. Kyoto: Rinsen shoten, 1967.
Chiritsuka monogatari. In *Kaitei shiseki shūran,* vol. 10, *Sanroku* 38, pp. 1–111. Kondō Keizō shuppanbu, 1901.
Chosŏn wangjo sillok (朝鮮王朝實錄). http://sillok.history.go.kr.
Chūgoku chiranki. Shinkō Gunsho ruijū. Vol. 17, *kassen bu* 2. Naigai shoseki kabushiki kaisha, 1930, pp. 432–48.
Chūgoku Chōsen no shiseki ni okeru Nihon shiryō shūsei. Richō jitsuroku no bu. 11 vols. Kokusho kankōkai, 1976–95.
Chūgoku shiryōshū. Edited by Yonehara Masao. Jinbutsu ōraisha, 1966.
Chūkun Sōtō shū zengoroku zensho Chūsei hen 8. Edited by Kawaguchi Kōfū et al. Shikisha, 2006.
Chūsei hōsei shiryōshū. 7 vols. Compiled by Satō Shin'ichi and Ikeuchi Yoshisuke. Iwanami shoten, 1955–2005.
Chūsei imoji shiryō. Edited by Nagoya daigaku bungakubu kokushi kenkyūshitsu. Hōsei daigaku shuppan kyoku, 1982.
Chūsei Masuda Masuda shi kankei shiryōshū. Compiled by Masuda shi kyōiku iinkai bunkazaika. Masuda, 2016.
Chūsei seiji shakai shisō. 2 vols. Edited by Satō Shin'ichi et al. Iwanami shoten, 1972.
Daijōin jisha zōjiki (Jinson). 12 vols. Edited by Takeuchi Rizō. Kyoto: Rinsen shoten, 1982.
Dainihon komonjo Hennen monjo. 25 vols. Compiled by Tōkyō daigaku shiryōhen sanjo. Tōkyō daigaku shuppankai, 1901–40.

Dainihon komonjo iewake 13. Aso monjo. 3 vols. Compiled by Tōkyō daigaku shiryōhen sanjo. Tōkyō daigaku shuppankai, 1932–34.

Dainihon komonjo iewake 19. Daigoji monjo. 17 vols. to date. Compiled by Tōkyō daigaku shiryōhen sanjo. Tōkyō daigaku shuppankai, 1955–.

Dainihon komonjo iewake 3. Date ke monjo. 10 vols. Compiled by Tōkyō daigaku shiryōhen sanjo. Tōkyō daigaku shuppankai, 1908–14.

Dainihon komonjo iewake 9. Kikkawa ke monjo. 3 vols. Compiled by Tōkyō daigaku shiryōhen sanjo. Tōkyō daigaku shuppankai, 1925–32.

Dainihon komonjo iewake 11. Kobayakawa ke monjo. 2 vols. Compiled by Tōkyō daigaku shiryōhen sanjo. Tōkyō daigaku shuppankai, 1927.

Dainihon komonjo iewake 14. Kumagai ke monjo Miura ke monjo, Hiraga ke monjo. Compiled by Tōkyō daigaku shiryōhen sanjo. Tōkyō daigaku shuppankai, 1937.

Danihon komonjo iewake 22. Masuda ke monjo. 4 vols. Compiled by Tōkyō daigaku shiryō hensanjo. Tōkyō daigaku shuppankai, 2000–2012.

Dainihon komonjo iewake 8. Mōri ke monjo. 4 vols. Compiled by Tōkyō daigaku shiryōhen sanjo. Tōkyō daigaku shuppankai, 1920–24.

Dainihon komonjo iewake 21. Ninagawa ke monjo. 6 vols. Compiled by Tōkyō daigaku shiryōhen sanjo. Tōkyō daigaku shuppankai, 1981–96.

Dainihon komonjo iewake 5. Sagara ke monjo. 2 vols. Compiled by Tōkyō daigaku shiryōhen sanjo. Tōkyō daigaku shuppankai, 1917–18.

Dainihon komonjo iewake 16. Shimazu ke monjo. 6 vols. Compiled by Tōkyō daigaku shiryōhen sanjo. Tōkyō daigaku shuppankai, 1952–2019.

Dainihon shiryō series 6. Compiled by Tōkyō daigaku shiryōhen sanjo. 50 vols. to date. Tōkyō daigaku shuppankai, 1901–.

Dainihon shiryō series 7. Compiled by Tōkyō daigaku shiryōhen sanjo. 34 vols. to date. Tōkyō daigaku shuppankai, 1927–.

Dainihon shiryō series 8. Compiled by Tōkyō daigaku shiryōhen sanjo. 42 vols. to date. Tōkyō daigaku shuppankai, 1913–.

Dainihon shiryō series 9. Compiled by Tōkyō daigaku shiryōhen sanjo. 28 vols. to date. Tōkyō daigaku shuppankai, 1928–.

Dainihon shiryō series 10. Compiled by Tōkyō daigaku shiryōhen sanjo. 29 vols. to date. Tōkyō daigaku shuppankai, 1968–.

Dazaifu Dazaifu Tenmangū shiryō. Compiled by Takeuchi Rizō and Kawazoe Shōji. 16 vols. to date. Dazaifu, 1989–.

Dazaifu shishi chūsei shiryōhen. Dazaifu, 2002.

Egakarata wakō "Wakō zukan" to "Kōwa zukan. Edited by Tōkyō daigaku shiryōhen sanjo. Yoshikawa kōbunkan, 2014.

Egara Tenjinsha kyūhyakunen. Edited by Kamakura kokuhōkan. Yokohama hōsōkyoku, 2004.

Ehime ken shi shiryōhen kodai (I-II) *chūsei.* 2 vols. Ehime, 1983–84.

Eikanshi danki nenroku. Edited by Awa kyōdokai. Tokushima, 2001.

Emakimonoshū Habikinoshishi bunkazaihen bessatsu. Compiled by Habikinoshi shiryō hensaniinkai. Habikino City, 1991.

Entairyaku (Toin Kinkata). 7 vols. Edited by Iwahashi Koyata and Saiki Kazuma. Zoku gunsho ruijū kanseikai, 1970–86.

Fudōsan Yōkōji no jihō. Iwakuni, 2010.

Fukuhara ke monjo. Vol. 1. Edited by Watanabe-ō kinen bunka kyōkai. Ube-shiritsu toshokan, 1983.

Fukuoka shishi shiryōhen chūsei 1. *Shinai shōzai monjo.* Fukuoka-shi, 2010.

Fusaaki oboegaki. Hiroshima kenshi kodai chūsei shiryōhen. Vol. 3. Hiroshima, 1978, 1107–54.

Gakuenji monjo. Edited by Gakuenji monjo kenkyūkai. Kyoto: Hōzōkan, 2015.

Gaun nikken roku batsuyū (Zuikei Shūhō). Edited by Tōkyō daigaku shiryō hensanjo. Iwanami shoten, 1961.

Genjo daisōjōki (Genjo). In *Zoku gunsho ruijū*, vol. 30, *Zatsubu* 1, pp. 1–69. Zoku gunsho ruijū kanseikai, 1957.

Gogumaiki (Sanjō Kintada). 4 vols. Edited by Tōkyō daigaku shiryōhen sanjo. In *Dainihon kokiroku.* Iwanami shoten, 1980–92.

Gohōjōji kanpakuki (Konoe Hisamichi). 3 vols. Edited by Atsuta Kō. Kyoto: Shibunkaku shuppan, 1985.

Gohōkō'inki (Konoe Masaie). 4 vols. Edited by Takeuchi Rizō. Kyoto: Rinsen shoten, 1978.

Gukanshō (Jien). Edited by Okami Masao and Akamatsu Toshihide. In *Nihon koten bungaku taikei.* Iwanami shoten, 1967.

Go-Nara tennō jitsuroku. 3 vols. *Tennō kōzoku jitsuroku* 96–98. Edited by Fujii Jōji. Yumani shobō, 2010.

Hagi han batsu etsu roku. 6 vols. Compiled by Yamaguchi ken monjokan. Yamaguchi ken monjokan, 1994.

Hakozakigū shiryō. Edited and compiled by Hakozakigū. Fukuoka: Hakozakigū, 1970.

Harutomi Sukuneki. Compiled by Kunaichō shoryōbu. Meiji shoin, 1971.

Heian ibun. 15 vols. Compiled by Takeuchi Rizō. Tōkyōdō shuppan, 1963–80.

Heisei 30 (2018) nendo monjokan komonjo jissen kōza, Chūsei-Kinsei no buke monjo o yomu-Nagata hiroku "shoka shōmon utsushi." http://archives.pref.yamaguchi.lg.jp/user_data/upload/File/kouza-kaidoku/h30-03yamagata.pdf.

Hekizan Nichiroku (Unkei Daikyoku). 2 vols. Edited by Tōkyō daigaku shiryō hensanjo. In *Dainihon kokiroku.* Iwanami shoten, 2013–17.

Hiesha shintō himitsuki. Gunshō ruijū, vol. 2, *Jingibu*, pp. 85–125. 3rd ed. Zoku gunsho ruijū kanseikai, 1983.

Himeji shishi. Vol. 2, *Honhen kodai chūsei.* Himeji-shi, 2018.

Hirai ke monjo-Dazaifu shi. www.city.dazaifu.lg.jp › group › hirai-familydocuments_s.

Hiroshima kenshi kodai chūsei shiryōhen. 5 vols. Hiroshima, 1974–80.

Hizen no kuni Kanzaki shōen shiryō. Compiled by Seno Sei'ichirō. Yoshikawa kōbunkan, 1975.

Hōfu shishi tsūshi I *Genshi kodai chūsei.* Compiled by Hōfu shishi hensan iinkai. Hōfu shi, 2004.

Hōfu shishi shiryōhen II *Kōko shiryō.* Compiled by Hōfu shishi hensan iinkai. Hōfu shi, 2004.

Hōfu Tenmangūten: Nihon saisho no Tenjin-sama: Matsugasaki Tenjin engi emaki nanahyakunen kinen. Yamaguchi: Yamaguchi bijutsukan, 2011.

Hyōgo kenshi. vol. 3. Hyōgo. Compiled by kenshi henshū senmon iinkaii. Hyōgo, 1978.

Hyōgo kenshi shiryōhen chūsei. 9 vols. Compiled by kenshi henshū senmon iinkaii. Kobe, 1983–97.

"Ichimon Ōno Mōri ke." *Kinsei Bōchō shokeizu shūran.* Compiled by Tamura Tetsuo. Reprint ed. Shōnan-shi: Matsuzono, 1980.

Inryōken nichiroku. 5 vols. *Dainihon bukkyō zensho.* Bukkyō kankōkai, 1912–13.

"Inu ya kame no shokuyō uratsuke? Ōuchi shi yakata no ato shūhen kara setsudan sareta hone Mōri shi jidai to suisoku." *Asahi Shinbun,* evening edition, August 15, 2006.

Intoku Taiheiki. 6 vols. Edited by Yonehara Masayoshi. Tōyō shoin, 1980–84.

Ise Matsuki monjo. Kyōto daigaku bungakubu kakubutsukan no komonjo no. 12. Kyōto daigaku bungakubu kakubutsukan, 6.1994.

Ishikawa ken maizō bunka hōkoku, no. 5 (2000), p. 45. http://www.ishikawa-maibun.jp/wp-content/uploads/2018/03/jouhou_05.pdf.

Itsukushima Jinja Kokuhōten-Taifu higai fukō shien. Itsukushima shrine. Hatsukaichi-shi, 2005.

Iwakuni shishi shiryōhen 1. Compiled by Iwakuni shi hensan iinkai. Iwakuni, 2001.

Iwami ginzan iseki hakkutsu chōsa gaiyō Kobuyamatani Munaoka jūtaku machinami hozon chiku. Vol. 23. Compiled by Shimane ken Ōta shi kyōiku iinkai. 3.2015.

Iwami ginzan iseki sōgō chōsa hōkokusho 6. Shimane ken kyōiku iinkai, 1999.

Iwami ginzan kaidō: Tomogaura, Yunotsu, Okinohamadō chōsa hōkokusho. Shimane ken kyōiku iinkai, 2004.

Iwami ginzan kankei hennen shiryō mokuroku. Shimane ken Shimane ken Ōta shi kyōiku iinkai, 2003.

Iwami ginzan kankei rekishi nenpyō 1334–1710. Iwami ginzan no 5 Kaiteiban. Shimane kyōiku iinkai, 2003.

Iwami Ginzan shiryō kaidai Ginzan kyūki. Edited by Tottori ken kyōiku chō bunka ka zaika sekai isan toroku suishin shitsu. Shimane, 2003.

Iwami jōseki: tenzen no yōgai ni kyoten kizuku." *Online News Sanin Chūō Shinpō,* 2.7.2006. https://www.sanin-chuo.co.jp/www/contents/1493222555197/index.html.

Iwami no kuni imoji tōryōYamane shi shiryō chōsa hōkokusho. Compiled by Sakurae-chō kyōiku iinkai. Sakurae-shi, 3.1992. http://www.ishikawa-maibun.jp/wp-content/uplo ads/2018/03/jouhou_05.pdf.

Jige monjo. See *Kyōto gosho Higashiyama gobunko shozō Jige monjo.*

Jōeiji shiryō. Yamaguchi, 1978.

Jōfukuji ato. 3 vols. Compiled by Yamaguchi shi kyōiku iinkai. Yamaguchi, 2001–4.

Jurin'in naifuki (Nakano'in Michihide). Edited by Okuno Takahiro et al. Zoku gunsho ruijū kanseikai, 1972.

Kaei sandaiki. Gunshō ruijū. Vol. 26, *Zatsubu,* 66–142. 3rd ed. Zoku gunsho ruijū kanseikai, 1983.

Kagoshima kenshiryō kyūki zatsuroku zenhen. 2 vols. Kagoshma ken ishinshi shiryōsanjo, 1979.

Kaitō shokokuki (Shin Sukchu). Edited by Tanaka Takeo. Iwanami bunko, 1991.

Kakitsuki. Gunsho ruijū,. Vol. 20, *Kassenbu,* 317–26. Zoku gunsho ruijū kanseikai, 1959.

Kamakura ibun. Compiled by Takeuchi Rizō. 51 vols. Tōkyōdō shuppan, 1971–97.

Kanagawa kenshi shiryō hen. Kodai-chūsei. Compiled by Kanagawa ken. Yokohama, 1973.

Kanagawa kenshi tsūshi hen. Genshi kodai chūsei. Compiled by Kanagawa ken. Yokohama, 1981.

Kanenobu kōki (Hirohashi Kanenobu). 2 vols. Edited by Murata Masashi. Zoku gunsho ruijū kanseikai, 1973–2012.

Kanmon gyōki (Fushimi no miya Sadafusa; Go-Sukō'in). 2 vols. Zoku gunsho ruijū kanseikai, hoi, 1930.

Kanmon nikki. (Fushimi no miya Sadafusa; Go-Sukō'in). 7 vols. Compiled by Kunaichō shoryōbu. 2002–14.

Kanō shiryō Sengoku. 16 vols. Compiled by Kanō shiryōhen iinkai. Ishikawa, 1998–2018.

Kasuga Taisha monjo. Compiled by Nagashima Fukutarō. 6 vols. Kasuga taisha, 1981–86.

Kennaiki. (Madenokōji Tokifusa). 10 vols. Edited by Tōkyō daigaku shiryōhen sanjo. In *Dainihon kokiroku.* Iwanami shoten, 1963–86.

Kita Kyūshū shiritsu rekishi kakubutsukan kenkyū kiyō 1 *Tokushū Buzen Shugendō. Kubotesan, Hikoyama.* Kita Kyūshū Shiritsu Rekishi Hakubutsukan, 1979.

Kōbunsō. Catalogue 44. 1.1973.

Kobunsō. Catalogue 35. 3.1960.

Kokuhō Onjōji Kondō hozon shūri kōji hōkokusho. Compiled by Shiga ken kyōiku iinkai. Shiga, 2009.

Kokuhō Tenjin sama. Fukuoka: Kyūshū National Museum, 2008.

Kōno ke monjo. Edited and compiled by Kageura Tsutomu. Matsuyama: Iyo shiryō shūsei, 1967.

Kōtei Kyōdaibon Taiheiki. Edited by Koakimoto Dan et al. Bensei shuppan, 2011.

Kōya shunshū hennen shūroku. Dainihon Bukkyō zensho. 161 vols. Bussho kankōkai, 1912–22, vol. 131 (1912).

Kōyasan Kongō sanmaiin monjo. Edited by Kōyasan shi hensanjo. Wakayama: Kōyasan monjo kankōkai, 1936.

Kujō ke monjo 6 Shoji'in kankei monjo. Kunaichō shoryōbu, 1976.

Kujō ke Rekidai kiroku 2. Kunaichō shoryōbu, 1990.

Kumamoto ken shiryō chūsei hen 2. Kumamoto, 1962.

Kyōgaku shiyōshō (Kyōgaku). 10 vols. Iwanami shoten, 1971–2018.

Kyōto gosho Higashiyama gobunko shozō Jige monjo. Edited by Suegara Yutaka. Yagi shoten, 2009.

Kyōtofu iseki chōsa hōkokushū, no. 176. Kyōtofu maizō bunkazai chōsa kenkyū sentaa, 2018.

Manzei jugō nikki (Manzei). 2 vols. In *Zoku gunsho ruijū hōi 1.* Zoku gunsho ruijū kanseikai, 1928.

"Maruyama iseki daisen chōsa." *Yamaguchi bunkazai nenpō* 4 (2009). Yamaguchi kyōiku iinkai, 2011.

Matsuratō kankei shiryōshū. 5 vols. Compiled by Seno Sei'ichirō and Murai Shōsuke. Zoku gunsho ruijū kanseikai/Yagi shoten, 1996–2020.

"Masuda Saneuji shozō shinshutsu chūsei monjo no shōkai." Edited by Tanaka Hiroki, Nakajima Keiichi, Nakatsukasa Ken'ichi, Nishida Tomohiro, and Watanabe Hiroki. *Kokuritsu rekishi minzoku hakubutsukan kenkyū hōkoku* 212 (12.2018), pp. 101–66.

Meiō kyūnen sangatsu itsuka Shōgun onnari kenritsu (Yamaguchi meibutsu ryori soshutsu suishin kaigi, 2017). https://yamaguchi-city.jp/informations/Download/110303_oou tigozen.pdf.

Meitokuki. Edited by Tomikura Tokujirō. Iwanami bunko, 1941.

Mibu ke monjo. 10 vols. Edited by Kunaichō shoryōbu. Meiji shoin, 1979–88.

Mie kenshi shiryōhen chūsei, vols. 1, pt. 1-2, 2, 3, pt. 1-3 (6 vols). Compiled by Mie ken. Mie, 1997–2018.

Miyazaki kenshi shiryōhen kinsei 1. Miyazaki prefecture, 1991.

"Miyoshi Nagayoshi, Nobunaga yori saki ishigaki dōnyū ka? Imorijō de tairyō ni hakken." *Asahi News,* 6.26.2019. https://www.asahi.com/articles/ASM6T5TH8M6TPPTB 00G.html.

Moji monjo. Kita Kyūshū: Kita Kyūshū shizenshi rekishi hakubutsukan, 2005.

Morimitsu kōki (Hirohashi Morimitsu). 1 vol. to date. *Shiryōsanshu kokirokū hen.* Yagi shoten, 2018–.

Munakata shishi shiryōhen chūsei 2. Compiled by Munakata shishi hensan iinkai. Munakata shi, 1996.

Munakata shishi tsūshihen. Compiled by Munakata shishi hensan iinkai. Munakata shi, 1997.

Muromachi bakufu hikitsuke shiryōshū shūsei. 2 vols. Compiled by Kuwayama Kōnen. Kondō shuppansha, 1980.

Muromachi bunka no naka ni miru Ōuchi bunka no ihōten. Yamaguchi kenritsu bijutsukan, 1989.

Muromachi ke gonaisho an. In *Kaitei shiseki shūran,* vol. 27, maki 108, 620–704. Kondō Keizō shuppanbu, 1926.

Nagaoki Sukuneki (Otsuki Nagaoki). *Shiryō sanshū kokiroku hen.* Edited by Iikura Harutake. Zoku gunsho ruijū, 1998.

Nagato no kuni shugo Kotōshi hakkyū monjo. Compiled by Nagato no kuni shugo Kotōshi hakkyū monjo henshū iinkai. Yamaguchi shi: Yamaguchi-shi chihōshi gakkai, 2014.

Nakatsu kyokan ato. 2 vols. Compiled by Iwakuni-shi Kyōiku iinkai. Iwakuni-shi, 2012–16.

Nanbokuchō ibun Chūgoku Shikoku hen. 6 vols. Compiled by Matsuoka Hisatō. Tōkyōdō shuppan, 1987–95.

Nanbokuchō ibun Kyūshū hen. 7 vols. Compiled by Seno Sei'ichirō. Tōkyōdō shuppan, 1985–92.

Nankai chiranki (Kasai Shigesuke). 3 vols. Edited by Ii Haruki. Kyōikusha, 1981.

Nankai tsūki. (Kasai Shigesuke). In *Kaitei shiseki shūran,* vol. 7, maki 30, pp. 1–496. 3rd printing, Kondō Keizō shuppanbu, 1932.

Nanpō kiden. In *Kaitei shiseki shūran,* vol. 3, maki 11, pp. 1–64. 3rd printing, Kondō Keizō shuppanbu, 1932.

Nantaiheiki (Imagawa Ryōshun). In *Gunsho ruijū,* vol. 17, *Kassen bu* no. 2, *Buke bu* no. 1, pp. 305–21. Naigai shoseki kabushiki kaisha, 1930.

Nanzan junshūroku. In *Kaitei shiseki shūran,* vol. 4, maki 21. 3rd printing, Kondō Keizō shuppanbu, 1906.

Nihon gaishi (Rai Sanyō). 3 vols. Edited by Rai Sei'ichi. Iwanami bunko, 2016.

Nihon kankei kaigai shiryō Iezusukai Nihon shokanshū Yakubun hen. Compiled by Tōkyō daigaku shiryōhen sanjo. Tōkyō daigaku shuppankai, 1990–.

Nihon sandai jitsuroku. Shintei zōho kokushi taikei 4. Compiled by Kuroita Katsumi. Yoshikawa kōbunkan, 1966.

Niigata kenshi shiryōhen 3 chūsei 1. Niigata, 1982.

Ninnaji shiryō jishihen 2. Nara: Nara Kokuritsu bunkazai kenkyūjo shiryō, 1967.

Nochi kagami (Narushima Chikuzan). *Shintei zōho kokushi taikei* 34–37. 4 vols. Compiled by Kuroita Katsumi. Yoshikawa kōbunkan, 1932.

Obama shishi shaji monjo hen. Obama, 1976.

Ōga ke monjo. Nakatsukasa Ken'ichi. "Bunken kara mita chūsei no Iwami no minato to ryūtsū." In *Nihon no kōeki to umi,* Compiled by Chūsei toshi kenkyūkai hen, pp. 93–114. Yamakawa shuppankai, 2016.

Ogori shishi 2. Tsūshihen chūsei kinsei kindai. Ogori, 2003.

Ogori shishi 5 shiryōhen. Ogori, 1999.

Ōita ken sentetsu sōsho Ōtomo Sōrin shiryōshū. 5 vols. Compiled Ōita ken kyōikuchō bunkaka. Ōita, 1993–94.

Ōita ken shiryō 32 dai 2 bu hoi 4 Ōtomo ke monjoroku 2. Ōita, 1980.

Ōita kenritsu rekishi hakubutsukan kenkyū kiyō 12 (2011).

Ōmagaki. In *Zoku gunsho ruijū Kuji bu,* vol. 10, no. 2, pp. 714–35. 3rd ed. Zoku gunsho ruijū kanseikai, 1981.

Ōnin kōki (應仁後記). In *Kaitei shiseki shūran,* vol. 3, maki 19, pp. 1–74. 3rd printing, Kondō Keizō shuppanbu, 1932.

Ōnin no ran. Compiled by Kyōto fūritsu sōgo shiryōkan. Kyōto fūritsu sōgo shiryōkan, 1989.

Ōsaka fushi 3 *chūseihen* 1. Ōsaka fu, 1979.

Ōtomoki. Gunsho ruijū. Vol. 21, *kassen-bu*, pp. 554–607. 3rd ed. Zoku gunsho ruijū kanseikai, 1994.

Ōtomo ke monjo hoi 2 *Ōita ken shiryō.* Vol. 26. Ōita, 1974.

Ōuchi bunka to Kita Kyūshū. Compiled by Kita Kyūshū shiritsu shizenshi rekishi hakubutsukan. Kita Kyūshū, 2012.

Ōuchi shi jitsuroku. Compiled by Kondō Kiyoshi. 1885. 3rd reprint ed., Tokuyama: Matsuno shoten, 1984.

Ōuchi shi kanren machinami iseki 8. Edited by Yamaguchi shi kyōiku iinkai. Yamaguchi shi kyōiku iinkai, 2014.

Ōuchi shi kanseki chisen teien. Yamaguchi kyōiku iinkai, 2016. https://www.city.yamagu chi.lg.jp/uploaded/attachment/35940.pdf.

Ōuchi shi no tobira: Yamaguchi o tsukutta saikoku daimyō. Yamaguchi shi rekishi minzoku shiryōkan, 10.2019.

Ōuchi shi yakata ato 1-15. Compiled by Yamaguchi shi kyōiku iinkai. Yamaguchi, 1981–2014.

Ōuchi yakata hōkokusho 11-13. Yamaguchi shi maizō bunka chōsa hōkoku 11-13. Yamaguchi, 2010–12.

Ōunki. In *Kaitei shiseki shūran*, vol. 3, maki 10, pp. 1–66. 2nd printing, Kondō Keizō shuppanbu, 1906.

Oyudono no ue no nikki. 11 vols. 3rd revised printing, Zoku gunsho ruijū kanseikai, 1995.

Rekidai koan. Edited by Haga Norihiko. *Shiryō sanshū komonjo hen.* 5 vols. Zoku gunsho ruijū kanseikai, 1993–2002.

Rokuonji (Kinkakuji) Teien. Tokubetsu shiseki tokubetsu meishō Rokuonji (Kinkakuji). Kyoto: Kyōto maizō bunkazai kenkyūjo, 2003.

Rōmōki (Nakarai Yasufusa). Zoku shiryō taisei, vol. 18. Edited by Takeuchi Rizō, pp. 97–134. Kyoto: Rinsen shoten, 1967.

Ryōunji ato 1-2. Compiled by Yamaguchi kyōiku iinkai. *Yamaguchi shi maizō bunkazai chōsha hōkokusho*, nos. 115, 121. Yamaguchi, 2015, 2019.

Saga ken shiryō shūsei. Komonjo hen. 30 vols. Compiled by Saga kenshi hensan iinkai. Saga kenritsu toshokan, 1955–90.

Sakaiki (Sonkeikaku bunkozō). Edited by Kansai daigaku chūsei bungaku kenkyūkai. Ōsaka: Izumi shoin, 1990.

Sakai shishi. Vol. 1. Sakai, 1929.

Sakkaiki (Nakayama Sadachika). 6 vols. *Dainihon kokiroku* 26. Edited by Tōkyō daigaku shiryōhen sanjo. Iwanami shoten, 2000–2016.

Sankō Taiheiki. Edited by Imai Kōsai et al. Rev. ed. Kokusho kankōkai, 1943.

Sakugen Nyūminki no kenkyū. 2 vols. Edited by Makita Tairyō. Bukkyō bunka kenkyūjo, 1955.

"Sea Lords: Documents (komonjo) of the Ōuchi and the Kōno." *Komonjo.* http://komo njo.princeton.edu/kono_ouchi/.

Sekai isan toroku kinen Kagayaki futatabi Iwami Ginzan ten. Shimane, 2007.

Sengoku bushō no hokori to inori: Kyūshū no haken to yukue. Fukuoka: Kyūshū rekishi shiryōkan, 2013.

Sengoku daimyō no komonjo Nishinihon hen. Edited by Yamamoto Hirofumi et al. Kashiwa shobō, 2013.

Sengoku ibun Ōuchi shi hen. 3 vols. to date. Compiled by Wada Shūsaku. Tōkyōdō shuppan, 2016–.

Sengoku jidai no kin to garasu-Kirameku Ichijōdani no bunka to gijutsu. Edited by Fukui kenritsu Ichijōdani Asakura shi iseki shiryōkan. Fukui, 2014.

Shimonoseki shishi shiryōhen 6. Shimonoseki, 2001.

Shinsen Chōroku Kanshōki. Gunsho ruijū, vol. 20. *Kassen bu,* pp. 327–47. Zoku gunsho ruijū kanseikai, 1959.

Shinshū Izumi Sanno shishi 4 *Shiryōhen kodai chūsei* 1. Seibundō, 2004.

Shinshū Izumi Sanno shishi 1 *Tsūshihen shizen chūsei.* Seibundō, 2008.

Shinkō sōsho. Edited by Hayakawa Junsaburō. Kokusho kankōkai, 1915.

Shiryōshū Mikita monjo. Edited by Iida Toshikuni. In *Komonjo ni Mikita no hitobito,* compiled and edited by Iida Kunio. Izumisano no rekishi to ima o shiru kai. Izumi, 2015.

Shizokuka kenshi chūsei shiryō 2. Shizuoka, 1994.

Shoku Nihongi. Edited by Kuroita Katsumi. Shintei zōho kokushi taikei. Yoshikawa kōbunkan, 1982.

Shōzui jidai Miyoshi Nagayoshi Tenka o seisu. Shōzuijōkanseki Kokushiseki shitei kinen tokubetsu ten, Tokushimajō hakubutsukan. Tokushima, 2001.

Sonkeikaku bunko zō Sakaiki. Edited by Kansai daigaku chūsei bungaku kenkyūkai. Ōsaka: Izumi shoin, 1990.

Sonpi bunmyaku (Tōin Kinsada). 5 vols. In *Shintei zōho kokushi taikei.* Yoshikawa kōbunkan, 1964.

Sugi ke monjo. In Inoue Minoru. *Hagi Hakubutsukan kitaku Sugi ke monjo, Hagi hakubutsukan kenkyū hōkoku,* no. 3 (3.2008), pp. 1–20.

Sumário de las Cosas de Japón (Alessandro Valignano, 1583). Edited by Alvarez-Taladriz. Sophia University Press, 1954.

Taiheiki (*Seigenin bon*). 6 vols. Edited by Hyōdō Hiromi. Iwanami bunko, 2014–16.

Tenryūji monjo no kenkyū. Compiled and edited by Harada Masatoshi. Kyoto: Shibunkaku, 2011.

Tōdaiji hokkedō yōroku. Zoku zoku gunsho ruijū, vol. 5, pp. 361–408. Ichishima Kenkichi, 1909.

Tōdaiji yōroku (Kangon). Edited by Tsutsui Eshun. Ōsaka: Zenkoku Shobō, 1944.

Tōji hyakugo monjo. 13 vols. to date. Edited by Kyōto furitsu sōgo shiryōkan. Kyoto: Kyōto furitsu sōgo shiryōkan, 2004–.

Tōji nijūikku kusōkata hyōjō hikitsuke. Vol. 1. Kyoto: Shibunkaku, 2002.

Tokitsugu kyōki. 7 vols. Zoku gunsho ruijū kanseikai, 1998.

Tokubetsuten Kamakura gokenin Tairako shi no seisen • hokusen. Yokohama: Yokohama shi rekishi hakubutsukan, 2003.

Tokubetsu kikakuten Sengoku Kyūshū to Takeo Gotō Takaaki Ienobu no jidai. Takeo shi toshokan Rekishi shiryōkan, 2009.

Tokubetsu ten Masuda shi vs. Yoshimi shi—Iwami no Sengoku jidai. Shimane kenritsu Iwami bijutsukan, 9.2019.

Tokushi yoron (Arai Hakuseki). Edited by Muraoka Tsunesugu. Iwanami shoten, 1995.

Tokuyama shishi. 2nd printing, Tokuyama, 1971.

Tōyō bunko no meihin. Tōyō bunko, 2007.

Tsukiyamabon Kōno kefu. "Chūsei Iyo no Yamagata Ryōshu to Kōno shi kenryoku." Edited by Kawaoka Tsutomu, pp. 15–36. *Ehime daigaku kyōiku gakubu kiyō jinbun shakai kagaku,* vol. 36 no. 1 (2003).

Tsuwano chōshi. Vol. 1. Tsuwano, 1970.

Umi o koeta chūsei no okane: "Bita ichimon" ni himerareta rekishi. Bank of Japan, 2009.

Ura ke monjo. See *Dainihon komonjo iewake* 11, *Kobayakawa ke monjo,* vol. 2.

Usa jingūshi shiryōhen. 16 vols. Compiled by Takeuchi Rizō and Nakano Hatayoshi. Usa-shi: Usa jingūchō, 1984–2011.

"Wakamiya Hachimangū monjo kiroku." *Gerin* 27.4–5 (8.1978), pp. 3–52.

Wakasa no kuni Saisho Imatomi myō ryōshu daidai shidai. Gunsho ruijū 4, *buninbu*, pp. 345–54. 3rd revised printing, Zoku gunsho ruijū kanseikai, 1991.

Yamada Sōjiki (Yamada Sōji). Iwanami bunko, 2006.

Yamada Shōei jikki (Yamada Shōei). *Kagoshima ken shiryōshū*, vol. 7. Edited by Kagoshima ken kankō iinkai. Kagoshima, 1967.

Yamaguchi jukkyōshi kō. Edited by Aramaki Daisetsu. Yamaguchi, Sakura printo, 1999.

Yamaguchi kan nyūsu, no. 49 (2015).

Yamaguchi ken shitei mukei minzoku bunkazai Sagi no mai. Yamaguchi shi kyōiku iinkai, 1981.

Yamaguchi kenshi shiryōhen chūsei. 4 vols. Compiled by Yamaguchi kenshi hensanshitsu. Yamaguchi, 1996–2008.

Yamaguchi kenshi shiryōhen kodai Compiled by Yamaguchi kenshi hensanshitsu. Yamaguchi, 2001.

Yamaguchi kenshi tsūshihen chūsei. Compiled by Yamaguchi kenshi hensanshitsu. Yamaguchi, 2012.

Yamaguchi kenshi tsūshihen furoku CD-ROM. Yamaguchi kenshi hensanshitsu. Yamaguchi, 2012.

Yamaguchi shishi shiryōhen Ōuchi bunka. Compiled by Yamaguchi shi kyōiku iinkai. Yamaguchi, 2010.

Yamaguchi shishi shiryōhen chūsei. Compiled byYamaguchi shi kyōiku iinkai. Yamaguchi, 2016.

Yamanouchi Sudō ke monjo. In *Dainihon komonjo iewake*, vol. 15, compiled by Tōkyō daigaku shiryōhen sanjo. Tōkyō daigaku shuppankai, 1940.

Yomigaeru akagane: Nanbanfuku to Sumitomo dōfukusho. Ōsaka: Ōsaka rekishi hakubutsukan, 2003.

Yoshida bunko Shintōsho mokuroku. Tenri daigaku shuppanbu, 1965. https://www.tcl. gr.jp/archive/catalog/yoshida/yoshida.pdf.

Yoshitakaki. Shinkō Gunsho ruijū 21 *kassen bu* 2, pp. 407–32. 3rd revised printing, Zoku gunsho ruijū kanseikai, 1994.

Yoshōki. Shinkō Gunsho ruijū 21 *kassen bu* 2, pp. 497–553. 3rd revised printing, Zoku gunsho ruijū kanseikai, 1994.

Yunotsu shi. Yunotsu chō, 1994.

Zenrin kokuhōki. Shintei Zenrin kokuhōki. Edited by Tanaka Takeo. Shūeisha, 1995.

Zenyaku Furoisu Nihonshi Shōgun Yoshiteru no saigō oyobi jiyū toshi Sakai: Oda Nobunaga hen 1. Translated by Matsuda Kiichi and Kawasaki Momota. Chūō kōron shinsha, 2000.

Zōho teisei Hennen Ōtomo shiryō. 35 vols. Compiled by Takita Manabu et al. Ōita, 1962–75.

Zoku gunsho ruijū. Keizubu. 7 vols. Zoku gunsho ruijū kanseikai, 1975.

Zoku Ōnin kōki. In *Kaitei shiseki shūran*, vol. 3, maki 20, pp. 1–208. 3rd printing, Kondō Keizō shuppanbu, 1900.

Secondary Sources in Japanese and Korean

Akamatsu Toshihide. "Jishi." In *Rokuon*, compiled by Rokuonji, pp. 1–41. Kyoto: Kinkakuji Rokuonji, 1955.

Akiyama Nobutaka. "Muromachi Sengokuki ni okeru Aki Iwami kōtsū." *Shigaku kenkyū* 218 (10.1997), pp. 1–15.

Amano Tadayuki. *Miyoshi ichizoku-Sengoku saisho no "tenkajin".* Chūkō shinsho, 2021.

Amano Tadayuki. "Sengokuki no shūkyō jitsujō no henyō to Miyoshi shi." *Shokuhōki kenkyū* 12 (10.2010), pp. 21–38.

Arikawa Nobuhiro. "Aso Takazane to Aso shi tatekeizu." *Kita kyūshū shiritsu shizenshi rekishi hakubutsukan kenkyū hōkoku* B, no. 4 (2007), pp. 1–18.

Arikawa Nobuhiro. "Buzen Kōkokuji no rekishi." *Buzen Agano Kōkokuji Kyūshū no jisha shirizu* no. 17 *Kyūshū rekishi shiryōkan* (3.2000), pp. 27–28.

Arikawa Nobuhiro. "Buzen Nagano shi ni tsuite." *Kita Kyūshū shiritsu rekishi hakubutsukan kenkyū kiyō* no. 3 (3.1995), pp. 39–81.

Ch'ung Sung-il. "Chosŏn ŭi dongjŏn kwa Ilbon ŭi ŭnhwa: hwap'ye ŭi yut'ong ŭl t'onghae bon 15~17 segi Hanil gwan'gye" (Korean Copper and Japanese Silver Money: Korean-Japanese Relations and the Circulation of Money between Chosŏn Korea and Japan from the Fifteenth Century to the Seventeenth Century). *Hanil gwangyesa yŏngu (Korea-Japan Historical Review)* 20 (4.2004), pp. 5–50.

Conlan, Thomas. "Ōuchi Yoshitaka no sento keikaku." *Yamaguchi ken chihōshi kenkyū* 123 (6.2020), pp. 14–28.

Conlan, Thomas. "Shiryō shōkai: Yoshida Kanemigi ga utsushita Ōuchi keizu." *Yamaguchi kenshi kenkyū* 21 (3.2013), pp. 65–70.

Ebina Nao and Fukuda Toyohiko. "Shiryō shōkai: 'Rokujō Hachimangū zōei chūmon' ni tsuite." *Kokuritsu rekishi minzoku hakubutsukan kenkyū hōkoku* 45 (12.1992), pp. 345–98.

Endō Keisuke. "Kofun no jōkaku riyō ni kan suru ikkōsatsu." *Jōkan shiryō gaku*, vol. 3. Jōkan shiryō gakkai. (7.2005), pp. 1–22.

Era Hiroshi. "Ise oshi to Usa no miya." *Ōita ken chihōshi* 130 (6.1988), pp. 1–10.

Frank, Bernard. *Nihon bukkyō mandala.* Fujiwara shoten, 2002.

Fujii Masako. "Ōnin Bunmei no rango ni okeru Daigoji no saikō." *Nihon rekishi* 764 (1.2012), pp. 125–26.

Fujii Takashi. *Ōuchi Yoshitaka.* Minerva shobō, 2019.

Fujii Takashi. *Ōuchi Yoshioki.* Ebisu kōshō, 2014.

Fujii Takashi. *Muromachiki daimyō kenryokuron.* Dōseisha, 2013.

Fujii Takashi. "Nanbokuchōki Nagato no kuni ni okeru Kotō shi kenryoku to Hiroyo ki Ōuchi shi kenryoku." *Kamakura ibun kenkyū* 21 (4.2008), pp. 56–87.

Fujii Takashi. "Norihiro ki Ōuchi shi no bunkoku shihai to gokenin sei." *Rekishi hyōron* 700 (8.2008), pp. 56–68.

Fujimori Terunobu and Maebashi Shigeji. *Gojūnotō nyūmon.* Shinchōsha, 2012.

Fujimoto Yukio. "Chōsenban Tō Raku Hinō shishū kō." *Chōsen gakuhō* 199–200 (2006), pp. 265–90.

Fukuda Ikuo. "Yokohama shiritsu daigaku toshokanzō no monjo ni tsuite, sono san Yoshimi." *Yokohama shiritsu daigaku ronsō jinbun kakagu keiretsu* 2–3 (3.1979), pp. 313–47.

Fukuo Takeichirō. *Ōuchi Yoshitaka.* Yoshikawa kōbunkan, 1959.

Fukuyama Toshio. *Jinja kenchiku no kenkyū.* Chūō kōron bijutsu shuppan, 1984.

Futaki Ken'ichi. *Sengoku bushō no tegami o yomu.* Kadokawa shoten, 1991.

Haga Kōshirō. *Sanjōnishi Sanetaka.* Yoshikawa kōbunkan, 1960.

Hagihara Daisuke. "Chūsei kōki Ōuchi shi no zaikyō." *Nihon rekishi* 786 (11.2013), pp. 17–32.

Hagihara Daisuke. "Chūsei 'na o komeru' monjo ron." *Shirin* 93.6 (11.2010), pp. 814–36.

Hagihara Daisuke. "Ōuchi shi no sodehan kudashibumi to gokenin sei." *Komonjo kenkyū* 68 (1.2010), pp. 80–102.

Hagiwara Tatsuo. *Chūsei Saishi soshiki no kenkyū*. Yoshikawa kobunkan, 1975.

Harada Masatoshi. "Mannen-san Shōkoku Jōtenzen-ji Ekō narabini sho to Ashikaga Yoshimitsu." *Kansai daigaku Tōzaigakujutsu kenkyū*, no. 46 (4.2013), pp. 17–31. http://www.kansai-u.ac.jp/Tozaiken/publication/asset/bulletin/46/kiyo4602.pdf.

Hasegawa Hiroshi. *Ōuchi shi no kōbō to nishi Nihon shakai*. Yoshikawa kōbunkan, 2020.

Hasegawa Hiroshi. *Sengoku Daimyō Amako shi no kenkyū*. Yoshikawa kōbunkan, 2000.

Hashimoto Yū. *Chūka gensō: Karamono to gaikō no Muromachi jidaishi*. Bensei shuppan, 2011.

Hashimoto Yū. *Chūsei Nihon no kokusai kankei—Higashi Ajia tsūkōken to gishi mondai*. Yoshikawa kōbunkan, 2005.

Hashimoto Yū. "Muromachi sengokuki no shōgun kenryoku to gaikōken." *Rekishigaku kenkyū* 708 (3.1998), pp. 1–18.

Hashimoto Yū. "Erizeni rei to rettō naigai no senka ryūtsū—'Zeni no michi'ko Ryūkyū o ichizukeru kokoromi." *Shutsudo senka* 9 (1998), pp. 99–100.

Hata Yasunori. "Bunmei jū-hachinen no Ōuchi shi to Sesshū Tōyō." In *Sesshū Tōyō: Sesshū e no tabi kenkyū zuroku*, pp. 247–51. Yamaguchi, 2006.

Hatakeyama Satoshi. "Chūsei kōki ni okeru Suō no kuni kokuga kei'ei." *Nihon rekishi* 627 (8.2000), pp. 17–33.

Hatakeyama Satoshi. "Muromachiki ni okeru jige kanjinryō to shugo daimyō." *Chihōshi kenkyū* 50.2 (4.2000), pp. 26–42.

Hayashi On. "Myōken Bosatsu." In *Myōken Bosatsu to hoshi mandara*. Nihon no bijutsu 377, pp. 48–51. Chibundō, 1997.

Hayashiya Tatsusaburō. *Hyōgo kitaseki irifune nōchō*. Chūō kōron bijutsu shuppan, 1981.

Hirase Naoki. *Ōuchi shi no ryōgoku shihai to shūkyō*. Hanawa shobō, 2017.

Hirasae Naoki. *Ōuchi Yoshihiro*. Minerva shobō, 2017.

Hirase Naoki. "Nanbokuchōki Ōuchi shi no honkyochi: Hiroyo ki o chūshin ni." *Nihon rekishi* 810 (11.2015), pp. 13–27.

Hirase Naoki. "Nanbokuchō ki Ōuchi shi ni mieru chiiki shihai kenryoku no kakuritsu." *Kamakura ibun kenkyū*, no. 34 (10.2014), pp. 41–56.

Hirase Naoki. "Kinsei no bungaku engeki ni egakareta Ōuchi shi." *Yamaguchi ken chihōshi kenkyū* 112 (10.2014), pp. 1–12.

Hirase Naoki. "Muromachiki ni okeru Ōuchi shi no Myōken shinkō to sosen densetsu." *Shirin* 97.5 (9.2014), pp. 33–64.

Hirase Naoki. "Ōei no ran to Sakai: Ōuchi Yoshihiro no kyoten ni tsuite." *Hokuriku toshi shigaku kaishi* 18 (8.2012), pp. 10–18.

Hirase Naoki. "Chūsei toshi no kūkan kōzō—Suō no kuni Yamaguchi o chūshin ni." *Hokuriku toshi shigaku kaishi* 8 (2001), pp. 1–14.

Hirase Naoki. "Kyū chōshū hanshi Izuwa ke monjo oyobi Naitō ke monjo." *Yamaguchi monjokan kenkyū kiyō* 22 (1995), pp. 69–81.

Hirase Naoki. "Shugo daimyō Ōuchi shi to kaihen no busō seiryoku: kaizoku, keigoshū, wakō." *Yamaguchi ken chihōshi kenkyū* 71 (6.1994), pp. 23–32.

Hirase Naoki. "Kōryūji no Tendai mikkyō to ujigami-Myōken no henshitsu." *Yamaguchi kenshi kenkyū* 2 (1994), pp. 111–21.

Hirase Naoki. "Ōuchi shi sadamegaki (Ōuchi *shoheki*) no denpon rokushū." *Yamaguchi ken monjokan kenkyū kiyō* 18 (3.1991), pp. 65–84.

Hironaga Tasuo. "Ōuchi shi no jinja sūkei." *Yamaguchi ken kyōwa ronsō* 1.1 (1942), pp. 1–31.

Horimoto Kazushige. "1550 nendai ni okeru Ōtomo shi no hokubu Kyūshū shihai no shinten-Ōuchi Yoshinaga no chiseiki o chūshin ni." *Kyūshū shigaku* 162 (8.2012), pp. 30–45.

Horimoto Kazushige. "Sengokuki Hizen no seiji dōkō to Gotōshi." In *Sengoku no Kyūshū to Takeo*, pp. 5–9. Takeo shi toshokan rekishi shiryōkan, 2009.

Horimoto Kazushige. "Sengoku jidai no Ogori." In *Ogori shishi*, vol. 2, *Tsūshihen chūsei kinsei kindai*, pp. 172–80. Ogori, 2003.

Hyakuda Masao. "Ōuchi Yoshihiro bōdaiji kōsekiji no jūzō." *Yamaguchi ken monjokan kenkyū kiyō*, 26 (3.1999), pp. 57–72.

Ichihara Michihiro. *Shintei Gishi Wajinden*. Iwanami bunko, 1994.

Ichikawa Mototarō. *Nihon jukyōshi 3 Chūsei hen*. Tōa gakujutsu kenkyūkai, 1992.

Ichimura Takao, ed. *Chūsei Tosa no sekai to Ichijō shi*. Kōshi shoin, 2010.

Ienaga Junji. "Sairon Gunki Ōninki to Ōnin no ran." In *Rekishi yūgaku shiryō o yomu*, pp. 57–71. Yamakawa shuppan, 2011.

Ienaga Junji. "Gunki Ōninki to Ōnin no ran." In *Rekishi yūgaku shiryō o yomu*, pp. 61–78. Yamakawa shuppan, 2001.

Ienaga Junji. *Muromachi bakufu shōgun kenryoku no kenkyū*. Tokyo daigaku nihon shigaku kenkyūshitsu, 1995.

Ienaga Junji. "Horigoe kubōfu metsubō no saikentō." *Sengokushi kenkyū* 27 (1994), pp. 1–10.

Iinuma Kenji, "Nihon Chūsei ni shiyō sareta Chūgokusen no mayō to idomu." In *Daikōkai no Nihon to kinzoku kōeki*, 3–17. Kyoto: Shibunkaku, 2014.

Ikeda Yoshifumi. "Kodai no Mine." In *Mitōchō shi Tsūshi hen*, pp. 72–90. Mitō-chō, 2004.

Imaeda Aishin. "Ashikaga Yoshimitsu no Shōkokuji sōken." In *Chūsei zenshūshi no kenkyū*, pp. 471–82. Tōkyō daigaku shuppan, 1970.

Imaoka Norikazu. "Ashikaga Yoshitane seiken to Ōuchi Yoshioki." In *Chūsei kōbu kenryoku no kōzō to tenkai*, edited by Uwayokote Masataka, pp. 190–202. Yoshikawa kōbunkan, 2001.

Imatani Akira et al., eds. *Miyoshi Nagayoshi*. Kyoto: Miyaobi shoten, 2013.

Imatani Akira. *Sengoku daimyō to tennō*. Kōdansha gakujutsu bunko, 2001.

Imatani Akira. *Shugo ryōgoku shihai kikō no kenkyū*. Hōsei daigaku shuppankai, 1986.

Imatani Akira. "Ōuchi Yoshioki no Yamashiro no kuni shihai." *Yamaguchi ken chihōshi kenkyū* 51 (6.1984), pp. 1–11.

Imatani Akira. "Seto naisei kaigen no sui-i to irifune nōchō." In *Hyōgo kitaseki irifune nōchō*. Edited by Hayashiya Tatsusaburō, 272–88. Chūō kōron bijutsu shuppan, 1981.

Inoue Atsushi. "Rigei (Yiye) to Iwami no tsunagari: Chosŏn kōchō jitsuroku, Dōbunikō, Hyōnin ryōraitōroku (Pyo-In Yong-Nae Dung-nok) o tegakari to shite." *Hokutō AJIA kenkyū* 27 (3.2016), pp. 25–48.

Inoue Hiroshi. *Nihon Chūsei kokka to shokoku Ichinomiya sei*. Iwata shoin, 2009.

Inoue Hiroshi. "Chūsei shokoku Ichinomiyasei no rekishiteki kōzō to toskushitsu: Chūsei kōki Nagato no kuni no jirei o chūshin ni." *Kokuritsu rekishi minzoku hakubutsukan kenkyū hōkoku*, no. 148 (12.2008), pp. 193–238.

Inoue Hiroshi, ed. *Shiryōshū Masuda Kanemi to sono jidai: Masuda ke monjo no kataru chūsei no Masuda 1*. Masuda kyōiku iinkai, 1994.

Inoue Hiroshi. *Shiryōshū Masuda Kanetaka to sono jidai: Masuda ke monjo no kataru chūsei no Masuda 1*. Masuda kyōiku iinkai, 1996.

Inoue Hiroshi. "Suō Ōuchi shi no Iwami gun Nima gun bun chigyō." *Nanbokuchō geppō* (1.1989), pp. 3–6.

Inoue Minoru. *Hagi hakubutsukan kitaku Sugi ke monjo. Hagi hakubutsukan kenkyū hōkoku*, no. 3 (3.2008), pp. 1–20.

Inoue Satoshi. "Bunmei gonen izen no Yoshida Kanetomo Saijōsho: Toku ni sōgen jiki o megutte." *Waseda daigaku daigakuin bungaku kenkyūka kiyō. Tetsugaku, shigaku hen* 17 (1990), pp. 43–54.

Inoue Tomokatsu. *Kinsei no jinja to chōtei ken'i*. Yoshikawa kōbunkan, 2007.

Ishibashi Kazuhiro. "Ashikaga Mitsukane to Muromachi bakufu." In *Ashikaga Mitsukane to sono jidai*, edited by Kuroda Motoki, pp. 6–23. Ebisu kōshō, 2015.

Itō Isato. *Usagūki no kenkyū*. Kōgakkan daigaku shuppan, 2011.

Itō Kenji. "Ōuchi shi no Iwami no kuni shihai no Nimagun bungun chigyō." In *Yunotsu chōshi jōkan*. Yunotsu, pp. 595–615. Yunotsu chō, 1994.

Itō Kenji. "Suō Ōuchi shi no Iwami no kuni Nimagun bungun chigyō." In *Nanbokuchō ibun Chūgoku Shikoku hen*, vol. 2 *furoku*, 1989, pp. 3–6.

Itō Kiyoshi. *Ashikaga Yoshimochi*. Yoshikawa kōbunkan, 2008.

Itō Kōji. *Chūsei no Hakata to Ajia*. Bensei shuppan, 2021.

Itō Kōji. "Higo Sagara shi to Higashi Ajia." In *Chūsei Sagara shi no tenkai to chiiki shakai*, edited by Inaba Tsuguhara et al., pp. 268–78. Ebisu kōshō, 2020.

Itō Kōji and Wada Shūsaku, eds. *Ōuchi shi no sekai o saguru*. Bensei shuppan, 2019.

Itō Kōji. "Ōuchi shi no potenshiyaru." In *Ōuchi shi no sekai o saguru*, compiled by Ōuchi shi rekishi bunka kenkyūkai, pp. 1–22. Bensei shuppan, 2019.

Itō Kōji. "Chūsei bushi no keifu—Suō Ōuchi shi no jirei to shite." *Rekishi to chiri Nihonshi no kenkyū*, no. 717 (9.2018), pp. 33–38.

Itō Kōji. "*Nyūminki* kara mita Higashi Ajia no kaiiki kōryū—kōro kōkai gijutsu kōkaishin shinkō funatabi to shi ni tsuite." In *Higashi Ajia Kaiiki sōsho*, vol. 2, *Hakata to Ninpō*, edited by Itō Kōji et al., pp. 191–230. Kyūko shoin, 2013.

Itō Kōji. "Ōuchi shi to Hakata." *Shishi kenkyū Fukuoka* 8 (3.2013), pp. 3–17.

Itō Kōji. "Ōuchi Norihiro, Masahiro to Higashi Ajia." *Kyūshū shigaku* no. 161 (7.2012), pp. 1–28.

Itō Kōji. "Ōuchi no sosen shinwa." *Tōhokugaku*, series 2, 37 (2011), pp. 94–107.

Itō Kōji, ed. *Daigakuteki Yamaguchi gaido*. Shōwadō, 2011.

Itō Kōji. "Ōei no gaikō o meguru kaii genshō." In *Nichō kōryū to sōkoku no rekishi*. Edited by Murai Shōsuke et. al., pp. 191–208. Asakura shobō, 2009.

Itō Kōji. "Gi-Ōuchi dono shikō-Ōuchi shi no Chōsen tsūkō to gishi mondai." *Nihon rekishi* 731 (4.2009), pp. 16–34.

Itō Kōji. "Chūsei saikoku shoshi no keifu ninshiki." In *Kyōkai aidentiti*, compiled by Kyūshū shigaku kenkyūkai, pp. 107–39. Fukuoka: Kyūshū shigakukai, 2008.

Itō Kōji. "Ōuchi shi no kokusai hatten: juyon seiki han juroku seiki han no Yamaguchi chiiki to Higashi Ajia sekai." *Yamaguchi kenritsu daigaku kokusai bunka gakubu kiyo*, no. 11 (2005), pp. 69–80.

Itō Kōji. "Ōuchi shi no Ryūkyū kotsū." *Nenpō chūseishi kenkyū* no. 28 (2003), pp. 187–210.

Itō Kōji. *Chūsei Nihon no gaikō to zenshū*. Yoshikawa kōbunkan, 2002.

Itō Kōji. "Chūsei kōki chiiki kenryoku to taigai kōshō to zenshū monha, Ōuchi shi to Tōfukuji shō-ichi ha no kakawari o chūshin ni." *Komonjo kenkyū*, no. 48 (10.1998), pp. 20–40.

Itō Satoshi. "Tenbun nenkan ni okeru Yoshida Kanemigi no Yamaguchi gekō o megutte." *Bungaku* 13.5 (9–10.2012), pp. 104–19.

Iwai Tomoji. "Yamaguchi-shi Manpukuji Jizō bosatsuzō ni tsuite." *Yamaguchi kenritsu bijutsukan kenkyū kiyō* 1 (1996), pp. 1–14.

Iwasaki Toshihiko. *Kōryūji monjo o yomu*. 2 vols. Yamaguchi: Ōuchi shi kabegaki kenkyūkai, 2004–5.

Iwasaki Toshihiko. *Ōuchi shi kabegaki o yomu*. Yamaguchi. Ōuchi shi kabegaki kenkyūkai, 1997.

Kage Toshio. *Sengoku daimyō no kaigai kōeki*. Bensei shuppan, 2019.

Kage Toshio. ""Kōwa zukan" "Wakō zukan" to Ōuchi Yoshinaga Ōtomo Sōrin." In *Sengoku daimyō no kaigai kōeki*, pp. 269–93. Bensei shuppan, 2019.

Kage Toshio. "'Kōji' nenki wakōsen to Sengoku daimyō suigun." In *Wakō zukan" "Kōwa zukan" o yomu*, edited by Suda Makiko, pp. 269–94. Bensei shuppan, 2016.

Kage Toshio, Editor. *Ōuchi to Ōtomo: Chūsei nishi Nihon no nidai daimyō*. Bensei shuppan, 2013.

Kage Toshio. "Ōuchi Ōtomo shi no 'kōji' kenminsen." *Tōkyō daigaku shiryōhen sanjo kenkyū kiyō* 23 (3.2013), pp. 296–307.

Kage Toshio. "Kenminsen to Sagara Ōuchi Ōtomo shi." *Nihonshi kenkyū* 610 (6.2013), pp. 3–28.

Kan Takako. "Sengokuki Yamaguchi jōka ni okeru jōkan to yashiki kami." *Yamaguchi ken chihōshi kenkyū* 74 (10.1995), pp. 1–12.

Kanaya Masato. "Ōuchi shi ni okeru Myōken shinkō no danpen." *Yamaguchi ken monjo kan kenkyū kiyō* 19 (1992), pp. 23–42.

Kanzaki Zen. "Nakazu kyokan ato hakkutsu chōsha ni tsuite." *Yamaguchi ken chihōshi kenkyū* 112 (10.2014), pp. 58–61.

Kashiwara Shōzō. "Nichimin kangō bōeki ni okeru Hosokawa Ōuchi no kyōsō." *Shigaku zasshi* 26.2–3 (1915), pp. 172–201.

Kawai Masaharu. *Chūsei buke shakai no kenkyū*. Yoshikawa kōbunkan, 1973.

Kawamura Kimiaki. *Hagi Abu no chūsei fūdoki*. Hagi: Mashiyama insatsu, 2010.

Kawamura Shō'ichi. *Aki Takeda shi*. Ebisu kōshō, 2010.

Kawaoka Tsutomu. "Muromachi bakufu shugo taisei to saikoku shugo." In *Saikoku no kenryoku to senran*, edited by Kawaoka et al., pp. 37–66. Seibundō shuppan, 2010.

Kawaoka Tsutomu. *Yamana Sōzen*. Yoshikawa kōbunkan, 2009.

Kawaoka Tsutomu, "Ōuchi shi no chigyōsei to gokenin sei." *Nihonshi kenkyū*, no. 254 (10.1983), pp. 1–29.

Kawase Kazuma. *Kokatsuji ban no kenkyū*. Antiquarian Booksellers of Japan, 1967.

Kawato Takashi. *Sengokuki no kahei to keizai*. Yoshikawa kōbunkan, 2008.

Kawato Takashi. "Sengoku daimyō Ōuchi shi no ishi dentatsu shisutemu." *Nihon rekishi* 713 (10.2007), pp. 53–75.

Kawato Takashi. "Chūsei kōki no ryūtsū kōzō to sensen." *Chūseishi kenkyū*, no. 32 (2007), pp. 177–200.

Kawazoe Shōji. "*Masatōki* ni mieru Ōuchi Masahiro to Hakata jisha." *Seiji Keizai shigaku* 401 (1.2000), pp. 1–15.

Kawazoe Shōji. "Kurushima monjo to Hizen Ōshima shi: Nanbokuchō ikō." *Matsuratō no kenkyū* 8 (1985), pp. 10–30.

Kawazoe Shōji. *Chūsei bungei no chihōshi*. Heibonsha, 1982.

Kawazoe Shōji. "Muromachi bakufu hōkōshū Chikuzen Aso shi ni tsuite." In Kawazoe Shōji, *Kyūshū chūseishi no kenkyū*, pp. 185–235. Yoshikawa kōbunkan, 1983.

Kawazoe Shōji. *Imagawa Ryōshun*. Yoshikawa kōbunkan, 1964.

"Kinkakuji ni Ashikaga Yoshimitsu ga zōei shita maboroshii no ike." *Kyōto shinbun*. https://headlines.yahoo.co.jp/hl?a=20181011-00000050-kyt-l26. Accessed 10.11.2018.

Kim Ilgŭn. *Ch'inp'il ŏn'gan ch'ongnam* (親筆諺簡總攬). Seoul: Unknown publisher, 1974.

Kimura Tadao. "Shihon bokuga tansai Jōfukuji garanzu kaisetsu." In *Yamaguchi kenshi shiryōhen chūsei 2 furoku*. Yamaguchi 2001.

Kinoshita Meiki. *Zusetsu Yamaguchi Hōfu no rekishi*. Yamaguchi: Kyōdo shuppansha, 2005.

Kira Kunimitsu. "Tenbun nenkan Ōuchi shi to Ōtomo." *Kyūshū shigaku* 162 (2012), pp. 4–29.

Kirita Takashi. "Tenri daigaku fuzoku toshokan shozō 'Kyōto gotaiji gokōmon.'" *Shintōshi kenkyū* 69.1 (2021), pp. 102–117.

Kirita Takashi. "'Kyōto gotaiji gokōmon' ni mieru Ashikaga Yoshimitsu no jingi kitō." *Komonjo kenkyū* 90 (12.2020), pp. 43–62.

Kishida Hiroshi. "Sakaime no dōshu Mōri Motonari no 'kokka' zukuri." In *Mōri Motonari to chiiki shakai*, edited by Kishida Hiroshi, pp. 13–43. Hiroshima: Chūgoku shinbunsha, 2007.

Kishida Hiroshi. "Ōuchi shi metsubō go no Bōchō kyūshinzō to Mōri shi." *Shigaku kenkyū* 200 (3.1993), pp. 3–25.

Kitajima Daisuke. "Ōuchi yakata to Yamaguchi." In *Saikoku no kenryoku to senran*, edited by Kawaoka Tsutomu and Koga Nobuyuki, pp. 181–222. Seibundō, 2010.

Kitajma Daisuke. "Ōuchi shi no machi zukuri: Chūsei toshi Yamaguchi no 'genten' no hakken." In *Sengoku daimyō no doboku jigyō*, edited by Kage Toshio, pp. 124–42. Ebisu kōshō, 2018.

Kitajima Daisuke. "Chūsei Yamaguchi ni okeru kinzoku seisan." *Yamaguchi shi maizō bunkazai chōsa hōkoku* 112 *Ōuchi shi kanren machinami iseki* 8. Edited by Yamaguchi shi kyōiku iinkai, pp. 254–61. Yamaguchi shi kyōiku iinkai, 2014.

Kitajima Daisuke. "Kinzoku seisan kanren ibutsu no bunrui." *Yamaguchi shi maizō bunkazai chōsa hōkoku* 112 *Ōuchi shi kanren machinami iseki* 8. Edited by Yamaguchi shi kyōiku iinkai, pp. 141–79. Yamaguchi shi kyōiku iinkai, 2014.

Ko Jyonyon. "Yamaguchi Jōfukuji ato shutsudo kawara no kentō." In *Kitani Yoshinobu sensei koki kinen ronshū*, edited by Kitani Yoshinobu sensei koki kinen ronshūkai, pp. 437–50. Ōsaka: Kitani Yoshinobu sensei koki kinen ronshū kankōkai, 2006.

Kobata Atsushi. "Nihonkai kaiun to minato machi." In *Fukui kenshi tsūshihen* vol. 2 *Chūsei*, pp. 839–869. Fukui, 1994.

Kobata Atsushi. *Nihon Kōzanshi no kenkyū*. Iwanami shoten, 1968.

Kobata Atsushi. *Chūsei Nisshi tsūkō bōekishi no kenkyū*. Tōkō shoin, 1941.

Kobata Atsushi. *Nihon kahei ryūtsūshi*. Tōkō shoin, 1930.

Kobayashi Takeo. "Sengoku daimyōke zaikyō zasshō o megutte: Ōuchi shi no bai." *Komazawa shigaku* nos. 39–40 (9.1988), pp. 225–38.

Kobayashi Yukio. *Kodai no gijutsu*. Hanawa shobo, 1962.

Koga Nobuyuki. "Ōuchi shi to Hakata." In *Chūsei toshi Hakata o horu*. Edited by Ōba Yasutoki, Saeki Kōji, Suganami Masato, Tagami Yūichirō, pp. 61–64. Fukuoka: Kaichōsha, 2008.

Koga Nobuyuki. "Suō no kuni Yamaguchi no sengokuki shugosho." In *Shugosho to Sengoku jōkamachi*, edited by Niki Hiroshi et al., pp. 371–86. Takashi shoin, 2006.

Koga Nobuyuki. "Bōshū Yamaguchi ni okeru shiro, tate, tera." In *Toshi no kyūshin roku*, compiled by Chūsei toshi kenkyū, pp. 99–119. Shinjinbutsu ōraishia, 2000.

Kōno Ryōsuke. "Nagato no yakimono." In *San'in, Nihon yakimono shūsei* 8, edited by Mitsuoka Tadanari, Narasaki Shōichi, and Hayashiya Seizō, p. 123. Heibonsha, 1981.

Kunihara Misako. "Jūgō seiki no nichōkan de juju shita sanju." *Shiron*, no. 54 (2001), pp. 119–54.

Kuratsune Kōichi. "Iwami no kuni ni tsutawatta chūsei imoji shiryō." *Nihon rekishi* 841 (6.2018), pp. 82–84.

Kurushima Noriko. "Ōnin Bunmei no ran to Masuda shi—Shiryōhen sanjo shozō Masuda ke monjochū no sashidashi fumei kana shojō no kōsatsu." *Daikibo Buke monjogun ni yoru chū kinsei shirōgaku no sōgōteki kenkyū Hagi han karo Masuda ke monjo o sozai ni*. Kagaku kenkyūhi hojokin kiban kenkyū A 5202018 (3.2008), pp. 69–91.

Kuwata Kazuaki. *Chūsei Munakatashi to Munakata sha.* Iwata shoin, 2003.

Kuwata Kazuyuki. "Ōuchi Yoshitaka no metsubō to Chikuzen Munakata shi." *Kyūshū shigaku* 105 (9.1992), pp. 23–40.

Kuwata Tadachika. *Nihon kassen zenshū: Ōnin Muromachi hen.* Akita shoten, 1973.

Maeda Yoshiaki. "Kitayama tei to Kitayamadono no kokōgaku kenkyū no genjō." In *Muromachi Seiken no shufu kōsō to Kyōto Muromachi Kitayama Higashiyama: Heiankyō Kyōto kenkyū sōsho,* edited by Momosaki Yūichirō and Yamada Kunikazu, pp. 219–37. Kyoto: Bunrikaku, 2016.

Maeda Yūya. "Ōuchi Yoshihiro to Chōsen." *Kōgakkan shigaku,* 24 (3.2009), pp. 69–94.

Maki Takayuki. "Suō no kuni Hikamisan Kōryūji no kyūkōnai to sono dōsha haichi." *Yamaguchi daigaku bunkakaishi* 65 (3.2015), pp. 41–61.

Maki Takayuki. "Kinsei Hikamisan kyōnai no kōiki sashizu to sono saibu kōsei." *Yamaguchigaku no kōchiku,* 7 (2015), pp. 107–45.

Maki Takayuki. "Suō no kuni Ōuchi shi to sono ujidera Kōryūji no shitsuteki henyō." In *Saikoku no bunka to gaikō,* edited by Kawaoka Tsutomu and Koga Nobuyuki, pp. 87–150. Seibundō, 2011.

Maki Takayuki. "Ōuchi Masahiro no haha ni kansuru oboegaki." *Yamaguchigaku no kōchiku* 1 (3.2005), pp. 51–60.

Maruo Kōsuke. "Ōuchi yakata Tsukiyama yakata o horu." In *Ōuchi shi no sekai o saguru,* compiled by Ōuchi shi rekishi bunka kenkyūkai, pp. 142–49. Bensei shuppan, 2019.

Machinaka daigaku jikō iinkai Ōuchi bunka kaidō machinami kyōgikai, comp. *Chizu no nenpyō de tadoru Ōdono kaiwai.* Yamaguchi, 3.2018.

Mashino Shinji. "Chūsei no Yamaguchi." In *Chūsei nishi Nihon no nidai daimyō,* edited by Kage Toshio, pp. 245–84. Bensei shuppan, 2013.

Matsubayashi Yasuaki. *Muromachi gunki no kenkyū.* Ōsaka: Izumi shoin, 1995.

Matsuda Kiichi. "Ōuchi Yoshinaga no Daidōji saikyojō ni tsuite." *Komonjo kenkyū* 4 (1970), pp. 20–36.

Matsui Naoto. "Yoshioki Yoshitakaki Ōuchi shi kenryoku no kōzōteki tokushitsu: Ōuchi shi hikan Numa shi no dōkō o tegakari ni." *Nihon rekishi* 822 (11.2016), pp. 17–33.

Matsumoto Takuya. "Chūsei Usagū no zōei shisutemu to Ōuchi shi." *Kamakura ibun kenkyū,* no. 31 (4.2013), pp. 55–90.

Matsuoka Hisatō. "Kamakura makki Suō no kuni kokugaryo shihai no dōkō to Ōuchi shi." In *Ōuchi shi no kenkyū.* Edited by Kishida Hiroshi, pp. 121–48. Seibundō, 2011.

Matsuoka Hisatō. *Ōuchi shi no kenkyū.* Edited by Kishida Hiroshi. Seibundō, 2011.

Matsuoka Hisato. *Ōuchi Yoshihiro.* Jinbutsu ōraisha, 1966.

Mimura Kōsuke. "Chūsei kōki ni okeru Ōuchi shi no chokkakuryō." *Kyūshū Shigaku* 136 (9.2003), pp. 1–29.

Mimura Kōsuke. "Ōuchi shi no hanzeisei." *Komonjo kenkyū* 56 (11.2002), pp. 1–18.

Miyachi Naokazu. "Muromachi bakufu no shūki." In *Jingi shi no kenkyū,* pp. 159–200. Kokon shoin, 1924.

Miyachi Naokazu. "Ōuchi Yoshitaka no Shintōkan." In *Jingi shi no kenkyū,* pp. 200–220. Kokon shoin, 1924.

Miyajima Shin'ichi. "Tosoku Tenjinzō to Totō tenjinzō." *Bungaku kaishaku to kanshō* 67.4 (4.2002), pp. 148–56.

Miyakami Shigetaka. "Higashiyama dono no kenchiku to sono haichi." In *Muromachi Seiken no shufu kōsō to Kyōto Muromachi Kitayama,* edited by Momosaki Yūichirō and Yamada Kunikazu, pp. 270–301. Kyoto: Bunrikaku, 2016.

Miyakami Shigetaka. *Kinkakuji Ginkakuji Nihon meikenchiku shashin senshū* 11. Shinchōsha, 1992.

Miyata Itsumi. "Hironaka shi ni tsuite." In *Nakatsu kyokan ato* II, compiled by Iwakuni-shi kyōiku iinkai, pp. 78–84. Iwakuni-shi, 2016.

Miyoshi Yukitaka. "Chūsei Kagoshima no minato to Sengoku jōkamachi no keisei." *Shirin* 101.5 (9.2018), pp. 95–115.

Mizuno Tomoyuki, *Muromachi jidai kōbu kankei no kenkyū*. Yoshikawa kōbunkan, 2005.

Momosaki Yūichirō. *Muromachi no hasha: Ashikaga Yoshimitsu*. Chikuma shobō, 2020.

Mori Michihiko. "Muromachiki ni okeru Takauji kachūzō no juyō to shōzōga seisaku: Ōuchi Yoshiokizō no shōkai o kanete." *Suzaku: Kyōto hakubutsukan kenkyū kiyō* 25 (2013), pp. 1–23.

Mori Shigeaki. "Ōuchi Masahiro no seishin sekai." *Sengoku ibun geppō* 1 Ōuchi shi hen (7.2016), pp. 1–3.

Mori Shigeaki. *Muromachi bakufu hōkai: Shōgun Yoshinori no yabō to zasetsu*. Kadokawa gakugei shuppan, 2011.

Mori Shigeaki, "Ōuchi shi no kōryū to sosen denju." *Yamaguchi kenshi kenkyū* 11 (3.2003), pp. 93–117.

Mori Shigeaki. "Suō no kuni Hikamisan Kōryūji shunigatsu-e ni tsuite no ikkōsatsu." *Fukuoka daigaku jinbun ronsō* 30.3, no. 118 (12.1998), pp. 1–59.

Mori Shigeaki. "Godanhō shūhō ichiran." *Fukuoka daigaku jinbun ronsō* 30, no 1. Fukuoka daigaku sōgōkenkyū (6.1998), pp. 785–847.

Mori Shigeaki. *Yami no rekishi Gonanchō*. Kadokawa shoten, 1997.

Mori Shigeaki. "Ōuchi shi to onyōdō-Ōuchi Masahiro to Kamo Akimune to no kankei o chūshin ni." *Nihon rekishi* 583 (12.1996), pp. 1–15.

Mori Shigeaki. "Godanhō no shiteki kenkyū." *Kyūshū bunkashi kenkyū kiyō* 39 (3.1994), pp. 111–56.

Moriyama Tsuneyo. "Shiryō shōkai Ihara ke monjo." *Kyūshū shigaku* 17 (1.1961), pp. 53–58.

Murai Yūki. "Tōkyō daigaku shiryōhen sanjo eishabon 'Tenbun jūyonen nikki.'" *Tōkyō daigaku shiryōhen sanjo kenkyū kiyō* 28 (3.2018), pp. 140–46.

Murakami Ryū. *Kin gin dō no Nihonshi*. Iwanami shoten, 2007.

Mutō Tadashi. "Chūsei no Hyōgo to seto naikai suiun." In *Hyōgo kitaseki irifune nōchō*. Edited by Hayashiya Tatsusaburō, 232–71. Chūō kōron bijutsu shuppan, 1981.

Nagae Shō'ichi. *Miyoshi Nagayoshi*. Yoshikawa kōbunkan, 1968.

Nagashima Fukutarō. *Ōnin no ran*. Shibundō, 1968.

Nagata Tadayasu. "Chūsei kōki ni okeru Buzen Ichinomiya Usagū no dōkō-Ōuchi shi to no kankei o chūshin ni." *Kokuritsu rekishi minzoku hakubutsukan kenkyū hōkoku*, no. 148 (12.2008), pp. 239–47.

Nakajima Junji. "Shinkei no shinjitsu: Sesshū hitsu Amanohashidate zu no seiritsu eizaite." *Museum* 472 (7.1990), pp. 4–17.

Nakajima Keiichi. "Chūsei kahei no fuhensei to chiikisei." In *Kōkogaku to chūseishi kenkyū*, edited by Amino Yoshihiko, pp. 173–89. Meicho shuppan, 1997.

Nakamura Hidetaka. *Nichō kankeishi no kenkyū jō*. Yoshikawa kōbunkan, 1965.

Nakatsukasa Ken'ichi. "Yoshimi Masayori." In *Shimane ken no kassen*. Edited by Yamane Masaaki, pp. 120–21. Iki shuppan, Shimane, 2018.

Nakatsukasa Ken'ichi. "Chūsei kōki Iwami no kuni kokujin dōkō to Muromachi bakufu, daimyō." *Iwami no chūsei ryōshu no seisui to Higashi Ajia kai-iki sekai*. Tottori ken kodai bunka sentaa kenkyū ronshū no. 18. Tottori (3.2018), pp. 65–76.

Nakatsukasa Ken'ichi. "Bunken kara mita chūsei no Iwami no minato to ryūtsū." In *Nihon no kōeki to umi*, compiled by Chūsei toshi kenkyūkai hen, pp. 93–114. Yamakawa shuppankai, 2016.

Nakatsuka Ken'ichi. "Ōuchi tōshugawa kinsō no keisei to tenkai." In *Ōuchi to Ōtomo: Chūsei nishi Nihon no nidai daimyō*, edited by Kage Toshio, pp. 115–39. Bensei shuppan, 2013.

Nakatsuka Ken'ichi. "Sue shi no ryōshu zaisei 1." *Shigaku kenkyū* 265 (8.2009), pp. 37–52.

Nakatsuka Ken'ichi. "Sue shi no ryōshu zaisei 2." *Shigaku kenkyū* 266 (9.2009), pp. 1–14.

Nomura Shinjō. "Sengoku ki ni okeru shōen yori toshi e no hatten." *Shakai eizai shigaku* 4.11 (1935), pp. 88–99.

Noshita Toshiki. "Ōuchi Dōjun no hanran to Ōuchi shi 'rusu-shū' Ōnin no ran to Ōuchi shi no ryōgoku shihai." *Shichikuma shigaku* no. 19 (2017), pp. 49–74.

Nozuki Michio. "*Meitokuki* to *shugo daimyō*." *Yagoto bunka* no. 4. Chūkyō daigaku chūsei bungaku kenkyūkai (3.1998), pp. 28–40.

Ōba Kōji. *Hakata no kōkogaku: Chūsei no bōeki toshi o horu*. Kōshi shoin, 2019.

Ōba Yasutoki. "Hakata to Iwami ginzan-minato no shiten kara." *Iwami ginzan Iwami ginzan iseki te-ma betsu chosa kenkyū hōkokusho* 1 (3.2011), pp. 97–110.

Ogawa Makoto. *Ashikaga ichimon shugo hattenshi no kenkyū*. Yoshikawa kōbunkan, 1980.

Ogawa Takeo. *Ashikaga Yoshimitsu*. Chūkō shinsho, 2012.

Ogawa Takeo, "Ryōshin kara mita Ashikaga Yoshimitsu." In *ZEAMI Chūsei no geijutsu to bunka: Tokushū: Ashikaga Yoshimitsu no jidai roppyaku nen kikinen*, edited by Ogawa Takeo et al., pp. 155–71. Shinwasha, 2007.

Okada Akio. *Kirishitan bateren*. Shibundō, 1955.

Okamoto Makoto. "'Sakai kentōshi' to Sengokuki no kenminsen hakken." *Shigaku zasshi* 124 (3.2015), pp. 38–61.

Okamoto Nin. "Nanbokuchō Muromachi shoki Ōuchi shi no shihai kōzō hōsha no bunseki o chūshin to shite." *Yamaguchi kenshi kenkyū*, no. 22 (3.2014), pp. 1–22.

Okuda Isao. *Sōgi*. Yoshikawa kōbunkan, 1998.

Ōmori Mihoko. "Ōuchi shi *hekisho* no jittai o megutte." *Historia* 108 (10.1985), pp. 43–63.

Ōta Junzō. "Ōuchi shi no Hikamisan nigatsu-e shinji to tokusei." In *Kyūshū chūsei shakai no kenkyū*, compiled by Watanabe Sumio sensei koki kinen jigyōkai, pp. 205–42. Daiichi hōki, 1981.

Ōta Takahiko. "Masaki bijutsukan zō 'Sansōzu' ni tsuite." *MUSEUM*. Tōkyō kokuritsu hakubutsukan, no. 450 (9.1998), pp. 4–12.

Saeki Arikiyo. *Shinsen Shōjiroku no kenkyū*. 10 vols. Yoshikawa kōbunkan, 2001.

Saeki Kōji. "Chūsei toshi Hakata no sōchinju to Hakozakigū." *Shien* 149 (3.2012), pp. 1–20.

Saeki Kōji. "Hakata shōnin Kameya Jūtei no jitsuzō." *Kyōkai kara mita uchi to soto "Kyūshū shigaku" sōkan 50 shūnen kinren ronbunshū ge*. Edited by Kyūshū shigaku kenkyūkai, pp. 147–65. Iwata shoin, 2009.

Saeki Kōji, "Muromachi kōki no Hakata shōnin Dōan to Higashi Ajia." *Shien* 140 (2003), pp. 31–49.

Saeki Kōji. "Muromachiki no Hakata shōnin Sōkin to Higashi Ajia." *Shien* 136 (1999), pp. 106–21.

Saeki Kōji. "Muromachi jidai ni okeru Ōuchi shi to Shōni shi-Ninagawa ke monjo Ōuchi Norihiro jōsho an no kentō." *Shien* 130 (3.1993), pp. 1–26.

Saeki Kōji. "Muromachi jidai no kenminsen keigo ni tsuite." In *Kodai Chūseishi ronshū*, compiled by Kyūshū daigaku kokushigaku kenkyūshitsu, pp. 461–80. Yoshikawa kōbunkan, 1990.

Saeki Kōji. "Chūsei toshi Hakata no hatten to Ikinohama." In *Nihon Chūsei ronkō*, edited by Kawazoe Shōji sensei kanreki kinenkai, pp. 419–50. Fukuoka: Bunken shuppan, 1987.

Saeki Kōji. "Chūsei kōki no Hakata to Ōuchi shi." *Shien* 121 (1984), pp. 1–28.

Saeki Kōji. "Ōuchi shi no Chikuzen no kuni gundai." In *Kyūshū daimyō no kenkyū*, edited by Kimura Tadao, pp. 310–46. Yoshikawa kōbunkan, 1983.

Saeki Kōji. "Ōuchi shi no Chikuzen no kuni shugo dai." In *Kyūshū chūsei shi kenkyū*, vol. 2, edited by Kawazoe Shōji, pp. 281–354. Fukuoka: Bunken shuppan, 1980.

Saeki Kōji. "Ōuchi shi no Chikuzen no kuni shihai: Yoshihiro ki kara Masahiro ki made." In *Kyūshū chūseishi kenkyū*, vol. 1, edited by Kawazoe Shōji, pp. 243–381. Fukuoka: Bunken shuppan, 1978.

Saeki Kōji. "Ōuchi shi to Ryūkyū." http://www.tulips.tsukuba.ac.jp/limedio/dlam/B95/B952214/1/dai-1/mokuji/5113.pdf, Accessed 11.10.2018.

Saeki Noriya. *Izumo no chūsei: chiiki to kokka no hazama*. Yoshikawa kōbunkan, 2017.

Sakurai Eiji. "Chūsei no gijutsu to rōdō." In *Iwanami kōza Nihon rekishi*, vol. 4, edited by Sakurai Eiji et al., pp. 279–314. Iwanami shoten, 2015.

Sakurai Eiji. *Muromachibito no seishin*. Kōdansha, 2001.

Sangnam Lee and Jaewon Ahn. "Mōri hakubutsukan shozō no Kankoku ibutsu o tsūshite mita Kankoku ōchō shoki busshitsu bunka no kōryū- Ōuchi shi to Mōri shi o chūshin ni." *Bijutsu kenkyū* 415 (3.2015), pp. 1–20.

Sasaki Takahiro. "Shugo daimyō Ōuchi kanren waka tanzaku shūsei (kō)." *Keiō Gijuku daigaku fuzoku kenkyūjō Shidō bunko* 50 (2015), pp. 99–143.

Sasaki Takahiro. "'Ōshimabon Genji monogatari' ni kansuru shoshigakuteki kōsatsu." *Keiō Gijuku daigaku fuzoku kenkyūjō Shidō bunko* 41 (2006), pp. 165–200.

Sasamoto Shōji. "Kinsei shoki ni okeru Matsugi ke no imoji shihai." *Nagoya daigaku bungakubu kenkyū ronshū Shigaku* 30 (3.1984), pp. 187–208.

Satō Chikara. "Suō no kuni Jōfukuji ato shutsudo kawara no saikentō." In *Ōuchi to Ōtomo: Chūsei nishi Nihon no nidai daimyō*, edited by Kage Toshio, pp. 367–98. Bensei shuppan, 2013.

Satō Shin'ichi. *Muromachi bakufu shugo seido no kenkyū*. 2 vols. Tōkyō daigaku shuppan, 1967–88.

Satō Shin'ichi. *Nanbokuchō no dōran*. Chūō kōronsha, 1974.

Satō Tsutomu. "Jōfukuji no kawara to Tomitajō no kawara." In *Yamaguchi daigaku kōkogaku ronshū*. Edited by Nakamura Tomohiro sensei taikan kinen jigyōkai, pp. 321–38. Yamaguchi, 2003.

Seki Shūichi. *Chūsei Nichō kai-iki shi no kenkyū*. Yoshikawa kōbunkan, 2002.

Seno Sei'ichirō. *Ashikaga Tadafuyu*. Yoshikawa kōbunkan, 2005.

Shimai Kiyoshi. "Yoshida Bunko no Kanemigi jihitsu hon ni tsuite 1." *Biblia*, no. 25 (6.1963), pp. 22–33.

Shimai Kiyoshi. "Yoshida Bunko no Kanemigi jihitsu hon ni tsuite 2." *Biblia*, no. 27 (3.1964), pp. 46–58,

Shimai Kiyoshi. "Yoshida Bunko no Kanemigi jihitsu hon ni tsuite 3." *Biblia*, no. 29 (10.1964), pp. 34–45.

Shimatani Kazuhiko. *Toshi o kiru*. Edited by Chūsei toshi kenkyūkai. Yamakawa shuppan, 2010.

Shindō Tōru. *Sengoku no toshokan*. Tōkyōdō shuppan, 2020.

Shinkawa Takashi. "Tōjiki kara mita Iwami ginzan shūhen chiiki Nima chō shutsudo shiryō o chūshin ni." *Sekai isan Iwami ginzan iseki no chōsa kenkyū* 3 (3.2013), pp. 1–15.

Shinjō Tsunezō. *Chūsei suiunshi no kenkyū*. Hanawa shobō, 1994.

Suda Makiko. "Ōuchi Masahiro no 'seitō' sōshutsu." *Rekihaku* 217 (11.2019), p. 6.

Suda Makiko. "'Kōwa zukan' no hakken 'Wakō zukan' no saikō." In *"Wakō zukan" "Kōwa zukan" o yomu*, edited by Suda Makiko, pp. 38–42. Bensei shuppan, 2016.

Suda Makiko. "Ōuchi shi no zaikyō katsudō." *Ōuchi to Ōtomo: Chūsei nishi Nihon no nidai daimyō*. Edited by Kage Toshio, pp. 97–113. Bensei shuppan, 2013.

Suda Makiko. *Chūsei Nichō kankei to Ōuchi shi*. Tōkyō daigaku shuppan, 2011.

Suda Makiko. "Kaga no Ōuchi shi ni tsuite." *Yamaguchi ken chihōshi kenkyū* 99 (6.2008), pp. 1–18.

Suda Makiko. "Chūsei koki ni okeru Ōuchi shi no daizōkyō yunyū." *Nenpō chūseishi kenkyū* 32 (2007), pp. 139–200.

Sugawara Masako. "Sengoku daimyō no bikkaihō to fūfu." *Rekishi hyōron*, no. 679 (11.2006), pp. 3–19.

Sugihara Takatoshi. *Myōkensama*. Kudamatsu: Myōkengū Washizuji, 1985.

Sukigara Toshio. *Chūsei Kyōto no kiseki*. Yuzankaku, 2008.

Sumitomo Shiryōkan, comp. *Kodō zuroku no kenkyū-Shoshi to keifu*. Kyoto: Sumitomo Shiryōkan, 2015.

Tajima Isao, ed. *Kinri kuge bunko kenkyū*. 4 vols. Kyoto: Shibunkaku, 2003–12.

Takagi Hisashi. *Nihon Chūsei kahei shiron*. Kōkura shobō, 2010.

Takahashi Ken. "Sengoku daimyō Mōri shi no Bōchō shihai to genki sannnen Ryūfukuji no 'saikō.'" *Yamaguchi ken chihōshi kenkyū* 99 (6.2008), pp. 19–33.

Takahashi Satoshi. *Muromachi jidai no koshōhon "Rongo Shūge" no kenkyū*. Kyūko shoin, 2008.

Takahashi Shinichirō. *Bushi no sadame: "Michi" o meguru Kamakura sengoku bushi no mō hitotsu to tatakai*. Shinjinbutsu ōraisha, 2012.

Takano Nobuharu. *Bushi shinkakuka no kenkyū*. Yoshikawa kōbunkan, 2018.

Takeda Osamu, ed. *Ashikaga Yoshimitsu to Tōji*. Kyoto: Kyōto furitsu sōgō shiryōkan rekishi shiryōka, 2004.

Takeuchi Ryō. "Kanei saidō jigyō to chiiki shakai no henyō." In *Kodai Nihon to sono shūhen chiiki ni okeru shukō gyōseisan no kisō kenkyū*. Edited by Takahashi Teruhiko, Nakakubo Tatsuo, and Ueda Naoya, pp. 261–74. Ōsaka daigaku daigakuin bungaku kenkyūka, 3.2016.

Tamamura Takeji. "Ashikaga Yoshimochi no Zenshū shinkō ni tsuite." In *Nihon zenshūshi ronshū ge*, no. 2, edited by Tamamura Takeji, pp. 57–84. Kyoto: Shibunkaku, 1981.

Tamamura Takeji. "Shoki Myōshinjishi no ni, san giten." In *Nihon zenshūshi ronshū ge*, no. 2, edited by Tamamura Takeji, pp. 267–310. Kyoto: Shibunkaku, 1981.

Tamura Masataka. "Ōuchi shi Hirai kashin Hirai Dōjo kō." *Nanakuma shigaku* 17 (3.2015), pp. 23–40.

Tamura Masataka. "Muromachiki ni okeru Usa no miya no saiki zōei saikō." *Chūsei shi kenkyū* 32 (2007), pp. 117–40.

Tamura Tetsuo. "Ōuchi no bushō Sugi shi monjo ni tsuite." *Yamaguchi chihōshi kenkyū*, no. 16 (11.1966), pp. 28–37.

Tanabe Hisako. *Uesugi Norizane*. Yoshikawa kōbunkan, 1999.

Tanaka Kōji. "Nihon chūsei ni okeru seni no shakaiteki kinō o megutte." Nōgaya shutsudo zeni chōsa kai Machida shi kyōiku iinkai, comp. *Nōgaya shutsudo chōsa hōkokusho* (3.1996), pp. 102–23.

Tanaka Ryōkō. *Kyōto no omogake*. Kyodo shumisha, 1931.

Tanaka Takeo. *Wakō*. Kōdansha, 2012.

Tanibayashi Hiroshi. "Ōuchi Morimi to sonōeisō." *Kokubungaku* 9.1 (1.1964), pp. 141–45.

Tasaka Yasuyuki. "Muromachiki Kyōto no kūkan kōzō to shakai." In *Muromachi Seiken no shufu kōsō to Kyōto Muromachi Kitayama Higashiyama: Heiankyō Kyōto kenkyū sōsho*, edited by Momosaki Yūichirō and Yamada Kunikazu, pp. 44–78. Kyoto: Bunrikaku, 2016.

Toma Shi'ichi. "Hiya ni tsuite." *Nantō kōko*, no. 14 (12.1994), pp. 123–52.

Tomita Masahiro. "Sengokuki no kugeshū." *Ritsumeikan bungaku* no. 509 (1988), pp. 249–88.

Ueda Jun'ichi. *Ashikaga Yoshimitsu to zenshū*. Kyoto: Hōzōkan, 2011.

Ueno Toshizō. "'Kudara ōke Mimatsu shi keizu' no shiryō kachi ni tsuite." In *Ritsuryō jidai no kikajin no kisoteki kenkyū*. Edited by Keiō daigaku hōgakubu, pp. 385–407. Keiō daigaku hōgakubu, 10.1983.

Uoya Shōhei. "Sue Harukata no kaimei jiki ni tsuite." *Yamaguchi ken chihōshi kenkyū* 115 (6.2016), pp. 64–68.

Villion, A. *Yamaguchi Daidōjji no hakken to saikyojō ni tsuite*. *Taiyōsha* 1926. http://dl.ndl. go.jp/info:ndljp/pid/1019433

Wada Hidemichi. "Sonkeikaku bunkozō *Towazu monogatari*." *Atomi gakuen jōshi daigaku kiyō* 16 (3.1983), pp. 61–90.

Wada Hidemichi. "Kunaichō shoryōbuzō *Meitokui* honkoku." *Atomi gakuen joshi daigaku kiyō* 12 (3.1979), pp. 35–70.

Wada Shūsaku. "Yoshida Kanemigi 'Bōshū gekōki' ni mieru Ōuchi shi kankei kiji." *Yamaguchi ken chihōshi kenkyū* 123 (6.2020), pp. 106–7.

Wada Shūsaku. "Ōuchi Masahiro no hakkyū monjo." *Sengoku ibun geppō* 1 *Ōuchi shi hen* (7.2016), pp. 3–5.

Wada Shūsaku. "Chūsei no Washizu shi ni tsuite." *Kudamatsu chihōshi kenkyū* 50 (4.2014), pp. 3–26.

Wada Shūsaku. "Suō Migita shi no sōden monjo ni tsuite." *Yamaguchi ken monjokan kenkyū kiyō* 41 (3.2014), pp. 93–119.

Wada Shūsaku. "Ōuchi shi no sōsho kankei o megutte." In *Ōuchi to Ōtomo: Chūsei nishi Nihon no nidai daimyō*, edited by Kage Toshio, pp. 25–61. Bensei shuppan, 2013.

Wada Shūsaku, ed. "Furoku Sasaki Shichibei no suke Yoshiie no honkoku to shōkai." *Yamaguchi monjokan kiyō* 39 (3.2012), pp. 121–28.

Wada Shūsaku. "Ōuchi shi no monjo kanri ni tsuite." *Yamaguchi monjokan kenkyū kiyō* 37 (3.2010), pp. 69–83.

Wada Shūsaku. "Ōuchi shi no ryōgoku shihai soshiki to jinzai tōyō." In *Mōri Motonari to chiiki shakai*, edited by Kishida Hiroshi, pp. 197–223. Hiroshima: Chūgoku shinbunsha, 2007.

Wada Shūsaku, "Yamaguchi denchū bunko." In *Mōri Motonari to chiiki shakai*, edited by Kishida Hiroshi, pp. 220–21. Hiroshima: Chūgoku shinbunsha, 2007.

Wada Shūsaku. "Yamaguchi de kurashita Ashikaga shōgun." In *Mōri Motonari to chiiki shakai*, edited by Kishida Hiroshi, pp. 222–23. Hiroshima: Chūgoku shinbunsha, 2007.

Wada Shūsaku. "Hagi hanshi Uno ke to Sue shi no keifu-'Uno Yoichi Uemon ke monjo' no saikentō." *Shigaku kenkyū*, no. 254 (10.2006), pp. 1–20.

Wada Shūsaku. "Ōuchi Takaharu oyobi sono kankei shiryō." *Yamaguchi monjokan kenkyū kiyō* 30 (2003), pp. 1–24.

Wada Shūsaku. "Ōuchi shi kashin Yasutomi shi no kankei shiryō ni tsuite I." *Yamaguchi ken monjo kan kenkyū kiyō* 27 (3.2000), pp. 55–84.

Wada Shūsaku. "Ōuchi shi kashin Yasutomi shi no kankei shiryō ni tsuite II." *Yamaguchi ken monjo kan kenkyū kiyō* 28 (3.2001), pp. 67–81.

Wada Shūsaku. "'Sue shi no coup d'état to Iwami kokujin Sufu shi no dōkō' Sufu ke monjo no shōkai." *Yamaguchi ken chihōshi kenkyū* 70 (10.1993), pp. 63–72.

Watanabe Daimon. *Sengoku no binbō tennō*. Kashiwa shobō, 2012.

Watanabe Shigeru. "Kokuritsu rekishi minzoku hakubutsukan shozō no kodai shiryō ni kansuru shoshiteki kentō." *Kokuritsu rekishi minzoku hakubutsukan kenkyū hōkoku* 153 (2009), pp. 169–392.

Yagita Ken. *Shiryō ni miru Chūsei no Moji.* Revised printing, Kita Kyūshū, 2010.

Yamada Kuniaki. "Sengoku no sōran." In *Iwanami kōza Nihon rekishi,* vol. 4, edited by Sakurai Eiji et al., pp. 3–36. Iwanami shoten, 2015.

Yamada Takashi. *Chūsei kōki buke kan'iron.* Ebisu kōshō, 2015.

Yamada Takashi. "Chūsei koki chiiki kenryoku ni yoru bushi no shinkakuka." *Nenpō Chūseishi kenkyū* 33 (2008), pp. 61–84.

Yamada Takashi. "Shiryō shōkai Kunaichō shoryōbu zō Sagara Taketō shōsatsu maki no shōkai to honyaku." *Yamaguchi kenshi kenkyū,* no. 18 (3.2010), pp. 72–89.

Yamada Yasuhiro. *Ashikaga Yoshitane.* Ebisu kōshō, 2016.

Yamagata Kinya. *Rekishi no umi o hashiru: Chūgoku zōsen gijutsu no kōseki.* Nōsan gyoson bunka kyōkai, 2004.

Yamaguchi Takamasa. "Sasaki monjo-Chūsei Hizen no kuni kankei shiryō jui." *Kyūshū shigaku* 124 (9.1999), pp. 52–67.

Yamamoto Benya. *Hagi no tōjiki.* Hagi, 1978.

Yamamoto Hiroki. *Saikoku no sengoku kassen. Sensō no Nihonshi* 12. Yoshikawa kōbunkan, 2007.

Yamamoto Hiroko. *Chūsei shinwa.* Iwanami shoten, 1998.

Yamamoto Hiroko. *Ishin Chūsei Nihon no hikyōteki sekai.* Heibonsha, 1998.

Yamamoto Hiroko. "Kokoro no mihashira to chūseiteki sekai." *Shunjū,* nos. 302–39 (10.1988–6.1992).

Yamamura Aki. "Chūsei toshi no kūkan kōzō." In *Yamaguchi kenshi tsūshi hen chūsei,* pp. 670–98. Yamaguchi, 2012.

Yanagi Tomoko. "Nisennen shutsudo no mokkan: Yamaguchi Suō kokufu no ato." *Mokkan kenkyū,* no. 23 (11.2001), pp. 143–49.

Yanbe Kōki. "Muromachi bakufu shugo no zaikyō to zaikoku." *Rekishi to chiri* 527 (1999), pp. 18–25.

Yonehara Masayoshi. *Sengoku bushi no bungei no kenkyū.* Ōfūsha, 1994.

Yonehara Masayoshi. *Ōuchi Yoshitaka. Nihon no bushō* 28. Jinbutsu ōraisha, 1967.

Yonetani Hitoshi. "Jūrokuseiki Nichō kankei ni okeru gishi hakken no kōzō to jittai." *Rekishigaku kenkyū* 697 (1997), pp. 1–18.

Yoshida Kenji. "Muromachi bakufu no shugo kokujin no rengō gun." *Chūsei shi kenkyū* 34 (2009), pp. 29–52.

Yoshida Yutaka. "Chūsei no Sakai." In *Kōwan to chūsei toshi Sakai Masuda Takamatsu Ōsaka 12.23.2011 Symposium.* Edited by Ōsaka rekishi hakubutsukan, pp. 29–35. Ōsaka rekishi hakubutsukan. 2011.

Yoshikawa Shinji. *Asuka no Miyako.* Iwanami shoten, 2011.

Yoshimura Kazuhisa, Ikeda Yoshifumi, et al. "Akiyoshidai Naganobori dōzan Ogirikō seki ni kiroku sareta ryūka kōseiren." *Gekkan Chikyū* 35.10 (2013), pp. 594–602.

Yoshino Hiroko. *Kakusareta kamigami: kodai shinkō to inyō gogyō.* Jinbun shoin, 1992.

Yoshino Hiroko. *Tennō no matsuri.* Kōdansha, 2000.

Yoshitake Masaaki. "Matsugi Hisanao to imojishi soshiki no musubituski ni okeru Yanagihara Sukesada to Ōuchi shi no yakuwari." *Ryūkoku kenkyū* 38 (3.2015), pp. 18–46.

Yoshizawa Hajime. "Ōeiki ni okeru Totō Tenjin setsuwa no tenkai." *Shigaku zasshi* 120.10 (2011), pp. 37–58.

Yugawa Toshiharu. "Ashikaga Yoshiharu shōgun ki no Konoe ke no dōkō." *Nihon rekishi* 604 (9.1998), pp. 64–80.

Yutani Yūzō. "Kinkakuji wa Kinkakuji to shite taterareta: 'Nihon kokuō Minamoto Dōgi' koto Ashikaga Yoshimitsu to Godaisan (Wu-Tai-Shan) no Bukkyō setsuwa." *Nagoya gaikokugo daigaku kokugo gakubu kiyō* 42 (2.2012), pp. 1–28.

Secondary Sources in European Languages

Ackroyd, Joyce. *Lessons from History: The Tokushi Yoron.* St. Lucia: University of Queensland Press, 1982.

Adolphson, Mikael. *The Gates of Power: Monks, Courtiers, and Warriors in Premodern Japan.* Honolulu: University of Hawaii Press, 2000.

Aikins, C. Melvin, Barnes, Gina L., and Rhee, Song-nai. *Archaeology and History of Toraijin: Human, Technical, and Cultural Flow from the Korean Peninsula to the Japanese Archipelago c. 800 BC–AD 600.* Oxford: Archaeopress Publishing, 2021.

Alesina, Alberto F., Easterly, William, Devleeschauwer, Arnaud, Kurlat, Sergio, and Wacziarg, Romain T. "Fractionalization." *Journal of Economic Growth* 8.2 (6.2002), pp. 155–94. Available at SSRN: https://ssrn.com/abstract=319762 or http://dx.doi.org/10.2139/ssrn.319762.

Althoff, Gerd. *Family, Friends and Followers: Political and Social Bonds in Medieval Europe.* Translated by Christopher Carroll. Cambridge: Cambridge University Press, 2004.

Amino, Yoshihiko. *Rethinking Japanese History.* Translated by Alan S. Christy. Ann Arbor: Center for Japanese Studies, University of Michigan, 2012.

Andreeva, Anna. *Assembling Shinto: Buddhist Approaches to Kami Worship in Medieval Japan.* Cambridge, MA: Harvard University Asian Center, 2017.

App, Urs. *The Cult of Emptiness: The Western Discovery of Buddhist Thought and the Invention of Oriental Philosophy.* Kyoto: University Media, 2012.

App, Urs. "St. Francis Xavier's Discovery of Japanese Buddhism: A Chapter in the European Discovery of Buddhism (Part 2: From Kagoshima to Yamaguchi, 1549–1551)." *Eastern Buddhist,* new series, 30.2 (1997), pp. 214–44.

Arichi, Meri. "Seven Stars of Heaven and Seven Shrines on Earth: The Big Dipper and the Hie Shrine in the Medieval Period." *Culture and Cosmos* 10.1 (2006), pp. 195–216.

Arnesen, Peter Judd. *The Medieval Japanese Daimyō: The Ōuchi Family's Rule of Suō and Nagato.* New Haven: Yale University Press, 1979.

Asao, Naohiro. "*Shōgun* and *Tennō.*" In *Japan before Tokugawa: Political Consolidation and Economic Growth, 1500–1650,* edited by John Whitney Hall, Nagahara Keiji, and Kozo Yamamura, pp. 248–71. Princeton: Princeton University Press, 1981.

Atwell, William. "International Bullion Flows and the Chinese Economy, circa 1530–1650." *Past and Present* 95 (5.1982), pp. 68–90.

Atwell, William. "Time, Money, and the Weather: Ming China and the 'Great Depression' of the Mid-Fifteenth Century." *Journal of Asian Studies* 61.1 (2.2002), pp. 83–113.

Barth, Fredrik. *Ethnic Groups and Boundaries: The Social Organization of Culture Difference.* Long Grove, IL: Waveland Press, 1998.

Batten, Bruce. "Foreign Threat and Domestic Reform: The Emergence of the Ritsuryō State." *Monumenta Nipponica* 41.2 (Summer 1986), pp. 199–219.

Batten, Bruce. *Hakata in War and Peace, 500–1300.* Honolulu: University of Hawaii Press, 2006.

Batten, Bruce. *To the Ends of Japan: Premodern Frontiers, Boundaries, and Interactions.* Honolulu: University of Hawaii Press, 2003.

Bennett, Steffani. "The Other Shore: Sesshū Tōyō (1420–ca. 1506) and the Sino-Japanese Cultural Sphere in the Fifteenth Century." PhD dissertation, Harvard University, 2020.

Berry, Mary Elizabeth. *The Culture of Civil War in Kyōto.* Berkeley: University of California Press, 1994.

Berry, Mary Elizabeth. "Public Official or Feudal Lord?" *Monumenta Nipponica* 36.2 (Summer 1981), pp. 187–93.

Berry, Mary Elizabeth. "Public Peace and Private Attachment: The Goals and Conduct of Power in Early Modern Japan." *Journal of Japanese Studies* 12.2 (Summer 1986), pp. 238–71.

Best, Jonathan. *A History of the Early Korean Kingdom of Paekche, together with Annotated Translation of the Paekche Annals of the Samguk Sagi.* Cambridge, MA: Harvard University East Asia Center, 2007.

Blair, Heather. "Rites and Rule: Kiyomori at Itsukushima and Fukuhara." *Harvard Journal of Asiatic Studies* 73.1 (2013), pp. 1–42.

Borgen, Robert. *Sugawara Michizane and the Early Heian Court.* Cambridge, MA: Harvard University Asia Center, 1986.

Boscaro, Adreana. "Toyotomi Hideyoshi and the 1587 Edicts Against Christianity." *Oriens Extremus* 20 (12.1973), pp. 219–41.

Bowring, Richard. *The Religious Traditions of Japan, 500–1600.* New York: Cambridge University Press, 2005.

Boxer, Charles. *The Great Ship from Amacon: Annals of Macao and the Old Japan Trade.* Lisbon: Centro de Estudos Históricos Ultramarinos, 1963.

Brightwell, Erin L. *Reflecting the Past: Place, Language, and Principle in Japan's Medieval Mirror Genre.* Cambridge, MA: Harvard University Asia Center, 2020.

Brown, Delmer. *Future and The Past: Translation and Study of the Gukanshō.* Berkeley: University of California Press, 1979.

Brown, Delmer. *Money Economy in Medieval Japan: A Study in the Use of Coins.* New Haven: Institute of Far Eastern Languages, Yale University, 1951.

Brubaker, Rogers. *Ethnicity without Groups.* Cambridge, MA: Harvard University Press, 2006.

Buhrman, Kristina. "The Stars and the State: Astronomy, Astrology, and the Politics of Natural Knowledge in Early Medieval Japan." PhD dissertation, University of Southern California, 2012.

Butler, Lee. *Emperor and Aristocracy in Japan, 1467–1680.* Cambridge, MA: Harvard University Asia Center, 2002.

Byington Mark. *Early Korea: The Rediscovery of Kaya in History and Archaeology.* Cambridge, MA: Korea Institute, Harvard University, 2012.

Carter, Steven. *Regent Redux.* Ann Arbor: Center for Japanese Studies, University of Michigan, 1996.

Celebrating the Arts of Japan: The Mary Griggs Burke Collection. New York: Metropolitan Museum of Art, 2015.

Church, Sally K. "Zhen He: An Investigation into the Plausibility of 450-ft Treasure Ships." *Monumenta Serica* 53 (2005), pp. 1–43.

Clark, Christopher. *Iron Kingdom: The Rise and Downfall of Prussia, 1600–1947.* Cambridge, MA: Harvard University Press, 2006.

Clulow, Adam. *The Company and the Shogun: The Dutch Encounter with Tokugawa Japan.* New York: Columbia University Press, 2014.

Collcutt, Martin. *Five Mountains: The Rinzai Zen Monastic Institution in Medieval Japan.* Cambridge, MA: Council of East Asian Studies, Harvard University, 1981.

Collcutt, Martin. "Religion in the Formation of the Kamakura Bakufu: As Seen through the *Azuma kagami.*" *Japan Review* 5 (1994), pp. 55–86.

Como, Michael. "Immigrant Gods on the Road to Jindō." "Rethinking Medieval Shintō." Edited by Bernard Faure, Michael Como, and Iyanaga Nobumi. *Cahiers d'Extrême-Asie* 16 (2009), pp. 49–69.

Como, Michael. *Weaving and Binding: Immigrant Gods and Female Immortals in Ancient Japan.* Honolulu: University of Hawaii Press, 2009.

Conlan, Thomas D. "The Failed Attempt to Move the Emperor to Yamaguchi and the Fall of the Ōuchi." *Japanese Studies* 35.2 (9.2015), pp. 1–19.

Conlan, Thomas D. *From Sovereign to Symbol: An Age of Ritual Determinism in Fourteenth Century Japan.* New York: Oxford University Press, 2011.

Conlan, Thomas D. "Instruments of Change: Organizational Technology and the Consolidation of Regional Power in Japan 1333–1600." In *War and State Building in Medieval Japan*, edited by John Ferejohn and Frances Rosenbluth, pp. 124–58. Stanford: Stanford University Press, 2010.

Conlan, Thomas D. "Largesse and the Limits of Loyalty in the Fourteenth Century." In *The Origins of Japan's Medieval World: Courtiers, Clerics, Warriors, and Peasants in the Fourteenth Century*, edited by Jeffrey P. Mass, pp. 39–64. Stanford: Stanford University Press, 1997.

Conlan, Thomas D. "Layered Sovereignties and Contested Seas: Recent Histories of Maritime Japan." *Journal of Asian Studies* 76.2 (5.2017), pp. 518–29.

Conlan, Thomas D. "The 'Ōnin War' as Fulfillment of Prophecy." *Journal of Japanese Studies* 46.1 (Winter 2020), pp. 31–60.

Conlan, Thomas D. *Samurai and the Warrior Culture of Japan, 471–1877: A Sourcebook.* Indianapolis: Hackett, 2022.

Conlan, Thomas D. *State of War: The Violent Order of Fourteenth Century Japan.* Ann Arbor: Center for Japanese Studies, University of Michigan, 2003.

Conlan, Thomas D. "Warfare in Japan 1200–1550." In *The Cambridge History of War*, vol. 2, edited by Anne Curry and David A. Graff, pp. 523–53. Cambridge: Cambridge University Press, 2020.

Conlan, Thomas D. "When Men Become Gods: Apotheosis, Sacred Space, and Political Authority in Japan 1486–1599." *Quaestiones Medii Aevi Novae*, no. 21 (2016), pp. 89–106.

Cooper, Michael, trans. *This Island of Japon: Joao Rodrigues' Account of 16th Century Japan.* Rutland, VT: Tuttle, 1973.

Costelloe, M. Joseph, S.J. *The Letters and Instructions of Francis Xavier.* St. Louis, MO: Institute of Jesuit Sources, 1992.

Curtis, Paula. "An Entrepreneurial Aristocrat: Matsugi Hisanao and the Forging of Imperial Service in Late Medieval Japan." *Monumenta Nipponica* 75.2 (2020), pp. 241–79.

Curtis, Paula. "Forgery in Motion: Cross-Status Networks, Authority, and Documentary Culture in Medieval Japan." PhD dissertation, University of Michigan, 2019.

Damien, Michelle M. "As Estates Faded: Late Medieval Maritime Shipping in the Seto Inland Sea." In *Land, Power, and the Sacred*, edited by Janet Goodwin and Joan Piggott, pp. 351–74. Honolulu: University of Hawaii Press, 2018.

Damien, Michelle M. "Late Medieval Japan's Seto Inland Seascape: Shipping, Sailors and Seafaring." PhD dissertation, University of Southern California, 2015.

Dolce, Lucia. "The Worship of Celestial Bodies in Japan: Politics, Rituals, and Icons." *Culture and Cosmos* 10.1–2 (2006), pp. 3–47.

Duthie, Torquil, *Man'yōshū and the Imperial Imagination in Early Japan*. Leiden: Brill, 2014.

Elison, George and Smith, Bardwell, eds., *Warlords, Artists, and Commoners: Japan in the Sixteenth Century*. Honolulu: University of Hawaii Press, 1981.

Elisonas, Jurgis. "Christianity and the Daimyo." In *The Cambridge History of Japan*, edited by John Whitney Hall et al., pp. 301–72. New York: Cambridge University Press, 1991.

Farris, William Wayne. "Shipbuilding and Nautical Technology in Japanese Maritime History: Origins to 1600." *The Mariner's Mirror* 95.3 (8.2009), pp. 260–83.

Farris, William Wayne. *Japan to 1600: A Social and Economic History*. Honolulu: University of Hawaii Press, 2009.

Farris, William Wayne. *Japan's Medieval Population: Famine, Fertility, and Warfare in a Transformative Age*. Honolulu: University of Hawaii Press, 2006.

Faure, Bernard. *The Fluid Pantheon: Gods of Medieval Japan*. Vol. 1. Honolulu: University of Hawaii Press, 2016.

Gay, Suzanne. *The Moneylenders of Late Medieval Kyōto*. Honolulu: University of Hawaii Press, 2001.

Gilbert, Megan. "Conciliators and Fixed Points: Dispute Resolution in Fifteenth Century Japan." PhD dissertation, Princeton University, 2022.

Golas, Peter S. *Science and Technology in China*. Vol. 5, *Chemistry and Chemical Technology*. Part 13, *Mining*. New York: Cambridge University Press, 1999.

Gouge, Kevin. "The Ties that Bind: Kinship, Inheritance, and the Environment in Medieval Japan." PhD dissertation, University of Michigan, 2017.

Grapard, Allan. "Flying Mountains and Walkers of Emptiness: Toward a Definition of Sacred Space in Japanese Religions." *History of Religions* 21.3 (2.1982), pp. 195–221.

Grapard, Allan. "Institution, Ritual and Ideology: The Twenty-Two Shrine-Temple Multiplexes of Heian Japan." *History of Religions* 27.3 (2.1988), pp. 246–69.

Grapard, Allan. *Mountain Mandalas: Shugendō in Kyushu*. New York: Bloomsbury, 2016.

Grapard, Allan. "The Shintō of Yoshida Kanetomo." *Monumenta Nipponica* 47.1 (Spring 1992), pp. 27–58.

Grossberg, Kenneth A., and Kanamoto Nobuhisa, trans. *The Laws of the Muromachi Bakufu: Kemmu Shikimoku (1336) and Muromachi Bakufu Tsuikahō*. Monumenta Nipponica and Sophia University Press, 1981.

Hall, John Whitney. "Foundations of the Modern Japanese Daimyō." *Journal of Asian Studies* 20.3 (1961), pp. 317–29.

Hall, John Whitney. *Government and Local Power in Japan 500 to 1700: A Study Based on the Bizen Province*. Princeton: Princeton University Press, 1966.

Hall, John Whitney, and Toyoda Takeshi, eds. *Japan in the Muromachi Age*. Ithaca, NY: Cornell East Asia Series, 2001; first published, 1977.

Hardacre, Helen. *Shinto: A History*. New York: Oxford University Press, 2016.

History of the Empire of Japan: Compiled and Translated for the Imperial Japanese Commission of the World's Columbia Exposition. Chicago, U.S.A., 1893. Dai Nippon tosho kabushiki kwaisha, 1893.

Hoffmann, Yoel. *Japanese Death Poems: Written by Zen Monks and Haiku Poets on the Verge of Death*. Rutland, Vt.: Tuttle 1998.

Horton, J. Mack. *The Journal of Sōchō*. Stanford: Stanford University Press, 2002.

Howell, David. "Ainu Ethnicity and the Boundaries of the Early Modern Japanese State." *Past and Present* 142 (2.1994), pp. 69–93.

Howell, David. *Geographies of Identity in Nineteenth Century Japan*. Berkeley: University of California Press, 2005.

Hudson, Mark J. *Ruins of Identity: Ethnogenesis in the Japanese Islands*. Honolulu: University of Hawaii Press, 1999.

Itō, Kōji. "Hakata Merchants and Bogus Embassies in the Fifteenth and Sixteenth Centuries." *Nenpō Mita chūseishi kenkyū* 14 (10.2007), pp. 115–33.

Itō, Kōji. "Studies of Medieval Ryukyu within Asia's Maritime Network." *Acta Asiatica* 95 (2008), pp. 79–99.

"Japanese First as Ancient Roman Coins Found in Okinawa Ruins." *Asahi Shimbun*, 9.27.2016.

Kanagawa, Nadia. "Making the Realm, Transforming the People: Foreign Subjects in Seventh-through Ninth-century Japan." PhD dissertation, University of Southern California, 2019.

Kang, Etsuko Hae-Jin. *Diplomacy and Ideology in Japanese-Korean Relations: From the Fifteenth to the Eighteenth Century*. London: Palgrave Macmillan, 1997.

Katsumata, Shizuo. "The Development of Sengoku Law." In *Japan before Tokugawa: Political Consolidation and Economic Growth, 1500–1650*, edited by John Whitney Hall, Nagahara Keiji, and Kozo Yamamura, pp. 101–24. Princeton: Princeton University Press, 1981.

Keene, Donald. *Yoshimasa and the Silver Pavilion: The Creation of the Soul of Japan*. New York: Columbia University Press, 2003.

Kim, Youn-mi. "(Dis)assembling the National Canon: Seventh-Century 'Esoteric' Buddhist Ritual, the Samguk yusa, and Sach'onwang-sa." In *New Perspectives on Early Korean Art: From Silla to Koryŏ*, edited by Youn-mi Kim, pp. 123–91. Cambridge, MA: Korea Institute, Harvard University, 2013.

Kitagawa, Anne Rose. "Behind the Scenes of Harvard's *Tale of Genji Album*." *Apollo* 154, no. 477 (11.2001), pp. 28–35.

Kobata, Atsushi. "The Production and Uses of Gold and Silver in Sixteenth- and Seventeenth-Century Japan." *Economic History Review*, 2nd series, 18.1–3 (1965), pp. 245–66.

Kobayashi, Hiroshi. "Domain Laws (*Bunkoku-hō*) in the Sengoku Period with Special Emphasis on the Date House Code, the *Jinkaishū*." *Acta Asiatica* 35 (11.1978), pp. 30–45.

Kornicki, Peter. "Korean Books in Japan: From the 1590s to the End of the Edo Period." *Journal of the American Oriental Society* 133.1 (2013), pp. 71–92.

Kuroda, Akinobu. "Copper Coins Chosen and Differentiated: Another Aspect of the 'Silver Century' in East Asia." *Acta Asiatica* 88 (2005), pp. 65–86.

Kuroda, Akinobu. *A Global History of Money: Routledge Explorations in Economic History*. New York: Routledge, 2020.

Kuroda, Toshio. "Discourse on the 'Land of Kami' (Shinkoku) in Medieval Japan." *Japanese Journal of Religious Studies* 23.3–4 (1996), pp. 353–85.

Lach, Donald. *Japan in the Eyes of Europe*. Chicago: University of Chicago Press, 1968.

Lee, Sangnam. "The Joseon Court and the Ōuchi clan: A Case Study of the Interregional Circulation of Material Culture." *Artibus Asiae* 78.2 (2018), pp. 151–80.

Lee, Sangnam. "Traces of a Lost Landscape Tradition and Cross-Cultural Relationships between Korea, China, and Japan in the Early Joseon Period (1392–1550)." PhD dissertation, University of Kansas, 2014.

Li, Yiwen. "Networks of Profit and Faith: Spanning the Sea of Japan and the East China Sea, 838–1403." PhD dissertation, Yale University, 2017.

Lieberman, Victor B. *Strange Parallels: Southeast Asia in Global Context c. 800–1830.* Vol. 2, *Mainland Mirrors: Europe, Japan, China, South Asia, and the Islands.* Cambridge: Cambridge University Press, 2012.

Lippit, Yukio. *Painting of the Realm: The Kanō House Painters in 17th Century Japan.* Seattle: University of Washington Press, 2012.

Lopez, Robert S. *The Commercial Revolution of the Middle Ages.* New York: Cambridge University Press, 1976.

Mass, Jeffrey P. *Antiquity and Anachronism in Japanese History.* Stanford: Stanford University Press, 1992.

Mass, Jeffrey P. *The Kamakura Bakufu: A Study in Documents.* Stanford: Stanford University Press, 1976.

MacGregor, Neil. *Germany: Memories of a Nation.* New York: Vintage books, 2014.

Marques, Alfredo Pinheiro. "Japan in Early Portuguese Maps." In *The UNESCO Courier: A Window Open on the World* vol. 42 no. 4, *Camões and the Portuguese Voyages of Discovery*, pp. 14–16. Paris, 4.1989. https://unesdoc.unesco.org/ark:/48223/pf0000083172.

Matsuda, Wataru. *Japan and China: Mutual Representations in the Modern Era.* Translated by Joshua Fogel. Surrey: Curzon, 2000.

Matsuoka, Hisatō. "The Sengoku Daimyo of Western Japan: The Case of the Ōuchi." In *Japan before Tokugawa: Political Consolidation and Economic Growth, 1500–1650*, edited by John Whitney Hall, Nagahara Keiji, and Kozo Yamamura, pp. 64–100. Princeton: Princeton University Press, 1981.

Mayo, Christopher M. "Mobilizing Deities: Deus, Gods, Buddhas, and the Warrior Band in Sixteenth-Century Japan." PhD dissertation, Princeton University, 2013.

Mayo, Christopher M. "The Ōtomo and Competition in the Ritual Marketplace." In *Ōuchi to Ōtomo: Chūsei nishi Nihon no nidai daimyō*, edited by Kage Toshio, pp. 1–30. Bensei shuppan, 2013.

Mayo, Christopher M. *Swearing Oaths and Waging War: People, Place, and Ritual Practice within the Ōtomo Warrior Band in Sixteenth-Century Japan.* Ise: Kōgakkan University Press, 2019.

McClain, James. "Japan's Pre-modern Urbanism." In *The Oxford Handbook of Cities in World History*, edited by Peter Clark, pp. 328–45. New York: Oxford University Press, 2013.

McCormick, Melissa. "Genji Goes West: The 1510 *Genji Album* and the Visualization of Court and Capital." *Art Bulletin* 85.1 (3.2003), pp. 54–85.

McCormick, Melissa. *The Tale of Genji: A Visual Companion.* Princeton: Princeton University Press, 2018.

Miyamoto, Kazuo. *Vikings of the Far East.* New York: Vantage Press, 1975.

Mohan, Pankaj. "The Controversy over the Ancient Korean State of Gaya: A Fresh Look at the Korea-Japan History War." In *"History Wars" and Reconciliation in Japan and Korea: The Roles of Historians, Artists and Activists*, edited by Michael Lewis, pp. 107–24. New York: Palgrave Macmillan, 2016.

Morris-Suzuki, Tessa. *The Technological Transformation of Japan: From the Seventeenth to the Twenty-First Century.* Cambridge: Cambridge University Press, 1994.

Murdoch, James. *A History of Japan.* 3 vols. London: K. Paul, Trench, Trubner, 1925.

Nikaido, Yoshihiro. "Chapter 3: Cultural Interaction: Myōken Bosatsu (妙見菩薩) and the God Zhenwu (真武)." *Asian Folk Religion and Cultural Interaction*, pp. 115–28. Göttingen: Vandenhoech & Ruprecht, 10.2015.

"Ōnin War: Visualizing Twelve Years of War in Japan, 1465–1478." http://commons. princeton.edu/onin/.

Ooms, Herman. *Tokugawa Ideology: Early Constructs, 1570–1680*. Princeton: Princeton University Press, 1985.

Parker, John. *Zen Buddhist Landscape Arts of Early Muromachi Japan (1336–1573)*. New York: SUNY Press, 1999.

Parrott, David. *Business of War: Military Enterprise and Military Revolution in Early Modern Europe*. Cambridge: Cambridge University Press, 2012.

Pearson, Richard. "Japanese Medieval Trading Towns: Sakai and Tosaminato." *Japanese Journal of Archaeology* 3 (2016), pp. 89–116.

Pitelka, Morgan. *Reading Medieval Ruins: Urban Life and Destruction in Sixteenth-Century Japan*. Cambridge: Cambridge University Press, 2022.

Pohl, Walter. "Introduction: Strategies of Identification—a Methodological Profile." In *Strategies of Identification: Ethnicity and Religion in Early Medieval Europe*. Edited by Walter Pohl, pp. 1–64. Turnhout: Brepols, 2013.

Pohl, Walter, et al., eds. *Meanings of Community across Medieval Eurasia: Comparative Approaches*. Leiden: Brill, 2016.

Rambelli, Fabio. "Iconoclasm and Religious Violence in Japan: Practices and Rationalizations." In *Buddhism and Iconoclasm in East Asia: A History*, edited by Fabio Rambelli and Eric Reinders, pp. 47–88. New York: Bloomsbury Academic, 2012.

Rambelli, Fabio. "Sea Theologies: Elements for a Conceptualization of Maritime Religiosity in Japan." In *The Sea and the Sacred in Japan: Aspects of Maritime Religion*, edited by Fabio Rambelli, pp. 181–99. New York: Bloomberg Academic, 2018.

Reid, Anthony. *Southeast Asia in the Age of Commerce*. 2 vols. New Haven: Yale University Press, 1988.

Reyes, Alexander K. "Flowers on the Battlefield: Intimacy and Hierarchy in the Construction of Japanese Warrior Masculinities, 1507–1636." PhD dissertation, Columbia University, 2022.

Ribeiro, Madalena. *Samurais Cristãos. Os Jesuítas e a Nobreza Cristã do Sul do Japão no Século XVI*. Lisbon: Centro de História de Além-Mar, 2009.

Roberts, Luke. *Performing the Great Peace: Political Space and Open Secrets in Tokugawa Japan*. Honolulu: University of Hawaii Press, 2012.

Robinson, David. *Martial Spectacle of the Ming Court*. Cambridge, MA: Harvard Yenching Monograph Series, 2013.

Robinson, Kenneth R. "An Island's Place in History: Tsushima in Japan and Chosŏn, 1392–1592." *Korean Studies* 30 (2006), pp. 40–66.

Robinson, Kenneth R. "A Japanese Trade Mission to Chosŏn Korea, 1537–1540: The Sonkai tokai nikki and the Korean Tribute System." In *Tools of Culture: Japan's Cultural, Intellectual, Medical, and Technological Contacts in East Asia, 1000–1500s*, edited by Andrew Goble, Kenneth R. Robinson, and Haruko Nishioka Wakabayashi, pp. 71–101. Ann Arbor, MI: Association for Asian Studies, 2009.

Robinson, Kenneth R. "Korean Chronicles of Japanese Emperors and Kings: An Annotated Translation from *Haedong chegukki*." *Journal of Northeast Asian History* 8.2 (2011), pp. 137–213.

Robinson, Kenneth R. "Organizing Japanese and Jurchens in Tribute Systems in Early Chosŏn Korea." *Journal of East Asian Studies* 13.2 (2013), pp. 337–60.

Robinson, Kenneth R. "Pak Tonji and the Vagaries of Government Service in Koryŏ and Chosŏn, 1360–1412." *Korean Studies* 40 (2016), pp. 78–118.

Robinson, Kenneth R. "The Printed *Haedong chegukki* and Korean-Japanese Relations in the Early Sixteenth Century." *Ilbon sasang* 9 (10.2005), pp. 89–122.

Robinson, Kenneth R. "Treated as Treasures: The Circulation of Sutras in Maritime Northeast Asia from 1388 to the Mid-Sixteenth Century." *East Asian History* 21 (6.2001), pp. 33–54.

Romney, David. "Godly Politics: Ise, the Court, and Japanese Religion 1330–1615." PhD dissertation, Princeton University, 2023.

Rubiés, Joan-Pau. "Real and Imaginary Dialogues in the Jesuit Mission of Sixteenth-Century Japan." *Journal of the Economic and Social History of the Orient* 55 (2012), pp. 447–94.

Sakurai, Eiji. "Medieval Japan's Commercial Economy and the Estate System." In *Land, Power, and the Sacred*, edited by Janet Goodwin and Joan Piggott, pp. 37–57. Honolulu: University of Hawaii Press, 2018.

Satō, Hiroo. "Wrathful Deities and Saving Deities." In *Buddhas and Kami in Japan: Honji Suijaku as a Combinatory Paradigm*, edited by Mark Teeuwen and Fabio Rambelli, pp. 95–114. New York: Routledge, 2003.

Satow, Ernest. "Vicissitudes of the Church at Yamaguchi from 1550 through 1586." *Transactions of the Asiatic Society of Japan* 7 (1879), pp. 139–66.

Schafer, Edward. *Pacing the Void: T'ang Approaches to the Stars*. Berkeley: University of California Press, 1977.

Scheid, Bernhard. "Hachiman Worship among Japanese Pirates (*wakō*) of the Medieval Period: A Preliminary Study." In *The Sea and the Sacred in Japan: Aspects of Maritime Religion*, edited by Fabio Rambelli, pp. 89–100. New York: Bloomberg Academic, 2018.

Scheid, Bernhard. "Shinto as a Religion for the Warrior Class: The Case of Yoshikawa Koretaru." *Japanese Journal of religious Studies* 29.3–4 (2002), pp. 299–324.

Schurhammer, Georg. *Francis Xavier: His Life and Times*. 4 vols. Translated by M. Joseph Costelloe. Rome: Jesuit Historical Institute, 1973–82.

Scott, James. *Against the Grain: A Deep History of the Earliest States*. New Haven: Yale University Press, 2017.

Segal, Ethan. *Coins, Trade, and the State: Economic Growth in Early Medieval Japan*. Cambridge, MA: Harvard University Asia Center, 2011.

Selinger, Vyjayanthi. *Authorizing the Shogunate Ritual and Material Symbolism in the Literary Construction of Warrior Order*. Leiden: Brill, 2013.

Shapinsky, Peter. *Lords of the Sea: Pirates, Violence, and Commerce in Late Medieval Japan*. Ann Arbor: Center for Japanese Studies, University of Michigan, 2014.

Shigeno, Yasuyori (Yasutsugu) and Hoshino, Hisashi. *The History of the Empire of Japan: Compiled and Translated for the Imperial Japanese Commission of the World's Columbian Exposition, Chicago, U. S. A., 1893*. Yokohama: Dai Nippon Tosho Kabushiki Kwaisha, 1893.

Shimao, Arata. "The Stewards of Art in Muromachi Japan: Nōami, Geiami, and Sōami." *Chanoyu Quarterly* 84 (1996), pp. 7–36.

Simpson, Emily B. "An Empress at Sea: Sea Deities and Divine Union in the Legend of Empress Jingū." In *The Sea and the Sacred in Japan: Aspects of Maritime Religion*, edited by Fabio Rambelli, pp. 65–78. New York: Bloomberg Academic, 2018.

Smits, Gregory. *Maritime Ryūkyū, 1050–1650*. Honolulu: University of Hawaii Press, 2018.

Soranaka, Isao. "Obama: The Rise and Decline of a Seaport." *Monumenta Nipponica* 52.1 (Spring 1997), pp. 85–102.

Souyri, Pierre. *The World Turned Upside Down: Medieval Japanese Society.* New York: Columbia University Press, 2001.

Spafford, David. *A Sense of Place: The Political Landscape in Late Medieval Japan.* Cambridge, MA: Harvard University Asia Center, 2013.

Stavros, Matthew. "Locational Pedigree and Warrior Status in Medieval Kyōto: The Residences of Ashikaga Yoshimitsu." *Japanese Studies* 29.1 (5.2009), pp. 3–18.

Stavros, Matthew. "Monuments and Mandalas in Medieval Kyoto: Reading Buddhist Kingship in the Urban Plan of Ashikaga Yoshimitsu." *Harvard Journal of Asiatic Studies* 77.1 (12.2017), pp. 321–61.

Stavros, Matthew and Tomishima, Yoshiyuki. "The Shōkokuji Pagoda: Building the Infrastructure of Buddhist Kingship in Medieval Japan." *Japanese Journal of Religious Studies* 45.1 (2018), pp. 125–44.

Stone, Jacqueline. *Original Enlightenment and the Transformation of Medieval Japanese Buddhism.* Honolulu: University of Hawaii Press, 1999.

Strathern, Alan. "The Many Meanings of Iconoclasm: Warrior and Christian Temple-Shrine Destruction in Late Sixteenth Century Japan." *Journal of Early Modern History* 25.3 (2020), pp. 1–31.

Strathern, Alan. *Unearthly Powers: Religious and Political Change in World History.* New York: Cambridge University Press, 2019.

Takekoshi, Yosaburō. *Economic Aspects of the History of the Civilization of Japan.* 3 vols. London: George Allen & Unwin, 1930.

Tanaka, Takeo. "Relations with Overseas Countries." In *Japan in the Muromachi Age*, edited by John Whitney Hall and Toyoda Takeshi, pp. 159–78. Berkeley: University of California Press, 1977.

Teeuwen, Mark. "The Creation of a Honji Suijaku Deity: Amaterasu as the Judge of the Dead." In *Buddhas and Kami in Japan: Honji Suijaku as a Combinatory Paradigm*, edited by Mark Teeuwen and Fabio Rambelli, pp. 115–44. New York: Routledge, 2003.

Teeuwen, Mark. "The Imperial Shrines of Ise: An Ancient Star Cult?" "The Worship of Stars in Japanese Religious Practice." Edited by Lucia Dolce. *Cultural and Cosmos* 10.1–2 (2006), pp. 79–98.

Teeuwen, Mark and Scheid, Bernhard. "Tracing Shinto in the History of Kami Worship: Editor's Introduction." *Japanese Journal of Religious Studies* 29.3–4 (Fall 2002), pp. 195–207.

Thompson, Sarah E. "The War of the Twelve Animals." In *Monsters, Animals and Other Worlds: A Collection of Short Medieval Japanese Tales*, edited by Keller Kimbrough and Haruo Shirane, pp. 385–416. New York: Columbia University Press, 2018.

Thompson, Sarah E. "The War of the Twelve Animals (*Jūnirui kassen emaki*): A Medieval Japanese Illustrated Beast Fable." PhD dissertation, Columbia University, 1999.

Tilly, Charles. *The Formation of Nation States in Western Europe.* Princeton: Princeton University Press, 1975.

Toby, Ronald. *Engaging the Other: "Japan" and Its Alter-Egos, 1550–1850.* Leiden: Brill, 2019.

Toby, Ronald. *State and Diplomacy in Early Modern Japan: Asia in the Development of the Tokugawa Bakufu.* Princeton: Princeton University Press, 1984.

Tonomura, Hitomi. *Community and Commerce in Late Medieval Japan: The Corporate Villages of Tokuchin-ho.* Stanford: Stanford University Press, 1992.

Tsang, Carol. *War and Faith: Ikkō Ikki in Late Muromachi Japan.* Cambridge, MA: Harvard East Asian Monographs, 2007.

Tsunoda, Ryūsaku. *Japan in the Dynastic Histories*. Pasadena: P.D. and Iona Perkins, 1951.

Tyler, Royall. *Fourteenth Century Voices*. 3 vols. Middleton, DE: Blue Tongue Books, 2016–17.

Tyler, Royall. "Unoha." In *To Hallow Genji: A Tribute to Noh*, pp. 227–39. Createspace Independent Publishing, 2013.

von Glahn, Richard. "Chinese Coin and Changes in Monetary Preferences in Maritime East Asia in the Fifteenth–Seventeenth Centuries." *Journal of the Economic and Social History of the Orient* 57 (2014), pp. 629–68.

von Glahn, Richard. *Fountain of Fortune: Money and Monetary Policy in China, 1000–1700*. Berkeley: University of California Press, 1996.

von Glahn, Richard. "The Ningbo-Hakata Merchant Network and the Reorientation of East Asian Maritime Trade, 1150–1350." *Harvard Journal of Asiatic Studies* 74.2 (2014), pp. 249–79.

von Verschuer, Charlotte. *Across the Perilous Sea: Japanese Trade with China and Korea from the Seventh to the Sixteenth Centuries*. Ithaca, NY: Cornell East Asia Series, 2006.

von Verschuer, Charlotte. "Ashikaga Yoshimitsu's Foreign Policy 1398–1408: A Translation from *Zenrin Kokuhō ki*, the Cambridge Manuscript." *Monumenta Nipponica* 62.3 (2007), pp. 261–97.

Vovin, Alexander. "Origins of the Japanese Language." In *Oxford Research Encyclopedia: Linguistics* (2017). https://oxfordre.com/linguistics/view/10.1093/acref ore/9780199384655.001.0001/acrefore-9780199384655-e-277,

Wilson, Noell. *Defensive Positions: The Politics of Maritime Security in Tokugawa Japan*. Cambridge, MA: Harvard University Asia Center, 2015.

Yiengpruksawan, Mimi Hall. *Hiraizumi: Buddhist Art and Regional Politics in Twelfth-Century Japan*. Cambridge, MA: Harvard East Asian Monographs, 1998.

Yoshimura, Kazuhisa, et al. "Sulfide Ore Smelting at the Naganobori Copper Mine Recorded on Speleothems from the Ogiri No. 4 Pit on the Akiyoshi-dai Plateau, Yamaguchi, Japan." *ISIJ International (The Iron and Steel Institute of Japan)* 54.5 (5.2014), pp. 1147–54.

Index

For the benefit of digital users, indexed terms that span two pages (e.g., 52–53) may, on occasion, appear on only one of those pages.

Figures are indicated by *f* following the page number